MW01484237

THE

LIFE AND WORK

OF

ST. PAUL.

THE

LIFE AND WORK

OF

ST. PAUL

BY

F. W. FARRAR, D.D., F.R.S.

Late Fellow of Trinity College, Cambridge
Canon of Westminster
and Chaplain in Ordinary to the Queen

VOLUME I

NEW YORK
E. P. DUTTON & COMPANY
31 WEST 23D STREET
1902

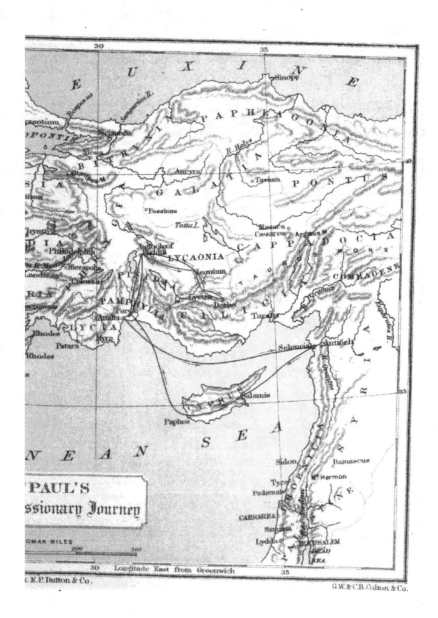

PAUL'S
ssionary Journey

PREFACE.

In the *Life of Christ* I endeavoured, to the best of my power, to furnish, in the form of a narrative, such a commentary upon the Gospels as should bring to bear the most valuable results of modern research. By studying every line and word of the Evangelists with close and reverent attention; by seeking for the most genuine readings and the most accurate translations; by visiting the scenes in the midst of which our Lord had moved; by endeavouring to form a conception at once true and vivid of the circumstances of the age in which He lived, and the daily conditions of religious thought and national custom by which He was surrounded—I thought that, while calling attention in large to His Divine Nature as the Incarnate Son of God, I might be enabled to set forth in clear outline the teaching and the actions of that human life which He lived for our example, and of that death which He died for us men and for our salvation.

In that work it was no small part of my object to enable readers to study the Gospels with a fuller under-standing of their significance, and with a more intense impression of their reality and truth. In the present volume I have undertaken a similar task for the Acts of

A

the Apostles and the thirteen Epistles of St. Paul. My first desire throughout has been to render some assistance towards the study of that large portion of the New Testament which is occupied with the labours and writings of the Apostle of the Gentiles; to show the grandeur of the work and example of one who was indeed a " vessel of election; ", and to bring his character and history to bear on the due comprehension of those Epistles, which have bequeathed to all subsequent ages an inestimable legacy of wisdom and knowledge. In order to accomplish this task, I can conscientiously say that I have used my best diligence and care. Circumstances have precluded me from carrying out my original intention of actually visiting the countries in which St. Paul laboured; and to do this was the less necessary because abundant descriptions of them may be found in the works of many recent travellers. This branch of the subject has been amply illustrated in the well-known volumes of Messrs. Conybeare and Howson, and Mr. Thomas Lewin. To those admirable works all students of St. Paul must be largely indebted, and I need not say that my own book is not intended in any way to come into competition with theirs. It has been written in great measure with a different purpose, as well as from a different point of view. My chief object has been to give a definite, accurate, and intelligible impression of St. Paul's teaching; of the controversies in which he was engaged; of the circumstances which educed his statements of doctrine and practice; of the inmost heart of his theology in each of its phases; of his Epistles as a whole, and of each Epistle in particular as complete and perfect in itself. The task is, I think, more necessary than might be generally supposed. In our custom of studying the Bible year after year in separate texts and isolated chapters, we are but too apt to lose sight of what the Bible is as a whole, and even of the special significance of its separate books. I thought, then, that if I could in any degree render each of the Epistles more thoroughly familiar, either in their general aspect or in their special particulars, I should be rendering some service—however humble—to the Church of God.

With this object it would have been useless merely to re-translate the Epistles. To do this, and to append notes to the more difficult expressions, would have been a very old, and a comparatively easy task. But to make the Epistles an integral part of the life—to put the reader in the position of those to whom the Epistles were first read in the infant communities of Macedonia and Proconsular Asia—was a method at once less frequently attempted, and more immediately necessary. I wish above all to make the Epistles comprehensible and real. On this account I have constantly deviated from the English version. Of the merits of that version, its incomparable force and melody, it would be impossible to speak with too much reverence, and it only requires the removal of errors which were inevitable to the age in which it was executed, to make it as nearly perfect as any work of man can be. But our very familiarity with it is often a barrier to our due understanding of many passages ; for "words," it has been truly said, "when often repeated, do ossify the very organs of intelligence." My object in translating with-

out reference to the honoured phrases of our English
Bible has expressly been, not only to correct where
correction was required, but also to brighten the edge
of expressions which time has dulled, and to reproduce,
as closely as possible, the exact force and form of the
original, even in those roughnesses, turns of expression,
and unfinished clauses which are rightly modified in
versions intended for public reading. To aim in these
renderings at rhythm or grace of style has been far from
my intention. I have simply tried to adopt the best
reading, to give its due force to each expression, tense,
and particle, and to represent as exactly as is at all compatible with English idiom what St. Paul meant in the
very way in which he said it.

With the same object, I have avoided wearying the
reader with those interminable discussions of often unimportant minutiæ—those endless refutations of impossible
hypotheses—those exhaustive catalogues of untenable
explanations which encumber so many of our Biblical
commentaries. Both as to readings, renderings, and explanations I have given at least a definite conclusion,
and indicated as briefly and comprehensively as possible
the grounds on which it is formed.

In excluding the enumeration of transient opinions,
I have also avoided the embarrassing multiplication of
needless references. When any German book has been
well translated I have referred to the translation of it
by its English title, and I have excluded in every way
the mere semblance of research. In this work, as in
the *Life of Christ*, I have made large use of illustrations from Hebrew literature. The Talmud is becoming

better known every day; the Mishna is open to the
study of every scholar in the magnificent work of
Surenhusius; and the most important treatises of the
Gemara—such as the *Berachôth* and the *Abhoda Zara*—
are now accessible to all, in French and German translations of great learning and accuracy. I have diligently
searched the works of various Jewish scholars, such as
Jost, Grätz, Schwab, Weill, Rabbinowicz, Deutsch,
Derenbourg, Munk, and others; but I have had two
great advantages—first, in the very full collection of
passages from every portion of the Talmud, by Mr. P.
J. Hershon, in his Talmudic Commentaries on Genesis
and Exodus—an English translation of the former of
which is now in the press—and, secondly, in the fact that
every single Talmudic reference in the following pages
has been carefully verified by a learned Jewish clergy-
man—the Rev. M. Wolkenberg, formerly a missionary
to the Jews in Bulgaria. All scholars are aware that
references to the Gemara are in general of a most inaccurate and uncertain character, but I have reason to
hope that, apart, it may be, from a few accidental errata,
every Hebraic reference in the following pages may be
received with absolute reliance.

The most pleasant part of my task remains. It is
to offer my heartfelt thanks to the many friends who
have helped me to revise the following pages, or have
given me the benefit of their kind suggestions. To
one friend in particular—Mr. C. J. Monro, late Fellow
of Trin. Coll., Cambridge—I owe the first expression of
my sincerest gratitude. To the Rev. J. Ll. Davies and the
Rev. Prof. Plumptre I am indebted for an amount of

labour and trouble such as it can be the happiness of few authors to receive from scholars at once so competent and so fully occupied by public and private duties. From the Very Rev. the Dean of Westminster; from Mr. Walter Leaf, Fell. of Trin. Coll., Cambridge, my friend and former pupil; from the Rev. J. E. Kempe, Rector of St. James's, Piccadilly; from Mr. R. Garnett, of the British Museum; and from my valued colleagues in the parish of St. Margaret's, the Rev. H. H. Montgomery and the Rev. J. S. Northcote, I have received valuable advice, or kind assistance in the laborious task of correcting the proof-sheets. The Bishop of Durham had kindly looked over the first few pages, and but for his elevation to his present high position, I might have derived still further benefit from his wide learning and invariable kindness. If my book fail to achieve the purposes for which it was written, I shall at least have enjoyed the long weeks of labour spent in the closest study of the Word of God, and next to this I shall value the remembrance that I received from so many friends, a self-sacrificing kindness which I had so little right to expect, and am so little able to repay.

I desire also to express my best obligations to my Publishers, and the gentlemen connected with their firm, who have spared no labour in seeing these volumes through the press.

After having received such ungrudging aid it would be ungrateful to dwell on the disadvantages in the midst of which this book has been written. I have done my best under the circumstances in which a task

of such dimensions was alone possible; and though I
have fallen far short of my own ideal—though I am
deeply conscious of the many necessary imperfections of
my work—though it is hardly possible that I should
have escaped errors in a book involving so many hundreds
of references, and necessitating the examination of so many
critical and exegetical questions—I still hope that these
volumes will be accepted as furnishing another part of a
humble but faithful endeavour to enable those who read
them to acquire a more thorough knowledge of a large
portion of the Word of God.

F. W. FARRAR.

TABLE OF CONTENTS.

Book I.

THE TRAINING OF THE APOSTLE.

CHAPTER I.

INTRODUCTORY.

PAGE

Various types of the Apostolate—St. Peter and St. John—The place of St. Paul in the History of the Church—His training in Judaism—What we may learn of his Life—Modern Criticism of the Acts of the Apostles—Authorities for the Biography of St. Paul—Records, though fragmentary, suffice for a true estimate—Grandeur of the Apostle's Work .   .   . 1

CHAPTER II.

BOYHOOD IN A HEATHEN CITY.

Date of his Birth—Question of Birthplace—Giscala or Tarsus?—The Scenery of Tarsus—Its History and Trade—Paul's indifference to the beauties of Nature—His Parentage—Early Education—Contact with Paganism—Paganism as seen at Tarsus—Paganism as it was—A decadent culture—Impressions left on the mind of St. Paul—St. Paul a Hebraist—His supposed familiarity with Classical Literature shown to be an untenable opinion 13

CHAPTER III.

THE SCHOOL OF THE RABBI.

Roman Citizenship—School Life at Tarsus and Jerusalem—Gamaliel—Permanent effects of Rabbinic training as traced in the Epistles—St. Paul's knowledge of the Old Testament—His method of quoting and applying the Scriptures—Instances—Rabbinic in form, free in spirit—Freedom from Rabbinic faults—Examples of his allegoric method—St. Paul a Hagadist—The Hagada and the Halacha 40

CHAPTER IV.

SAUL THE PHARISEE.

Early struggles—The minutiæ of Pharisaism—Sense of their insufficiency—Legal blamelessness gave no peace—Pharisaic hypocrisies—Troubled

PAGE

years—Memories of these early doubts never obliterated—Had Saul seen
Jesus?—It is almost certain that he had not—Was he a married man?
—Strong probability that he was 62

CHAPTER V.

ST. PETER AND THE FIRST PENTECOST.

Saul's First Contact with the Christians—Source of their energy—The Resurrection—The Ascension—First Meeting—Election of Matthias—The Upper
Room—Three Temples—The Descent of the Spirit at Pentecost—Earthquake, Wind, and Flame—Tongues—Nature of the Gift—Varying opinions—
Ancient and Modern Views—Glossolaly at Corinth—Apparent nature of the
sign—Derisive Comment—Speech of Peter—Immediate Effects on the
Progress of the Church 83

CHAPTER VI.

EARLY PERSECUTIONS.

Beauty and Power of the Primitive Christian Life—Alarm of the Sanhedrin—
Peter and John—Gamaliel—Toleration and Caution—Critical Arguments
against the Genuineness of his Speech examined—The Tübingen School on
the Acts 105

Book II.

ST. STEPHEN AND THE HELLENISTS.

CHAPTER VII.

THE DIASPORA: HEBRAISM AND HELLENISM.

Preparation for Christianity by three events—Spread of the Greek Language—
Rise of the Roman Empire—Dispersion of the Jews—Its vast Effects—
Its Influence on the Greeks and Romans—Its Influence on the Jews them-
selves—Worked in opposite directions—Pharisaic Jews—Growing Power
of the Scribes—Decay of Spirituality—Liberal Jews—Commerce Cosmo-
politan—Hellenes and Hellenists—Classes of Christians tabulated—Two
Schools of Hellenism—Alexandrian Hellenists—Hebraising Hellenists—
Hellenists among the Christians—Widows—The Seven—Stephen . . 114

CHAPTER VIII.

WORK AND MARTYRDOM OF ST. STEPHEN.

Success of the Seven—Pre-eminent faith of Stephen—Clear Views of the
Kingdom—Tardier Enlightenment of the Apostles—Hollow Semblance of
Union with Judaism—Relation of the Law to the Gospel—Ministry of St.
Stephen—Hellenistic Synagogues—Saul—Power of St. Stephen—Rabbinic
Views of Messiah—Scriptural View of a Suffering Messiah—Suspected
Heresies — Discomfiture and Violence of the Hellenists — St. Stephen

arrested—Charges brought against him—The Trial—" The Face of an
Angel "—The Speech delivered in Greek—Line of Argument—Its consum-
mate Skill—Proofs of its Authenticity—His Method of Refutation and
Demonstration—Sudden Outburst of Indignation—Lawless Proceedings—
" He fell asleep "—Saul 185

Book III.

THE CONVERSION.

CHAPTER IX.

SAUL THE PERSECUTOR.

Age of Saul—His Violence—Severity of the Persecution underrated—" Compelled them to blaspheme "—Flight of the Christians—Continued Fury of
Saul—Asks for Letters to Damascus—The High Priest Theophilus—Aretas 169

CHAPTER X.

THE CONVERSION OF SAUL.

The Commissioner of the Sanhedrin—The Journey to Damascus—Inevitable
Reaction and Reflection—Lonely Musings—Kicking against the Pricks—
Doubts and Difficulties—Noon—The Journey's End—The Vision and the
Voice—Change of Heart—The Spiritual Miracle—Sad Entrance into
Damascus—Ananias—The Conversion as an Evidence of Christianity . 180

CHAPTER XI.

THE RETIREMENT OF ST. PAUL.

Saul a " Nazarene "—Records of this Period fragmentary—His probable
Movements guided by Psychological Considerations—His Gospel not " of
man "—Yearnings for Solitude—Days in Damascus—Sojourn in Arabia—
Origin of the " Stake in the Flesh "—Feelings which it caused—Influence
on the Style of the Epistles—Peculiarites of St. Paul's Language—
Alternating Sensibility and Boldness 205

CHAPTER XII.

THE BEGINNING OF A LONG MARTYRDOM.

" To the Jew first "—Reappearance in Damascus—Saul in the Synagogues—
No ordinary Disputant—The Syllogism of Violence—First Plot to Murder
him—His Escape from Damascus—Journey to Jerusalem 222

CHAPTER XIII.

SAUL'S RECEPTION AT JERUSALEM.

Visit to Jerusalem—Apprehensions and Anticipations—St. Peter's Goodness
of Heart—Saul and James—Contrast of their Character and Epistles—

PAGE

The Intervention of Barnabas—Intercourse with St. Peter—Saul and the Hellenists—Trance and Vision of Saul at Jerusalem—Plot to Murder him —Flight—Silent Period at Tarsus 229

CHAPTER XIV.

GAIUS AND THE JEWS—PEACE OF THE CHURCH.

"Then had the Church rest"—Survey of the Period—Tiberius—Accession of Gaius (Caligula)—Herod Agrippa I.—Persecution of the Jews of Alexandria—Fall of Flaccus—Madness of Gaius—Determined to place his Statue in the Temple—Anguish of the Jews—The Legate Petronius— Embassy of Philo—Murder of Gaius—Accession of Claudius . . . 243

Book IV.

THE RECOGNITION OF THE GENTILES.

CHAPTER XV.

THE SAMARITANS—THE EUNUCH—THE CENTURION.

The brightening Dawn of the Church—"Other Sheep not of this Fold"—Conse- quence of Saul's Persecution—Philip in Samaria—Simon Magus—The Ethiopian Eunuch—Significance of his Baptism—St. Peter at Joppa— House of Simon the Tanner—Two Problems: (1) What was the Relation of the Church to the Gentiles (2) and to the Levitical Law?—Christ and the Mosaic Law—Utterances of the Prophets—Uncertainties of St. Peter —The Tanner's Roof—The Trance—Its Strange Significance and Appro- priateness—"This he said . . . making all meats pure"—Cornelius— "God is no respecter of persons"—Bold initiative of Peter—Ferment at Jerusalem—How it was appeased 256

Book V.

ANTIOCH.

CHAPTER XVI.

THE SECOND CAPITAL OF CHRISTIANITY.

Hellenists boldly preach to the Gentiles—Barnabas at Antioch—Need of a Colleague—He brings Saul from Tarsus—The Third Metropolis of the World, the Second Capital of Christianity—Site and Splendour of Antioch —Its Population—Its Moral Degradation—Scepticism and Credulity— Daphne and its Asylum—The Street Singon—The Name of "Christian"— Its Historic Significance—Given by Gentiles—Christiani and Chrestiani— Not at once adopted by the Church—Marks a Memorable Epoch—Joy of Gentile Converts 284

CHAPTER XVII.

A MARTYRDOM AND A RETRIBUTION.

PAGE

A Year of Happy Work—Another Vision—Agabus and the Famine—Collec-
tions for Poor Brethren of Jerusalem—Paul and Barnabas sent with the
Chaluka—The Royal Family of Adiabene—The Policy of Herod Agrippa I.
—Martyrdom of St James the Elder—Seizure and Escape of Peter—
Agrippa in his Splendour—Smitten of God—St. Mark   304

CHAPTER XVIII.

JUDAISM AND HEATHENISM.

The Church at Antioch—Stirrings of the Missionary Spirit—The Prophets and
the Gentiles—Difficulties of the Work—Hostility of the Jews to the
Gospel—Abrogation of the Law—A Crucified Messiah—Political Timidity
—Hatred of Gentiles for all Jews and especially for Christian Jews—
Depravity of the Heathen World — Influx of Oriental Superstitions—
Despairing Pride of Stoicism—The Voice of the Spirit   322

Book VI.

THE FIRST MISSIONARY JOURNEY.

CHAPTER XIX.

CYPRUS.

"Sent forth by the Holy Ghost"—Ancient Travelling—Prospects of the
Future—Paul, his Physical and Moral Nature—His Extraordinary Gifts—
Barnabas—Mark—Arrival at Cyprus—The Pagan Population—Salamis—
The Syrian Aphrodite—Paphos—Sergius Paulus—Elymas—Just Denuncia-
tion and Judgment—"Saul who also is called Paul"   336

CHAPTER XX.

ANTIOCH IN PISIDIA.

Perga—Defection of Mark—Passes of the Taurus—St. Paul's Absorption in
his one Purpose—Pisidian Antioch—Worship of the Synagogue—The
Parashah and Haphtarah—The Sermon in the Synagogue—Example of
Paul's Method—Power of his Preaching—Its Effect on the Jews—Immediate Results—"We turn to the Gentiles"—Driven from the City   .   . 357

CHAPTER XXI.

THE CLOSE OF THE JOURNEY.

Iconium—Persistent Enmity of the Jews—Lystra—Healing of the Cripple—
Unwelcome Honours—The Fickle Mob—The Stoning—Probable Meeting
with Timothy—Derbe—They Retrace their Steps—Return to Antioch—
Date of the Journey—Effects of Experience on St. Paul—The Apostle of
the Gentiles   377

CHAPTER XXII.

THE CONSULTATION AT JERUSALEM.

PAGE

"Certain from Judæa" visit Antioch—A Hard Dogma—Circumcision—A Crushing Yoke—Paul's Indignation—Reference to Jerusalem—The Delegates from Antioch—Sympathy with them in their Journey—The First Meeting—The Private Conference—The Three won over to St. Paul's Views—Their Request about the Poor—Titus—Was he Circumcised?—Strong Reasons for believing that he was—Motives of St. Paul—The Final Synod—Eager Debate—The Speech of St. Peter—St. James: his Character and Speech—His Scriptural Argument—Final Results—The Synod not a "Council"—The Apostolic Letter—Not a Comprehensive and Final "Decree"—Questions still Unsolved—Certain Genuineness of the Letter—Its Prohibitions 398

CHAPTER XXIII.

ST. PETER AND ST. PAUL AT ANTIOCH.

Joy at Antioch—Ascendency of St. Paul—St. Peter at Antioch—Arrival of "certain from James"—"He separated himself"—Want of Moral Courage —Unhappy Results—Arguments of St. Paul—Character of St. Peter—A Public Rebuke—Effects of the Rebuke—Malignity of the Pseudo Clementine Writings—Mission-Hunger—The Quarrel of Paul and Barnabas—Results of their Separation—Overruled for Good—Barnabas and Mark . 437

CHAPTER XXIV.

BEGINNING OF THE SECOND MISSIONARY JOURNEY—PAUL, SILAS, TIMOTHY—PAUL IN GALATIA.

Paul and Silas—The Route by Land—The Cilician Gates—Derbe—Where is Barnabas?—Lystra—"Timothy, my Son"—His Circumcision and Ordination—The Phrygian and Galatian District—Scanty Details of the Record—The Galatians—Illness of St. Paul—Kindness of the Galatians —Varied Forms of Religion—Pessinus, Ancyra, Tavium—Their course guided by Divine intimations—Troas—The Vision—"Come over into Macedonia and help us"—Meeting with St. Luke—His Character and Influence 454

Book VII.

CHRISTIANITY IN MACEDONIA.

CHAPTER XXV.

PHILIPPI.

The Sail to Neapolis—Philippi—The Place of Prayer—Lydia—Macedonian Women—Characteristics of Philippian Converts—The Girl with a Spirit of Python—The Philippian Prætors—Their Injustice—Scourging—The Dungeon and the Stocks—Prison Psalms—The Earthquake—Conversion of the Jailer—Honourably dismissed from Philippi 482

CHAPTER XXVI.

THESSALONICA AND BERŒA.

PAGE

Thessalonica and its History—Poverty of the Apostles—Philippian Generosity—Success among the Gentiles—Summary of Teaching—St. Paul's State of Mind—The Mob and the Politarchs—Attack on the House of Jason—Flight to Berœa—"These were more noble"—Sopater—Escape to Athens . 504

Book VIII.

CHRISTIANITY IN ACHAIA.

CHAPTER XXVII.

ST. PAUL AT ATHENS.

The Spell of Athens—Its Effect on St. Paul—A City of Statues—Heathen Art—Impression produced on the Mind of St. Paul—Altar "to the Unknown God"—Athens under the Empire—Stoics and Epicureans—Curiosity excited—The Areopagus—A Mock Trial—Speech of St. Paul—Its Power, Tact, and Wisdom—Its many-sided Applications—Mockery at the Resurrection—Results of St. Paul's Visit 521

CHAPTER XXVIII.

ST. PAUL AT CORINTH.

Corinth—Its Population and Trade—Worship of Aphroditè—Aquila and Priscilla—Eager Activity—Crispus—Character of the Corinthian Converts—Effect of Experience on St. Paul's Preaching—Rupture with the Jews—Another Vision—Gallio—Discomfiture of the Jews—Beating of Sosthenes—Superficial Disdain 553

CHAPTER XXIX.

THE FIRST EPISTLE TO THE THESSALONIANS.

Timothy with St. Paul—Advantages of Epistolary Teaching—Importance of bearing its Characteristics in Mind—Vivid Spontaneity of Style—St. Paul's Form of Greeting—The Use of "we" and "I"—Grace and Peace—The Thanksgiving—Personal Appeal against Secret Calumnies—Going off at a Word—Bitter Complaint against the Jews—Doctrinal Section—The Coming of the Lord—Practical Exhortations—Unreasonable Fears as regards the Dead—Be ready—Warning against Insubordination and Despondency—Its Reception—The Second Advent—Conclusion of the First Epistle . 574

CHAPTER XXX.

THE SECOND EPISTLE TO THE THESSALONIANS.

News from Thessalonica—Effects of the First Letter—A New Danger—Eschatological Excitement—"We which are alive and remain"—St. Paul's Meaning—The Day of the Lord—Destruction of the Roman and the

PAGE

Jewish Temples—Object of the Second Epistle—The Epistles Rich in
Details, but Uniform in Method—Consist generally of Six Sections—The
Greeting—Doctrinal and Practical Sections of the Epistle — Moral
Warnings—Autograph Authentication—Passage respecting " the Man of
Sin "—Mysterious Tone of the Language—Reason for this—Similar
Passage in Josephus—What is meant by " the Checker " and " the Check "
—The rest incapable of present explanation 599

APPENDIX.

Excursus I.—The Style of St. Paul as Illustrative of his Character . . 619

Excursus II.—The Rhetoric of St. Paul 625

Excursus III.—The Classic Quotations and Allusions of St. Paul . . . 630

Excursus IV.—St. Paul a Hagadist 638

Excursus V.—Gamaliel and the School of Tübingen 644

Excursus VI.—On Jewish Stoning 647

Excursus VII.—On the Power of the Sanhedrin to Inflict Capital Punishment 648

Excursus VIII.—Damascus under Hareth 650

Excursus IX.—Saul in Arabia 651

Excursus X.—St. Paul's "Stake in the Flesh" 652

Excursus XI.—On Jewish Scourgings 661

Excursus XII.—Apotheosis of Roman Emperors 664

Excursus XIII.—Burdens laid on Proselytes 666

Excursus XIV.—Hatred of the Jews in Classical Antiquity . . . 667

Excursus XV.—Judgment of Early Pagan Writers on Christianity . 669

Excursus XVI.—The Proconsulate of Sergius Paulus 671

Excursus XVII.—St. John and St. Paul 673

Excursus XVIII.—St. Paul in the Clementines 575

LIFE AND WORK OF ST. PAUL.

Book I.
THE TRAINING OF THE APOSTLE.

CHAPTER I.

INTRODUCTORY.

Σκεῦος ἐκλογῆς μοι ἐστὶν οὗτος.—ACTS ix. 15.

OF the twelve men whom Jesus chose to be His companions and heralds during the brief years of His earthly ministry, two alone can be said to have stamped upon the infant Church the impress of their own individuality. These two were John and Simon. Our Lord Himself, by the titles which He gave them, indicated the distinctions of their character, and the pre-eminence of their gifts. John was called a Son of Thunder; Simon was to be known to all ages as Kephas, or Peter, the Apostle of the Foundation stone.[1] To Peter was granted the honour of authoritatively admitting the first uncircumcised Gentile, on equal terms, into the brotherhood of Christ, and he has ever been regarded as the main pillar of the early Church.[2] John, on the other hand, is the Apostle of Love, the favourite Apostle of the Mystic, the chosen Evangelist of those whose inward adoration rises above the level of outward forms. Peter as the first to recognise

---

[1] 1 Pet. ii. 4—8.   [2] Gal. ii. 9.

B

the Eternal Christ, John as the chosen friend of the living Jesus, are the two of that first order of Apostles whose names appear to human eyes to shine with the brightest lustre upon those twelve precious stones, which are the foundations of the New Jerusalem.[1]

Yet there was another, to whom was entrusted a wider, a more fruitful, a more laborious mission; who was to found more numerous churches, to endure intenser sufferings, to attract to the fold of Christ a vaster multitude of followers. On the broad shoulders of St. Peter rested, at first, the support and defence of the new Society; yet his endurance was not tested so terribly as that of him on whom fell daily the "care of all the churches." St. John was the last survivor of the Apostles, and he barely escaped sharing with his brother the glory of being one of the earliest martyrs; yet even his life of long exile and heavy tribulations was a far less awful trial than that of him who counted it but a light and momentary affliction to "die daily," to be "in deaths oft."[2] A third type of the Apostolate was necessary. Besides the Apostle of Catholicity and the Apostle of Love, the Church of Christ needed also "the Apostle of Progress."

In truth it is hardly possible to exaggerate the extent, the permanence, the vast importance, of those services which were rendered to Christianity by Paul of Tarsus. It would have been no mean boast for the most heroic worker that he had toiled more abundantly than such toilers as the Apostles. It would have been a sufficient claim to eternal gratitude to have preached from Jerusalem to Illyricum, from Illyricum to Rome, and, it may be, even to Spain, the Gospel which gave new life to a weary and outworn world. Yet these are, perhaps, the least permanent of the benefits which mankind has reaped

---

[1] Rev. xxi. 14.   [2] 1 Cor. xv. 31; 2 Cor. xi. 23.

from his life and genius. For it is in his Epistles—casual
as was the origin of some of them—that we find the
earliest utterances of that Christian literature to which
the world is indebted for its richest treasures of poetry and
eloquence, of moral wisdom and spiritual consolation. It
is to his intellect, fired by the love and illuminated by
the Spirit of his Lord, that we owe the first systematic
statement, in their mutual connection and inter-depen-
dence, of the great truths of that Mystery of Godliness
which had been hidden from the ages, but was revealed in
the Gospel of the Christ. It is to his undaunted determination, his clear vision, his moral loftiness that we are
indebted for the emancipation of religion from the intolerable yoke of legal observances—the cutting asunder of the
living body of Christianity from the heavy corpse of an
abrogated Levitism.[1] It was he alone who was God's
appointed instrument to render possible the universal
spread of Christianity, and to lay deep in the hearts
of European churches the solid bases of Christendom.
As the Apostle of the Gentiles he was pre-eminently and
necessarily the Apostle of freedom, of culture, of the understanding; yet he has, if possible, a higher glory than
all this, in the fact that he too, more than any other, is
the Apostle who made clear to the religious consciousness
of mankind the "justification by faith" which springs
from the mystic union of the soul with Christ—the
Apostle who has both brought home to numberless Christians in all ages the sense of their own helplessness, and
pointed them most convincingly to the blessedness and
the universality of that redemption which their Saviour
wrought. And hence whenever the faith of Christ has
been most dimmed in the hearts of men, whenever its pure
fires have seemed in greatest danger of being stifled, as in

---

[1] Gal. iv. 9; Rom. viii. 3. (Heb. vii. 18.)

the fifteenth century—under the dead ashes of sensuality,
or quenched, as in the eighteenth century, by the chilling
blasts of scepticism, it is mostly by the influence of his
writings that religious life has been revived.[1]   It was one
of his searching moral precepts—"Let us walk honestly,
as in the day ; not in rioting and drunkenness, not in
chambering and wantonness, not in strife and envying "—
which became to St. Augustine a guiding star out of the
night of deadly moral aberrations.[2]   It was his prevailing
doctrine of free deliverance through the merits of Christ
which, as it had worked in the spirit of Paul himself
to shatter the bonds of Jewish formalism, worked once
more in the soul of Luther to burst the gates of brass,
and break the bars of iron in sunder with which the
Papacy had imprisoned for so many centuries the souls
which God made free.

It has happened not unfrequently in the providence
of God that the destroyer of a creed or system has been
bred and trained in the inmost bosom of the system
which he was destined to shake or to destroy.   Sakya
Mouni had been brought up in Brahminism; Luther had
taken the vows of an Augustinian; Pascal had been
trained as a Jesuit; Spinoza was a Jew; Wesley and
Whitefield were clergymen of the Church of England.   It
was not otherwise with St. Paul.   The victorious enemy
of heathen philosophy and heathen worship had passed his
boyhood amid the heathen surroundings of a philosophic
city.   The deadliest antagonist of Judaic exclusiveness
was by birth a Hebrew of the Hebrews.   The dealer
of the death-wound to the spirit of Pharisaism was a
Pharisee, a son of Pharisees ;[3] had been brought up from

---

[1] See Neander, *Planting*, E.T., p. 78.

[2] Aug. *Confess.* viii. 12—18 ; Krenkel, *Paulus der Ap. d. Heiden*, p. 1.

[3] Acts xxiii. 6 (Phil. iii. 5).   The true reading, υἱὸς Φαρισαίων (א. A, B, C,
Syr., Vulg.) ; he was a Pharisee of the third generation, τριφαρισαῖος.

his youth at Jerusalem at the feet of Gamaliel;[1] had been taught according to the perfect manner of the law of the fathers; had lived "after the most straitest sect" of the Jewish service.[2] As his work differed in many respects from that of the other Apostles, so his training was wholly unlike theirs. Their earliest years had been spent in the villages of Gennesareth and the fisher-huts on the shores of the Sea of Galilee; his in the crowded ghetto of a Pagan capital. They, with few exceptions, were men neither of commanding genius nor strongly marked characteristics; he was a man of intense individuality and marvellous intellectual power. They were "unlearned and ignorant," untrained in the technicalities, inexperienced in the methods, which passed among the Jews for theologic learning; he had sat as a "disciple of the wise "[3] at the feet of the most eminent of the Rabbis, and had been selected as the inquisitorial agent of Priests and Sanhedrists because he surpassed his contemporaries in burning zeal for the traditions of the schools.[4]

This is the man whose career will best enable us to understand the Dawn of Christianity upon the darkness alike of Jew and Gentile; the man who loosed Christianity from the cerements of Judaism, and inspired the world of Paganism with joy and hope. The study of his life will leave upon our minds a fuller conception of the extreme nobleness of the man, and of the truths which he lived and died to teach. And we must consider that life, as far as possible, without traditional bias, and with the determination to see it as it appeared to his contemporaries, as it appeared to Paul himself.

[1] Acts xxii. 3; xxvi. 4.
[2] Acts xxvi. 5. θρησκεία is rather " cult," " external service," than "religion."
[3] The חכם תלמיד, of whose praises and privileges the Talmud is full.
[4] Gal. i. 14, προέκοπτον ἐν τῷ Ἰουδαϊσμῷ (i.e., in Jewish observances), ὑπὲρ κ.τ.λ., περισσοτέρως ζηλωτὴς, κ.τ.λ.

"For if he was a Paul," says St. Chrysostom, "he also was a man,"—nay, more than this, his very infirmities enhanced his greatness. He stands infinitely above the need of indiscriminate panegyric. If we describe him as exempt from all human weakness—if we look at his actions as though it were irreverence to suppose that they ever fell short of his own ideal—we not only describe an impossible character, but we contradict his own reiterated testimonies. It is not a sinless example which we are now called upon to contemplate, but the life of one who, in deep sincerity, called himself "the chief of sinners;" it is the career of one whose ordinary life (βίος) was human, not divine—human in its impetuosity, human in its sensibilities, human, perhaps, in some of its concessions and accommodations; but whose inner life (ζωή) was truly divine in so far as it manifested the workings of the Spirit, in so far as it was dead to the world, and hid with Christ in God.[1] It is utterly alien to the purpose and manner of Scripture to present to us any of our fellow-men in the light of faultless heroes or unapproachable demi-gods. The notion that it is irreverent to suppose a flaw in the conduct of an Apostle is one of those instances of "false humility" which degrade Scripture under pretence of honouring it, and substitute a dead letter-worship for a living docility. From idealised presentments of the lives of our fellow-servants,[2] there would be but little for us to learn; but we *do* learn the greatest and most important of all lessons when we mark in a struggling soul the triumph of the grace of God—when we see a man, weak like ourselves, tempted like ourselves, erring like ourselves, enabled by the force of a sacred purpose to conquer temptation, to trample on selfishness, to rear even upon sins and failures the super-

[1] Βίος, *vita quam vivimus*; ζωή, *vita quâ vivimus*. (Gal. ii. 20.)
[2] Rev. xix. 10.

structure of a great and holy life,—to build (as it were) "the cities of Judah out of the ruined fortresses of Samaria." [1]

It may seem strange if I say that we know the heart of St. Paul to its inmost depths. It is true that, besides a few scattered remnants of ecclesiastical tradition, we have but two sources whence to derive his history— the Acts of the Apostles, and the Epistles of Paul himself; and the day has gone by when we could at once, and without further inquiry, *assume* that both of these sources, in the fullest extent, were absolutely and equally to be relied on. Since Baur wrote his *Paulus*, and Zeller his *Apostelgeschichte*, it has become impossible to make use of the Acts of the Apostles, and the thirteen Epistles commonly attributed to St. Paul, without some justification of the grounds upon which their genuineness is established. To do this exhaustively would require a separate volume, and the work has been already done, and is being done by abler hands than mine. All that is here necessary is to say that I should in no instance make use of any statement in those Epistles of which the genuineness can still be regarded as fairly disputable, if I did not hope to state some of the reasons which appear sufficient to justify my doing so; and that if in any cases the genuineness or proper superscription of any Epistle, or part of an Epistle, seems to me to be a matter of uncertainty, I shall feel no hesitation in expressing such an opinion. Of the Acts of the Apostles I shall have various opportunities to speak incidentally, and, without entering on any separate defence of the book against the assaults of modern critics, I will at present only express my conviction that, even if we admit that it was "an ancient Eirenicon," intended to check the strife of parties by showing that there had been no irreconcilable opposition

[1] Bossuet (1 Kings xv. 22). Acts xiv. 15.

between the views and ordinances of St. Peter and St.
Paul;—even if we concede the obvious principle that
whenever there appears to be any contradiction between
the Acts and the Epistles, the authority of the latter
must be considered paramount;—nay, even if we acknowledge that subjective and artificial considerations may
have had some influence in the form and construction
of the book;—yet the Acts of the Apostles is in all its
main outlines a genuine and trustworthy history. Let
it be granted that in the Acts we have a picture of
essential unity between the followers of the Judaic and
the Pauline schools of thought, which we might conjecture from the Epistles to have been less harmonious
and undisturbed; let it be granted that in the Acts we
more than once see Paul acting in a way which from the
Epistles we should à priori have deemed unlikely. Even
these concessions are fairly disputable; yet in granting them
we only say what is in itself sufficiently obvious, that both
records are confessedly fragmentary. They are fragmentary, of course, because neither of them even professes to
give us any continuous narrative of the Apostle's life.
That life is—roughly speaking—only known to us at
intervals during its central and later period, between the
years A.D. 36 and A.D. 66. It is like a manuscript of
which the beginning and the end are irrecoverably lost.
It is like one of those rivers which spring from unknown
sources, and sink into the ground before they have reached
the sea. But more than this, how incomplete is our
knowledge even of that portion of which these records and
notices remain! Of this fact we can have no more overwhelming proof than we may derive from reading that
"Iliad of woes," the famous passage of the Second Epistle
to the Corinthians, where, driven against his will by the
calumnies of his enemies to an appearance of boastfulness

of which the very notion was abhorrent to him, he is
forced to write a summary sketch of what he had done and
suffered.[1] That enumeration is given long before the end
of his career, and yet of the specific outrages and dangers
there mentioned no less than eleven are not once alluded
to in the Acts, though many others are there mentioned
which were subsequent to that sad enumeration. Not one,
for instance, of the five scourgings with Jewish thongs is
referred to by St. Luke; one only of the three beatings
with Roman rods; not one of the three shipwrecks, though
a later one is so elaborately detailed; no allusion to the
night and day in the deep; two only of what St. Clement
tells us were seven imprisonments.[2] There are even whole
classes of perils to which the writer of the Acts, though
he was certainly at one time a companion of St. Paul,
makes no allusion whatever—as, for instance, the perils of
rivers, the perils of robbers, the perils in the wilderness,
the perils among false brethren, the hunger, the thirst, the
fasting, the cold, the nakedness. And these, which are
thus passed over without notice in the Acts, are in the
Epistles mentioned only so cursorily, so generally, so un-
chronologically, that scarcely one of them can be dwelt
upon and assigned with certainty to its due order of
succession in St. Paul's biography. If this, then, is the
case, who can pretend that in such a life there is not room
for a series of events and actions—even for an exhibition
of phases of character—in the narrative, which neither did
nor could find place in the letters; and for events and
features of character in the letters which find no reflection
in the narrative? For of those letters how many are
preserved? Thirteen only—even if all the thirteen be

---

[1] 2 Cor. xi. 24—33, written about A.D. 57, nearly ten years before his
death.

[2] ἑπτάκις δεσμὰ φορέσας (Ep. 1 ad Cor. 5).

indisputably genuine—out of a much larger multitude which he must undoubtedly have written.[1] And of these thirteen some are separated from others by great intervals of time; some contain scarcely a single particular which can be made to bear on a consecutive biography; and not one is preserved which gives us the earlier stage of his views and experiences before he had set foot on European soil. It is, then, idle to assume that either of our sources must be rejected as untrustworthy because it presents us with fresh aspects of a myriad-sided character; or that events in the narrative must be condemned as scarcely honest inventions because they present no *primâ facie* accordance with what we might otherwise have expected from brief and scattered letters out of the multiplex correspondence of a varied life. If there were anything in the Acts which appeared to me irreconcilable with the certain indications of the Epistles, I should feel no hesitation in rejecting it. But most, if not all, of the objections urged against the credibility of the Acts appear to me—for reasons to be hereafter given—both frivolous and untenable. If there are any passages in that book which have been represented as throwing a shade of inconsistency over the character of the great Apostle, there is no such instance which, however interpreted, does not find its support and justification in his own undoubted works. If men of great learning, eminence, and acuteness had not assumed the contrary, it might have seemed superfluous to say that the records of history, and the experiences of daily life, furnish us with abundant instances of lives narrated with perfect honesty, though they have been presented from opposite points of view; and of events which appear to be contradictory

---

[1] I do not reckon the Epistle to the Hebrews, believing it to be the work of Apollos.

only because the point of reconcilement between them has been forgotten. Further than this, the points of contact between the Acts and the Epistles are numberless, and it must suffice, once for all, to refer to Paley's *Horæ Paulinæ* in proof that even the undesigned coincidences may be counted by scores. To furnish a separate refutation of all the objections which have been brought against the credibility of the Acts of the Apostles, would be a tedious and interminable task; but the actual narrative of the following pages should exhibit a decisive answer to them, unless it can be shown that it fails to combine the separate *data*, or that the attempt to combine them has led to incongruous and impossible results.

I believe, then, that we have enough, and more than enough, still left to us to show what manner of life Paul lived, and what manner of man he was. A biography sketched in outline is often more true and more useful than one that occupies itself with minute detail. We do not in reality know more of a great man because we happen to know the petty circumstances which made up his daily existence, or because a mistaken admiration has handed down to posterity the promiscuous commonplaces of his ordinary correspondence. We know a man truly when we know him at his greatest and his best; we realise his significance for ourselves and for the world when we see him in the noblest activity of his career, on the loftiest summit, and in the fullest glory of his life. There are lives which may be instructive from their very littleness, and it may be well that the biographers of such lives should enter into detail. But of the best and greatest it may be emphatically asserted that to know more about them would only be to know less of them. It is quite possible that if, in the case of one so sensitive and so impetuous as St. Paul, a minute and servile record had preserved for us every hasty expression, every fugitive note, every momentary fall below the loftiest standard, the small souls which ever rejoice at seeing the noblest of their race degraded, even for an instant, to the same dead level as themselves, might have found some things over which to glory.   That such must have been the result we may infer from the energy and sincerity of self-condemnation with which the Apostle recognises his own imperfections. But such miserable records, even had they been entirely truthful, would only have obscured for us the true Paul —Paul as he stands in the light of history; Paul as he is preserved for us in the records of Christianity; Paul ener- getic as Peter, and contemplative as John; Paul the hero of unselfishness; Paul the mighty champion of spiritual freedom; Paul a greater preacher than Chrysostom, a greater missionary than Xavier, a greater reformer than Luther, a greater theologian than St. Thomas of Aqui- num; Paul the inspired Apostle of the Gentiles, the slave of the Lord Jesus Christ.

CHAPTER II.

BOYHOOD IN A HEATHEN CITY.

Οὐκ ἀσήμου πόλεως πολίτης.—ACTS xxi. 39.

THOUGH we cannot state with perfect accuracy the date either of the birth or death of the great Apostle of the Gentiles, both may be inferred within narrow limits. When he is first mentioned, on the occasion of Stephen's martyrdom, he is called a young man,[1] and when he wrote the Epistle to Philemon he calls himself Paul the aged.[2] Now, although the words νεανίας and πρεσβύτης were used vaguely in ancient times, and though the exact limits of "youth" and "age" were as indeterminate then as they have ever been, yet, since we learn that immediately after the death of Stephen, Saul was intrusted with a most important mission, and was, in all probability, a member of the Sanhedrin, he must at that time have been a man of thirty. Now, the martyrdom of Stephen probably took place early in A.D. 37, and the Epistle to Philemon was written about A.D. 63. At the latter period, therefore, he would have been less than sixty years old, and this may seem too young to claim the title of "the aged." But "age" is a very relative term, and one who had

---

[1] Acts vii. 58.

[2] Philem., verse 9. It should, indeed, be mentioned that whether we read πρεσβύτης or πρεσβευτὴς, the meaning may be, "Paul an ambassador, ay, and now even a chained ambassador, of Jesus Christ." Compare the fine antithesis, ὑπὲρ οὗ πρεσβεύω ἐν ἁλύσει, "I am an ambassador in fetters" (Eph. vi. 20). The tone of his later writings is, however, that of an old man.

been scourged, and lashed, and stoned, and imprisoned, and shipwrecked—one who, for so many years, besides the heavy burden of mental anguish and responsibility, had been "scorched by the heat of Sirius and tossed by the violence of Euroclydon,"[1] might well have felt himself an old and outworn man when he wrote from his Roman prison at the age of threescore years.[2] It is, therefore, tolerably certain that he was born during the first ten years of our era, and probable that he was born about A.D. 3. Since, then, our received Dionysian era is now known to be four years too early, the birth of Christ's greatest follower happened in the same decade as that of our Lord Himself.[3]

But all the circumstances which surrounded the cradle and infancy of the infant Saul were widely different from those amid which his Lord had grown to boyhood. It was in an obscure and lonely village of Palestine, amid surroundings almost exclusively Judaic, that Jesus "grew in wisdom and stature and favour with God and man;" but Saul passed his earliest years in the famous capital of a Roman province, and must have recalled, with his first conscious reminiscences, the language and customs of the Pagan world.

There is no sufficient reason to doubt the entire accuracy of the expression " born in Tarsus," which is attributed to St. Paul in his Hebrew speech to the infuriated

[1] Jer. Taylor.

[2] Roger Bacon calls himself "senem," apparently at fifty-three, and Sir Walter Scott speaks of himself as a "grey old man" at fifty-five. (See Lightfoot, *Colossians*, p. 404.) According to Philo a man was *νεανίας* between twenty-one and twenty-eight; but his distinctions are purely artificial. It seems that a man might be called *νεανίας* and even *νεανίσκος* till forty. (Xen. *Mem.* i. 2, 35; Krüger, *Vit. Xen.* 12.)

[3] These dates agree fairly with the statement of the Pseudo-Chrysostom (*Orat. Encom. in Pet. et Paul.*, *Opp.* viii., ed. Montfaucon), that he had been for thirty-five years a servant of Christ, and was martyred at the age of sixty-eight.

multitude from the steps of the Tower of Antonia.[1] To assert that the speeches in the Acts could not have attained to verbal exactness may be true of some of them, but, on the other hand, those who on such grounds as these disparage the work of St. Luke, as a mere " treatise with an object," must bear in mind that it would, in this point of view, have been far more to the purpose if he had made St. Paul assert that he was born in a Jewish town. We must, therefore, reject the curious and twice-repeated assertion of St. Jerome,[2] that the Apostle was born at Giscala,[3] and had been taken to Tarsus by his parents when they left their native city, in consequence of its devastation by the Romans. The assertion is indeed discredited because it is mixed up with what appears to be a flagrant anachronism as to the date at which Giscala was destroyed.[4] It is, however, worthy of attention. St. Jerome, from his thorough familiarity with the Holy Land, in which he spent so many years of his life, has preserved for us several authentic fragments of tradition, and we may feel sure that he would not arbitrarily have set aside a general belief founded upon a distinct statement in the Acts of the Apostles. If in this matter

---

[1] Acts xxii. 3.

[2] Jer. de Viris Illustr. 5: "De tribu Benjamin et oppido Judaeae Giscalis fuit, quo a Romanis capto, cum parentibus suis Tarsum Ciliciae commigravit." It has been again and again asserted that St. Jerome rejects or discredits this tradition in his Commentary on Philemon (Opp. iv. 454), where he says that some understood the term "my fellow-prisoner" to mean that Epaphras had been taken captive at Giscala at the same time as Paul, and had been settled in Colossae. Even Neander (Planting, p. 79) follows this current error, on the ground that Jerome says, "Quis sit Epaphras concaptivus Pauli talem fabulam accepimus." But that fabula does not here mean "false account," as he translates it, is sufficiently proved by the fact that St. Jerome continues, "Quod si ita EST, possumus et Epaphram illo tempore captum suspicari, quo captus est Paulus," &c.

[3] Giscala, now El-Jish, was the last place in Galilee that held out against the Romans. (Jos. B. J. ii. 20, § 6; iv. 2, §§ 1—5.)

[4] It was taken A.D. 67.

pure invention had been at work, it is almost inconceivable that any one should have singled out for distinction so insignificant a spot as Giscala, which is not once mentioned in the Bible, and which acquired its sole notoriety from its connexion with the zealot Judas.[1] We may, therefore, fairly assume that the tradition mentioned by St. Jerome is so far true that the parents or grandparents of St. Paul had been Galilæans and had, from some cause or other—though it cannot have been the cause which the tradition assigned—been compelled to migrate from Giscala to the busy capital of Pagan Cilicia.

If this be the case, it helps, as St. Jerome himself points out, to explain another difficulty. St. Paul, on every possible occasion, assumes and glories in the title not only of "an Israelite,"[2] which may be regarded as a "name of honour," but also of "a Hebrew"—"a Hebrew of the Hebrews."[3] Now certainly, in its proper and technical sense, the word "Hebrew" is the direct opposite of "Hellenist,"[4] and St. Paul, if brought up at Tarsus, could only strictly be egarded as a Jew of the Dispersion—a Jew of that vast bdy who, even when they were not ignorant of Hebrew—as even the most learned of them sometimes were—still spoke Greek as their native tongue.[5] It may, of course, be said that St. Paul uses the word Hebrew only in its general sense, and that he meant to imply by it that he was not a Hellenist to the same extent that, for instance, even so learned and eminent a Jew as Philo was, who,

[1] Jos. A J. vi. 21, § 1; Vit. 10. He calls it Πολιχνη.
[2] John i. 47; Acts xiii. 16; Rom. ix. 4.
[3] 2 Cor. xi. 22; Phil. iii. 5.
[4] See Acts vi. 1, and infra, p. 125.
[5] "Parentum conditionem adolescentulum Paulum secutum, et sic posse stare illud, quod de se ipso testatur, 'Hebraei sunt?' et ego, &c., quae illum Judaeum magis indicant, quam Tarsensem" (Jer.).

with all his great ability, did not know either the Biblical
Hebrew or the Aramaic vernacular, which was still called
by that name.[1] Perhaps St. Paul spoke Aramaic with
equal or greater fluency than he spoke Greek itself;[2]
and his knowledge of Hebrew may be inferred from his
custom of sometimes reverting to the Hebrew scriptures
in the original when the LXX. version was less suitable
to his purpose. It is an interesting, though undesigned,[3]
confirmation of this fact, that the Divine Vision on the
road to Damascus spoke to him, at the supreme moment
of his life, in the language which was evidently the
language of his own inmost thoughts. As one, therefore, to whom the Hebrew of that day was a sort of
mother-tongue, and the Hebrew of the Bible an acquired
language, St. Paul might call himself a Hebrew, though
technically speaking he was also a Hellenist; and the
term would be still more precise and cogent if his parents
and forefathers had, almost till the time of his birth, been
Palestinian Jews.

The Tarsus in which St. Paul was born was very
different from the dirty, squalid, and ruinous Mohammedan
city which still bears the name and stands upon the site.
The natural features of the city, indeed, remain unchanged:
the fertile plain still surrounds it; the snowy mountains
of the chain of Taurus still look down on it; the bright
swift stream of the Cydnus still refreshes it.[4] But with
these scenes of beauty and majesty we are the less con-

[1] Philo's ignorance of Hebrew is generally admitted.

[2] Acts xxi. 40: τῇ Ἑβραΐδι διαλέκτῳ—i.e., of course, the Syriac. These
Jews of Palestine would for the most part be able to understand the Bible,
if not in the original Hebrew, at any rate through the aid of a paraphrast.

[3] E.g., in 1 Cor. iii. 19; 2 Cor. viii. 15; 2 Tim. ii. 19. Whether there
existed any Volksbibel of extracts besides the LXX. I will not discuss. See
Hilgenfeld, Zeitschr. xviii. (1875), p. 118.

[4] The Cydnus no longer, however, flows through Tersoos as it did (Strabo,
xiv. 5; Plin. H. N. vi. 22; Beaufort's Karamania, 271 sq.).

C

cerned, because they seem to have had no influence over
the mind of the youthful Saul. We can well imagine
how, in a nature differently constituted, they would have
been like a continual inspiration ; how they would have
melted into the very imagery of his thoughts; how, again
and again, in crowded cities and foul prisons, they would have

> " Flashed upon that inward eye
> Which is the bliss of solitude."

The scenes in which the whole life of David had been
spent were far less majestic, as well as far less varied,
than many of those in which the lot of St. Paul was
cast; yet the Psalms of David are a very handbook of
poetic description, while in the Epistles of St. Paul we
only breathe the air of cities and synagogues.   He alludes
indeed, to the Temple not made with hands, but never
to its mountain pillars, and but once to its nightly stars.[1]
To David the whole visible universe is but one vast House
of God, in which, like angelic ministrants, the fire and
hail, snow and vapour, wind and storm, fulfil His word.
With St. Paul—though he, too, is well aware that " the
invisible things of Him from the creation of the world
are clearly visible, being apprehended by the things that
He hath made, even His eternal power and divinity "—
yet to him this was an indisputable axiom, not a conviction constantly renewed with admiration and delight.
There are few writers who, to judge solely from their
writings, seem to have been less moved by the beauties
of the external world.   Though he had sailed again and
again across the blue Mediterranean, and must have been
familiar with the beauty of those Isles of Greece—

> " Where burning Sappho loved and sung,
> Where grew the arts of war and peace,
> Where Delos rose, and Phœbus sprung ; "

[1] Acts xvii. 24 ; 1 Cor. xv. 41.

though he had again and again traversed the pine-clad gorges of the Asian hills, and seen Ida, and Olympus, and Parnassus, in all their majesty; though his life had been endangered in mountain torrents and stormy waves, and he must have often wandered as a child along the banks of his native stream, to see the place where it roars in cataracts over its rocky course—his soul was so entirely absorbed in the mighty moral and spiritual truths which it was his great mission to proclaim, that not by one verse, scarcely even by a single expression, in all his letters, does he indicate the faintest gleam of delight or wonder in the glories of Nature. There is, indeed, an exquisite passage in his speech at Lystra on the goodness of "the living God, which made heaven and earth, and the sea, and all things that are therein," and "left not Himself without witness, in that He did good, and gave us rain from heaven, and fruitful seasons, filling our hearts with food and gladness."[1] But in this case Barnabas had some share in the address, which even if it do not, as has been conjectured,[2] refer to the fragment of some choral song, is yet, in tone and substance, directly analogous to passages of the Old Testament.[3] And apart from this allusion, I cannot find a single word which shows that Paul had even the smallest susceptibility for the works of Nature. There are souls in which the burning heat of some transfusing purpose calcines every other thought, every other desire, every other admiration; and St. Paul's was one. His life was absorbingly, if not solely and exclusively, the spiritual life—the life which is utterly dead to every other interest of the groaning and travailing creation, the life hid with Christ in God. He sees the universe of God only as it is reflected in the heart and life of man.

---

[1] Acts xiv. 17. [2] By Mr. Humphry, *ad loc.*
[3] Job v. 10; Ps. civ. 16, cxlvii. 8, 9.

It is true—as Humboldt has shown in his *Cosmos*—
that what is called the sentimental love of Nature is a
modern rather than an ancient feeling.[1] In St. Paul,
however, this indifference to the outer world is neither
due to his antiquity nor to his Semitic birth, but solely
to his individual character. The poetry of the Old Testament is full of the tenderness and life of the pastures
of Palestine. In the discourses and conversations of
our Lord we find frequent allusions to the loveliness of
the flowers, the joyous carelessness of birds, the shifting
winds, the red glow of morning and evening clouds.
St. Paul's inobservance of these things—for the total
absence of the remotest allusion to them by way of even
passing illustration amounts to a proof that they did not
deeply stir his heart—was doubtless due to the expulsive
power and paramount importance of other thoughts. It
may, however, have been due also to that early training
which made him more familiar with crowded assemblies
and thronged bazaars than with the sights and sounds of
Nature.[2] It is at any rate remarkable that the only
elaborate illustration which he draws from Nature, turns
not on a natural phenomenon but on an artificial process,
and that even this process—if not absolutely unknown

---

[1] Compare the surprise expressed by the Athenian youth at Socrates'
description of the lovely scene at the beginning of the *Phaedrus*, § 10,
Σὺ δέ γε ὦ θαυμάσιε ἀτοπώτατός τις φαίνει. There is an admirable chapter on this
subject in Friedländer, *Sittengesch. Roms.* vii. 5, § 3. The reader will recall
the analogous cases of St. Bernard riding all day along the Lake of Geneva,
and asking in the evening where it was; of Calvin showing no trace of delight
in the beauties of Switzerland; and of Whitefield, who seems not to have
borrowed a single impression or illustration from his thirteen voyages
across the Atlantic and his travels from Georgia to Boston.

[2] " For I was bred,
In the great city, pent 'mid cloisters dim,
And saw nought lovely save the sky and stars."
                                        Coleridge.

to the ancients—was the exact opposite of the one most commonly adopted.[1]

But if St. Paul derived no traceable influence from the scenery with which Tarsus is surrounded, if no voices from the neighbouring mountains or the neighbouring sea mingled with the many and varied tones of his impassioned utterance, other results of this providential training may be easily observed, both in his language and in his life.

The very position of Tarsus made it a centre of commercial enterprise and political power. Situated on a navigable stream by which it communicated with the eastern-most bay of the Mediterranean, and lying on a fruitful plain under that pass over the Taurus which was known as "the Cilician gates," while by the Amanid and Syrian gates it communicated with Syria, it was so necessary as a central emporium that even the error of its having embraced the side of Antony in the civil war hardly disturbed its fame and prosperity.[2] It was here that Cleopatra held

---

[1] I allude to the famous illustration of the wild olive graft (Rom. xi. 16—25). St. Paul's argument requires that a *wild* slip should have been budded upon a *fruitful* tree—viz., the ἀγριέλαιος of heathendom on the ἐλαία of Judaism. But it is scarcely needful to remark that this is never done, but the reverse—namely, the grafting of a fruitful scion on a wild stock. The olive shoot would be grafted on the oleaster, not the oleaster on the olive (Aug. *in* Ps. lxxii.). It is true that St. Paul here cares solely for the general analogy, and would have been entirely indifferent to its non-accordance with the ordinary method of ἐγκεντρισμός. Indeed, as he says that it is παρὰ φύσιν (xi. 24), it seems needless to show that this kind of grafting was ever really practised. Yet the illustration would, under these circumstances, hardly have been used by a writer more familiar with the facts of Nature. The notion that St. Paul alluded to the much rarer African custom of grafting oleaster (or Ethiopic olive) on olive, *to strengthen the latter* (cf. Plin. *H. N.* xvii. 18; Colum. *De re Rust.* v. 9; Palladius; &c.), is most unlikely, if only for the reason that it destroys the whole force of the truth which he is desiring to inculcate. (*See* Ewbank, ii. 112; Tholuck, *Rom.* 617; Meyer, 343.) He may have known the proverb, ἀκαρπότερον ἀγριελαίου. See, however, a somewhat different view in Thomson, *Land and Book*, p. 53.

[2] Tarsus resisted the party of Brutus and Cassius, but was conquered by

that famous meeting with the Roman Triumvir which Shakspeare has immortalised, when she rowed up the silver Cydnus, and

> " The barge she sat in like a burnished throne
> Burnt on the water; the poop was beaten gold,
> Purple the sails, and so perfumèd that
> The winds were love-sick with them."

Yet it continued to flourish under the rule of Augustus, and enjoyed the distinction of being both a capital and a free city—*libera* and *immunis*. It was from Tarsus that the vast masses of timber, hewn in the forests of Taurus, were floated down the river to the Mediterranean dockyards; it was here that the vessels were unladen which brought to Asia the treasures of Europe; it was here that much of the wealth of Asia Minor was accumulated before it was despatched to Greece and Italy. On the coins of the city she is represented as seated amid bales of various merchandise. The bright and busy life of the streets and markets must have been the earliest scenes which attracted the notice of the youthful Saul. The dishonesty which he had witnessed in its trade may have suggested to him his metaphors of "huckstering" and " adulterating" the word of life;[1] and he may have borrowed a metaphor from the names and marks of the owners stamped upon the goods which lay upon the quays,[2] and from the earnest-money paid by the purchasers.[3] It may even have been the assembly of the free city which made him more readily adopt from the Septuagint that name

Lucius Rufus, B.C. 43, and many Tarsians were sold as slaves to pay the fine of 1,500 talents which he inflicted on the city. (Appian, *Bell. Civ.* iv. 64.) Τάρσος . . γὰρ αὐτοῖς τῶν πόλεων ἀξιολογωτάτη μητρόπολις οὖσα (Jos. *Antt.* i. 6, § 1).

[1] 2 Cor. ii. 17, καπηλεύοντες; iv. 2, δολοῦντες.
[2] Eph. i. 13; iv. 30, ἐσφραγίσθητε.
[3] 2 Cor. i. 22, ἀρραβῶν.

of Ecclesia for the Church of Christ's elect of which his
Epistles furnish the earliest instances.[1]

It was his birth at Tarsus which also determined the
trade in which, during so many days and nights of toil
and self-denial, the Apostle earned his daily bread. The
staple manufacture of the city was the weaving, first into
ropes, then into tent-covers and garments, of the hair
which was supplied in boundless quantities by the goat
flocks of the Taurus.[2] As the making of these *cilicia* was
unskilled labour of the commonest sort, the trade of tent-
maker[3] was one both lightly esteemed and miserably paid.
It must not, however, be inferred from this that the family
of St. Paul were people of low position. The learning of
a trade was a duty enjoined by the Rabbis on the parents
of every Jewish boy.[4] The wisdom of the rule became
apparent in the case of Paul, as doubtless of hundreds
besides, when the changes and chances of life compelled
him to earn his own livelihood by manual labour. It is

[1] אַר. 1 Kings xii. 2 (LXX.) The word "Church," in its more technical
modern sense (as in Eph. and Col.), is developed out of the simpler meaning
of *congregation* in St. Paul's earlier Epistles.

[2] See Philo, *De Victim.* 836; Plin. *H. N.* v. 32.

[3] σκηνοποιὸς, Acts xviii. 3; σκηνορράφος, Ps. Chrys. *Orat. Encon.* (*Opp.* viii. 8,
Montfauc.). When Chrysostom calls him a σκυτοτόμος, "leather-cutter" (*Hom.*
iv. 3, p. 864, on 2 Tim. ii.), this can hardly be correct, because such a trade
would not be favoured by strict Pharisees. On the use of *cilicium* for tents
see Veget. *Milit.* iv. 6; Serv. ad Virg. *Georg.* iii. 313. It served for many
other purposes, as garden rugs, mantelets, shoes, and beds. (Colum. xii. 46;
Liv. xxxviii. 7; Mart. xiv. 140; Jer. *Ep.* 108.) To handle the "*olentis barba
mariti*" could not have been a pleasant trade. It was "bought from the
shepherds of Taurus, and sold to Greek shippers of the Levant." To this
day *cilice* means hair-cloth in French.

[4] On this subject see my *Life of Christ*, i. p. 82, *n.* Gamaliel himself
was the author of the celebrated aphorism, that "learning of any kind
(תורה כל, *i.e.*, even the advanced study of the Law) unaccompanied by a trade
ends in nothing, and leads to sin" (*Pirke Abhôth*, ii. 2). R. Judah said truly
that "labour honours the labourer" (*Nedarim*, f. 49, 2); R. Meir said, "Let a
man always teach his son pure and easy trades" (Toseft. in *Kidd.* f. 82, 1);
R. Judah says, that not to teach one's son a trade is like teaching him robbery
(*Kiddushin*, f. 30, 2).

clear, from the education provided for Paul by his parents,
that they could little indeed have conjectured how absolutely their son would be reduced to depend on a toil so
miserable and so unremunerative.[1] But though we see
how much he felt the burden of the wretched labour by
which he determined to earn his own bread rather than
trespass on the charity of his converts,[2] yet it had one
advantage in being so absolutely mechanical as to leave the
thoughts entirely free. While he plaited the black, strong-
scented goat's hair, he might be soaring in thought to the
inmost heaven, or holding high converse with Apollos or
Aquila, with Luke or Timothy, on the loftiest themes
which can engage the mind of man.

Before considering further the influence exercised by
his birthplace on the future fortunes of St. Paul, we must
pause to inquire what can be discovered about his immediate family. It must be admitted that we can ascertain
but little. Their possession, by whatever means, of the
Roman citizenship—the mere fact of their leaving Palestine, perhaps only a short time before Paul's birth, to
become units in the vast multitude of the Jews of the
Dispersion—the fact, too, that so many of St. Paul's
"kinsmen" bear Greek and Latin names,[3] and lived in
Rome or in Ephesus,[4] might, at first sight, lead us to suppose that his whole family were of Hellenising tendencies.
On the other hand, we know nothing of the reasons which

---

[1] The reason why he was taught this particular trade may have been
purely local. Possibly his father had been taught the same trade as a boy.
" A man should not change his trade, nor that of his father," says R. Yochanan;
for it is said, " Hiram of Tyre was a widow's son, . . . and his father was . . .
a worker in brass " (1 Kings vii. 13, 14); *Erechin*, f. 16, 2.

[2] 1 Thess. ii. 6, 9 ; 2 Thess. iii. 8; 1 Cor. ix. 12, 15.

[3] Rom. xvi. 7; Andronicus, Junia, or perhaps Junias (=Junianus); 11,
Herodion; 21, Lucius, Jason, Sosipater (συγγενεῖς).

[4] See *infra, ad loc.*, for the question whether ch. xvi. is a genuine portion
of the Epistle to the Romans.

may have compelled them to leave Palestine, and we
have only the vaguest conjectures as to their possession
of the franchise. Even if it be certain that συγγενεῖς
means "kinsmen" in our sense of the word, and not,
as Olshausen thinks, "fellow-countrymen,"[1] it was so
common for Jews to have a second name, which they
adopted during their residence in heathen countries,
that Andronicus and the others, whom he salutes in the
last chapter of the Epistle to the Romans, may all have
been genuine Hebrews. The real name of Jason, for
instance, may have been Jesus, just as the real name of
Paul was Saul.[2] However this may be, the thorough
Hebraism of the family appears in many ways. Paul's
father and grandfather had been Pharisees,[3] and were,
therefore, most strict observers of the Mosaic law. They
had so little forgotten their extraction from the tribe of
Benjamin—one of the two tribes which had remained
faithful to the covenant—that they called their son Saul,[4]
partly perhaps because the name, like Theætetus, means
"asked" (of God), and partly because it was the name of
that unfortunate hero-king of their native tribe, whose sad
fate seems for many ages to have rendered his very name
unpopular.[5] They sent him, probably not later than the age
of thirteen, to be trained at the feet of Gamaliel. They
seem to have had a married daughter in Jerusalem, whose
son, on one memorable occasion, saved Paul's life.[6] Though

---

[1] As in Rom. ix. 3.

[2] When a Greek or Roman name bore any resemblance in sound to a Jewish
one, it was obviously convenient for the Jew to make so slight a change. Thus
Dosthai became Dositheus; Tarphon, Tryphon; Eliakim, Alkimos, &c.

[3] Acts xxiii. 6.   [4] שָׁאוּל, Shaûl.

[5] It is found as a Hebrew name in the Pentateuch (Gen. xxxvi. 37;
xlvi. 10; Ex. vi. 15; Numb. xxvi. 13); but after the death of King Saul it
does not occur till the time of the Apostle, and again later in Josephus
(*Antt.* xx. 9, 4; *B. J.* ii. 17, 4; Krenkel, *Paulus*, p. 217).

[6] Acts xxiii. 16.

they must have ordinarily used the Septuagint version of the Bible, from which the great majority of the Apostle's quotations are taken,[1] and from which nearly his whole theological phraseology is derived, they yet trained him to use Aramaic as his native tongue, and to read the Scriptures —an accomplishment not possessed by many learned Jewish Hellenists—in their own venerable original Hebrew.[2]

That St. Paul was a "Hebraist" in the fullest sense of the word is clear from almost every verse of his Epistles. He reckons time by the Hebrew calendar. He makes constant allusion to Jewish customs, Jewish laws, and Jewish festivals. His metaphors and turns of expression are derived with great frequency from that quiet family life for which the Jews have been in all ages distinguished. Though he writes in Greek, it is not by any means in the Greek of the schools,[3] or the Greek which, in spite of its occasional antitheses and paronomasias, would have been found tolerable by the rhetoricians of his native city. The famous critic Longinus does indeed, if the passage be genuine, praise him as the master of a dogmatic style; but certainly a Tarsian professor or a philosopher of Athens would have been inclined to ridicule his Hebraic peculiarities, awkward anakolutha, harshly-mingled metaphors, strange forms, and irregular constructions.[4] St. Jerome, criticising the οὐ κατενάρκησα ὑμῶν of

---

[1] There are about 278 quotations from the Old Testament in the New. Of these 53 are identical in the Hebrew, Septuagint, and New Testament; in 10 the Septuagint is correctly altered; in 76 it is altered incorrectly—i.e., into greater divergence from the Hebrew; in 37 it is accepted where it differs from the Hebrew; in 99 all three differ; and there are 3 doubtful allusions. (See Turpie, *The Old Testament in the New*, p. 267, and *passim*.)

[2] V. *supra*, p. 16.

[3] Among numerous explanations of the πηλίκοις γράμμασιν of Gal. vi. 11, one is that his Greek letters were so ill-formed, from want of practice, as to look almost laughable.

[4] See *infra*, Excursus I., "The Style of St. Paul;" and Excursus II., "Rhetoric of St. Paul."

2 Cor. xi. 9, xii. 13—which in our version is rendered,
"I was not burdensome to you," but appears to mean
literally, "I did not benumb you"—speaks of the
numerous *cilicisms* of his style; and it is probable that
such there were, though they can hardly be detected with
certainty by a modern reader.[1]   For though Tarsus was
a city of advanced culture, Cilicia was as intellectually
barbarous as it was morally despicable.   The proper
language of Cilicia was a dialect of Phœnician,[2] and the
Greek spoken by some of the cities was so faulty as
to have originated the term "solecism," which has been
perpetuated in all languages to indicate impossible
constructions.[3]

The residence of a Jew in a foreign city might, of
course, tend to undermine his national religion, and make
him indifferent to his hereditary customs.   It might,
however, produce an effect directly the reverse of this.
There had been abundant instances of Hellenistic Jews
who Hellenised in matters far more serious than the
language which they spoke; but, on the other hand, the
Jews, as a nation, have ever shown an almost miraculous
vitality, and so far from being denationalised by a home

---

[1] "Multa sunt verba, quibus juxta morem urbis et provinciae suae, fami-
liarius Apostolus utitur: e quibus exempli gratiâ pauca ponenda sunt."
He refers to κατενάρκησα (2 Cor. xi. 9), ὑπὸ ἀνθρωπίνης ἡμέρας (1 Cor. iv. 3), and
καταβραβευέτω (Col. ii. 18); and adds, "Quibus, et aliis multis, usque hodie
utuntur Cilices" (Jer. *Ep. ad Algas*, qu. 10).   Wetstein, however, adduces
ἀπονάρκάω, from Plut. *De Liber. Educ.* p. 8, and ναρκάω occurs in the LXX.
(Gen. xxxii. 25, 32; Job xxxiii. 19) and in Jos. *Antt.* viii. 8, § 5; νάρκη is the
torpedo or *gymnotus*.   Since καταναρκάω is only found in Hippocrates, Dr.
Plumptre thinks it may have been a medical word in vogue in the schools of
Tarsus.   Gregory of Nyssa, on 1 Cor. xv. 28, quotes ἐκένωσεν (Phil. ii. 7),
ὁμειρόμενοι (1 Thess. ii. 8), περπερεύεται (1 Cor. xiii. 4), ἐριθείας (Rom. ii. 8), &c.,
as instances of St. Paul's autocracy over words.

[2] See Hdt. i. 74, vii. 91; Xen. *Anab.* b. ii. 26.

[3] Σολοικισμός.   See Strabo, p. 663; Diog. Laert. i. 51.   But the derivation
from Soli is not certain.

among the heathen, have only been confirmed in the intensity of their patriotism and their faith. We know that this had been the case with that numerous and important body, the Jews of Tarsus. In this respect they differed considerably from the Jews of Alexandria. They could not have been exempt from that hatred which has through so many ages wronged and dishonoured their noble race, and which was already virulent among the Romans of that day. All that we hear about them shows that the Cilician Jews were as capable as any of their brethren of repaying hate with double hatred, and scorn with double scorn. They would be all the more likely to do so from the condition of things around them. The belief in Paganism was more firmly rooted in the provinces than in Italy, and was specially vigorous in Tarsus—in this respect no unfitting burial-place for Julian the Apostate. No ages are worse, no places more corrupt, than those that draw the iridescent film of an intellectual culture over the deep stagnancy of moral degradation. And this was the condition of Tarsus. The seat of a celebrated school of letters, it was at the same time the metropolis of a province so low in universal estimation that it was counted among the τρία κάππα κάκιστα —the three most villainous k's of antiquity, Kappadokia, Kilikia, and Krete. What religion there was at this period had chiefly assumed an orgiastic and oriental character, and the popular faith of many even in Rome was a strange mixture of Greek, Roman, Egyptian, Phrygian, Phœnician, and Jewish elements. The wild, fanatical enthusiasms of the Eastern cults shook with new sensations of mad sensuality and weird superstition the feeble and jaded despair of Aryan Paganism. The Tarsian idolatry was composed of these mingled elements. There, in Plutarch's time, a generation after St. Paul, the sword of Apollo, miraculously preserved from decay and rust, was still displayed. Hermes Eriounios, or the luck-bringer, still appears, purse in hand, upon their coins. Æsculapius was still believed to manifest his power and presence in the neighbouring Ægæ.[1] But the traditional founder of the city was the Assyrian, Sardanapalus, whose semi-historical existence was confused, in the then syncretism of Pagan worship, with various representatives of the sun-god—the Asiatic Sandan, the Phœnician Baal, and the Grecian Hercules. The gross allusiveness and origin of this worship, its connection with the very types and ideals of luxurious effeminacy, unbounded gluttony, and brutal licence, were quite sufficient to awake the indignant loathing of each true-hearted Jew; and these revolts of natural antipathy in the hearts of a people in whom true religion has ever been united with personal purity would be intensified with patriotic disgust when they saw that, at the main festival of this degraded cult the effeminate Sardanapalus and the masculine Semiramis—each equally detestable—were worshipped with rites which externally resembled the pure and thankful rejoicings of the Feast of Tabernacles. St. Paul must have witnessed this festival. He must have seen at Anchiale the most defiant symbol of cynical contentment with all which is merely animal in the statue of Sardanapalus, represented as snapping his fingers while he uttered the sentiment engraved upon the pedestal—

"Eat, drink, enjoy thyself; the rest is nothing."[2]

The result which such spectacles and such sentiments

---

[1] *De Def. Orac.* 41; Hausrath, pp. 7—9. See, too, Plutarch, περὶ δεισιδαιμονίας καὶ ἀθεότητος, ii.; Neander, *Ch. Hist.* i. 15 sq.

[2] Strabo, xiv. 4; Athen. xii. p. 529; Cic. *Tusc. Disp.* v. 35. Hausrath, p. 7, finds a reminiscence of this in 1 Cor. xv. 32, which may, however, have been quite as probably derived from the wide-spread fable of the Epicurean fly dying in the honey-pot, καὶ βέβρωκα καὶ πέπωκα καὶ λέλουμαι κἂν ἀποθάνω οὐδὲν μέλει μοί.

had left upon his mind, had not been one of tolerance, or
of blunted sensibility to the horror of evil. They had
inspired, on the one hand, an overpowering sense of
disgust; on the other, an overwhelming conviction,
deepened by subsequent observation, that mental per-
versity leads to, and is in its turn aggravated by, moral
degradation; that error in the intellect involves an ultimate error in the life and in the will; that the darkening
of the understanding is inevitably associated with the
darkening of the soul and spirit, and that out of such
darkness spring the hidden things which degrade immoral lives. He who would know what was the aspect
of Paganism to one who had seen it from his childhood
upwards in its characteristic developments, must read that
most terrible passage of all Scripture, in which the full
blaze of scorching sunlight burns with its fiercest flame
of indignation upon the pollutions of Pagan wickedness.
Under that glare of holy wrath we see Paganism in all
its unnatural deformity. No halo of imagination surrounds it, no gleam of fancy plays over its glittering
corruption. We see it as it was. Far other may be
its aspect when the glamour of Hellenic grace is flung
over it, when "the lunar beam of Plato's genius" or the
meteoric wit of Aristophanes light up, as by enchantment,
its revolting sorceries. But he who would truly judge
of it—he who would see it as it shall seem when there
shall fall on it a ray out of God's eternity, must view
it as it appeared to the penetrating glance of a pure
and enlightened eye. St. Paul, furnished by inward chastity with a diviner *moly*, a more potent *haemony*, than
those of Homer's and Milton's song—unmoved, untempted,
unbewitched, unterrified—sees in this painted Circe no
laughing maiden, no bright-eyed daughter of the sun,
but a foul and baleful harlot; and, seizing her by the hair,

stamps deep upon her leprous forehead the burning titles
of her shame. Henceforth she may go for all time
throughout the world a branded sorceress. All may read
that festering stigma; none can henceforth deceive the
nations into regrets for the vanished graces of a world
which knew not God.[1]

But besides this unmitigated horror inspired by the
lowest aspect of heathen life, St. Paul derived from his
early insight into its character his deep conviction that
earthly knowledge has no necessary connection with
heavenly wisdom. If we may trust the romance of the
sophist Philostratus, and if he is not merely appropriating
the sentiments which he had derived from Christianity,
the youthful Apollonius of Tyana, who was afterwards held
up as a kind of heathen parallel to Christ, was studying
under the orator Euthydemus at Tarsus at the very time
when it must also have been the residence of the youthful
Paul;[2] and even Apollonius, at the age of thirteen, was so
struck with the contrast between the professed wisdom of
the city and its miserable morality, that he obtained leave
from his father to remove to Ægæ, and so pursue his
studies at a more serious and religious place.[3] The picture
drawn, so long afterwards, by Philostratus, of the luxury,
the buffoonery, the petulance, the dandyism, the gossip, of
the life at Tarsus, as a serious boy-philosopher is supposed
to have witnessed it, might have no historical value if it
were not confirmed in every particular by the sober narrative of the contemporary Strabo. "So great," he says, " is
the zeal of the inhabitants for philosophy and all other
encyclic training, that they have surpassed even Athens and

---

[1] V. infra, on Rom. i. 18—32.

[2] Philostrat. Vit. Apoll. i. 7.

[3] Ὁ δὲ τὸν μὲν διδάσκαλον εἶχετο τὸ δὲ τῆς πόλεως ἦθος ἄτοπόν τε ἡγεῖτο καὶ οὐ
χρηστὸν ἐμφιλοσοφῆσαι. τρυφῆς τε γὰρ οὐδαμοῦ μᾶλλον ἅπτονται, σκωπτόται τε καὶ
ὑβρισταὶ πάντες (Philostr. Vit. Apollon, i. p. 8, chap. 7, ed. Olear. 1709).

Alexandria, and every other place one could mention in
which philological and philosophical schools have arisen."[1]
The state of affairs resulting from the social atmosphere
which he proceeds to describe is as amusing as it is despicable.   It gives us a glimpse of the professorial world
in days of Pagan decadence; of a professorial world, not
such as it now is, and often has been, in our English and
German Universities, where Christian brotherhood and
mutual esteem have taken the place of wretched rivalism,
and where good and learned men devote their lives to
" gazing on the bright countenance of truth in the mild
and dewy air of delightful studies," but as it was also in the
days of the Poggios, Filelfos, and Politians of the Renaissance—cliques of jealous *savans*, narrow, selfish, unscrupulous, base, sceptical, impure—bursting with gossip, scandal,
and spite.   " The thrones " of these little " academic gods "
were as mutually hostile and as universally degraded as
those of the Olympian deities, in which it was, perhaps, a
happy thing that they had ceased to believe.   One illustrious professor cheated the State by stealing oil; another
avenged himself on an opponent by epigrams; another by a
nocturnal bespattering of his house; and rhetorical jealousies
often ended in bloody quarrels.   On this unedifying spectacle of littleness in great places the people in general looked
with admiring eyes, and discussed the petty discords of
these squabbling sophists as though they were matters
of historical importance.[2]   We can well imagine how unutterably frivolous this apotheosis of pedantism would
appear to a serious-minded and faithful Jew; and it may
have been his Tarsian reminiscences which added emphasis

---

[1] Strabo, xiv. 4, pp. 672, 673. See, too, Xen. *Anab.* i. 2, 23; Plin. v. 22;
Q. Curt. iii. 5, 1.   The Stoics, Athenodorus, tutor of Augustus, and Nestor,
tutor of Tiberius, lived at Tarsus ; and others are mentioned.

[2] Ποταμός τε αὐτοὺς διαῤῥεῖ Κύδνος, ᾧ παραχθηνται, κάθαπερ τῶν ὀρνίθων οἱ ὑγροί.
(Philostr. *ubi supr.*).

to St. Paul's reiterated warnings—that the wise men of
heathendom, "alleging themselves to be wise, became
fools;" that "they became vain in their disputings, and
their unintelligent heart was darkened;"[1] that "the wisdom
of this world is folly in the sight of God, for it is written,
He who graspeth the wise in their own craftiness." And
again, "the Lord knoweth the reasonings of the wise that
they are vain."[2] But while he thus confirms his tenet,
according to his usual custom, by Scriptural quotations
from Job and the Psalms, and elsewhere from Isaiah and
Jeremiah,[3] he reiterates again and again from his own experience that the Greeks seek after wisdom and regard the
Cross as foolishness, yet that the foolishness of God is wiser
than men, and the weakness of God stronger than men,
and that God hath chosen the foolish things of the world
to confound the wise, and the base things of the world
to confound the mighty; and that when, in the wisdom of
God, the world by wisdom knew not God, it pleased God
by "the foolishness of the proclamation"[4]—for in his strong
irony he loves and glories in the antitheses of his opponent's choosing—"by the foolishness of the thing preached"
to save them that believe.[5] If the boasted wisdom of
the Greek and Roman world was such as the young Saul
had seen, if their very type of senselessness and foolishness was that which the converted Paul believed, then
Paul at least—so he says in his passionate and scornful
irony—would choose for ever to be on the side of, to cast
in his lot with, to be gladly numbered among, the idiots
and the fools.

[1] Rom. i. 21, 22.
[2] 1 Cor. iii. 18—20.
[3] Job v. 13; Ps. xciv. 11; Is. xxix. 14; xxxiii. 18; xliv. 25; Jer. viii. 9;
1 Cor. i. 18—27.
[4] 1 Cor. i. 21, διὰ τῆς μωρίας τοῦ κηρύγματος.
[5] 1 Cor. i. 18 - 25; ii. 14; iii. 19; iv. 10; 2 Cor. xi. 16, 19.

D

" He who hath felt the Spirit of the Highest
　　Cannot confound, or doubt Him, or defy;
　　Yea, with one voice, O world, though thou deniest,
　　Stand thou on that side—for on this am I ! "

St. Paul, then, was to the very heart a Jew—a Jew in
culture, a Jew in sympathy, a Jew in nationality, a Jew in
faith.　His temperament was in no sense what we ordinarily regard as a poetic temperament; yet when we remember how all the poetry which existed in the moral
depths of his nature was sustained by the rhythms and
imagery, as his soul itself was sustained by the thoughts
and hopes, of his national literature—when we consider
how the star of Abraham had seemed to shine on his
cradle in a heathen land, and his boyhood in the dim
streets of unhallowed Tarsus to gain freshness and sweetness "from the waving and rustling of the oak of
Mamre "[1]—we can understand that though in Christ
there is neither Jew nor Greek, neither circumcision nor
uncircumcision, but a new creation,[2] yet for no earthly
possession would he have bartered his connection with
the chosen race.　In his Epistle to the Romans he
speaks in almost the very language of the Talmudist:
"Israel hath sinned (Josh. vii. 11), but although he hath
sinned," said Rabbi Abba bar Zavda, " he is still Israel.
Hence the proverb—A myrtle among nettles is still called
a myrtle."[3]　And when we read the numerous passages in
which he vaunts his participation in the hopes of Israel,
his claim to be a fruitful branch in the rich olive of
Jewish life ; when we hear him speak of their adoption,
their Shechinah, their covenants, their Law, their worship,
their promises, their Fathers, their oracles of God, their

[1] Hausrath, p. 20.
[2] κτίσις, Gal. vi. 15; iii. 28.
[3] Sanhedrin, f. 44, 1. Rom. iii. 2; ix., passim.

claim of kinsmanship with the humanity of Christ,[1] we can understand to the full the intense ejaculation of his patriotic fervour, when—in language which has ever been the stumbling-block of religious selfishness, but which surpasses the noblest utterances of heroic self-devotion— he declares that he could wish himself accursed from Christ[2] for his brethren, his kinsmen, according to the flesh.[3] The valiant spirit of the Jews of Tarsus sent them in hundreds to die, sword in hand, amid the carnage of captured Jerusalem, and to shed their last blood to slake, if might be, the very embers of the conflagration which destroyed the Temple of their love. The same patriotism burned in the spirit, the same blood flowed in the veins, not only of Saul the Pharisee, but of Paul the prisoner of the Lord.

It will be seen from all that we have said that we wholly disagree with those who have made it their favourite thesis to maintain for St. Paul the early acquisition of an advanced Hellenic culture. His style and his dialectic method have been appealed to in order to support this view.[4] His style, however, is that of a man who wrote in a peculiar and provincial Greek, but thought

---

[1] Rom. ix. 1—5; x. 1; xi. 1.

[2] Rom. ix. 3.

[3] Any one who wishes to see the contortions of a narrow exegesis struggling to extricate itself out of a plain meaning, which is too noble for its comprehension, may see specimens of it in commentaries upon this text. This, alas! is only one instance of the spirit which so often makes the reading of an ordinary variorum Pauline commentary one of the most tedious, bewildering, and unprofitable of employments. Strange that, with the example of Christ before their eyes, many erudite Christian commentators should know so little of the sublimity of unselfishness as to force us to look to the parallels of a Moses—nay, even of a Danton—in order that we may be able to conceive of the true nobleness of a Paul! But there are cases in which he who would obtain from the writings of St. Paul their true, and often quite simple and transparent, meaning, must tear away with unsparing hand the accumulated cobwebs of centuries of error.

[4] See Schaff, *Hist. of Anct. Christianity*, i. 68.

D 2

in Syriac; and his dialectical method is purely Rabbinic. As
for his deep knowledge of heathen life, we may be sure that
it was not derived from books, but from the fatal wickedness
of which he had been a daily witness. A Jew in a heathen
city needed no books to reveal to him the "depths of
Satan." In this respect how startling a revelation to the
modern world was the indisputable evidence of the ruins of
Pompeii! Who would have expected to find the infamies of
the Dead Sea cities paraded with such infinite shamelessness
in every street of a little provincial town? What innocent
snow could ever hide the guilty front of a life so unspeakably abominable? Could anything short of the earthquake
have engulfed it, or of the volcano have burnt it up?
And if Pompeii was like this, we may judge, from the
works of Aristophanes and Athenæus, of Juvenal and
Martial, of Petronius and Apuleius, of Strato and Meleager
—which may be regarded as the "*pièces justificatives*" of
St. Paul's estimate of heathendom—what Tarsus and
Ephesus, what Corinth and Miletus, were likely to have
been. In days and countries when the darkness was so
deep that the very deeds of darkness did not need to hide
themselves—in days and cities where the worst vilenesses
of idolatry were trumpeted in its streets, and sculptured
in its market-places, and consecrated in its worship, and
stamped upon its coins—did Paul need Greek study to tell
him the characteristics of a godless civilisation? The
notion of Baumgarten that, after his conversion, St. Paul
earnestly studied Greek literature at Tarsus, with a view
to his mission among the heathen—or that the "books"
and parchments which he asked to be sent to him from
the house of Carpus at Troas,[1] were of this description—is
as precarious as the fancy that his parents sent him to be
educated at Jerusalem in order to counteract the com-

[1] 2 Tim. iv. 13.

mencing sorcery exercised over his imagination by
Hellenic studies. Gamaliel, it is true, was one of the few
Rabbis who took the liberal and enlightened view about
the permissibility of the *Chokmah Jovanith*, or "wisdom
of the Greeks"—one of the few who held the desirability
of not wholly dissevering the white *tallith* of Shem from
the stained *pallium* of Japhet.[1] But, on the one hand,
neither would Gamaliel have had that false toleration
which seems to think that "the ointment of the apothe-
cary" is valueless without "the fly which causeth it to
stink;" and, on the other hand, if Gamaliel had allowed
his pupils to handle such books, or such parts of books, as
dwelt on the darker side of Paganism, Paul was not the
kind of pupil who would, for a moment, have availed
himself of such "ruinous edification."[2] The Jews were
so scrupulous, that some of them held concerning books of
their own hagiographa—such, for instance, as the Book of
Esther—that they were dubious reading. They would
not allow their youth even to open the Song of Solomon

[1] See *Life of Christ*, Exc. IV. vol. ii. 461. The study of Greek literature by the
House of Gamaliel is said to have been connived at by the Rabbis, on the plea
that they needed a knowledge of Greek in civil and diplomatic intercourse on
behalf of their countrymen (see Etheridge, *Heb. Lit.* p. 45). Rabban Shimon Ben
Gamaliel is said to have remarked that there were 1,000 children in his father's
house, of whom 500 studied the law, and 500 the wisdom of the Greeks, and that
of these all but two perished [in the rebellion of Bar-chocba?] (*Babha Kama*,
f. 83, 1). The author of the celebrated comparison, that "because the two sons of
Noah, Shem and Japhet, united to cover with one garment their father's nakedness, Shem obtained the fringed garment (*tallith*), and Japhet the philosopher's
garment (*pallium*), which ought to be united again," was R. Jochanan Ben
Napuchah (*Midr. Rabbah*, Gen. xxxvi.; Jer. *Sotah, ad f.*; Selden, *De Synedr.*
ii. 9, 2; Biscoe, p. 60). On the other hand, the narrower Rabbis identified Greek
learning with Egyptian thaumaturgy; and when R. Elieser Ben Dama asked
his uncle, R. Ismael, whether one might not learn Greek knowledge after
having studied the entire law, R. Ismael quoted in reply Josh. i. 8, and said,
"Go and find a moment which is neither day nor night, and then abandon
yourself in it to Greek knowledge" (*Menachôth*, 99, 2).

[2] 1 Cor. viii. 10, ἡ συνείδησις αὐτοῦ ἀσθενοῦς ὄντος οἰκοδομηθήσεται εἰς τὸ τὰ
εἰδωλόθυτα ἐσθίειν. *Ruinosa aedificatio*, Calv. ad loc.

before the age of twenty-one. Nothing, therefore, can be
more certain than that " a Pharisee of Pharisees," even
though his boyhood were spent in heathen Tarsus, would
not have been allowed to read—barely even allowed to
know the existence of—any but the sweetest and soundest
portions of Greek letters, if even these.[1] But who that
has read St. Paul can believe that he had ever studied
Homer, or Æschylus, or Sophocles? If he had done
so, would there—in a writer who often " thinks in
quotations "—have been no touch or trace of any reminiscence of, or allusion to, epic or tragic poetry in
epistles written at Athens and at Corinth, and beside
the very tumuli of Ajax and Achilles? Had Paul been
a reader of Aristotle, would he have argued in the style
which he adopts in the Epistles to the Galatians and the
Romans?[2] Had he been a reader of Plato, would the
fifteenth chapter of the first Epistle to the Corinthians
have carried in it not the most remotely faint allusion to
the splendid guesses of the Phaedo? Nothing can be more
clear than that he had never been subjected to a classic
training. His Greek is not the Greek of the Atticists, nor
his rhetoric the rhetoric of the schools, nor his logic the
logic of the philosophers. It is doubtful whether the incomparable energy and individuality of his style and of his

---

[1] See *Sota*, 49, 6; and the strong condemnation of all Gentile books by
R. Akibha, Bab. *Sanhedr.* 90, a. (Gfrörer, *Jahrh. d. Heils.* i. 114; Philo, ii.
350; Grätz, iii. 502; Derenbourg, *Palest.* 114.) In *Yadayim*, iv. 6, the
Sadducees complain of some Pharisees for holding that the Books of Eccle-
siastes and Canticles " defile the hands," while " the books of Homeros " do not.
The comment appended to this remark shows, however, the most astounding
ignorance. The two Rabbis (*in loco*) take " Meros " to be the proper name,
preceded by the article, and deriving Meros from *rasas*, to destroy, make
the poems of Homer into books which cavil against the Law and are doomed
to destruction! Grätz denies that חרם is Homer.

[2] " Melius haec sibi convenissent," says Fritzsche, in alluding to one of
St. Paul's antinomies, " si Apostolus Aristotelis non Gamalielis alumnus
fuisset."

reasoning would not have been merely enfeebled and conventionalised if he had gone through any prolonged course of the only training which the Sophists of Tarsus could have given him.[1]

[1] See Excursus I., "The Style of St. Paul;" Excursus II., "Rhetoric of St. Paul;" and Excursus III., "The Classic Quotations and Allusions of St. Paul." I may sum up the conclusion of these essays by stating that St. Paul had but a slight acquaintance with Greek literature, but that he had very probably attended some elementary classes in Tarsus, in which he had gained a tincture of Greek rhetoric, and possibly even of Stoic principles.

CHAPTER III.

THE SCHOOL OF THE RABBI.

'Ἠκούσατε γὰρ τὴν ἐμὴν ἀναστροφήν ποτε ἐν Ἰουδαϊσμῷ, ὅτι . . . προέκοπτον ἐν τῷ Ἰουδαϊσμῷ ὑπέρ πολλοὺς συνηλικιώτας ἐν τῷ γένει μου.—GAL. i. 13, 14.

"Let thy house be a place of resort for the wise, and cover thyself with the dust of their feet, and drink their words with thirstiness."—*Pirke Abhôth*, i. 4.

"The world was created for the sake of the Thorah."—*Nedarim*, 32, 1.

"Whoever is busied in the law for its own sake is worth the whole world."
—PEREK R. MEIR, 1.

So far, then, we have attempted to trace in detail, by the aid of St. Paul's own writings, the degree and the character of those influences which were exercised upon his mind by the early years which he spent at Tarsus, modified or deepened as they must have been by long intercourse with heathens, and with converts from heathendom, in later years. And already we have seen abundant reason to believe that the impressions which he received from Hellenism were comparatively superficial and fugitive, while those of his Hebraic training and nationality worked deep among the very bases of his life. It is this Hebraic side of his character, so important to any understanding of his life and writings, that we must now endeavour to trace and estimate.

That St. Paul was a Roman citizen, that he could go through the world and say in his own defence, when needful or possible, *Civis Romanus sum*, is stated so distinctly, and under circumstances so manifestly probable, that the fact stands above all doubt. There are, indeed, some difficulties about it which induce many German theologians quietly to deny its truth, and attribute the statement to a desire on the part of the author of the Acts "to recommend St. Paul to the Romans as a native Roman," or "to remove the reproach that the originators of Christendom had been enemies of the Roman State." It is true that, if St. Paul was a free-born Roman citizen, his legal rights as established by the Lex Porcia[1] must, according to his own statement, have been eight times violated at the time when he wrote the Second Epistle to the Corinthians ;[2] while a *ninth* violation of those rights was only prevented by his direct appeal. Five of these, however, were Jewish scourgings, and what we have already said, as well as what we shall say hereafter, may well lead us to suppose that, as against the Jews, St. Paul would have purposely abstained from putting forward a claim which, from the mouth of a Jew, would have been regarded as an odious sign that he was willing to make a personal advantage of his country's subjection. The Jewish authorities possessed the power to scourge, and it is only too sadly probable that Saul himself, when he was their agent, had been the cause of its infliction on other Christians. If so, he would have felt a strong additional reason for abstaining from the plea which would have exempted him from the authority of his countrymen; and we may see in this abstention a fresh and, so far as I am aware, a hitherto unnoticed trait of his natural nobleness. As to the Roman scourgings, it is clear that the author of the Acts, though well aware of the privileges which Roman citizenship entailed, was also aware that, on turbulent occasions and in remote places, the plea might be summarily set aside in the case of those who were too weak or too

---

[1] "Porcia lex virgas ab omnium civium Romanorum corpore amovet" (Cic. *pro Rab.* 3; Liv. x. 9).

[2] When he was about fifty-three years old.

obscure to support it. If under the full glare of publicity in Sicily, and when the rights of the "*Civitas*" were rare, a Verres could contemptuously ignore them to an extent much more revolting to the Roman sense of dignity than scourging was—then very little difficulty remains in reconciling St. Paul's expression, "Thrice was I beaten with rods," with the claim which he put forth to the praetors of Philippi and to the chiliarch at Jerusalem. How St. Paul's father or grandfather obtained the highly-prized distinction we have no means of ascertaining. It certainly did not belong to any one as a citizen of Tarsus, for, if so, Lysias at Jerusalem, knowing that St. Paul came from Tarsus, would have known that he had also the rights of a Roman. But Tarsus was not a *Colonia* or a *Municipium*, but only an *Urbs Libera;* and this privilege, bestowed upon it by Augustus, did not involve any claim to the *Civitas.* The franchise may either have been purchased by Paul's father, or obtained as a reward for some services of which no trace remains.[1] When Cassius punished Tarsus by a heavy fine for having embraced the side of Antony, it is said that many Tarsians were sold as slaves in order to pay the money; and one conjecture is that St. Paul's father, in his early days, may have been one of these, and may have been first emancipated and then presented with the *Civitas* during a residence at Rome. The conjecture is just possible, but nothing more.

At any rate, this Roman citizenship is not in any way inconsistent with his constant claim to the purest Jewish descent; nor did it appreciably affect his

---

[1] See for such means of acquiring it, Suet. *Aug.* 47; Jos. *B. J.* ii. 14; Acts xxii. 28. The possession of citizenship had to be proved by a "*diploma*," and Claudius punished a false assumption of it with death. (Suet. *Claud.* 25; *Calig.* 28; *Nero*, 12; Epictet. *Dissert.* iii. 24.)

character. The father of Saul may have been glad
that he possessed an inalienable right, transmissible to
his son, which would protect him in many of those
perils which were only too possible in such times;
but it made no difference in the training which he
gave to the young Saul, or in the destiny which he
marked out for him. That training, as we can clearly
see, was the ordinary training of every Jewish boy.
"The prejudices of the Pharisaic house," it has been
said, "surrounded his cradle; his Judaism grew like the
mustard-tree in the Gospel, and intolerance, fanaticism,
national hatred, pride, and other passions, built their nests
among its branches."[1] At the age of five he would begin
to study the Bible with his parents at home; and even
earlier than this he would doubtless have learnt the
Shema[2] and the Hallel (Psalms cxiii.—cxviii.) in whole
or in part. At six he would go to his "vineyard," as the
later Rabbis called their schools. At ten he would begin to
study those earlier and simpler developments of the oral
law, which were afterwards collected in the Mishna. At
thirteen he would, by a sort of "confirmation," become a
"Son of the Commandment."[3] At fifteen he would be
trained in yet more minute and burdensome halachôth,
analogous to those which ultimately filled the vast mass
of the Gemara. At twenty, or earlier, like every orthodox
Jew, he would marry. During many years he would be
ranked among the "pupils of the wise,"[4] and be mainly
occupied with "the traditions of the Fathers."[5]

[1] Hausrath, p. 19.
[2] Strictly Deut. vi. 4—9; but also xi. 13—27; Num. xv. 37—41.
[3] *Bar Mitsvah.*
[4] *Pirke Abhôth,* v. 21. See too Dr. Ginsburg's excellent article on
"Education" in Kitto's *Bibl. Cycl.*
[5] *Pirke Abhôth,* i. 1. The two favourite words of the Pharisees were
ἀκρίβεια and τὰ πάτρια ἔθη. See Acts xxvi. 5; xxii. 3; Jos. *B. J.* ii. 8, 14; i. 5,
2; *Antt.* xiii. 10, 6; xvii. 2, *ad fin.*

It was in studies and habits like these that the young Saul of Tarsus grew up to the age of thirteen, which was the age at which a Jewish boy, if he were destined for the position of a Rabbi, entered the school of some great master. The master among whose pupils Saul was enrolled was the famous Rabban Gamaliel, a son of Rabban Simeon, and a grandson of Hillel, "a doctor of the law had in reputation among all the people."[1] There were only seven of the Rabbis to whom the Jews gave the title of Rabban, and three of these were Gamaliels of this family, who each in turn rose to the high distinction of *Nasi*, or President of the School. Gamaliel I., like his grandfather Hillel, held the somewhat anomalous position of a liberal Pharisee. A Pharisee in heartfelt zeal for the traditions of his fathers,[2] he yet had none of the narrow exclusiveness which characterised Shammai, the rival of his grandfather, and the hard school which Shammai had founded. His liberality of intellect showed itself in the permission of Pagan literature; his largeness of heart in the tolerance which breathes through his speech before the Sanhedrin. There is no authority for the tradition that he was a secret Christian,[3] but we see from the numerous notices of him in the Talmud, and from the sayings there ascribed to him, that he was a man of exactly the character

---

[1] Acts v. 34, xxii. 3. See Grätz, *Gesch. d. Juden*, iii. 274.

[2] I have noticed farther on (see Excursus V.) the difficulty of being sure which of the Gamaliels is referred to when the name occurs in the Talmud. This, however, is less important, since they were all of the same school, and entirely faithful to Mosaism. We may see the utter change which subsequently took place in St. Paul's views if we compare Rom. xiv. 5, Col. ii. 16, Gal. iv. 10, with the following anecdote:—"Rabban Gamaliel's ass happened to be laden with honey, and it was found dead one Sabbath evening, because he had been unwilling to unload it on that day" (*Shabbath*, f. 154, c. 2).

[3] *Recogn. Clem.* i. 65; Phot. *Cod.* 171, p. 199; Thilo, *Cod. Apocr.* p. 501 (Meyer *ad* Acts v. 34).

which we should infer from the brief notice of him
and of his sentiments in the Acts of the Apostles.
In both sources alike we see a humane, thoughtful,
high-minded, and religious man—a man of sufficient
culture to elevate him above vulgar passions, and of
sufficient wisdom to see, to state, and to act upon the
broad principles that hasty judgments are dangerously
liable to error; that there is a strength and majesty in
truth which needs no aid from persecution; that a light
from heaven falls upon the destinies of man, and that by
that light God "shows all things in the slow history of
their ripening."

At the feet of this eminent Sanhedrist sat Saul of
Tarsus in all probability for many years;[1] and though for
a time the burning zeal of his temperament may have
carried him to excesses of intolerance in which he was
untrue to the best traditions of his school, yet, since the
sunlight of the grace of God ripened in his soul the latent
seeds of all that was wise and tender, we may believe that
some of those germs of charity had been implanted in his
heart by his eminent teacher. So far from seeing any
improbability in the statement that St. Paul had been
a scholar of Gamaliel, it seems to me that it throws a
flood of light on the character and opinions of the Apostle.
With the exception of Hillel, there is no one of the Jewish
Rabbis, so far as we see them in the light of history,
whose virtues made him better suited to be the teacher of a
Saul, than Hillel's grandson. We must bear in mind that
the dark side of Pharisaism which is brought before us
in the Gospels—the common and current Pharisaism, half

---

[1] Acts xxii. 3. The Jewish Rabbis sat on lofty chairs, and their pupils sat
at their feet, either on the ground or on benches. There is no sufficient
ground for the tradition that up till the time of Gamaliel's death it had been
the custom for the pupils to stand. (2 Kings ii. 3, iv. 38; Bab. Sanhedr.
vii. 2; Biscoe, p. 77.)

hypocritical, half mechanical, and wholly selfish, which
justly incurred the blighting flash of Christ's denunciation
—was not the *only* aspect which Pharisaism could wear.
When we speak of Pharisaism we mean obedience petri-
fied into formalism, religion degraded into ritual, morals
cankered by casuistry; we mean the triumph and per-
petuity of all the worst and weakest elements in religious
party-spirit.   But there were Pharisees and Pharisees.
The New Testament furnishes us with a favourable picture of the candour and wisdom of a Nicodemus and a
Gamaliel.   In the Talmud, among many other stately
figures who walk in a peace and righteousness worthy of
the race which sprang from Abraham, we see the lovable
and noble characters of a Hillel, of a Simeon, of a
Chaja, of a Juda " the Holy."   It was when he thought
of such as these, that, even long after his conversion, Paul could exclaim before the Sanhedrin with no
sense of shame or contradiction—" Men and brethren, I
am a Pharisee, a son of Pharisees."   He would be the
more able to make this appeal because, at that moment, he
was expressly referring to the resurrection of the dead,
which has been too sweepingly characterised as " the
one doctrine which Paul the Apostle borrowed from Saul
the Pharisee."

It is both interesting, and for the study of St. Paul's
Epistles most deeply important, to trace the influence
of these years upon his character and intellect.   Much
that he learnt during early manhood continued to be,
till the last, an essential part of his knowledge and experience.   To the day of his death he neither denied nor
underrated the advantages of the Jew; and first among
those advantages he placed the possession of " the oracles
of God."[1]   He had begun the study of these Scriptures

[1] Rom. iii. 2.

at the age of six, and to them, and the elucidations of them which had been gathered during many centuries in the schools of Judaism, he had devoted the most studious years of his life. The effects of that study are more or less traceable in every Epistle which he wrote; they are specially remarkable in those which, like the Epistle to the Romans, were in whole or in part addressed to Churches in which Jewish converts were numerous or predominant.

His profound knowledge of the Old Testament Scriptures shows how great had been his familiarity with them from earliest childhood. From the Pentateuch, from the Prophets, and above all from the Psalter, he not only quotes repeatedly, advancing at each step of the argument from quotation to quotation, as though without these his argument, which is often in reality quite independent of them, would lack authority; but he also quotes, as is evident, from memory, and often into one brief quotation weaves the verbal reminiscences of several passages.[1] Like all Hellenistic Jews, he uses the Greek version of the LXX., but he had an advantage over most Hellenists in that knowledge of the original Hebrew which sometimes stands him in good stead. Yet though he can refer to the original when occasion requires, the LXX. was to him as much " the Bible " as our English version is to us; and, as is the case with many Christian writers, he knew it so well that his sentences are constantly moulded by its rhythm, and his thoughts incessantly coloured by its expressions.

And the controversial use which he makes of it is very remarkable. It often seems at first sight to be wholly independent of the context. It often seems to read between

[1] *E.g.*, Rom. i. 24, iii. 6, iv. 17, ix. 33, x. 18, xi. 8; 1 Cor. vi. 2 ix. 7, xv. 45; &c.

the lines.[1] It often seems to consider the mere words of
a writer as of conclusive authority entirely apart from their
original application.[2] It seems to regard the word and
letter of Scripture as full of divine mysterious oracles,
which might not only be cited in matters of doctrine, but
even to illustrate the simplest matters of contemporary
fact.[3] It attaches consequences of the deepest importance
to what an ordinary reader might regard as a mere grammatical expression.[4] But if the general conception of
this style of argumentation was due to Paul's long
training in Rabbinic principles of exegesis, it should not
be forgotten that while these principles often modified
the form of his expressions, they cannot in any single
instance be said to have furnished the essential matter
of his thoughts. It was quite inevitable that one who
had undergone the elaborate training of a Rabbi—one
who, to full manhood, had never dreamt that any training
could be superior to it—would not instantly unlearn the
reiterated lessons of so many years. Nor was it in any
way necessary to the interests of religious truth that he
should do so. The sort of traditional culture in the
explanation of Scripture which he learnt at the feet of
Gamaliel was not only of extreme value in all his controversies with the Jews, but also enriched his style, and lent
fresh vividness to his arguments, without enfeebling his
judgment or mystifying his opinions. The ingenuity of

---

[1] Rom. ii. 24, iii. 10—18, ix. 15; 1 Cor. x. 1—4; Gal. iv. 24—31; &c. This
is the essence of the later Kabbala, with its *Pardes*—namely, *Peshat*, "explanation;" *Remes*, "hint;" *Derush*, "homily;" and *Sod*, "mystery." Yet in
St. Paul there is not a trace of the methods (*Geneth*) of Gematria, Notarikon,
or Themourah, which the Jews applied *very early* to Old Testament exegesis.
I have fully explained these terms in a paper on "Rabbinic Exegesis,"
Expositor, May, 1877.

[2] 1 Cor. xiv. 21; Rom. x. 6—9; 1 Cor. xv. 45
[3] See Rom. x. 15—21.
[4] Gal. iii. 16

the Jewish Rabbi never for one moment overpowers the vigorous sense and illuminated intellect of the Christian teacher. Although St. Paul's method of handling Scripture, undoubtedly, in its general features, resembles and recalls the method which reigns throughout the Talmud, yet the practical force, the inspired wisdom, the clear intuition, of the great Apostle, preserve him from that extravagant abuse of numerical, kabbalistic, esoteric, and impossibly inferential minutiæ which make anything mean anything—from all attempt to emulate the remarkable exegetical feats of those letter-worshipping Rabbis who prided themselves on suspending dogmatic mountains by textual hairs. He shared, doubtless, in the views of the later Jewish schools—the Tanaim and Amoraim—on the nature of inspiration. These views, which we find also in Philo, made the words of Scripture co-extensive and identical with the words of God, and in the clumsy and feeble hands of the more fanatical Talmudists often attached to the dead letter an importance which stifled or destroyed the living sense. But as this extreme and mechanical literalism—this claim to absolute infallibility even in accidental details and passing allusions—this superstitious adoration of the letters and vocables of Scripture as though they were the articulate vocables and immediate autograph of God—finds no encouragement in any part of Scripture, and very direct discouragement in more than one of the utterances of Christ, so there is not a single passage in which any approach to it is dogmatically stated in the writings of St. Paul.[1] Nay, more—the very point of his specific

---

[1] 2 Tim. iii. 16 is no exception ; even if θεόπνευστος be there regarded as a predicate, nothing would be more extravagant than to rest on that single adjective the vast hypothesis of literal dictation (see *infra, ad loc.*). On this great subject of inspiration I have stated what I believe to be the Catholic faith fully and clearly in the *Bible Educator*, i. 190 *sq.*

E

difference from the Judæo-Christians was his denial of
the permanent validity of the entire scheme of legislation
which it was the immediate object of the Pentateuch to
record. If it be asserted that St. Paul deals with the Old
Testament in the manner of a Rabbi, let it be said in
answer that he uses it to emancipate the souls which
Judaism enslaved ; and that he deduces from it, not the
Kabbala and the Talmud—" a philosophy for dreamers
and a code for mummies "[1]—but the main ideas of the
Gospel of the grace of God.

It will be easy for any thoughtful and unprejudiced
reader of St. Paul's Epistles to verify and illustrate for
himself the Apostle's use of Scripture. He adopts the
current mode of citation, but he ennobles and enlightens it.[2]
That he did not consider the method universally applicable
is clear from its omission in those of his Epistles which
were intended in the main for Gentile Christians,[3] as also
in his speeches to heathen assemblies. But to the Jews
he would naturally address a style of argument which was
in entire accordance with their own method of dialectics.
Many of the truths which he demonstrates by other considerations may have seemed to him to acquire additional
authority from their assonance with certain expressions of
Scripture. We cannot, indeed, be sure in some instances
how far St. Paul meant his quotation for an argument, and
how far he used it as a mere illustrative formula. Thus,
we feel no hesitation in admitting the cogency of his proof
of the fact that both Jews and Gentiles were guilty in God's
sight ; but we should not consider the language of David
about his enemies in the fourteenth and fifty-third Psalms,
still less his strong expressions " all " and " no, not one,"

---

[1] Reuss, *Théol. Chrét.* i. 268 and 408—421.
[2] See Jowett, *Romans,* i. 353—362.
[3] There are no Scriptural quotations in 1, 2 Thess., Phil., Col.

as adding any great additional force to the general argument. It is probable that a Jew would have done so; and St. Paul, as a Jew trained in this method of Scriptural application, may have done so too. But what has been called his "inspired Targum" of the Old Testament does not bind us to the mystic method of Old Testament commentary. As the Jews were more likely to adopt any conclusion which was expressed for them in the words of Scripture, St. Paul, having undergone the same training, naturally enwove into his style—though only when he wrote to them—this particular method of Scriptural illustration. To them an argument of this kind would be an *argumentum ex concessis*. To us its argumentative force would be much smaller, because it does not appeal to us, as to him and to his readers, with all the force of familiar reasoning. So far from thinking this a subject for regret, we may, on the contrary, be heartily thankful for an insight which could give explicitness to deeply latent truths, and find in an observation of minor importance, like that of Habakkuk, that "the soul of the proud man is not upright, but the just man shall live by his steadfastness"[1]—*i.e.*, that the Chaldeans should enjoy no stable prosperity, but that the Jews, here ideally represented as "the upright man," should, because of their fidelity, live secure—the depth of power and meaning which we attach to that palmary truth of the Pauline theology that "*the just shall live by his faith.*"[2]

A similar but more remarkable instance of this apparent subordination of the historic context in the illustrative

[1] Hab. ii. 4. (Heb. בֶאֱמוּנָתוֹ, by his trustworthiness.) See Lightfoot *ad Gal.* iii. 11, and p. 149.

[2] *Gal.* iii. 11; *Rom.* i. 17; also in Heb. x. 38. St. Paul omits the μου of the LXX., which is not in the Hebrew.

E 2

application of prophetic words is found in 1 Cor. xiv. 21.
St. Paul is there speaking of the gift of tongues, and speaking of it with entire disparagement in comparison with the
loftier gift of prophecy, *i.e.*, of impassioned and spiritual
teaching.   In support of this disparaging estimate, and as
a proof that the tongues, being mainly meant as a sign
to unbelievers, ought only to be used sparingly and under
definite limitations in the congregations of the faithful,
he quotes from Isaiah xxviii. 11[1] the verse—which he does
not in this instance borrow from the LXX. version—"*With
men of other tongues and other lips will I speak unto this people,
and yet for all that will they not hear me, saith the Lord.*"
The whole meaning and context are, in the original, very
interesting, and generally misunderstood.   The passage
implies that since the drunken, shameless priests and
prophets, chose, in their hiccoughing scorn, to deride the
manner and method of the divine instruction which came
to them,[2] God should address them in a wholly different
way, namely, by the Assyrians, who spake tongues which
they could not understand ; and yet even to that instruction—the stern and unintelligible utterance of foreign
victors—they should continue deaf.   This passage, in a
manner quite alien from any which would be natural
to us, St. Paul embodied in a pre-eminently noble and
able argument, as though it illustrated, if it did not
prove, his view as to the proper object and limitations
of those soliloquies of ecstatic spiritual emotion which
were known as Glossolalia, or " the Gift of Tongues."

One more instance, and that, perhaps, the most re-

---

[1] The quotation is introduced with the formula, " It has been written in *the
Law*," a phrase which is sometimes applied to the entire Old Testament.

[2] They ridiculed Isaiah's repetitions by saying they were all " bid and bid,
bid and bid, forbid and forbid, forbid and forbid," &c. (*Tsav la-tsav, tsav
la-tsav, kav la-kav, kav la-kav*, &c., Heb.). (See an admirable paper on this
passage by Rev. S. Cox, *Expositor*, i. p. 101).

markable of all, will enable us better to understand a
peculiarity which was the natural result of years of
teaching. In Gal. iii. 16 he says, "Now the promises
were spoken to Abraham and to his seed. He saith not,
AND TO SEEDS, as applying to many, but, as applying to
one, AND TO THY SEED—who is Christ." Certainly at
first sight we should say that an argument of immense
importance was here founded on the use of the Hebrew
word *zerá* in the singular,[1] and its representative the
σπέρμα of the LXX.; and that the inference which
St. Paul deduces depends solely on the fact that the
plural, *zeraím* (σπέρματα), is not used; and that, therefore,
the promise of Gen. xiii. 15 pointed from the first to a
special fulfilment in ONE of Abraham's descendants. This
primâ facie view must, however, be erroneous, because
it is inconceivable that St. Paul—a good Hebraist and
a master of Hellenistic Greek—was unaware that the
plural *zeraím*, as in 1 Sam. viii. 15, Dan. i. 12, and
the title of the Talmudic treatise, could not by any possibility have been used in the original promise, because
it could only mean "*various kinds of grain*"—exactly
in the sense in which he himself uses *spermata* in
1 Cor. xv. 38—and that the Greek *spermata*, in the
sense of "offspring," would be nothing less than an
impossible barbarism. The argument, therefore—if it
be an argument at all, and not what the Rabbis would
have called a *sod*, or "mystery"—does not, and cannot,
turn, as has been so unhesitatingly assumed, on the fact
that *sperma* is a *singular* noun, but on the fact that it is a
collective noun, and was deliberately used instead of "sons"
or "children;"[2] and St. Paul declares that this *collective*
term was meant from the first to apply to Christ, as
elsewhere he applies it spiritually to the servants of

[1] זֶרַע   [2] See Lightfoot, *ad loc.* p. 139.

Christ. In the interpretation, then, of this word, St.
Paul reads between the lines of the original, and is
enabled to see in it deep meanings which are the true,
but not the primary ones. He does not say at once that
the promises to Abraham found in Christ—as in the
purpose of God it had always been intended that they
should find in Christ [1]—their highest and truest fulfilment; but, in a manner belonging peculiarly to the
Jewish style of exegesis, he illustrates this high truth
by the use of a *collective noun* in which he believes it to
have been mystically foreshadowed.[2]

This passage is admirably adapted to throw light on
the Apostle's use of the Old Testament. Rabbinic in
form, it was free in spirit. Though he does not disdain
either Amoraic or Alexandrian methods of dealing with
Scripture, St. Paul never falls into the follies or extravagances of either. Treating the letter of Scripture with
intense respect, he yet made the literal sense of it bend
at will to the service of the spiritual consciousness.
On the dead letter of the Urim, which recorded the
names of lost tribes, he flashed a mystic ray, which made
them gleam forth into divine and hitherto undreamed-of
oracles. The actual words of the sacred writers became
but as the wheels and wings of the Cherubim, and
whithersoever the Spirit went they went. Nothing is
more natural, nothing more interesting, in the hands of
an inspired teacher nothing is more valuable, than this

---

[1] As in Gen. iii. 15. The Jews could not deny the force of the argument,
for they interpreted Gen. iv. 25, &c., of the Messiah. But St. Jerome's remark,
"Galatis, quos paulo ante stultos dixerat, factus est stultus," as though the
Apostle had purposely used an "accommodation" argument, is founded on
wrong principles.

[2] The purely illustrative character of the reference seems to be clear from
the different, yet no less spiritualised, sense given to the text in Rom. iv. 13,
16, 18 ; ix. 8; Gal. iii. 28, 29.

mode of application. We have not in St. Paul the frigid
spirit of Philonian allegory which to a great extent
depreciated the original and historic sense of Scripture,
and was chiefly bent on educing philosophic mysteries
from its living page; nor have we a single instance of
Gematria or Notarikon, of Atbash or Albam, of Hillel's
middoth or Akibha's method of hanging legal decisions
on the horns of letters. Into these unreal mysticisms
and exegetical frivolities it was impossible that a man
should fall who was intensely earnest, and felt, in the vast
mass of what he wrote, that he had the Spirit of the
Lord. In no single instance does he make one of
these general quotations the demonstrative *basis* of the
point which he is endeavouring to impress. In every
instance he states the solid argument on which he rests
his conclusion, and only adduces Scripture by way of
sanction or support. And this is in exact accordance
with all that we know of his spiritual history—of the
genuineness of which it affords an unsuspected confirmation. He had not arrived at any one of the truths of his
special gospel by the road of ratiocination. They came
to him with the flash of intuitive conviction at the miracle
of his conversion, or in the gradual process of subsequent
psychological experience. We hear from his own lips that
he had not originally found these truths in Scripture, or
been led to them by inductive processes in the course of
Scripture study. He received them, as again and again he
tells us, by revelation direct from Christ. It was only
when God had taught him the truth of them that he
became cognisant that they *must* be latent in the writings
of the Old Dispensation. When he was thus enlightened
to see that they existed in Scripture, he found that all
Scripture was full of them. When he knew that the
treasure lay hid in the field, he bought the whole field,

to become its owner. When God had revealed to him
the doctrine of justification by faith, he saw—as we may
now see, but as none had seen before him—that it
existed implicitly in the trustfulness of Abraham and
the "life" and "faith" of Habakkuk. Given the
right, nay, the necessity, to spiritualise the meaning of
the Scriptures—and given the fact that this right was
assumed and practised by every teacher of the schools in
which Paul had been trained and to which his countrymen looked up, as it has been practised by every great
teacher since—we then possess the key to all such
passages as those to which I have referred; and we also
see the cogency with which they would come home to the
minds of those for whom they were intended. In other
words, St. Paul, when speaking to Jews, was happily
able to address them, as it were, in their own dialect,
and it is a dialect from which Gentiles also have deep
lessons to learn.

It is yet another instance of the same method when
he points to the two wives of Abraham as types of
the Jewish and of the Christian covenant, and in the
struggles and jealousies of the two, ending in the ejection
of Agar, sees allegorically foreshadowed the triumph of
the new covenant over the old. In this allegory, by marvellous interchange, the physical descendants of Sarah
become, in a *spiritual* point of view, the descendants
of Agar, and those who were Agar's children become
Sarah's true spiritual offspring. The inhabitants of the
Jerusalem that now is, though descended from Sarah and
Abraham, are foreshadowed for rejection under the type
of the offspring of Ishmael; and the true children of
Abraham and Sarah are those alone who are so *spiritually*,
but of whom the vast majority were not of the chosen
seed. And the proof of this—if proof be in any case the

right word for what perhaps St. Paul himself may only have regarded as allegoric confirmation—is found in Isaiah liv. 1, where the prophet, addressing the New Jerusalem which is to rise out of the ashes of her Babylonian ruin, calls to her as to a barren woman, and bids her to rejoice as having many more children than she that hath a husband. The Jews become metamorphosed into the descendants of Agar, the Gentiles into the seed of Abraham and heirs of the Promise.[1]

This very ranging in corresponding columns of type and antitype, or of the actually existent and its ideal counterpart—this Systoichia in which Agar, Ishmael, the Old Covenant, the earthly Jerusalem, the unconverted Jews, &c., in the one column, are respective counterparts of their spiritual opposites, Sarah, Isaac, the New Covenant, the heavenly Jerusalem, the Christian Church, &c., in the other column—is in itself a Rabbinic method of setting forth a series of conceptions, and is, therefore, another of the many traces of the influence of Rabbinic training upon the mind of St. Paul. A part of the system of the Rabbis was to regard the earth as—

"But the shadow of heaven, and things therein
Each to the other like more than on earth is thought."

This notion was especially applied to everything connected

---

[1] Other specimens of exegesis accordant in result with the known views of the Rabbis may be found in Rom. ix. 33 (compared with Is. viii. 14, xxviii. 16; Luke ii. 34), since the Rabbis applied both the passages referred to—"the rock of offence," and "the corner-stone"—to the Messiah; and in 1 Cor. ix. 9, where by a happy analogy (also found in Philo, *De Victimas Offerentibus*, 1) the prohibition to muzzle the ox that treadeth out the corn is applied to the duty of maintaining ministers (1 Cor. ix. 4, 11; Eph. iv. 8). The expressions in Rom. v. 12; 1 Cor. xi. 10; 2 Cor. xi. 14; Gal. iii. 19; iv. 29, find parallels in the Targums, &c. To these may be added various images and expressions in 1 Cor. xv. 36; 2 Cor. xii. 2; 1 Thess. iv. 16. (See Immer, *Neut. Theol.* 210; Krenkel, p. 218.)

with the Holy People, and there was no event in the
wanderings of the wilderness which did not stand typi-
cally for matters of spiritual experience or heavenly
hope.[1] This principle is expressly stated in the First
Epistle to the Corinthians,[2] where, in exemplification of
it, not only is the manna made the type of the bread
of the Lord's Supper, but, by a much more remote
analogy, the passing through the waters of the Red Sea,
and the being guided by the pillar of cloud by day, is
described as "being baptised unto Moses in the cloud
and in the sea," and is made a prefigurement of Christian
baptism.[3]

But although St. Paul was a Hebrew by virtue of
his ancestry, and by virtue of the language which he
had learnt as his mother-tongue, and although he would
probably have rejected the appellation of "Hellenist,"
which is indeed never applied to him, yet his very
Hebraism had, in one most important respect, and one
which has very little attracted the attention of scholars,
an Hellenic bias and tinge. This is apparent in the
fact which I have already mentioned, that he was,
or at any rate that he became, to a marked extent,
in the technical language of the Jewish schools, an
Hagadist, not an Halachist.[4] It needs but a glance at
the Mishna, and still more at the Gemara, to see that
the question which mainly occupied the thoughts and
interests of the Palestinian and Babylonian Rabbis, and

[1] "Quicquid evenit patribus signum filiis," &c. (Wetstein, and Schöttgen
on 1 Cor. x. 11). (See Wisd. xi, xvi—xviii.)
[2] 1 Cor. x. 6. Ταῦτα δὲ τύποι ἡμῶν ἐγενήθησαν. On the manna (= θεῖος λόγος),
compare Philo, De Leg. Alleg. iv. 56; on the rock (= σοφία τοῦ θεο), id. ii. 21.
[3] So Greg. Naz. Orat. 39, p. 688, Jer. Ep. ad Fabiol. and most commentators,
followed by the collect in our baptismal service, "figuring thereby thy holy
baptism." But observe that the typology is quite incidental, the moral lesson
paramount (1 Cor. x. 6, 11).
[4] See Excursus IV., "St. Paul a Hagadist."

which almost constituted the entire education of their
scholars, was the *Halacha,* or "rule;" and if we compare
the Talmud with the Midrashim, we see at once that
some Jewish scholars devoted themselves to the Hagada
almost exclusively, and others to the Halacha, and that
the names frequent in the one region of Jewish literature are rarely found in the other. The two classes of
students despised each other. The Hagadist despised
the Halachist as a minute pedant, and was despised in
turn as an imaginative ignoramus. There was on the
part of some Rabbis a jealous dislike of teaching the
Hagadôth at all to any one who had not gone through
the laborious training of the *Halacha.* "I hold from
my ancestors," said R. Jonathan, in refusing to teach the
Hagada to R. Samlaï, "that one ought not to teach
the Hagada either to a Babylonian or to a southern
Palestinian, because they are arrogant and ignorant."
The consequences of the mutual dis-esteem in which
each branch of students held the other was that the
Hagadists mainly occupied themselves with the Prophets,
and the Halachists with the Law. And hence the latter
became more and more Judaic, Pharisaic, Rabbinic. The
seven rules of Hillel became the thirteen rules of Ishmael,[1]
and the thirty-three of Akibha, and by the intervention
of these rules almost anything might be added to or
subtracted from the veritable Law.[2] The letter of the
Law thus lost its comparative simplicity in boundless
complications, until the Talmud tells us how Akibha
was seen in a vision by the astonished Moses, drawing

---

[1] See Derenbourg, *Palest.* p. 397.

[2] Even R. Ishmael, who shares with R. Akibha the title of Father of the
World, admits to having found three cases in which the Halacha was contrary
to the letter of the Pentateuch. It would not be difficult to discover very
many more.

from every horn of every letter whole bushels of decisions.[1] Meanwhile the Hagadists were deducing from the utterances of the Prophets a spirit which almost amounted to contempt for Levitical minutiæ;[2] were developing the Messianic tradition, and furnishing a powerful though often wholly unintentional assistance to the logic of Christian exegesis. This was because the Hagadists were grasping the spirit, while the Halachists were blindly groping amid the crumbled fragments of the letter. It is not wonderful that the Jews got to be so jealous of the Hagada, as betraying possible tendencies to the heresies of the *minim*—*i.e.*, the Christians—that they imposed silence upon those who used certain suspected hagadistic expressions, which in themselves were perfectly harmless. "He who profanes holy things," says Rabbi Eliezer of Modin, in the *Pirke Abhôth*, "who slights the festivals, who causes his neighbour to blush in public, who breaks the covenant of Abraham, and discovers explanations of the Law contrary to the Halacha, even if he knew the Law and his works were good, would still lose his share in the life to come."[3]

It is easy to understand from these interesting particulars that if the Hagada and the Halacha were alike taught in the lecture-room of Gamaliel, St. Paul, whatever may have been his original respect for and study of the one, carried with him in mature years no trace of such studies, while he by no means despised the best parts of the other, and, illuminated by the Holy Spirit of God, found in the training with which it had furnished him at least an occasional germ, or illustration, of those

---

[1] *Menachôth*, 29, 2.
[2] Is. i. 11—15; lviii. 5—7; Jer. vii. 21.
[3] *Pirke Abhôth*, iii. 8; Grätz, iii. 79.

Christian and Messianic arguments which he addressed with such consummate force alike to the rigid Hebraists and the most bigoted Hellenists in after years.[1]

[1] See Derenbourg's *Hist. de la Palestine d'après les Thalmuds* (ch. xxi. and xxiii.), which seems to me to throw a flood of light on the views and early training of St. Paul.

CHAPTER IV.

SAUL THE PHARISEE.

Ζηλωτὴς ὑπάρχων τῶν πατρικῶν μου παραδόσεων.—GAL. i. 14; ACTS xxii. 3.
Κατὰ τὴν ἀκριβεστάτην αἵρεσιν τῆς ἡμετέρας θρησκείας ἔζησα Φαρισαῖος.—ACTS xxvi. 5.

IF the gathered lore of the years between the ages of thirteen and thirty-three has left, as it must inevitably have left, unmistakable traces on the pages of St. Paul, how much more must this be the case with all the moral struggles, all the spiritual experiences, all those inward battles which are not fought with earthly weapons, through which he must have passed during the long period in which "he lived a Pharisee"?

We know well the kind of life which lies hid behind that expression. We know the minute and intense scrupulosity of Sabbath observance wasting itself in all those *abhôth* and *toldôth*—those primary and derivative rules and prohibitions, and inferences from rules and prohibitions, and combinations of inferences from rules and prohibitions, and cases of casuistry and conscience arising out of the infinite possible variety of circumstances to which those combinations of inference might apply— which had degraded the Sabbath from "a delight, holy of the Lord and honourable," partly into an anxious and pitiless burden, and partly into a network of contrivances hypocritically designed, as it were, in the lowest spirit of heathenism, to cheat the Deity with the mere *semblance* of accurate observance.[1] We know the carefulness about the colour of fringes, and the tying of tassels, and the lawfulness of meats and drinks. We know the tithings, at once troublesome and ludicrous, of mint, anise, and cummin, and the serio-comic questions as to whether in tithing the seed it was obligatory also to tithe the stalk. We know the double fasts of the week, and the triple prayers of the day, and the triple visits to the Temple. We know the elaborate strainings of the water and the wine, that not even the carcase of an animalcula might defeat the energy of Levitical anxiety. We know the constant rinsings and scourings of brazen cups and pots and tables, carried to so absurd an extreme that, on the occasion of washing the golden candelabrum of the Temple, the Sadducees remarked that their Pharisaic rivals would wash the Sun itself if they could get an opportunity. We know the entire and laborious ablutions and bathings of the whole person, with carefully tabulated ceremonies and normal gesticulations, not for the laudable purpose of personal cleanliness, but for the nervously strained endeavour to avoid every possible and impossible chance of contracting ceremonial uncleanness. We know how this notion of perfect Levitical purity thrust itself with irritating recurrence into every aspect and relation of ordinary life, and led to the scornful avoidance of the very contact and shadow of fellow-beings, who might after all be purer and nobler than those who would not touch them with the tassel of a garment's hem. We know the obtrusive prayers,[2] the ostentatious almsgivings,[3] the broadened phylacteries,[4] the petty ritualisms,[5] the professorial arrogance,[6] the reckless proselytism,[7] the greedy

---

[1] See the rules about the mixtures (*Erubhin*), *Life of Christ*, i. 436, ii. 472.
[2] Matt. vi. 5.   [3] Matt. vi. 2.   [4] Matt. xxiii. 5.
[5] Mark vii. 4—8.   [6] John vii. 49.   [7] Matt. xxiii. 15.

avarice,[1] the haughty assertion of pre-eminence,[2] the ill-
concealed hypocrisy,[3] which were often hidden under this
venerable assumption of superior holiness. And we know
all this quite as much, or more, from the admiring records
of the Talmud—which devotes one whole treatise to hand-
washings,[4] and another to the proper method of killing a
fowl,[5] and another to the stalks of legumes[6]—as from
the reiterated "woes" of Christ's denunciation.[7] But
we may be sure that these extremes and degeneracies
of the Pharisaic aim would be as grievous and displeasing to the youthful Saul as they were to all the noblest
Pharisees, and as they were to Christ Himself. Of the
seven kinds of Pharisees which the Talmud in various
places enumerates, we may be quite sure that Saul of
Tarsus would neither be a "bleeding" Pharisee, nor a
"mortar" Pharisee, nor a "Shechemite" Pharisee, nor a
"timid" Pharisee, nor a "tumbling" Pharisee, nor a
"painted" Pharisee at all; but that the only class of
Pharisee to which he, as a true and high-minded Israelite,
would have borne any shadow of resemblance, and that not
in a spirit of self-contentment, but in a spirit of almost
morbid and feverish anxiety to do all that was commanded,
would be the Tell-me-anything-more-to-do-and-I-will-do-it
Pharisee ![8]

And this type of character, which bears no remote resemblance to that of many of the devotees of the monastic
life—however erroneous it may be, however bitter must be
the pain by which it must be accompanied, however deep the
dissatisfaction which it must ultimately suffer—is very far
from being necessarily ignoble. It is indeed based on the

[1] Luke xx. 47.   [2] Luke xviii. 11.   [3] Matt. xxii. 17.
[4] *Yadayim.*   [5] *Cholin.*   [6] *Ozekin.*
[7] See Schöttgen, *Hor. Hebr.* pp. 7, 160, 204.
[8] *Jer. Berachôth,* ix. 7, &c. See *Life of Christ,* vol. ii. p. 248, where
these names are explained.

enormous error that man can deserve heaven by care in external practices; that he can win by quantitative goodness
his entrance into the kingdom of God; that that kingdom
is meat and drink, not righteousness and peace and joy in
believing. Occasionally, by some flash of sudden conviction, one or two of the wisest Doctors of the Law
seem to have had some glimmering of the truth, that
it is *not* by works of righteousness, but only by God's
mercy, that man is saved. But the normal and all but
universal belief of the religious party among the Jews was
that, though of the 248 commands and 365 prohibitions
of the Mosaic Law some were "light" and some were
"heavy,"[1] yet that to one and all alike—not only in the
spirit but in the letter—not only in the actual letter, but
in the boundless inferences to which the letter might lead
when every grain of sense and meaning had been crushed
out of it under mountain loads of "decisions"—a rigidly
scrupulous obedience was due. This was what God
absolutely required. This, and this only, came up to the
true conception of the blameless righteousness of the Law.
And how much depended on it! Nothing less than
recovered freedom, recovered empire, recovered pre-eminence
among the nations; nothing less than the restoration of
their national independence in all its perfectness, of their
national worship in all its splendour; nothing less than
the old fire upon the altar, the holy oil, the sacred ark,
the cloud of glory between the wings of the cherubim;
nothing less, in short, than the final hopes which for many
centuries they and their fathers had most deeply cherished.
If but one person could only for one day keep the whole Law

---

[1] See *Life of Christ*, ii. 239. All these distinctions were a part of the
Seyyag, the "hedge of the Law," which it was the one *raison d'être* of
Rabbinism to construct. The object of all Jewish learning was to make a
mishmereth ("ordinance," Lev. xviii. 30) to God's *mishmereth* (*Yebhamoth*,
f. 21, 1.)

F

and not offend in one point—nay, if but one person could but keep that one point of the Law which affected the due observance of the Sabbath—then (so the Rabbis taught) the troubles of Israel would be ended, and the Messiah at last would come.[1]

And it was at nothing less than this that, with all the intense ardour of his nature, Saul had aimed. It is doubtful whether at this period the utter nullity of the Oral Law could have dawned upon him. It sometimes dawned even on the Rabbis through the dense fogs of sophistry and self-importance, and even on their lips we sometimes find the utterances of the Prophets that humility and justice and mercy are better than sacrifice. "There was a flute in the Temple," says the Talmud, "preserved from the days of Moses; it was smooth, thin, and formed of a reed. At the command of the king it was overlaid with gold, which ruined its sweetness of tone until the gold was taken away. There were also a cymbal and a mortar, which had become injured in course of time, and were mended by workmen of Alexandria summoned by the wise men; but their usefulness was so completely destroyed by this process, that it was necessary to restore them to their former condition."[2] Are not these things an allegory? Do they not imply that by overlaying the written Law with what they called the gold, but what was in reality the dross and tinsel of tradition, the Rabbis had destroyed or injured its beauty and usefulness? But probably Saul had not realised this. To him there was no distinction between the relative importance of the Written and Oral, of the moral and ceremonial Law. To every precept—and they were countless—obedience was

---

[1] See Acts iii. 19, where ὅπως ἂν is "in order that haply," not "when," as in E. V. (*Shabbath*, f. 118, b).

[2] *Birachin*, f. 10, 2.

due. If it *could* be done, he would do it. If on him, on his accuracy of observance, depended the coming of the Messiah, then the Messiah should come. Were others learned in all that concerned legal rectitude? he would be yet more learned. Were others scrupulous? he would be yet more scrupulous. Surely God had left man free?[1] Surely He would not have demanded obedience to the Law if that obedience were not possible! All things pointed to the close of one great *aeon* in the world's history, and the dawn of another which should be the last. The very heathen yearned for some deliverer, and felt that there could be no other end to the physical misery and moral death which had spread itself over their hollow societies.[2] Deep midnight was brooding alike over the chosen people and the Gentile world. From the East should break forth a healing light, a purifying flame. Let Israel be true, and God's promise would not fail.

And we know from his own statements that if external conformity were all—if obedience to the Law did not mean obedience in all kinds of matters which escaped all possibility of attention—if avoidance of its prohibitions did not involve avoidance in matters which evaded the reach of the human senses—then Saul was, touching the righteousness of the Law, *blameless*, having lived in all good conscience towards God.[3] Had *he* put the question to the Great Master, "What shall I do to be saved?" or been bidden to "keep the commandments," it is certain that he would have been able to reply with the youthful ruler, "All these have I kept from my youth," and—he might have added—"very much besides." And

---

[1] The Rabbis said, "Everything is in the hands of heaven, except the fear of heaven." "All things are ordained by God, but a man's actions are his own." (Barclay, *Talmud*, 18.)

[2] Virg. Ecl. iv. Suet. *Aug.* 94; *Vesp.* 4.

[3] 2 Cor. xi. 22; Rom. xi. 1; Acts xxii. 3, xxiii. 1 6.

F 2

yet we trace in his Epistles how bitterly he felt the hollowness of this outward obedience—how awful and how burdensome had been to him "the curse of the Law." Even
moral obedience could not silence the voice of the conscience, or satisfy the yearnings of the soul; but these
infinitesimal Levitisms, what could they do? Tormenting
questions would again and again arise. Of what use was
all this? from what did the necessity of it spring? to
what did the obedience to it lead? Did God indeed care
for the exact size of a strip of parchment, or the particular number of lines in the texts which were upon it,
or the way in which the letters were formed, or the shape
of the box into which it was put, or the manner in which
that box was tied upon the forehead or the arm?[1]   Was
it, indeed, a very important matter whether "between
the two evenings" meant, as the Samaritans believed, between sunset and darkness, or, as the Pharisees asserted,
between the beginning and end of sunset? Was it a matter worth the discussion of two schools to decide whether
an egg laid on a festival might or might not be eaten?[2]
Were all these things indeed, and in themselves, important? And even if they were, would it be errors as to
these littlenesses that would really kindle the wrath of a
jealous God? How did they contribute to the beauty of
holiness? in what way did they tend to fill the soul
with the mercy which was better than sacrifice, or to edu-
cate it in that justice and humility, that patience and
purity, that peace and love, which, as some of the prophets
had found grace to see, were dearer to God than thousands
of rams and ten thousands of rivers of oil? And behind

---

[1] I have adduced abundant illustrations from Rabbinic writers of the extravagant importance attached to minutiæ in the construction of the two
phylacteries of the hand (*Tephillin shel Yad*) and of the head (*Teph. shel
Rôsh*), in the *Expositor*, 1877, No. xxvii.

[2] See Bîtsah, 1 *ad in.*

all these questions lay that yet deeper one which agitated the schools of Jewish thought—the question whether, after all, man could reach, or with all his efforts must inevitably fail to reach, that standard of righteousness which God and the Law required? And if indeed he failed, what more had the Law to say to him than to deliver its sentence of unreprieved condemnation and indiscriminate death?[1]

Moreover, was there not mingled with all this nominal adoration of the Law a deeply-seated hypocrisy, *so* deep that it was in a great measure unconscious? Even before the days of Christ the Rabbis had learnt the art of straining out gnats and swallowing camels. They had long learnt to nullify what they professed to defend. The ingenuity of Hillel was quite capable of getting rid of any Mosaic regulation which had been found practically burdensome. Pharisees and Sadducees alike had managed to set aside in their own favour, by the devices of the "mixtures," all that was disagreeable to themselves in the Sabbath scrupulosity. The fundamental institution of the Sabbatic year had been stultified by the mere legal fiction of the *prosbol*. Teachers who were on the high road to a casuistry which could construct "rules" out of every superfluous particle had found it easy to win credit for ingenuity by elaborating prescriptions to which Moses would have listened in mute astonishment.[1] If there be one thing more definitely laid down in the Law than another it is the uncleanness of creeping things, yet the Talmud assures us that "no one is appointed a member of the Sanhedrin who does not possess sufficient ingenuity to prove from the written Law that a creeping thing is ceremonially clean;"[2] and that

---

[1] Rom. x. 5; Gal. iii. 10.   [2] *Sanhedr.* f. 17, 1.

there was an unimpeachable disciple at Jabne who could adduce one hundred and fifty arguments in favour of the ceremonial cleanness of creeping things.[1] Sophistry like this was at work even in the days when the young student of Tarsus sat at the feet of Gamaliel; and can we imagine any period of his life when he would not have been wearied by a system at once so meaningless, so stringent, and so insincere? Could he fail to notice that they "hugely violated what they trivially obeyed?"

We may see from St. Paul's own words that these years must have been very troubled years. Under the dignified exterior of the Pharisee lay a wildly-beating heart; an anxious brain throbbed with terrible questionings under the broad phylactery. Saul as a Pharisee believed in eternity, he believed in the resurrection, he believed in angel and spirit, in voices and appearances, in dreaming dreams and seeing visions. But in all this struggle to achieve his own righteousness—this struggle so minutely tormenting, so revoltingly burdensome—there seemed to be no hope, no help, no enlightenment, no satisfaction, no nobility—nothing but a possibly mitigated and yet inevitable curse. God seemed silent to him, and heaven closed. No vision dawned on his slumbering senses, no voice sounded in his eager ear. The sense of sin oppressed him; the darkness of mystery hung over him; he was ever falling and falling, and no hand was held out to help him; he strove with all his soul to be obedient, and he was obedient—and yet the Messiah did not come.

The experience of Saul of Tarsus was the heartrending experience of all who have looked for peace elsewhere than in the love of God. All that Luther suffered at Erfurdt Saul must have suffered in Jerusalem; and the record of

[1] *Erubhin,* f. 13, 2.

the early religious agonies and awakenment of the one is
the best commentary on the experience of the other.
That the life of Saul was free from flagrant transgressions
we see from his own bold appeals to his continuous
rectitude. He was not a convert from godlessness or
profligacy, like John Bunyan or John Newton. He
claims integrity when he is speaking of his life in
the aspect which it presented to his fellow-men, but he
is vehement in self-accusation when he thinks of that
life in the aspect which it presented to his God. He
found that no external legality could give him a clean
heart, or put a right spirit within him. He found that
servile obedience inspired no inward peace. He must
have yearned for some righteousness, could he but know
of it, which would be better than the righteousness of the
Scribes and Pharisees. The Jewish doctors had imagined
and had directed that if a man did not feel inclined to do
this or that, he should force himself to do it by a direct
vow. "Vows," said Rabbi Akibha,[1] "are the enclosures
of holiness." But Saul the Pharisee, long before he
became Paul the Apostle, must have proved to the very
depth the hollowness of this direction. Vows might be
the enclosures of formal practice; they were not, and
could not be, the schooling of the disobedient soul; they
could not give calm to that place in the human being
where meet the two seas of good and evil impulse[2]—to
the heart, which is the battle-field on which passionate
desire clashes into collision with positive command.

Even when twenty years of weariness, and wandering,
and struggle, and suffering, were over, we still catch in the
Epistles of St. Paul the mournful echoes of those days of
stress and storm—echoes as of the thunder when its fury

---

[1] סְיָג לַחָכְמָה סְיָג, *Pirke Abhôth*, iii. 10.
[2] The *Yetser tôbh* and the *Yetser ha-râ* of the Talmud.

is over, and it is only sobbing far away among the distant
hills.   We hear those echoes most of all in the Epistle to
the Romans.   We hear them when he talks of "the curse
of the law."   We hear them when, in accents of deep
self-pity, he tells us of the struggle between the flesh and
the spirit; between the law of sin in his members, and
that law of God which, though holy and just and good
and ordained to life, he found to be unto death.   In the
days, indeed, when he thus writes, he had at last found
peace ; he had wrung from the lessons of his life the hard
experience that by the works of the law no man can be
justified in God's sight, but that, being justified by faith,
we have peace with God through our Lord Jesus Christ.
And though, gazing on his own personality, and seeing it
disintegrated by a miserable dualism, he still found a law
within him which warred against that inward delight
which he felt in the law of God—though groaning
in this body of weakness, he feels like one who is imprisoned in a body of death, he can still, in answer to the
question, "Who shall deliver me?" exclaim with a burst
of triumph, "I thank God, through Jesus Christ our
Lord."[1]   But if the Apostle, after he has found Christ,
after he has learnt that "there is no condemnation to
them that are in Christ Jesus"[2] still felt the power
and continuity of the inferior law striving to degrade
his life into that captivity to the law of sin from which
Christ had set him free, through what hours of mental
anguish must he not have passed when he knew of no
other dealing of God with his soul than the impossible,
unsympathising, deathful commandment, "This *do*, and
thou shalt live!"   *Could* he "this do"?   And, if he could

[1] See Rom. vi., vii., viii., *passim*.
[2] Rom. viii. 1.   The rest of this verse in our E. V. is probably a gloss, or a
repetition, since it is not found in ℵ, B, C, D, F, G.

not, what hope, what help? Was there any voice of pity among the thunders of Sinai?[1] Could the mere blood of bulls and goats be any true propitiation for wilful sins?

But though we can see the mental anguish through which Saul passed in his days of Pharisaism, yet over the events of that period a complete darkness falls; and there are only two questions, both of them deeply interesting, which it may, perhaps, be in our power to answer.

The first is, Did Saul in those days ever see the Lord Jesus Christ?

At first sight we might suppose that the question was answered, and answered affirmatively, in 1 Cor. ix. 1, where he asks, "Am I not an Apostle? Have I not seen Jesus, our Lord?" and still more in 2 Cor. v. 16, where he says, "Yea, though we have known Christ after the flesh, yet now henceforth know we Him no more."[2]

But a little closer examination of these passages will show that they do not necessarily involve any such meaning. In the first of them, St. Paul cannot possibly be alluding to any knowledge of Jesus before His crucifixion, because such mere external sight, from the position of one who disbelieved in Him, so far from being a confirmation of any claim to be an Apostle, would rather have been a reason for rejecting such a claim. It can only apply to the appearance of Christ to him on the way to Damascus,

---

[1] "That man that overtook you," said Christian, "was Moses. He spareth none, neither knoweth he how to show mercy to them that transgress his law." (Pilgrim's Progress.)

[2] εἰ καὶ ἐγνώκαμεν. It is perfectly true that εἰ καὶ (quamquam, "even though," wenn auch) in classical writers—though perhaps less markedly in St. Paul—concedes a fact, whereas καὶ εἰ (etiam si, "even if,") puts an hypothesis; but the explanation here turns, not on the admitted force of the particles, but on what is meant by "knowing Christ after the flesh."

or to some similar and subsequent revelation.[1] The
meaning of the second passage is less obvious. St. Paul
has there been explaining the grounds of his Apostolate in
the constraining love of Christ for man. He has shown
how that love was manifested by His death for all, and
how the results of that death and resurrection are
intended so utterly to destroy the self-love of His children,
so totally to possess and to change their individuality,
that "if any man be in Christ he is a new creation."
And the Christ of whom he is here speaking is the
risen, glorified, triumphant Christ, in whom all things
are become new, because He has reconciled man to God.
Hence the Apostle will know no man, judge of no
man, in his mere human and earthly relations, but
only in his union with their risen Lord. The partisans
who used, and far more probably abused, the name of
James, to thrust their squabbling Judaism even into the
intercourse between a Paul and a Peter, and who sowed
the seeds of discord among the converts of the Churches
which St. Paul had founded, were constantly under-
rating the Apostolic dignity of Paul, because he had not
been an eye-witness of the human life of Christ. The
answer of the Apostle always was that he too knew Christ
by an immediate revelation, that "it had pleased God
to reveal His Son in him that he might preach Christ among
the Gentiles."[2] The day had been when he had known
"Christ according to the flesh"—not indeed by direct

---

[1] Cf. Acts xviii. 9, xxii. 18; 2 Cor. xii. 1. The absence of such *personal* references to Jesus in St. Paul's Epistles as we find in 1 Pet. ii. 21 *sq.*,
iii. 18 *sq.*; 1 John i. 1—confirms this view (Ewald, *Gesch.* vi. 389).

[2] Gal. i. 16. I cannot agree with Dr. Lightfoot (following Jerome,
Erasmus, &c.) that ἐν ἐμοί means "a revelation *made through Paul to others*,"
as in ver. 24, 1 Tim. i. 16, and 2 Cor. xiii. 3; because, as a friend points out,
there is an *exact* parallelism of clauses between i. 11, 12 and 13—17, and
ἀποκαλύψαι τὸν υἱὸν αὐτοῦ ἐν ἐμοί balances δι' ἀποκαλύψεως Ἰησοῦ Χριστοῦ in ver. 12.

personal intercourse with Him in the days of His earthly ministry, but by the view which he and others had taken of Him. In his unconverted days he had regarded Him as a *mesith*—an impostor who deceived the people, or at the very best as a teacher who deceived himself. And after his conversion he had not perhaps, at first, fully learnt to apprehend the *Plenitude* of the glory of the risen Christ as rising far above the conception of the Jewish Messiah. All this was past. To apprehend by faith the glorified Son of God was a far more blessed privilege than to have known a living Messiah by earthly intercourse. Even if he had known Christ as a living man, that knowledge would have been less near, less immediate, less intimate, less eternal, in its character, than the closeness of community wherewith he now lived and died in Him; and although he had known Him first only by false report, and then only with imperfect realisation as Jesus of Nazareth, the earthly and human conception had now passed away, and been replaced by the true and spiritual belief. The Christ, therefore, whom now he knew was no " Christ after the flesh," no Christ in the days of His flesh, no Christ in any earthly relations, but Christ sitting for ever at the right hand of God. To have seen the Lord Jesus with the eyes was of itself nothing —it was nothing to boast of. Herod had seen Him, and Annas, and Pilate, and many a coarse Jewish mendicant and many a brutal Roman soldier. But to have seen Him with the eye of Faith—to have spiritually apprehended the glorified Redeemer—that was indeed to be a Christian.

All the other passages which can at all be brought to bear on the question support this view, and lead us to believe that St. Paul had either not seen at all, or at the best barely seen, the Man Christ Jesus. Indeed, the

question, "Who art Thou, Lord?"[1] preserved in all three
narratives of his conversion, seems distinctly to imply that
the personal appearance of the Lord was unknown to him,
and this is a view which is confirmed by the allusion to
the risen Christ in 1 Cor. xv. St. Paul there says that
to him, the least of the Apostles, and not meet to be called
an Apostle, Christ had appeared last of all, as to the
abortive-born of the Apostolic family.[2] And, indeed, it is
inconceivable that Saul could in any real sense have seen
Jesus in His lifetime. That ineffaceable impression produced by His very aspect; that unspeakable personal
ascendency, which awed His worst enemies and troubled
the hard conscience of His Roman judge; the ineffable
charm and power in the words of Him who spake as never
man spake, could not have appealed to him in vain. We
feel an unalterable conviction, not only that, if Saul had
seen Him, Paul would again and again have referred to
Him, but also that he would in that case have been saved
from the reminiscence which most of all tortured him in
after days—the undeniable reproach that he had persecuted
the Church of God. If, indeed, we could imagine that
Saul had seen Christ, and, having seen Him, had looked on
Him only with the bitter hatred and simulated scorn of
a Jerusalem Pharisee, then we may be certain that that
Holy Face which looked into the troubled dreams of Pilate's
wife—that the infinite sorrow in those eyes, of which one
glance broke the repentant heart of Peter—would have
recurred so often and so heartrendingly to Paul's remembrance, that his sin in persecuting the Christians would
have assumed an aspect of tenfold aggravation, from the
thought that in destroying and imprisoning them he had

---

[1] Acts ix. 5 (xxii. 8, xxvi. 15). There is not the shadow of probability in
the notion of Ewald, that St. Paul was the young man clad in a *sindōn*, of
Mark xiv. 52.   [2] 1 Cor. xv. 9.

yet more openly been crucifying the Son of God afresh, and putting Him to an open shame. The intense impressibility of Paul's mind appears most remarkably in the effect exercised upon him by the dying rapture of St. Stephen. The words of Stephen, though listened to at the time with inward fury, not only lingered in his memory, but produced an unmistakable influence on his writings. If this were so with the speech of the youthful Hellenist, how infinitely more would it have been so with the words which subdued into admiration even the alien disposition of Pharisaic emissaries? Can we for a moment conceive that Paul's Pharisaism would have lasted unconsumed amid the white lightnings of that great and scathing denunciation which Christ uttered in the Temple in the last week of His ministry, and three days before His death? Had St. Paul heard one of these last discourses, had he seen one of those miracles, had he mingled in one of those terrible and tragic scenes to which he must have afterwards looked back as events the most momentous in the entire course of human history, is there any one who can for a moment imagine that no personal reminiscence of such scenes would be visible, even ever so faintly, through the transparent medium of his writings?

We may, then, regard it as certain that when the gloom fell at mid-day over the awful sacrifice of Golgotha, when the people shouted their preference for the murderous brigand, and yelled their execration of the Saviour whose day all the noblest and holiest of their fathers had longed to see, Saul was not at Jerusalem. Where, then, was he? It is impossible to answer the question with any certainty. He may have been at Tarsus, which, even after his conversion, he regarded as his home.[1] Or perhaps the

---

[1] Acts ix. 30, xi. 25; Gal. i. 21.

explanation of his absence may be seen in Gal. v. 11.
He there represents himself as having once been a preacher
of circumcision.   Now we know that one of the characteristics of the then Pharisaism was an active zeal in
winning proselytes.   " Ye compass sea and land," said
Christ to them, in burning words, " to make one proselyte;
and when he is made, ye make him twofold more the
child of Gehenna than yourselves."[1]   The conversion
which changed Paul's deepest earlier convictions left
unchanged the natural impulse of his temperament.
Why may not the same impetuous zeal, the same restless desire to be always preaching some truth and
doing some good work which marked him out as the
Apostle of the Gentiles,[2] have worked in him also in these
earlier days, and made him, as he seems to imply, a missionary of Pharisaism?   If so, he may have been absent
on some journey enjoined upon him by the party whose
servant, heart and soul, he was, during the brief visits to
Jerusalem which marked the three years' ministry of Christ
on earth.

2. The other question which arises is, Was Saul married?   Had he the support of some loving heart during
the fiery struggles of his youth?   Amid the to-and-fro contentions of spirit which resulted from an imperfect and
unsatisfying creed, was there in the troubled sea of his
life one little island home where he could find refuge from
incessant thoughts?

Little as we know of his domestic relations, little as
he cared to mingle mere private interests with the great
spiritual truths which occupy his soul, it seems to me
that we must answer this question in the affirmative.   St.
Paul, who has been very freely charged with egotism, had

---

[1] Matt. xxiii. 15.   [2] Gal. i. 16.   (See Krenkel, p. 18.)

not one particle of that egotism which consists in attaching any importance to his personal surroundings. The circumstances of his individual life he would have looked on as having no interest for any one but himself. When he speaks of himself he does so always from one of two reasons—from the necessity of maintaining against detraction his apostolic authority, or from the desire to utilise for others his remarkable experience. The things that happened to him, the blessings and privations of his earthly condition, would have seemed matters of supreme indifference, except in so far as they possessed a moral significance, or had any bearing on the lessons which he desired to teach.

It is, then, only indirectly that we can expect to find an answer to the question as to his marriage. If, indeed, he was a member of the Sanhedrin, it follows that, by the Jewish requirements for that position, he must have been a married man. His official position will be examined hereafter; but, meanwhile, his marriage may be inferred as probable from passages in his Epistles. In 1 Cor. ix. 5 he asks the Corinthians, "Have we not power to lead about a sister, a wife, as well as other Apostles, and as the brethren of the Lord, and Kephas?" This passage is inconclusive, though it asserts his right both to marry, and to take a wife with him in his missionary journeys if he thought it expedient.[1] But from 1 Cor. vii. 8 it seems a distinct inference that he classed himself among *widowers;* for, he says, "I say, therefore, to the *unmarried* and widows, it is good for them if they *abide* (μείνωσιν) even as I." That by "the unmarried"

---

[1] The notion that the "true yokefellow" (γνήσιε σύζυγε) of Phil. iv. 3 has any bearing on the question is an error as old as Clemens Alexandrinus. (See *Strom.* iii. 7; Ps. Ignat. *ad Philad.* 4, 'Ως Πέτρου καὶ Παύλου καὶ τῶν ἄλλων ἀποστόλων τῶν γάμοις ὁμιλησάντων.)

he here means " widowers "—for which there is no special
Greek word—seems clear, because he has been already
speaking, in the first seven verses of the chapter, to those
who have never been married.[1] To them he concedes, far
more freely than to the others, the privilege of marrying
if they considered it conducive to godliness, though, in
the present state of things, he mentions his own personal
predilection for celibacy, in the case of all who had the grace
of inward purity.   And even apart from the interpretation
of this passage, the deep and fine insight of Luther had
drawn the conclusion that Paul knew by experience what
marriage was, from the wisdom and tenderness which
characterise his remarks respecting it.   One who had
never been married could hardly have written on the
subject as he has done, nor could he have shown
the same profound sympathy with the needs of all,
and received from all the same ready confidence.   To
derive any inference from the loving metaphors which
he draws from the nurture of little children [2] would
be more precarious.   It is hardly possible that Paul
ever had a child who lived.   Had this been the case,
his natural affection could hardly have denied itself
some expression of the tender love which flows out
so freely towards his spiritual children.   Timothy would
not have been so exclusively "his own true child"
in the faith if he had had son or daughter of his own.
If we are right in the assumption that he was married,

---

[1] If so, Chaucer is mistaken when he says, " I wot wel the Apostle was a
mayd," i.e., παρθένος, Rev. xiv. 4 (Prologue to *Wife of Bath's Tales*).   Ver. 7
does not militate against this view, because there he is alluding, not to his
condition, but to the grace of continence. It is not true, as has been said, that
early tradition was unanimous in saying that he had never married.   Tertullian (*De Monogam.* 3) and Jerome (*Ep.* 22) says so; but Origen is doubtful,
and Methodius (*Conviv.* 45), as well as Clemens Alex. and Ps. Ignatius
(v. *supra*), say that he was a widower.

[2] 1 Cor. iii. 2, vii. 14, iv. 15; 1 Thess. ii. 7; v. 3.

it seems probable that it was for a short time only, and that his wife had died.

But there is one more ground which has not, I think, been noticed, which seems to me to render it extremely probable that Saul, before the time of his conversion, had been a married man. It is the extraordinary importance attached by the majority of Jews in all ages to marriage as a moral duty, nay, even a positive command, incumbent on every man.[1] The Mishna fixes the age of marriage at eighteen,[2] and even seventeen was preferred. The Babylonist Jews fixed it as early as fourteen.[3] Marriage is, in fact, the first of the 613 precepts. They derived the duty partly from the command of Gen. i. 28, partly from allusions to early marriage in the Old Testament (Prov. ii. 17; v. 18), and partly from allegorising explanations of passages like Eccl. xi. 6; Job v. 24.[4] The Rabbis in all ages have laid it down as a stringent duty that parents should marry their children young;[5] and the one or two who, like Ben Azai, theoretically placed on a higher level the duty of being more free from incumbrance in order to study the Law, were exceptions to the almost universal rule. But even these theorists were themselves married men. If St. Paul had ever evinced the smallest sympathy with the views of the Therapeutæ and Essenes

---

[1] "A Jew who has no wife is not a man" (Gen. v. 2, *Yebhamoth,* f. 63, 1).

[2] *Pirke Abhôth,* v. 21.

[3] God was supposed to curse all who at twenty were unmarried (*Kiddushin,* 29, 1; 30; *Yebhamoth,* 62, 63). (See Hamburger, Talmud. Wörterb. *s.v. Ehe, Verheirathung;* Weill, *La Morale du Judaisme,* 49, seq.) The precept is inferred from "He called *their* name *man* (sing.)," and is found in the Rabbinic digest *Tur-Shulchan Aruch.*

[4] See Ecclus. vii. 25; xlii. 9; cf. 1 Cor. vii. 36.

[5] Early marriages are to this day the curse of the Jews in Eastern countries. Sometimes girls are married at ten, boys at fourteen (Frankl. *Jews in East,* ii. 18, 84). Not long ago a Jewish girl at Jerusalem, aged fourteen, when asked in school why she was sad, replied that she h'd been three times divorced.

—if his discountenancing of marriage, under certain immediate conditions, had been tinged by any Gnostic fancies about its essential inferiority—we might have come to a different conclusion. But he held no such views either before or after his conversion;[1] and certainly, if he lived unmarried as a Jerusalem Pharisee, his case was entirely exceptional.

[1] 1 Cor. vii. 9, 36; 1 Tim. iv. 3; v. 14.

CHAPTER V.

ST. PETER AND THE FIRST PENTECOST.

Ἔκκριτος ἦν τῶν ἀποστόλων, καὶ στόμα τῶν μαθητῶν, καὶ κορυφὴ τοῦ χοροῦ.—
CHRYS. *In Joan. Hom.* 88.

Πέτρος ἡ ἀρχὴ τῆς ορθοδοξίας, ὁ μέγας τῆς ἐκκλησίας ἱεροφάντης.—PS. CHRYS.
Orat. Encom. 9.

WHATEVER may have been the cause of Saul's absence
from Jerusalem during the brief period of the ministry of
Jesus, it is inevitable that, on his return, he must have
heard much respecting it. Yet all that he heard would be
exclusively from the point of view of the Pharisees, who
had so bitterly opposed His doctrines, and of the Sadducees, who had so basely brought about His death. But
he would have abundant opportunities for seeing that the
Infant Church had not, as the Jews of Jerusalem had
hoped, been extinguished by the murder of its founder.
However much the news might fill him with astonishment and indignation, he could not have been many days
in Jerusalem without receiving convincing proofs of the
energy of what he then regarded as a despicable sect.

Whence came this irresistible energy, this inextinguish-
able vitality? The answer to that question is the history
of the Church and of the world.

For the death of Jesus had been followed by a succession of events, the effects of which will be felt to the
end of time—events which, by a spiritual power at once
astounding and indisputable, transformed a timid handful
of ignorant and terror-stricken Apostles into teachers of

G 2

unequalled grandeur, who became in God's hands the instruments to regenerate the world.

The Resurrection of Christ had scattered every cloud from their saddened souls. The despair which, for a moment, had followed the intense hope that this was He who would redeem Israel, had been succeeded by a joyous and unshaken conviction that Christ had risen from the dead. In the light of that Resurrection, all Scripture, all history, all that they had seen and heard during the ministry of Jesus, was illuminated and transfigured. And though during the forty days between the Resurrection and the Ascension, the intercourse held with them by their risen Lord was not continuous, but brief and interrupted,[1] yet—as St. Peter himself testifies, appealing, in confirmation of his testimony, to the scattered Jews to whom his Epistle is addressed—God had begotten them again by the Resurrection unto a lively hope, to an inheritance incorruptible, and undefiled, and that fadeth not away.[2] But besides this glorious truth, of which they felt themselves to be the chosen witnesses,[3] their Risen Lord had given them many promises and instructions, and spoken to them about the things which concerned the Kingdom of God. In His last address He had specially bidden them to stay in Jerusalem, and there await the outpouring of the Spirit of which they had already heard.[4] That promise was to be fulfilled to them, not only individually, but as a body, as a Church; and it was to be fulfilled in the same city in which they had witnessed His

---

[1] Acts i. 3, δι' ἡμερῶν τεσσαράκοντα ὀπτανόμενος αὐτοῖς. This is the only passage in Scripture which tells us the interval which elapsed between the Resurrection and the Ascension.

[2] 1 Pet. i. 3, 4.

[3] Acts ii. 32; iii. 15; iv. 33; v. 32; x. 40, 41; Luke xxiv. 48, &c. On this fact St. Luke dwells repeatedly and emphatically. (See Meyer on Acts i. 22.)

[4] Acts i. 4; Luke xxiv. 49.

uttermost humiliation. And they were assured that they should not have long to wait. But though they knew that they should be baptised with the Holy Ghost and with fire "not many days hence," yet, for the exercise of their faith and to keep them watchful, the exact time was not defined.[1]

Then came the last walk towards Bethany, and that solemn parting on the Mount of Olives, when their Lord was taken away from them, and "a cloud received Him out of their sight." But even in His last discourse He had rendered clear to them their position and their duties. When, with lingerings of old Messianic fancies, they had asked Him whether He would at that time re-constitute[2] the kingdom for Israel, He had quenched such material longings by telling them that it was not for them to know "the times or the seasons,"[3] which the Father placed in His own authority.[4] But though these secrets of God were not to be revealed to them or to any living man, there *was* a power which they should receive when the Holy Ghost had fallen upon them—a power to be witnesses to Christ, His sufferings, and His Resurrection, first in the narrow limits of the Holy Land, then to all the world.

---

[1] Chrys. *ad loc.* "Numerus dierum non definitus exercebat fidem apostolorum" (Bengel). The reading ἕως τῆς πεντηκοστῆς of D and the Sahidic version is a mere gloss.

[2] Acts i. 6, ἀποκαθιστάνεις.

[3] Acts i. 7, χρόνους ἢ καιρούς, "periods or crises."

[4] The E.V. passes over the distinction between ἐξουσία here and δύναμις in the next verse, and a neglect of this distinction has led Bengel and others to understand οὐχ ὑμῶν ἐστι in the sense that it was not *yet* their prerogative to know these things ("quae apostolorum nondum erat nosse"—Beng.), but that it should be so hereafter. That *this*, however, was not the error of our translators appears from their marginal gloss to δύναμις in ver. 8, "the power of the Holy Ghost coming upon you." We shall see hereafter that St. Paul, in common with all the early Christians (1 Thess. iv. 16, 17; 2 Thess. ii. 8; Rom. xiii. 12; 1 Cor. xvi. 22; Phil. iv. 5; 1 Pet. iv. 5; James v. 8; Heb. x. 37), hoped for the near return of Christ to earth.

From the mountain slopes of Olivet they returned that Sabbath-day's journey[1] to Jerusalem, and at once assembled in the upper chamber,[2] which was so suitable a place for their early gatherings. It was one of those large rooms under the flat roof of Jewish houses, which, for its privacy, was set apart for religious purposes; and in the poverty of these Galilæan Apostles, we can scarcely doubt that it was the same room of which they had already availed themselves for the Last Supper, and for those gatherings on the "first day of the week,"[3] at two of which Jesus had appeared to them. Hallowed by these divine associations, it seems to have been the ordinary place of sojourn of the Apostles during the days of expectation.[4] Here, at stated hours of earnest prayer, they were joined by the mother of Jesus[5] and the other holy women who had attended His ministry; as well as by His brethren, of whom one in particular[6] plays henceforth an important part in the history of the Church. Hitherto these "brethren of the Lord" had scarcely been numbered among those who believed in Christ,[7] or, if they had believed in Him, it had only been in a secondary and material sense, as a human Messiah. But now, as we might naturally conjecture, even apart from tradition, they had been convinced and converted by "the power of His Resurrection." Even in these earliest meetings of the whole Church of Christ at Jerusalem it is interesting to see that, though the Apostles

---

[1] 2,000 cubits, between five and six furlongs, the distance between the Tabernacle and the farthest part of the camp (cf. Numb. xxxv. 5). This is the only place in which it is alluded to in the N.T.

[2] Not "*an* upper room," as in E.V. It is probably the רֶגֶג, or topmost room of the house, which is called ἀνώγεον in Mark xiv. 15.

[3] John xx. 19, 26.

[4] Acts i. 13, οὗ ἦσαν καταμένοντες ὅ τε Πέτρος, κ.τ.λ.

[5] Here last mentioned in the N.T.

[6] James, the Lord's brother.

[7] Matt. xii. 46; xiii. 55; Mark vi. 3; 1 Cor. xv. 7.

were still Jews in their religion, with no other change as
yet beyond the belief in Jesus as the Christ, the Son of the
Living God,[1] they yet suffered the women to meet with
them in prayer, not in any separate court, as in the Temple
services, not with dividing partitions, as in the worship
of the synagogue,[2] but in that equality of spiritual communion, which was to develop hereafter into the glorious
doctrine that among Christ's redeemed "there is neither
Jew nor Greek, there is neither bond nor free, there is
neither male and female," but that, in Christ Jesus, all
are one.[3]

During the ten days which elapsed between the
Ascension and Pentecost, it was among the earliest
cares of the Apostles to fill up the vacancy which had
been caused in their number by the death of Judas.
This was done at a full conclave of the believers in
Jerusalem, who, in the absence of many of those five
hundred to whom Christ had appeared in Galilee, numbered about one hundred and twenty. The terrible circumstances of the traitor's suicide, of which every varied
and shuddering tradition was full of horror, had left upon
their minds a deeper faith in God's immediate retribution upon guilt. He had fallen from his high charge
by transgression, and had gone to his own place.[4] That

---

[1] "The Church, so to speak, was but half born; the other half was still in
the womb of the synagogue. The followers of Jesus were under the guidance
of the Apostles, but continued to acknowledge the authority of the chair of
Moses in Jerusalem" (Dr. Döllinger, *First Age*, p. 43).

[2] Jos. *Antt.* xv. 11, § 5; Philo, ii. 476.

[3] Gal. iii. 28.

[4] Acts i. 25, εἰς τὸν τόπον τὸν ἴδιον (al. δίκαιον). This profound and reverent
euphemism is one of the many traces of the reticence with which the early
Church spoke of the fate of those who had departed. The reticence is all the
more remarkable if the word "place" be meant to bear allusive reference to
the same word in the earlier part of the text, where the true reading is
τόπον τῆς διακονίας (A, B, C, D), not κλῆρον, as in E.V. The origin of this

his place should be supplied appeared reasonable, both
because Jesus Himself had appointed twelve Apostles
—the ideal number of the tribes of Israel—and also
because Peter, and the Church generally, saw in Judas
the antitype of Ahitophel, and applying to him a passage of the 109th Psalm, they wished, now that his
habitation was desolate, that another should take his
office.[1] The essential qualification for the new Apostle was
that he should have been a witness of the Resurrection,
and should have companied with the disciples all the time
that the Lord Jesus went in and out among them.   The
means taken for his appointment, being unique in the
New Testament, seem to result from the unique position
of the Church during the few days between the Ascension and the Descent of the Holy Ghost.   As though
they felt that the swift power of intuitive discernment
was not yet theirs, they selected two, Joseph Barsabbas,
who in Gentile circles assumed the common surname of
Justus, and Matthias.[2]   They then, in accordance with
Old Testament analogies[3] and Jewish custom,[4] prayed to

---

striking expression may perhaps be the Rabbinic comments on Numb. xxiv. 25,
where "Balaam went to his own place" is explained to mean "to Gehenna."
Cf. Judg. ix. 55, וישבו, and Targ. Eccles. vi. 6.; v. Schöttgen, p. 407; and cf.
Clem. Rom. ad Cor. i. 5; Polyc. ad Phil. 9; Ignat. ad Magnes. 5 (Meyer).
See too Dan. xii. 13.

[1] Ps. xli. 9; cix. 8.   The alteration of the LXX. αὐτὸν into αὐτοῦ is a
good illustration of the free method of quotation and interpretation of the
Old Testament, which is universally adopted in the New.   The 109th has
been called the Iscariotic Psalm.

[2] Of these nothing is known, unless it be true that they were among the
Seventy (Euseb. H. E. i. 12; Epiphan. Haer. i. 20); and that Joseph drank
poison unharmed (Papias ap. Euseb. H. E. iii. 39).   On the uncertain derivation
of Barsabbas (so in א, A, B, E), see Lightfoot, Hor. Hebr., ad loc.   There is
a Judas Barsabbas in Acts xv. 22.   Matthias is said to have been martyred
(Niceph. ii. 60), and there were apocryphal writings connected with his name
(Euseb. H. E. iii. 23; Clem. Alex. Strom. ii. 163).

[3] Numb. xxvi. 55, 56; Josh. vii. 14; 1 Sam. x. 20; Prov. xvi. 33.

[4] Luke i. 9.

God that He would appoint[1] the one whom He chose. The names were written on tablets and dropped into a vessel. The vessel was shaken, and the name of Matthias leapt out. He was accordingly reckoned among the twelve Apostles.[2]

We are told nothing further respecting the events of the ten days which elapsed between the Ascension and Pentecost. With each of those days the yearning hope, the keen expectation, must have grown more and more intense, and most of all when the day of Pentecost had dawned.[3] It was the first day of the week, and the fiftieth day after Nisan 16. The very circumstances of the day would add to the vividness of their feelings. The Pentecost was not only one of the three great yearly feasts, and the Feast of Harvest, but it came to be identified—and quite rightly—in Jewish consciousness with the anniversary of the giving of the Law on Sinai.[4]

[1] ἀνάδειξον, "appoint," not "show": Luke x. 1, μετὰ δὲ ταῦτα ἀνέδειξεν ὁ Κύριος ἑτέρους, ἑβδομήκοντα. The word is peculiar in the N.T. to St. Luke. For ἐξελέξω, see Acts i. 2, τοῖς ἀποστόλοις .... οὓς ἐξελέξατο. I need hardly notice the strange view that the election of St. Matthias was a sheer mistake made before the gift of the Spirit, and that Paul was in reality the destined twelfth Apostle! (Stier, Reden d. Apostl. i. 15.)

[2] The method in which the lot was cast (see Lev. xvi. 8; Ezek. xxiv. 6) is not certain, but the expression ἔδωκαν, rather than ἔβαλον κλήρους αὐτοῖς, goes against the notion of their casting dice as in Luke xxiii. 34. "The lot fell on Matthias" is a common idiom in all languages (Hom. Il. v. 316; Od. E. 209; Ps. xxii. 18; Jon. i. 7, &c.; ut cujusque sors exciderat; Liv. xxi. 42). From the use of the word κλῆρος in this passage, in ver. 17 and in viii. 21, xxvi. 18, is probably derived the Latin clerus and our clergy, clerici, κλῆρος = τὸ σύστημα τῶν διακόνων καὶ πρεσβυτέρων. (Suid.) (Wordsworth, ad loc.)

[3] This is the obvious meaning of συμπληροῦσθαι, not "was drawing near" (cf. Eph. i. 10), or "had passed."

[4] It is true that this point is not adverted to by either Philo or Josephus. The inference arises, however, so obviously from the comparison of Ex. xii. 2; xix. 1, that we can hardly suppose that it was wholly missed. (See Schöttgen, ad loc.; Jer. Ep. ad Fabiolam, xii.; Aug. c. Faustum, xxxii. 12; Maimon. Mor. Nevoch. iii. 41.) The Simcath Thorah, or "Feast of the Joy of the Law," is kept on the last day of the Feast of Tabernacles, when the last Haphtarah from the Pentateuch is read.

The mere fact that another solemn festival had come round, and that at the last great festival their Lord had been crucified in the sight of the assembled myriads who thronged to the Passover, would be sufficient on this solemn morning to absorb their minds with that over-whelming anticipation which was the forecast of a change in themselves and in the world's history—of a new and eternal consecration to the service of a new law and the work of a new life.

It was early morning. Before "the third hour of the day" summoned them to the Temple for morning prayer,[1] the believers, some hundred and twenty in number, were gathered once more, according to their custom, in the upper room. It has been imagined by some that the great event of this first Whit-Sunday must have taken place in the Temple. The word rendered "house"[2] might equally well mean a "chamber," and is actually used by Josephus of the thirty small chambers which were attached to the sides of Solomon's Temple, with thirty more above them.[3] But it is supremely im-probable that the poor and suspected disciples should have been able to command the use of such a room; and further, it is certain that if, in the Herodian Temple, these rooms were no larger than those in the Temple of Solomon, the size of even the lower ones would have been wholly inadequate for the accommodation of so large a number. The meeting was probably one of those holy and simple meals which were afterwards known among Christians as the *Agapæ*, or Love Feasts. It need hardly be added that any moral significance which might attach to the occurrence of the event in the Temple would be no less striking if we think of the sign of a new era as having

---

[1] *i.e.*, 9 o'clock in the morning (cf. Luke xxiv. 53; Acts ii. 46; iii. 1).
[2] Acts ii. 2, οἶκον.   [3] Jos. *Antt.* viii. 3, § 2.

hallowed the common street and the common dwelling-place; as the visible inauguration of the days in which neither on Zion nor on Gerizim alone were men to worship the Father, but to worship Him everywhere in spirit and in truth.[1]

It is this inward significance of the event which constitutes its sacredness and importance. Its awfulness consists in its being the solemn beginning of the new and final phase of God's dealings with mankind. To Abraham He gave a promise which was the germ of a religion. When He called His people from Egypt He gave them the Moral Law and that Levitical Law which was to serve as a bulwark for the truths of the theocracy. During the two thousand years of that Mosaic Dispensation the Tabernacle and the Temple had been a visible sign of His presence. Then, for the brief period of the life of Christ on earth, He had tabernacled among men, dwelling in a tent like ours and of the same material.[2] That mortal body of Christ, in a sense far deeper than could be true of any house built with hands, was a Temple of God. Last of all, He who had given to mankind His Son to dwell among them, gave His Spirit into their very hearts. More than this He could not give; nearer than this He could not be. Henceforth His Temple was to be the mortal body of every baptised Christian, and His Spirit was to prefer

"Before all temples the upright heart and pure."

He who believes this in all the fulness of its meaning, he whose heart and conscience bear witness to its truth, will consider in its true aspect the fulfilment of Christ's promise in the effusion of His Spirit; and regarding the

---

[1] John iv. 21—23.
[2] Archbishop Leighton, John i. 14, ὁ λόγος σὰρξ ἐγένετο καὶ ἐσκήνωσεν ἐν ἡμῖν.

outward wonder as the *least* marvellous part of the Day of Pentecost, will not, as Neander says, be tempted to explain the greater by the less, or "consider it strange that the most wonderful event in the inner life of mankind should be accompanied by extraordinary outward appearances as sensible indications of its existence."[1]

Suddenly, while their hearts burned within them with such ardent zeal, and glowed with such enkindled hope—suddenly on the rapt and expectant assembly came the sign that they had desired—the inspiration of Christ's promised Presence in their hearts—the baptism with the Holy Ghost and with fire—the transforming impulse of a Spirit and a Power from on high—the eternal proof to them, and through them, in unbroken succession, to all who accept their word, that He who had been taken from them into heaven was still with them, and would be with them always to the end of the world.

It came from heaven with the sound as of a rushing mighty wind, filling the whole house where they were sitting, and with a semblance as of infolded flame,[2] which, parting itself in every direction,[3] played like a tongue of lambent light over the head of every one of them. It was not wind, but "a sound as of wind in its rushing violence;" it was not fire, but something which seemed to them like quivering tongues of a flame which gleamed but did not burn—fit symbol of that Holy Spirit which, like the wind, bloweth where it listeth, though we know not whence it cometh or whither it goeth; and, like

---

[1] Neander, p. 3.

[2] Acts ii. 2, 3, ὥσπερ πνοῆς . . . ὡσεὶ πυρὸς. (Cf. Luke iii. 22, ὡσεὶ περιστερὰν; Ezek. i. 24; xliii. 2; 1 Kings xix. 11.)

[3] γλῶσσαι διαμεριζόμεναι, not "cloven tongues," as in the E.V., though this view of the word is said to have determined the symbolic shape of the Episcopal mitre. The expression "tongue of fire" is found also in Isa. v. 24, but there it is a devouring flame.

the kindled fire of love, glowing on the holy altar of every
faithful heart, utters, not seldom, even from the stammering
lips of ignorance, the burning words of inspiration.

And that this first Pentecost marked an eternal
moment in the destiny of mankind, no reader of history
will surely deny. Undoubtedly in every age since then
the sons of God have, to an extent unknown before,
been taught by the Spirit of God. Undoubtedly since
then, to an extent unrealised before, we may know that
the Spirit of Christ dwelleth in us. Undoubtedly we
may enjoy a nearer sense of union with God in Christ
than was accorded to the saints of the Old Dispensation,
and a thankful certainty that we see the days which kings
and prophets desired to see and did not see them, and
hear the truths which they desired to hear and did not
hear them. And this New Dispensation began henceforth
in all its fulness. It was no exclusive consecration to a
separated priesthood, no isolated endowment of a narrow
Apostolate. It was the consecration of a whole Church
—its men, its women, its children—to be all of them
"a chosen generation, a royal priesthood, a holy nation,
a peculiar people;" it was an endowment, of which the
full free offer was meant ultimately to be extended to
all mankind. Each one of that hundred and twenty was
not the exceptional recipient of a blessing and witness
of a revelation, but the forerunner and representative of
myriads more. And this miracle was not merely transient,
but is continuously renewed. It is not a rushing sound
and gleaming light, seen perhaps only for a moment, but
it is a living energy and an unceasing inspiration. It is
not a visible symbol to a gathered handful of human souls
in the upper room of a Jewish house, but a vivifying wind
which shall henceforth breathe in all ages of the world's
history; a tide of light which is rolling, and shall roll,

from shore to shore until the earth is full of the knowledge of the Lord as the waters cover the sea.

And if this be the aspect under which it is regarded, the outward symbol sinks into subordinate importance. They who hold the truths on which I have been dwelling will not care to enter into the voluminous controversy as to whether that which is described as audible and visible was so in seeming only—whether the something which sounded like wind, and the something which gleamed like flame,[1] were external realities, or whether they were but subjective impressions, so vivid as to be identified with the things themselves. When the whole soul is filled with a spiritual light and a spiritual fire—when it seems to echo, as in the Jewish legend of the great Lawgiver, with the music of other worlds—when it is caught up into the third heaven and hears words which it is not possible for man to utter—when, to the farthest horizon of its consciousness, it seems as it were filled with the "rush of congregated wings"—when, to borrow the language of St. Augustine, the natural life is dead, and the soul thrills, under the glow of spiritual illumination, with a life which is supernatural—what, to such a soul, is objective and what is subjective? To such questions the only answer it cares to give is, "Whether in the body or out of the body, I cannot tell. God knoweth."[2]

But when from these mysterious phenomena we turn to the effects wrought by them in those for whom they were manifested, we are dealing with things more capable of being defined. Here, however, it is necessary to distinguish between the immediate result and the permanent inspiration. The former astounded a

---

[1] Acts ii. 2, 3, ἦχος . . . ὥσει.

[2] "It did me much harm that I did not then know it was possible to see anything otherwise than with the eyes of the body" (St. Teresa, Vida, vii. 11).

multitude; the latter revived a world. The former led to an immediate conversion; the latter is the power of a holy life. The former was a new and amazing outburst of strange emotion; the latter was the sustaining influence which enables the soul to soar from earth heavenwards in steady flight on the double wings of Faith and Love.

Yet, though there be no manner of comparison between the real importance of the transient phenomenon and the continuous result, it is necessary to a true conception of the age of the Apostles that we should understand what is told us of the former. "And they were all immediately filled," it is said, " with the Holy Spirit, and began to speak with other tongues as the Spirit gave them to utter."[1]

The *primâ facie* aspect of the narrative which follows —apart from the analogy of other Scriptures—has led to the belief that the outpouring of the Holy Spirit at Pentecost was succeeded by an outburst of utterance, in which a body of Galilæans spoke a multitude of languages which they had never learned; and this has led to the inference that throughout their lives the Apostles possessed the power of speaking languages which they had not acquired.[2]

---

[1] Acts ii. 4. λαλεῶ, " to speak," as distinguished from λέγειν, " to say," points rather to the actual articulations than to the thoughts which words convey; ἀποφθέγγεσθαι, *eloqui*, implies a brief forcible utterance. Neither ἑτεραί nor γλῶσσαι throw light on the nature of the phenomena, except as referring to Isa. xxviii. 11.

[2] Against this view (which, with the contrast with Babel, &c., is not found, I think, earlier than the Fathers of the fourth and fifth centuries), see Herder, *Die Gabe d. Sprache*; Bunsen, *Hippol.* ii. 12; Ewald, *Gesch. Isr.* vi. 110; Neander, *Planting*, 13, 14; De Wette, *Einleit.* 27—37; Hilgenfeld, *Einleit.* 275; Reuss, *Hist. Apol.* 50—55; Olshausen, *ad loc.*; De Pressensé, *Trois prem. Siècles*, i. 355; and almost every unbiassed modern commentator. Meyer (*ad loc.*) goes so far as to say that "the sudden communication of the gift of speaking in foreign languages is neither logically possible nor psychologically and morally conceivable."

But if we examine other passages where the same phenomenon is alluded to or discussed, they will show us that this view of the matter is at least questionable. In Mark xvi. 17—waiving all argument as to the genuineness of the passage—the word καιναῖς, "new," is omitted in several uncials and versions;[1] but if retained, it goes against the common notion, for it points to strange utterances, not to foreign languages. In the other places of the Acts[2] where the gift of the Spirit is alluded to, no hint is given of the use of unknown languages. In fact, that view of the subject has chiefly been stereotyped in the popular conception by the interpolation of the word "*unknown*" in 1 Cor. xiv.[3] The glossolalia, or "speaking with a tongue," is connected with "prophesying"—that is, exalted preaching—and magnifying God. The sole passage by which we can hope to understand it is the section of the First Epistle to the Corinthians to which I have just alluded.[4] It is impossible for any one to examine that section carefully without being forced to the conclusion that, at Corinth at any rate, the gift of tongues had not the least connexion with foreign languages. Of such a knowledge, if this single passage of the Acts be not an exception, there is not the shadow of a trace in Scripture. That this passage is *not* an exception seems to be clear from the fact that St. Peter, in rebutting the coarse insinuation that the phenomenon was the result of drunkenness, does not so much as make

[1] C, L, Δ, Copt., Arm. Apart from these questions, the unlimited universality of the promise leads us to believe that our Lord here, as elsewhere, is using the language of spiritual metaphor. Many a great missionary and preacher has, in the highest sense, spoken " with new tongues " who has yet found insuperable difficulty in the acquisition of foreign languages.

[2] x. 46; xix. 6 (cf. xi. 15).

[3] 1 Cor. xiv. 4, 13, 14, 27.

[4] 1 Cor. xii.—xiv. 33.

the most passing allusion to an evidence so unparalleled; and that the passage of Joel of which he sees the fulfilment in the outpouring of Pentecost, does not contain the remotest hint of foreign languages. Hence the fancy that *this* was the immediate result of Pentecost is unknown to the first two centuries, and only sprang up when the true tradition had been obscured. The inference that the gift of unlearnt languages was designed to help the Apostles in their future preaching is one that unites a mass of misconceptions. In the first place, such a gift would be quite alien to that law of God's Providence which never bestows on man that which man can acquire by his own unaided efforts. In the second place, owing to the universal dissemination at that time of Greek and Latin, there never was a period in which such a gift would have been more absolutely needless.[1] In the third place, though all other miracles of the New Testament found their continuance and their analogies, for a time at any rate, after the death of the Apostles, there is no existing allusion, or even early legend, which has presumed the existence of this power.[2] In the fourth place, although Paul 'spoke with a tongue'[3] more than all his converts, it is clear from the narrative of what occurred at Lycaonia, that at a most crucial moment he did not understand the Lycaonian dialect. In the fifth place, early

---

[1] For instance, the whole multitude from fifteen countries which heard the Apostles speak " in their own tongues " the wonderful works of God, yet *all* understood the speech which St. Peter addressed to them in Greek. Hence such a power of speaking unlearnt foreign languages would have been a "Luxus-wunder" (Immer, *Neut. Theol.* 195). Far different was it with the true glossolaly which in its controlled force involved a spiritual power of stirring to its inmost depths the heart of unbelief. (1 Cor. xiv. 22.)

[2] Middleton, *Mirac. Powers*, 120. The passage of Irenæus (*Haer.* v. 6, 1) usually quoted in favour of such a view, tells the other way, since the object of the παντοδαπαὶ γλῶσσαι is there explained to be τὰ κρύφια τῶν ἀνθρώπων εἰς φανερὸν ἄγειν.

[3] 1 Cor. xiv. 18, γλώσσῃ (א, A, D, E, F, G).

H

Christian tradition distinctly asserts that the Apostles did *not* possess a supernatural knowledge of foreign tongues, since Papias tells us that Mark accompanied St. Peter as an "interpreter" (ἑρμηνευτὴς), and Jerome that Titus was useful to St. Paul from his knowledge of Greek.[1] We are, therefore, forced to look for some other aspect of the utterance of that inspiration which accompanied the heavenly signs of Pentecost. The mistaken explanation of it has sprung from taking too literally St. Luke's dramatic reproduction of the vague murmurs of a throng, who mistook the *nature* of a gift of which they witnessed the *reality*. I do not see how any thoughtful student who has really considered the whole subject can avoid the conclusion of Neander, that "any foreign languages which were spoken on this occasion were only something accidental, and not the essential element of the language of the Spirit."[2]

In ancient times—especially before Origen—there seems to have been an impression that only one language was spoken, but that the miracle consisted in each hearer imagining it to be his own native tongue.[3] The explanation is remarkable as showing an early impression that the passage had been misunderstood. The modern view, developed especially by Schneckenburger (following St.

---

[1] Papias, *ap.* Euseb. *H. E.* iii. 30; cf. Iren. iii. 1; interpres. Tert. *adv. Marc.* iv. 5.

[2] *Planting*, 13, 14. I have not touched on any modern analogies to these spiritual manifestations, but agree with the view of Dr. Döllinger, who says that they have occurred "in a lower sphere, and without any miraculous endowment . . . an unusual phenomenon, but one completely within the range of natural operations, which the gift of the Apostolic age came into to exalt and ennoble it " (*First Age of Church*, 315).

[3] Greg. Nyss. *De Spir. Sanct.* Bp. Martensen, *Christl. Dogm.* 381; Overbeck, *Apg.*, p. 26, and many others. The often-repeated objection of Gregory of Nazianzus (*Orat.* xliv.) that this is to transfer the miracle to the hearers, has no weight whatever. The effect on the hearers was solely due to the power of the new spiritual "tongue."

Cyprian and Erasmus), is that the "tongue" was, from its own force and significance, intelligible equally to all who heard it. That such a thing is possible may be readily admitted, and it derives some probability from many analogies in the history of the Church. The stories of St. Bernard, St. Anthony of Padua, St. Vincent Ferrer, St. Louis Bertrand, St. Francis Xavier, and others who are said to have been endowed with the spiritual power of swaying the passions, kindling the enthusiasm, or stirring the penitence of vast multitudes whom they addressed in a language unintelligible to the majority of the hearers, are so far from being inventions, that any one who has been present at the speech of a great orator, though beyond the range of his voice, can readily understand the nature and the intensity of the effect produced.[1] But neither of these theories taken alone seems adequate to account for the language used by St. Peter and St. Paul. Almost all the theories about the glossolalia are too partial. The true view can only be discovered by a combination of them. The belief that languages were used which were unknown, or only partially known, or which had only been previously known to the speaker; that the tongue was a mystic, exalted, poetic, unusual style of phraseology and utterance;[2] that it was a dithyrambic outpouring of strange and rhythmic praise; that it was the impassioned use of ejaculatory words and sentences of Hebrew Scripture; that it was a wild, unintelligible, inarticulate succession of sounds, which either conveyed no impression to the ordinary hearer, or could

---

[1] See *Chapters on Language*, p. 63; Marsh, *Lect. on Lang.* 486—488; Cic. *de Orat.* iii. 216.

[2] Γλῶσσα sometimes means "an unusual expression" (Arist. *Rhet.* iii. 2, 14). Cf. our "gloss," "glossology." See especially Bleek, *Stud. u. Krit.* 1829. "Linguam esse cum quis loquatur obscuras et mysticas significationes" (Aug. *de Gen. ad litt.* xii. 8).

H 2

only be interpreted by one whose special gift it was to understand the rapt and ecstatic strain—none of these views is correct separately, all may have some elements of truth in their combination. This is the meaning of St. Paul's expression "*kinds* of tongues." If we assume, as must be assumed, that the glossolalia at Corinth and elsewhere was identical with the glossolalia at Pentecost, then we must interpret the narrative of St. Luke by the full and earnest discussion of the subject—written, be it remembered, at a far earlier period, and in immediate contact with, and even experience of, the manifestation— by St. Paul. That the glossolaly at Corinth was not a speaking in foreign languages is too clear to need proof. St. Paul in speaking of it uses the analogies of the clanging of a cymbal, the booming of a gong,[1] the indistinct blare of a trumpet,[2] the tuneless strains of flute or harp.[3] We learn that, apart from interpretation, it was not for the edification of any but the speaker;[4] that even the speaker did not always understand it;[5] that it was sporadic in its recurrences;[6] that it was excited, inarticulate, astonishing,[7] intended as a sign to unbelievers rather than as an aid to believers, but even on unbelievers liable, when not under due regulation, to leave an impression of madness;[8] lastly, that, though controllable by all who were truly and nobly under its influence, it often led to spurious and disorderly outbreaks.[9]

---

[1] 1 Cor. xiii. 1, χαλκὸς ἠχῶν, κύμβαλον ἀλαλάζον.

[2] 8, ἐὰν ἄδηλον φωνὴν σάλπιγξ δῷ. St. Chrysostom uses language equally disparaging of analogous outbreaks in Constantinople (*Hom. in Ps.* vi. 12 see Dr. Plumptre's interesting article in Smith's *Dict.* iii. 1560).

[3] xiv. 7, ὅμως τὰ ἄψυχα φωνὴν διδόντα, κ.τ.λ., ἐὰν διαστολὴν τοῖς φθόγγοις μὴ δῷ.

[4] xiv. 2, οὐκ ἀνθρώποις λαλεῖ. 4, ἑαυτὸν οἰκοδομεῖ. Cf. 11. The proper meaning of the words λαλεῖν, γλῶσσα, φωνή, all point in this direction. In St. Luke's phraseology the word for a language is not γλῶσσα, but διάλεκτος.

[5] xiv. 19. [6] xiv. 27. [7] xiv. 2. [8] xiv. 23, οὐκ ἐροῦσιν ὅτι μαίνεσθε;

[9] xiv. 9, 11, 17, 20—23, 26—28, 33, 40.

Any one who fairly ponders these indications can hardly doubt that, when the consciousness of the new power came over the assembled disciples, they did not speak as men ordinarily speak. The voice they uttered was awful in its range, in its tone, in its modulations, in its startling, penetrating, almost appalling power;[1] the words they spoke were exalted, intense, passionate, full of mystic significance; the language they used was not their ordinary and familiar tongue, but was Hebrew, or Greek, or Latin, or Aramaic, or Persian, or Arabic, as some overpowering and unconscious impulse of the moment might direct; the burden of their thoughts was the ejaculation of rapture, of amazement, of thanksgiving, of prayer, of empassioned psalm, of dithyrambic hymn; their utterances were addressed not to each other, but were like an inspired soliloquy of the soul with God. And among these strange sounds of many voices, all simultaneously raised in the accordance of ecstatic devotion,[2] there were some which none could rightly interpret, which rang on the air like the voice of barbarous languages, and which, except to those who uttered them, and who in uttering them felt carried out of themselves, conveyed no definite significance beyond the fact that they were reverberations of one and the same ecstasy—echoes waked in different consciousnesses by the same immense emotion. Such—as we gather from the notices of St. Luke, St. Peter, and St. Paul—was the " Gift of Tongues." And thus regarded, its strict accord-

---

[1] So we infer from St. Paul's allusions, which find illustration in modern analogies. Archd. Stopford describes the "unknown tongue" of the Irish Revivalists in 1859 as " a sound such as I never heard before, unearthly and unaccountable."

[2] This simultaneity of utterance by people under the same impressions is recorded several times in the Acts of the Apostles. It was evidently analogous to, though not perhaps identical with " glossolalia "—the eloquence of religious transport thrilling with rapture and conviction.

ance with the known laws of psychology [1] furnishes us
with a fresh proof of the truthfulness of the history, and
shows us that no sign of the outpouring of the Holy
Spirit could have been more natural, more evidential, or
more intense.

The city of Jerusalem at that moment was crowded
by a miscellaneous multitude of Jews and Proselytes.
It was inevitable that the awful sound [2] should arrest
the astonished attention, first of one, then of more,
lastly of a multitude of the inhabitants and passers-by.
The age—an age which was in keen expectation of some
divine event; the day—the great anniversary of Pentecost
and of Sinai; the hour—when people were already beginning to throng the streets on their way to the Temple
service—would all tend to swell the numbers, and in-
tensify the feelings of the crowd. Up the steps which
led outside the house to the "upper room" they would
first begin to make their way in twos and threes, and
then to press in larger numbers, until their eagerness,
their obtrusion, their exclamations of fear, surprise, admiration, insult, could not fail to break the spell. The
Church for the first time found itself face to face with
the world—a world loud in its expressions of perplexity,
through which broke the open language of hate and
scorn. That which fixed the attention of all the better
portion of the crowd was the fact that these " Galilæans "
were magnifying, in strange tongues, the mercies and
power of God. But most of the spectators were filled

---

[1] Compare in the Old Testament the cases of Saul, &c. (1 Sam. x. 11;
xviii. 10; xix. 23, 24). "C'est le langage brûlant et mystérieux de l'extase"
(De Pressensé, i. 355).

[2] In Acts ii. 6 the words γενομένης δὲ τῆς φωνῆς ταύτης do not mean (as
in the E.V.) "now when this was noised abroad," but "when this sound
occurred " (cf. ἦχος, ver. 2; John iii. 8; Rev. vi. 1). It is evidently an allusion
to the *Bath Kol*. (See Herzog, *Real. Encycl.*, *s.v.*)

with contempt at what seemed to them to be a wild
fanaticism. "These men," they jeeringly exclaimed,
"have been indulging too freely in the festivities of
Pentecost.[1] They are drunk with sweet wine."[2]

It was the prevalence of this derisive comment which
forced upon the Apostles the necessity of immediate explanation.[3] "The spirits of the prophets," as St. Paul
says, with that masculine practical wisdom which in
him is found in such rare combination with burning
enthusiasm, "are subject unto the prophets."[4] The
Apostles were at once able not only to calm their own
exaltation, but also, even at this intense moment, to hush
into absolute silence the overmastering emotion of their
brethren. They saw well that it would be fatal to
their position as witnesses to a divine revelation if anything in their worship could, however insultingly, be
represented as the orgiastic exhibition of undisciplined
fervour. It was a duty to prove from the very first that
the Christian disciple offered no analogy to the fanatical
fakeer. Clearing the room of all intruders, making a
space for themselves at the top of the steps, where they
could speak in the name of the brethren to the surging
throng who filled the street, the Apostles came forward,
and Peter assumed the office of their spokesman. Standing in an attitude, and speaking in a tone, which
commanded attention,[5] he first begged for serious attention, and told the crowd that their coarse suspicion

---

[1] See Deut. xvi. 11.

[2] γλεῦκος cannot be "new wine," as in E.V., for Pentecost fell in June, and
the vintage was in August.

[3] Acts ii. 15, ὡς ὑμεῖς ὑπολαμβάνετε. There is a slight excuse for this insult,
since spiritual emotion may produce effects similar to those which result
from intoxication (Eph. v. 18; 1 Sam. x. 10, 11; xviii. 10—Heb., "raved").
Compare the German expression, "Ein Gott-trunkener Mann."

[4] 1 Cor. xiv. 32.

[5] Acts ii. 14, σταθείς . . . ἐπῆρε τὴν φωνήν.

was refuted at once by the fact that it was but nine
o'clock. He then proceeded to explain to them that this
was the fulfilment of the prophecy of Joel that, among
other signs and portents of the last days, there should be
a special effusion of the Spirit of God, like that of which
they had witnessed the manifestations. It was the object
of the remainder of his speech to prove that this Spirit
had been outpoured by that same Jesus of Nazareth[1]
whom they had nailed to the cross, but whose resurrection
and deliverance from the throes of death were foreshadowed
in the Psalms of His glorious ancestor.

The power with which this speech came home to the
minds of the hearers; the force and fearlessness with
which it was delivered by one who, not two months
before, had been frightened, by the mere question of a
curious girl, into the denial of his Lord; the insight
into Scripture which it evinced in men who so recently
had shown themselves but 'fools and slow of heart'
to believe all that the prophets had spoken concerning
Christ;[2] the three thousand who were at once baptised
into a profession of the new faith—were themselves the
most convincing proofs—proofs even more convincing
than rushing wind, and strange tongues, and lambent
flames—that now indeed the Promise of the Paraclete
had been fulfilled, and that a new æon had begun in God's
dealings with the world.

[1] Acts ii. 22, Ναζωραῖος, the Galilæan form of Ναζαρηνός.
[2] Luke xxiv. 25.

CHAPTER VI.

EARLY PERSECUTIONS.

"It fills the Church of God; it fills
The sinful world around;
Only in stubborn hearts and wills
No place for it is found."—KEBLE.

THE life of these early Christians was the poetic childhood
of the Church in her earliest innocence. It was marked by
simplicity, by gladness, by worship, by brotherhood. At
home, and in their place of meeting, their lives were a perpetual prayer, their meals a perpetual love-feast and a perpetual eucharist. In the Temple they attended the public
services with unanimous zeal. In the first impulses of
fraternal joy many sold their possessions to contribute to
a common stock. The numbers of the little community
increased daily, and the mass of the people looked on them
not only with tolerance, but with admiration and esteem.

The events which followed all tended at first to
strengthen their position. The healing of the cripple
in Solomon's porch; the bold speech of Peter afterwards;
the unshaken constancy with which Peter and John faced
the fury of the Sadducees; the manner in which all the
disciples accepted and even exulted in persecution, if it
came in the fulfilment of their duties;[1] the power with

[1] It is a very interesting fact that on the first summons of Peter and
John before the Hierarchs, they were dismissed, with threats, indeed, and
warnings, but unpunished, because the Council became convinced (καταλαβόμενοι)
that they were "unlearned and ignorant men" (Acts iv. 13). The words,
however, convey too contemptuous a notion to English readers. Ἀγράμματοι

which they witnessed to the resurrection of their Lord;
the beautiful spectacle of their unanimity; the awful
suddenness with which Ananias and Sapphira had been
stricken down; the signs and wonders which were wrought
by the power of faith; the zeal and devotion which marked
their gatherings in Solomon's porch, caused a rapid advance
in the numbers and position of the Christian brothers.
As their influence increased, the hierarchic clique, which
at that time governed the body which still called itself
the Sanhedrin, grew more and more alarmed. In spite
of the populace, whose sympathy made it dangerous at
that time to meddle with the followers of Jesus, they at
last summoned the two leading Apostles before a solemn
conclave of the Sanhedrin and senate.[1] Probably, as at
the earlier session, the whole priestly party were there—
the crafty Annas, the worldly Caiaphas,[2] the rich, unscrupulous, money-loving body of Kamhiths, and Phabis, and
Kantheras, and Boethusîm,[3] the Pharisaic doctors of the
law, with Gamaliel at their head; John, perhaps the cele-

simply means that their knowledge of Jewish culture was confined to the Holy
Scriptures; ἰδιῶται, that they had never studied in rabbinic schools. The
word *Hediot* (ἰδιώτης) occurs frequently in the Talmud, and expresses a position
far superior to that of the *am-haarets*. The *Hediot* is one who, though not a
frequenter of the schools, still pays deference to the authority of the Rabbis;
the *am-haarets* is one who hates and despises that authority. Hillel was distinguished for his forbearing condescension towards the ignorance of *Hediots*
(*Babha Metsia*, f. 104, 1). Compare John vii. 15, "How knoweth this man
letters, *having never learned?*"

[1] "Populus sanior quam qui praesunt" (Bengel). The use of the word
γερουσία in Acts v. 21 is somewhat perplexing, because we know nothing of
any Jewish "senate" apart from the Sanhedrin, and because if γερουσία be
taken in an etymological rather than a political sense, the Sanhedrin *included*
the elders (iv. 8; xxv. 15). It is impossible, in the obscurity of the subject, to
distinguish between the *political* and the *Talmudic* Sanhedrin. See Derenbourg (*Palestine*, 213), who thinks that Agrippa had been the first to introduce
Rabbis into the Sanhedrin.

[2] Both of these are mentioned as having been at the earlier meeting, and
we are probably intended to understand they were also present at this.

[3] On these, see *Life of Christ*, ii., pp. 329—342.

brated Johanan Ben Zakkai;[1] Alexander, perhaps the
wealthy brother of the learned Philo;[2] the same body
who had been present at those secret, guilty, tumultuous,
illegal meetings in which they handed over the Lord Jesus
to their Roman executioners—were again assembled, but
now with something of misgiving and terror, to make one
more supreme effort to stamp out the Galilæan heresy.

The Apostles, when first brought before the Sanhedrin, had been arrested in the evening by the
Captain of the Temple, and had been released with strong
threats, partly because the Sadducees affected to despise
them, but still more because they did not know how to
gainsay the miracle of the healing of the cripple. The
Apostles had then openly declared that they should be
compelled by the law of a higher duty to disregard these
threats, and they had continued to teach to increasing thousands that doctrine of the resurrection which
filled the Sadducees with the greatest jealousy. It was
impossible to leave them unmolested in their career,
and by the High Priest's order they were thrust
into prison. The Sanhedrin met at dawn to try them;
but when they sent for them to the prison they found
that the Apostles were not there, but that, delivered by
" an angel of the Lord," they were calmly teaching in
the Temple. In the deepest perplexity, the Sanhedrists
once more despatched the Levitical officer to arrest them,
but this time without any violence, which might lead to
dangerous results. They offered no resistance, and were
once more placed where their Lord had once stood—in
the centre of that threatening semicircle of angry judges.
In reply to the High Priest's indignant reminder of the
warning they had received, St. Peter simply laid down the

---

[1] Lightfoot, *Cent. Chor.* in Matt., *cap.* 15.
[2] Jos. *Antt.* xviii. 8, § 1.

principle that when our duty to man clashes with our duty to God, it is God that must be obeyed.[1] The High Priest had said, "Ye want to bring upon us the blood of this man." The words are an awful comment on the defiant cry, "His blood be on us, and on our children." *Then* the Sanhedrin had not been afraid of Jesus; now they were trembling at the vengeance which might yet be brought on them by two of the despised disciples. The phrase is also remarkable as furnishing the first instance of that avoidance of the name of Christ which makes the Talmud, in the very same terms, refer to Him most frequently as *Peloni*[2]—"so and so." Peter did not aggravate the Priests' alarm. He made no allusion to the charge of an intended vengeance; he only said that the Apostles, and the Holy Spirit who wrought in them, were witnesses to the resurrection and exaltation of Him whom they had slain. At these words the Sanhedrin ground their teeth with rage, and began to advise another judicial murder, which would, on their own principles, have rendered them execrable to their countrymen, as an assembly given to deeds of blood.[3] This disgrace was averted by the words of one wise man among them. How far the two Apostles were protected by the animosities between the rival sects of Sadducees and Pharisees we do not know, but it was certainly the speech of Gamaliel which saved them from worse results than that scourging by Jewish thongs—those forty stripes save one—which they received, and in which they exulted.[4]

---

[1] Cf. Plat. *Apol.* 29. πείσομαι δὲ Θεῷ μᾶλλον ἢ ὑμῖν. "It were better for me to be called 'fool' all the days of my life, than to be made wicked before *Ha-Makom*," i.e., God; literally "the Place" (*Edioth*, ch. v. 6).

[2] In Spanish and Portuguese *fulano* (through the Arabic). The designation *otho haish*, "that man," is still more contemptuous. יש׳ו (*Yeshu*) is used as the contraction for יש׳ו, and is composed of the initial letters of an imprecation.

[3] "The Sanhedrin is not to save, but to destroy life" (*Sanhedr.* 42 b). (See *Life of Christ*, ii. 352, and *infra*, Excursus VII. [4] Deut xxv. 2.

That speech of Gamaliel was not unworthy of a grand-son of Hillel—of one of those seven who alone won the supreme title of Rabbanîm [1]—of one who subsequently became a President of the Sanhedrin. It has been strangely misunderstood. The supposed anachronism of thirty years in the reference to Theudas has led the school of Baur to deny altogether the genuineness of the speech, but it has yet to be proved that the allusion may not have been perfectly correct. The notion that the speech was due to a secret leaning in favour of Christianity, and the tradition of the Clementine Recognitions, that Gamaliel was in heart a Christian,[2] have no shadow of probability in their favour, since every allusion to him in the Talmud shows that he lived and died a Pharisee. Nor, again, is there the least ground for Schrader's indignation against his supposed assertion of the principle that the success of a religion is a sufficient test of its truth. We must remember that only the briefest outline of his speech is given, and all that Gamaliel seems to have meant was this—'Let these men alone at present. As far as we can see, they are only the victims of a harmless delusion. There is nothing seditious in their practice, nothing subversive in their doctrines. Even if there were we should have nothing to fear from them, and no need to adopt violent measures of precaution. Fanaticism and imposture are short-lived, even when backed by popular insurrection; but in the views of these men there may be something more than at present appears. Some germ of truth, some gleam of revelation, may inspire their singular enthusiasm, and to fight against this may be to fight against God.' Gamaliel's

---

[1] All the Rabbans except Johanan Ben Zakkai were descendants of Gamaliel.

[2] Thilo, *Cod. Apocr.*, p. 501.

plea was not so much a plea for systematic tolerance as for temporary caution.[1] The day of open rupture between Judaism and Christianity was indeed very near at hand, but it had not yet arrived. His advice is neither due to the quiescence of Pharisaic fatalism, nor to a 'fallacious *laisser aller* view of the matter, which serves to show how low the Jews had sunk in theology and political sagacity if such was the counsel of their wisest.'[2] There was time, Gamaliel thought, to wait and watch the development of this new fraternity. To interfere with it might only lead to a needless embroilment between the people and the Sanhedrin. A little patience would save trouble, and indicate the course which should be pursued. Gamaliel was sufficiently clear-sighted to have observed that the fire of a foolish fanaticism dies out if it be neglected, and is only kindled into fury by premature opposition. Let those who venture to arraign the principle of the wise Rabbi remember that it is practically identical with the utterance of Christ, "Every plant, which my heavenly Father planted not, shall be plucked up by the roots."[3]

The advice was too sound, and the authority of the speaker too weighty, to be altogether rejected. The Priests and Rabbis, tortured already with guilty anxiety as to the consequences of their judicial murder, renewed their futile command to the Apostles to preach no more in the name of Jesus, and scourging them for disobedience

---

[1] Too much has, perhaps, been made of the ἐὰν ᾖ ἐξ ἀνθρώπων as contrasted with εἰ δὲ ἐκ Θεοῦ ἐστιν, vv. 38, 39; cf. Gal. i. 8, 9—(Beng. ἐὰν ᾖ si fit, conditionaliter; εἰ ἐστιν si est, categorice)—as though Gamaliel leaned to the latter view—"wornach der gesetzte *Zweite* Fall als der dem Gamaliel wahrscheinlichere erscheint" (Meyer). It merely means—'If it should be from men, as results will show,' and, 'if, a case which I at present suppose, from God.' (See Winer.)

[2] Alford, following Schrader, *Der Apostel Paulus.*

[3] See Matt. xv. 13. It was in this sense that Luther urged the advice of Gamaliel upon the Elector of Trèves.

to their former injunctions, let them go. Neither in public nor in private did the Apostles relax their exertions. The gatherings still continued in Solomon's porch; the *agapæ* were still held in the houses of the brethren. So far from being intimidated, the two Apostles only rejoiced that they were counted worthy of the honour of being dishonoured for the name of Him on whom they believed.

And here I must pause for a moment to make a remark on the grounds which have led many modern critics to reject the authority of the Acts of the Apostles, and to set it down as a romance, written in the cause of reconciliation between Judaising and Pauline Christians. My object in these volumes is not controversial. It has been my endeavour here, as in my *Life of Christ*, to diffuse as widely as I can a clear knowledge of the Dawn of the Christian Faith, and to explain as lucidly as is in my power the bearing of its earliest documents. But I have carefully studied the objections urged against the authenticity and the statements of the New Testament writings; and I cannot forbear the expression of my astonishment at the baselessness of many of the hypotheses which have been accepted in their disparagement. Honesty of course demands that we should admit the existence of an error where such an error can be shown to exist; but the same honesty demands the rejection of all charges against the accuracy of the sacred historian which rest on nothing better than hostile prepossession. It seems to me that writers like Baur and Zeller—in spite of their wide learning and great literary acumen—often prove, by captious objections and by indifference to counter considerations, the fundamental weakness of their own system.[1]

---

[1] See Baur, *Paul.* i. 35; Zeller, *Die Apostelgesch.*, p. 134. Baur asserts that Gamaliel could not have delivered the speech attributed to him because of "the striking chronological error in the appeal to the example of Theudas."

Hausrath altogether rejects the statement that Paul was
"brought up at the feet of Gamaliel," on the ground that
Paul calls himself "a zealot" for the traditions of the
fathers, and must therefore have belonged far rather to
the school of Shammai.   He could not, according to this

And yet he does not offer any proof either that the Theudas here alluded to
is *identical* with the Theudas of Josephus, or that Josephus must *necessarily
be right* and St. Luke necessarily wrong. Zeller, while entering more fully
into the discussion, seems only to be struck by the resemblance between the
two impostors, without allowing for the obvious differences in the accounts of
them; and he attaches an extravagant importance to the silence of Josephus
about the unimportant movement of the earlier fanatic to whom Gamaliel
is supposed to allude; nor does he notice the possibility, admitted even by a
Jewish writer (Jost, *Gesch. d. Jud.* ii. 76), that the Theudas of Gamaliel may
be the Simon, a slave of Herod, of Jos. *Antt.* xvii. 10, § 6; Tac. *H.* v. 9. On this
identification, see Sonntag, *Stud. u. Krit.*, 1837, p. 622; and Hackett, *ad loc.*
Again, critics of the Tübingen school point out the supposed absurdity of
believing that the Sanhedrin would admit "a notable miracle" and yet
punish the men who had performed it. But this is to reason from the standpoint of modern times. The Jews have never denied the miracles of Jesus,
but they have not on that account believed in His mission. Just as a modern
Protestant, familiar with the peculiarities of nervous maladies, might accept
the narrative of wonderful cures performed at La Salette, without for a
moment admitting the reality of the vision which is supposed to have consecrated the place, so the Jews freely admitted the possibility of inconclusive
miracles, which they attributed generally to *kishouf* (*i.e.*, thaumaturgy, miracles
wrought by unhallowed influence), or to עינים אחיזת, phantasmagoria, or de-
ception of the eyes. (Derenbourg, *Palest.* 106, n. 3; 361, n. 1.) Thus they
allowed miraculous power to idols (*Abhoda Zara*, f. 54, 2). There is a
Talmudic anecdote (perhaps a sort of allegory on Eccles. x. 8) which
exactly illustrates this very point. R. Eliezer ben Dama was bitten by
a serpent, and Jacob the *min* (*i.e.*, Christian) *offered to heal him in the
name of Jesus*. "Ben Dama, it is forbidden!" said his uncle, R. Ismael.
"Let me do it," urged Jacob; "I will prove to you by the Law that it is
allowable." Before the argument was over the sick man died. "Happy Ben
Dama!" exclaimed his uncle; "thou hast yielded thy soul in purity, without
violating a precept of the wise" (*Abhoda Zara*, cf. 27, 6; 55, 1; *Jer.
Shabbath*, 14, 4).—When St. Luke makes Gamaliel speak of "Judas of
Galilee," whereas Judas was born at Gamala, and commonly known as Judas
the Gaulonite (Γαυλανίτης ἀνήρ, Jos. *Antt.* xviii. 1, § 1), this trivial peculiarity
would unquestionably have been paraded by German critics as a proof of the
unhistorical character of the speech, but for the fortunate accident that
Josephus, with reference to the sphere of his activity, thrice calls him
ὁ Γαλιλαῖος (*Antt.* xviii. 1, § 6; xx. 5, § 2; *B. J.* ii. 8, § 1).

writer, have been trained by a Rabbi who was remarkable
for his mildness and laxity. He accordingly assumes that
the author of the Acts only invents the relations between
St. Paul and Gamaliel in order to confer a sort of distinction upon the former, when the fame of Gamaliel the
Second, founder of the school of Jabne, kept alive, in
the second century, the fame of his grandfather, Gamaliel
the Elder.[1] Now of what value is a criticism which contemptuously, and I may even say calumniously, contradicts a writer whose accuracy, in matters where it can be
thoroughly tested, receives striking confirmation from the
most opposite sources? It would have been rightly considered a very trivial blot on St. Luke's accuracy if he
had fallen into some slight confusion about the enrolment
of Quirinus, the tetrarchy of Abilene, the Ethnarch under
Aretas, the Asiarchs of Ephesus, the "Prætors" of Philippi,
the "Politarchs" of Thessalonica, the "Protos" of Malta, or
the question whether "Proprætor," or "Pro-consul," was,
in the numerous changes of those days, the exact official
title of the Roman Governor of Cyprus or Corinth. On
several of these points he has been triumphantly charged
with ignorance and error; and on all these points his
minute exactitude has been completely vindicated or
rendered extremely probable. In every historical allusion
—as, for instance, the characters of Gallio, Felix, Festus,
Agrippa II., Ananias, the famine in the days of Claudius,
the decree to expel Jews from Rome, the death of
Agrippa I., the rule of Aretas at Damascus, the Italian
band, &c.—he has been shown to be perfectly faithful
to facts. Are we to charge him with fraudulent
assertions about Paul's relation to Gamaliel on the
questionable supposition that, after reaching the age of

---

[1] Ha-zaken, as he is usually called.

I

manhood, the pupil deviated from his teacher's doctrines?[1] Are we, on similar grounds, to charge Diogenes Laertius with falsehood when he tells us that Antisthenes, the Cynic, and Aristippus, the Cyrenaic, were both of them pupils of Socrates? A remarkable anecdote, which will be quoted farther on, has recorded the terrible quarrel between the parties of Rabbi Eliezer and Rabbi Joshua, of whom the former is called a Shammaite, and the latter a Hillelite;[2] and yet both of them were pupils of the same Rabbi, the celebrated Hillelite, R. Johanan Ben Zaccai. Such instances might be indefinitely multiplied. And if so, what becomes of Hausrath's criticism? Like many of the Tübingen theories, it crumbles into dust.[3]

---

[1] Turning to Buddæus, *Philos. Hebraeorum* (1720), I find that he answered this objection long ago. An interesting anecdote in *Berachôth*, f. 16, 2, shows that the natural kindness of Gamaliel was too strong for the severity of his own teaching.

[2] *Jer. Shabbath*, i. 7.

[3] See Excursus V.: "Gamaliel and the School of Tübingen."

Book II.

ST. STEPHEN AND THE HELLENISTS.

CHAPTER VII.

THE DIASPORA: HEBRAISM AND HELLENISM.

"Τόπον οὐκ ἔστι ῥᾳδίως εὑρεῖν τῆς οἰκουμένης ὃς οὐ παραδέδεκται τοῦτο τὸ φῦλον, μηδ' (sic) ἐπικρατεῖται ὑπ' αὐτοῦ.—STRABO, *ap. Jos. Antt.* xiv. 7, § 2. (Cf. Philo, *Leg. ad Gaium,* xxxvi.)

THE gradual change of relation between the Jews and the Christians was an inevitable result of the widening boundaries of the Church. Among the early converts were "Grecians," as well as "Hebrews," and this fact naturally led to most important consequences, on which hinged the historic future of the Christian Faith.

It is not too much to say that any real comprehension of the work of St. Paul, and of the course of events in the days after Christ must depend entirely on our insight into the difference between these two classes of Jews. And this is a point which has been so cursorily treated that we must here pause while we endeavour to see it in its proper light.

When the successive judgments, first of the Assyrian, then of the Babylonian captivity, had broken all hopes of secular power and all thoughts of secular pride in the hearts of the Jews, a wholly different impulse was given to the current of their life. Settled in the countries to which they had been transplanted, allowed the full rights

I 2

of citizenship, finding free scope for their individual
energies, they rapidly developed that remarkable genius
for commerce by which they have been characterised in
all succeeding ages. It was only a wretched handful
of the nation—compared by the Jewish writers to the
chaff of the wheat—who availed themselves of the free
permission of Cyrus, and subsequent kings of Persia, to
return to their native land.[1] The remainder, although
they jealously preserved their nationality and their traditions, made their homes in every land to which they had
been drifted by the wave of conquest, and gradually
multiplying until, as Josephus tells us,[2] they crowded
every corner of the habitable globe, formed that great and
remarkable body which continues to be known to this day
as "the Jews of the Dispersion."[3]

This Dispersion of the Chosen People was one of
those three vast and world-wide events in which a
Christian cannot but see the hand of God so ordering the
course of history as to prepare the world for the Revelation of His Son. (i.) The immense field covered by the

[1] Of the whole nation only 42,360 returned; and as the separate items of
the returning families given by Ezra and Nehemiah only amount to 30,000,
it was precariously conjectured by the Jews that the surplus consisted of
members of the ten tribes. As a body, however, the ten tribes were finally
and absolutely absorbed into the nations—not improbably of Semitic origin—
among whom they were scattered (Jos. *Antt.* xi. 5, § 2; 2 Esdr. xiii. 45).
Such expressions as τὸ δωδεκάφυλον of James i. 1; Acts xxvi. 7, point rather to
past reminiscences, to patriotic yearnings, and to the sacredly-treasured genea-
logical records of a very few families, than to any demonstrable reality. Of
the priestly families only four courses out of the twenty-four returned (Ezr.
ii. 36—39).

[2] Jos. *Antt.* xiv. 7, § 2.

[3] The word is first found in this sense in Deut. xxviii. 25; Ps. cxlvii. 2,
"He shall gather together the outcasts (נִדְחֵי; LXX., τὰς διασπορὰς) of Israel."
It is also found in 2 Macc. i. 27, "Gather together those that are scattered
from us, deliver them that serve among the heathen." They were originally
called *Beni Galootha* (Ezr. vi. 16.) In John vii. 35, τὴν διασπορὰν τῶν Ἑλλήνων
means the Jews scattered over the Greek world. The only other passages
where it occurs in the N.T. are James i. 1; 1 Pet. i. 1.

conquests of Alexander gave to the civilised world a Unity of Language, without which it would have been, humanly speaking, impossible for the earliest preachers to have made known the good tidings in every land which they traversed. (ii.) The rise of the Roman Empire created a Political Unity which reflected in every direction the doctrines of the new faith. (iii.) The dispersion of the Jews prepared vast multitudes of Greeks and Romans for the Unity of a pure Morality and a monotheistic Faith. The Gospel emanated from the capital of Judæa; it was preached in the tongue of Athens; it was diffused through the empire of Rome: the feet of its earliest missionaries traversed, from the Euphrates to the Pillars of Hercules, the solid structure of undeviating roads by which the Roman legionaries— "those massive hammers of the whole earth"[1] — had made straight in the desert a highway for our God. Semite and Aryan had been unconscious instruments in the hands of God for the spread of a religion which, in its first beginnings, both alike detested and despised. The letters of Hebrew and Greek and Latin inscribed above the cross were the prophetic and unconscious testimony of three of the world's noblest languages to the undying claims of Him who suffered to obliterate the animosities of the nations which spoke them, and to unite them all together in the one great Family of God.

This contact of Jew with Greek was fruitful of momentous consequences both to the Aryan and the Semitic race. It is true that the enormous differences between the morals, the habits, the tendencies, the religious systems, the whole tone of mind and view of life in these two great human families, inspired them with feelings of mutual aversion and almost detestation. Out of the chaos

---

[1] Shairp, *Mod. Culture.*

of struggling interests which followed the death of
Alexander, there gradually emerged two great kingdoms,
the Egyptian and the Syrian, ruled respectively by the
Ptolemies and the Seleucids. These dynasties had in-
herited the political conceptions of the great Macedonian
conqueror, and desired to produce a fusion of the heterogeneous elements included in their government. Both
alike turned their eyes to Palestine, which became
the theatre of their incessant contentions, and which
passed alternately under the sway of each. The Ptolemies
continuing the policy of Alexander, did their utmost to
promote the immigration of Jews into Egypt. The
Seleucids, both by force and by various political induce-
ments, settled them as largely as they could in their
western cities. Alike the Lagidæ and the Seleucidæ knew
the value of the Jews as quiet and order-loving citizens.
To the shores of the Mediterranean flocked an ever-
increasing multitude of Greek merchants and Greek
colonists. "The torrent of Greek immigration soon met
the torrent of Jewish emigration. Like two rivers which
poured their differently coloured waves into the same
basin without mixing with one another, these two peoples
cast themselves on the young Macedonian cities, and
there simultaneously established themselves without
intermixture, continually separated by the irreconcilable diversity of their beliefs and customs, though continually flung into connexion by community of business
and by the uniform legislation which protected their
interests." [1]

The effect of this on the Greek was less marked and
less memorable than its effect on the Jew. Judaism was
more Hellenised by the contact than Hellenism was

[1] Reuss, *Théol. Chrét.* L i. 93; and in Herzog, *Cyclop.*, *s.v.* "Hellenism."
On this isopolity see *Jos. c. Ap.* ii. 4.

Judaised. There can be no more striking proof of this fact than the total loss by the "Sons of the Dispersion" of their own mother tongue. That the effects on the Pagan world were less beneficial than might have been anticipated was, in great measure, the fault of the Jews themselves. That sort of obtrusive humility which so often marks a race which has nothing to live on but its memories, was mingled with an invincible prejudice, a rooted self-esteem, an unconcealed antipathy to those of alien race and religion, which, combined as it was with commercial habits by no means always scrupulous, and a success by no means always considerate, alienated into disgust the very sympathies which it should have striven to win. The language in which the Jews are spoken of by the writers of the Empire—a language expressive of detestation mingled with curiosity—sufficiently accounts for the outbreaks of mob violence, from which in so many ages they have been liable to suffer. These outbreaks, if not connived at by the governing authorities, were too often condoned. Yet, in spite of this, the influence insensibly exercised by the Jews over the heathen among whom they lived was full of important consequences for Christianity. "*Victi*," says Seneca, "*victoribus leges dederunt.*" The old Paganism was, in intellectual circles, to a great extent effete. Great Pan was dead. Except in remote country districts, the gods of Olympus were idle names. In Rome the terrors of Tartarus were themes for a schoolboy's laughter. Religion had sunk into a state machinery.[1] The natural consequences followed. Those minds which were too degraded to feel the need of a religion were content to wallow, like natural brute beasts, in the Stygian pool of a hideous immorality. Others became the votaries

---

[1] See Juv. ii. 149; Boissier, *La Religion Romaine*, i. 374—450 and *contra* Friedländer, *Sittengesch. Roms.* (who goes too far).

of low foreign superstitions,[1] or the dupes of every variety
of designing charlatans. But not a few were attracted
into the shadow of the synagogue, and the majority of
these were women,[2] who, restricted as was their influence,
yet could not fail to draw the attention of their domestic
circles to the belief which they had embraced. In every
considerable city of the Roman Empire the service of the
synagogue was held in Greek, and these services were
perfectly open to any one who liked to be present at
them. Greek, too, became emphatically the language
of Christianity. Multitudes of early converts had been
Jewish proselytes before they became Christian disciples.
They passed from the synagogue of Hellenists into the
Church of Christ.

The influences exercised by the Dispersion on the Jews
themselves were, of course, too varied and multitudinous to
be summed up under one head; yet we may trace two consequences which, century after century, worked in opposite
directions, but each of which was deeply marked. On the
one hand they became more faithful to their religion; on the
other more cosmopolitan in their views. Although they
made their home in the heathen countries to which they had
been removed by conquest, or had wandered in pursuit of
commerce, it must not be supposed that they were at all

[1] Because these presented vaguer and more shadowy conceptions of the
Divine, more possible to grasp than gross concrete images (see Hausrath,
Neut. Zeitg. ii. 76), and because Greek religion was too gay for a sick and
suffering world (Apul. *Metam.* xi. *passim*). See Cat. x. 26; Ov. *F.* iv. 309;
A. A. i. 78; Juv. vi. 489, 523; Tac. *Ann.* xvi. 6, &c.

[2] The important part played by these proselytes (who are also called
σεβόμενοι, εὐσεβεῖς, εὐλαβεῖς) may be seen in Acts x. 2; xiii. 43; xvi. 14, &c., and
passim. Owing to the painful and, to Hellenic imagination, revolting rite of
circumcision, women were more frequently converted to Judaism than men.
Josephus (*B. J.* ii., xx. 2) tells us that nearly all the women of Damascus had
adopted Judaism; and even in the first century three celebrated Rabbis were
sons of heathen mothers who had embraced the faith of Moses (Derenbourg,
Palest., p. 223).

ready to forfeit their nationality or abandon their traditions. On the contrary, the great majority of them clung to both with a more desperate tenacity. In the destruction of their independence they had recognised the retribution threatened in that long-neglected series of prophecies which had rebuked them for their idolatries. Of all polytheistic tendencies the Jew was cured for ever, and as though to repair past centuries of rebellion and indifference—as though to earn the fulfilment of that great promise of an Anointed Deliverer which was the centre of all their hopes—they devoted themselves with all the ardour of their self-conscious pride to keep the minutest observances of their Law and ritual. Their faithfulness—a complete contrast to their old apostasies—was due to the work of the *Sopherim*, or Scribes. It was towards Jerusalem that they worshipped; it was to the Sanhedrin of Jerusalem that they looked for legal decisions; it was from the *Amoraim* and *Tanaim* of Jerusalem that they accepted all solutions of casuistical difficulties; it was from Jerusalem that were flashed the fire-signals which announced over many lands the true date of the new moons; it was into the treasury of Jerusalem that they poured, not only the stated Temple-tribute of half a shekel, but gifts far more costly, which told of their unshaken devotion to the church of their fathers. It was in Jerusalem that they maintained a special synagogue, and to Jerusalem that they made incessant pilgrimages.[1] The hatred, the suspicion, the contempt created in many countries by the exclusiveness of their prejudices, the peculiarity of their institutions, the jealousy of their successes, only wedded them more fanatically to the observance of their Levitical rules by giving a tinge of

[1] See Philo, *Legat.* 36; *in Flacc.* 7; Jos. *Antt.* xvi. 6; xviii. 9, § 1; Cic. *pro Flacc.* xxviii.; Shekalim, 7, 4; Rosh Hashana, 2, 4.

martyrdom to the fulfilment of obligations. It became
with them a point of conscience to maintain the institutions which their heathen neighbours attacked with
every weapon of raillery and scorn. But these very
circumstances tended to produce a marked degeneracy of
the religious spirit. The idolatry, which in old days
had fastened on the visible symbols of alien deities,
only assumed another form when concentrated on the
dead-letter of documents, and the minute ritualism of
service. Gradually, among vast masses of the Jewish
people, religion sank almost into fetichism. It lost all
power over the heart and conscience, all its tender love,
all its inspiring warmth, all its illuminating light. It
bound the nation hand and foot to the corpse of meaningless traditions. Even the ethics of the Mosaic legislation
were perverted by a casuistry which was at once timid
in violating the letter, and audacious in superseding the
spirit. In the place of moral nobleness and genial bene-
volence, Judaism in its decadence bred only an incapacity
for spiritual insight, a self-satisfied orthodoxy, and an
offensive pride. It enlisted murder and falsity in defence
of ignorant Shibboleths and useless forms. The difference
between the ideal Jew of earlier and later times can only
be measured by the difference between the moral principles
of the Law and the dry precedents of the Mishna—by
the difference which separates the Pentateuch from the
Talmud, the Book of Exodus from the Abhoda Zara.[1]

But while it produced these results in many of the
Jewish communities, there were others, and there were
special individuals in all communities, in whom the
influence of heathen surroundings worked very differently.
There were many great and beautiful lessons to be learnt

[1] "The author of the Pentateuch and the Tanaim moved in different
worlds of ideas" (Kuenen, iii. 291).

from the better aspects of the heathen world. If there was a grace that radiated from Jerusalem, there were also gifts which brightened Athens. The sense of beauty—the exquisiteness of art—the largeness and clearness of insight—the perfection of literary form which characterised the Greek of the age of Pericles, had left the world an immortal heritage; and Rome had her own lessons to teach of dignity, and law, and endurance, and colonisation, and justice. Commerce is eminently cosmopolitan. The Jewish Captivity, with the events which followed it, made the Jews a commercial people. This innate tendency of the race had been curbed, first by the Mosaic legislation,[1] then by the influence of the prophets. But when these restrictions had been providentially removed, the Jew flung himself with ardour into a career from which he had been hitherto restrained. So far from regarding as identical the notions of "merchant" and "Canaanite,"[2] the Rabbis soon began to sing the praises of trade. "There can be no worse occupation than agriculture!" said R. Eleazar. "All the fanning in the world will not make you so remunerative as commerce," said Rabh[3] as he saw a cornfield bowing its golden ears under the summer breeze.[4] So easy is it for a people to get over an archaic legislation if it stands in the way of their interests or inclinations! The Mosaic

---

[1] Deut. xvi. 16, 17; Lev. xxv.; Ps. cvii. 23. See Jos. c. Ap. i. 12. The chapter begins with the remark, ἡμεῖς τοίνυν οὔτε χώραν οἰκοῦμεν παράλιον οὔτ ἐμπορίαις χαίρομεν, οὐδὲ ταῖς πρὸς ἄλλους διὰ τούτων ἐπιμιξίαις. Munk (Palest., p. 393) makes some excellent remarks on this subject, showing that commerce would not only have encouraged intercourse with the heathen, but would also have disturbed the social equilibrium at which Moses aimed, so that it was impossible as long as the Law was rigidly observed (Hos. xii. 8; Amos viii. 4—6, &c.).

[2] Targum of Jonathan (Zech. xiv. 21).

[3] Rabh was a contemporary of Rabbi (Judah the Holy), and was "Head of the Captivity."

[4] Yebhamôth, f. 63, 1.

restrictions upon commerce were, of course, impracticable
in dealing with Gentiles, and in material successes the
Jews found something, at any rate, to make up to them
for the loss of political independence. The busy intercourse of cities wrought a further change in their opinions.
They began to see that God never meant the nations of
the world to stand to each other in the position of
frantic antagonism or jealous isolation.   A Jerusalem
Rabbi, ignorant of everything in heaven and earth and
under the earth, except his own *Halacha*, might talk of
all the rest of the world promiscuously as an "elsewhere"
of no importance; [1] but an educated Alexandrian Jew
would be well aware that the children of heathen lands
had received from their Father's tenderness a share in
the distribution of His gifts. The silent and imperceptible
influences of life are often the most permanent, and no
amount of exclusiveness could entirely blind the more
intelligent sons of the Dispersion to the merits of a
richer civilisation.   No Jewish boy familiar with the
sights and sounds of Tarsus or Antioch could remain
unaware that all wisdom was not exhausted in the trivial
discussions of the Rabbis; that there was something
valuable to the human race in the Greek science which
Jewish nescience denounced as thaumaturgy ; that there
might be a better practice for the reasoning powers than
an interminable application of the *Middôth* of Hillel; in
short, that the development of humanity involves larger
and diviner duties than a virulent championship of the
exclusive privileges of the Jew.[2]

---

[1] ץראל הצוח ' outside the land ' (Frankl. *Jews in the East*, ii. 34). Something like the French *là-bas*.

[2] Many of the Rabbis regarded the Gentiles as little better than so much
fuel for the fires of Gehenna. R. Jose construes Isa. xxxiii. 12, " And the
peoples shall be a *burning like* lime." Rabh Bar Shilo explained it "that they
should be burnt because of their neglect of the Law, which was written upon

We might naturally have conjectured that these wider sympathies would specially be awakened among those Jews who were for the first time brought into close contact with the great peoples of the Aryan race. That contact was first effected by the conquests of Alexander. He settled 8,000 Jews in the Thebais, and the Jews formed a third of the population of his new city of Alexandria. Large numbers were brought from Palestine by Ptolemy I., and they gradually spread from Egypt, not only over "the parts of Libya about Cyrene," but along the whole Mediterranean coast of Africa.[1] Seleucus Nicator, after the battle of Ipsus, removed them by thousands from Babylonia, to such cities as Antioch and Seleucia; and, when their progress and prosperity were for a time shaken by the senseless persecutions of Antiochus Epiphanes, they scattered themselves in every direction until there was hardly a seaport or a commercial centre in Asia Minor, Macedonia, Greece, or the Islands of the Ægean, in which Jewish communities were not to be found. The vast majority of these Jewish settlers adopted the Greek language, and forgot that Aramaic dialect which had been since the Captivity the language of their nation.

It is to these Greek-speaking Jews that the term Hellenist mainly and properly refers. In the New Testament there are two words, *Hellen* and *Hellenistes*, of which the first is rendered "Greek," and the second "Grecian." The word "Greek" is used as an antithesis either to

lime." (See the curious *Hagadah* in *Sotah*, f. 35, 2.) But the Hellenist would soon learn to feel that—

> "All knowledge is not couch'd in Moses' Law,
> The Pentateuch, or what the Prophets wrote ;
> The Gentiles also know, and write, and teach
> To admiration, taught by Nature's light."—MILTON, *Par. Reg.* iv. 225.

[1] See Philo, *c. Fl.* ii. 523; Jos. *Antt.* xvi. 7, § 2; Dr. Deutsch in Kitto's *Cycl., s.v.* "Dispersion;" and Canon Westcott in Smith's *Bible Dict.*

"barbarians" or to "Jews." In the first case it means all nations which spoke the Greek language;[1] in the second case it is equivalent to "Gentiles."[2] The meaning of the word Hellenist or "Grecian" is wholly different. As far as the form is concerned, it means, in the first instance, one who "Græcises" in language or mode of life, and it points to a difference of training and of circumstances, not to a difference of race.[3] It is therefore reserved as the proper antithesis, not to "Jews,"—since vast numbers of the Hellenists were Jews by birth,—but to strict "Hebrews." The word occurs but twice in the New Testament,[4] and in both cases is used of Jews who had embraced Christianity but who spoke Greek and used the Septuagint version of the Bible instead of the original Hebrew or the Chaldaic Targum of any Interpreter.[5]

Now this Hellenism expressed many shades of differ-

---

[1] See Acts xviii. 17; 1 Cor. i. 22, 23; Rom. i. 14. The emissaries of Abgarus—if such they were—who applied to Philip when they wished to see Jesus were "Greeks," not "Grecians" (John xii. 20).

[2] Rom. i. 16; ii. 9; iii. 9; 1 Cor. x. 32; Gal. ii. 3, &c. Thus in 2 Macc. iv. 13, Ἑλληνισμὸς is equivalent to ἀλλοφυλισμός; and in iv. 10, 15; vi. 9, τὰ Ἑλληνικὰ ἤθη means "Paganism;" and in Isa. ix. 12, "Philistines" is rendered by the LXX. Ἕλληνας.

[3] Cf. Xen. Anab. vii. 3, 12.

[4] Acts vi. 1; ix. 29. In xi. 20 the true reading is Ἕλληνας.

[5] Some of the Hebraising Hellenists hated even the Septuagint (Geiger, Urschr, 419, 439; Zunz, Gottesd. Vort. 95). The various classes of Christians may be tabulated as follows:—

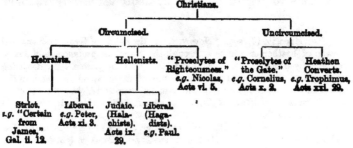

ence, and therefore the exact meaning of the word Hellenist varies with the circumstances under which it is used. The accident of language might make a man, technically speaking, a Hellenist, when politically and theologically he was a Hebrew: and this must have been the condition of those Hellenist who disputed against the arguments of St. Paul in his fi· t visit to Jerusalem.[1] On the other hand, the name ʟ..ght imply that alienation from the system of Judaism, which in some Jews extended into positive apostasy, and into so deep a shame of their Jewish origin, as to induce them, not only in the days of Jason and Menelaus,[2] but even under the Herods, to embrace the practices of the Greeks, and even to obliterate the external sign of their nationality.[3] Others again, like the astute Herodian princes, were hypocrites, who played fast and loose with their religion, content to be scrupulous Jews at Jerusalem, while they could be shameless heathen at Berytus or Cæsarea. But the vast majority of Hellenists lay between these extremes. Contact with the world had widened their intelligence and enabled them so far to raise their heads out of the heavy fog of Jewish scholasticism as to distinguish between that which was of eternal and that which was but of transient significance. Far away from Jerusalem, where alone it was *possible* to observe the Levitical law, it was a natural result that they came to regard outward symbols as merely valuable

---

[1] Acts ix. 29.

[2] See 2 Macc. iv. 13, *seqq.*, "Now such was the height of Greek fashions, and increase of heathenish manners, through the exceeding profaneness of Jason, that ungodly wretch, and no high p.iest, . . . that the priests, . . . despising the temple, . . . hastened to be partakers of the unlawful allowance in the place of exercise, after the game of Discus called them forth," &c. מלכות יון הרשעה, "the abominable kingdom of Javan" is an expression which stereotypes the hatred for Greek fashions.

[3] ἐπισπασμὸς (1 Cor. vii. 18). The condition of a משוך (1 Macc. i. 15; Jos. *Antt.* xii. 5, § 1). (On Judaic Hellenism, see Ewald, *Gesch.* v. § ii. 4.)

for the sake of inward truths. To this class belonged the
wisest members of the Jewish Dispersion. It is to them
that we owe the Septuagint translation, the writings of
Philo and Josephus, and a large cycle of historical, poetic,
and apocryphal literature. Egypt was the main centre of
this Græco-Jewish activity, and many of the Jews of
Alexandria distinguished themselves in the art, the learning, and the accomplishments of the Greeks.[1] It is hardly
to be wondered at that these more intellectual Jews were
not content with an infructuose Rabbinism. It is not
astonishing that they desired to represent the facts of
their history, and the institutions of their religion, in
such an aspect as should least waken the contempt of the
nations among whom they lived.[2] But although this
might be done with perfect honesty, it tended, no doubt,
in some to the adoption of unauthorised additions to their
history, and unauthorised explanations of their Scriptures
—in one word, to that style of exegesis which, since it
deduced anything out of anything, nullified the real significance of the sacred records.[3] Nor can we be surprised

---

[1] Thus, an Ezekiel wrote a tragedy on Moses; another, Philo, wrote an Epic
on Jerusalem; Theodotus, a tragedy on the Rape of Dina; Demetrius and
Eupolemos wrote secular history. The story of Susanna is a novelette. But
the feeling of stricter Jews was sternly opposed to these forms of literary
activity. In the letter of Aristeas we are told that Theopompus was struck
with madness, and Theodektes with blindness, for offences in this direction
(Hausrath, *Neut. Zeitg.* ii. 130).

[2] Such was the main object of Josephus in his *Antiquities.*

[3] The views of these liberal Hellenists may be seen represented in the works
of the pseudo-Aristeas, the pseudo-Aristobulus, and in the verses of Pho-
cylides (Kuenen, *Religion of Israel,* iii. 180). It was the aim of an entire
cycle of literature to prove that all Greek wisdom was derived from Jewish
sources, and the names of Orpheus and the Sibyl were frequently given to
Jewish forgeries and interpolations (Clem. Alex. *Strom.* v. 4; Euseb. *Praep.
Evang.* vii. 14; viii. 10; xiii. 12). Bel and the Dragon, the Epistle of Jeremiah,
the letter of pseudo-Heraclitus, &c., belong to this class of writings. See too
Wisd. of Solomon x.—xii.; Jos. *c. Ap.* ii. 39; Hausrath, *N. Zeitgesch.* ii. 100, *sq.*
Josephus says that Pythagoras borrowed from Moses (*c. Ap.* i. 22).

that this Alexandrian theosophy—these allegoric interpretations—this spirit of toleration for the Pagan systems by which they were surrounded—were regarded by the stricter Jews as an incipient revolt from Mosaism thinly disguised under a hybrid phraseology.[1] Hence arose the the antagonism between advanced Hellenists and the Hebrews, whose whole patriotic existence had concentrated itself upon the Mosaic and Oral Law. The severance between the two elements became wider and wider as the Jews watched the manner in which Christianity spread in the Gentile world. The consciousness that the rapidity of that diffusion was due, not only to the offer of a nobler faith, but also to the loosening of an intolerable yoke, only made their exclusiveness more obstinate. It was not long before the fall of Jerusalem that there took place in the school of R. Hananiah Ben Hiskiah Ben Garon, that memorable meeting at which eighteen ordinances were resolved upon, of which it was the exclusive object to widen the rift of difference between Jews and Pagans. These ordinances, to which the Mishna only alludes, are found in a *baraita* ("supplemental addition") of R. Simeon Ben Johai in the second century, and they consist of prohibitions which render impossible any interchange of social relations between Jews and heathen. It was in vain that R. Joshua and the milder Hillelites protested against so dangerous a bigotry. The quarrel passed from words to blows. The followers of Hillel were attacked with swords and lances, and some of them were killed. "That day," says the Jerusalem Talmud, "was as dis-

---

[1] Such Hebraising Hellenists are the author of "the Epistle of Jeremiah," and (on the whole) of Wisdom (see vii. 22, *seq.*, xiii.—xix.). "The Liberal Hellenists spiritualised and volatilised the wall of partition between Jews and Pagans," so that, although Philo said that the wall should still be kept up, it is not surprising to find that his nephew, the Procurator Tiberius Alexander, had abandoned Judaism (Jos. *Antt.* xx. 5, § 2; Kuenen, *Rel. of Israel*, iii.).

J

astrous to Israel as the one on which they made the
golden calf; " but it seemed to be a general opinion that
the eighteen resolutions could not be rescinded even by
Elias himself, because the discussion had been closed by
bloodshed; and they were justified to the national conscience by the savage massacres which had befallen the
Jews at Beth-shan, Cæsarea, and Damascus.[1]   The
feelings of Jews towards Pagans were analogous to the
hatred of Hebrews to Hellenists.   In later days the Christians absorbed the entire fury of that detestation which
had once burned in the Jewish heart against Hellenism.
When a question arose as to the permissibility of burning the Gospels and other books of the Christians (*Minim*),
considering how frequently they contained the name of
God, "May I lose my son," exclaimed Rabbi Tarphon,
"if I do not fling these books into the fire when they
come into my hands, name of God and all.   A man
chased by a murderer, or threatened by a serpent's bite,
ought rather to take refuge in an idol's temple than in
the houses of the *Minim*, for these latter know the truth
and deny it, whereas idolaters deny God because they
know Him not."[2]

Such, then, being the feelings of the Palestinian Jews
with regard to every approach towards idolatry, the
antagonism between them and the more liberal Hellenists
rose from the very nature of things, and was so deeply
rooted that we are not surprised to find a trace of it
even in the history of the Church;—for the earliest
Christians—the Apostles and disciples of Jesus—were
almost exclusively Hebrews and Israelites,[3] the former

---

[1] *Shabbath*, i. 7; Grätz, iii. 494; Derenbourg, *Palest.*, p. 274.

[2] *Shabbath*, 116 a; Derenbourg, p. 380.

[3] The Hellenic names of Philip and Andrew prove nothing, because at this
epoch such names were common among the Jews.   But they may have had
Hellenic connexions.   (John xii. 20.)

being a general, and the latter a religious designation. Their feelings towards those who were Hellenists in principles as well as in language would be similar to that of other Jews, however much it might be softened by Christian love. But the jealousies of two sections so widely diverse in their sympathies would be easily kindled; and it is entirely in accordance with the independent records of that period that, "when the number of the disciples was being multiplied," there should have arisen, as a natural consequence, "a murmuring of the Grecians against the Hebrews."

The special ground of complaint was a real or fancied neglect of the widows of Hellenists in the daily ministration of food and assistance. There might be some jealousy because all the offices of the little Church were administered by Hebrews, who would naturally have been more cognisant of the claims of their immediate compatriots. Widows, however, were a class who specially required support. We know how full a discussion St. Paul applies to their general position even at Corinth, and we have already mentioned that some of the wisest regulations attributed to Gamaliel were devoted to ameliorating the sufferings to which they were exposed. In the seclusion to which centuries of custom had devoted the Oriental woman, the lot of a widow, with none to plead her cause, might indeed be bitter. Any inequalities in the treatment of the class would awaken a natural resentment, and the more so because previous to their conversion these widows would have had a claim on the *Corban*, or Temple treasury.[1]

But the Apostles met these complaints in that spirit of candour and generosity which is the best proof how

---

[1] 2 Macc. iii. 10, "Then the high priest told him (Heliodorus) that there was such money laid up for the relief of widows and fatherless children."

J 2

little they were responsible for any partiality which may
have been shown to the widows of the Hebrews. Summoning a meeting of the disciples, they pointed out to
them that the day had now come in which it was inconvenient for the Apostles to have anything further to do
with the apportionment of charity[1]—a routine task which
diverted them from more serious and important duties.
They therefore bade the meeting elect seven men of
blameless character, high spiritual gifts, and practical
wisdom, to form what we should call a committee of
management, and relieve the Apostles from the burden,
in order that they might devote their energies to prayer
and pastoral work. The advice was followed, and seven
were presented to the Apostles as suitable persons. They
were admitted to the duties of their position with prayer
and the laying on of hands, which have been thenceforth
naturally adopted in every ordination to the office of a
deacon.[2]

The seven elected were Stephen, Philip, Prochorus,
Nicanor, Timon, Parmenas, and Nicolas, a proselyte of
Antioch. The fact that every one of them bears a Greek

---

[1] Acts vi. 2, διακονεῖν τραπέζαις. That τράπεζα has not here its meaning of
"bank" (Jos. Antt. xii. 1, § 2; cf. τραπεζίταις, Matt. xxv. 27; τράπεζαν, Luke
xix. 23), is clear from the context.

[2] The seven officers were not, however, "deacons" in the modern sense of
the word, nor were they mere almoners. The only special title given to any
one of them is Evangelist (Acts xxi. 8). Alike their gifts and their functions
are loftier than those required for deacons in 1 Tim. iii. Deacons in the
modern sense find their nearer prototypes in the νεώτεροι and νεανίσκοι (Acts
v. 5, 10; cf. Luke xxii. 26), and in the Chazzanîm of the synagogue (Luke iv. 20).
The seven, as St. Chrysostom observes, rather had the duties of presbyters,
and must be regarded as a body chosen only for a special purpose—πρὸς ἓν εἰς
τοῦτο ἐχειροτονήθησαν. Another analogy for this appointment was furnished
by the existing institution of three almoners (Parnasîm), who undertook the
collection and distribution of the "alms of the cup" (see Dr. Ginsburg in
Kitto, s.v. "Synagogue") and "alms of the box" in the Jewish synagogues;
and these were always chosen by the entire congregation of the synagogue,
as the Apostles here suggest should be done in the case of the new func-
tionaries.

name has often been appealed to as a proof of the conciliatoriness of the Apostles, as though they had elected
every one of their committee from the very body which
had found some reason to complain. This, however, would
have been hardly just. It would have been to fly into an
opposite extreme. The frequency with which the Jews of
this time adopted Greek names prevents us from drawing
any conclusion as to their nationality. But although we
cannot be certain about the conjecture of Gieseler that
three of them were Hebrews, three of them Hellenists,
and one a proselyte, it is only natural to suppose that
the choice of them from different sections of the Church
would be adopted as a matter of fairness and common
sense. And the fact that a Gentile like Nicolas should
thus have been selected to fill an office so honourable and
so responsible is one of the many indications which mark
the gradual dawn of a new conception respecting the
Kingdom of God.

Though two alone[1] of the seven are in any way

[1] Nicolas is no exception. If, as early tradition asserted, Luke was
himself "a proselyte of Antioch" (Euseb. *H. E.* iii. 4; Jer. *De Vir. Illustr.* 7),
this may have suggested the passing reference to him. The evidence which
connects him with " the sect of the Nicolaitanes " (Rev. ii. 6, 15), and the story
that they adopted both their name and their abominable doctrines from a
perversion of his remark that we ought παραχρῆσθαι τῇ σαρκὶ are insufficient.
παραχρῆσθαι, though used of unrestrained indulgence (Suid.), has also the sense
of διαχρῆσθαι, to mortify (Just. M. *Apol.* 49). Irenaeus (*c. Haer.* i. 47), followed
by many of the Fathers (Hippolytus, *R. H.* vii. 36; Tertullian, *De praescr.
haeret.* c. 46), accepts the tradition of his connexion with the sect. Clemens
of Alexandria, while defending him from the charge of personal immorality,
and admitting that the meaning of his words (which, to say the least, were
unfortunately chosen) had been entirely misunderstood (τὴν ἐγκράτειαν τῶν περι-
σπουδάστων ἡδονῶν τὸ " παραχρῆσθαι τῇ σαρκὶ " ἐδίδασκει, *Strom.* iii. iv. 26, ed. Pott.,
p. 523), yet tells a dubious, and probably mistaken, story about his conduct
when charged with jealousy of his wife. This story is repeated by Eusebius
(*H. E.* iii. 29), and other Fathers. For further information on the subject,
and on the identification by Cocceius of Nicolas with Balaam in Rev. ii., see
Gieseler, *Ecc. Hist.* i. 86, E.T.; Mansel, *Gnostic Her.*, p. 72; Derenbourg,
p. 363.

known to us, yet this election was a crisis in the history of the Church. At the work of Philip we shall glance hereafter, but we must now follow the career of Stephen, which, brief as it was, marked the beginning of a memorable epoch. For St. Stephen must be regarded as the immediate predecessor of him who took the most prominent part in bringing about his martyrdom; he must be regarded as having been, in a far truer sense than Gamaliel himself, the Teacher of St. Paul. St. Paul has, indeed, been called a " colossal St. Stephen;" but had the life of St. Stephen been prolonged—had he not been summoned, it may be, to yet loftier spheres of activity —we know not to what further heights of moral grandeur he might have attained. We possess but a single speech to show his intellect and inspiration, and we are suffered to catch but one glimpse of his life. His speech influenced the whole career of the greatest of the Apostles, and his death is the earliest martyrdom.

CHAPTER VIII.

WORK AND MARTYRDOM OF ST. STEPHEN.

Παύλου.ὁ διδάσκαλος.—BASIL SELEUC. Orat. de S. Steph.

Καὶ ἴδοι τις ἂν τὸ λεγόμενον σαφῶς εἰ τὴν σοφίαν τοῦ Στεφάνου, εἰ τὴν Πέτρου γλῶτταν, εἰ τὴν Παύλου ῥύμην ἐννοήσειε, πῶς οὐδὲν αὐτοὺς ἔφερεν οὐδὲν ὑφίστατο, οὐ δημῶν θυμὸς, οὐ τυράννων ἐπαναστάσεις, οὐ δαιμόνων ἐπιβουλὴ, οὐ θάνατοι καθημερινοί. ἀλλ' ὥσπερ ποταμοὶ πολλῷ τῷ ῥοίζῳ φερόμενοι οὕτω πάντα παρασύροντες ἀπῄεσαν.—S. CHRYS. in Joan. Hom. li. Opp. viii. 30.

"This farther only have I to say, my lords, that like as St. Paul was present and consenting to the death of the proto-martyr St. Stephen, and yet they be now twain holy saints in heaven, ... so I verily trust we may hereafter meet in heaven merrily together, to our everlasting salvation."—*Last Words of Sir T. More to his Judges.*

THE appointment of the Seven, partly because of their zeal and power, and partly because of the greater freedom secured for the Apostles, led to marked successes in the progress of the Church. Not only was the number of disciples in Jerusalem greatly multiplied, but even a large number of the priests [1] became obedient to the faith. Up to this time the acceptance of the Gospel, so far from

---

[1] Cf. John xii. 42. Commentators have resorted to extraordinary shifts to get rid of this simple statement, which, as I have shown in the text, involves no improbability. Some would adopt the wholly worthless v. l. Ἰουδαίων found in a few cursive MSS. and the Philoxenian Syriac. Others accept Beza's conjectural emendation, πολύς τε ὄχλος καὶ ἱερέων (sc. τινες). Others, again, follow Heinsius and Elsner in the suggestion that ὄχλος τῶν ἱερέων means "priests of the common order," "plebeian priests," what the Jews might have called עם הארץ or "people-of-the-land priests," as distinguished from the *Thalmídí hachachámím,* or "learned priests;" but there is no trace that any such distinction existed, although it is in itself all but certain that none of these converts came from the families of the lordly and supercilious Boethusím, Kamhíts, &c. But neither here nor in i. 15, ὄχλος ὀνομάτων, has ὄχλος a contemptuous sense.

involving any rupture with Judaism, was consistent with
a most scrupulous devotion to its observances. It must
be borne in mind that the priests in Jerusalem, and a few
other cities, were a multitudinous body,[1] and that it was
only the narrow aristocratic clique of a few alien families
who were Sadducees in theology and Herodians in politics.
Many of the lower ranks of the priesthood were doubtless
Pharisees, and as the Pharisees were devoted to the
doctrine of the Resurrection, there was nothing inconsistent with their traditions in admitting the Messiahship
of a Risen Saviour. Such a belief would at this time, and,
indeed, long afterwards, have made little difference in their
general position, although if they were true believers it
would make a vast difference in their inward life. The
simplicity, the fervour, the unity, the spiritual gifts of
the little company of Galilæans, would be likely to
attract the serious and thoughtful. They would be won
by these graces far more than by irresistible logic, or
by the appeals of powerful eloquence. The mission
of the Apostles at this time was, as has been well
observed, no mere apostolate of rhetoric, nor would they
for a moment pretend to be other than they were—
illiterate men, untrained in the schools of technical
theology and rabbinic wisdom. Had they been otherwise, the argument for the truth of Christianity, which
is derived from the extraordinary rapidity of its dissemination, would have lost half its force. The weapons
of the Apostolic warfare were not carnal. Converts
were won, not by learning or argument, but by the
power of a new testimony and the spirit of a new life.

Up to this period the name of Stephen has not occurred
in Christian history, and as the tradition that he had been

---

[1] 4,289 had returned with Ezra (ii. 36—39).

one of the seventy disciples is valueless,[1] we know nothing
of the circumstances of his conversion to Christianity.
His recognition, however, of the glorified figure, which
he saw in his ecstatic vision, as the figure of Him who
on earth had called Himself "the Son of Man," makes
it probable that he was one of those who had enjoyed
the advantage of hearing the living Jesus, and of drawing from its very fountain-head the river of the water
of life.[2] We would fain know more of one who, in so
brief a space of time, played a part so nobly wise. But
it was with Stephen as it has been with myriads of others
whose names have been written in the Book of Life; they
have been unknown among men, or known only during
one brief epoch, or for one great deed. For a moment,
but for a moment only, the First Martyr steps into the
full light of history. Our insight into his greatness is
derived almost solely from the record of a single speech
and a single day—the last speech he ever uttered—the
last day of his mortal life.

It was the *faith* of Stephen, together with his loving
energy and blameless sanctity which led to the choice of
him as one of the Seven. No sooner was he elected than
he became the most prominent of them all. The grace
which shone in his colleagues shone yet more brightly in
him,[3] and he stood on a level with the Apostles in the
power of working wonders among the people. Many a
man, who would otherwise have died unknown, has re-

---

[1] Epiphan. *Haer.* xl. p. 50.

[2] That he was a Hellenist is not merely a precarious inference from the
Greek form of his name, which may merely have been a rendering of the
Aramaic Kelîl, but is implied by the narrative itself, and is rendered certain
by the character of his speech; but whether he was trained at Alexandria,
or was a Roman freedman (Plumptre on Acts vi. 5), and what had brought
him to Jerusalem, we cannot tell.

[3] χάριτος (א, A,B,D, &c.), not πίστεως, is the true reading in Acts vi. 8

vealed to others his inherent greatness on being entrusted
with authority. The immense part played by Stephen
in the history of the Church was due to the development of powers which might have remained latent but for
the duties laid on him by his new position. The distribution of alms seems to have been a part only of the task
assigned him. Like Philip, he was an Evangelist as well
as a Deacon, and the speech which he delivered before
the Sanhedrin, showing as it does the logical force and
concentrated fire of a great orator and a practised controversialist, may explain the stir which was caused by
his preaching.

The scenes of that preaching were the Hellenistic
synagogues of Jerusalem. To an almoner in a city
where so many were poor, and to a Hellenist of unusual
eloquence, opportunities would constantly recur in which
he was not only permitted, but urged, to explain the
tenets of the new society. Hitherto that society was
in full communion with the Jewish Church. Stephen
alone was charged with utterances of a disloyal tendency
against the tenets of Pharisaism, and this is a proof
how different was his preaching from that of the Twelve,
and how much earlier he had arrived at the true appreciation of the words of Jesus respecting the extent and
nature of His Kingdom. That which, in the mind of a
Peter, was still but a grain of mustard seed, sown in the
soil of Judaism, had already grown, in the soul of a
Stephen, into a mighty tree. The Twelve were still
lingering in the portals of the synagogue. For them
the new wine of the kingdom of heaven had not yet
burst the old wine-skins. As yet they were only regarded as the heads of a Jewish sect,[1] and although

---

[1] Acts xxiv. 5; xxviii. 22, αἵρεσις.

they believed that their faith would soon be the
faith of all the world, there is no trace that, up to this
time, they ever dreamed of the abrogation of Mosaism,
or the free admission of uncircumcised Gentiles into a
full equality of spiritual privileges. A proselyte of
righteousness—one who, like Nicolas of Antioch, had
accepted the sign of circumcision—might, indeed, be
held worthy of honour; but one who was only a "proselyte of the gate,"[1] one who held back from the seal of
the covenant made to Abraham, would not be regarded as
a full Christian any more than he would be regarded
as a full Jew.

Hence, up to this time, the Christians were looked
on with no disfavour by that Pharisaic party which regarded the Sadducees as intriguing apostates. They were
even inclined to make use of the Resurrection which the
Christians proclaimed, as a convenient means of harassing
their rivals. Nor was it they who had been guilty of the
murder of Jesus. They had not, indeed, stirred one
finger for His deliverance, and it is probable that many
of them—all those hypocrites of whom both Jesus and
John had spoken as a viper brood—had looked with
satisfaction on the crime by which their political opponents had silenced their common enemy. Yet they did
not fear that His blood would be brought on *them*, or that
the Apostles would ever hurl on them or their practices
His terrible denunciations. Though the Christians
had their private meetings on the first day of the
week, their special tenets, their sacramental institutions,
and their common meal, there was nothing reprehensible
in these observances, and there was something attractive
even to Pharisees in their faithful simplicity and enthu-

[1] The name did not arise till later, but is here adopted for convenience'
sake.

siastic communism.[1] In all respects they were "devout
according to the Law." They would have shrunk with
horror from any violation of the rules which separated
clean from unclean meats; they not only observed the
prescribed feasts of the Pentateuch and its single fast,
but even adopted the fasts which had been sanctioned
by the tradition of the oral law; they had their children duly circumcised; they approved and practised the
vows of the Nazarites; they never omitted to be on
their knees in the Temple, or with their faces turned
towards it, at the three stated hours of prayer.[2] It
needs but a glance at the symbolism of the Apocalypse
to see how dear to them were the names, the reminiscences,
the Levitical ceremonial, the Temple worship of their
Hebrew fellow-citizens. Not many years later, the "many
myriads of Jews who believed were *all* zealous of the Law,"
and would have thought it a disgrace to do otherwise than
"to walk orderly."[3] The position, therefore, which they
held was simply that of one synagogue more, in a city
which, according to the Rabbis, could already boast that
it possessed as many as 480. They might have been
called, and it is probable that they were called, by
way of geographical distinction, "the Synagogue of the
Nazarenes."

But this acceptance with the people could only be
temporary and deceptive. If, indeed, the early believers

---

[1] The Jews would have regarded them at that time as *Chaberim*, a body
of people associated, quite harmlessly, for a particular object.

[2] Called שחרית, *shacrith*, at 9; מנחה, *minchah*, at 3.30; and מערב, *mearib*
at dark (Acts ii. 1; iii. 1; x. 30).

[3] Acts xxi. 20, 24. See for the facts in the previous paragraphs, Acts x.
9, 14, 30; xiii. 2, 3; xviii. 18, 21; xx. 6, 16; xxii. 3; Rom. xiv. 5; Gal.
iv. 10; v. 2; Phil. iii. 2; Rev. ii. 9; iii. 9; vii. 15; xi. 19, &c.; Reuss, *Théol.
Chrét.* i. 291, who quotes Sulpic. Sever. ii. 31, "Christum Deum sub legis
observatione credebant."

had never advanced beyond this stand-point, Christianity might have been regarded to the last as nothing more than a phase of Pharisaism, heretical for its acceptance of a crucified Messiah, but worthy of honour for the scrupulosity of its religious life. But had Christianity never been more than this, then the olive branch would have died with the oleaster on which it was engrafted. It was as necessary for the Church as for the world that this hollow semblance of unison between religions which, in their distinctive differences, were essentially antagonistic, should be rudely dissipated. It was necessary that all Christians, whether Jews or Gentiles, should see how impossible it was to put a new patch on an old garment.

This truth had been preached by Jesus to His Apostles, but, like many other of His words, it lay long dormant in their minds. After some of His deepest utterances, in full consciousness that He could not at once be understood, He had said, "He that hath ears to hear, let him hear." And as they themselves frankly confess, the Apostles had not always been among those "who had ears to hear." Plain and reiterated as had been the prophecies which He had addressed to them respecting His own crucifixion and resurrection, the first of these events had plunged them into despair and horror, the second had burst upon them with a shock of surprise. He who commanded the light to shine out of darkness had, indeed, shined in their hearts "to give the light of the knowledge of the glory of God in the face of Jesus Christ;"[1] but still they were well aware that they had this treasure "in earthen vessels." To attribute to them an equality of endowments, or an entire unanimity of opinion, is to contradict their plainest

---

[1] 2 Cor. iv. 6, 7.

statements. To deny that their knowledge gradually widened is to ignore God's method of revelation, and to set aside the evidence of facts. To the last they "knew in part, and they prophesied in part."[1] Why was James the Lord's brother so highly respected by the people as tradition tells us that he was? Why was Paul regarded by them with such deadly hatred? Because St. Paul recognised more fully than St. James the future universal destiny of a Christianity separated from Judaic institutions. The Crucifixion had, in fact, been the protest of the Jew against an isopolity of faith. "From that moment the fate of the nation was decided. Her religion was to kill her. But when the Temple burst into flames, that religion had already spread its wings and gone out to conquer an entire world."[2]

Now, as might have been expected, and as was evidently designed by their Divine Master, the *last* point on which the Galilæan Apostles attained to clearness of view and consistency of action was the fact that the Mosaic law was to be superseded, even for the Jew, by a wider revelation. It is probable that this truth, in all its fulness, was never finally apprehended by all the Apostles. It is doubtful whether, humanly speaking, it would ever have been grasped by any of them if their powers of insight had not been quickened, in God's appointed method, by the fresh lessons which came to them through the intellect and faith of men who had been brought up in larger views. The obliteration of natural distinctions is no part of the divine method. The inspiration of God never destroys the individuality of those holy souls which it has made into sons of God and prophets. There are, as St. Paul so earnestly tried to impress upon the infant Churches,

---

[1] 1 Cor. xiii. 9.   [2] Kuenen, *Rel. of Isr.* iii. 281.

diversities of gifts, diversities of ministrations, diversities of operations, though it is the same Spirit, the same Lord, the same God, who worketh all things in all.[1] The Hellenistic training of a Stephen and a Saul prepared them for the acceptance of lessons which nothing short of an express miracle could have made immediately intelligible to a Peter and a James.

Now the relation of the Law to the Gospel had been exactly one of those subjects on which Jesus, in accordance with a divine purpose, had spoken with a certain reserve. His mission had been to found a kingdom, not to promulgate a theology; He had died not to formulate a system, but to redeem a race. His work had been not to construct the dogmas of formal creeds, but to purify the soul of man, by placing him in immediate relation to the Father in Heaven. It required many years for Jewish converts to understand the meaning of the saying that "He came not to destroy the Law but to fulfil." Its meaning could indeed only become clear in the light of other sayings of which they overlooked the force. The Apostles had seen Him obedient to the Law; they had seen Him worship in the Temple and the Synagogues, and had accompanied Him in His journeys to the Feasts. He had never told them in so many words that the glory of the Law, like the light which lingered on the face of Moses, was to be done away. They had failed to comprehend the ultimate tendency and significance of His words and actions respecting the Sabbath,[2] respecting outward observances,[3] respecting divorce,[4] respecting the future universality of spiritual worship.[5] They remembered, doubtless, what He had said about the permanence of every yod and horn of a letter in the Law,[6] but

---

[1] 1 Cor. xii. 4—6. [2] Matt. ix. 13; xii. 7. [4] John iv. 22.
[3] Mark ii. 27; John v. 17. [4] Matt. xix. 3, 6, 8; v. 32. [6] Matt. v. 18.

they had not remarked that the assertion of the pre-eminence of moral over ceremonial duties is one unknown to the Law itself. Nor had they seen that His fulfilment of the Law had consisted in its spiritualisation; that He had not only extended to infinitude the range of its obligations, but had derived their authority from deeper principles, and surrounded their fulfilment with diviner sanctions. Nor, again, had they observed how much was involved in the emphatic quotation by Christ of that passage of Hosea, "I will have mercy and not sacrifice."[1] They were not yet ripe for the conviction that to attach primary importance to Mosaic regulations after they had been admitted into the kingdom of Heaven, was to fix their eyes upon a waning star while the dawn was gradually broadening into boundless day.

About the early ministry of Stephen we are told comparatively little in the Acts, but its immense importance has become more clear in the light of subsequent history. It is probable that he himself can never have formed the remotest conception of the vast results—results among millions of Christians through centuries of progress — which in God's Providence should arise from the first clear statement of those truths which he was the first to perceive. Had he done so he would have been still more thankful for the ability with which he was inspired to support them, and for the holy courage which prevented him from quailing for an instant under the storm of violence and hatred which his words awoke.

What it was which took him to the synagogues of Jewish Hellenists we do not know. It may have been the same missionary zeal which afterwards carried to so many regions the young man of Tarsus who at this time was

---

[1] Matt. ix. 13; xii. 7.

among his ablest opponents. All that we are told is that
" there arose some of the synagogue which is called the
synagogue of the Libertines and Cyrenians, and Alexandrians, and those of Cilicia and Asia disputing with
Stephen." The form of the sentence is so obscure that it
is impossible to tell whether we are meant to understand
that the opponents of Stephen were the members of *one*
synagogue which united these widely-scattered elements; of
five separate synagogues; of *three* synagogues—namely, that
of the Freedmen, that of the African, and that of the Asiatic
Hellenists; or of *two* distinct synagogues, of which one
was frequented by the Hellenists of Rome, Greece, and
Alexandria; the other by those of Cilicia and Proconsular
Asia. The number of synagogues in Jerusalem was (as I
have already mentioned) so large that there is no difficulty in believing that each of these bodies had their
own separate place of religious meeting,[1] just as at this
day in Jerusalem there are separate synagogues for the
Spanish Sephardim, the Dutch Anshe hod, and the
German and Polish Ashkenazim.[2] The freedmen may
have been the descendants of those Jews whom
Pompey had sent captive to Italy, and Jews were to be
counted by myriads in Greece, in Alexandria, and in the
cities of Asia. But to us the most interesting of all these
Greek-speaking Jews was Saul of Tarsus, who, beyond all
reasonable doubt, was a member of the synagogue of the

---

[1] The assertion of the Talmud (cf. *Sanhedr.* f. 58, 1) that there were 480
synagogues in Jerusalem is indeed valueless, because the remarks of the
Rabbis about Jerusalem, Bethyr, and indeed Palestine generally, are mere
hyperbole; but, as Renan remarks (*Les Apôtres*, p. 109), it does not seem
at all impossible to those who are familiar with the innumerable mosques of
Mahommedan cities. We are informed in the Talmud that each synagogue
had not only a school for the teaching of Scripture, but also for the teaching
of traditions (בית תלמוד למשנה, *Megillah*, f. 73, 4).

[2] See Frankl, *Jews in the East*, ii. 21, E. T.

K

Cilicians,[1] and who in that case must not only have taken his part in the disputes which followed the exhortations of the fervid deacon,[2] but as a scholar of Gamaliel and a zealous Pharisee, must have occupied a prominent position as an uncompromising champion of the traditions of the fathers.

Though the Saul of this period must have differed widely from that Paul, the slave of Jesus Christ, whom we know so well, yet the main features of his personality must have been the same. He could not have failed to recognise the moral beauty, the dauntless courage, the burning passion latent in the tenderness of Stephen's character. The white ashes of a religion which had smouldered into formalism lay thickly scattered over his own heart, but the fire of a genuine sincerity burned below. Trained as he had been for years in Rabbinic minutiæ, he had not yet so far grown old in a deadening system as to mistake the painted cere-cloths of the mummy for the grace and flush of healthy life. While he listened to St. Stephen, he must surely have felt the contrast between a dead theology and a living faith; between a kindling inspiration and a barren exegesis; between a minute analysis of unimportant ceremonials and a preaching that stirred the inmost depths of the troubled heart. Even the rage which is often intensified by the unconscious rise of an irresistible conviction could not wholly prevent him from perceiving that these preachers of a gospel which he disdained as an execrable superstition, had found " in Christ" the secret of a light and joy, and love and peace, compared with which his own condition was that of one who was chained indissolubly to a corpse.

[1] He may have been a *Libertinus* also.
[2] Acts vi. 9, συζητοῦντες.

We catch but a single glimpse of these furious controversies. Their immediate effect was the signal triumph of St. Stephen in argument. The Hellenists were unable to withstand the wisdom and the spirit with which he spake. Disdainful Rabbinists were at once amazed and disgusted to find that he with whom they now had to deal was no rude provincial, no illiterate *am ha-arets*, no humble *hediot*, like the fishermen and tax-gatherers of Galilee; but one who had been trained in the culture of heathen cities as well as in the learning of Jewish communities—a disputant who could meet them with their own weapons, and speak Greek as fluently as themselves. Steeped in centuries of prejudice, engrained with traditions of which the truth had never been questioned, they must have imagined that they would win an easy victory, and convince a man of intelligence how degrading it was for him to accept a faith on which, from the full height of their own ignorance, they complacently looked down. How great must have been their discomfiture to find that what they had now to face was not a mere personal testimony which they could contemptuously set aside, but arguments based on premisses which they themselves admitted, enforced by methods which they recognised, and illustrated by a learning which they could not surpass! How bitter must have been their rage when they heard doctrines subversive of their most cherished principles maintained with a wisdom which differed not only in degree, but even in kind, from the loftiest attainments of their foremost Rabbis—even of those whose merits had been rewarded by the flattering titles of "Rooters of Mountains" and "Glories of the Law!"

At first the only discussion likely to arise would be as to the Messiahship of Jesus, the meaning of His death, the fact of His Resurrection. These would be points on

K 2

which the ordinary Jew would have regarded argument as
superfluous condescension. To him the stumbling-block
of the Cross would have been insurmountable. In all
ages the Messianic hope had been prominent in the
minds of the most enlightened Jews, but during the
Exile and the Restoration it had become the central
faith of their religion. It was this belief which, more
than any other, kindled their patriotism, consoled their
sorrows, and inspired their obedience. If a Shammai
used to spend the whole week in meditating how he
could most rigidly observe the Sabbath—if the Pharisees
regarded it as the main function of their existence to
raise a hedge around the Law—the inspiring motive was
a belief that if only for one day Israel were entirely
faithful, the Messiah would come. And what a coming!
How should the Prince of the House of David smite the
nations with the sword of his mouth! How should He
break them in pieces like a potter's vessel! How should
He exalt the children of Israel into kings of the earth,
and feed them with the flesh of Behemoth, and Leviathan,
and the bird Bar Juchne, and pour at their feet the
treasures of the sea! And to say that *Jesus of Nazareth*
was the promised Messiah—to suppose that all the splendid
prophecies of patriarchs, and seers, and kings, from the
Divine Voice which spoke to Adam in Paradise, to the last
utterance of the Angel Malachi—all pointed to, all centred
in, One who had been the carpenter of Nazareth, and
whom they had seen crucified between two brigands—
to say that their very Messiah had just been "hung"[1] by
Gentile tyrants at the instance of their own priests;—
this, to most of the hearers in the synagogue, would have
seemed wicked if it had not seemed too absurd. Was
there not one sufficient and decisive answer to it all in the

[1] תלה.

one verse of the Law—"Cursed by God is he that hangeth on a tree?"[1]

Yet this was the thesis which such a man as Stephen —no ignorant Galilæan, but a learned Hellenist—undertook to prove, and *did* prove with such power as to produce silence if not assent, and hatred if not conviction. For with all their adoration of the letter, the Rabbis and Pharisees had but half read their Scriptures, or had read them only to use as an engine of religious intolerance, and to pick out the views which most blended with their personal preconceptions. They had laid it down as a principle of interpretation that the entire books of the · Canon prophesied of nothing else but the days of the Messiah. How, under these circumstances, they could possibly miss the conception of a *suffering* as well as of a *triumphant* Messiah,[2] might well amaze us, if there had not been proof in all ages that men may entirely overlook the statements and pervert the meaning of their own sacred books, because, when they read those books, the veil of obstinate prejudice is lying upon their hearts. But when the view of ancient prophecy, which proved that it behoved Christ thus to suffer and to enter into His glory,[3] was forcibly presented to them by the insight and eloquence of one who was their equal in learning and their superior in illumination, we can understand the difficulties to

---

[1] Deut. xxi. 23, κεκατηραμένος ὑπὸ τοῦ Θεοῦ. The later view of this, "He that is hanged is an insult to God" arose from the fact that Jewish patriots in the Jewish War were crucified by scores. St. Paul, in quoting the verse, omits the ὑπὸ Θεοῦ (Gal. iii. 13; and Lightfoot, p. 133).

[2] Of the notion of a suffering Messiah, Ben Joseph, as distinguished from the triumphant son of David (Rashi on Isa. xxiv. 18; *Succah*, 52, 1, 2, where reference is made to Zech. xii. 10, and Ps. ii., &c.; see Otho, *Lex. Rab.* s. v. Messiah), there is no trace in Jewish literature till long afterwards. St. Paul's witness from Moses and the Prophets—εἰ παθητὸς ὁ Χριστὸς, Acts xxvi. 23—only woke a sneer from Agrippa II.

[3] Luke xxiv. 26.

which they were reduced. How, for instance, could
they elude the force of the 53rd chapter of Isaiah, to
which their Rabbis freely accorded a Messianic interpretation? The Messianic application of what is there
said about the Servant of Jehovah, and the deep humiliation borne for the sake of others, is not only found
in the Targum of Jonathan and in many Rabbinic allusions, down even to the Book Zohar, but seems to have
remained entirely undisputed until the mediæval Rabbis
found themselves inconvenienced by it in their controversies with Christians.[1] Yet this was but an isolated prophecy, and the Christians could refer to passage after
passage which, on the very principles of their adversaries,
not only justified them in accepting as the Christ One
whom the rulers of the Jews had crucified, but even
distinctly foreshadowed the mission of His Forerunner;
His ministry on the shores of Gennesareth; His humble
entry into Jerusalem; His rejection by His own people;
the disbelief of His announcements; the treachery of
one of His own followers; the mean price paid for His
blood; His death as a malefactor; even the bitter and
stupefying drinks that had been offered to Him; and
the lots cast upon His clothes—no less than His victory
over the grave by Resurrection, on the third day, from
the dead, and His final exaltation at the right hand of
God.[2] How tremendous the cogency of such arguments
would be to the hearers of Stephen cannot be shown more

[1] Proofs of this statement may be found in Dr. A. Wünsche's *Die Leiden
des Messias*, and several quotations from his book may be found in the
Speaker's Commentary, ad loc.

[2] See Is. xl. 3; Mark i. 3; Mal. iii. 1; Matt. xi. 10; Is. viii. 14; ix. 1;
Matt. iv. 14; Is. lxi. 1; Luke iv. 18; Ps. lxxviii. 2; Matt. xiii. 35; Ps. cxviii. 22;
Luke ii. 34; Acts iv. 11; xiii. 41; Ps. xli. 9; Zech. xi. 12; John xiii. 18;
Matt. xxvi. 15; xxvii. 9—10; Zech. xii. 10; John xix. 37; Isa. liii. 9; Ps. xvi.
10; Matt. xii. 40; Acts ii. 27; Ps. cx. 1; Acts ii. 33; Heb. i. 13, &c. (See
Davison *On Prophecy, passim*; *Hausrath*, p. 112, seqq.)

strikingly than by the use made of them by St. Paul
after the conversion which they doubtless helped to bring
about. It must have been from St. Stephen that he heard
them first, and they became so convincing to him that he
constantly employs the same or analogous arguments in
his own reasonings with his unconverted countrymen.[1]

It is clear that, in the course of argument, Stephen
was led to adduce some of those deep sayings as to the
purpose of the life of Christ which the keen insight of
hate had rendered more intelligible to the enemies of our
Lord than they had been in the first instance to His
friends. Many of those priests and Pharisees who had
been baptised into the Church of Christ with the notion
that their new belief was compatible with an unchanged
loyalty to Judaism, had shown less understanding of the
sayings of their Master, and less appreciation of the
grandeur of His mission, than the Sadducees whose hatred
had handed Him over to the secular arm. It did lie
within the natural interpretation of Christ's language
that the Law of Moses, which the Jews at once idolised
and evaded, was destined to be disannulled; not, indeed,
those moral sanctions of it which were eternal in obligation, but the complicated system wherein those moral
commandments were so deeply imbedded. The Jewish
race were right to reverence Moses as an instrument in
the hands of God to lay the deepest foundations of a
national life. As a Lawgiver whose Decalogue is so
comprehensive in its brevity as to transcend all other
codes—as the sole Lawgiver who laid his prohibition
against the beginnings of evil, by daring to forbid an
evil thought—as one who established for his people a
monotheistic faith, a significant worship, and an unde-

---

[1] Eph. ii. 20; Rom. ix. 34, &c.

finable hope—he deserved the gratitude and reverence
of mankind. That this under-official of an obscure
sect of yesterday should dare to move his tongue
against that awful name, and prophesy the abolition of
institutions of which some had been delivered to their
fathers of old from the burning crags of Sinai, and
others had been handed down from the lips of the
mighty teacher through the long series of priests and
prophets, was to them something worse than folly and
presumption—it was a blasphemy and a crime!

And how did he dare to speak one word against, or
hint one doubt as to the permanent glory of, the Temple?
The glowing descriptions of the Talmud respecting its
colossal size and royal splendour are but echoes of the
intense love which breathes throughout the Psalms. In
the heart of Saul any word which might sound like a
slight to "the place where God's honour dwelt" would
excite a peculiar indignation. When the conflagration
seized its roofs of cedar-wood and melted its golden tables,
every Jew in the city was fired with a rage which
made him fight with superhuman strength—

> " Through their torn veins reviving fury ran,
> And life's last anger warmed the dying man."

Among those frenzied combatants was a body of Tarsian
youths who gladly devoted their lives to the rescue of
Jerusalem. What they felt at that supreme moment may
show us what such a zealot as Saul of Tarsus would feel,
when he heard one who called himself a Jew use language
which sounded like disparagement of "the glory of the
whole earth."

Foiled in argument, the Hellenists of the synagogues
adopted the usual resource of defeated controversialists
who have the upper hand. They appealed to violence for

the suppression of reason. They first stirred up the people—whose inflammable ignorance made them the ready tools of any agitator—and through them aroused the attention of the Jewish authorities. Their plot was soon ripe. There was no need of the midnight secrecy which had marked the arrest of Jesus. There was no need to secure the services of the Captain of the Temple to arrest Stephen at twilight, as he had arrested Peter and John. There was no need even to suppress all semblance of violence, lest the people should stone them for their unauthorised interference. The circumstances of the day enabled them to assume unwonted boldness, because they were at the moment enjoying a sort of interregnum from Roman authority. The approval of the multitude had been alienated by the first rumour of defective patriotism. When every rank of Jewish society had been stirred to fury by false witnesses whom these Hellenists had suborned, they seized a favourable moment, suddenly came upon Stephen,[1] either while he was teaching in a synagogue, or while he was transacting the duties of an almoner, and led him away—apparently without a moment's pause—into the presence of the assembled Sanhedrin. Everything was ready; everything seemed to point to a foregone conclusion. The false witnesses were at hand, and confronted their victim with the charge of incessant harangues against "this Holy Place"—the expression seems to show that the Sanhedrin were for this time sitting in their famous "Hall of Squares,"—and against the Law.[2] In support of this general accusation, they testified that they had heard him say that Jesus— "this Nazarene,"[3] as they indignantly add to distinguish Him from others who bore that common name—"shall

---

[1] Acts vi. 12, ἐπιστάντες; cf. xvii. 5.   [2] Acts vi. 13, οὐ παύεται ῥήματα λαλῶν.
[3] Acts vi. 14, Ἰησοῦς, ὁ Ναζωραῖος οὗτος.

destroy this place, and shall change the customs which
Moses handed down to us." It is evident that these false
witnesses made some attempt to base their accusation
upon truth. There was good policy in this, as false
witnesses in all ages have been cunning enough to see.
Half truths are often the most absolute of lies, because

> " A lie which is half a truth is ever the blackest of lies ;
> For a lie which is all a lie may be met and fought with outright,
> But a lie which is part a truth is a harder matter to fight."

It is certain that if Stephen had not used the very
expressions with which they charged him, he had used
others not unlike them. It is his immortal glory to have
remembered the words of Jesus, and to have interpreted
them aright. Against the moral Law—the great Ten
Words of Sinai, or any of those precepts of exquisite
humanity and tenderness which lie scattered amid the
ceremonial observances—he is not even falsely accused
of having uttered a word. But against the permanent
validity of the ceremonial Law he may have spoken
with freedom; for, as we have seen, its destined
abrogation was involved in the very slight importance
which Jesus had attached to it. And for the Oral
Law it is probable that Stephen, whose training would
have rendered impossible any minute fulfilment of its
regulations, neither felt nor professed respect. The
expression used by the witnesses against him seems to
show that it was mainly, though not perhaps exclusively,
of this Oral Law that he had been thinking.[1] It was
not, perhaps, any doubt as to its authenticity which made
him teach that Jesus should change its customs, for in
those days the critical spirit was not sufficiently developed

---

[1] Acts vi. 14, τὰ ἔθη ἃ παρέδωκεν ἡμῖν Μωϋσῆς. (Cf. Jos. *Antt.* xiii. 10, § 6,
and 16, § 2.)

to give rise to any challenge of a current assertion; but he had foreseen the future nullity of these "traditions of the fathers," partly from their own inherent worthlessness, and partly because he may have heard, or had repeated to him, the stern denunciation which the worst of these traditions had drawn from the lips of Christ Himself.[1]

But though Stephen must have seen that the witnesses were really false witnesses, because they misrepresented the tone and the true significance of the language which he had used — although, too, he was conscious how dangerous was his position as one accused of blasphemy against Moses, against the Temple, against the traditions, and against God—it never occurred to him to escape his danger by a technicality or a compromise. To throw discredit even upon the Oral Law would not be without danger in the presence of an assembly whose members owed to its traditions no little of the authority which they enjoyed.[2] But Stephen did not at all intend to confine his argument to this narrow range. Rather the conviction came upon him that now was the time to speak out—that this was the destined moment in which, even if need be to the death, he was to bear witness to the inner meaning of the Kingdom of his Lord. That conviction—an inspiration from on high—gave unwonted grandeur and heavenliness to his look, his words, his attitude. His whole bearing was ennobled, his whole being was transfigured by a consciousness which illuminated his very countenance. It is probable that the unanimous tradition of the Church is correct in representing him as youthful and beautiful; but now there was something about him far more beautiful than youth or beauty could bestow.

[1] Matt. xv. 2—6; Mark vii. 3, 5, 8, 9, 13.
[2] Maimon. Pref. to the *Yad Hachazakah*; McCaul, *Old Paths*, p. 335.

In the spiritual light which radiated from him he
seemed to be overshadowed by the Shechinah, which
had so long vanished from between the wings of the
Temple cherubim. While the witnesses had been delivering
their testimony, no one had observed the sudden brightness which seemed to be stealing over him; but when the
charge was finished, and every eye was turned from the
accusers to a fixed gaze on the accused,[1] all who were seated
in the Sanhedrin—and one of the number, in all probability, was Saul of Tarsus—"saw his face as it had been
the face of an angel."

In the sudden hush that followed, the voice of the
High Priest Jonathan was heard putting to the accused
the customary and formal question—

"Are these things so?"[2]

In reply to that question began the speech which is
one of the earliest, as it is one of the most interesting,
documents of the Christian Church. Although it was
delivered before the Sanhedrin, there can be little doubt that
it was delivered in Greek, which, in the bilingual condition
of Palestine—and, indeed, of the civilised world in general
—at that time, would be perfectly understood by the
members of the Sanhedrin, and which was perhaps the
only language which Stephen could speak with fluency.[3]
The quotations from the Old Testament follow the

---

[1] Acts vi. 15, ἀτενίσαντες εἰς αὐτὸν ἅπαντες.

[2] St. Chrysostom sees in the apparent mildness of the question an indication that the High Priest and the Sanhedrin were awed by the supernatural
brightness of the martyr's look—ὁρᾷς ὡς μετὰ ἐπιεικείας ἡ ἐρώτησις καὶ οὐδὲν
τέως φορτικὸν ἔχουσα; (Homil. xv. in Act.). But the question appears to have
been a regular formula of interrogation. It was, in fact, the "Guilty or Not
Guilty?" of the Jewish Supreme Court.

[3] Against this view are urged—(1) the unlikelihood that St. Stephen
would have pleaded in Greek before the Sanhedrin; (2) the use of the
Hebraism ὄυρανοὶ in Acts vii. 56. But as to 1, if even Philo knew no Hebrew,
Stephen may have known none; and, 2, the word οὐρανοὶ points to a special
Jewish belief, independent of language.

Septuagint, even where it differs from the Hebrew, and the individuality which characterises almost every sentence of the speech forbids us to look on it as a mere conjectural paraphrase. There is no difficulty in accounting for its preservation. Apart from the fact that two secretaries were always present at the judicial proceedings of the Sanhedrin,[1] there are words and utterances which, at certain times, are branded indelibly upon the memory of their hearers; and since we can trace the deep impression made by this speech on the mind of St. Paul, we find little difficulty in adopting the conjecture that its preservation was due to him. The *Hagadóth* in which it abounds, the variations from historical accuracy, the free citation of passages from the Old Testament, the roughness of style, above all the concentrated force which makes it lend itself so readily to differing interpretations, are characteristics which leave on our minds no shadow of doubt that whoever may have been the reporter, we have here at least an *outline* of Stephen's speech. And this speech marked a crisis in the annals of Christianity. It led to consequences that changed the Church from a Judaic sect at Jerusalem, into the Church of the Gentiles and of the world. It marks the commencing severance of two institutions which had not yet discovered that they were mutually irreconcilable.

Since the charge brought against St. Stephen was partly false and partly true, it was his object to rebut what was false, and justify himself against all blame for what was true. Hence apology and demonstration are subtly blended throughout his appeal, but the apology is only secondary, and the demonstration is mainly

---

[1] See Jahn, *Archaeol. Bibl.* § 248. He quotes no authority, and I at first felt some doubt about the assertion, but I find it so stated in the Mishna, *Sanhedr.* iv. 2.

meant to rouse the dormant consciences of his hearers.
Charged with blasphemous words, he contents himself
with the incidental refutation of this charge by the
entire tenor of the language which he employs. After
his courteous request for attention, his very first words are
to speak of God under one of His most awful titles of
majesty, as the God of the Shechinah. On the history of
Moses he dwells with all the enthusiasm of patriotic
admiration. To the Temple he alludes with entire
reverence. Of Sinai and the living oracles he uses
language as full of solemnity as the most devoted Rabbi
could desire. But while he thus shows how impossible it
must have been for him to have uttered the language of a
blasphemer, he is all the while aiming at the establish-
ment of facts far deeper than the proof of his own
innocence. The consummate art of his speech consists
in the circumstance that while he seems to be engaged in
a calm, historical review, to which any Jewish patriot might
listen with delight and pride, he is step by step leading up
to conclusions which told with irresistible force against
the opinions of his judges. While he only seems to be
reviewing the various migrations of Abraham, and the
chequered fortunes of the Patriarchs, he is really showing
that the covenants of God with His chosen people,
having been made in Ur and Haran and Egypt, were
all parts of one progressive purpose, which was so little
dependent on ceremonials or places as to have been
anterior not only to the existence of the Tabernacle
and Temple, not only to the possession of the Holy
Land, but even to the rite of circumcision itself.[1]

---

[1] What fruit the argument bore in the mind of St. Paul we may see
in the emphasis with which he dwells on "that faith of our father Abraham
which he had being yet uncircumcised" (Rom. iv. 12). How necessary it was
to point this out will be seen from the opinions of succeeding Rabbis.

While sketching the career of Joseph, he is pointing allusively to the similar rejection of a deliverer greater than Joseph. While passing in review the triple periods of forty years which made up the life of Moses, he is again sketching the ministry of Christ, and silently pointing to the fact that the Hebrew race had at every stage been false alike to Moses and to God. This is why he narrates the way in which, on the first appearance of Moses to help his suffering countrymen, they rudely spurned his interference; and how in spite of their rejection he was chosen to lead them out of the house of bondage. In defiance of this special commission—and it is well worth notice how, in order to conciliate their deeper attention, this palmary point in his favour is not triumphantly paraded, but quietly introduced as an incident in his historic summary — Moses had himself taught them to regard his own legislation as provisional, by bidding them listen to a Prophet like unto himself who should come hereafter. But the history of Moses, whom they trusted, was fatal to their pretence of allegiance. Even when he was on Sinai they had been disloyal to him, and spoken of him as "this Moses," and as one who had gone they knew not where.[1] And, false to Moses, they had been yet more false to God. The Levitical sacrifices had been abandoned from the very time of their institution, for sacrifices to the host of heaven; and the tabernacle of Moloch, and the star of Remphan,[2] had been dearer to

---

"Abraham," says Rabbi—as "Juda the Holy," the compiler of the *Mishna*, is called, κατ' ἐξοχήν—"was not called perfect until he was circumcised, and by the merit of circumcision a covenant was made with him respecting the giving of the land" (*Joreh Deah*, 260, ap. McCaul, *Old Paths*, p. 451 ; *Nedarim*, f. 31, 2). It is superfluous to add that the latter statement is a flat contradiction of Gen. xv. 18.

[1] Perhaps there is a passing allusion to the expression, " Jesus, this Nazarene," which they had just heard from the lips of the false witnesses.

[2] The LXX. reading for the Hebrew *Chiun*.

them than the Tabernacle of Witness and the Shechinah
of God. At last a Jesus—for, in order that he might
be heard to due purpose, Stephen suppresses the name of
that Jesus of whom his thoughts were full—led them and
their Tabernacle into the land of which he dispossessed the
Gentiles. That Tabernacle, after an obscure and dishonoured history, had passed away, and it may perhaps be
intimated that this was due to their indifference and neglect.
David—their own David—had indeed desired to replace it
by another, but the actual building of the House was carried
out by the less faithful Solomon.[1] But even at the very
time the House was built it had been implied in the Prayer
of David, and in the dedication prayer of Solomon,[2] that
"the Most High dwelleth not in temples made with
hands." And to guard against the dangerous superstition into which the reverence paid to material places
is apt to degenerate — to obviate the trust in lying
words which thought it sufficient to exclaim, " The Temple
of the Lord, the Temple of the Lord, the Temple of the
Lord are these "—the great Prophet had cried, in God's
name,[3] " Heaven is my throne, and earth is my footstool;
what house will ye build for me, saith the Lord, or what
is the place of my abiding? Did not my hand make all
these things?" The inference from this—that the day
must come, of which Jesus had prophesied to the woman
of Samaria, in which neither in Gerizim nor yet in Jerusalem should men worship the Father, constituted a perfect defence against the charge that anything which he had
said could be regarded as a blasphemy against the Temple.
Thus far he had fulfilled all the objects of his speech,

---

[1] It must remain doubtful whether any contrast is intended between the
σκήνωμα (v. Suid, *s.v.*) designed by David, and the οἶκος built by Solomon.

[2] 1 Kings viii. 27; 1 Chron. xxix. 11; quoted by St. Paul, Acts xvii. 24.

[3] Isa. lxvi. 1, 2.

and had shown that injurious words had been as far as possible from his thoughts. It had become clear also from his summary of the national story that the principles which he had advocated were in accordance with the teaching of those past ages; that the rejection of Christ by the rulers of His nation was no argument against His claims; that the Temple *could* not have been meant to be the object of an endless honour; lastly, that if he had said that Jesus should change the customs which Moses had delivered, Moses himself had indicated that in God's due time his entire dispensation was destined to pass away. And he had stated the grounds from which these conclusions followed, rather than urged upon them the inferences themselves. He had done this in deference to their passions and prejudices, and in the hope of bringing the truth gently into their hearts. He might have continued the story through centuries of weak or apostate kings, stained with the blood of rejected prophets, down to the great retribution of the exile; and he might have shown how, after the exile, the obsolete idolatry of gods of wood and stone had only been superseded by the subtler and more self-complacent idolatry of formalism and letter-worship; how the Book had been honoured to the oblivion of the truths which it enshrined; how in the tithing of mint and anise and cummin there had been a forgetfulness of the weightier matters of the Law; how the smoke of dead sacrifices had been thought of more avail than deeds of living mercy; how circumcision and Sabbatism had been elevated above faith and purity; how the long series of crimes against God's messengers had been consummated in the murder of the Lord of glory. A truth which is only suggested, often comes home to the heart with more force than one which is put in words, and it may have

L

been his original design to guide rather than to refute. But if so, the faces of his audience showed that his object had failed. They were listening with stolid self-complacency to a narrative of which the significant incidents only enabled them to glory over their fathers. It was, I think, something in the aspect of his audience —some sudden conviction that to such invincible obstinacy his words were addressed in vain—which made him suddenly stop short in his review of history, and hurl in their faces the gathered thunder of his wrath and scorn.

"Stiff-necked!" he exclaimed, "and uncircumcised in your heart and in your ears, *ye* are ever in conflict with the Holy Spirit; as your fathers, so ye! Which of the prophets did not your fathers persecute? and they killed those who announced before respecting the coming of the Just, of whom ye now proved yourselves betrayers and murderers; ye who received the Law at the ordinance of angels,[1] and kept it not!"[2]

A denunciation so scathing and so fearless, from the lips of a prisoner whose life depended on their will, might well have startled them; and this strong burst of righteous indignation against those whom he had addressed as "brethren and fathers," can only be accounted for by the long-pent feelings of one whose patience has been exhausted. But he could hardly have addressed them in words more calculated to kindle their fury. The very terms in which he characterised their bearing, being borrowed from their own Law and Prophets, added force to the previous epitome of their history;[3] and to call them

---

[1] Acts vii. 52; leg. ἐγένεσθε, A, B, C, D, E.

[2] Acts vii. 53, ἐλάβετε τὸν νόμον εἰς διαταγὰς ἀγγέλων; Gal. iii. 19, ὁ νόμος διαταγεὶς δι ἀγγέλων; Deut. xxxiii. 2; LXX., ἐκ δεξιῶν αὐτοῦ ἄγγελοι μετ᾽ αὐτοῦ; Ps. lxvii. 18; Heb. ii. 2. In Ps. lxviii. 12 they read, מלאך "angels," for מלך, "kings." (*Shabbath*, f. 88, 2.)

[3] Deut. ix. 6, 13; x. 16; xxx. 6; Neh. ix. 16; Ezek. xliv. 7; Jer. ix. 26.

uncircumcised *in heart and ears* was to reject with scorn the idle fancies that circumcision alone was enough to save them from God's wrath, and that uncircumcision was worse than crime.[1] To convict them of being the true sons of their fathers, and to brand consciences, already ulcerated by a sense of guilt, with a murder worse than the worst murder of the prophets, was not only to sweep away the prestige of an authority which the people so blindly accepted, but it was to arraign his very judges and turn upon them the tables of accusation. And this he did, not only in the matter of their crucifixion of the Messiah, but also in the matter of disobedience to that Law ordained by angels of which they were at that very moment professing to vindicate the sanctity and the permanence.

It would be difficult in the entire range of literature to find a speech more skilful, more pregnant, more convincing; and it becomes truly astonishing when we remember that it seems to have been delivered on the spur of the moment.[2]

---

[1] Rabbi [Juda the Holy] said "that circumcision is equivalent to all the Commandments which are in the Law" (*Nedarim*, f. 32, 1).

[2] The impression which it made on the heart of St. Paul is nowhere noticed by St. Luke, or by the Apostle himself; but the traces of that impression are a series of coincidences which confirm the genuineness of the speech. In his earliest recorded speech at Antioch he adopts the same historic method so admirably suited to insinuate truth without shocking prejudice; he quotes the same texts in the same striking phraseology and application (compare Acts vii. 48, 51, with Acts xvii. 24, Rom. ii. 29); alludes to the same tradition (Acts vii. 53, Gal. iii. 19); uses the same style of address (Acts vii. 2, xxii. 1); and gives the same marked significance to the faith of Abraham (Rom. iv. 9, Gal. iii. 7), and to God's dealings with him before the covenant of circumcision (Acts vii. 5—8, Rom. iv. 10—19). Nor can we doubt that 2 Tim. iv. 16 was an echo of the last prayer of Stephen, breathed partly on his own behalf. There are at least seven *Hagadôth* in the speech of Stephen—Acts vii. 2 (call of Abraham); 4 (death of Terah); 14 (seventy-five souls); 16 (burial of Patriarchs at Shechem); 22 (Egyptian training of Moses); 23 (forty years); 42 (desert idolatry); 53 (angels at Sinai). As for the slight instances of σφάλμα μνημονικόν in 6, 7, 14, 16, they are mere "obiter dicta, auctoris aliud agentis." The attempt to square them rigidly with the Old Testament has led

But the members of the Sanhedrin were roused to fury
by the undaunted audacity of Stephen's final invective.
The most excitable of Western nations can hardly imagine
the raging passion which maddens a crowd of Eastern
fanatics.[1]   Barely able to continue the semblance of a
judicial procedure, they expressed the agony of hatred
which was sawing their hearts asunder, by outward
signs which are almost unknown to modern civilisation
—by that grinding and gnashing of the teeth only possible
to human beings in whom "the ape and the tiger" are
not yet quite dead.   To reason with men whose passions
had thus degraded them to the level of wild beasts would
have been worse than useless.   The flame of holy anger
in the breast of Stephen had died away as suddenly as
the lightning.   It was a righteous anger; it was aimed
not at them but at their infatuation; it was intended not
to insult but to awaken.[2]   But he saw at a glance that
it had failed, and that all was now over.   In one instant
his thoughts had passed away to that heaven from which
his inspiration had come.   From those hateful faces,
rendered demoniac by evil passion, his earnest gaze was
turned upward and heavenward.   There, in ecstacy of vision,
he saw the Shechinah—the Glory of God—and Jesus
"standing" as though to aid and receive him "at the right
hand of God."   Transported beyond all thought of peril by
that divine epiphany, he exclaimed as though he wished
his enemies to share his vision: "Lo! I behold the
heavens parted asunder,[3] and the Son of Man standing at

to much dishonest exegesis.   The speech of St. Stephen has been called "a
compendium of the Old Testament drawn up in fragments of the Septuagint"
(Greenfield, *Apol. for the LXX.*, 103).   "He had regard to the meaning, not
to the words" (Jerome).

[1] Acts vii. 54, διεπρίοντο ταῖς καρδίαις αὐτῶν, καὶ ἔβρυχον τοὺς ὀδόντας ἐπ' αὐτόν.

[2] "Non fratri irascitur qui peccato fratris irascitur" (Aug.).

[3] Acts vii. 56, loq., διηνεγμένους, א, A, B, C.

the right hand of God." At such a moment he would not pause to consider, he would not even be able to consider, the words he spoke ; but whether it was that he recalled the Messianic title by which Jesus had so often described himself on earth, or that he remembered that this title had been used by the Lord when He had prophesied to this very Sanhedrin that hereafter they should see the Son of Man sitting on the right hand of power—certain it is that this is the only passage of the New Testament where Jesus is called the Son of Man by lips other than His own.[1]

But those high words were too much for the feelings of his audience. Stopping their ears as though to shut out a polluting blasphemy, they rose in a mass from both sides of the semi-circular range in which they sat, and with one wild yell[2] rushed upon Stephen. There was no question any longer of a legal decision. In their rage they took the law into their own hands, and then and there dragged him off to be stoned outside the city gate.[3]

We can judge how fierce must have been the rage which turned a solemn Sanhedrin into a mob of murderers. It was true that they were at this moment under Sadducean influence, and that this influence, as at the Trial of Christ, was mainly wielded by the family of Hanan, who were the most merciless members of that least merciful sect. If, as there is reason to believe, the martyrdom took place A.D. 37, it was most probably during the brief presidency of the High Priest Jonathan, son of Hanan. Unhappy family of the man whom Josephus pronounces to have been so exceptionally blest! The hoary father, and his son-in-law Caiaphas, imbrued their hands in the blood of

---

[1] See, however, Rev. i. 13; xiv. 14.
[2] Acts vii. 57, πράξαντες φωνῇ μεγάλῃ.
[3] See Excursus VI., "Capital Punishments."

Jesus; Jonathan during his few months' term of office
was the Nasî of the Sanhedrin which murdered Stephen;
Theophilus, another son, was the High Priest who, during
the utmost virulence of the first persecution gave Saul his
inquisitorial commission to Damascus; Matthias, another
son, must, from the date of his elevation, have been one of
those leading Jews whom Herod Agrippa tried to conciliate by the murder of James the son of Zebedee; and
another Hanan, the youngest son of the " viper brood "
brought about with illegal violence the murder of James
the brother of the Lord.[1]   Thus all these judicial murders
—so rare at this epoch—were aimed at the followers of
Jesus, and all of them directed or sanctioned by the
cunning, avaricious, unscrupulous members of a single
family of Sadducean priests.[2]

Stephen, then, was hurried away to execution with a
total disregard of the ordinary observances.   His thoughts
were evidently occupied with the sad scene of Calvary; it
would come home to him with all the greater vividness
because he passed in all probability through that very gate
through which Jesus, four short years before, had borne
His cross.   It was almost in the words of his Master[3]
that when the horrid butchery began—for the precautions
to render death speedy seem to have been neglected in
the blind rage of his murderers—he exclaimed, "Lord
Jesus receive my spirit."[4]   And when bruised and bleeding he was just able to drag himself to his knees it

---

[1] Jos. *Antt.* xviii. 4, 3; 5, 3; xix. 6, 2; xx. 9, 1.

[2] Every epithet I have used is more than justified by what we know of
this family from the New Testament, from Josephus, and, above all, from the
Talmud. See Excursus VII., "The Power of the Sanhedrin to Inflict
Death."

[3] Luke xxiii. 34, 46.

[4] ἐπικαλούμενον means "calling on Jesus." There is no need for the
ingenious conjecture of Bentley that ΘΝ is lost by homoeoteleuton of the ΟΝ.

was again in the spirit of that Lord that he prayed for his murderers, and even the cry of his anguish rang forth in the forgiving utterance—showing how little malice there had been in the stern words he had used before—" Lord, lay not to their charge this sin."[1] With that cry he passed from the wrath of men to the peace of God. The historian ends the bloody tragedy with one weighty and beautiful word, " He fell asleep."[2]

To fulfil their dreadful task, the witnesses had taken off their garments;[3] and they laid them " at the feet of a young man whose name was Saul."

It is the first allusion in history to a name, destined from that day forward to be memorable for ever in the annals of the world. And how sad an allusion! He stands, not indeed actively engaged in the work of death; but keeping the clothes, consenting to the violence, of those who, in this brutal manner, dimmed in blood the light upon a face which had been radiant as that of an angel with faith and love.

Stephen was dead, and it might well have seemed that all the truth which was to be the glory and the strength of Christianity had died with him. But the

---

[1] This—not as in the received text—is the proper order of the words (א, A, B, C, D). "Saevire videbatur Stephanus: lingua ferox, cor lene" (Aug. *Serm.* 315). " Si Stephanus non orasset ecclesia Paulum non habuisset." With the expression itself comp. Rev. xiv. 13. Perhaps in the word στήσης we may see an allusion to the Jewish notion that a man's sins actually followed and stood by him in the world to come (1 Tim. v. 24; *Sotah*, f. 3, 2.).

[2] So in a beautiful epigram of the Anthology, we find the lines, ἱερὸν ὕπνον κοιμᾶται· θνήσκειν μὴ λέγε τοὺς ἀγαθούς. It is the *Neshikah* of the Jews (Deut. xxxiv. 8). That the solemn rhythmical epitrite ἐκοιμήθη is not wholly unintentional seems to be clear from the similar weighty 'ἀκωλύτως with which, as Bishop Wordsworth points out, the Acts of the Apostles ends. St. Luke is evidently fond of paronomasia, as well as St. Paul (cf. κατηξιώθησαν ἀτιμασθῆναι, Acts v. 41). This is the third recorded death in the Christian community: the first had been a suicide, the second a judgment, the third a martyrdom.

[3] This custom is not alluded to in the Mishna or Gemara.

deliverance of the Gentiles, and their free redemption by the blood of Christ, were truths too glorious to be quenched. The truth may be suppressed for a time, even for a long time, but it always starts up again from its apparent grave. Fra Dolcino was torn to pieces, and Savonarola and Huss were burnt, but the Reformation was not prevented. Stephen sank in his blood, but his place was taken by the young man who stood there to incite his murderers. Four years after Jesus had died upon the cross of infamy, Stephen was stoned for being His disciple and His worshipper; thirty years after the death of Stephen, his deadliest opponent died also for the same holy faith.

THE CONVERSION.

CHAPTER IX.

SAUL THE PERSECUTOR.

ποτὶ κέντρον δέ τοι λακτίζεμεν
τελέθει ὀλίσθηρος οἶμος.—PIND. *Pyth.* ii. 173.

"AT a young man's feet." The expression is vague, but there is good reason to believe that Saul was now not less than thirty years old.[1] The reverence for age, strong among all Orientals, was specially strong among the Jews, and they never entrusted authority to those who had not attained to full years of discretion. We may regard it as certain that even a scholar of Gamaliel, so full of genius and of zeal as Saul, would not have been appointed a commissioner of the Sanhedrin to carry out a responsible inquisition earlier than the age of thirty; and if we attach a literal meaning to the expression, "When they were being condemned to death, I gave a vote against them,"[2] this implies that Saul was a member of the Sanhedrin. If so, he was at this time, by the very condition of that dignity, a married man.[3]

[1] Josephus uses νεανίας of Agrippa I. when he must have been at least forty (*Antt.* xviii. 6, 7; *v. supra*, p. 18).

[2] Acts xxvi. 10, ἀναιρουμένων τε αὐτῶν κατήνεγκα ψῆφον.

[3] Selden, *De Synedr.* ii. 7, 7. In the Mishna the only qualifications mentioned for membership of the Sanhedrin are that a man must not be a dicer, usurer, pigeon-flyer, or dealer in the produce of the Sabbatical year (*Sanhedr.*

But if the regulation that a Sanhedrist must be a married man was intended to secure the spirit of gentleness,[1] the rule had failed of its purpose in the case of Saul. In the terrible persecution of the Christians which ensued—a persecution far more severe than the former attacks of the Sadducees on the Apostles—he was the heart and soul of the endeavour to stamp out the Christian faith. Not content with the flagging fanaticism of the Sanhedrin, he was at once the prime mover and the chief executor of religious vengeance. The charge which had cost St. Stephen his life must have been partially valid against others of the Hellenistic Christians, and although their views might be more liberal than those of the Galilæan disciples, yet the bonds of affection between the two branches of the Church were still so close that the fate of one section could not be dissevered from that of the other. The Jews were not naturally fond of persecution. The Sanhedrin of this period had incurred the charge of disgraceful laxity. The *Sicarii* were not suppressed; the red heifer was slain no longer;[2] the ordeal of the bitter water had been done away, *because* the crime of adultery had greatly increased.[3] Rabbi Joshua Ben Korcha, when R. Elieser had arrested some thieves, reproached him

iii. 3); but in the Gemara, and in later Jewish writers, we find that, besides the qualification mentioned in Exod. xviii. 21, and Deut. i. 13–16, a candidate must be free from every physical blemish, stainless in character, learned in science, acquainted with more than one language, and with a family of his own, because such were supposed to be less inclined to cruelty, and more likely to sympathise with domestic affections. (*Horajoth*, i. 4; *Sanhedr.* f. 17, 1, 36, b.; *Menachôth*, f. 65, 1; Maimon. *Sanhedr.* ii.; Otho, *Lex Rabb.* s. v.) Whatever may be thought of the other qualifications, it is probable that this one, at any rate, was insisted on, and it adds force to our impression that St. Paul had once been a married man (1 Cor. vii. 8; *v. supra*, p. 79, sq. See Ewald, *Sendschr. d. Ap. Paul*, p. 161; *Gesch. d. Apost. Zeitalt.*, p. 371.)

[1] See Surenhus. *Mishna*, iv. *Praef.*   [2] *Sotah*, f. 47, 1.

[3] Maimon. in *Sotah*, c. 3. They quoted Hos. iv. 14 in favour of this abolition of Num. v. 18; cf. Matt. xii. 39; xvi. 4.

with the words, "How long will you hand over the people of God to destruction? Leave the thorns to be plucked up by the Lord of the vineyard."[1] But to the seducer (*mesitk*), the blasphemer (*megadeph*), and the idolater, there was neither leniency nor compassion.[2] By the unanimous testimony of the Jews themselves, Christians could not be charged with the crime of idolatry ;[3] but it was easy to bring them under the penalty of stoning, which was attached to the former crimes. The minor punishments of flagellation and excommunication seem to have been in the power, not only of the Sanhedrin, but even of each local synagogue. Whatever may have been the legal powers of these bodies, whatever licences the temporary relaxation of Roman supervision may have permitted,[4] they were used and abused to the utmost by the youthful zealot. The wisdom of the toleration which Gamaliel himself had recommended appears in the fact that the great persecution, which broke up the Church at Jerusalem, was in every way valuable to the new religion. It dissipated the Judaism which would have endangered the spread of Christianity, and showed that the disciples had a loftier mission than to dwindle down into a Galilæan synagogue. The sacred fire, which might have burnt low on the hearth of the upper chamber at Jerusalem, was kindled into fresh heat and splendour when its brands were scattered over all Judæa and Samaria, and uncircumcised Gentiles were admitted by baptism into the fold of Christ.

The solemn burial of Stephen by holy men—whether Hellenist Christians or Jewish proselytes—the beating of

---

[1] *Babha Metzia*, f. 82, 2; Otho, *Lex Rabb.*, s. v. Synedrium.

[2] Deut. xiii. 8, 9; *Sanhedr.* f. 29, 1; 32, 3.

[3] There is not one word about the Christians in the tract, *Abhôda Zara*, or on "alien worship."

[4] Marcellus, who was at this time an *ad interim* governor, held the rank, not of Procurator, ἡγεμών, but only of ἐπιμελητής (Jos. *Antt.* xviii. 4, § 2).

the breast, the wringing of the hands with which they lamented him,[1] produced no change in the purpose of Saul. The sight of that dreadful execution, the dying agonies and crushed remains of one who had stood before the Sanhedrin like an angel in the beauty of holiness, could hardly have failed to produce an impression on a heart so naturally tender. But if it was a torture to witness the agony of others, and to be the chief agent in its infliction, then that very torture became a more meritorious service for the Law. If his own blameless scrupulosity in all that affected legal righteousness was beginning to be secretly tainted with heretical uncertainties, he would feel it all the more incumbent on him to wash away those doubts in blood. Like Cardinal Pole, when Paul IV. began to impugn his orthodoxy, he must have felt himself half driven to persecution, in order to prove his soundness in the faith.

The part which he played at this time in the horrid work of persecution has, I fear, been always underrated. It is only when we collect the separate passages—they are no less than eight in number—in which allusion is made to this sad period—it is only when we weigh the terrible significance of the expressions used—that we feel the load of remorse which must have lain upon him, and the taunts to which he was liable from malignant enemies. He "made havoc of"—literally, "he was ravaging"—the Church.[2] No stronger metaphor could well have been used. It occurs nowhere else in the New Testament, but in the Septuagint, and in classical Greek, is applied to the wild boars which uproot a vineyard.[3] Not

---

[1] Acts viii. 2, κοπετὸς μέγας. The word is found in the LXX., Gen. l. 10, &c., but here alone in the New Testament.

[2] Acts viii. 3, ἐλυμαίνετο τὴν ἐκκλησίαν.

[3] Ps. lxxix. 14; Callim. *Hymn in Dian.* 156. σύες ἔργα σύες φυτὰ λυμαίνονται.

content with the visitation of the synagogues, he got authority for an inquisitorial visit from house to house, and even from the sacred retirement of the Christian home he dragged not only men, but women, to judgment and to prison.[1] So thorough was his search, and so deadly were its effects, that, in referring to it, the Christians of Damascus can only speak of Saul as "he that *devastated* in Jerusalem them that call on this name,"[2] using the strong word which is strictly applicable to an invading army which scathes a conquered country with fire and sword. So much St. Luke tells us, in giving a reason for the total scattering of the Church, and the subsequent blessings which sprang from their preaching the Word in wider districts. The Apostles, he adds, remained. What was the special reason for this we do not know; but as the Lord's direct permission to the seventy to fly before persecution[3] would have sanctioned their consulting their own safety, it may have been because Jesus had bidden them stay in Jerusalem till the end of twelve years.[4] If, as St. Chrysostom imagines, they stayed to support the courage of others, how was it that the shepherds escaped while the flock was being destroyed? Or are we to infer that the main fury of the persecution fell upon those Hellenists who shared the views of the first martyr, and that the Apostles were saved from molestation by the blameless Mosaism of which one of the leading brethren—no less a person than James, the Lord's brother—was so conspicuous an example? Be

---

[1] These hostile measures are summed up in the ὅσα κακὰ ἐποίησε τοῖς ἁγίοις of Ananias, who says that the rumour had reached him from many sources (Acts ix. 13).

[2] Acts ix. 21, ὁ πορθήσας.

[3] Matt. x. 23.

[4] A brief visit to Samaria " to confirm the churches " (Acts viii. 14) would not militate against this command.

that as it may, at any rate they did not fall victims
to the rage which was so fatal to many of their companions.

In two of his speeches and four of his letters does
St. Paul revert to this crime of an erring obstinacy. Twice
to the Galatians does he use the same strong metaphor
which was applied to his conduct by the Damascene
believers.[1] He tells the Corinthians[2] that he was "the
least of the Apostles, not meet to be called an Apostle,
because he persecuted the Church of God." He reminds
the Philippians[3] that his old Hebraic zeal as a Pharisee
had shown itself by his "persecuting the Church."
And even when the shadows of a troubled old age were
beginning to close around him, keen in the sense that he
was utterly forgiven through Him who "came into the
world to save sinners, of whom I am chief," he cannot
forget the bitter thought that, though in ignorance, he
had once been "a blasphemer, and persecutor, and injurious."[4] And when he is speaking to those who knew
the worst—in his speech to the raging mob of Jerusalem, as he stood on the steps of the Tower of
Antonia—he adds one fact more which casts a lurid
light on the annals of the persecution. He shows
there that the blood of Stephen was not the only blood
that had been shed—not the only blood of which the
stains had incarnadined his conscience. He tells the mob
not only of the binding and imprisonment of women as
well as men, but also that he "persecuted this way
unto the death."[5] Lastly, in his speech at Cæsarea,
he adds what is perhaps the darkest touch of all, for he
says that, armed with the High Priest's authority, he

---

[1] Gal. i. 13, where he also says that he persecuted them beyond measure
(καθ᾽ ὑπερβολήν); and i. 23.

[2] 1 Cor. xv. 9.   [3] Phil. iii. 6.   [4] 1 Tim. i. 13.   [5] Acts xxii. 4.

not only fulfilled unwittingly the prophecy of Christ[1] by
scourging the Christians "often" and "in every synagogue," but that, *when it came to a question of death*, he
gave his vote against them, and that he *did his best to
compel them to blaspheme*.[2] I say "did his best," because
the tense he uses implies effort, but not necessarily success.
Pliny, in a passage of his famous letter to Trajan from
Bithynia,[3] says that, in questioning those who, in anonymous letters, were accused of being "Christians," he
thought it sufficient to test them by making them offer
wine and incense to the statues of the gods and the bust
of the emperor, and to blaspheme the name of Christ;
and, if they were willing to do this, he dismissed them
without further inquiry, because he had been informed
that to no one of these things could a genuine Christian
ever be impelled.

We do not know that in all the sufferings of the
Apostle any attempt was ever made to compel him to
blaspheme. With all the other persecutions which he
made the Christian suffer he became in his future life
too sadly familiar. To the last dregs of lonely and
unpitied martyrdom he drank the bitter cup of merciless
persecution. Five times—in days when he was no longer
the haughty Rabbi, the self-righteous Pharisee, the fierce
legate of the Sanhedrin armed with unlimited authority
for the suppression of heresy, but was himself the scorned,

---

[1] Matt. x. 17; Mark xiii. 9.

[2] Acts xxvi. 11, ἠνάγκαζον βλασφημεῖν. There is a possibility that in the
ἄχρι θανάτου of the previous passage, and the κατήνεγκα ψῆφον of this, St. Paul
may allude to his own endeavour (cf. Gal. vi. 12) to have them capitally
punished, without implying that the vote was carried. I have translated
the ἀναιρουμένων so as to admit of this meaning, which, perhaps, acquires a
shade of additional probability from Heb. xii. 4, "Ye have not yet resisted
unto blood," if that Epistle was specially addressed to Palestinian Jews.

[3] Plin. *Ep.* x. 97 . . . . "praeterea maledicere Christo; *quorum nihil
cogi posse dicuntur* qui sunt revera Christiani."

hunted, hated, half-starved missionary of that which was branded as an apostate sect—five times, from the authority of some ruler of the synagogue, did he receive forty stripes save one. He, too, was stoned, and betrayed, and many times imprisoned, and had the vote of death recorded against him; and in all this he recognised the just and merciful flame that purged away the dross of a once misguided soul—the light affliction which he had deserved, but which was not comparable to the far more eternal weight of glory. In all this he may have even rejoiced that he was bearing for Christ's sake that which he had made others bear, and passing through the same furnace which he had once heated sevenfold for them. But I doubt whether any one of these sufferings, or all of them put together, ever wrung his soul with the same degree of anguish as that which lay in the thought that he had used all the force of his character and all the tyranny of his intolerance to break the bruised reed and to quench the smoking flax—that he had endeavoured, by the infamous power of terror and anguish, to compel some gentle heart to blaspheme its Lord.

The great persecution with which St. Paul was thus identified—and which, from these frequent allusions, as well as from the intensity of the language employed, seems to me to have been more terrible than is usually admitted—did not spend its fury for some months. In Jerusalem it was entirely successful. There were no more preachings or wonders in Solomon's Porch; no more throngs that gathered in the streets to wait the passing shadow of Peter and John; no more assembled multitudes in the house of Mary, the mother of St. Mark. If the Christians met, they met in mournful secrecy and diminished numbers, and the Love-feasts, if held at all, must have been held as in the early days

before the Ascension, with doors closed, for fear of the
Jews. Some of the Christians had suffered cruelly for
their religion; the faithless members of the Church
had doubtless apostatised; the majority had fled at once
before the storm.[1]

It is, perhaps, to indicate the *continuance* of this
active hostility that St. Luke here inserts the narrative
of Philip's preaching as a fitting prelude to the work
of the Apostle of the Gentiles. At this narrative we
shall glance hereafter; but now we must follow the career
of Saul the Inquisitor, and see the marvellous event which,
by one lightning flash, made him "a *fusile* Apostle"—
which in one day transformed Saul the persecutor into
Paul the slave of Jesus Christ.

His work in Jerusalem was over. The brethren who remained had either eluded his search-warrant, or been rescued
from his power. But the young zealot was not the man
to do anything by halves. If he had smitten one head of
the hydra,[2] it had grown up in new places. If he had
torn up the heresy by the roots from the Holy City, the
winged seeds had alighted on other fertile ground, and
the rank weed was still luxuriant elsewhere; so that, in
his outrageous madness—it is his own expression[3]—he
began to pursue them even to foreign cities. Damascus,
he had heard, was now the worst nest of this hateful delusion, and fortunately in that city he could find scope for
action; for the vast multitude of Jews which it contained
acknowledged allegiance to the Sanhedrin. To the High
Priest, therefore, he went—unsated by all his previous
cruelties, and in a frame of mind so hot with rage that

---

[1] This is implied in the *ἐν ἐκείνῃ τῇ ἡμέρᾳ*, and in the aorist *διεσπάρησαν* of
Acts viii. 1.

[2] Domitian and Maximin struck medals of Hercules and the Hydra with
the inscription " Deletâ religione Christianâ quae orbem turbabat."

[3] Acts xxvi. 11, *περισσῶς ἐμμαινόμενος αὐτοῖς.*

M

again it can only be described by the unparalleled phrase that he was "breathing threats and slaughter against the disciples of the Lord."[1] The High Priest—in all probability Theophilus, who was promoted by Vitellius at the Pentecost of A.D. 37[2]—was a Sadducee, and a son of the hated house of Hanan. Yet it was with Saul, and not with Theophilus, that the demand originated, to pursue the heresy to Damascus.[3] Not sorry to find so thorough an instrument in one who belonged to a different school from his own—not sorry that the guilty responsibility for "this man's blood" should be shared by Sadducees with the followers of Hillel—Theophilus gave the letters which authorised Saul to set up his court at Damascus, and to bring from thence in chains all whom he could find, both men and women, to await such mercy as Stephen's murder might lead them to hope for at the hands of the supreme tribunal.[4] In ordinary times— when that Jewish autonomy, which always meant Jewish intolerance, was repressed within stern limits by the Roman government—it would have been impossible to carry out so cruel a commission. This might have been urged as an insuperable difficulty if an incidental expression in 2 Cor. xi. 32 had not furnished a clue in explanation of the circumstances. From this it appears

---

[1] Acts ix. 1, ἐμπνέων ἀπειλῆς καὶ φόνου.

[2] Jos. *Antt.* xviii. 5, § 3.

[3] Acts ix. 2, "If he should find any of *the way*." The word Χριστιανισμός was invented later (*infra*, p. 297). The Jewish writers similarly speak of the "*derek* ha-Notserim," or "way of the Nazarenes."

[4] The repeated allusions to the punishment of women shows not only the keenness of the search, but also the large part played by Christian women in the spread of that religion which first elevated their condition from the degradation of the harem and the narrowness of the gynaeceum. These women-martyrs of the great persecution were the true predecessors of those Saints Catherine, and Barbara, and Lucia, and Agnes, and Dorothea, and Caecilia, and Felicitas, who leave the light of their names on the annals of Christian heroism.

that at this time the city was more or less in the hands
of Aretas or Hareth, the powerful Emîr of Petra.[1]
Now there are notices in the Talmud which prove
that Hareth stood in friendly relations to the Jewish
High Priest,[2] and we can see how many circumstances
thus concurred to create for Saul an exceptional opportunity to bring the Christians of Damascus under the
authority of the Sanhedrin. Never again might he find
so favourable an opportunity of eradicating the heresy of
these hated Nazarenes.

[1] See Excursus VIII.: " Damascus under Hareth."
[2] A story is told that on one occasion the High Priest Simeon Ben
Kamhith was incapacitated from performing the duties of the Day of
Atonement, because, while familiarly talking with Hareth on the previous
evening, a drop of the Emir's saliva had fallen on the High Priest's dress
(cf. *Niddah*, f. 33, 2).

CHAPTER X.

THE CONVERSION OF SAUL.

. . . κατελήφθην ὑπὸ τοῦ Χριστοῦ Ἰησοῦ.—PHIL. iii. 12.

"Opfert freudig aus was ihr besessen
Was ihr einst gewesen, was ihr seyd ;
Und in einem seligen Vergessen
Schwinde die Vergangenheit."—SCHILLER.

ARMED with his credentials Saul started from Jerusalem
for his journey of nearly 150 miles. That journey would
probably be performed exactly as it is now performed with
horses and mules, which are indispensable to the traveller
along those rough, bad roads, and up and down those
steep and fatiguing hills. Saul, it must be remembered,
was travelling in a manner very different from that of our
Lord and His humble followers. They who, in preaching
the Gospel to the poor, assumed no higher earthly dignity
than that of the carpenter of Nazareth and the fishermen
of Galilee, would go on foot with staff and scrip from
village to village, like the other "people of the land" whom
long-robed Scribes despised. Saul was in a very different
position, and the little retinue which was assigned him
would treat him with all the deference due to a Pharisee
and a Rabbi—a legate à latere of Theophilus, the powerful
High Priest.

But, however performed, the journey could not occupy
less than a week, and even the fiery zeal of the persecutor
would scarcely enable him to get rid of the habitual
leisureliness of Eastern travelling. And thus, as they

made their way along the difficult and narrow roads, Saul
would be doomed to a week of necessary reflection.
Hitherto, ever since those hot disputes in the synagogues
of Cilician Hellenists, he had been living in a whirl of
business which could have left him but little time for
quiet thought. That active inquisition, those domiciliary
visits, those incessant trials, that perpetual presiding over
the scourgings, imprisonments, perhaps even actual stonings
of men and women, into which he had been plunged,
must have absorbed his whole energies, and left him no
inclination to face the difficult questions, or to lay the
secret misgivings, which had begun to rise in his
mind.[1] Pride—the pride of system, the pride of nature,
the rank pride of the self-styled theologian, the exclusive
national Pharisaic pride in which he had been trained—
forbade him to examine seriously whether he might not
after all be in the wrong. Without humility there can
be no sincerity; without sincerity, no attainment of the
truth. Saul felt that he could not and would not let
himself be convinced; he could not and would not admit
that much of the learning of his thirty years of life
was a mass of worthless cobwebs, and that all the

[1] See Rom. vii. 8, 9, 10. This picture of St. Paul's mental condition is no
mere imaginative touch; from all such, both in this work and in my *Life of Christ*,
I have studiously abstained. It springs as a direct and inevitable conclusion
from his own epistles and the reproof of Jesus, "It is hard for thee to kick
against the goads." These words, following the "Why persecutest thou me?"
imply, with inimitable brevity, "Seest thou not that *I* am the pursuer and *thou*
the pursued?" What were those goads? There were no conceivable goads for
him to resist, except those which were wielded by his own conscience. The
stings of conscience, the anguish of a constant misgiving, inflicted wounds
which should have told him long before that he was advancing in a wrong
path. They were analogous to the warnings, both inward and outward, which
"forbade the madness" of the Mesopotamian sorcerer. Balaam, too, was
taught by experience how terrible a thing it is "to kick against the pricks."
The resisted inward struggles of St. Paul are also implied in the "calling"
of Gal. i. 15, preceding the "revelation." (See Monod, *Cinq Discours*, p. 168;
Stier, *Reden d. Apost.* ii. 299; De Pressensé, *Trois Prem. Siècles*, i. 434.)

righteousness with which he had striven to hasten the coming of the Messiah was as filthy rags. He could not and would not admit the possibility that people like Peter and Stephen could be right, while people like himself and the Sanhedrin could be mistaken; or that the Messiah could be a Nazarene who had been crucified as a malefactor; or that after looking for Him so many generations, and making their whole religious life turn on His expected Advent, Israel should have been found sleeping, and have murdered Him when at last He came. If haunting doubts could for a moment thrust themselves into his thoughts, the vehement self-assertion of contempt would sweep them out, and they would be expiated by fresh zeal against the seductive glamour of the heresy which thus dared to insinuate itself like a serpent into the very hearts of its avengers. What could it be but diabolic influence which made the words and the arguments of these blasphemers of the Law and the Temple fasten involuntarily upon his mind and memory? Never would he too be seduced into the position of a *mesith!* Never would he degrade himself to the ignorant level of people who knew not the Law and were accursed!

But the ghosts of these obstinate questionings would not always be so laid. As long as he had work to do he could crush by passion and energy such obtruding fancies. But when his work was done—when there were in Jerusalem no more Hellenists to persecute—when even the Galilæans had fled or been silenced, or been slain—then such doubts would again thicken round him, and he would hear the approach of them like the sound of a stealthy footfall on the turf. Was it not this that kindled his excessive madness—this that made him still breathe out threats and blood? Was not this a part of the motive which had driven him to the wily Sadducee with the demand for a fresh commission? Would not this work for the Law protect him from the perplexing complications of a will that plunged and struggled to resist the agonising goad-thrusts of a ruinous misgiving?

But now that he was journeying day after day towards Damascus, how could he save himself from his own thoughts? He could not converse with the attendants who were to execute his decisions. They were mere subordinates—mere apparitors of the Sanhedrin—members, perhaps, of the Temple guard—ignorant Levites, whose function it would be to drag with them on his return the miserable gang of trembling heretics. We may be sure that the vacuity of thought in which most men live was for Saul a thing impossible. He could not help meditating as the sages bade the religious Jew to meditate, on the precepts and promises of his own Law. For the first time perhaps since he had encountered Stephen he had the uninterrupted leisure to face the whole question calmly and seriously, in the solitude of thoughts which could no longer be sophisticated by the applause of Pharisaic partisans. He was forced to go up into the dark tribunal of his own conscience and set himself before himself. More terrible by far was the solemnity, more impartial the judgment of that stern session, than those either of the Jewish Sanhedrin, or of that other Areopagus in which he would one day stand. If there be in the character any seriousness at all; if the cancer of conceit or vice have not eaten out all of the heart that is not frivolous and base, then how many a man's intellectual conclusions, how many a man's moral life has been completely changed—and for how many would they not at this moment be completely changed—by the *necessity* for serious reflection during a few days of unbroken leisure?

And so we may be quite sure that day after day, as he rode on under the morning sunlight or the bright stars of an Eastern night, the thoughts of Saul would be overwhelmingly engaged. They would wander back over the past; they would glance sadly at the future. Those were happy years in Tarsus; happy walks in childhood beside "the silver Cydnus;" happy hours in the school of Gamaliel, where there first dawned upon his soul the glories of Moses and Solomon, of the Law and the Temple, of the Priesthood and the chosen race. Those were golden days when he listened to the promised triumphs of the Messiah, and was told how near was that day when the Holy Land should be exalted as the Lady of kingdoms, and the vaunted strength of Rome, which now lay so heavy on his subjugated people, be shattered like a potsherd! But had not something of the splendour faded from these more youthful dreams? What had the righteousness of the Law done for him? He had lived, as far as men were concerned, an honourable life. He had been exceedingly zealous, exceedingly blameless in the traditions of the fathers; but what inward joy had he derived from them?—what enlightenment?—what deliverance from that law of his members, which, do what he would, still worked fatally against the law in his mind? His sins of pride and passion, and frailty—would not a jealous God avenge them? Was there any exemption at all from the Law's curse of "death?" Was there any deliverance at all from this ceaseless trouble of a nature dissatisfied with itself, and therefore wavering like a wave of the troubled sea?

Would the deliverance be secured by the coming of the Messiah? That advent for the nation would be triumph and victory; would it be for the individual also, peace of conscience, justification, release from heavy bondage, forgiveness of past sins, strength in present weakness?

And then it must have flashed across him that these Nazarenes, at any rate, whom he had been hunting and slaying, said that it would. For them the Messiah had come, and certainly they had found peace. It was true that their Messiah was despised and rejected; but was not that the very thing which had been said of the Servant of Jehovah in that prophecy to which they always appealed, and which also said that which his troubled conscience needed most:—

"Surely He hath borne our griefs and carried our sorrows : yet we did esteem Him stricken, smitten of God, and afflicted. But He was wounded for our transgressions, He was bruised for our iniquities : the chastisement of our peace was upon Him; and with His stripes we are healed. All we like sheep have gone astray ; we have turned every one to his own way ; and the Lord hath laid on Him the iniquity of us all."[1]

This passage certainly gave a very different aspect to the conception of the Messiah from any which he had been taught to contemplate. Yet the Rabbis had said that *all* prophecies were Messianic. Jesus had been crucified. A crucified Messiah was a horrible thought; but was it worse than a Messiah who should be a leper? Yet here the ideal servant of Jehovah was called a leper.[2] And if His physical condition turned out to be meaner than Israel had always expected, yet surely the moral conception, the spiritual conception, as he had heard it from these hated Galilæans, was infinitely lovelier! They spoke—and oh, undeniably those were blessed words!—of a Messiah through whom they obtained forgiveness of sins.

If this were true, what infinite comfort it brought!

[1] Isa. liii. 4—6.
Isa. lii. 14, liii. 4, "*stricken*" Heb., cf. Lev. xiii. 13, Sanhedr. f. 98.

how it ended the hopelessness of the weary struggle!
The Law, indeed, promised life to perfect obedience.[1]   But
who ever had attained, who *could* attain, to that perfect
obedience?[2]   Did he see it in the Gentile world, who,
though they had not the Law of Moses, had their own law
of nature?   Did he see it in the Jewish world?—alas,
what a depth of disappointment was involved in the very
question!   Was Hanan, was Caiaphas, was Theophilus,
was Ishmael Ben Phabi a specimen of the righteousness of
the Law?   And if, as was too true, Israel had not attained
—if he himself had not attained—to the law of righteousness, what hope was there?[3]   Oh, the blessedness of him
whose unrighteousness was forgiven, whose sin was
covered!   Oh, the blessedness of him to whom the Lord
would not impute sin!   Oh, to have the infinite God who
seemed so far away brought near, and to see His face not
darkened by the cloud, not glaring through the pillar of
fire, but as a man seeth the face of his friend!   Oh that a
Man were a hiding-place from the wind, and a covert from
the tempest, as the shadow of a great rock in a weary
land![4]

And so, again and again, he would realise with a sense
of remorse that he was yearning for, that he was gliding
into, the very doctrines which he was persecuting to the
death.   For to these Nazarenes their Son of Man was
indeed the image of the Invisible God.   Could he be
right in thus striving to stamp out a faith so pure, so

---

[1] Lev. xviii. 5; Gal. iii. 12.

[2] Rom. x. 5.

[3] Rom. ix. 31. When Rabbi Eleazar was sick, and Akibha rejoiced because
he feared that Eleazar had been receiving his good things in this life, "Akibha,"
exclaimed the sufferer, "is there anything in the whole Law which I have
failed to fulfil?"   "Rabbi," replied Akibha, "thou hast taught me 'There is
not a just man upon earth that doeth good, and sinneth not.'" Eccles. vii. 20.
(*Sanhedr.*, f. 101, 1.)

[4] Isa. xxxii. 2.

ennobling? For, whether it was heresy or not, that it was pure and ennobling he could not fail to acknowledge. That face of Stephen which he had seen bathed as with a light from heaven until it had been dimmed in blood, must have haunted him then, as we know it did for long years afterwards. Would the Mosaic law have inspired so heavenly an enthusiasm? would it have breathed into the sufferers so infinite a serenity, so bright a hope? And where in all the Holy Pentateuch could he find utterances so tender, lessons so divine, love so unspeakable, motives which so mastered and entranced the soul, as these had found in the words and in the love of their Lord? Those beatitudes which he had heard them speak of, the deeds of healing tenderness which so many attested, the parables so full of divine illumination — the moral and spiritual truths of a Teacher who, though His nation had crucified Him, had spoken as never man spake — oh, Who was this who had inspired simple fishermen and ignorant publicans with a wisdom unattainable by a Hillel or a Gamaliel? Who was this to whom His followers turned their last gaze and uttered their last prayer in death; who seemed to breathe upon them from the parted heavens a glory as of the Shechinah, a peace that passed all understanding? Who was this who, as they declared, had risen from the dead; whose body certainly had vanished from the rock-hewn sepulchre in which it had been laid; whom these good Galilæans — these men who would rather die than lie — witnessed that they had seen, that they had heard, that He had appeared to them in the garden, in the upper chamber, on the public road, to four of them upon the misty lake, to more than five hundred of them at once upon the Galilæan hill? Could that have been a right path which led him to

persecute these? could it be God's will which had driven
him so fiercely along a road that was stained in blood?
could he be required to pass through those scenes of horror
in which he had haled the wife and the mother to prison,

MAP SHOWING THE ROADS FROM JERUSALEM TO DAMASCUS.

and seen the coarse menials of the synagogue remorselessly
scourge men whose whole life was love and humility and
holiness? Had he after all been mistaking pride for
faithfulness, and rage for zeal? Had he been murdering
the saints that were upon the earth, and them that ex-
celled in virtue? Was Gamaliel right in suggesting the

possibility that in meddling with these men they might haply be fighting against God?

So day by day, his mind filled more and more with distracting doubts, his imagination haunted by sights of cruelty which, in spite of all zeal, harrowed up his soul, he journeyed on the road to Damascus. Under ordinary circumstances he might have felt an interest in the towns and scenes through which he passed—in Bethel and Shiloh—in the soft green fields that lie around the base of Mount Gerizim—in Jacob's tomb and Jacob's well —in Bethshean, with its memories of the miserable end of that old king of his tribe whose name he bore—in the blue glimpses of the Lake of Galilee with its number-less memorials of that Prophet of Nazareth whose followers he was trying to destroy. But during these days, if I judge rightly, his one desire was to press on, and by vehement action to get rid of painful thought.

And now the journey was nearly over. Hermon had long been gleaming before them, and the chain of Anti-libanus. They had been traversing a bare, bleak, glaring, undulating plain, and had reached the village of Kaukab, or "the Star." At that point a vision of surpassing beauty bursts upon the eye of the weary traveller. Thanks to the "golden Abana" and the winding Pharpar, which flow on either side of the ridge, the wilderness blossoms like the rose. Instead of brown and stony wastes, we begin to pass under the flickering shadows of ancient olive-trees. Below, out of a soft sea of verdure—amid masses of the foliage of walnuts and pomegranates and palms, steeped in the rich haze of sunshine—rise the white terraced roofs and glittering cupolas of the immemorial city of which the beauty has been compared in every age to the beauty of a Paradise of God. There amid its gardens of rose, and groves of delicious fruit, with the gleam of waters that flowed through it, flooded with the gold of breathless morn, lay the eye of the East.[1] To that land of streams, to that city of fountains, to that Paradise of God, Saul was hastening—not on messages of mercy, not to add to the happiness and beauty of the world—but to scourge and to slay and to imprison, those perhaps of all its inhabitants who were the meekest, the gentlest, the most pure of heart. And Saul, with all his tenacity of purpose, was a man of almost emotional tenderness of character.[2] Though zeal and passion might hurry him into acts of cruelty, they could not crush within him the instincts of sympathy; and the horror of suffering and blood. Can we doubt that at the sight of the lovely glittering city—like (if I may again quote the Eastern metaphor) "a handful of pearls in its goblet of emerald "—he felt one more terrible recoil from his unhallowed task, one yet fiercer thrust from the wounding goad of a reproachful conscience?

It was high noon—and in a Syrian noon the sun shines fiercely overhead in an intolerable blaze of boundless light; —the cloudless sky glows like molten brass; the white earth under the feet glares like iron in the furnace; the whole air, as we breathe it, seems to quiver as though it were pervaded with subtle flames. That Saul and his comrades should at such a moment have still been pressing forward on their journey would seem to argue a troubled impatience, an impassioned haste. Generally at that time of day the traveller will be resting in his khan, or lying under the shelter of his tent. But it was Saul who would regulate the movements of his little company; and Saul was pressing on.

Then suddenly all was ended—the eager haste, the

---

[1] See Porter's *Syria*, p. 435.
[2] See Adolphe Monod's sermon, *Les Larmes de St. Paul.*

agonising struggle, the deadly mission, the mad infatuation, the feverish desire to quench doubt in persecution.
Round them suddenly from heaven there lightened a great
light.[1] It was not Saul alone who was conscious of it. It
seemed as though the whole atmosphere had caught fire,
and they were suddenly wrapped in sheets of blinding
splendour. It might be imagined that nothing can
outdazzle the glare of a Syrian sun at noon; but this light
was more vivid than its brightness, more penetrating than
its flame. And with the light came to those who
journeyed with Saul an awful but unintelligible sound. As
though by some universal flash from heaven, they were
all struck to earth together, and when the others had
arisen and had partially recovered from their terror,
Saul was still prostrate there. They were conscious that
something awful had happened. Had we been able to
ask them what it was, it is more than doubtful whether
they could have said. Had it been suggested to them that
it was some overwhelmingly sudden burst of thunder, some
inexpressibly vivid gleam of electric flame—some blinding,
suffocating, maddening breath of the sirocco—some rare
phenomenon unexperienced before or since—they might
not have known. The vision was not for them. They
saw the light above the noonday—they heard, and heard
with terror, the unknown sound which shattered the dead
hush of noon; but they were not converted by this
epiphany. To the Jew the whole earth was full of God's
visible ministrants. The winds were His spirits, the
flaming fires His messengers; the thunder was the voice
of the Lord shaking the cedars, yea, shaking the cedars
of Libanus. The *bath-kol* might come to him in sounds

---

[1] Acts ix. 3, περιήστραψεν, "lightened round." The word is again used
in xxii. 6, but is not found in the LXX., and is unknown to classical
Greek.

which none but he could understand: others might say it thundered when to him an angel spake.[1]

But that which happened was not meant for those who journeyed with Saul:[2] it was meant for him; and of that which he saw and which he heard he confessedly could be the only witness. They could only say that a light had shone from heaven, but to Saul it was a light from Him who is the light of the City of God—a ray from the light which no man can approach unto.[3]

And about that which he saw and heard he never wavered. It was the secret of his inmost being; it was the most unalterable conviction of his soul; it was the very crisis and most intense moment of his life. Others might hint at explanations or whisper doubt:[4] Saul *knew*. At that instant God had shown him His secret and His covenant. God had found him; had flung him to the ground in the career of victorious outrage, to lead him henceforth in triumph, a willing spectacle to angels and to men.[5] God had spoken to him, had struck him into darkness out of the noonday, only that He might kindle a noon in the midnight of his heart. From that moment Saul was converted. A change total, utter, final had passed over him, had transformed him. God had called him, had

---

[1] John xii. 29.

[2] Acts ix. 7, εἱστήκεισαν μηδένα θεωροῦντες. Cf. Dan. x. 7, " I Daniel alone saw the vision; for the men that were with me saw not the vision; but a great quaking fell upon them, so that they fled to hide themselves." So in *Shemôth Rabba*, sect. 2, f. 104, 3, it is said that others were with Moses, but that he alone saw the burning bush (Exod. iii. 2). Similarly Rashi, at the beginning of his commentary on Leviticus, says that when God called Moses the voice was heard by him alone.

[3] 1 Tim. vi. 14—16; 2 Cor. xii. 1.

[4] We trace a sort of hesitating sneer in the Clementine *Homilies*, xvii. 13, "He who believes a vision . . . . may indeed be deceived by an evil demon, ... which really is nothing, and if he asks who it is that appears " (with an allusion to τίς εἶ, Κύριε, ix. 5), " it can answer what it will;"—with very much more to the same effect.

[5] 2 Cor. ii. 14.

revealed His Son in him,[1] had given him grace and power
to become an Apostle to the Gentiles, had sent him forth
to preach the faith which he had once destroyed, had
shone in his heart to give " the light of the knowledge of
the glory of God in the face of Jesus Christ." [2]

And the means of this mighty change all lay in this
one fact:—at that awful moment *he had seen the Lord
Jesus Christ.*[3] To him the persecutor—to him as to the
abortive-born of the Apostolic family[4]—the risen, the
glorified Jesus had appeared. He had " been apprehended
by Christ." On that appearance all his faith was
founded; on that pledge of resurrection—of immortality to himself, and to the dead who die in Christ,—
all his hopes were anchored.[5] If that belief were un-
substantial, then all his life and all his labours were a
delusion and a snare—he was a wretch more to be pitied
than the wretchedest of the children of the world. But if
an angel from heaven preached a different doctrine it was
false, for he had been taught by the revelation of Jesus
Christ, and if this hope were vain, then to him

> " The pillared firmament was rottenness,
> And earth's base built on stubble."

The strength of this conviction became the leading
force in Paul's future life. He tells us that when the
blaze of glory lightened round him he was struck to the
earth, and there he remained till the voice bade him rise,
and when he rose his eyes were blinded ;—he opened them
on darkness. Had he been asked about the long controversies which have arisen in modern days, as to whether
the appearance of the Risen Christ to him was objective
or subjective, I am far from sure that he would even have

---

[1] Acts xxii. 21; xxvi. 17, 18; Gal. i. 15, 16.
[2] 2 Cor. iv. 6.   [4] 1 Cor. xv. 8.
[3] 1 Cor. ix. 1; xv. 8; *v. supra*, p.73 *seq.* [5] 1 Cor. xv. 10—29.

understood them.[1]   He uses indeed of this very event the
term " vision."   " I was not disobedient," he says to King
Agrippa, " to the heavenly vision."[2]   But the word used
for vision means "a waking vision," and in what conceivable respect could St. Paul have been more overpoweringly
convinced that he had in very truth seen, and heard, and
received a revelation and a mission from the Risen Christ?
Is the essential miracle rendered less miraculous by a
questioning of that objectivity to which the language
seems decidedly to point?   Are the eye and the ear the
only organs by which definite certainties can be conveyed
to the human soul?   are not rather these organs the
poorest, the weakest, the most likely to be deceived?
To the eyes of St. Paul's companions, God spoke by
the blinding light; to their ears by the awful sound ;
but to the soul of His chosen servant He was visible
indeed in the excellent glory, and He spoke in the
Hebrew tongue; but whether the vision and the voice
came through the dull organs of sense or in presen-
tations infinitely more intense, more vivid, more real,
more unutterably convincing to the spirit by which only
things spiritual are discerned—this is a question to which
those only will attach importance to whom the soul is

---

[1] See 2 Cor. xii. 1.

[2] Acts xxvi. 19. τῇ οὐρανίῳ ὀπτασίᾳ.   When Zacharias came out of the
Temple speechless, the people recognised that he had seen an ὀπτασία (Luke i.
22).   The women returning from the tomb say they have seen an ὀπτασία
ἀγγέλων (Luke xxiv. 23).   The word, then, is peculiar to Luke and the Acts, as
are so many words.   It is, however, the word used in the passage of the
Corinthians just quoted, and the ὀπτασία there leaves him no certainty as to
whether it was corporeal or spiritual.   The LXX. use it (Dan. ix. 23, &c.)
to render מַרְאֶה, which is used of a night vision in Gen. xlvi. 2.   Phavorinus
distinctly says that δραμα, whether by day or by night, is distinct from
ἐνύπνιον " dream," and it seems as if St. Luke, at any rate, meant by ὀπτασία
something more objective than he meant by δραμα (Acts ix. 10—12; xi. 5;
xii. 9; xvi. 9; xviii. 9) or ἔκστασις (Acts xi. 5; xxii. 17).   Ὅρασις, in the N. T.,
only occurs in Rev. iv. 3; ix. 17; and in a quotation, Acts ii. 17.

nothing but the material organism—who know of no
indubitable channels of intercourse between man and his
Maker save those that come clogged with the imperfections
of mortal sense—and who cannot imagine anything real
except that which they can grasp with both hands. One
fact remains upon any hypothesis—and that is, that the
conversion of St. Paul was in the highest sense of
the word a miracle, and one of which the spiritual
consequences have affected every subsequent age of the
history of mankind.[1]

For though there may be trivial variations, obviously
reconcilable, and · absolutely unimportant, in the thrice-
repeated accounts of this event, yet in the narration of
the *main* fact there is no shadow of variation, and no
possibility of doubt.[2] And the main fact as St. Paul
always related and referred to it was this—that, after
several days' journey, when they were now near Damascus,
some awful incident which impressed them all alike as an
infolding fire and a supernatural sound arrested their
progress, and in that light, as he lay prostrate on the earth,

---

[1] At such moments the spirit only lives, and the ψυχὴ, the animal life, is
hardly adequate as an ὄργανον ληπτικὸν to apprehend such revelations. See
Augustine, *De Genesi ad Litt.* xii. 8. "La chose essentielle est que nous ne
perdions pas de vue le grand principe évangélique d'un contact direct de
l'esprit de Dieu avec celui de l'homme, contact qui échappe à l'analyse du
raisonnement . . . . Le mysticisme évangélique en révélant au sens chrétien
un monde de miracles incessants, lui épargne la peine de se préoccuper du
petit nombre de ceux qu' analysent contradictoirement le rationalisme critique
et le rationalisme orthodoxe " (Reuss, *Hist. Apostolique*, p. 114). "Christ
stood before me," said St. Teresa. "*I saw Him with the eyes of the soul more
distinctly than I could have seen Him with the eyes of the body*" (*Vida*,
vii. 11).

[2] It is superfluous to repeat the reconciliation of these small apparent contradictions, because they are all reconciled and accounted for in the narrative
of the text. Had they been of the smallest importance, had they been such
as one moment of common sense could fail to solve, a writer so careful as
St. Luke would not have left them side by side.

N 2

Saul saw a mortal shape[1] and heard a human voice saying
to him, " Shaûl, Shaûl "—for it is remarkable how the
vividness of that impression is incidentally preserved in
each form of the narrative[2]—" why persecutest thou Me ?
It is hard for thee to kick against the goads."[3] But at
that awful moment Saul did not recognise the speaker,
whom on earth he had never seen. " Who art Thou,
Lord ? " he said. And He—" I am Jesus of Nazareth
whom thou persecutest."

" Jesus of Nazareth ! " Why did the glorified speaker
here adopt the name of his obscurity on earth ? Why, as
St. Chrysostom asks, did He not say, " I am the Son of
God ; the Word that was in the beginning ; He that sitteth
at the right hand of the Father ; He who is in the form of
God ; He who stretched out the heaven ; He who made
the earth ; He who levelled the sea ; He who created
the angels ; He who is everywhere and filleth all things ;

---

[1] This, though not in the Acts asserted in so many words in the direct
narrative, seems to be most obviously implied in the ὤφθην σοί of xxvi. 16, in
the contrast of the μηδένα θεωροῦντες of ix. 7, in the 'Ιησοῦς ὁ ὀφθείς σοι ἐν τῇ
ὁδῷ of ver. 17, in the πῶς ἐν τῇ ὁδῷ εἶδεν τὸν κύριον of verse 27, and in the already
quoted references (1 Cor. ix. 1 ; xv. 8). The remark of Chrysostom, καὶ μὴν
οὐκ ὤφθη ἀλλὰ διὰ πραγμάτων ἔφθη, is meant to be perfectly sincere and honest,
but when compared with the above passage, seems to show less than the great
orator's usual care and discrimination.

[2] Elsewhere he is always called Σαῦλος, but here Σαούλ.

[3] This addition is genuine in Acts xxvi. 14 ; and ὁ Ναζωραῖος certainly in
xxii. 8. Of the many illustrations quoted by Wetstein, and copied from
him by subsequent commentators, the most apposite and interesting are
Æsch. Agam. 1633, Prom. 323, Eur. Bacch. 791, Ter. Phorm. i. 22, 7. It
is, however, remarkable that though ox-goads were commonly used in the
East, not one single Eastern or Semitic parallel can be adduced. The
reference to Deut. xxxii. 15 is wholly beside the mark, though goads are
alluded to in Judg. iii. 31 ; Ecclus. xxxviii. 25. St. Paul would have been
naturally familiar with the common Greek proverbs, and those only will be
startled that a Greek proverb should be addressed to him by his glorified Lord,
who can never be brought to understand the simple principle that Inspiration
must always speak (as even the Rabbis saw) "in the tongue of the sons
of men."

He who was pre-existent and was begotten?" Why did He not utter those awful titles, but, "I am Jesus of Nazareth whom thou persecutest"—from the earthly city, from the earthly home? Because His persecutor knew Him not; for had he known Him he would not have persecuted Him. He knew not that He had been begotten of the Father, but that He was from Nazareth he knew. Had He then said to him, "I am the Son of God, the Word that was in the beginning, He who made the heaven," Saul might have said, "That is not He whom I am persecuting." Had He uttered to him those vast, and bright, and lofty titles, Saul might have said, "This is not the crucified." But that he may know that he is persecuting Him who was made flesh,[1] who took the form of a servant, who died, who was buried, naming Himself from the earthly place, He says, "I am Jesus of Nazareth whom thou persecutest." This, then, was the Messiah whom he had hated and despised—this was He who had been the Heavenly Shepherd of his soul;—He who to guide back his wandering footsteps into the straight furrow had held in His hand that unseen goad against which, like some stubborn ox, he had struggled and kicked in vain.

And when the Voice of that speaker from out of the unapproachable brightness had, as it were, smitten him to the very earth with remorse by the sense of this awful truth,—"But rise," it continued, "and stand upon thy feet, and go into the city, and it shall be told thee what thou must do."

This is the form in which the words are, with trivial differences, given in St. Luke's narrative, and in St. Paul's speech from the steps of Antonia. In his speech before

---

[1] Chrysostom adds, τὸν μὲτ' αὐτοῦ συνασταγραφέντα, but this I believe to be a mistake.

Agrippa, it might seem as if more had been spoken then
But in this instance again it may be doubted whether,
after the first appalling question, "Shaûl, Shaûl, why
persecutest thou Me?" which remained branded so vividly
upon his heart, Paul could himself have said how much
of the revelation which henceforth transfigured his life
was derived from the actual moment when he lay blinded
and trembling on the ground, and how much from the
subsequent hours of deep external darkness and brightening inward light. In the annals of human lives, there
have been other spiritual crises analogous to this in their
startling suddenness, in their absolute finality. To many
the resurrection from the death of sin is a slow and lifelong process; but others pass with one thrill of conviction,
with one spasm of energy, from death to life, from the
power of Satan unto God. Such moments crowd eternity
into an hour, and stretch an hour into eternity.

> " At such high hours
> Of inspiration from the Living God
> Thought is not."

When God's awful warnings burn before the soul in
letters of flame, it can read them indeed, and know
their meaning to the very uttermost, but it does not
know, and it does not care, whether it was Perez or
Upharsin that was written on the wall. The utterances
of the Eternal Sibyl are inscribed on records scattered and
multitudinous as are the forest leaves. As the anatomist
may dissect every joint and lay bare every nerve of the
organism, yet be infinitely distant from any discovery of
the principle of life, so the critic and grammarian may
decipher the dim syllables and wrangle about the disputed
discrepancies, but it is not theirs to interpret. If we
would in truth understand such spiritual experiences, the

records of them must be read by a light that never was on land or sea.

Saul rose another man: he had fallen in death, he rose in life: he had fallen in the midst of things temporal, he rose in awful consciousness of the things eternal: he had fallen a proud, intolerant, persecuting Jew; he rose a humble, broken-hearted, penitent Christian. In that moment a new element had been added to his being. Henceforth—to use his own deep and dominant expression—he was "in Christ." God had found him; Jesus had spoken to him, and in one flash changed him from a raging Pharisee into a true disciple—from the murderer of the saints into the Apostle of the Gentiles. It was a new birth, a new creation. As we read the story of it, if we have one touch of reverence within our souls, shall we not take off our shoes from off our feet, for the place whereon we stand is holy ground?

Saul rose, and all was dark. The dazzling vision had passed away, and with it also the glittering city, the fragrant gardens, the burning noon. Amazed and startled, his attendants took him by the hand and led him to Damascus. He had meant to enter the city in all the importance of a Commissioner from the Sanhedrin, to be received with distinction, not only as himself a great "pupil of the wise," but even as the representative of all authority which the Jews held most sacred. And he had meant to leave the city, perhaps, amid multitudes of his applauding countrymen, accompanied by a captive train of he knew not how many dejected Nazarenes. How different were his actual entrance and his actual exit! He is led through the city gate, stricken, dejected, trembling, no longer breathing threats and slaughter, but longing only to be the learner and the suppliant, and the lowest brother among those whom he had intended to destroy.

He was ignominiously let out of the city, alone, in imminent peril of arrest or assassination, through a window, in a basket, down the wall.

They led him to the house of Judas, in that long street which leads through the city and is still called Straight; and there, in remorse, in blindness, in bodily suffering, in mental agitation, unable or unwilling to eat or drink, the glare of that revealing light ever before his darkened eyes, the sound of that reproachful voice ever in his ringing ears, Saul lay for three days. None can ever tell what things in those three days passed through his soul; what revelations of the past, what lessons for the present, what guidance for the future. His old life, his old self, had been torn up by the very roots, and though now he was a new creature, the crisis can never pass over any one without agonies and energies—without earthquake and eclipse. At last the tumult of his being found relief in prayer; and, in a vision full of peace, he saw one of those brethren for a visit from whom he seems hitherto to have yearned in vain, come to him and heal him. This brother was Ananias, a Christian, but a Christian held in respect by all the Jews, and therefore a fit envoy to come among the Pharisaic adherents by whom we cannot but suppose that Saul was still surrounded. It was not without shrinking that Ananias had been led to make this visit. He had heard of Saul's ravages at Jerusalem, and his fierce designs against the brethren at Damascus; nay, even of the letters of authority from the High Priest which were still in his hand. He had heard, too, of what had befallen him on the way, but it had not wholly conquered his not unnatural distrust. A divine injunction aided the charity of one who, as a Christian, felt the duty of believing all things, and hoping all things. The Lord, appearing to him in a dream, told him that the zeal which had burned so fiercely in the cause of Sadducees should henceforth be a fiery angel of the Cross,—that this pitiless persecutor should be a chosen vessel to carry the name of Christ before Gentiles, kings, and the children of Israel. "For I will show him," said the vision, "how much he must suffer for My name."[1] The good Ananias, hesitated no longer. He entered into the house of Judas, and while his very presence seemed to breathe peace, he addressed the sufferer by the dear title of brother, and laying his hands upon the clouded eyes, bade him rise, and see, and be filled with the Holy Ghost. "Be baptised," he added, "and wash away thy sins, calling on the name of the Lord." The words of blessing and trust were to the troubled nerves and aching heart of the sufferer a healing in themselves. Immediately "there fell from his eyes as it had been scales."[2] He rose, and saw, and took food and was strengthened, and received from the hands of his humble brother that sacrament by which he was admitted into the full privileges of the new faith. He became a member of the Church of Christ, the extirpation of which had been for months the most passionate desire and the most active purpose of his life.

Fruitful indeed must have been the conversation which he held with Ananias, and doubtless with other brethren, in the delicious calm that followed this heart-shaking moment of conviction. In those days Ananias must more and more have confirmed him in the high destiny which the voice of revelation had also marked out to himself. What became of his commission; what he did with the

---

[1] " Fortia agere Romanum est; fortia pati Christianum " (Corn. à Lap.).

[2] There is a remarkable parallel in Tob. xi. 13, καὶ ἐλεπίσθη ἀπὸ τῶν κάνθων τῶν ὀφθαλμῶν αὐτοῦ τὰ λευκώματα.

High Priest's letters; how his subordinates demeaned themselves; what alarming reports they took back to Jerusalem; with what eyes he was regarded by the Judaic synagogues of Damascus,—we do not know; but we do know that in those days, whether they were few or many, it became more and more clear to him that "God had chosen him to know His will, and see that Just One, and hear the voice of His mouth, and be His witness unto all men of what he had seen and heard."[1]

And here let me pause to say that it is impossible to exaggerate the importance of St. Paul's conversion as one of the evidences of Christianity. That he should have passed, by one flash of conviction, not only from darkness to light, but from one direction of life to the very opposite, is not only characteristic of the man, but evidential of the power and significance of Christianity. That the same man who, just before, was persecuting Christianity with the most violent hatred, should come all at once to believe in Him whose followers he had been seeking to destroy, and that in this faith he should become a "new creature"—what is this but a victory which Christianity owed to nothing but the spell of its own inherent power? Of all who have been converted to the faith of Christ, there is not one in whose case the Christian principle broke so immediately through everything opposed to it, and asserted so absolutely its triumphant superiority. Henceforth to Paul Christianity was summed up in the one word Christ. And to what does he testify respecting Jesus? To almost every single primarily important fact respecting His Incarnation, Life, Sufferings, Betrayal, Last Supper, Trial, Crucifixion, Resurrection, Ascension, and Heavenly

---

[1] Acts xxii. 14, 15.

Exaltation.[1] We complain that nearly two thousand years have passed away, and that the brightness of historical events is apt to fade, and even their very outline to be obliterated, as they sink into the " dark backward and abysm of time." Well, but are we more keen-sighted, more hostile, more eager to disprove the evidence, than the consummate legalist, the admired rabbi, the commissioner of the Sanhedrin, the leading intellect in the schools—learned as Hillel, patriotic as Judas of Gaulon, burning with zeal for the Law as intense as that of Shammai? He was not separated from the events, as we are, by centuries of time. He was not liable to be blinded, as we are, by the dazzling glamour of a victorious Christendom. He had mingled daily with men who had watched from Bethlehem to Golgotha the life of the Crucified,—not only with His simple-hearted followers, but with His learned and powerful enemies. He had talked with the priests who had consigned Him to the cross; he had put to death the followers who had wept beside His tomb. He had to face the unutterable horror which, to any orthodox Jew, was involved in the thought of a Messiah who "had hung upon a tree." He had heard again and again the proofs which satisfied an Annas and a Gamaliel that Jesus was a deceiver of the people.[2] The events on which the Apostles relied, in proof of His divinity, had taken place in the full blaze of contemporary knowledge. He had not to deal with uncertainties of criticism or assaults on authenticity. He could question, not ancient documents, but living men; he could analyse, not fragmentary records, but existing evidence.

---

[1] See, among other passages, Rom. viii. 3, 11; 1 Tim. iii. 16; Rom. ix. 5; 2 Cor. i. 5; Col. i. 20; 1 Cor. i. 23; ii. 2; v. 7; x. 16; Gal. vi. 19; Eph. ii. 13; Rom. v. 6; vi. 4, 9; viii. 11; xiv. 15; xv. 3; 1 Cor. xv. *passim*; Rom. x. 6; Col. iii. 1; Eph. ii. 6; 1 Tim. iii. 16, &c.

[2] John vii. 12, 47; ix. 16; x. 20.

He had thousands of means close at hand whereby to test the reality or unreality of the Resurrection in which, up to this time, he had so passionately and contemptuously disbelieved. In accepting this half-crushed and wholly execrated faith he had everything in the world to lose— he had nothing conceivable to gain; and yet, in spite of all—overwhelmed by a conviction which he felt to be irresistible—Saul, the Pharisee, became a witness of the Resurrection, a preacher of the Cross.

CHAPTER XI.

THE RETIREMENT OF ST. PAUL.

"Thou shalt have joy in sadness soon,
The pure calm hope be thine,
That brightens like the eastern moon
When day's wild lights decline."—*Keble.*

SAUL was now a "Nazarene," but many a year of thought and training had to elapse before he was prepared for the great mission of his life.

If, indeed, the Acts of the Apostles were our only source of information respecting him, we should have been compelled to suppose that he instantly plunged into the work of teaching. "He was with the disciples in Damascus certain days," says St. Luke; "and immediately in the synagogues he began to preach Jesus, that He is the Son of God;"[1] and he proceeds to narrate the amazement of the Jews, the growing power of Saul's demonstrations, and, after an indefinite period had elapsed, the plot of the Jews against him, and his escape from Damascus.

But St. Luke neither gives, nor professes to give, a complete biography. During the time that he was the companion of the Apostle his details, indeed, are numerous and exact; but if even in this later part of his career he never mentions Titus, or once alludes to the fact that St. Paul wrote a single epistle, we cannot be surprised that his notices of the Apostle's earlier career are fragmentary,

[1] Acts ix. 19, 20.

either because he knew no more, or because, in his brief space, he suppresses all circumstances that did not bear on his immediate purpose.

Accordingly, if we turn to the biographic retrospect in the Epistle to the Galatians, in which St. Paul refers to this period to prove the independence of his apostolate, we find that in the Acts the events of three years have been compressed into as many verses, and that, instead of immediately beginning to preach at Damascus, he immediately retired into Arabia.[1] For " when," he says, " He who separated me from my mother's womb, and called me by His grace, was pleased to reveal His Son in me, that I might preach ` Him among the Gentiles, immediately I did not communicate with flesh and blood, nor went I up to Jerusalem to those who were Apostles before me, but I went away into Arabia, and again I returned to Damascus."

[1] I understand the εὐθέως of Gal. i. 16 as immediately succeeding St. Paul's conversion; the εὐθέως of Acts ix. 20 as immediately succeeding his return to Damascus. The retirement into Arabia must be interpreted as a lacuna either at the middle of Acts ix. 19, or at the end of that verse, or after verse 21. The reasons why I unhesitatingly assume the first of these alternatives are given in the text. There is nothing to be said for supposing with Kuinoel and Olshausen that it was subsequent to the *escape* from Damascus, which seems directly to contradict, or at any rate to render superfluous, the πάλιν of Gal. i. 17. We may be quite sure that St. Paul did not talk promiscuously about this period of his life. No man, even with familiar friends, will make the most solemn crises of his life a subject of common conversation; and Paul was by no means a man to wear his heart upon his sleeve. How many hundreds who read this passage will by a moment's thought become aware that apart from written memoranda, and possibly even with their aid, there is no one living who could write his own biography with any approach to accuracy? What reason is there for supposing that it would have been otherwise with St. Paul? What reason is there for the supposition that he entrusted St. Luke with all the important facts which had occurred to him, when we see that what St. Luke was able to record about him neither portrayed one-fourth of his character nor preserved a memorial of one tithe of his sufferings? And it is to be observed that in Acts xxii. 16, 17, where it had no bearing on his immediate subject, St. Paul himself omits all reference to this retirement into Arabia.

No one, I think, who reads this passage attentively can deny that it gives the impression of an intentional retirement from human intercourse. A multitude of writers have assumed that St. Paul first preached at Damascus, then retired to Arabia, and then returned, with increased zeal and power, to preach in Damascus once more. Not only is St. Paul's own language unfavourable to such a view, but it seems to exclude it. What would all psychological considerations lead us to think likely in the case of one circumstanced as Saul of Tarsus was after his sudden and strange conversion? The *least* likely course —the one which would place him at the greatest distance from all deep and earnest spirits who have passed through a similar crisis—would be for him to have plunged at once into the arena of controversy, and to have passed, without pause or breathing-space, from the position of a leading persecutor into that of a prominent champion. In the case of men of shallow nature, or superficial convictions, such a proceeding is possible; but we cannot imagine it of St. Paul. It is not thus with souls which have been arrested in mid-career by the heart-searching voice of God. Just as an eagle which has been drenched and battered by some fierce storm will alight to plume its ruffled wings, so when a great soul has "passed through fire and through water" it needs some safe and quiet place in which to rest. The lifelong convictions of any man may be reversed in an instant, and that sudden reversion often causes a marvellous change; but it is never in an instant that the whole *nature* and *character* of a man are transformed from what they were before. It is difficult to conceive of any change more total, any rift of difference more deep, than that which separated Saul the persecutor from Paul the Apostle; and we are sure that— like Moses, like Elijah, like our Lord Himself, like almost

every great soul in ancient or modern times to whom has
been entrusted the task of swaying the destinies by mould-
ing the convictions of mankind—like Sakya Mouni, like
Mahomet in the cave of Hira, like St. Francis of Assisi
in his sickness, like Luther in the monastery of Erfurdt—
he would need a quiet period in which to elaborate his
thoughts, to still the tumult of his emotions, to com-
mune in secrecy and in silence with his own soul. It
was necessary for him to understand the Scriptures; to
co-ordinate his old with his new beliefs. It is hardly
too much to say that if Saul—ignorant as yet of many
essential truths of Christianity, alien as yet from the experience of its deepest power—had begun at once to argue
with and to preach to others, he could hardly have done the
work he did. To suppose that the truths of which afterwards he became the appointed teacher were all revealed
to him as by one flash of light in all their fulness, is to
suppose that which is alien to God's dealings with the
human soul, and which utterly contradicts the phenomena
of that long series of Epistles in which we watch the
progress of his thoughts. Even on grounds of historic
probability, it seems unlikely that Saul should at once
have been able to substitute a propaganda for an inquisition. Under such circumstances it would have been
difficult for the brethren to trust, and still more difficult
for the Jews to tolerate him. The latter would have
treated him as a shameless renegade,[1] the former would
have mistrusted him as a secret spy.

We might, perhaps, have expected that Saul would
have stayed quietly among the Christians at Damascus,
mingling unobtrusively in their meetings, listening to
them, learning of them, taking at their love-feasts the

---

[1] They would have called him a משומד, one who had abandoned his religious
convictions.

humblest place. We can hardly suppose that he cherished, in these first days of his Christian career, the developed purpose of preaching an independent Gospel. Assailed, as he subsequently was, on all sides, but thwarted most of all by the espionage of false brethren, and the calumnies of those who desired to throw doubt on his inspired authority, it was indeed a providential circumstance that the events which followed his conversion were such as to separate him as far as possible from the appearance of discipleship to human instructors. As a Pharisee he had sat at the feet of Gamaliel; as a Christian he called no man his master. He asserts, with reiterated earnestness, that his teaching as well as his authority, "his Gospel" no less than his Apostleship, had been received immediately from God. Indeed, the main object of that intensely interesting and characteristic narrative which occupies the two first chapters of the Epistle to the Galatians is to establish the declaration which he felt it necessary to make so strongly, that "the Gospel preached by him was not a human gospel, and that he did not even receive it from any human being, nor was he taught it, but through revelation of Jesus Christ."[1] Had he not been able to assure his converts of this—had he not been able to appeal to visions and revelations of the Lord—he might have furnished another instance of one whose opinions have been crushed and silenced by the empty authority of names. It was from no personal feeling of emulation—a feeling of which a soul so passionately in earnest as his is profoundly incapable—but it was from the duty of ensuring attention to the truths he preached that he felt it to be so necessary to convince the churches which he had founded how deep would be their folly if they allowed

[1] Gal. i. 11, 12.

O

themselves to be seduced from the liberty of his Gospel
by the retrograde mission of the evangelists of bondage.
It was indispensable for the dissemination of the truth
that he should be listened to as an Apostle "neither of
man, nor by any man, but by Jesus Christ, and God, who
raised Him from the dead." Had his Apostleship
emanated from ($\dot{a}\pi\dot{o}$) the Twelve, or been conferred on
him by the consecrating act of ($\delta\iota\dot{a}$) any one of them,[1] then
they might be supposed to have a certain superior com-
mission, a certain coercive power. If, as far as he was
concerned, they had no such power, it was because he
had received his commission directly from his Lord. And
to this independence of knowledge he often refers. He
tells the Thessalonians, "by the Word of the Lord,"[2]
that those who were still alive at the Second Advent
should not be beforehand with—should gain no advantage
or priority over—those that slept. He tells the Ephesians[3] that it was by revelation that God "made known
to him the mystery which in other generations was not
made known to the sons of men—namely, that the Gentiles are co-heirs and co-members and co-partakers[4] of the
promise in Christ Jesus, through the Gospel of which he
became a minister according to the gift of the grace of
God, which was given him according to the mighty working of His power." He tells the Colossians[5] that he
became a minister of the Church "in accordance with the
stewardship of God given to him for them, that he might
fully preach the Word of God, the mystery hidden from the
ages and the generations." From these and from other
passages it seems clear that what St. Paul meant to represent as special subjects of the revelation which he had

---

[1] Gal. i. 1, οὐκ ἀπ' ἀνθρώπων οὐδὲ δι' ἀνθρώπου.

[2] 1 Thess. iv. 15, ἐν λόγῳ Κυρίου.   [3] Eph. iii. 3—6.

[4] συγκληρονόμα καὶ σύσσωμα καὶ συμμέτοχα   [5] Col. i. 25.

received were partly distinct views of what rule ought to be followed by Christians in special instances, partly great facts about the resurrection,[1] partly the direct vision of a Saviour not only risen from the dead, but exalted at the right hand of God; but especially the central and peculiar fact of his teaching "the mystery of Christ"—the truth once secret, but now revealed—the deliverance which He had wrought, the justification by faith which He had rendered possible, and, most of all, the free offer of this great salvation to the Gentiles, without the necessity of their incurring the yoke of bondage, which even the Jew had found to be heavier than he could bear.[2]

It can hardly, therefore, be doubted that after his recovery from the shock of conviction with which his soul must long have continued to tremble, Paul only spent a few quiet days with Ananias, and any other brethren who would hold out to him the right hand of friendship. He might talk with them of the life which Jesus had lived on earth. He might hear from them those reminiscences of the

> "Sinless years
> Which breathed beneath the Syrian blue,"

of which the most precious were afterwards recorded by the four Evangelists. In listening to these he would have been fed with "the spiritual guileless milk."[3] Nor can we doubt that in those days more than ever he would refrain his soul and keep it low—that his soul was even as a weaned child. But of the mystery which he was afterwards to preach—of that which emphatically he called "his Gospel"[4]—neither Ananias (who was himself

---

[1] See 1 Cor. xv. 22; 1 Thess. iv. 15.

[2] See Col. iv. 3; Eph. iii. 3; vi. 19; Rom. xvi. 25.

[3] 1 Pet. ii. 2, τὸ λογικὸν ἄδολον γάλα.

[4] 1 Cor. ix. 17; Gal. ii. 2, 7; 2 Thess. ii. 14; 2 Tim. ii. 8.

o 2

a rigid Jew), nor any of the disciples, could tell him
anything. That was taught him by God alone. It
came to him by the illuminating power of the Spirit
of Christ, in revelations which accompanied each step
in that Divine process of education which constituted
his life.

But he could not in any case have stayed long in
Damascus. His position there was for the present untenable. Alike the terror with which his arrival must
have been expected by the brethren, and the expectation
which it had aroused among the Jews, would make him
the centre of hatred and suspicion, of rumour and curiosity.
He may even have been in danger of arrest by the very
subordinates to whom his sudden change of purpose must
have seemed to delegate his commission. But a stronger
motive for retirement than all this would be the yearning
for solitude; the intense desire, and even the overpowering
necessity, to be for a time alone with God. He was a
stricken deer, and was impelled as by a strong instinct to
leave the herd. In solitude a man may trace to their
hidden source the fatal errors of the past; he may pray
for that light from heaven—no longer flaming with more
than noonday fierceness, but shining quietly in dark places
—which shall enable him to understand the many mysteries
of life; he may wait the healing of his deep wounds by
the same tender hand that in mercy has inflicted them;
he may

> " Sit on the desert stone
> Like Elijah at Horeb's cave alone;
> And a gentle voice comes through the wild,
> Like a father consoling his fretful child,
> 'hat banishes bitterness, wrath, and fear,
> Saying, ' MAN IS DISTANT, BUT GOD IS NEAR.'"

And so Saul went to Arabia—a word which must, I think,

be understood in its popular and primary sense to mean the Sinaitic peninsula.[1]

He who had been a persecutor in honour of Moses, would henceforth be himself represented as a renegade from Moses. The most zealous of the living servants of Mosaism was to be the man who should prove most convincingly that Mosaism was to vanish away. Was it not natural, then, that he should long to visit the holy ground where the bush had glowed in unconsuming fire, and the granite crags had trembled at the voice which uttered the fiery law? Would the shadow of good things look so much of a shadow if he visited the very spot where the great Lawgiver and the great Prophet had held high communings with God? Could he indeed be sure that he had come unto the Mount Sion, and unto the city of the living God, the heavenly Jerusalem, and to Jesus the Mediator of a new covenant, until he had visited the mount that might be touched and that burned with fire, where amid blackness, and darkness, and tempest, and the sound of a trumpet and the voice of words, Moses himself had exceedingly feared and quaked?

How long he stayed, we do not know. It has usually been assumed that his stay was brief; to me it seems far more probable that it occupied no small portion of those "three years"[2] which he tells us elapsed before he visited Jerusalem. Few have doubted that those "three years" are to be dated from his conversion. It seems clear that after his conversion he stayed but a few days (ἡμέραι τινές) with the disciples; that then—at the earliest practicable moment—he retired into Arabia; that after his return he began to preach, and that this ministry in Damascus was

---

[1] See Excursus IX., "Saul in Arabia."   [2] Gal. i. 18.

interrupted after a certain period (ἡμέραι ἱκαναί) by the conspiracy of the Jews. The latter expression is translated "many days" in the Acts; but though the continuance of his preaching may have occupied days which in comparison with his first brief stay might have been called "many," the phrase itself is so vague that it might be used of almost any period from a fortnight to three years.[1] As to the general correctness of this conclusion I can feel no doubt; the only point which must always remain dubious is whether the phrase "three years" means three complete years, or whether it means one full year, and a part, however short, of two other years. From the chronology of St. Paul's life we can attain no certainty on this point, though such lights as we have are slightly in favour of the longer rather than of the shorter period.

Very much depends upon the question whether physical infirmity, and prostration of health, were in part the cause of this retirement and inactivity. And here again we are on uncertain ground, because this at once opens the often discussed problem as to the nature of the affliction to which St. Paul so pathetically alludes as his "stake in the flesh." I am led to touch upon that question here, because I believe that this dreadful affliction, whatever it may have been, had its origin at this very time.[2] The melancholy through which, like a fire at midnight, his enthusiasm burns its way—the deep despondency which sounds like an undertone even amid the bursts of exultation which triumph over it, seem

---

[1] It actually is used of three years in 1 Kings ii. 38.

[2] There is nothing to exclude this in the ἐδόθη μοι of 2 Cor. xii. 7. The affliction might not have arrived at its *full intensity* till that period, which was some years after his conversion, about A.D. 43, when St. Paul was at Antioch or Jerusalem or Tarsus.

to me to have been in no small measure due to this. It gave to St. Paul that painful self-consciousness which is in itself a daily trial to any man who, in spite of an innate love for retirement, is thrust against his will into publicity and conflict. It seems to break the wings of his spirit, so that sometimes he drops as it were quite suddenly to the earth, checked and beaten down in the very midst of his loftiest and strongest flights.

No one can even cursorily read St. Paul's Epistles without observing that he was aware of something in his aspect or his personality which distressed him with an agony of humiliation—something which seems to force him, against every natural instinct of his disposition, into language which sounds to himself like a boastfulness which was abhorrent to him, but which he finds to be more necessary to himself than to other men. It is as though he felt that his appearance was against him. Whenever he has ceased to be carried away by the current of some powerful argument, whenever his sorrow at the insidious encroachment of errors against which he had flung the whole force of his character has spent itself in words of immeasurable indignation—whenever he drops the high language of apostolical authority and inspired conviction— we hear a sort of wailing, pleading, appealing tone in his personal addresses to his converts, which would be almost impossible in one whose pride of personal manhood had not been abashed by some external defects, to which he might indeed appeal as marks at once of the service and the protection of his Saviour, but which made him less able to cope face to face with the insults of opponents or the ingratitude of friends. His language leaves on us the impression of one who was acutely sensitive, and whose sensitiveness of temperament has been aggravated by a meanness of presence which is indeed forgotten by the friends who know him, but which raises in strangers a prejudice not always overcome Many, indeed, of the brethren in the little churches. which he founded, had so "grappled him to their souls with hooks of steel," that he could speak in letter after letter of their abounding love and tenderness and gratitude towards him[1]— that he can call them "my little children "—that he can assume their intense desire to see him, and can grant that desire as an express favour to *them;*[2] and that he is even forced to soothe those jealousies of affection which were caused by his acceptance of aid from one church which he would not accept from others. But he is also well aware that he is hated with a perfect virulence of hatred, and (which is much more wounding to such a spirit) that with this hatred there is a large mixture of unjust contempt. From this contempt even of the contemptible, from this hatred even of the hateful he could not but shrink, though he knew that it is often the penalty with which the world rewards service, and the tribute which virtue receives from vice.

It is this which explains the whole style and character of his Epistles.[3] The charges which his enemies made against him have their foundation in facts about his method and address, which made those charges all the more dangerous and the more stinging by giving them a certain plausibility. They were, in fact, yet another instance of those half-truths which are the worst of lies. Thus—adopting the taunts of his adversaries, as he often does—he says that he is in presence " humble" among them,[4] and "rude in speech,"[5] and he quotes their own reproach that " his bodily presence was weak, and his

---

[1] Phil. *passim.*   [2] 2 Cor. i. 15, 23.
[3] See Excursus X., "The Style of St. Paul as illustrative of his Character."
[4] 2 Cor. x. 1, 2.   [5] 2 Cor. xi. 6, ἰδιώτης ἐν λόγῳ.

speech contemptible."[1] Being confessedly one who strove
for peace and unity, who endeavoured to meet all men
half-way, who was ready to be all things to all men
if by any means he might save some, he has more than
once to vindicate his character from those charges of insincerity, craftiness, dishonesty, guile, man-pleasing and
flattery,[2] which are, perhaps, summed up in the general
depreciation which he so indignantly rebuts that "he
walked according to the flesh,"[3] or in other words that his
motives were not spiritual, but low and selfish. He has,
too, to defend himself from the insinuation that his self-
abasements had been needless and excessive;[4] that even
his apparent self-denials had only been assumed as a cloak
for ulterior views;[5] and that his intercourse was so
marked by levity of purpose, that there was no trusting to his promises.[6] Now how came St. Paul to be
made the butt for such calumnies as these? Chiefly, no
doubt, because he was, most sorely against his will, the
leader of a party, and because there are in all ages
souls which delight in lies—men "whose throat is an
open sepulchre, and the poison of asps is under their lips;"
but partly, also, because he regarded tact, concession,
conciliatoriness, as Divine weapons which God had permitted him to use against powerful obstacles; and
partly because it was easy to satirise and misrepresent a
depression of spirits, a humility of demeanour, which were
either the direct results of some bodily affliction, or which
the consciousness of this affliction had rendered habitual.
We feel at once that this would be natural to the bowed
and weak figure which Albrecht Dürer has represented;
but that it would be impossible to the imposing orator

---

[1] 2 Cor. x. 10.
[2] 2 Cor. ii. 17, iv. 2; 1 Thess. ii. 3—5.
[3] 2 Cor. x. 2.
[4] 2 Cor. xi. 7.
[5] 2 Cor. xii. 16.
[6] 2 Cor. i. 17.

whom Raphael has placed on the steps of the Areopagus.[1]

And to this he constantly refers. There is hardly a
letter in which he does not allude to his mental trials, his
physical sufferings, his persecutions, his infirmities. He
tells the Corinthians that his intercourse with them had
been characterised by physical weakness, fear, and much
trembling.[2] He reminds the Galatians that he had
preached among them in consequence of an attack of
severe sickness.[3] He speaks of the inexorable burden of
life, and its unceasing moan.[4] The trouble, the perplexity,
the persecution, the prostrations which were invariable
conditions of his life, seem to him like a perpetual carrying about with him in his body of the mortification—
the putting to death—of Christ;[5] a perpetual betrayal
to death for Christ's sake—a perpetual exhibition of the
energy of death in his outward life.[6] He died daily, he
was in deaths oft;[7] he was being killed all the day long.[8]

And this, too—as well as the fact that he seems to
write in Greek and think in Syriac—is the key to the peculiarities of St. Paul's language. The feeling that he was
inadequate for the mighty task which God had specially
entrusted to him; the dread lest his personal insignificance
should lead any of his hearers at once to reject a doctrine
announced by a weak, suffering, distressed, overburdened
man, who, though an ambassador of Christ, bore in his
own aspect so few of the credentials of an embassy; the
knowledge that the fiery spirit which "o'erinformed its
tenement of clay" was held, like the light of Gideon's

---

[1] Hausrath, p. 51.   [2] 1 Cor. ii. 3.   [3] Gal. iv. 13.
[4] 2 Cor. v. 4, οἱ ὄντες ἐν τῷ σκήνει στενάζομεν βαρούμενοι.
[5] 2 Cor. iv. 8—10, θλιβόμενοι . . . ἀπορούμενοι . . . διωκόμενοι . . . κατα-
βαλλόμενοι . . . πάντοτε τὴν νέκρωσιν τοῦ Ἰησοῦ ἐν τῷ σώματι περιφέροντες.
[6] Id. 11, ἀεὶ γὰρ ἡμεῖς οἱ ζῶντες, εἰς θάνατον παραδιδόμεθα.
[7] 2 Cor. xi. 23; 1 Cor. xv. 31.   [8] Rom. viii. 36.

pitchers, in a fragile and earthen vessel,[1] seems to be so constantly and so oppressively present with him, as to make all words too weak for the weight of meaning they have to bear. Hence his language, in many passages, bears the traces of almost morbid excitability in its passionate alternations of humility with assertions of the real greatness of his labours,[2] and of scorn and indignation against fickle weaklings and intriguing calumniators with an intense and yearning love.[3] Sometimes his heart beats with such quick emotion, his thoughts rush with such confused impetuosity, that in anakoluthon after anakoluthon, and parenthesis after parenthesis, the whole meaning becomes uncertain.[4] His feeling is so intense that his very words catch a life of their own—they become "living creatures with hands and feet."[5] Sometimes he is almost contemptuous in his assertion of the rectitude which makes him indifferent to vulgar criticism,[6] and keenly bitter in the sarcasm of his self-depreciation.[7] In one or two instances an enemy might almost apply the word "brutal" to the language in which he ridicules, or denounces, or unmasks the impugners of his gospel;[8] in one or two passages he speaks with a tinge of irony, almost of irritation, about those "accounted to be pillars"—the "out-and-out Apostles," who even if they were Apostles ten times over added nothing to him:[9] —but the storm of passion dies away in a moment; he is sorry even for the most necessary and justly-deserved

[1] 2 Cor. iv. 7.   [2] 1 Cor. xv. 10.   [3] Gal. and 2 Cor. *passim*.
[4] Gal. iv. 12.   [5] Gal. iv. 14; 1 Cor. iv. 13; Phil. iii. 8.
[6] 1 Cor. iv. 3.   [7] 1 Cor. iv. 10; x. 15; 2 Cor. xi. 16—19; xii. 11.
[8] Gal. iii. 1; iv. 17 (in the Greek).
[9] Gal. ii. 6, τῶν δοκούντων εἶναί τι,—ὁποῖοί ποτε ἦσαν οὐδέν μοι διαφέρει; 9, οἱ δοκοῦντες στύλοι εἶναι; 11, κατεγνωσμένος ἦν. 1 Cor. xv. 9; 2 Cor. xi. 5 τῶν ὑπερλίαν ἀποστόλων. 2 Cor. xii. 11, οὐδὲν ὑστέρησα τῶν ὑπερλίαν ἀποστόλων εἰ καὶ οὐδέν εἰμι.

severity, and all ends in expressions of tenderness and, as it were, with a burst of tears.[1]

Now it is true that we recognise in Saul of Tarsus the restlessness, the vehemence, the impetuous eagerness which we see in Paul the Apostle; but it is hard to imagine in Saul of Tarsus the nervous shrinking, the tremulous sensibility, the profound distrust of his own gifts and powers apart from Divine grace, which are so repeatedly manifest in the language of Paul, the fettered captive of Jesus Christ. It is hard to imagine that such a man as the Apostle became could ever have been the furious inquisitor, the intruder even into the sacred retirement of peaceful homes, the eager candidate for power to suppress a heresy even in distant cities, which Saul was before the vision on the way to Damascus. It is a matter of common experience that some physical humiliation, especially if it take the form of terrible disfigurement, often acts in this very way upon human character.[2] It makes the bold shrink; it makes the arrogant humble; it makes the self-confident timid; it makes those who once loved publicity long to hide them-

---

[1] Gal. iv. 19; 2 Cor. ii. 4; Rom. ix. 1—3. As bearing on this subject, every one will read with interest the verses of Dr. Newman—

> "I dreamed that with a passionate complaint
> I wished me born amid God's deeds of might,
> And envied those who had the presence bright
> Of gifted prophet or strong-hearted saint,
> Whom my heart loves, and fancy strives to paint.
> I turned, when straight a stranger met my sight,
> Came as my guest, and did awhile unite
> His lot with mine, and lived without restraint.
> Courteous he was, and grave ; *so meek in mien,*
> *It seemed untrue, or told a purpose weak ;*
> *Yet, in the mood, could he with aptness speak*
> *Or with stern force, or show of feeling keen,*
> *Marking deep craft, methought, and hidden pride ;*
> Then came a voice, ' St. Paul is at thy side !'"

[2] The ἰσόη of 2 Cor. xii. 7, shows that the "stake in the flesh" was nothing congenital.

selves from the crowd; it turns every thought of the heart from trust in self to humblest submission to the will of God. Even a dangerous illness is sometimes sufficient to produce results like these; but when the illness leaves its physical marks for life upon the frame, its effects are intensified; it changes a mirthful reveller, like Francis of Assisi, into a squalid ascetic; a favourite of society, like Francis Xavier, into a toilsome missionary; a gay soldier, like Ignatius Loyola, into a rigid devotee.

What was the nature of this stake in the flesh, we shall examine fully in a separate essay;[1] but that, whatever it may have been, it came to St. Paul as a direct consequence of visions and revelations, and as a direct counteraction to the inflation and self-importance which such exceptional insight might otherwise have caused to such a character as his, he has himself informed us. We are, therefore, naturally led to suppose that the *first* impalement of his health by this wounding splinter accompanied, or resulted from, that greatest of all his revelations, the appearance to him of the risen Christ as he was travelling at noonday nigh unto Damascus. If so, we see yet another reason for a retirement from all exertion and publicity, which was as necessary for his body as for his soul.

[1] See Excursus X., "St. Paul's 'Stake in the Flesh.'"

CHAPTER XII

THE BEGINNING OF A LONG MARTYRDOM.

"Be bold as a leopard, swift as an eagle, bounding as a stag, brave as a lion, to do the will of thy Father which is in heaven."—PESACHIM, f. 112, 2.

CALMED by retirement, confirmed, it may be, by fresh revelations of the will of God, clearer in his conceptions of truth and duty, Saul returned to Damascus. We need look for no further motives of his return than such as rose from the conviction that he was now sufficiently prepared to do the work to which Christ had called him.

He did not at once begin his mission to the Gentiles. "To the Jew first" was the understood rule of the Apostolic teaching,[1] and had been involved in the directions given by Christ Himself.[2] Moreover, the Gentiles were so unfamiliar with the institution of preaching, their whole idea of worship was so alien from every form of doctrinal or moral exhortation, that to begin by preaching to them was almost impossible. It was through the Jews that the Gentiles were most easily reached. The proselytes, numerous in every city, were specially numerous at Damascus, and by their agency it was certain that every truth propounded in the Jewish synagogue would, even if only by the agency of female proselytes, be rapidly communicated to the Gentile agora.

It was, therefore, to the synagogues that Saul natu-

[1] Rom. i. 16; Acts iii. 26; xiii. 38, 39, 46; John iv. 22.
[2] Luke xxiv. 47; cf. Isa. ii. 2, 3; xlix. 6; Mic. iv. 2.

rally resorted, and there that he first began to deliver his
message. Since the Christians were still in communion
with the synagogue and the Temple—since their leader,
Ananias, was so devout according to the law as to have
won the willing testimony of all the Jews who lived in
Damascus[1]—no obstacle would be placed in the way of the
youthful Rabbi; and as he had been a scholar in the most
eminent of Jewish schools, his earliest appearances on the
arena of controversy would be awaited with attention and
curiosity. We have no reason to suppose that the animosity
against the Nazarenes, which Saul himself had kept alive
in Jerusalem, had as yet penetrated to Damascus. News is
slow to travel in Eastern countries, and those instantaneous
waves of opinion which flood our modern civilisation
were unknown to ancient times. In the capital of Syria,
Jews and Christians were still living together in mutual
toleration, if not in mutual esteem. They had been
thus living in Jerusalem until the spark of hatred had
been struck out by the collision of the Hellenists of the
liberal with those of the narrow school — the Christian
Hellenists of the *Hagadóth* with the Jewish Hellenists of
the *Halacha*. To Saul, if not solely, yet in great measure,
this collision had been due; and Saul had been on his way
to stir up the same wrath and strife in Damascus, when
he had been resistlessly arrested[2] on his unhallowed mission
by the vision and the reproach of his ascended Lord.

But the authority, and the letters, had been entrusted
to him alone, and none but a few hot zealots really desired
that pious and respectable persons like Ananias—children
of Abraham, servants of Moses—should be dragged, with
a halter round their necks, from peaceful homes, scourged
by the people with whom they had lived without any

---

[1] Acts xxii. 12.   [2] Phil. iii. 12, κατελήφθην ὑπὸ τοῦ Χριστοῦ Ἰησοῦ.

serious disagreement, and haled to Jerusalem by fanatics who would do their best to procure against them the fatal vote which might consign them to the revolting horrors of an almost obsolete execution.

So that each Ruler of a Synagogue over whom Saul might have been domineering with all the pride of superior learning, and all the intemperance of flaming zeal, might be glad enough to see and hear a man who could no longer hold in terror over him the commission of the Sanhedrin, and who had now rendered himself liable to the very penalties which, not long before, he had been so eager to inflict.

And had Saul proved to be but an ordinary disputant, the placidity of Jewish self-esteem would not have been disturbed, nor would he have ruffled the sluggish stream of legal self-satisfaction. He did not speak of circumcision as superfluous ; he said nothing about the evanescence of the Temple service, or the substitution for it of a more spiritual worship. He did not breathe a word about turning to the Gentiles. The subject of his preaching was that "Jesus is the Son of God."[1] At first this preaching excited no special indignation. The worshippers in the synagogue only felt a keen astonishment[2] that this was the man who had ravaged in Jerusalem those who called on "this name,"[3] and who had come to Damascus for the express purpose of leading them bound to the High Priest. But when once self-love is seriously wounded, toleration rarely survives. This was the case with the Jews of Damascus. They very soon discovered that it was no mere Ananias with whom they had to deal. It was, throughout life, Paul's unhappy fate to kindle the most virulent animosities, because, though conciliatory and courteous by temperament, he yet carried into

[1] Ἰησοῦν, not Χριστὸν, is here the true reading (א, A, B, C, E).
[2] Acts ix. 21, ἐξίσταντο.   [3] V. supra, p. 108.

his arguments that intensity and forthrightness which awaken dormant opposition. A languid controversialist will always meet with a languid tolerance. But any controversialist whose honest belief in his own doctrines makes him terribly in earnest, may count on a life embittered by the anger of those on whom he has forced the disagreeable task of re-considering their own assumptions. No one likes to be suddenly awakened. The Jews were indignant with one who disturbed the deep slumber of decided opinions. Their accredited teachers did not like to be deposed from the papacy of infallible ignorance. They began at Damascus to feel towards Saul that fierce detestation which dogged him thenceforward to the last day of his life. Out of their own Scriptures, by their own methods of exegesis, in their own style of dialectics, by the interpretation of prophecies of which they did not dispute the validity, he simply confounded them. He could now apply the very same principles which in the mouth of Stephen he had found it impossible to resist. The result was an unanswerable proof that the last *æon* of God's earthly dispensations had now dawned, that old things had passed away, and all things had become new.

If arguments are such as cannot be refuted, and yet if those who hear them will not yield to them, they inevitably excite a bitter rage. It was so with the Jews. Some time had now elapsed since Saul's return from Arabia,[1] and they saw no immediate chance of getting rid of this dangerous intruder. They therefore took refuge in what St. Chrysostom calls "the syllogism of violence." They might at least plead the excuse—and how bitter was the remorse which such a plea would excite in Saul's own conscience—that they were only treating him

---

[1] Acts ix. 23, ἡμέραι ἱκαναί.

P

in the way in which he himself had treated all who held
the same opinions. Even-handed justice was thus com-
mending to his own lips the ingredients of that poisoned
chalice of intolerance which he had forced on others
It is a far from improbable conjecture that it was at this
early period that the Apostle endured one, and perhaps
more than one, of those five Jewish scourgings which he
tells the Corinthians that he had suffered at the hands of
the Jews. For it is hardly likely that they would resort
at once to the strongest measures, and the scourgings
might be taken as a reminder that worse was yet to
come. Indeed, there are few more striking proofs of the
severity of that life which the Apostle so cheerfully—
nay, even so joyfully—endured, than the fact that in his
actual biography not one of these five inflictions, terrible
as we know that they must have been, is so much as
mentioned, and that in his Epistles they are only recorded,
among trials yet more insupportable, in a passing and
casual allusion.[1]

But we know from the example of the Apostles at
Jerusalem that no such pain or danger would have put a
stop to his ministry. Like them, he would have seen an
honour in such disgrace. At last, exasperated beyond all
endurance at one whom they hated as a renegade, and
whom they could not even enjoy the luxury of despising
as a heretic, they made a secret plot to kill him.[2] The
conspiracy was made known to Saul, and he was on his
guard against it. The Jews then took stronger and more
open measures. They watched the gates night and day to
prevent the possibility of his escape. In this they were
assisted by the Ethnarch who supplied them with the

---

[1] See Excursus XI., " On Jewish Scourgings."

[2] These secret plots were fearfully rife in these days of the Sicarii (Jos.
Antt. xx. 8, § 5).

means of doing it. This Ethnarch was either the Arab
viceroy of Hareth, or the chief official of the Jews themselves,[1] who well might possess this authority under a
friendly prince.

There was thus an imminent danger that Saul would
be cut off at the very beginning of his career. But this
was not to be. The disciples "took Saul"[2]—another of
the expressions which would tend to show that he was exceptionally in need of help—and putting him in a large
rope basket,[3] let him down through the window of a house
which abutted on the wall.[4] It may be that they chose
a favourable moment when the patrol had passed, and had
not yet turned round again. At any rate, the escape was
full of ignominy; and it may have been this humiliation,
or else the fact of its being among the earliest perils which
he had undergone, that fixed it so indelibly on the memory
of St. Paul. Nearly twenty years afterwards he mentions
it to the Corinthians with special emphasis, after agonies
and hair-breadth escapes which to us would have seemed
far more formidable.[5]

Here, then, closed in shame and danger the first page
in this chequered and sad career. How he made his way
to Jerusalem must be left to conjecture. Doubtless, as
he stole through the dark night alone—above all, as he
passed the very spot where Christ had taken hold of him,

[1] 2 Cor. xi. 32, ὁ ἐθνάρχης ἐφρούρει τὴν πόλιν; Acts ix. 24, οἱ Ἰουδαῖοι παρετήρουν
τὰς πύλας. Ethnarch, as well as Alabarch, was a title of Jewish governors in
heathen cities.

[2] Acts ix. 25. The reading οἱ μαθηταὶ αὐτοῦ, though well attested, can
hardly be correct.

[3] On σπυρίς see my Life of Christ, i. 403, 480. In 2 Cor. xi. 33 it is called
σαργάνη, which is defined by Hesych. as πλέγμα τι ἐκ σχοινίου.

[4] Such windows are still to be seen at Damascus. For similar escapes, see
Josh. ii. 15; 1 Sam. xix. 12.

[5] 2 Cor. xi. 32. St. Paul's conversion was about A.D. 37. The Second
Epistle to the Corinthians was written A.D. 57, or early in A.D. 58.

P 2

and into one moment of his life had been crowded a
whole eternity—his heart would be full of thoughts too
deep for words. It has been supposed, from the expression
of which he makes use in his speech to Agrippa, that he
may have preached in many synagogues on the days which
were occupied on his journey to Jerusalem.[1] But this
seems inconsistent with his own statement that he was
"unknown by face to the churches of Judæa which were
in Christ."[2]   It is not, however, unlikely that he may
sometimes have availed himself of the guest-chambers
which were attached to Jewish synagogues; and if such
was the case, he might have taught the first truths of the
Gospel to the Jews without being thrown into close contact
with Christian communities.

In any case, his journey could not have been much
prolonged, for he tells us that it was his express object to
visit Peter, whose recognition must have been invaluable
to him, apart from the help and insight which he could
not but derive from conversing with one who had long
lived in such intimate friendship with the Lord.

[1] Acts xxvi. 20.   [2] Gal. i. 22.

CHAPTER XIII.

SAUL'S RECEPTION AT JERUSALEM.

" Cogitemus ipsum Paulum, licet caelesti voce prostratum et instructum, ad hominem tamen missum esse, ut sacramenta perciperet."—Aug. *De Doctr. Christ., Prol.*

To re-visit Jerusalem must have cost the future Apostle no slight effort. How deep must have been his remorse as he neared the spot where he had seen the corpse of Stephen lying crushed under the stones! With what awful interest must he now have looked on the scene of the Crucifixion, and the spot where He who was now risen and glorified had lain in the garden-tomb! How dreadful must have been the revulsion of feeling which rose from the utter change of his present relations towards the priests whose belief he had abandoned, and the Christians whose Gospel he had embraced! He had left Jerusalem a Rabbi, a Pharisee, a fanatic defender of the Oral Law; he was entering it as one who utterly distrusted the value of legal righteousness, who wholly despised the beggarly elements of tradition. The proud man had become unspeakably humble; the savage persecutor unspeakably tender; the self-satisfied Rabbi had abandoned in one moment his pride of nationality, his exclusive scorn, his Pharisaic pre-eminence, to take in exchange for them the beatitude of unjust persecution, and to become the suffering preacher of an execrated faith. What had he to expect from Theophilus, whose letters he had perhaps destroyed? from the Sanhedrists, whose zeal he had fired? from his old fellow-

pupils in the lecture-room of Gamaliel, who had seen in
Saul of Tarsus one who in learning was the glory of the
school of Hillel, and in zeal the rival of the school of
Shammai? How would he be treated by these friends of
his youth, by these teachers and companions of his life,
now that proclaiming his system, his learning, his convictions, his whole life—and therefore theirs no less than his
—to have been irremediably wrong, he had become an
open adherent of the little Church which he once ravaged
and destroyed?

But amid the natural shrinking with which he could
not but anticipate an encounter so full of trial, he would
doubtless console himself with the thought that he would
find a brother's welcome among those sweet and gentle
spirits whose faith he had witnessed, whose love for each
other he had envied while he hated. How exquisite
would be the pleasure of sharing that peace which he had
tried to shatter; of urging on others those arguments
which had been bringing conviction to his own mind even
while he was most passionately resisting them; of hearing
again and again from holy and gentle lips the words
of Him whom he had once blasphemed! Saul might
well have thought that the love, the nobleness, the
enthusiasm of his new brethren would more than com-
pensate for the influence and admiration which he had
voluntarily forfeited; and that to pluck with them the fair
fruit of the Spirit—love, joy, peace, long-suffering, gentleness, goodness, faith, meekness, temperance—would be a
bliss for which he might cheerfully abandon the whole
world beside. No wonder that "he assayed to join himself
to the disciples."[1] His knowledge of human nature might
indeed have warned him that "confidence is a plant of slow

---

[1] Acts ix. 26.

growth"—that such a reception as he yearned for was hardly possible. It may be that he counted too much on the change wrought in human dispositions by the grace of God. The old Adam is oftentimes too strong for young Melancthon.

For, alas! a new trial awaited him. Peter, indeed, whom he had expressly come to see, at once received him with the large generosity of that impulsive heart, and being a married man, offered him hospitality without grudging.[1] But at first that was all. It speaks no little for the greatness and goodness of Peter—it is quite in accordance with that natural nobleness which we should expect to find in one whom Jesus Himself had loved and blessed—that he was the earliest among the brethren to rise above the influence of suspicion. He was at this time the leader of the Church in Jerusalem. As such he had not been among those who fled before the storm. He must have known that it was at the feet of this young Pharisee that the garments of Stephen's murderers had been laid. He must have feared him, perhaps even have hidden himself from him, when he forced his way into Christian homes. Nay, more, the heart of Peter must have sorely ached when he saw his little congregation slain, scattered, destroyed, and the cœnobitic community, the faith of which had been so bright, the enthusiasm so contagious, the common love so tender and so pure, rudely broken up by the pitiless persecution of a Pupil of the Schools. Yet, with the unquestioning trustfulness of a sunny nature—with that spiritual insight into character by which a Divine charity not only perceives real worth, but even creates worthiness where it did not before exist—Peter opens his door to one whom a meaner man might well have excluded as still too possibly a wolf amid the fold.

[1] Gal. i. 18.

But of the other leaders of the Church—if there were
any at that time in Jerusalem—not one came near the new
convert, not one so much as spoke to him. He was met
on every side by cold, distrustful looks. At one stroke he
had lost all his old friends; it seemed to be too likely that
he would gain no new ones in their place. The brethren
regarded him with terror and mistrust; they did not
believe that he was a disciple at all.[1] The *facts* which
accompanied his alleged conversion they may indeed have
heard of; but they had occurred three years before. The
news of his recent preaching and recent peril in Damascus
was not likely to have reached them; but even if it had,
it would have seemed so strange that they might be
pardoned for looking with doubt on the persecutor turned
brother—for even fearing that the asserted conversion
might only be a ruse to enable Saul to learn their secrets,
and so entrap them to their final ruin. And thus at
first his intercourse with the brethren in the Church of
Jerusalem was almost confined to his reception in the
house of Peter. "Other of the Apostles saw I none,"
he writes to the Galatians, "save James the Lord's
brother." But though he *saw* James, Paul seems to
have had but little communion with him. All that we
know of the first Bishop of Jerusalem shows us the
immense dissimilarity, the almost antipathetic peculiarities which separated the characters of the two men.
Even with the Lord Himself, if we may follow the
plain language of the Gospels,[2] the eldest of His brethren
seems, during His life on earth, to have had but little
communion. He accepted indeed His Messianic claims,
but he accepted them in the Judaic sense, and was

---

[1] Acts ix. 26, ἐπειρᾶτο κολλᾶσθαι τοῖς μαθηταῖς (the imperfect marks an unsuc-
cessful effort) καὶ πάντες ἐφοβοῦντο αὐτόν, μὴ πιστεύοντες ὅτι ἐστὶν μαθητής.

[2] Matt. xii. 46; Mark iii. 31; Luke viii. 19; John vii. 5.

displeased at that in His life which was most unmis-
takably Divine. If he be rightly represented by tradition as a Legalist, a Nazarite, almost an Essene, spending
his whole life in prayer in the Temple, it was his obedience
to Mosaism—scarcely modified in any external particular
by his conversion to Christianity—which had gained for
him even from the Jews the surname of "the Just." If,
as seems almost demonstrable, he be the author of the
Epistle which bears his name, we see how slight was the
extent to which his spiritual life had been penetrated by
those special aspects of the one great truth which were to
Paul the very breath and life of Christianity. In that
Epistle we find a stern and noble morality which raises it
infinitely above the reproach of being "a mere Epistle of
straw;"[1] but we nevertheless do not find one direct word
about the Incarnation, or the Crucifixion, or the Atonement, or Justification by Faith, or Sanctification by the
Spirit, or the Resurrection of the Dead. The notion that
it was written to counteract either the teaching of St.
Paul, or the dangerous consequences which might sometimes be deduced from that teaching, is indeed most
extremely questionable; and all that we can say of that
supposition is, that it is not quite so monstrous a chimera
as that which has been invented by the German theologians,
who see St. Paul and his followers indignantly though
covertly denounced in the Balaam and Jezebel of the
Churches of Pergamos and Thyatira,[2] and the Nicolaitans
of the Church of Ephesus,[3] and the "synagogue of Satan,
which say they are Jews, and are not, but do lie," of the
Church of Philadelphia.[4] And yet no one can read the
Epistle of James side by side with any Epistle of St. Paul's

---

[1] "Ein recht strohern Epistel, denn sie doch kein evangelisch Art an ihm
hat" (Luther, Praef. N. T., 1522); but he afterwards modified his opinion.
[2] Rev. ii. 20.   [3] Rev. ii. 6.   [4] Rev. iii. 9.

without perceiving how wide were the differences between
the two Apostles. St. James was a man eminently inflexible; St. Paul knew indeed how to yield, but then
the very points which he was least inclined to yield
were those which most commanded the sympathy of
James. What we know of Peter is exactly in accordance
with the kind readiness with which he received the suspected and friendless Hellenist. What we know of James
would have led us *à priori* to assume that his relations
with Paul would never get beyond the formal character
which they wear in the Acts of the Apostles, and still
more in the Epistle to the Galatians. But let it not be
assumed that because there was little apparent sympathy
and co-operation between St. Paul and St. James, and
because they dwell on apparently opposite aspects of the
truth, we should for one moment be justified in disparaging either the one or the other. The divergences which
seem to arise from the analysis of truth by individual
minds are merged in the catholicity of a wider syn-
thesis. When St. Paul teaches that we are "justified by
faith," he is teaching a truth infinitely precious; and St.
James is also teaching a precious truth when, with a different shade of meaning in both words, he says that "by
works a man is justified."[1] The truths which these two
great Apostles were commissioned to teach were comple-
mentary and supplementary, but not contradictory of each
other. Of both aspects of truth we are the inheritors. If
it be true that they did not cordially sympathise with each
other in their life-time, the loss was theirs; but, even in
that case, they were not the first instances in the Church
of God—nor will they be the last—in which two good
men, through the narrowness of one or the vehemence

---

[1] James ii. 24. It is hardly a paradox to say that St. James meant by
"faith" something analogous to what St. Paul meant by works.

of the other, have been too much beset by the spirit of human infirmity to be able, in all perfectness, to keep the unity of the spirit in the bond of peace.

The man who saved the new convert from this humiliating isolation—an isolation which must at that moment have been doubly painful—was the wise and generous Joseph. He has already been mentioned in the Acts as a Levite of Cyprus who, in spite of the prejudices of his rank, had been among the earliest to join the new community, and to sanction its happy communism by the sale of his own possessions. The dignity and sweetness of his character, no less than the sacrifices which he had made, gave him a deservedly high position among the persecuted brethren; and the power with which he preached the faith had won for him the surname of Barnabas, or "the son of exhortation."[1] His intimate relations with Paul in after-days, his journey all the way to Tarsus from Antioch to invite his assistance, and the unity of their purposes until the sad quarrel finally separated them, would alone render it probable that they had known each other at that earlier period of life during which, for the most part, the closest intimacies are formed. Tradition asserts that Joseph had been a scholar of Gamaliel, and the same feeling which led him to join a school of which one peculiarity was its permission of Greek learning, might have led him yet earlier to take a few hours' sail from Cyprus to see what could be learnt in the University of Tarsus. If so, he would naturally have come into contact with the family of Saul, and the friendship thus commenced would be continued

---

[1] נבואה בר, "son of prophecy." That he had been one of the Seventy is probably a mere guess. (Euseb. *H. E.* i. 12; Clem. Alex. *Strom.* ii. 176.) "Παράκλησις late patet; ubi desides excitat est *hortatio*, ubi tristitiae medetur est *solatium*" (Bengel).

at Jerusalem. It had been broken by the conversion of Barnabas, it was now renewed by the conversion of Saul.

Perhaps also it was to this friendship that Saul owed his admission as a guest into Peter's house. There was a close link of union between Barnabas and Peter in the person of Mark, who was the cousin[1] of Barnabas, and whom Peter loved so tenderly that he calls him his son. The very house in which Peter lived may have been the house of Mary, the mother of Mark. It is hardly probable that the poor fisherman of Galilee possessed any dwelling of his own in the Holy City. At any rate, Peter goes to this house immediately after his liberation from prison, and if Peter lived in it, the relation of Barnabas to its owner would have given him some claim to ask that Saul should share its hospitality. Generous as Peter was, it would have required an almost super-human amount of confidence to receive at once under his roof a man who had tried by the utmost violence to extirpate the very fibres of the Church. But if one so highly honoured as Barnabas was ready to vouch for him, Peter was not the man to stand coldly aloof. Thus it happened that Saul's earliest introduction to the families of those whom he had scattered would be made under the high auspices of the greatest of the Twelve.

The imagination tries in vain to penetrate the veil of two thousand years which hangs between us and the intercourse of the two Apostles. Barnabas, we may be sure, must have been often present in the little circle, and must have held many an earnest conversation with his former friend. Mary, the mother of Mark, would have something to tell.[2] Mark may have been an eye-

[1] Col. iv. 10.

[2] St. John and other Apostles were probably absent, partly perhaps as a consequence of the very persecution in which Paul had been the prime mover.

witness of more than one pathetic scene. But how boundless would be the wealth of spiritual wisdom which Peter must have unfolded! Is it not certain that from those lips St. Paul must have heard about the Divine brightness of the dawning ministry of Jesus during the Galilæan year—about the raising of Jairus' daughter, and the Transfiguration on Hermon, and the discourse in the synagogue of Capernaum, and the awful scenes which had occurred on the day of the Crucifixion? And is it not natural to suppose that such a hearer— a hearer of exceptional culture, and enlightened to an extraordinary degree by the Holy Spirit of God—would grasp many of the words of the Lord with a firmness of grasp, and see into the very inmost heart of their significance with a keenness of insight, from which his informant might, in his turn, be glad to learn?

It must be a dull imagination that does not desire to linger for a moment on the few days during which two such men were inmates together of one obscure house in the city of Jerusalem. But however fruitful their intercourse, it did not at once secure to the new disciple a footing among the brethren whose poverty and perse-cutions he came to share. Then it was that Barnabas came forward, and saved Saul for the work of the Church. The same discrimination of character, the same charity of insight which afterwards made him prove Mark to be a worthy comrade of their second mission, in spite of his first defection, now made him vouch unhesi-tatingly for the sincerity of Saul. Taking him by the hand, he led him into the presence of the Apostles—the term being here used for Peter,[1] and James the Lord's

---

[1] Acts ix. 27; Gal. i. 19. The true reading in Gal. i. 18 seems to be "Kephas" (א, A, B, and the most important versions); as also in ii. 9, 11, 14. This Hebrew form of the name also occurs in 1 Cor. ix. 5. Although else-

brother,[1] and the elders of the assembled church—and there
narrated to them the circumstances, which either they had
never heard, or of the truth of which they had not yet
been convinced. He told them of the vision on the road
to Damascus, and of the fearlessness with which Saul had
vindicated his sincerity in the very city to which he had
come as an enemy. The words of Barnabas carried weight,
and his confidence was contagious. Saul was admitted
among the Christians on a footing of friendship, "going
in and out among them." To the generosity and clear-
sightedness of Joseph of Cyprus, on this and on a later
occasion, the Apostle owed a vast debt of gratitude.
Next only to the man who achieves the greatest and
most blessed deeds is he who, perhaps himself wholly
incapable of such high work, is yet the first to help and
encourage the genius of others. We often do more good
by our sympathy than by our labours, and render to the
world a more lasting service by absence of jealousy, and
recognition of merit, than we could ever render by the
straining efforts of personal ambition.

No sooner was Saul recognised as a brother, than he
renewed the ministry which he had begun at Damascus.
It is, however, remarkable that he did not venture to
preach to the Hebrew Christians. He sought the synagogues of the Hellenists in which the voice of Stephen
had first been heard, and disputed with an energy not

where (e.g., ii. 7, 8) St. Paul uses "Peter" indifferently with Cephas, as is
there shown by the unanimity of the MSS., it seems clear that St. Paul's conception of St. Peter was one which far more identified him with the Judaic
Church than with the Church in general. In the eyes of St. Paul, Simon
was *specially* the Apostle of the Circumcision.

[1] Gal. i. 19, ἕτερον δὲ τῶν ἀποστόλων οὐκ εἶδον εἰ μὴ Ἰάκωβον . . . It is impossible from the form of the words to tell whether James is here regarded as in
the *strictest* sense an Apostle or not. The addition of "the Lord's brother"
—τὸ σεμνολόγημα, as Chrysostom calls it—distinguishes him from James the
brother of John, and from James the Less, the son of Alphæus.

inferior to his. It was incumbent on him, though it was a duty which required no little courage, that his voice should be uplifted in the name of the Lord Jesus in the places where it had been heard of old in blasphemy against Him. But this very circumstance increased his danger. His preaching was again cut short by a conspiracy to murder him.[1]

It was useless to continue in a place where to stay was certain death. The little Galilæan community got information of the plot. To do the Jews justice, they showed little skill in keeping the secret of these deadly combinations. It was natural that the Church should not only desire to save Saul's life, but also to avoid the danger of a fresh outbreak. Yet it was not without a struggle, and a distinct intimation that such was the will of God, that Saul yielded to the solicitations of his brethren. How deeply he felt this compulsory flight, may be seen in the bitterness with which he alludes to it[2] even after the lapse of many years. He had scarcely been a fortnight in Jerusalem when the intensity of his prayers and emotions ended in a trance,[3] during which he again saw the Divine figure and heard the Divine voice which had arrested his mad progress towards the gates of Damascus. "Make instant haste, and depart in speed from Jerusalem," said Jesus to him; "for they will not receive thy testimony concerning Me." But to Saul it seemed incredible that his testimony could be resisted. If the vision of the risen Christ by which he had been converted was an argument which, from the

---

[1] Acts ix. 29, ἐπεχείρουν αὐτὸν ἀνελεῖν. We know of at least ten such perils of assassination in the life of St. Paul.

[2] 1 Thess. ii. 15, "who both killed the Lord Jesus, and their own prophets, and drove us out" (ἡμᾶς ἐκδιωξάντων).

[3] Acts xxii. 17.

nature of the case, could not, alone, be convincing to
others, yet it seemed to Saul that, knowing what they
did know of his intellectual power, and contrasting his
present earnestness with his former persecution, they
could not but listen to such a teacher as himself. He
longed also to undo, so far as in him lay, the misery and
mischief of the past havoc he had wrought. But however deep may have been his yearnings, however ardent
his hopes, the answer came brief and peremptory, "Go!
for I will send thee forth afar to the Gentiles."[1]

All reluctance was now at an end ; and we can see
what at the time must have been utterly dark and
mysterious to St. Paul,—that the coldness with which he
was received at Jerusalem, and the half-apparent desire
to precipitate his departure—events so alien to his own
plans and wishes, that he pleads even against the Divine
voice which enforced the indications of circumstance—
were part of a deep providential design. Years afterward,
when St. Paul "stood pilloried on infamy's high stage," he
was able with one of his strongest asseverations to appeal
to the brevity of his stay in Jerusalem, and the paucity
of those with whom he had any intercourse, in proof
that it was not from the Church of Jerusalem that he
had received his commission, and not to the Apostles at
Jerusalem that he owed his allegiance. But though at
present all this was unforeseen by him, he yielded to the
suggestions of his brethren, and scarcely a fortnight after
his arrival they—not, perhaps, wholly sorry to part with

---

[1] Acts xxii. 17—21. The omission of this vision in the direct narrative of
Acts ix. is a proof that silence as to this or that occurrence in the brief narrative of St. Luke must not be taken as a proof that he was unaware of the
event which he omits. We may also note, in this passage, the first appearance
of the interesting word μάρτυς. Here doubtless it has its primary sense of
"witness;" but it contains the germ of its later sense of one who testified to
Christ by voluntary death.

one whose presence was a source of many embarrassments —conducted him to the coast town of Cæsarea Stratonis[1] to start him on his way to his native Tarsus. Of his movements on this occasion we hear no more in the Acts of the Apostles; but in the Epistle to the Galatians he says that he came into the regions of Syria and Cilicia, but remained a complete stranger to the churches of Judæa that were in Christ, all that they had heard of him being the rumours that their former persecutor was now an evangelist of the faith of which he was once a destroyer; news which gave them occasion to glorify God in him.[2]

Since we next find him at Tarsus, it might have been supposed that he sailed there direct, and there remained. The expression, however, that "he came into the regions of Syria and Cilicia," seems to imply that this was not the case.[3] Syria and Cilicia were at this time politically separated, and there is room for the conjecture that the ship in which the Apostle sailed was destined, not for Tarsus, but for Tyre, or Sidon, or Seleucia, the port of Antioch. The existence of friends and disciples of Saul in the Phœnician towns, and the churches of Syria as well as

---

[1] That he was not sent to Cæsarea *Philippi* is almost too obvious to need argument. Neither κατήγαγον, which means a going downwards—*i.e.*, to the coast—nor ἐξαπέστειλαν, would at all suit the long journey northwards to Cæsarea Philippi; nor is it probable that Saul would go to Tarsus by land, travelling in the direction of the dangerous Damascus, when he could go so much more easily by sea. It is a more interesting inquiry whether, as has been suggested, these words κατήγαγον and ἐξαπέστειλαν, imply a more than ordinary amount of *passivity* in the movements of Paul; and whether in this case the passiveness was due to the attacks of illness which were the sequel of his late vision.

[2] Gal. i. 21—24, ἤμην ἀγνοούμενος . . . ἀκούοντες ἦσαν . . . εὐαγγελίζεται . . . ἐπόρθει.

[3] Gal. i. 21. The expression is not indeed decisive, since Cilicia might easily be regarded as a mere definitive addition to describe the part of Syria to which he went. (Ewald, *Gesch. d. Apost. Zeitalt.*, p. 439.)

Q

Cilicia,[1] point, though only with dim uncertainty, to the possibility that he performed part of his journey to Tarsus by land, and preached on the way. There is even nothing impossible in Mr. Lewin's suggestion[2] that his course may have been determined by one of those three shipwrecks which he mentions that he had undergone. But the occasions and circumstances of the three shipwrecks must be left to the merest conjecture. They occurred during the period when St. Luke was not a companion of St. Paul, and he has thought it sufficient to give from his own journal the graphic narrative of that later catastrophe of which he shared the perils. The active ministry in Syria and Cilicia may have occupied the period between Saul's departure in the direction of Tarsus, and his summons to fresh fields of labour in the Syrian Antioch. During this time he may have won over to the faith some of the members of his own family, and may have enjoyed the society of others who were in Christ before him. But all is uncertain, nor can we with the least confidence restore the probabilities of a period of which even the traditions have for centuries been obliterated. The stay of Saul at Tarsus was on any supposition a period mainly of waiting and of preparation, of which the records had no large significance in the history of the Christian faith. The fields in which he was to reap were whitening for the harvest; the arms of the reaper were being strengthened, and his heart prepared.

[1] Acts xxi. 2; xxvii. 3; xv. 23, 41.   [2] St. Paul, i. 77.

CHAPTER XIV.

GAIUS AND THE JEWS.—PEACE OF THE CHURCH.

"Reliqua ut de monstro narranda sunt."—SUET. *Calig.*

IMMEDIATELY after the hasty flight of Saul from Jerusalem, St. Luke adds,[1] "Then had the church rest throughout the whole of Judæa, and Galilee, and Samaria, being built up, and walking in the fear of the Lord; and by the exhortation of the Holy Spirit was multiplied." At first sight it might almost seem as though this internal peace, which produced such happy growth, was connected in the writer's mind with the absence of one whose conversion stirred up to madness the prominent opponents of the Church. It may be, however, that the turn of his expression is simply meant to resume the broken thread of his narrative. The absence of molestation, which caused the prosperity of the faith, is sufficiently accounted for by the events which were now happening in the Pagan world. The pause in the recorded career of the Apostle enables us also to pause and survey some of the conflicting conditions of Jewish and Gentile life as they were illustrated at this time by prominent events. It need hardly be said that such a survey has an immediate bearing on the conditions of the Days after Christ, and on the work of His great Apostle.

A multitude of concurrent arguments tend to show

[1] Acts ix. 31, ἡ μὲν οὖν ἐκκλησία (א, A, B, C, and the chief versions). I follow what seems to me to be the best punctuation of the verse.

that Saul was converted early in A.D. 37, and this brief stay
at Jerusalem must therefore have occurred in the year 39.
Now in the March of A.D. 37 Tiberius died, and Gaius—
whose nickname of Caligula, or " Bootling," given him in
his infancy by the soldiers of his father Germanicus, has
been allowed to displace his true name—succeeded to the
lordship of the world. Grim as had been the despotism of
Tiberius, he extended to the religion of the Jews that contemptuous toleration which was the recognised principle of
Roman policy. When Pilate had kindled their fanaticism
by hanging the gilt shields in his palace at Jerusalem,[1]
Tiberius, on an appeal being made to him, reprimanded
the officiousness of his Procurator, and ordered him to
remove the shields to Cæsarea. It is true that he allowed
four thousand Jews to be deported from Rome to Sardinia, and punished with remorseless severity those who,
from dread of violating the Mosaic law, refused to take
military service.[2] This severity was not, however, due to
any enmity against the race, but only to his indignation
against the designing hypocrisy which, under pretence of
proselytising, had won the adhesion of Fulvia, a noble
Roman lady, to the Jewish religion; and to the detestable
rascality with which her teacher and his companions had
embezzled the presents of gold and purple which she had
entrusted to them as an offering for the Temple at Jerusalem. Even this did not prevent him from protecting
the Jews as far as he could in their own country; and
when Vitellius, the Legate of Syria, had decided that there
was *primá facie* cause for the complaints which had been
raised against the Procurator in all three divisions of his
district, it is probable that Pilate, who was sent to Rome
to answer for his misdemeanours, would have received

---

[1] *Life of Christ*, ii. 362. [2] Jos. *Antt.* xviii. 3—5; Suet. *Tib.* xxxvi.

strict justice from the aged Emperor. But before Pilate arrived, Tiberius had ended his long life of disappointment, crime, and gloom.

The accession of Gaius was hailed by the whole Roman world with a burst of rapture,[1] and there were none to whom it seemed more likely to introduce a golden era of prosperity than to the Jews. For if the young Emperor had any living friend, it was Herod Agrippa. That prince, if he could command but little affection as a grandson of Herod the Great, had yet a claim to Jewish loyalty as a son of the murdered Aristobulus, a grandson of the murdered Mariamne, and therefore a direct lineal descendant of that great line of Asmonæan princes whose names recalled the last glories of Jewish independence. Accordingly, when the news reached Jerusalem that Tiberius at last was dead, the Jews heaved a sigh of relief, and not only took with perfect readiness the oath of allegiance to Gaius, which was administered by Vitellius to the myriads who had thronged to the Feast of Pentecost, but offered speedy and willing holocausts for the prosperity of that reign which was to bring them a deeper misery, and a more absolute humiliation, than any which had been inflicted on them during the previous dominion of Rome.[2]

Gaius lost no time in publicly displaying his regard for the Herodian prince, who, with remarkable insight, had courted his friendship, not only before his accession was certain, but even in spite of the distinct recommendation of the former Emperor.[3]

[1] Suet. *Calig.* 13, 14.

[2] Compare for this entire narrative Suet. *Caligula;* Philo, *Leg. ad Gaium,* and *in Flaccum;* Jos. *Antt.* xviii. 9; *B. J.* ii. 10; Dio Cass. lix. 8, *seq.;* Grätz, iii. 270—277; Jahn, *Hebr. Commonwealth,* 174.

[3] The adventures of Herod Agrippa I. form one of the numerous romances which give us so clear a glimpse of the state of society during the early Empire. Sent to Rome by his grandfather, he had breathed from early

One day, while riding in the same carriage as Gaius, Agrippa was imprudent enough to express his wish for the time when Tiberius would bequeath the Empire to a worthier successor. Such a remark might easily be construed into a crime of high treason, or *laesa majestas*. In a court which abounded with spies, and in which few dared to express above a whisper their real thoughts, it was natural that the obsequious slave who drove the chariot should seek an audience from Tiberius to communicate what he had heard; and when by the influence of Agrippa himself he had gained this opportunity, his report made the old Emperor so indignant, that he ordered the Jewish prince to be instantly arrested. Clothed as he was in royal purple, Agrippa was seized, put in chains, and taken off to a prison, in which he languished for the six remaining months of the life of Tiberius. Almost the first thought of Gaius on his accession was to relieve the friend who had paid him such assiduous court before his fortunes were revealed. Agrippa was at once released from custody. A few days after, Gaius sent for him, put a diadem on his head, conferred on him the tetrarchies of Herod Philip, and of Lysanias, and presented him with a golden chain of equal weight with the iron one with which he had been bound.

Now, although Agrippa was a mere unprincipled adventurer, yet he had the one redeeming feature of respect for the external religion of his race. The Edomite admixture in his blood had not quite effaced the more generous instincts of an Asmonæan prince,

youth the perfumed and intoxicating atmosphere of the Imperial court as a companion of Drusus, the son of Tiberius. On the death of Drusus he was excluded from Court, and was brought to the verge of suicide by the indigence which followed a course of extravagance. Saved from his purpose by his wife Cypros, he went through a series of debts, disgraces, and escapades, until he was once more admitted to favour by Tiberius at Capreæ.

nor had the sty of Capreæ altogether made him forget that he drew his line from the Priest of Modin. The Jews might well have expected that, under an Emperor with whom their prince was a bosom friend, their interests would be more secure than they had been even under a magnanimous Julius and a liberal Augustus. Their hopes were doomed to the bitterest disappointment; nor did any reign plunge them into more dreadful disasters than the reign of Agrippa's friend.

In August, A.D. 38, Agrippa arrived at Alexandria on his way to his new kingdom. His arrival was so entirely free from ostentation—for, indeed, Alexandria, where his antecedents were not unknown, was the last city in which he would have wished to air his brand-new royalty—that though he came in sight of the Pharos about twilight, he ordered the captain to stay in the offing till dark, that he might land unnoticed.[1] But the presence in the city of one who was at once a Jew, a king, an Idumæan, a Herod, and a favourite of Cæsar, would not be likely to remain long a secret; and if it was some matter of exultation to the Jews, it exasperated beyond all bounds the envy of the Egyptians. Flaccus, the Governor of Alexandria, chose to regard Agrippa's visit as an intentional insult to himself, and by the abuse which he heaped in secret upon the Jewish prince, encouraged the insults in which the mob of Alexandria were only too ready to indulge. Unpopular everywhere, the Jews were regarded in Alexandria with special hatred. Their wealth, their numbers, their usuries, their exclusiveness, the immunities which the two first Cæsars had granted them,[2] filled the worthless

---

[1] Derenbourg is therefore mistaken (p. 222) that Agrippa " se donna la puérile satisfaction d'étaler son luxe royal dans l'endroit où naguère il avait traîné une si honteuse misère."

[2] Jos. *Antt.* xiv. 7, 2; xix. 5, 2, and xiv. 10, *passim* (Decrees of Julius).

populace of a hybrid city with fury and loathing. A Jewish *king* was to them a conception at once ludicrous and offensive. Every street rang with lampoons against him, every theatre and puppet-show echoed with ribald farces composed in his insult. At last the wanton mob seized on a poor naked idiot named Carabbas, who had long been the butt of mischievous boys, and carrying him off to the Gymnasium, clothed him in a door-mat, by way of tallith, flattened a papyrus leaf as his diadem, gave him a stalk of papyrus for a sceptre, and surrounding him with a mimic body-guard of youths armed with sticks, proceeded to bow the knee before him, and consult him on state affairs. They ended the derisive pageant by loud shouts of *Maris! Maris!* the Syriac word for "Lord."

Encouraged by impunity and the connivance of the Præfect, they then bribed him to acquiesce in more serious outrages. First they raised a cry to erect images of Gaius in the synagogues, hoping thereby to provoke the Jews into a resistance which might be interpreted as treason. This was to set an example which might be fatal to the Jews, not only in Egypt, but in all other countries. Irritated, perhaps, by the determined attitude of the Jews, Flaccus, in spite of the privileges which had long been secured to them by law and charter, published an edict in which he called them "foreigners and aliens," and drove them all into a part of a single quarter of the city in which it was impossible for them to live. The mob then proceeded to break open and plunder the shops of the deserted quarter, blockaded the Jews in their narrow precincts, beat and murdered all who in the pangs of hunger ventured to leave it, and burnt whole families alive, sometimes with green fuel, which added terribly to their tortures. Flaccus, for his part, arrested thirty-eight leading members of their Council, and after having stripped them of all their possessions, had them beaten, not with rods by the lictors, but with scourges by the lowest executioners, with such severity that some of them died in consequence. Their houses were rifled, in the hope of finding arms; but though nothing whatever was found, except common table-knives, men and women were dragged into the theatre, commanded to eat swine's flesh, and tortured if they refused.[1]

But neither these attempts to win popularity among the Gentile inhabitants by letting loose their rage against their Jewish neighbours, nor his ostentatious public loyalty and fulsome private flatteries saved Flaccus from the fate which he deserved. These proceedings had barely been going on for two months, when Gaius sent a centurion with a party of soldiers, who, landing after dark, proceeded at once to the house of Stephanion, a freed-man of Tiberius, with whom Flaccus happened to be dining, arrested him without difficulty, and brought him to Rome. Here he found that two low demagogues, Isidorus and Lampo, who had hitherto been among his parasites, and who had constantly fomented his hatred of the Jews, were now his chief accusers. He was found guilty. His property was confiscated, and he was banished, first to the miserable rock of Gyara, in the Ægean, and then to Andros. In one of those sleepless nights which were at once a symptom and an aggravation of his madness, Gaius, meditating on the speech of an exile whom he had restored, that during his banishment he used to pray for the death of Tiberius, determined to put an end to the crowd of distinguished criminals which imperial tyranny had collected on the barren islets of the Mediterranean. Flaccus was among

---

[1] There seem to be distinct allusions to these troubles in 3 Macc. (*passim*).

the earliest victims, and Philo narrates with too gloating a vindictiveness the horrible manner in which he was hewn to pieces in a ditch by the despot's emissaries.[1]

Gaius had begun his reign with moderation, but the sudden change from the enforced simplicity of his tutelage to the boundless luxuries and lusts of his autocracy —the sudden plunge into all things which, as Philo[2] says, "destroy both soul and body and all the bonds which unite and strengthen the two"—brought on the illness which altered the entire organism of his brain. Up to that time he had been a vile and cruel man; thenceforth he was a mad and sanguinary monster. It was after this illness, and the immediately subsequent murders of Tiberius Gemellus, Macro, and Marcus Silanus, which delivered him from all apprehension of rivalry or restraint, that he began most violently to assert his godhead. His predecessors would have regarded it as far less impious to allow themselves or their fortunes to be regarded as divine, than to arrogate to themselves the actual style and attributes of existing deities.[3] But disdaining all mere demi-gods like Trophonius and Amphiaraus, Gaius began to appear in public, first in the guise of Hercules, or Bacchus, or one of the Dioscuri, and then as Apollo, or Mars, or Mercury, or even Venus (!), and demanded that choruses should be sung in his honour under these attributes; and, lastly, he did not hesitate to assert his perfect equality with Jupiter

---

[1] It is not impossible that Herod Antipas may have perished in consequence of this same order of Gaius. It is true that Suetonius (*Calig.* 28) only says, "Misit circum *insulas* qui omnes (exsules) trucidarent;" but the *cause* would apply as much to all political exiles, and Dion (lix. 18) distinctly says that he put Antipas to death (κατέσφαξε). The trial of Antipas took place at Puteoli shortly before the Philonian embassy, A.D. 39.

[2] *De Leg.* 2.

[3] See Excursus XII., "Apotheosis of Roman Emperors."

himself. The majority of the Romans, partly out of abject terror, partly out of contemptuous indifference, would feel little difficulty in humouring these vagaries; but the Jews, to their eternal honour, refused at all costs to sanction this frightful concession of divine honours to the basest of mankind. As there were plenty of parasites in the Court of Gaius who would lose no opportunity of indulging their spite against the Jews, an ingrained hatred of the whole nation soon took possession of his mind. The Alexandrians were not slow to avail themselves of this antipathy. They were well aware that the most acceptable flattery to the Emperor, and the most overwhelming insult to the Jews, was to erect images of Gaius in Jewish synagogues, and they not only did this, but even in the superb and celebrated Chief Synagogue of Alexandria [1] they erected a bronze statue in an old gilt quadriga which had once been dedicated to Cleopatra.

Of all these proceedings Gaius was kept informed, partly by his delighted study of Alexandrian newspapers, which Philo says that he preferred to all other literature, and partly by the incessant insults against the Jews distilled into his ears by Egyptian buffoons like the infamous Helicon.[2]

The sufferings of the Jews in Alexandria at last became so frightful that they despatched the venerable Philo with four others on an embassy to the insane youth whom they refused to adore. Philo has left us an account of this embassy, which, though written with his usual rhetorical diffuseness, is intensely interesting as a record of the times. It opens for us a little window into the daily life of the Imperial Court at Rome within ten years of the death of Christ.

---

[1] The Diapleuston.   [2] Philo, *Leg. John* xxv.

The first interview of the ambassadors with Gaius took place while he was walking in his mother's garden on the banks of the Tiber, and the apparent graciousness of his reception deceived all of them except Philo himself. After having been kept waiting for some time, the Jews were ordered to follow him to Puteoli, and there it was that a man with disordered aspect and bloodshot eyes rushed up to them, and with a frame that shivered with agony and in a voice broken with sobs, barely succeeded in giving utterance to the horrible intelligence that Gaius had asserted his intention of erecting a golden colossus of himself with the attributes of Jupiter in the Holy of Holies at Jerusalem. After giving way to their terror and agitation, the ambassadors asked the cause of this diabolical sacrilege, and were informed that it was due to the advice of "that scorpion-like slave," Helicon, who with "a poisonous Ascalonite" named Apelles—a low tragic actor—had made the suggestion during the fit of rage with which Gaius heard that the Jews of Jamnia had torn down a trumpery altar which the Gentiles of the city had erected to his deity with no other intention than that of wounding and insulting them.

So far from this being a transient or idle threat, Gaius wrote to Petronius, the Legate of Syria, and ordered him to carry it out with every precaution and by main force; and though the legate was well aware of the perilous nature of the undertaking, he had been obliged to furnish the necessary materials for the statue to the artists of Sidon.

No sooner had the miserable Jews heard of this threatened abomination of desolation, than they yielded themselves to such a passion of horror as made them forget every other interest. It was no time to be per-secuting Christians when the most precious heritage of their religion was at stake. Flocking to Phœnicia in myriads, until they occupied the whole country like a cloud, they divided themselves into six companies of old men, youths, boys, aged women, matrons, and virgins, and rent the air with their howls and supplications, as they lay prostrate on the earth and scattered the dust in handfuls upon their heads. Petronius, a sensible and honourable man, was moved by their abject misery, and with the object of gaining time, ordered the Sidonian artists to make their statue very perfect, intimating not very obscurely that he wished them to be as long over it as possible. Meanwhile, in order to test the Jews, he went from Acre to Tiberias, and there the same scenes were repeated. For forty days, neglecting the sowing of their fields, they lay prostrate on the ground, and when the legate asked them whether they meant to make war against Cæsar, they said, No, but they were ready to die rather than see their temple desecrated, and in proof of their sincerity stretched out their throats. Seeing the obstinacy of their resolution, besieged by the entreaties of Aristobulus and Helcias the elder, afraid, too, that a famine would be caused by the neglect of tillage, Petronius, though at the risk of his own life, promised the Jews that he would write and intercede for them, if they would separate peaceably and attend to their husbandry. It was accepted by both Jews and Gentiles as a sign of the special blessing of God on this brave and humane decision, that no sooner had Petronius finished his speech than, after long drought, the sky grew black with clouds, and there was an abundant rain. He kept his word. He wrote a letter to Gaius, telling him that if the affair of the statue were pressed, the Jews would neglect their harvest and there would be great danger lest he should find the whole country in a state of staivation, which might be even dangerous for himself and his suite, if he carried out his intended visit.

Meanwhile, in entire ignorance of all that had taken place, Agrippa had arrived at Rome, and he at once read in the countenance of the Emperor that something had gone wrong. On hearing what it was, he fell down in a fit, and lay for some time in a deep stupor. By the exertion of his whole influence with Gaius, he only succeeded in procuring a temporary suspension of the design ; and it was not long before the Emperor announced the intention of taking with him from Rome a colossus of gilded bronze—in order to cut off all excuse for delay—and of personally superintending its erection in the Temple, which would henceforth be regarded as dedicated to " the new Jupiter, the illustrious Gaius." Even during his brief period of indecision he was so angry with Petronius for the humanity that he had shown that he wrote him a letter commanding him to commit suicide if he did not want to die by the hands of the executioner.

These events, and the celebrated embassy of Philo to Gaius, of which he has left us so painfully graphic a description, probably took place in the August of the year 40. In the January of the following year the avenging sword of the brave tribune Cassius Chærea rid the world of the intolerable despot.[1] The vessel which had carried to Petronius the command to commit suicide, was fortunately delayed by stormy weather, and only arrived twenty-seven days after intelligence had been received that the tyrant was dead. From Claudius — who owed his throne entirely to the subtle intrigues of Agrippa—the

---

[1] The Jews believed that a *Bath Kôl* from the Holy of Holies had announced his death to the High Priest (Simon the Just), and the anniversary was forbidden to be ever observed as a fast day (*Megillath Taanith*, § 26 ; *Sotah*, f. 33, 1 ; Derenbourg, *Palest.*, p. 207).

Jews received both kindness and consideration. Petronius was ordered thenceforth to suppress and punish all attempts to insult them [1] in the quiet exercise of their religious duties; and Claudius utterly forbad that prayers should be addressed or sacrifices offered to himself.[2]

[1] See the decree of Claudius against the inhabitants of Dor, who had set up his statue in a Jewish synagogue.

[2] Dion, lx. 5.

Book IV.

THE RECOGNITION OF THE GENTILES.

CHAPTER XV.

THE SAMARITANS—THE EUNUCH—THE CENTURION.

"Whenever I look at Peter, my very heart leaps for joy. If I could paint a portrait of Peter I would paint upon every hair of his head 'I believe in the forgiveness of sins.'"—LUTHER.

"Quel Padre vetusto
Di santa chiesa, a cui Cristo le chiavi
Raccommandó di questo fior venusto."
DANTE, *Paradiso*, xxxii. 124.

"Blessed is the eunuch, which with his hands hath wrought no iniquity, nor imagined wicked things against God: for unto him shall be given the special gift of faith, and an inheritance in the temple of the Lord more acceptable to his mind. For glorious is the fruit of good labours: and the root of wisdom shall never fall away."—WISD. iii. 14, 15.

THE peace, the progress, the edification, the holiness of the Church, were caused, no doubt, by that rest from persecution which seems to have been due to the absorption of the Jews in the desire to avert the outrageous sacrilege of Gaius. And yet we cannot but ask with surprise whether the Christians looked on with indifference at the awful insult which was being aimed at their national religion. It would mark a state of opinion very different from what we should imagine if they had learnt to regard the unsullied sanctity of Jehovah's Temple as a thing in which they had no longer any immediate concern. Can we for one moment suppose that James the Lord's brother, or

Simon the Zealot, were content to enjoy their freedom from
molestation, without caring to take part in the despairing
efforts of their people to move the compassion of the
Legate of Syria? Is it conceivable that they would have
stayed quietly at home while the other Jews in tens of
thousands were streaming to his headquarters at Cæsarea,
or flinging the dust upon their heads as they lay prostrate
before him at Tiberias? Or was it their own personal
peril which kept them from mingling among masses of
fanatics who indignantly rejected their co-operation? Were
they forced to confine their energies to the teaching of the
infant churches of Palestine because they were not even
allowed to participate in the hopes and fears of their
compatriots? We may fairly assume that the Jewish
Christians abhorred the purposed sacrilege; but if the
schools of Hillel and Shammai, and the cliques of
Hanan and Herod, hated them only one degree less than
they hated the minions of Gaius, it is evident that there
could have been nothing for the Apostles to do but to
rejoice over their immediate immunity from danger, and
to employ the rest thus granted them for the spread of
the Kingdom of God. The kings of the earth might rage,
and the princes imagine vain things, but *they*, at least,
could kiss the Son,[1] and win the blessing of those who
trusted in the Lord. It was the darkest midnight of the
world's history, but the Goshen of Christ's Church was
brightening more and more with the silver dawn.

To this outward peace and inward development was
due an event which must continue to have the most
memorable importance to the end of time—the admission
of Gentiles, as Gentiles, into the Church of Christ. This

---

[1] Ps. ii. 12, נַשְּׁקוּ־בַר, either " kiss the Son," or " worship purely." Which
rendering is right has been a disputed point ever since Jerome's day (*Adv.
Ruff.* i.). See Perowne, *Psalms*, i. 116.

R

great event must have seemed inevitable to men like
St. Stephen, whose training as Hellenists had emancipated
them from the crude spirit of Jewish isolation. But the
experience of all history shows how difficult it is for the
mind to shake itself free from views which have become
rather instinctive than volitional; and though Jesus had
uttered words which could only have one logical explanation, the older disciples, even the Apostles themselves,
had not yet learnt their full significance. The revelation
of God in Christ had been a beam in the darkness.
To pour suddenly upon the midnight a full flood of
spiritual illumination would have been alien to the
method of God's dealings with our race. The dayspring
had risen, but many a long year was to elapse before it
broadened into the boundless noon.

But the time had now fully come in which those other
sheep of which Jesus had spoken—the other sheep which
were not of this fold [1]—must be brought to hear His voice.
Indirectly, as well as directly, the result was due to St.
Paul in a degree immeasurably greater than to any other
man. To St. Peter, indeed, as a reward for his great confession, had been entrusted the keys of the Kingdom of
Heaven; and, in accordance with this high metaphor,
to him was permitted the honour of opening to the
Gentiles the doors of the Christian Church. And that
this was so ordained is a subject for deep thankfulness.
The struggle of St. Paul against the hostility of Judaism
from without, and the leaven of Judaism from within,
was severe and lifelong, and even at his death faith alone
could have enabled him to see that it had not been in
vain. But the glorious effort of his life must have been
fruitless had not the principle at stake been publicly

[1] John x. 16. In this verse it is a pity that the English version makes no
distinction between αὐλή, "fold," and ποίμνη, "flock."

conceded—conceded in direct obedience to sanctions which none ventured to dispute—by the most eminent and most authoritative of the Twelve. And yet, though St. Peter was thus set apart by Divine foresight to take the initiative, it was to one whom even the Twelve formally recognised as the Apostle of the Uncircumcision, that the world owes under God the development of Christian faith into a Christian theology, and the emancipation of Christianity from those Judaic limitations which would have been fatal to its universal acceptance.[1] To us, indeed, it is obvious that "it would have been impossible for the Gentiles to adopt the bye-laws of a Ghetto." If the followers of Christ had refused them the right-hand of fellowship on any other conditions, then the world would have gone its own way, and Mammon and Belial and Beelzebub would have rejoiced in the undisturbed corruption of a Paganism which was sinking deeper and deeper into the abyss of shame.

And as this deliverance of the Gentiles was due directly to the letters and labours of St. Paul, so the first beginnings of it rose indirectly from the consequences of the persecutions of which he had been the most fiery agent. The Ravager of the Faith was unconsciously proving himself its most powerful propagator. When he was making havoc of the Church, its members, who were thus scattered abroad, went everywhere preaching the word. To the liberal Hellenists this was a golden opportunity, and Philip, who had been a fellow-worker with Stephen, gladly seized it to preach the Gospel to the hated Samaritans. The eye of Jesus had already gazed in that country on fields whitening to the harvests, and

---

[1] Immer, *Neut. Theol.* 206.

s 2

the zeal of Philip, aided by high spiritual gifts, not only won a multitude of converts, but even arrested the influence of a powerful *goés*, or sorcerer, named Simon.[1] Justin Martyr calls him Simon of Gitton, and he has been generally identified with Simon Magus, the first heresiarch,[2] and with Simon the Cyprian, whom Felix employed to entrap the wandering affections of the Queen Drusilla. This man, though, as afterwards appeared, with the most interested and unworthy motives, went so far as to receive baptism; and the progress of the faith among his former dupes was so remarkable as to require the immediate presence of the Apostles. St. Peter and St. John went from Jerusalem to confirm the converts, and their presence resulted not only in the public discomfiture of Simon,[3] but also in that outpouring of special manifestations which accompanied the gift of the promised Comforter.

But Philip had the honour of achieving yet another great conversion, destined to prove yet more decisively that the day was at hand when the rules of Judaism were to be regarded as obsolete. Guided by divine impressions

[1] As I have no space to give an account of the strange career and opinions of this "hero of the Romance of Heresy," as given in the Pseudo-Clementine *Homilies* and *Recognitions*, I must content myself by referring to Hippolyt. *Philosoph.*, p. 161 *seq.*; Iren. *Haer.* i. 23; Neander, *Ch. Hist.* i. 454; *Planting*, 51—64; Gieseler, *Eccl. Hist.* i. 49; Mansel, *Gnostic Heresies*, 91—94; De Pressensé, i. 396 *seq.* The stories about him are fabulous (Arnob. *Adv. Gent.*, 11, 12), and the supposed statue to him (Just. Mart. *Apol.* i. 26, 56; Iren. *Adv. Haer.* i. 23; Tert. *Apol.* 13) is believed, from a tablet found in 1574 on the Insula Tiberina, to have been a statue to the Sabine God *Semo Sancus* (Baronius, *in ann.* 44; Burton, *Bampt. Lect.* 375). A typical impostor of this epoch was Alexander of Abonoteichos (see Lucian, *Pseudo-mantis*, 10—51, and on the general prevalence of magic and theurgy, Döllinger, *Judenth. u. Heidenth.* viii. 2, § 7).

[2] Πάσης αἱρέσεως εὑρετής (Cyril. Iren. *adv. Hær.* i. 27; ii. *praef.*). "Gitton" may very likely be a confusion with Citium, whence "Chittim," &c.

[3] From his endeavour to obtain spiritual functions by a bribe is derived the word *simony*.

and angel voices he had turned his steps southward along
the desert road which leads from Eleutheropolis to Gaza,[1]
and there had encountered the retinue of a wealthy
Ethiopian eunuch, who held the high position of treasurer
to the Kandake of Meroe.[2] There seems to be some reason
for believing that this region had been to a certain extent
converted to Judaism by Jews who penetrated into it from
Egypt in the days of Psammetichus, whose descendants
still exist under the name of Falâsyán.[3] The eunuch, in
pious fulfilment of the duties of a Proselyte of the Gate—
and his very condition rendered more than this impossible
—had gone up to Jerusalem to worship, and not improbably
to be present at one of the great yearly festivals. As he
rode in his chariot at the head of his retinue he occupied
his time, in accordance with the rules of the Rabbis, in
studying the Scriptures, and he happened at the moment
to be reading aloud in the LXX. version[4] the prophecy
of Isaiah, " He was led as a sheep to slaughter, and
as a lamb before his shearer is dumb, so he openeth
not his mouth. In his humiliation his judgment was
taken away, and his generation who shall declare? for
his life is being taken from the earth."[5] Philip asked

---

[1] The αὕτη ἐστὶν ἔρημος of viii. 26 probably refers to the *road*. Gaza was
not destroyed till A.D. 65 (Robinson, *Bibl. Res.* ii. 640). Lange's notion
(*Apost. Zeit.* ii. 109) that ἔρημος means " a moral desert" is out of the question.
Although paronomasia is so frequent a figure in the N. T., yet I cannot think
that there is anything intentional in the εἰς Γάζαν of 26, and the τῆς γάζης of 27.

[2] The title of the Queen of Meroe (Pliny, *H. N.* vi. 35 ; Dio Cass. liv. 5).
(For the " treasure" of Ethiopia see Isa. xlv. 14). Ethiopian tradition gives
the eunuch the name of Indich. On the relation of the Jews with Ethiopia
see Zeph. iii. 10; Ps. lxviii. 31 ; and for another faithful Ethiopian eunuch,
also a " king's servant " (Ebed-melech), Jer. xxxviii. 7; xxxix. 16.

[3] Renan, *Les Apôtres*, p. 158.

[4] Isa. liii. 7, 8. The quotation in Acts viii. 33 is from the LXX. We
might have supposed that the eunuch was reading the ancient Ethiopic version
founded on the LXX. ; but in that case Philip would not have understood him.

[5] This passage differs in several respects from our Hebrew text.

him whether he understood what he was reading? The
eunuch confessed that it was all dark to him, and after
having courteously invited Philip to take a seat in
his chariot, asked who it was to whom the prophet
was referring.　Philip was thus enabled to unfold the
Christian interpretation of the great scheme of prophecy,
and so completely did he command the assent of his
listener, that on their reaching a spring of water—possibly
that at Bethsoron, not far from Hebron[1]—the eunuch
asked to be baptised.　The request was addressed to a
large-hearted Hellenist, and was instantly granted, though
there were reasons which might have made a James or a
Simon hesitate.　But in spite of the prohibition of
Deuteronomy,[2] Philip saw that the Christian Church was
to be an infinitely wider and more spiritual communion
than that which had been formed by the Mosaic ritual.
Recalling, perhaps, the magnificent prediction of Isaiah,[3]
which seemed to rise above the Levitical prohibition—
recalling, perhaps, also some of the tender words and
promises of his Master, Christ—he instantly stepped
down with the eunuch into the water.　Without any
recorded confession of creed or faith—for that which is
introduced into Acts viii. 37 is one of the early instances
of interpolation[4]—he administered to one who was not
only (as is probable) a Gentile by birth, but a eunuch

[1] Josh. xv. 58; Neh. iii. 16; Jer. *Ep.* ciii.　The spring is called *Ain edh-Dhirweh.*　But Dr. Robinson fixes the site near Tell el-Hasy (*Bibl. Res.* ii.
641).　The tradition which fixes it at Ain Haniyeh, near Jerusalem, is much
later.

[2] Deut. xxiii. 1.　As for the nationality of the Ethiopian it must be borne
in mind that even Moses himself had once married an Ethiopian wife (Numb.
xii. 1).

[3] Isa. lvi. 3, 8.

[4] It is not found in א, A, B, C, G, H, and the phrase τὸν Ἰησοῦν Χριστόν is
unknown to St. Luke.　It is moreover obvious that while there was to some a
strong temptation to insert something of the kind, there was no conceivable
reason to omit it if it had been genuine.

by condition, the rite of baptism. The law of Deuteronomy forbade him to become a member of the Jewish Church, but Philip admitted him into that Christian communion[1] in which there is neither Jew nor Greek, neither male nor female, neither bond nor free.[2]

The subsequent work of Philip in the towns of Philistia and the sea-coast, as well as during his long subsequent residence at Cæsarea[3] was doubtless fruitful, but for Christian history the main significance of his life lay in his successful mission to detested Samaritans, and in that bold baptism of the mutilated alien. Deacon though he was, he had not shrunk from putting into effect the divine intimations which foreshadowed the ultimate obliteration of exclusive privileges. We cannot doubt that it was the fearless initiative of Philip which helped to shape the convictions of St. Peter, just as it was the avowed act of St. Peter which involved a logical concession of all those truths that were dearest to the heart of St. Paul.

In the peaceful visitation of the communities which the undisturbed prosperity of the new faith rendered both possible and desirable, Peter had journeyed westward, and, encouraged by the many conversions caused by the healing of Æneas and the raising of Tabitha, he had fixed his home at Joppa, in order to strengthen

---

[1] The significance of the act on those grounds is probably the main if not the sole reason for its narration ; and if εὐνοῦχος had merely meant "chamberlain," there would have been no reason to add the word δυνάστης in v. 27. Dr. Plumptre (*New Testament Commentary, in loc.*) adduces the interesting parallel furnished by the first decree of the first Œcumenical Council (Conc. Nic. *Can.* 1).

[2] Gal. iii. 28. In Iren. *Haer.* iii. 12; Euseb. *H. E.* ii. 1, he is said to have evangelised his own country.

[3] Acts xxi. 8, 9. Observe the undesigned coincidence in his welcome of the Apostle of the Gentiles. At this point he disappears from Christian history. The Philip who died at Hierapolis (Euseb. *H. E.* iii. 31) is probably Philip the Apostle.

the young but flourishing churches on the plain of Sharon. That he lodged in the house of Simon, a tanner, is merely mentioned as one of those incidental circumstances which are never wanting in the narratives of writers familiar with the events which they describe. But we may now see in it a remarkable significance. It shows on the one hand how humble must have been the circumstances of even the chiefest of the Apostles, since nothing but poverty could have induced the choice of such a residence. But it shows further that Peter had already abandoned Rabbinic scrupulosities, for we can scarcely imagine that he would have found it impossible to procure another home,[1] and at the house of a tanner no strict and uncompromising follower of the Oral Law could have been induced to dwell. The daily contact with the hides and carcases of various animals necessitated by this trade, and the materials which it requires, rendered it impure and disgusting in the eyes of all rigid legalists. If a tanner married without mentioning his trade, his wife was permitted to get a divorce.[2] The law of levirate marriage might be set aside if the brother-in-law of the childless widow was a tanner. A tanner's yard must be at least fifty cubits distant from any town,[3] and it must be even further off, said Rabbi Akibha, if built to the west of a town, from which quarter the effluvium is more easily blown. Now, a trade that is looked on with disgust tends to lower the self-respect of all who undertake it, and although Simon's yard may not have been

---

[1] Lydda and Joppa were thoroughly Judaic (Jos. *B. J.* ii. 19, § 1).

[2] *Ketubhôth*, f. 77, 1.

[3] *Babha Bathra*, f. 25, 1, 16, 2 (where the remark is attributed to Bar Kappara). "No trade," says Rabbi, "will ever pass away from the earth; but happy be he whose parents belong to a respectable trade . . . . The world cannot exist without tanners, ... but woe unto him who is a tanner" (*Kiddushîn*, f. 82, 2).

contiguous to his house, yet the choice of his house as a residence not only proves how modest were the only resources which Peter could command, but also that he had learnt to rise superior to prejudice, and to recognise the dignity of honest labour in even the humblest trade.

It is certain that two problems of vast importance must constantly have been present to the mind of Peter at this time: namely, the relation of the Church to the Gentiles, and the relation alike of Jewish and Gentile Christians to the Mosaic, or perhaps it would be more accurate to say—though the distinction was not then realised—to the Levitical law. In the tanner's house at Joppa these difficulties were to meet with their divine and final solution.

They were problems extremely perplexing. As regards the first question, if the Gentiles were now to be admitted to the possession of full and equal privileges, then had God cast off His people? had the olden promises failed? As regards the second question, was not the Law divine? had it not been delivered amid the terrors of Sinai? Could it have been enforced on *one* nation if it had not been intended for all? Had not Jesus himself been obedient to the commandments? If a distinction were to be drawn between commandments ceremonial and moral, where were the traces of any distinction in the legislation itself, or in the words of Christ? Had He not bidden the leper go show himself to the priest, and offer for his cleansing such things as Moses has commanded for a testimony unto them?[1] Had He not said, " Think not that I am come to destroy the Law and the Prophets; I am not come to destroy, but to *fulfil?* "[2] Had He not even said, "Till heaven and earth shall pass away, one jot or

---

[1] Matt. viii. 4; Mark i. 44.   [2] Matt. v. 17.

one tittle shall in no wise pass from the law till all be fulfilled ? " [1]

These perplexing scruples had yet to wait for their removal, until, by the experience of missionary labour, God had ripened into its richest maturity the inspired genius of Saul of Tarsus. At that period it is probable that no living man could have accurately defined the future relations between Jew and Gentile, or met the difficulties which rose from these considerations. St. Stephen, who might have enlightened the minds of the Apostles on these great subjects, had passed away. St. Paul was still a suspected novice. The day when, in the great Epistles to the Galatians and the Romans, such problems should be fully solved, was still far distant. There is no hurry in the designs of God. It is only when the servitude is at its worst that Moses is called forth. It is only when the perplexity is deepest that Saul enters the arena of controversy. It was only in the fulness of time that Christ was born.

But even at this period St. Peter—especially when he had left Jerusalem—must have been forced to see that the objections of the orthodox Jew to the equal participation of the Gentiles in Gospel privileges could be met by counter objections of serious importance; and that the arguments of Hebraists as to the eternal validity of the Mosaic system were being confronted by the logic of facts with opposing arguments which could not long be set aside.

For if Christ had said that He came to fulfil the Law, had He not also said many things which showed that those words had a deeper meaning than the *primâ facie* application which might be attached to them ? Had He

---

[1] Matt. v. 18 ; Luke xvi. 17.

not six times vindicated for the Sabbath a larger freedom than the scribes admitted?[1] Had He not poured something like contempt on needless ceremonial ablutions?[2] Had He not Himself abstained from going up thrice yearly to Jerusalem to the three great festivals? Had He not often quoted with approval the words of Hoshea: "I will have mercy and not sacrifice?"[3] Had He not repeatedly said that all the Law and the Prophets hang on two broad and simple commandments?[4] Had He not, both by word and action, showed His light estimation of mere ceremonial defilement, to which the Law attached a deep importance?[5] Had He not refused to sanction the stoning of an adulteress? Had He not even gone so far as to say that Moses had conceded some things, which were in themselves undesirable, only because of the hardness of Jewish hearts? Had He not said, "The Law and the Prophets were UNTIL JOHN?"[6]

And, besides all this, was it not clear that He meant His Church to be an Universal Church? Was not this universality of the offered message of mercy and adoption clearly indicated in the language of the Old Testament? Had not the Prophets again and again implied the ultimate calling of the Gentiles?[7] But if the Gentiles were to be admitted into the number of saints and brethren; if, as Jesus Himself had prophesied, there was to be at last one flock and one Shepherd,[8] how could this be if the Mosaic Law was to be considered as of permanent and universal validity? Was it not certain that the Gentiles, as a body, never would accept the whole system

---

[1] Luke xiv. 1—6; John v. 10; Mark ii. 28; Matt. xii. 10; John ix. 14; Luke xiii. 14; xvi. 16. (See *Life of Christ*, ii. 114.)

[2] Matt. xv. 20.

[3] Mark xii. 33; Matt. ix. 13; xii. 7.

[4] Matt. xxii. 40.

[5] Matt. xv. 17; Mark vii. 19.

[6] Matt. xix. 8; Mark x. 5—9.

[7] See Rom. xv. 9, 10, 11.

[8] John x. 16, ποίμνη.

of Mosaism, and never would accept, above all, the crucial
ordinance of circumcision? Would not such a demand
upon them be a certain way of insuring the refusal of
the Gospel message? Or, if they did embrace it, was it
conceivable that the Gentiles were never to be anything
but mere Proselytes of the Gate, thrust as it were outside
the portals of the True Spiritual Temple? If so, were not
the most primary conceptions of Christianity cut away at
the very roots? were not its most beautiful and essential
institutions rendered impossible? How could there be
love-feasts, how could there be celebrations of the Lord's
Supper, how could there be the beautiful spectacle of
Christian love and Christian unity, if the Church was to
be composed, not of members joined together in equal
brotherhood, but of a proletariate of tolerated Gentiles,
excluded even from the privilege of eating with an aristocracy of superior Jews? Dim and dwarfed and maimed
did such an ideal look beside the grand conception of the
redeemed nations of the world coming to Sion, singing,
and with everlasting joy upon their heads !

And behind all these uncertainties towered a yet vaster
and more eternal question. Christ had died to take away
the sins of the world; what need, then, could there be of
sacrifices? What significance could there be any more in
the shadow, when the substance had been granted?[1]
Where was the meaning of types, after they had been fulfilled in the glorious Antitype? What use was left for the
lamp of the Tabernacle when the Sun of Righteousness
had risen with healing in His wings?

Such thoughts, such problems, such perplexities, pressing for a decided principle which should guide men in
their course of action amid daily multiplying difficulties,

---

[1] 1 Cor. xiii. 10; Col. ii. 17; Heb. x. i.

must inevitably have occupied, at this period, the thoughts of many of the brethren. In the heart of Peter they must have assumed yet more momentous proportions, because on him in many respects the initiative would depend.[1] The destinies of the world during centuries of history—the question whether, ere that brief *aeon* closed, the inestimable benefits of the Life and Death of Christ should be confined to the sectaries of an obsolete covenant and a perishing nationality, or extended freely to all the races of mankind—the question whether weary generations should be forced to accept the peculiarities of a Semitic tribe, or else look for no other refuge than the shrines of Isis or the Stoa of Athens—all depended, humanly speaking, on the line which should be taken by one who claimed no higher earthly intelligence than that of a Jewish fisherman. But God always chooses His own fitting instruments. In the decision of momentous questions, rectitude of heart is a far surer guarantee of wisdom than power of intellect. When the unselfish purpose is ready to obey, the supernatural illumination is never wanting. When we desire only to do what is right, it is never long before we hear the voice behind us saying, "This is the way, walk ye in it," however much we might be otherwise inclined to turn aside to the right hand or to the left.

With such uncertainties in his heart, but also with such desire to be guided aright, one day at noon Peter mounted to the flat roof of the tanner's house for his mid-day prayer.[2] It is far from impossible that the house may have been on the very spot with the one with which it has long been identified. It is at the

---

[1] "Lo maggior Padre di famiglia" (Dante, *Parad.* xxxii. 136).

[2] Matt. x. 27; xxiv. 17; Luke xvii. 31. House-tops in old days had been the common scenes of idol-worship (Jer. xix. 13; Zeph. i. 5, &c.).

south-west corner of the little town, and the spring in the
courtyard would have been useful to the tanner if he
carried on his trade in the place where he lived. A fig-
tree now overshadows it, and there may have been one
even then to protect the Apostle from the Syrian sun. In
any case his eyes must have looked on identically the
same scene which we may now witness from that spot; a
small Oriental town with the outline of its flat roofs and
low square houses relieved by trees and gardens; a line
of low dunes and sandy shore; a sea stretching far
away to the Isles of the Gentiles—a golden mirror burning under the rays of the Eastern noon in unbroken light,
except where it is rippled by the wings of the sea-birds
which congregate on the slippery rocks beneath the town,
or where its lazy swell breaks over the line of reef which
legend has connected with the story of Andromeda. It is
a meeting-point of the East and West. Behind us lie
Philistia and the Holy Land. Beyond the Jordan, and
beyond the purple hills which form the eastern ramparts
of its valley, and far away beyond the Euphrates, were the
countries of those immemorial and colossal despotisms—
the giant forms of empires which had passed long ago
" on their way to ruin: " before us—a highway for the
nations—are the inland waters of the sea whose shores
during long ages of history have been the scene of all
that is best and greatest in the progress of mankind. As
he gazed dreamily on sea and town did Peter think of that
old prophet who, eight centuries before, had been sent by
God from that very port to preach repentance to one of
those mighty kingdoms of the perishing Gentiles, and
whom in strange ways God had taught?[1]

It was high noon, and while he prayed and meditated,

---

[1] Jonah i 8.

the Apostle, who all his life had been familiar with the scanty fare of poverty, became very hungry. But the midday meal was not yet ready, and, while he waited, his hunger, his uncertainties, his prayers for guidance, were all moulded by the providence of God, to the fulfilment of His own high ends. There is something inimitably natural in the way in which truths of transcendent importance were brought home to the seeker's thoughts amid the fantastic crudities of mental imagery. The narrative bears upon the face of it the marks of authenticity, and we feel instinctively that it is the closest possible reflection of the form in which divine guidance came to the honest and impetuous Apostle as, in the hungry pause which followed his mid-day supplications, he half-dozed, half meditated on the hot flat roof under the blazing sky, with his gaze towards the West and towards the future, over the blazing sea.

A sort of trance came over him.[1]

The heaven seemed to open. Instead of the burning radiance of sky and sea there shone before him something like a great linen sheet,[2] which was being let down to him from heaven to earth by ropes which held it at the four corners.[3] In its vast capacity, as in the hollow of some great ark, he saw all the four-footed beasts, and reptiles of the earth, and fowls of the air,[4] while a voice said to him, "Rise, Peter, slay and eat." But even in his hunger, kindled yet more keenly by the sight of food, Peter did not forget

---

[1] Acts x. 10, ἐγένετο ἐπ' αὐτὸν ἔκστασις (א, A, B, C, E, &c.).

[2] ὀθόνη (cf. John xix. 40).

[3] This seems to be implied in the ἀρχαῖς (see Eur. *Hippol.* 762, and Wetst. *ad loc.*). But δεδεμένον καὶ are wanting in א, A, B, E. The Vulgate has "quatuor initiis submitti de caelo."

[4] Acts x. 12, πάντα τὰ, "all the," not "all kinds of," which would be παντοῖα. Augustine uses the comparison of the ark (*c. Faust.* xii. 15); omit καὶ τὰ θηρία (, A, B, &c.).

the habits of his training.   Among these animals and
creeping things were swine, and camels, and rabbits, and
creatures which did not chew the cud or divide the hoof—
all of which had been distinctly forbidden by the Law
as articles of food.   Better die of hunger than violate
the rules of the *Kashar*, and eat such things, the very
thought of which caused a shudder to a Jew.[1]   It
seemed strange to Peter that a voice from heaven
should bid him, without exception or distinction, to
slay and eat creatures among which the unclean were
thus mingled with the clean;—nay, the very presence
of the unclean among them seemed to defile the entire
sheet.[2]   Brief as is the narrative of this trance in which
bodily sensations assuming the grotesque form of objective
images became a medium of spiritual illumination,[3] it is
clearly implied that though pure and impure animals were
freely mingled in the great white sheet, it was mainly on
the latter that the glance of Peter fell, just as it was
with " sinners " of the Gentiles, and their admission to the
privileges of brotherhood, that his thoughts must have
been mainly occupied.   Accordingly, with that simple and
audacious self-confidence which in his character was so
singularly mingled with fits of timidity and depression, he
boldly corrects the Voice which orders him, and reminds

[1] On the *Kashar*, see *infra*, p. 434. The example of Daniel (i. 8—16)
made the Jews more particular. Josephus (*Vit.* 3) tells us that some priests
imprisoned at Rome lived only on figs and nuts.

[2] In the Talmud (*Sanhedr.* f. 59, col. 2) there is a curious story about
unclean animals supernaturally represented to R. Shimon Ben Chalaphtha, *who
slays them for food.* This leads to the remark, "*Nothing unclean comes down
from heaven.*" Have we here an oblique argument against the significance of
St. Peter's vision? R. Ishmael said that the care of Israel to avoid creeping
things would alone have been a reason why God saved them from Egypt
(*Babha Metzia*, f. 61, 2). Yet every Sanhedrist must be ingenious enough to
prove that a creeping thing is clean (*Sanhedrin*, f. 17, 1).

[3] See some excellent remarks of Neander, *Planting*, i. 78.

the Divine Interlocutor that he must, so to speak, have made an oversight.[1]

"By no means, Lord!"—and the reader will immediately recall the scene of the Gospel, in which St. Peter, emboldened by Christ's words of praise, took Him and began to rebuke Him, saying, "Be it far from Thee, Lord,"—"for," he added, with a touch of genuine Judaic pride, "I never ate anything profane or unclean." And the Voice spake a second time: "What God cleansed, 'profane' not thou;" or, in the less energetic periphrasis of our Version, "What God hath cleansed, that call not thou common." This was done thrice, and then the vision vanished. The sheet was suddenly drawn up into heaven. The trance was over. Peter was alone with his own thoughts; all was hushed; there came no murmur more from the blazing heaven; at his feet rolled silently the blazing sea.

What did it mean? St. Peter's hunger was absorbed in the perplexity of interpreting the strange symbols by which he felt at once that the Holy Spirit was guiding him to truth—to truth on which he must act, however momentous were the issues, however painful the immediate results. Was that great linen sheet in its whiteness the

---

[1] Cf. John xiii. 8. Increased familiarity with Jewish writings invariably deepens our conviction that in the New Testament we are dealing with truthful records. Knowing as we do the reverence of the Jews for divine intimations, we might well have supposed that not even in a trance would Peter have raised objections to the mandate of the Bath Kol. And yet we find exactly the same thing in Scripture (1 Kings xix. 14; Jonah iv. 1, 9; Jer. i. 6), in the previous accounts of Peter himself (Matt. xvi. 22); of St. Paul (Acts xxii. 19); and in the Talmudic writings. Few stories of the Talmud convey a more unshaken conviction of the indefeasible obligatoriness of the Law than that of the resistance even to a voice from heaven by the assembled Rabbis, in *Babha Metsia*, f. 59, 2 (I have quoted it in the *Expositor*, 1877). It not only illustrates the point immediately before us, but also shows more clearly than anything else could do the overwhelming forces against which St. Paul had to fight his way.

8

image of a world washed white,[1] and were its four corners
a sign that they who dwelt therein were to be gathered
from the east and from the west, from the north and from
the south; and were all the animals and creeping things,
clean and unclean, the image of all the races which
inhabit it? And if so, was the permission—nay, the
command—to eat of the unclean no less than of the clean
an indication that the Levitical Law was now "ready
to vanish away;"[2] and that with it must vanish away,
no less inevitably, that horror of any communion with
Gentile races which rested mainly upon its provisions?
What else could be meant by a command which directly
contradicted the command of Moses?[3] Was it really
meant that all things were to become new? that even
these unclean things were to be regarded as let down
from heaven? and that in this new world, this pure
world, Gentiles were no longer to be called "dogs," but
Jew and Gentile were to meet on a footing of perfect
equality, cleansed alike by the blood of Christ?

Nor is the connexion between the symbol and the
thing signified quite so distant and arbitrary as has been
generally supposed. The distinction between clean and
unclean meats was one of the insuperable barriers between
the Gentile and the Jew—a barrier which prevented all
intercourse between them, because it rendered it impossible for them to meet at the same table or in social
life. In the society of a Gentile, a Jew was liable at
any moment to those ceremonial defilements which
involved all kinds of seclusion and inconvenience; and
not only so, but it was mainly by partaking of unclean
food that the Gentiles became themselves so unclean
in the eyes of the Jews. It is hardly possible to put

---

[1] So Œcumenius.   [2] Heb. viii. 13.   [3] Lev. xi. 7; Deut. xiv. 8.

into words the intensity of horror and revolt with which the Jew regarded swine.[1] They were to him the very ideal and quintessence of all that must be looked upon with an energetic concentration of disgust. He would not even mention a pig by name, but spoke of it as *dabhar achèer*, or "the other thing." When, in the days of Hyrcanus, a pig had been surreptitiously put into a box and drawn up the walls of Jerusalem, the Jews declared that a shudder of earthquake had run through four hundred parasangs of the Holy Land.[2] Yet this filthy and atrocious creature, which could hardly even be thought of without pollution, was not only the chief delicacy at Gentile banquets,[3] but was, in one form or other, one of the commonest articles of Gentile consumption. How could a Jew touch or speak to a human being who of deliberate choice had banqueted on swine's flesh, and who might on that very day have partaken of the abomination? The cleansing of all articles of food involved far more immediately than has yet been noticed the acceptance of Gentiles on equal footing to equal privileges.

And doubtless, as such thoughts passed through the soul of Peter, he remembered also that remarkable "parable" of Jesus of which he and his brother disciples had once asked the explanation. Jesus in a few words, but with both of the emphatic formulæ which He adopted to call special attention to any utterance of more than ordinary depth and solemnity—"*Hearken unto me, every one of you, and understand ;*" "*If any man hath ears to hear, let him*

---

[1] Isa. lxv. 4; lxvi. 3; 2 Macc. vi. 18, 19; Jos. *C. Ap.* ii. 14. The abhorrence was shared by many Eastern nations (*Hdt.* ii. 47; Pliny, *H. N.* viii. 52; Koran). This was partly due to its filthy habits (2 Pet. ii. 22).

[2] *Jer. Berachôth*, iv. 1; Derenbourg, *Palest.* 114; Grätz. iii. 480. (The story is also told in *Babha Kama*, f. 82, 2; *Menachoth*, f. 64, 2; *Sotah*, f. 49, 2.)

[3] *Sumen*, in Plaut. *Curc.* ii. 3, 44; Pers. i. 53; Plin. *H. N.* xi. 37.

s 2

hear,"[1]—had said, "There is nothing from without a man entering into him which can defile him." What He had proceeded to say—that what truly defiles a man is that which comes out of him—was easy enough to understand, and was a truth of deep meaning; but so difficult had it been to grasp the first half of the clause, that they had asked Him to explain a "parable" which seemed to be in direct contradiction to the Mosaic Law. Expressing His astonishment at their want of insight, He had shown them that what entered into a man from without did but become a part of his material organism, entering, "not into the heart, but into the belly, and so passing into the draught." THIS, HE SAID—as now for the first time, perhaps, flashed with full conviction into the mind of Peter—MAKING ALL MEATS PURE;[2]—as he proceeded afterwards to develop those weighty truths about the inward character of all real pollution, and the genesis of all crime from evil thoughts, which convey so solemn a warning. To me it seems that it was the trance and vision of Joppa which first made Peter realise the true meaning of Christ in one of those few *distinct* utterances in which he had intimated the coming annulment of the Mosaic Law. It is, doubtless, due to the fact that St. Peter, as the informant of St. Mark in writing his Gospel, and the sole ultimate authority for this vision in the Acts, is the source of *both* narratives,

---

[1] Mark vii. 14, 16.

[2] Mark vii. 19. This interpretation, due originally to the early Fathers—being found in Chrysostom, *Hom. in Matt.* li. p. 526, and Gregory Thaumaturgus—was revived, forty years ago, by the Rev. F. Field, in a note of his edition of St. Chrysostom's *Homilies* (iii. 112). (See *Expositor* for 1876, where I have examined the passage at length.) Here, however, it lay unnoticed, till it gained, quite recently, the attention which it deserved. The true reading is certainly καθαρίζων, not the καθαρίζον of our edition—a reading due, in all probability, to the impossibility of making καθαρίζων agree with ἀφεδρῶνα. The loss of the true interpretation has been very serious. Now, however, it is happily revived. It has a more direct bearing than any other on the main practical difficulty of the Apostolic age.

that we owe the hitherto unnoticed circumstance that the two verbs "*cleanse*" and "*profane*"—both in a peculiarly pregnant sense—are the two most prominent words in the narrative of both events.

While Peter thus pondered—perplexed, indeed, but with a new light dawning in his soul—the circumstance occurred which gave to his vision its full significance. Trained, like all Jews, in unquestioning belief of a daily Providence exercised over the minutest no less than over the greatest events of life, Peter would have been exactly in the mood which was prepared to accept any further indication of God's will from whatever source it came. The recognised source of such guidance at this epoch was the utterance of voices apparently accidental which the Jews reckoned as their sole remaining kind of inspired teaching, and to which they gave the name of *Bath Kol*.[1] The first words heard by Peter after his singular trance were in the voices of Gentiles. In the courtyard below him were three Gentiles, of whom one was in the garb of a soldier. Having asked their way to the house of Simon the Tanner, they were now inquiring whether a certain Simon, who bore the surname of Peter, was lodging there. Instantly there shot through his mind a gleam of heavenly light. He saw the divine connexion between the vision of his trance and the inquiry of these Gentiles, and a Voice within him warned him that these men had come in accordance with an express intimation of God's will, and that he was to go with them without question or hesitation. He instantly obeyed. He descended from the roof, told the messengers he was the person whom they were seeking, and asked their business. They were the bearers of a strange message. "Cornelius," they said, " a

---

[1] *Life of Christ*, i. 118.

centurion, a just man, and a worshipper of God, to whose virtues the entire Jewish nation bore testimony, had received an angelic intimation to send for him, and hear his instructions. Peter at once offered them the free and simple hospitality of the East; and as it was too hot and they were too tired to start at once on their homeward journey, they rested there until the following morning. Further conversation would have made Peter aware that Cornelius was a centurion of the Italian band;[1] that not only he, but all his house, "feared God;" that the generosity of his almsgiving and the earnestness of his prayers were widely known; and that the intimation to send for Peter had been given to him while he was fasting on the previous day at three o'clock. He had acted upon it so immediately that, in spite of the heat and the distance of thirty miles along shore and plain, his messengers had arrived at Joppa by the following noon.

The next morning they all started on the journey which was to involve such momentous issues. How deeply alive St. Peter himself was to the consequences which might ensue from his act is significantly shown by his inviting no fewer than six of the brethren at Joppa to accompany him, and to be witnesses of all that should take place.[2]

The journey—since Orientals are leisurely in their movements, and they could only travel during the cool hours—occupied two days. Thus it was not until the fourth day after the vision of Cornelius that, for the first time during two thousand years, the Jew and the Gentile met on the broad grounds of perfect religious equality

---

[1] The Italian cohort was probably one composed of "*Velones*," Italian volunteers. "Cohors militum voluntaria, quae est in Syria" (Gruter, *Inscr.* i. 434; Akerman, *Num. Illustr.* 84). It would be specially required at Cæsarea.

[2] Compare Acts x. 23 with xi. 12.

before God their Father. Struck with the sacredness of the occasion—struck, too, it may be, by something in the appearance of the chief of the Apostles—Cornelius, who had risen to meet Peter on the threshold, prostrated himself at his feet,[1] as we are told that, three hundred years before, Alexander the Great had done at the feet of the High Priest Jaddua,[2] and, six hundred years afterwards, Edwin of Deira did at the feet of Paulinus.[3] Instantly Peter raised the pious soldier, and, to the amazement doubtless of the brethren who accompanied him, perhaps even to his own astonishment, violated all the traditions of a lifetime, as well as the national customs of many centuries, by walking side by side with him in free conversation into the presence of his assembled Gentile relatives. This he did, not from the forgetfulness of an enthusiastic moment, but with the avowal that he was doing that which had been hitherto regarded as irreligious,[4] but doing it in accordance with a divine revelation. Cornelius then related the causes which had led him to send for Peter, and the Apostle began his solemn address to them with the memorable statement that now he perceived with undoubted certainty that "GOD IS NO RESPECTER OF PERSONS, BUT IN EVERY NATION HE THAT FEARETH HIM AND WORKETH RIGHTEOUSNESS IS ACCEPTABLE TO HIM."[5] Never were

[1] D and the Syr. have the pragmatic addition, "And when Peter drew near to Cæsarea, one of the slaves running forward gave notice that he had arrived; and Cornelius springing forth, and meeting him, falling at his feet, worshipped him."

[2] See Jos. Antt. xi. 8, § 5.

[3] The story is told in Bede, Eccl. Hist. Angl. ii. 12.

[4] Acts x. 28, ἀθέμιτον; cf. John xviii. 28. Lightf. Hor. Hebr. ad. Matt. xviii. 17.

[5] St. Peter's words are the most categorical contradiction of the Rabbinic comments on Prov. xiv. 34, which asserted that any righteous acts done by the Gentiles were sin to them. Such was the thesis maintained even by

words more noble uttered. But we must not interpret
them to mean the same proposition as that which is so
emphatically repudiated by the English Reformers, "That
every man shall be saved by the law or sect which he
professeth, so that he be diligent to frame his life according to that law and the light of Nature." Had this
been the meaning of the Apostle—a meaning which it
would be an immense anachronism to attribute to him—
it would have been needless for him to preach to Cornelius, as he proceeded to do, the leading doctrines of the
Christian faith; it would have been sufficient for him to
bid Cornelius continue in prayer and charity without un-
folding to him "only the name of Jesus Christ whereby
men must be saved." The indifference of nationality was
the thought in Peter's mind; not by any means the
indifference of religions. All who, to the utmost of the
opportunities vouchsafed to them, fear and love God with
sincerity of heart, shall be saved by Christ's redemption;
some of them—many of them—will He lead to a knowledge of Him in this life; all of them shall see Him and
know Him in the life to come.[1]

Accordingly Peter proceeded to recall to these Gentiles
all that they had heard[2] of the preaching of peace by
Jesus Christ the Lord of all; of His life and ministry
after the baptism of John; how God anointed Him
with the Holy Spirit and with power; how He went
about doing good, and healing all who were under the
tyranny of the devil; and then of the Crucifixion and
Resurrection from the dead, of which the disciples were
the appointed witnesses, commissioned by the Voice of

Hillelites like Gamaliel II. and R. Eliezer of Modin, *Babha Bathra*, f. 10, 2
(v. *infra*, ii., pp. 135, 176.)

[1] Cf. Rom. ii. 6, 10, 14, 15.

[2] Acts x. 36. To understand τὸν λόγον here in the Johannine sense
seems to me utterly uncritical.

their risen Lord to testify that He is the destined Judge
of quick and dead. And while Peter was proceeding to
show from the Prophets that all who believed on Him
should through His name receive remission of sins,
suddenly on these unbaptised Gentiles no less than on
the Jews who were present, fell that inspired emotion
of superhuman utterance which was the signature of
Pentecost. "The Holy Ghost fell upon them." The six
brethren who had accompanied Peter from Joppa might
well be amazed. Here were men unbaptised, uncircumcised, unclean—men who had been idolators, dogs of the
Gentiles, eaters of the unclean beast, whose touch involved ceremonial pollution—speaking and praising God
in the utterances which could only come from hearts
stirred by divine influence to their most secret depth.
With bold readiness Peter seized the favourable moment.
The spectacle which he had witnessed raised him above
ignoble prejudices, and the rising tide of conviction swept
away the dogmas and habits of his earlier years. Appealing to this proof of the spiritual equality of the Gentile
with the Jew, he asked "whether any one could forbid
water for their baptism?" No one cared to dispute the
cogency of this proof that it was God's will to admit
Cornelius and his friends to the privileges of Christian
brotherhood. Peter not only commanded them to be
baptised in the name of the Lord, but even freely
accepted their invitation "to tarry with them certain
days."

The news of a revolution so astounding was not long
in reaching Jerusalem, and when Peter returned to the
Holy City he was met by the sterner zealots who had
joined Christianity, by those of whom we shall henceforth
hear so often as "those of the circumcision," with the
fierce indignant murmur, "*Thou wentest into the house of*

men uncircumcised, and didst EAT WITH THEM!" [1] To
associate with them, to enter their houses, was not that
pollution enough? to touch in familiar intercourse men
who had never received the seal of the covenant, to be in
daily contact with people who might, no one knew how
recently, have had "broth of abominable things in their
vessels"—was not this sufficiently horrible? But *"to eat
with them"*—to eat food prepared by Gentiles—to taste
meat which had been illegally killed by Gentile hands—
to neglect the rules of the *Kashar*—to take food from
dishes which any sort of unclean insect or animal, nay
even "the other thing," might have defiled—was it to
be thought of without a shudder? [2]

Thus Peter was met at Jerusalem by something very like
an impeachment, but he confronted the storm with perfect
courage. [3] What he had done he had not done arbitrarily,
but step by step under direct divine guidance. He detailed to them his vision on the roof at Joppa, and the
angelic appearance which had suggested the message of
Cornelius. Finally he appealed to the outpouring of the
Holy Spirit, which had been manifested in these Gentiles
by the very same signs as in themselves. Was not this
the promised baptism with the Holy Ghost? was it not
a proof that God accepted these Gentiles no less fully
than He accepted *them?* "What was I that I could
withstand God?"

The bold defence silenced for a time the adversaries of

---

[1] "He who eats with an uncircumcised person, eats, as it were, with a
dog; he who touches him, touches, as it were, a dead body; and he who
bathes in the same place with him, bathes, as it were, with a leper" (*Pirke
Rabbi Elieser*, 29).

[2] To this day orthodox Jews submit to any inconvenience rather than
touch meat killed by a Gentile butcher (McCaul, *Old Paths*, 397, *sq.*). This
leads sometimes not only to a monopoly, but even to a downright tyranny on
the part of the butcher who has the *kadima* (Frankl, *Jews in the East*, ii.).

[3] Acts xi. 2, διεκρίνοντο πρὸς αὐτόν; cf. Jud. 9.

what they regarded as an unscriptural and disloyal innovation. They could not dispute facts authenticated by the direct testimony of their six brethren,—whom Peter, conscious of the seriousness of the crisis, had very prudently brought with him from Joppa,—nor could they deny the apparent approval of heaven. The feeling of the majority was in favour of astonished but grateful acquiescence. Subsequent events prove only too plainly that there was at any rate a displeased minority, who were quite unprepared to sacrifice their monopoly of precedence in the equal kingdom of God. Even in the language of the others[1] we seem to catch a faint echo of reluctance and surprise. Nor would they admit any general principle. The only point which they conceded was—not that the Gentiles were to be admitted, without circumcision, to full communion, still less that Jews would be generally justified in eating with them, as Peter had done—but only that "God had, it seemed, to the Gentiles also granted repentance unto life."

Meanwhile, and, so far as we are aware, in entire independence of these initial movements, the Church had been undergoing a new and vast development in Syria, which transferred the position of the metropolis of Christianity from Jerusalem to Antioch, as completely as it was to be afterwards transferred from Antioch to Rome.

[1] Acts xi. 18, ἄραγε καὶ τοῖς ἔθνεσιν.

Book V

ANTIOCH.

CHAPTER XVI.

THE SECOND CAPITAL OF CHRISTIANITY.

"Quos, per flagitia invisos, vulgus *Christianos* appellabat."— TAC. *Ann.* xv. 44.

Χριστιανός εἰμί.—*Mart. Polyc.* iii.

Εὐχαριστοῦμεν σοι ὅτι τὸ ὄνομα τοῦ Χριστοῦ σου ἐπικέκληται ἐφ᾽ ἡμᾶς, καὶ σοὶ προσφκειφμεθα.—CLEM. ROM.

Οὐκ αὐτοὶ βλασφημοῦσι τὸ καλὸν ὄνομα τὸ ἐπικληθέν ἐφ᾽ ὑμᾶς;—JAS. ii. 7.

Εἰ ὀνειδίζεσθε ἐν ὀνόματι Χριστοῦ, μακάριοι.—1 PET. iv. 14.

"Nomen . . . quod sicut unguentum diffusum longe lateque redolet."—GAL. *Tyr.* iv. 9.

"Oditur ergo in hominibus innocuis etiam nomen innocuum."—TERT. *Apol.* 3.

THE overruling Providence of God is so clearly marked in the progress of human events that the Christian hardly needs any further proof that "there is a hand that guides." In the events of his own little life the perspective of God's dealings is often hidden from him, but when he watches the story of nations and of religions he can clearly trace the divine purposes, and see the lessons which God's hand has written on every page of history. What seems to be utter ruin is often complete salvation; what was regarded as cruel disaster constantly turns out to be essential blessing.

It was so with the persecution which ensued on the death of Stephen. Had it been less inquisitorial, it would not have accomplished its destined purpose. The Saul who laid in ruins the Church of Jerusalem was unconsciously deepening the foundations of circumstance on which hereafter—the same and not the same—he should rear the superstructure of the Church of God. Saul the persecutor was doing, by opposite means, the same work as Paul the Apostle.

For when the members of the infant Church fled terror-stricken from the Holy City, they carried with them far and wide the good tidings of the Jerusalem above. At first, as was natural, they spoke to Jews alone. It would be long before they would hear how Philip had evangelised Samaria, and how, by his baptism of the eunuch, he had admitted into the Church of Christ one whom Moses had excluded from the congregation of Israel. The baptism of the pious soldier had taken place still later, and the knowledge of it could not at once reach the scattered Christians. In Phœnicia, therefore, and in Cyprus their preaching was confined at first within the limits of Judaism; nor was it until the wandering Hellenists had reached Antioch that they boldly ventured *TO PREACH TO THE GENTILES*.[1] Whether these

[1] Acts xi. 20. There can be no doubt that Ἕλληνας, and not Ἑλληνιστὰς (which is accepted by our version, and rendered " Grecians ") is the true reading. (1) External evidence in favour of Ἕλληνας is indeed defective, since it is only found in A (which also has Ἕλληνας, even in ix. 29, where Ἑλληνιστὰς is the only *possible* reading) and D. א has εὑαγγελιστὰς, which has been altered into Ἕλληνας; but both א and B read καὶ before ἐλάλουν, which indicates a new and important statement. Some of the most important versions are valueless as evidence of reading in this instance, because they have no specific word by which to distinguish Ἑλληνισταὶ and Ἕλληνες. Œcumenius and Theophylact read Ἑλληνιστὰς, and so does Chrysostom in his text, but in his commentary he accepts Ἕλληνας, as does Eusebius. But (2) if we turn to internal evidence it is clear that " Greeks," not " Grecians "—*i.e., Gentiles*, not Greek-speaking Jews—is the only admissible reading; for (i.) Hellenists were, of course, Jews, and as it is perfectly certain that the Ἰουδαίοις of the previous verse cannot mean only Hebraists, this verse 20 would add nothing whatever to the narrative if " Hellenists " were the right reading.

Gentiles were such only as had already embraced the "Noachian dispensation," or whether they included others who had in no sense become adherents of the synagogue, we are not told. Greek proselytes were at this period common in every considerable city of the Empire,[1] and it is reasonable to suppose that they furnished a majority, at any rate, of the new converts. However this may have been, the work of these nameless Evangelists was eminently successful. It received the seal of God's blessing, and a large multitude of Greeks turned to the Lord. The fact, so much obscured by the wrong reading followed by our English Version, is nothing less than the beginning, on a large scale, of the *conversion of the Gentiles*. It is one of the great *moments* in the ascensive work begun by Stephen, advanced by Philip, authorised by Peter, and finally culminating in the life, mission, and Epistles of St. Paul.

When the news reached Jerusalem, it excited great attention, and the members of the Church determined to despatch one of their number to watch what was going on.

(ii.) The statement comes as the sequel and crowning point of narratives, of which it has been the express object to describe the admission of *Gentiles* into the Church. The reading "*Hellenists*" obscures the verse on which the entire narrative of the Acts hinges. (iii.) The conversion of a number of Hellenists at Antioch would have excited no special notice, and required no special mission of inquiry, seeing that the existing Church at Jerusalem itself consisted largely of Hellenists. The entire context, therefore, conclusively proves that "Ελληνας is the right reading, and it has accordingly been received into the text, in spite of the external evidence against it, by all the best editors —Griesbach, Lachmann, Scholz, Tischendorf, Meyer, Alford, &c. The reason for the corruption of the text seems to have been an assumption that this narrative is retrospective, and that to suppose the admission of Gentiles into the faith before Peter had opened to them the doors of the kingdom would be to derogate from his authority. But this preaching at Antioch may have been subsequent to the conversion of Cornelius ; and it was, in any case, the authority of Peter which for the majority of the Church incontrovertibly settled the claim of the Gentiles.

[1] See Acts xiv. 1; xviii. 4; John xii. 20.

Their choice of an emissary showed that as yet the counsels of the party of moderation prevailed, for they despatched the large-hearted and conciliatory Barnabas. His Levitical descent, and the sacrifice which he had made of his property to the common fund, combined with his sympathetic spirit and liberal culture to give him a natural authority, which he had always used on the side of charity and wisdom.

The arrival of such a man was an especial blessing. This new church, which was so largely composed of Gentiles, was destined to be a fresh starting-point in the career of Christianity. Barnabas saw the grace of God at work, and rejoiced at it, and justified his happy title of "the son of exhortation," by exhorting the believers to cleave to the Lord with purpose of heart. His ministry won over converts in still larger numbers, for, as Luke adds with emphatic commendation, "he was a good man, and full of the Holy Ghost and faith."

The work multiplied in his hands, and needed so much wisdom, knowledge, and energy, that he soon felt the need of a colleague. Doubtless, had he desired it, he could have secured the co-operation of one of the Apostles, or of their trusted adherents. But Barnabas instinctively perceived that a fresher point of view, a clearer insight, a wider culture, a more complete immunity from pre-judices were needed for so large and delicate a task. Himself a Grecian, and now called upon to minister not only to Grecians but to Greeks, he longed for the aid of one who would maintain the cause of truth and liberality with superior ability and more unflinching con-viction. There was but one man who in any degree met his requirements—it was the delegate of the San-hedrin, the zealot of the Pharisees, the once persecuting Saul of Tarsus. Since his escape from Jerusalem, Saul had been more or less unnoticed by the leading Apostles. We lose sight of him at Cæsarea, apparently starting on his way to Tarsus, and all that Barnabas now knew about him was that he was living quietly at home, waiting the Lord's call. Accordingly he set out, to seek for him, and the turn of expression seems to imply that it was not without difficulty that he found him. Paul readily accepted the invitation to leave his seclusion, and join his friend in this new work in the great capital of Syria. Thus, twice over, did Barnabas save Saul for the work of Christianity. To his self-effacing nobleness is due the honour of recognising, before they had yet been revealed to others, the fiery vigour, the indomitable energy, the splendid courage, the illuminated and illuminating intellect, which were destined to spend themselves in the high endeavour to ennoble and evangelise the world.

No place could have been more suitable than Antioch for the initial stage of such a ministry. The queen of the East, the third metropolis of the world, the residence of the imperial Legate of Syria, this vast city of perhaps 500,000 souls must not be judged of by the diminished, shrunken, and earthquake-shattered Antakieh of to-day.[1] It was no mere Oriental town, with low flat roofs and dingy narrow streets, but a Greek capital enriched and enlarged by Roman munificence. It is situated at the point of junction between the chains of Lebanon and Taurus. Its natural position on the northern slope of Mount Silpius, with a navigable river, the broad, historic Orontes, flowing at its feet, was at once commanding and beautiful. The windings of the river enriched the whole well-wooded plain, and as the city was but sixteen miles from the shore, the sea-

---

[1] It is now a fifth-rate Turkish town of 6,000 inhabitants. (Porter's *Syria*, p. 568.)

breezes gave it health and coolness. These natural advantages had been largely increased by the lavish genius of ancient art. Built by the Seleucidæ [1] as the royal residence of their dynasty, its wide circuit of many miles was surrounded by walls of astonishing height and thickness, which had been carried across ravines and over mountain summits with such daring magnificence of conception as to give the city the aspect of being defended by its own encircling mountains, as though those gigantic bulwarks were but its natural walls. The palace of the kings of Syria was on an island formed by an artificial channel of the river. Through the entire length of the city, from the Golden or Daphne gate on the west, ran for nearly five miles a fine corso adorned with trees, colonnades, and statues. Originally constructed by Seleucus Nicator, it had been continued by Herod the Great, who, at once to gratify his passion for architecture, and to reward the people of Antioch for their good-will toward the Jews, had paved it for two miles and a half with blocks of white marble.[2] Broad bridges spanned the river and its various affluents; baths, aqueducts, basilicas, villas, theatres, clustered on the level plain, and, overshadowed by picturesque and rugged eminences, gave the city a splendour worthy of its fame as only inferior in grandeur to Alexandria and Rome. Mingled with this splendour were innumerable signs of luxury and comfort. Under the spreading plane-trees that shaded the banks of the river, and among gardens brightened with masses of flowers, sparkled amid groves of laurel and myrtle the gay villas of the wealthier inhabitants, bright with Greek frescoes, and adorned with every refinement which Roman wealth had borrowed from Ionian luxury. Art had lent

---

[1] B.C. 301, Apr. 23.   [2] Jos. *Antt.* xvi. 5, § 3.

T

its aid to enhance the beauties of nature, and one colossal crag of Mount Silpius, which overlooked the city, had been carved into human semblance by the skill of Leïos. In the days of Antiochus Epiphanes, a pestilence had ravaged the kingdom, and to appease the anger of the gods, the king had ordered the sculptor to hew the mountain-mass into one vast statue. The huge grim face, under the rocky semblance of a crown, stared over the Forum of the city, and was known to the Antiochenes as the Charonium, being supposed to represent the head of

> "That grim ferryman which poets write of,"

who conveyed the souls of the dead in his dim-gleaming boat across the waters of the Styx.

It was natural that such a city should attract a vast multitude of inhabitants, and those inhabitants were of very various nationalities. The basis of the population was composed of native Syrians, represented to this day by the Maronites;[1] but the Syrian kings had invited many colonists to people their Presidence, and the most important of these were Greeks and Jews. To these, after the conquest of Syria by Pompey, had been added a garrison of Romans.[2] The court of the Legate of Syria, surrounded as it was by military pomp, attracted into its glittering circle, not only a multitude of rapacious and domineering officials, but also that large retinue of flatterers, slaves, artists, literary companions, and general hangers-on, whose presence was deemed essential to the state of an imperial viceroy. The autonomy of the city, and its consequent freedom from the property tax, made it a pleasant place of abode to many others. The soft, yielding, and voluptuous

---

[1] Renan, *Les Apôtres*, p. 228.

[2] Syria was made a Roman province B.C. 64. M. Æmil. Scaurus went there as *Quaestor pro Praetore*, B.C. 62.

Syrians, the cunning, versatile, and degraded Greeks, added their special contributions to the general corruption engendered by an enervating climate and a frivolous society. Side by side with these—governed, as at Alexandria, by their own Archon and their own mimic Sanhedrin, but owning allegiance to the central government at Jerusalem —lived an immense colony of Jews. Libanius could affirm from personal experience that he who sat in the agora of Antioch might study the customs of the world.

Cities liable to the influx of heterogeneous races are rarely otherwise than immoral and debased. Even Rome, in the decadence of its Cæsarism, could groan to think of the dregs of degradation—the quacks, and pandars, and musicians, and dancing-girls—poured into the Tiber by the Syrian Orontes. Her satirists spoke of this infusion of Orientalism as adding a fresh miasma even to the corruption which the ebbing tide of glory had left upon the naked sands of Grecian life.[1] It seems as though it were a law of human intercourse, that when races are commingled in large masses, the worst qualities of each appear intensified in the general iniquity. The mud and silt of the combining streams pollute any clearness or sweetness they may previously have enjoyed. If the Jews had been less exclusive, less haughtily indifferent to the moral good of any but themselves, they might have checked the tide of immorality. But their disdainful isolation, either prevented them from making any efforts to ameliorate the condition of their fellow-citizens, or rendered their efforts nugatory. Their synagogues—

---

[1] " Jam pridem Syrus in Tiberim defluxit Orontes
Et linguam, et mores, et cum tibicine chordas
Obliquas, necnon gentilia tympana secum
Vexit, et ad circum jussas prostare puellas."

Juv. Sat. iii. 62—65.

T 2

one, at least, of which was a building of some pretensions, adorned with brazen spoils which had once
belonged to the Temple of Jerusalem,[1] and had been
resigned by Antiochus Epiphanes, in a fit of remorse,
to the Jews of Antioch—rose in considerable numbers
among the radiant temples of the gods of Hellas.   But
the spirit of those who worshipped in them rendered
them an ineffectual witness; and the Jews, absorbed in the
conviction that they were the sole favourites of Jehovah,
passed with a scowl of contempt, or "spat, devoutly brutal,
in the face" of the many statues which no classic beauty
could redeem from the disgrace of being "dumb idols."
There were doubtless, indeed, other proselytes besides
Nicolas and Luke; but those proselytes, whether few or
many in number, had, up to this period, exercised no
appreciable influence on the gay and guilty city.   And
if the best Jews despised all attempts at active propa-
gandism, there were sure to be many lewd and wicked
Jews who furthered their own interests by a propaganda
of iniquity.   If the Jewish nationality has produced some
of the best and greatest, it has also produced some of the
basest and vilest of mankind.   The Jews at Antioch were
of just the same mixed character as the Jews at
Alexandria, or Rome, or Paris, or London; and we may
be quite sure that there must have been many among
them who, instead of witnessing for Jehovah, would only
add a tinge of original wickedness to the seething mass of
atheism, idolatry, and polluted life.

And thus for the great mass of the population in
Antioch there was nothing that could be truly called a
religion to serve as a barrier against the ever-rising flood
of Roman   sensuality   and   Græco-Syrian   suppleness.

[1] Jos. B. J vii. 3, § 3.

What religion there was took the form of the crudest
nature-worship, or the most imbecile superstition.   A few
years before the foundation of a Christian Church at
Antioch, in the year 37, there had occurred one of those
terrible earthquakes to which, in all ages, the city had
been liable.[1] It might have seemed at first sight incredible that an intellectual and literary city like Antioch
—a city of wits and philosophers, of casuists and rhetoricians, of poets and satirists—should at once have
become the dupes of a wretched quack named Debborius,
who professed to avert such terrors by talismans as
ludicrous as the famous earthquake-pills which so often
point an allusion in modern literature.   Yet there is in
reality nothing strange in such apparent contrasts.   History
more than once has shown that the border-lands of
Atheism reach to the confines of strange credulity.[2]

[1] Our authorities for the description and condition of Antioch are unusually rich.   The chief are Josephus, *B. J.* vii. 3, § 3; *Antt.* xii. 3, § 1;
xvi. 5, § 3; *c. Ap.* ii. 4; 1 Macc. iii. 37; xi. 13; 2 Macc. iv. 7—9, 33; v. 21;
xi. 36; Philostr. *Vit. Apollon.* iii. 58; Libanius, *Antioch.* pp. 355, 356;
Chrysost. *Homil. ad Pop. Antioch.* vii., *in* Matth., *et passim*; Julian. *Misopogon*; Pliny, *H. N.* v. 18; and, above all, the *Chronographia* of John of
Antioch, better known by his Syriac surname of Malala, or the Orator.
O. O. Müller, in his *Antiquitates Antiochenae* (Gött. 1830), has diligently
examined all these and other authorities.   Some accounts of modern Antioch,
by travellers who have visited it, may be found in Pocock's *Descript. of the
East*, ii. 192; Chesney, *Euphrates Expedition*, i. 425, seqq.; Ritter, *Paläst.
u. Syria*, iv. 2. Its hopeless decline dates from 1268, when it was reconquered
by the Mohammedans.

[2] The state of the city has been described by a master-hand. "It was,"
says M. Renan—rendered still more graphic in his description by familiarity
with modern Paris—"an unheard-of collection of jugglers, charlatans, pan-
tomimists, magicians, thaumaturgists, sorcerers, and priestly impostors; a
city of races, of games, of dances, of processions, of festivals, of bacchanalia,
of unchecked luxury; all the extravagances of the East, the most unhealthy
superstitions, the fanaticism of orgies. In turns servile and ungrateful,
worthless and insolent, the Antiochenes were the finished model of those
crowds devoted to Cæsarism, without country, without nationality, without
family honour, without a name to preserve. The great Corso which traversed
the city was like a theatre, in which all day long rolled the waves of a

Into this city of Pagan pleasure—into the midst of a
population pauperised by public doles, and polluted by the
indulgences which they procured—among the intrigues
and ignominies of some of the lowest of the human race
at one of the lowest periods of human history[1]—passed the
eager spirit of Saul of Tarsus. On his way, five miles from
the city, he must have seen upon the river-bank at least the
fringe of laurels, cypresses, and myrtles that marked

> "—— that sweet grove
> Of Daphne by Orontes,"[2]

and caught sight, perhaps, of its colossal statue of Apollo,[3]
reared by Seleucus Nicator. But it was sweet no longer,
except in its natural and ineffaceable beauty, and it is
certain that a faithful Jew would not willingly have entered its polluted precincts. Those precincts, being endowed
with the right of asylum, were, like all the asylums of ancient and modern days, far more a protection to outrageous
villany than to persecuted innocence;[4] and those um-

population empty, frivolous, fickle, turbulent, sometimes witty, absorbed in
songs, parodies, pleasantries, and impertinences of every description. It was,"
he continues, after describing certain dances and swimming-races, which, if we
would understand the depravity of Gentile morals we are forced to mention'
"like an intoxication, a dream of Sardanapalus, in which all pleasures, all
debaucheries, unfolded themselves in strange confusion, without excluding
certain delicacies and refinements" (*Les Apôtres*, p. 221). The Orontes never
flowed with fouler mud than when there began to spring up upon its banks
the sweet fountain of the river of the water of life.

[1] Ausonius says of Antioch and Alexandria,
> "Turbida vulgo
> Utraque et amentis populi malesana tumultu" (*Ordo Nob. Urb.* iii.).

[2] See the celebrated passage in Gibbon's *Decline and Fall*, ch. xxiii.

[3] Now *Beit-al-Ma'a*—a secluded glen. A few dilapidated mills mark a spot
where the shrine of Apollo once gleamed with gold and gems. When Julian
the Apostate paid it a solemn visit, he found there a solitary goose! The Bab
Bolos, or "Gate of Paul," is on the Aleppo road. The town still bears a bad
name for licentiousness, and only contains a few hundred Christians. (See
Carne's *Syria*, i. 5, &c.)

[4] 2 Macc. iv. 33.

brageous groves were the dark haunts of every foulness.
For their scenic loveliness, their rich foliage, their fragrant
herbage, their perennial fountains, the fiery-hearted convert had little taste. He could only have recalled with
a sense of disgust how that grove had given its title to
a proverb which expressed the superfluity of naughtiness,[1]
and how its evil haunts had flung away the one rare chance
of sheltering virtue from persecution, when the good Onias
was tempted from it to be murdered by the governor of
its protecting city.[2]

Such was the place where, in the street Singon, Saul
began to preach. He may have entered it by the gate
which was afterwards called the Gate of the Cherubim,
because twenty-seven years later[3] it was surmounted
by those colossal gilded ornaments which Titus had
taken from the Temple of Jerusalem. It was a populous quarter, in close proximity to the Senate House,
the Forum, and the Amphitheatre; and every time
that during his sermon he raised his eyes to the lower
crags of Mount Silpius, he would be confronted by the
stern visage and rocky crown of the choleric ferryman
of Hades. But the soil was prepared for his teaching.
It is darkest just before the dawn. When mankind has
sunk into hopeless scepticism, the help of God is often
very nigh at hand. "Bitter with weariness, and sick
with sin," there were many at any rate, even among the
giddy and voluptuous Antiochenes, who, in despair of all
sweetness and nobleness, were ready to hail with rapture
the preaching of a new faith which promised forgiveness
for the past, and brought ennoblement to the present.
The work grew and prospered, and for a whole year the
Apostles laboured in brotherly union and amid constant

---

[1] "Daphnici mores."   [2] Jos. *Antt.* xii. 5, § 1.   [3] A.D. 70.

encouragement. The success of their labours was most
decisively marked by the coinage of a new word, destined
to a glorious immortality;—the disciples were first called
CHRISTIANS at Antioch.

It is always interesting to notice the rise of a new
and memorable word, but not a few of those which have
met with universal acceptance have started into accidental life. It is not so with the word " Christian."
It indicates a decisive epoch, and was the coinage
rather of a society than of any single man. More,
perhaps, than any word which was ever invented, it
marks, if I may use the expression, the watershed of all
human history. It signalises the emergence of a true
faith among the Gentiles, and the separation of that faith
from the tenets of the Jews. All former ages, nations,
and religions contribute to it. The conception which
lies at the base of it is Semitic, and sums up centuries of expectation and of prophecy in the historic
person of One who was anointed to be for all mankind
a Prophet, Priest, and King. But this Hebrew conception is translated by a Greek word, showing that the
great religious thoughts of which hitherto the Jewish
race had been the appointed guardians, were henceforth
to be the common glory of mankind, and were, therefore,
to be expressed in a language which enshrined the world's
most perfect literature, and which had been imposed on
all civilised countries by the nation which had played
by far the most splendid part in the secular annals of
the past. And this Greek rendering of a Hebrew idea
was stamped with a Roman form by receiving a Latin
termination,[1] as though to foreshadow that the new name

---

[1] The Greek adjective from Χριστὸς would have been Χριστεῖος. It is true
that ηνὸς and ινὸς are Greek terminations, but anus is mainly Roman, and
there can be little doubt that it is due—not to the Doric dialect!—but to the

should be coextensive with the vast dominion which swayed the present destinies of the world. And if the word was thus pregnant with all the deepest and mightiest associations of the past and of the present, how divine was to be its future history! Henceforth it was needed to describe the peculiarity, to indicate the essence, of all that was morally the greatest and ideally the most lovely in the condition of mankind. From the day when the roar of the wild beast in the Amphitheatre was interrupted by the proud utterance, *Christianus sum*— from the days when the martyrs, like "a host of Scævolas," upheld their courage by this name as they bathed their hands without a shudder in the bickering fire—the idea of all patience, of all heroic constancy, of all missionary enterprise, of all philanthropic effort, of all cheerful self-sacrifice for the common benefit of mankind is in that name. How little thought the *canaille* of Antioch, who first hit on what was to them a convenient nickname, that thenceforward their whole city should be chiefly famous for its "Christian" associations; that the fame of Seleucus Nicator and Antiochus Epiphanes should be lost in that of Ignatius and Chrysostom; and that long after the power of the imperial legates had been as utterly crumbled into the dust of oblivion as the glittering palace of the Seleucidae in which they dwelt, the world would linger with unwearied interest on every detail of the life of the obscure Cypriot, and the afflicted Tarsian, whose preaching only evoked their wit and laughter! How much less could they have conceived it

prevalence of Roman terminology at Antioch, even if it be admitted that the spread of the Empire had by this time made *anus* a familiar termination throughout the East (cf. Mariani, Pompeiani, &c.). "Christianity" (Χρισ-τιανισμὸς) first occurs in Ignatius (*ad Philad.* 6), as was natural in a Bishop of *Antioch*; and probably "Catholic" (Ignat. *ad Smyrn.* 8) was invented in the same city (*id.* 78). See Bingham, *Antt.* II. i. § 4.

possible that thenceforward all the greatest art, all the
greatest literature, all the greatest government, all the
greatest philosophy, all the greatest eloquence, all the
greatest science, all the greatest colonisation—and more
even than this—all of what is best, truest, purest, and
loveliest in the possible achievements of man, should be
capable of no designation so distinctive as that furnished by
the connotation of what was intended for an impertinent
sobriquet! The secret of the wisdom of the Greek, and the
fervour of the Latin fathers, and the eloquence of both,
is in that word; and the isolation of the hermits, and
the devotion of the monks, and the self-denial of the
missionaries, and the learning of the schoolmen, and the
grand designs of the Catholic statesmen, and the chivalry of the knights, and the courage of the reformers,
and the love of the philanthropists, and the sweetness
and purity of northern homes, and everything of divine
and noble which marks—from the squalor of its cata-
combs to the splendour of its cathedrals—the story
of the Christian Church.   And why does all this lie
involved in this one word?   Because it is the standing witness that the world's Faith is centred not in
formulæ, but in historic realities—not in a dead system,
but in the living Person of its Lord.   An ironic inscription on the Cross of Christ had been written in letters
of Greek, of Latin, and of Hebrew; and that Cross, im-
plement as it was of shame and torture, became the symbol
of the national ruin of the Jew, of the willing allegiance
of the Greeks and Romans, of the dearest hopes and
intensest gratitude of the world of civilisation.   An
hybrid and insulting designation was invented in the
frivolous streets of Antioch, and around it clustered
for ever the deepest faith and the purest glory of mankind.

I have assumed that the name was given by Gentiles, and given more or less in sport. It could not have been given by the Jews, who preferred the scornful name of "Galilæan,"[1] and who would not in any case have dragged through the mire of apostasy—for so it would have seemed to them—the word in which centred their most cherished hopes. Nor was it in all probability a term invented by the Christians themselves. In the New Testament, as is well known, it occurs but thrice; once in the historical notice of its origin, and only in two other places as a name used by enemies. It was employed by Agrippa the Second in his half-sneering, half-complimentary interpellation to St. Paul;[2] and it is used by St. Peter as the name of a charge under which the brethren were likely to be persecuted and impeached.[3] But during the life-time of the Apostles it does not seem to have acquired any currency among the Christians themselves,[4] and they preferred those vague and loving appellations of "the brethren,"[5] "the disciples,"[6] "the believers,"[7] "the saints,"[8] "the Church of Christ,"[9] "those of the way,"[10] "the elect,"[11] "the faithful,"[12] which had been sweetened to them by so much tender and hallowed intercourse during so many heavy trials and persecutions. Afterwards, indeed, when the name Christian had acquired a charm so potent that the very sound of it was formidable, Julian tried to forbid

---

[1] Or, Nazarene. Acts xxiv. 5 (cf. John i. 46; Luke xiii. 2). Cyril, Catech. x.
[2] Acts xxvi. 28. This (which was twenty years later) is the first subsequent allusion to the name. Epiphanius (Haer. 29, n. 4) says that an earlier name for Christian was 'Ιεσσαῖοι.   [3] 1 Pet. iv. 16.
[4] The allusion to it in Jas. ii. 7 is, to say the least, dubious.
[5] Acts xv. 1; 1 Cor. vii. 12.   [6] Acts ix. 26; xi. 29.
[7] Acts v. 14.   [8] Rom. viii. 27; xv. 25.   [9] Eph. v. 25.
[10] Acts xix. 9, 23. Compare the name Methodist.   [11] 2 Tim. ii. 10, &c.
[12] Eph. i. 1, &c. Later names like pisciculi, &c., had some vogue also.

its use by edict,[1] and to substitute for it the more ignominious term of "Nazarene," which is still universal in the East. A tradition naturally sprang up that the name had been invented by Evodius, the first Bishop of Antioch, and even adopted at a general synod.[2] But what makes it nearly certain that this is an error, is that up to this time "Christ" was not used, or at any rate was barely beginning to be used, as a proper name; and the currency of a designation which marked adherence to Jesus, as though Christ were His *name* and not His title, seems to be due only to the ignorance and carelessness of Gentiles, who without further inquiry caught up the first prominent word with which Christian preaching had made them familiar.[3] And even this word, in the prevalent itacism, was often corrupted into the shape *Chrestiani*, as though it came from the Greek *Chrêstos*, "excellent," and not from *Christos*, "anointed."[4] The latter term—arising from customs and conceptions which up to this time were almost exclusively Judaic—would convey little or no meaning to Greek or Roman ears. We may therefore regard it as certain that the most famous of all noble words was invented by the wit for which the Antiochenes

---

[1] Greg. Naz. *Orat.* iii. 81; Julian, *Epp.* vii., ix.; Gibbon, v. 312, ed. Milman; Renan, *Les Apôtres*, 235.

[2] Suid. ii. 3930 a, ed. Gaisford; Malala, *Chronogr.* 10, p. 318, ed. Mill. Dr. Plumptre (*Paul in Asia*, 74) conjectures that Evodius and Ignatius may have been contemporary presbyter-episcopi of the Judaic and Hellenist communities at Antioch. Babylas the martyr and Paul of Samosata, the heresiarchs, were both Bishops of Antioch, as was Meletius, who baptised St. Chrysostom.

[3] "Christus non proprium nomen est, sed nuncupatio potestatis et regni" (Lact. *Div. Instt.* iv. 7; see *Life of Christ*, i. 287, n.). The name "Christian" expressed contemptuous indifference, not definite hatred. Tacitus uses it with dislike—"quos *vulgus* Christianos appellabat" (*Ann.* xv. 44).

[4] In 1 Pet. ii. 3, some have seen a sort of allusion to "the Lord" being both χριστος and χρηστος, just as there seems to be a play on ἰᾶται and Ἰησοῦς in Acts ix. 34; x. 38.

were famous in antiquity, and which often displayed itself
in happy appellations.[1] But whatever may have been the
spirit in which the name was given, the disciples would
not be long in welcoming so convenient a term. Bestowed
as a stigma, they accepted it as a distinction. They who
afterwards gloried in the contemptuous reproaches which
branded them as *sarmenticii* and *semaxii*,[2] from the fagots
to which they were tied and the stakes to which they were
bound, would not be likely to blush at a name which was
indeed their robe of victory, their triumphal chariot.[3]
They gloried in it all the more because even the ignorant
mispronunciations of it which I have just mentioned were
a happy *nomen et omen*. If the Greeks and Romans spoke
correctly of *Christus*, they gave unwilling testimony to the
Universal King; if they ignorantly said *Chrestus*, they
bore witness to the Sinless One. If they said *Christiani*,
they showed that the new Faith centred not in a dogma,
but in a Person; if they said *Chrestiani*, they used a
word which spoke of sweetness and kindliness.[4] And
beyond all this, to the Christians themselves the name
was all the dearer because it constantly reminded them
that they too were God's *anointed ones*—a holy generation, a royal priesthood; that they had an unction from

---

[1] See Julian, *Misopogon* (an answer to their insults about his beard);
Zosim, iii. 11; Procop. *B. P.* ii. 8. γελοίοις τε καὶ ἀταξίᾳ ἱκανῶς ἔχονται.
Philostr. *Vit. Apollon.* iii. 16; Conyb. and Hows. i. 130.

[2] Tert. *Apol.* 50.

[3] 1 Pet. iv. 16, εἰ δὲ ὡς Χριστιανός, μὴ αἰσχυνέσθω, δοξαζέτω δὲ τὸν θεὸν ἐπὶ τῷ
ὀνόματι (A, B, &c., not μέρει as in E. V.) τούτῳ. The mere name became a
crime. Διώκουσι τοίνυν ἡμᾶς οὐκ ἀδίκους εἶναι καταλαβόντες ἀλλ' αὐτῷ μόνῳ τῷ
Χριστιανοὺς εἶναι τὸν βίον ἀδικεῖν ὑπολαμβάνοντες. κ. τ. λ. Clem. Alex. *Strom.* iv.
11, § 81.

[4] "Sed quum et perperam Chrestiani nuncupamur a vobis (nam nec
nominis certa est notitia penes vos) *de suavitate et benignitate compositum
est*" (Tert. *Apol.* 3). Οἱ εἰς Χριστὸν πεπιστευκότες χρηστοί τε εἰσι καὶ λέγονται
(Clem. Alex. *Strom.* ii. 4, § 18). See Just. Mart. *Apol.* 2.

the Holy One which brought all truth to their remembrance.[1]

The name marks a most important advance in the progress of the Faith. Hitherto, the Christians had been solely looked upon as the obscure sectarians of Judaism. The Greeks in their frivolity, the Romans in their superficial disdain for all "execrable" and "foreign superstitions," never troubled themselves to learn the difference which divided the Jew from the Christian, but idly attributed the internal disturbances which seemed to be agitating the peace of these detested fanaticisms to the instigations of some unknown person named Chrêstus.[2] But meanwhile, here at Antioch, the inhabitants of the third city in the Empire had seen that there was between the two systems an irreconcilable divergence, and had brought that fact prominently home to the minds of the Christians themselves by imposing on them a designation which seized upon, and stereotyped for ever, the very central belief which separated them from the religion in which they had been born and bred.

The necessity for such a name marks clearly the success which attended the mission work of these early

---

[1] This was a beautiful after-thought. τούτου ἕνεκεν καλούμεθα Χριστιανοὶ ὅτι χριόμεθα ἔλαιον Θεοῦ. (Theoph. ad Autol. i. 12; Tert. Apol. 3.) Compare the German Christen (Jer. Taylor, Disc. of Confirm., § 3). There are similar allusions in Ambr. De Obit. Valent., and Jerome on Ps. cv. 15 ("Nolite tangere Christos meos"). See Pearson on the Creed, Art. ii.

[2] Even in Epictetus (Dissert. iv. 7, 6) and Marcus Aurelius (xi. 3), Renan (Les Apôtres, 232) thinks that "Christians" means sicarii. This seems to me very doubtful. Sulpicius Severus (ii. 30) preserves a phrase in which Tacitus says of Christianity and Judaism, "Has superstitiones, licet con trarias sibi, 'usdem tamen auctoribus profectas.' Christianos a Judaeis enstitisse" (Bermays, Ueber die Chronik Sulp. Sev., p. 57). See Spartianus, Sept. Sever. 16; Caracalla, 1; Lampridius, Alex. Sev. 22—45, 51. Vopiscus, Saturn. 8. The confusion was most unfortunate, and peaceful Christians were constantly persecuted while turbulent Jews were protected. (Tert. Apol. 2, Ad Nat. i. 3; Justin, Apol. i. 4—7, n.)

Evangelists. They could not have tilled a soil which was more likely to be fruitful. With what a burst of joy must the more large-hearted even of the Jews have hailed the proclamation of a Gospel which made them no longer a hated colony living at drawn daggers with the heathen life that surrounded them! How ardently must the Gentile whose heart had once been touched, whose eyes had once been enlightened, have exulted in the divine illumination, the illimitable hope! How must his heart have been stirred by the emotions which marked the outpouring of the Spirit and accompanied the grace of baptism! How with the new life tingling through the dry bones of the valley of vision must he have turned away—with abhorrence for his former self, and a divine pity for his former companions—from the poisoned grapes of Heathendom, to pluck the fair fruits which grow upon the Tree of Life in the Paradise of God! How, in one word, must his heart have thrilled, his soul have dilated, at high words like these:—"Such things *were* some of you; but ye washed yourselves, but ye are sanctified, but ye are justified, by the name of the Lord Jesus, and by the Spirit of our God."[1]

[1] 1 Cor. vi. 11. Ταῦτά τινες ἦτε ἀλλ' ἀπελούσασθε, κ.τ.λ.

CHAPTER XVII.

"O great Apostle! rightly now
  Thou readest all thy Saviour meant,
What time His grave yet gentle brow
  In sweet reproof on thee was bent."—KEBLE.

THUS it was that at Antioch the Church of Christ was enlarged, and the views of its members indefinitely widened. For a whole year—and it may well have been the happiest year in the life of Saul—he worked here with his beloved companion. The calm and conciliatory tact of Barnabas tempered and was inspirited by the fervour of Saul. Each contributed his own high gifts to clear away the myriad obstacles which still impeded the free flow of the river of God's grace. In the glory and delight of a ministry so richly successful, it is far from impossible that Saul may have enjoyed that rapturous revelation which he describes in the Epistle to the Corinthians, during which he was caught up into Paradise as far as the third heaven,[1] and heard unspeakable words which man neither could nor ought to utter. It was one of those ecstasies which the Jews themselves regarded as the highest form of revelation—one of those moments of inspiration in which the soul, like Moses on Sinai, sees God face to

---

[1] The "third heaven" is called "Zevul" by Rashi (cf. *Chagigah*, f. 12, 2). In such visions the soul "hath no eyes to see, nor ears to hear, yet sees and hears, and is all eye, all ear." St. Teresa, in describing her visions as *indescribable*, says, "The restless little butterfly of the memory has its wings burnt now, and it cannot fly." (*Vida*, xviii. 18.)

face and does not die. St Paul, it must be remembered, had a work to perform which required more absolute self-sacrifice, more unwavering faith, more undaunted courage, more unclouded insight, more glorious superiority to immemorial prejudices, than any man who ever lived. It needed moments like this to sustain the nameless agonies, to kindle the inspiring flame of such a life. The light upon the countenance of Moses might die away, like the radiance of a mountain peak which has caught the colour of the dawn, but the glow in the heart of Paul could never fade. The utterance of the unspeakable words might cease to vibrate in the soul, but no after-influence could obliterate the impression of the eternal message. Amid seas and storms, amid agonies and energies, even when all earthly hopes had ceased, we may be sure that the voice of God still rang in his heart, the vision of God was still bright before his spiritual eye.

The only recorded incident of this year of service is the visit of certain brethren from Jerusalem, of whom one, named Agabus, prophesied the near occurrence of a general famine. The warning note which he sounded was not in vain. It quickened the sympathies of the Christians at Antioch, and enabled the earliest of the Gentile Churches to give expression to their reverence for those venerable sufferers in the Mother Church of Jerusalem who "had seen and heard, and whose hands had handled the Word of Life."[1] A contribution was made for the brethren of Judæa. The inhabitants of that country, and more especially of the Holy City, have been accustomed in all ages, as they are in this, to rely largely on the *chaluka*,[2] or alms, which are willingly

[1] 1 John i. 1.

[2] According to Dr. Frankl (*Jews in the East*, ii. 31) a sum of 818,000 piastres finds its way annually to Jerusalem, for a Jewish population of some 5,700 souls. It is distributed partly as *chaluka—i.e.*, at so much per head,

U

contributed to their poverty by Jews living in other
countries. The vast sums collected for the Temple
tribute flowed into the bursting coffers of the *Beni
Hanan*—much as they now do, though in dwindled rills,
into those of a few of the leading *Ashkenazim* and
Ansche hod. But there would be little chance that any
of these treasures would help to alleviate the hunger of
the struggling disciples. Priests who starved their own
coadjutors[1] would hardly be inclined to subsidise their
impoverished opponents. The Gentiles, who had been
blessed by the spiritual wealth of Jewish Christians,
cheerfully returned the benefit by subscribing to the
supply of their temporal needs.[2] The sums thus gathered
were entrusted by the Church to Barnabas and Saul.

The exact month in which these two messengers of
mercy arrived to assist their famine-stricken brethren
cannot be ascertained, but there can be but little doubt
that it was in the year 44. On their arrival they found
the Church in strange distress from a 'new persecution.
It is not impossible that the fury of the onslaught may
once more have scattered the chief Apostles, for we hear
nothing of any intercourse between them and the two
great leaders of the Church of Antioch. Indeed, it is
said that the alms were handed over, not to the Apostles,
but to the Elders. It is true that Elders may include
Apostles, but the rapid and purely monetary character of
the visit, and the complete silence as to further details,
seem to imply that this was not the case.

The Church of Antioch was not the sole contributor
to the distresses of Jerusalem. If they helped their
Christian brethren, the Jews found benefactors in the

without distinction of age or sex—and partly as *kadima*, according to the
rank of the recipient.

[1] Derenbourg, p. 232 *seq.*   [2] Rom. xv. 26, 27.

members of an interesting household, the royal family of Adiabene, whose history is much mingled at this time with that of Judæa, and sheds instructive light on the annals of early Christianity.

Adiabene, once a province of Assyria, now forms part of the modern Kurdistan. Monobazus, the king of this district, had married his sister Helena, and by that marriage had two sons, of whom the younger, Izates, was the favourite of his parents.[1] To save him from the jealousy of his other brothers, the king and queen sent him to the court of Abennerig, king of the Charax-Spasini, who gave him his daughter in marriage. While he was living in this sort of honourable exile, a Jewish merchant, named Hananiah, managed to find admission into the harem of Abennerig, and to convert some of his wives to the Jewish faith. In this way he was introduced to Izates, of whom he also made a proselyte. Izates was recalled by his father before his death, and endowed with the princedom of Charrae; and when Monobazus died, Helena summoned the leading men of Adiabene, and informed them that Izates had been appointed successor to the crown. These satraps accepted the decision, but advised Helena to make her elder son, Monobazus, a temporary sovereign until the arrival of his brother, and to put the other brothers in bonds preparatory to their assassination in accordance with the common fashion of Oriental despotism.[2] Izates, however, on his arrival, was cheerfully acknowledged by his elder brother, and set all his other brothers free, though he sent them as hostages to Rome and various neighbouring courts.

[1] Josephus (*Antt.* xx. 2, § 1) attributes this partiality to a prophetic dream.

[2] Hence we are told that "'King' Mumbaz made golden handles for the vessels used in the Temple on the Day of Atonement" (*Yoma*, 37 a).

u 2

I shall subsequently relate the very remarkable circumstances which led to his circumcision.[1]   At present I need only mention that his reign was long and prosperous, and that he was able to render such important services to Artabanus, the nineteenth Arsacid, that he received from him the kingdom of Nisibis, as well as the right to wear the peak of his tiara upright, and to sleep in a golden bed—privileges usually reserved for the kings of Persia. Even before these events, Helena had been so much struck with the prosperity and piety of her son, that she too had embraced Judaism, and at this very period was living in Jerusalem.   Being extremely wealthy, and a profound admirer of Jewish institutions, she took energetic measures to alleviate the severity of the famine; and by importing large quantities of corn from Alexandria, and of dried figs from Cyprus, she was happily able to save many lives.   Her royal bounty was largely aided by the liberality of Izates,[2] whose contributions continued to be of service to the Jews long after the arrival of Saul and Barnabas with the alms which they had brought from Antioch for their suffering brethren.

It is clear that they arrived shortly before the Passover, or towards the end of March; for St. Luke fixes their visit about the time of Herod's persecution, which began just before, and would, but for God's Providence, have been consummated just after, that great feast. Indeed, it was *à priori* probable that the Apostles would time their visit by the feast, both from a natural desire to be present at these great annual celebrations, and

---

[1] *Infra*, ii., p. 136.

[2] Oros. vii. 6; Jos. *Antt.* xx. 2, § 5. Helena is also said to have given to the Temple a golden candlestick, and a golden tablet inscribed with the "trial of jealousy" (*Yoma*, 37 *a*).

also because that was the very time at which the vast concourse of visitors would render their aid most timely and indispensable.

They arrived, therefore, at a period of extreme peril to the little Church at Jerusalem, which had now enjoyed some five years of unbroken peace.[1]

Herod Agrippa I., of whom we have already had some glimpses, was one of those singular characters who combine external devotion with moral laxity. I have elsewhere told the strange story of the part which on one memorable day he played in Roman history,[2] and how his supple address and determination saved Rome from a revolution and placed the uncouth Claudius on his nephew's throne. Claudius, who with all his pedantic and uxorious eccentricity was not devoid either of kindness or rectitude, was not slow to recognise that he owed to the Jewish prince both his life and his empire. It was probably due, in part at least, to the influence of Agrippa that shortly after his accession he abolished the law of "Impiety" on which Gaius had so vehemently insisted,[3] and which attached the severest penalties to any neglect of the imperial cult. But the further extension of the power of Agrippa was fraught with disastrous consequences to the Church of Christ. For the Jews were restored to the fullest privileges which they had ever enjoyed, and Agrippa set sail for Palestine in the flood-tide of imperial favour and with the splendid additions of Judæa and Samaria, Abilene, and the district of Lebanon[4] to Herod Philip's tetrarchy of Trachonitis, which he had received at the accession of Gaius.[5]

---

[1] Caligula's order to place his statue in the Temple was given in A.D. 39. Herod Agrippa died in A.D. 44.

[2] *Seekers after God*, p. 76.   [3] Dion. lx. 3, 5.

[4] Jos. *Antt.* xix. 5, §§ 2, 3.   [5] *Id.* xviii. 5, § 10.

It is natural that a prince of Asmonæan blood,[1] who thus found himself in possession of a dominion as extensive as that of his grandfather Herod the Great, should try to win the favour of the people whom he was sent to govern. Apart from the subtle policy of facing both ways so as to please the Jews while he dazzled the Romans, and to enjoy his life in the midst of Gentile luxuries while he affected the reputation of a devoted Pharisee, Agrippa seems to have been sincere in his desire to be—at any rate at Jerusalem—an observer of the Mosaic Law. St. Luke, though his allusions to him are so brief and incidental, shows remarkable fidelity to historic facts in presenting him to us in both these aspects. In carrying out his policy, Agrippa paid studious court to the Jews, and especially to the Pharisees. He omitted nothing which could win their confidence or flatter their pride, and his wife, Cypros,[2] seems also to have been as

---

[1] Agrippa I. was the grandson of Herod the Great and Mariamne. Mariamne was the granddaughter of Hyrcanus II., who was a grandson of Hyrcanus I., who was a son of Simon, the elder brother of Judas Maccabæus. Some of the Rabbis were, however, anxious to deny any drop of Asmonæan blood to the Herodian family. They relate that Herod the Great had been a slave to one of the Asmonæans, and one day heard a Bath Kol saying, "Every slave that now rebels will succeed." Accordingly, he murdered all the family, except one young maiden, whom he reserved for marriage. But she mounted to the roof, cried out that "any one who asserted himself to be of the Asmonæan house henceforth would be a slave, for that she alone of that house was left;" and flinging herself down was killed. Some say that for seven years Herod preserved her body in honey, to make people believe that he was married to an Asmonæan princess. Angry with the Rabbis, who insisted on Deut. xvii. 15, he killed them all, except Babha Ben Buta (whom he blinded by binding up his eyes with the skin of a hedgehog), that he might have one counsellor left. Having disguised himself, and tried in vain to tempt Babha Ben Buta to say something evil of him, he revealed himself, and asked what he ought to do by way of expiation. The blind man answered, "Thou hast extinguished the light of the world (see Matt. v. 14); rekindle it by building the Temple" (*Babha Bathra*, f. 3, 2, *seqq.*).

[2] Cypros was the name of the wife of Antipater and mother of Herod the Great. She was descended from a Nabathean family; her name, which is probably connected with כֵּנָא, (*kenna*), was borne by several Herodian princesses (Derenbourg, *Palest.*, p. 210).

much attached to the party as her kinswoman, Salome, sister of Herod the Great.[1]

It is clear that such a king—a king who wished to foster the sense of Jewish nationality,[2] to satisfy the Sadducees, to be supported by the Pharisees, and to be popular with the multitude—could not have lived long in Jerusalem, which was his usual place of residence,[3] without hearing many complaints about the Christians. At this time they had become equally distasteful to every section of the Jews, being regarded not only as fanatics, but as apostates, some of whom sat loosely to the covenant which God had made with their fathers. To extirpate the Christians would, as Agrippa was well aware, be the cheapest possible way to win general popularity. It was accordingly about the very time of the visit of the two Apostles to the Passover, as delegates from Antioch, that "he laid hands on certain of the Church to injure them; and he slew James, the brother of John, with the sword; and seeing that it was pleasing to the Jews, proceeded to arrest Peter also."[4] Thus in a single touch does St. Luke strike the keynote of Agrippa's policy, which was an unscrupulous desire for such popularity as could be earned by identifying himself with Jewish prejudices. In the High Priests of the day he would find willing coadjutors. The priest for the time being was probably Elionæus, whom Josephus calls a son of Kanthera, but whom the Talmud calls a son of Caiaphas.[5] If so, he would have been animated with an hereditary fury against the followers of Christ, and would have been an eager instrument in the hands of Herod. When such allies were

---

[1] See Excursus XIII, "Herod Agrippa I. in the Talmud and in Secular History."

[2] Jos. *Antt.* xx. 1, § 1.

[3] *Id.* xix. 7, § 3.   [4] Acts xii. 1—3.

[5] Jos. *B. J.* xix. 8, § 1, *Para,* iii. 5; *Ben Hakkaiph;* Derenbourg, p. 215.

in unison, and Agrippa in the very plenitude of his power,
it was easy to strike a deadly blow at the Nazarenes.
It was no bold Hellenist who was now singled out as a
victim, no spirited opponent of Jewish exclusiveness.
James, as the elder brother of the beloved disciple, perhaps
as a kinsman of Christ Himself, as one of the earliest and
one of the most favoured Apostles, as one not only of the
Twelve, but of the Three, as the son of a father apparently of higher social position than the rest of the little
band, seems to have had a sort of precedence at Jerusalem;
and for this reason alone—not, so far as we are aware,
from being personally obnoxious—he was so suddenly
seized and martyred that no single detail or circumstance
of his martyrdom has been preserved. Two words[1] are all
the space devoted to recount the death of the first Apostle
by the historian who had narrated at such length the
martyrdom of Stephen.   It may be merely due to a sense
of inadequacy in this brief record that Christian tradition
told how the constancy and the harangues of James converted his accuser, and caused him to become a voluntary
sharer of his death.[2]   But perhaps we are meant to see a
spiritual fitness in this lonely and unrecorded end of the
son of Thunder.   He had stood by Jesus at the bedside
of the daughter of Jairus, and on the holy mount, and in
the agony of the garden; had once wished to call down
fire from heaven on those who treated his Lord with
incivility; had helped to urge the claim that he might
sit in closest proximity to His throne of judgment.
There is a deep lesson in the circumstance that he should,
meekly and silently, in utter self-renouncement, with no

---

[1] Acts xii. 2, ἀνεῖλε . . . μαχαίρῃ.

[2] Clem. Alex. ap. Euseb. H. E. ii. 9. The Apostle, it is said, looked at
him for a little time, and then kissed him, with the words, "Peace be with
you," just before they both were killed.

visible consolation, with no elaborate eulogy, amid no
pomp of circumstance, with not even a recorded burial,
perish first of the faithful few who had forsaken all to
follow Christ, and so be the first to fulfil the warning
prophecy that he should drink of His bitter cup, and be
baptised with His fiery baptism.

It was before the Passover that James had been
doomed to feel the tyrant's sword. The universal approbation of the fact by the Jews—an approbation which
would be all the more conspicuous from the presence of
the vast throngs who came to Jerusalem to celebrate the
Passover—stimulated the king, to whom no incense was so
sweet as the voice of popular applause, to inflict a blow
yet more terrible by seizing the most prominent of all the
Apostles. Peter was accordingly arrested, and since there
was no time to finish his trial before the Passover, and the
Jews were not inclined to inflict death by their own act
during the Feast, he was kept in prison till the seven
sacred days had elapsed that he might then be put to
death with the most ostentatious publicity.[1] Day after
day the Apostle remained in close custody, bound by
either arm to two soldiers, and guarded by two others.
Aware how irreparable would be the loss of one so brave,
so true, so gifted with spiritual fervour and wisdom, the
Christians of Jerusalem poured out their hearts and souls
in prayer for his deliverance. But it seemed as if all
would be in vain. The last night of the Feast had come ;
the dawn of the morning would see Peter brought forth
to the mockery of trial, and the certainty of death. It
seemed as if the day had already come when, as his Lord
had told him, another should gird him, and carry him
whither he would not. But in that last extremity God
had not forsaken His Apostle or His Church. On that

---

[1] Acts xii. 4, ἀνάγειν.

last night, by a divine deliverance, so sudden, mysterious, and bewildering, that to Peter, until he woke to the sober certainty of his rescue, it seemed like a vision,[1] the great Apostle was snatched from his persecutors. After briefly narrating the circumstances of his deliverance to the brethren assembled in the house of Mary, the mother of John Mark the Evangelist, he entrusted them with the duty of bearing the same message to James, the Lord's brother, and to the other Christians who were not present, and withdrew for a time to safe retirement, while Herod was left to wreak his impotent vengeance on the unconscious quaternion of soldiers.

It might well seem as though the blood of martyrdom brought its own retribution on the heads of those who cause it to be spilt. We have seen Agrippa in the insolent plenitude of his tyranny; the next scene exhibits him in the horrible anguish of his end. It was at the beginning of April, A.D. 44, that he had slain James and arrested Peter; it was probably the very same month which ended his brief and guilty splendour, and cut him off in the flower of his life.

Versatile and cosmopolitan as was natural in an adventurer whose youth and manhood had experienced every variety of fortune, Agrippa could play the heathen at Cæsarea with as much zeal as he could play the Pharisee at Jerusalem. The ordinary herd of Rabbis and hierarchs had winked at this phase of his royalty, and had managed to disintegrate in their imaginations the Herod who offered holocausts in the Temple, from the Herod who presided in amphitheatres at Berytus; the Herod who wept, because he was only half a Jew, in the Temple at the Passover, and the Herod who presided at Pagan spectacles at Cæsarean

---

[1] Acts xii. 9.

jubilees.[1] One bold Pharisee—Simon by name—did indeed venture for a time to display the, courage of his opinions. During an absence of Agrippa from Jerusalem, he summoned an assembly and declared the king's actions to be so illegal that, on this ground, as well as on the ground of his Idumæan origin, he ought to be excluded from the Temple. As it was not Agrippa's object to break with the Pharisees, he merely sent for Simon to Cæsarea, made him sit by his side in the theatre, and then asked him gently "whether he saw anything there which contradicted the law of Moses?" Simon either was or pretended to be convinced that there was no overt infraction of Mosaic regulations, and after begging the king's pardon was dismissed with a small present.

It was in that same theatre that Agrippa met his end. Severe troubles had arisen in the relations between Judæa and the Phœnician cities of Tyre and Sidon, and since that maritime strip of coast depends entirely for its subsistence on the harvests of Palestine, it was of the extremest importance to the inhabitants of the merchant cities that they should keep on good terms with the little autocrat.[2] The pressure of the famine, which would fall on them with peculiar severity, made them still more anxious to bring about a reconciliation, and the visit of Agrippa to Cæsarea on a joyful occasion furnished them with the requisite opportunity.

That occasion was the news that Claudius had returned in safety from his expedition to Britain, and had been welcomed at Rome with an outburst of flattery, in which the interested princelings of the provinces thought

---

[1] Jos. *Antt.* xix. 7, § 4.
[2] Cf. 1 Kings v. 9; Ezek. xxvii. 17; Ezra iii. 7.

it politic to bear their part.[1] Agrippa was always glad
of any excuse which enabled him to indulge his passion
for gladiatorial exhibitions and the cruel vanities of
Roman dissipation. Accordingly he hurried to Cæsarea,
which was the Roman capital of Palestine, and ordered
every preparation to be made for a splendid festival. To
this town came the deputies of Tyre and Sidon, taking
care to secure a friend at court in the person of Blastus,
the king's groom of the bedchamber.[2]

It was on the second morning of the festival, at the
early dawn of a burning day in the Syrian spring, that
Agrippa gave audience to the Phœnician embassy. It
was exactly the time and place and occasion in which
he would be glad to display his magnificence and
wealth. Accordingly he entered the theatre with his
royal retinue in an entire robe of tissued silver, and
taking his seat on the *bêma*, made to the Tyrians and
Sidonians a set harangue. As he sat there the sun blazed
on his glittering robe, and seemed to wrap him in a
sheet of splendour. The theatre was thronged with his
creatures, his subjects, the idle mob whose amusement
he was supplying with profuse liberality, and the people
whose prosperity depended on his royal favour. Here and
there among the crowd a voice began to be heard shouting
that it was a god who was speaking to them,[3] a god
whose radiant epiphany was manifested before their eyes.
In the prime of life, and of the manly beauty for which
his race was remarkable, at the zenith of his power, in the
seventh year of his reign, in the plenitude of his wealth,[4]

---

[1] Dion. lx. 23; Suet. *Claud.* 17; Philo, *Leg.* 45. See Lewin, *Fasti Sacri*, §§ 1668, 1674; and *contra* Wieseler, *Chron. d. Apost. Zeit.* 130.

[2] ἐπὶ τοῦ κοιτῶνος, *cubicularius*, praefectus cubiculi.

[3] See Jos. *Antt.* xix. 8, § 2, which closely confirms the narrative of Acts xii.

[4] His revenue is stated to have been 12,000,000 of drachmæ, or more than £425,000, a year.

an autocrat by his own position, and an autocrat rendered
all but irresistible by the support of the strange being
whom his supple address had saved from the dagger to
seat him on the imperial throne—surrounded, too, at this
moment by flatterers and parasites, and seated in the very
midst of the stately buildings which Jews and Gentiles
alike knew to have been conferred upon the city by the
architectural extravagance of his race—the feeble intellect of Agrippa was turned by this intoxicating incense.
He thought himself to be the god whom they declared.
Why should not *he* accept the apotheosis so abjectly
obtruded on a Caligula or a Claudius? He accepted the
blasphemous adulation, which, as a King of the Jews,
he ought to have rejected with indignant horror. At
that very moment his doom was sealed. It was a fresh
instance of that irony of heaven which often seems to
place men in positions of superlative gorgeousness at the
very moment when the fiat is uttered which consigns
them to the most pitiable and irrecoverable fall.[1]

There was no visible intervention. No awful voice
sounded in the ears of the trembling listeners. No awful
hand wrote fiery letters upon the wall. St. Luke says
merely that the angel of God smote him. Josephus
introduces the grotesque incident of an owl seated above
him on one of the cords which ran across the theatre,
which Agrippa saw, and recognised in it the predicted
omen of impending death.[2] Whether he saw an owl or
not, he was carried from the theatre to his palace a
stricken man—stricken by the hand of God. In five
days from that time—five days of internal anguish and

---

[1] See Bishop Thirlwall's *Essay on the Irony of Sophocles.*

[2] He says that an owl was sitting on a tree on the day of Agrippa's arrest
at Capreae, and that a German soothsayer had foretold that he should become
a king, but should be near his death when he saw that owl again. See also
Euseb. *H. E.* ii. 10, who substitutes the angel for the owl.

vain despair,[1] in the fifty-fourth year of his age, and
the fourth of his reign over the entire dominion of his
grandfather—Agrippa died.   And whatever may be the
extent to which he had won the goodwill of the Jews
by his lavish benefactions, the Gentiles hated him all the
more because he was not only a Jew but an apostate.
A consistent Jew they could in some measure tolerate,
even while they hated him; but for these hybrid rene-
gades they always express an unmitigated contempt.   The
news of Agrippa's death was received by the population, and especially by the soldiers, both at Cæsarea and
Sebaste with feastings, carousals, and every indication
of indecent joy.   Not content with crowning themselves
with garlands, and pouring libations to the ferryman of
the Styx, they tore down from the palace the statues
of Agrippa's daughters, and subjected them to the most
infamous indignities.   The foolish inertness of Claudius
left the insult unpunished, and these violent and dissolute
soldiers contributed in no small degree to the evils which
not many years afterwards burst over Judæa with a storm
of fire and sword.[2]

   Of these scenes Saul and Barnabas may have been

---

[1] Jos. *Antt.* xix. 8, § 2, γαστρὸς ἀλγήμασι διεργασθεὶς: Acts xii. 23, σκωληκόβρωτος ἀπέθανεν.   Whether there be any disease which can strictly be
described as the phthiriasis, *morbus pedicularis*, is, as I have mentioned in
my *Life of Christ*, i. 47, more than doubtful.   The death of Herod Agrippa,
like that of his grandfather, has been so called, but not by the sacred historians.   It is, however, an historic fact that many cruel tyrants have died
of ulcerous maladies, which the popular rumour described much as Lactan-
tius describes them in his tract *De Mortibus persecutorum*.   Instances are
Pheretima (Herod. iv. 205, εὐλέων ἐξέζεσεν, where the retributive appropriate-
ness of the disease is first pointed out); Antiochus Epiphanes (2 Macc. v. 9);
Herod the Great (Jos. *Antt.* xvii. 6, § 5, *B. J.* i. 33, §§ 8, 9); Maximius Galerius
(Euseb. *H. E.* viii. 16); Maximin (*id.* ix. 10, 11; Lact. *De Mort. persec.*
xxxiii.); Claudius Lucius Herminianus (Tertull. *ad Scap.* iii. cum vivus ver-
mibus ebulliisset "Nemo sciat" dicebat, "ne gaudeant Christiani"); Duke
of Alva, &c.

[2] Jos. *Antt.* xix. 9, § 2.

eye-witnesses on their return journey from Jerusalem to Antioch. The order of events in St. Luke may indeed be guided by the convenience of narrating consecutively all that he had to say about Herod Agrippa, and above all of showing how the sudden onslaught on the Church, which seemed to threaten it with nothing short of extermination, was checked by the deliverance of Peter, and arrested by the retribution of God. This would be the more natural if, as there seems to be good reason to believe, the ghastly death of Herod took place in the very same month in which, by shedding the blood of the innocent in mere pursuit of popularity, he had consummated his crimes.[1] If Saul and Barnabas were at Jerusalem during Peter's imprisonment, they may have been present at the prayer meeting at the house of Mary, the mother of Mark, and the kinswoman of Barnabas. If so we can at once account for the vivid minuteness of the details furnished to St. Luke respecting the events of that memorable time.[2]

In any case, they must have heard the death of Agrippa discussed a thousand times, and must have recognised in it a fresh proof of the immediate governance of God. But this was to them a truth of the most elementary character. Their alleged indifference to public

---

[1] Saul and Barnabas seem to have started from Antioch with the intention of arriving at Jerusalem for the Passover of April 1, A.D. 44. The martyrdom of James immediately preceded the Passover, and the imprisonment of Peter took place during the Paschal week (Acts xii. 3—6). It was immediately afterwards that Herod started for Cæsarea ; and if the object of his visit was to celebrate the return of Claudius from Britain, it must have been in this very month. For Claudius returned early in A.D. 44, and it would take some little time for the news to reach Jerusalem. Further, Josephus says that Agrippa reigned seven years (*Antt.* xix. 8, § 2), and as he was appointed in April, A.D. 37, these seven years would end in April, A.D. 44. See the question fully examined in Lewin, *Fasti Sacri*, p. 280.

[2] In D is mentioned even the number of steps from Peter's prison to the street.

questions simply arose from their absorption in other
interests. Their minds were full of deeper concerns
than the pride and fall of kings; and their visit to Jerusalem was so purely an episode in the work of St. Paul
that in the Epistle to the Galatians he passes it over
without a single allusion.[1] There is nothing surprising
in the omission. It is the object of the Apostle to show
his absolute independence of the Twelve. This second
visit to Jerusalem had, therefore, no bearing on the
subject with which he was dealing. More than eleven
years had already elapsed since the Crucifixion, and a very
ancient tradition says that twelve years (which to the
Jews would mean anything above eleven years) was the
period fixed by our Lord for the stay of the Apostles
in the Holy City.[2] Even if we attach no importance
to the tradition, it is certain that it approximates to
known facts, and we may therefore assume that, about
this time, the Apostles began to be scattered in various
directions. St. Paul passes over this eleemosynary visit,
either because in this connexion it did not occur to his
memory, or because the mention of it was wholly unimportant for his purpose.

Yet there was one circumstance of this visit which was
fraught with future consequences full of sadness to both
the Apostles. Barnabas, as we have seen, was nearly
related to John Mark, son[3] of that Mary in whose house
was the upper room. It would be most natural that he,
and therefore that Saul, should, during their short visit,
be guests in Mary's house, and the enthusiasm of her son
may well have been kindled by the glowing spirit of his

---

[1] Gal. ii. 1.

[2] See Apollon. *ap.* Euseb. *H. E.* v. 18; Clem. Alex. *Strom.* vi. p. 762, ed.
Potter.

[3] Col. iv. 10, ὁ ἀνέψιος means " cousin," not " sister's son," which would be
ἀδελφιδοῦς.

cousin and the yet more fiery ardour of his great companion. The danger of further persecution seemed to be over, but Peter, Mark's close friend and teacher, was no longer in Jerusalem, and, in spite of any natural anxieties which the prevalent famine may have caused, the Christian mother consented to part with her son, and he left Jerusalem in the company of the Apostle of the Gentiles.

V

CHAPTER XVIII.

JUDAISM AND HEATHENISM.

" Whoso breaketh a hedge [applied by the Rabbis to their *Seyyag la Thorah,*
or 'hedge for the Law'], a serpent shall bite him."—ECCLES. x. 8.

" ' Gods of Hellas! Gods of Hellas! '
　Said the old Hellenic tongue;
　Said the hero-oaths, as well as
　Poets' songs the sweetest sung!
' Have ye grown deaf in a day?
Can ye speak not yea or nay—
　　Since Pan is dead?' "—E. BARRETT BROWNING.

" Die Götter sanken vom Himmelsthron
　Es stürzten die Herrlichen Saülen,
Und geboren würde der Jungfrau Sohn
　Die Gebrechen der Erde zu heilen;
Verbannt war der Sinne flüchtige Lust
Und der Mensch griff denkend in seine Brust."
　　　　　　　　　　SCHILLER.

WHEN Barnabas and Saul returned to Antioch they found
the Church still animated by the spirit of happy activity
It was evidently destined to eclipse the importance of
the Holy City as a centre and stronghold of the Faith.
In the Church of Jerusalem there were many sources of
weakness which were wanting at Antioch. It was ham-
pered by depressing poverty. It had to bear the brunt
of the earliest persecutions. Its lot was cast in the very
furnace of Jewish hatred; and yet the views of its most
influential elders were so much identified with their old
Judaic training that they would naturally feel less interest
in any attempt to proselytise the Gentiles.

At Antioch all was different. There the prejudices of
the Jews wore an aspect more extravagant, and the claims
of the Gentiles assumed a more overwhelming importance.

At Jerusalem the Christians had been at the mercy of a petty Jewish despot. At Antioch the Jews were forced to meet the Christians on terms of perfect equality, under the impartial rule of Roman law.[1]

Of the constitution of the early Church at Antioch nothing is said, but we are told of a little group of prophets and teachers[2] who occupied a prominent position in their religious services. These were Barnabas, Simeon (surnamed, for distinction's sake, Niger, and possibly, therefore, like Lucius, a native of Cyrene), Manaen, and Saul. Of Simeon and Lucius nothing whatever is known, since the suggestion that Lucius may be the same person as Luke the Evangelist is too foundationless to deserve a refutation. Of Manaen, or, to give him his proper Jewish name, Menahem, we are told the interesting circumstance that he was the foster-brother of Herod Antipas. It has, therefore, been conjectured that he may have been a son of the Essene who lent to Herod the Great the influence of his high authority,[3] and who, when Herod was a boy at school, had patted him on the back and told him he should one day be king.[4] If so, Menahem must have been one of the few early converts who came from

---

[1] "Eruditissimis hominibus liberalissimisque studiis affluens" (Cic. Pro Archid, iii.).

[2] The accurate distinction between "prophets" and "teachers" is nowhere laid down, but it is clear that in the Apostolic age it was well understood (1 Cor. xii. 28; Eph. iv. 11). But the question naturally arises whether it is meant that Barnabas and Saul were "prophets" or "teachers"—or whether they were both. The latter, perhaps, is the correct view. The prophet stood higher than the teacher, was more immediately inspired, spoke with a loftier authority; but the teacher, whose functions were of a gentler and humbler nature, might, at great moments, and under strong influences, rise to the power of prophecy, while the prophet also might on ordinary occasions fulfil the functions of a teacher. (See Neander, Planting, p. 133, seqq.)

[3] Jos. Antt. xv. 10, § 5.

[4] Incidents of this kind are also told of Galba (Tac. Ann. vi. 20; Suet. Galb. 4; Jos. Antt. xviii. 6, § 9); of Henry VII.; and of Louis Philippe.

v 2

wealthy positions; but there is nothing to prove that he was thus connected with the celebrated Essene, and in any case he can hardly have been his son.[1]

It was during a period of special service, accompanied by fasting, that the Holy Spirit brought home to their souls the strong conviction of the new work which lay before the Church, and of the special commission of Barnabas and Saul.[2] The language in which this Divine intimation is expressed seems to imply a sudden conviction following upon anxious deliberation; and that special prayer and fasting[3] had been undertaken by these prophets and teachers in order that they might receive guidance to decide about a course which had been already indicated to the two Apostles.

St. Paul, indeed, must long have yearned for the day in which the Lord should see fit to carry out His own promise "to send him far hence to the Gentiles."[4] The more deeply he thought over his predicted mission, the more would he realise that it had been predestined in the councils of God. Gentiles worshipped idols, but so had their own fathers done when they dwelt beyond Euphrates. Jewish Rabbis had admitted that, after all, Abraham himself was but the earliest

---

[1] Because Manaen, the Essene, must have attained middle age when Herod the Great was a boy, and since we have now reached A.D. 45, this Manaen could only have been born when the other was in extreme old age.

[2] Acts xiii. 2, 'Αφορίσατε δή, " Come, set apart at once." The meaning of the λειτουργούντων (hence our word "liturgy") is probably general. Chrysostom explains it by κηρυττόντων. For other instances of the word, see Luke i. 23; Rom. xv. 16; 2 Cor. ix. 12; Phil. ii. 30. The δ προσκέκλημαι αὐτοὺς implies, of course, that Barnabas and Saul had already received a summons to the work (cf. Acts ix. 15; xxii. 21; Rom. i. 1; Gal. i. 1). Hooker thinks that Paul was made an Apostle because James could not leave Jerusalem; and Barnabas to supply the place of James, the brother of John (Eccl. Pol. vii. 4, 2).

[3] On fasting in Ember weeks, see Bingham, xxi., ch. 2.

[4] Acts ix. 15, 16.

of the proselytes.[1]   If, as legend told, Terah had been
a maker of idols, and if Abraham had received his first
call, as Stephen had said, while yet living in Ur of the
Chaldees, why should not thousands of the heathen be
yet numbered among the elect of God?   Had not God
made of one blood all the nations upon earth?   Had
not the aged Simeon prophesied that the infant Jesus
should be a light to lighten the Gentiles, no less than the
glory of His people Israel?   And were there not to be
reckoned among His human ancestors Rahab, the harlot
of Jericho, and Ruth, the loving woman of the accursed
race of Moab?   Had not Hadassah been a sultana in the
seraglio of Xerxes?   Had not Moses himself married a
woman of Ethiopia?[2] And among the great doctors of recent days was it not asserted that Shammai was descended
from Haman, the Amalekite?[3]   And, however necessary
had been the active hostility to mixed marriages, and all
other close intercourse with the heathen in the reforming
period of Ezra and Nehemiah, had not Zephaniah declared
in the voice of prophecy that "men should worship Jehovah
every one from his place, even all the isles of the heathen?"[4]
Nay, did no deeper significance than was suggested in the
vulgar exegesis lie in the ancient promise to Abraham, that
"in him all families of the earth should be blessed?"[5]
Did the prophecy that all the ends of the earth should see
the salvation of our God[6] merely mean that they should

---

[1] Josh. xxiv. 2. The apologue of the gazelle feeding among a flock of sheep,
found in the Talmud, and attributed to Hillel, beautifully expresses the toleration of the wiser and more enlightened Rabbis; but the proselytism contemplated is, of course, that purchased by absolute conformity to Jewish precepts.

[2] The Rabbis, to get over this startling fact, interpreted *Koosith* ("Ethiopian woman") by *Gematria*, and made it mean "fair of face;" since *Koosith*
=736=the Hebrew words for "fair of eyes."

[3] Similarly it was said that Akibha descended from Sisera.

[4] Zeph. ii. 11.   [5] Gen. xii. 3; Gal. iii. 14.

[6] Isa. lii. 10.

see it as excluded aliens, or as wanderers doomed to perish ?
If the Gentiles were to come to the light of Zion, and kings
to the brightness of her dawn—if the isles were to wait
for God, and the ships of Tarshish [1] — did this merely
mean that the nations were but to be distant admirers
and tolerated servants, admitted only to the exoteric doctrines and the less peculiar blessings, and tolerated only
as dubious worshippers in the Temple's outmost courts?
Would not this be to them a blessing like the blessing of
Esau, which was almost like a curse, that their dwelling
should be away from the fatness of the earth, and away
from the dew of blessing from above?[2] Or, after all, if
such reasonings were inconclusive—if, however conclusive,
they were still inadequate to break down that barrier of
prejudice which was an obstacle more difficult to surmount
than the middle wall of partition—was any argument
needful, when they had heard so recently the *command*
of their Lord that they were to *go into all the world and
preach the Gospel to every creature*,[3] and the *prophecy* that
they should be witnesses unto the uttermost parts of the
earth?[4]

Such convictions may have been in the heart of Paul
long before he could persuade others to join in giving
effect to them. It is matter of daily experience that the
amount of reasoning which ought to be sufficient to produce immediate action is often insufficient to procure even
a languid assent. But the purpose of the Apostle was
happily aided by the open-hearted candour of Barnabas,
the intellectual freshness of the Church of Antioch, and the
immense effect produced by the example of Peter, who

---

[1] Isa. lx. 3, 9.

[2] Gen. xxvii. 39, "Behold, *without* the fatness of the earth shall be thy
dwelling, and *without* the dew of heaven from above" (v. Kalisch, *in loc.*).

[3] Mark xvi. 15.   [4] Acts i. 8.

had won even from the Church of Jerusalem a reluctant acquiescence in the baptism of Cornelius.

And apart from the all but ineradicable dislike towards the heathen which must have existed in the minds of Jews and Jewish Christians, as a legacy of six centuries of intolerance—even supposing this dislike to be removed from *within*—yet the attempt to win over to the new faith the vast opposing forces of Judaism and heathenism *without* the fold might well have seemed fantastic and impossible. Could any but those whose hearts were lit with a zeal which consumed every difficulty, and dilated with a faith to which it seemed easy to remove mountains, listen without a smile to the proposal of evangelising the world which was then being advanced by two poor Jews—Jews who, as Jews by birth, were objects of scorn to the Gentiles, and as Jews who sat loose to what had come to be regarded as the essence of Judaism, were objects of detestation to Jews themselves? Is it possible to imagine two emissaries less likely to preach with acceptance "to the Jew first, and afterwards to the Greek?" And if the acceptance of such a mission required nothing short of the religious genius and ardent faith of Paul, surely nothing short of the immediate aid of the Holy Spirit of God could have given to that mission so grand and eternal a success.

For even had the mission been to the Jews exclusively, the difficulties which it presented might well have seemed insuperable. It must utterly fail unless the Jew could be persuaded of two things, of which one would be most abhorrent to his pride, the other most opposed to his convictions, and both most alien to his deepest prejudices. To become a Christian he would be forced to admit that all his cherished conceptions

of the Messiah had been carnal and erroneous, and that
when, after awaiting His advent for twenty centuries, that
Lord had come suddenly to His Temple, the Jews had not
only rejected but actually crucified Him, and thereby filled
up the guilt which their fathers had incurred by shedding
the blood of the Prophets. Further, he would have to
acknowledge that not only his "hereditary customs," but
even the Law—the awful fiery Law which he believed
to have been delivered by God Himself from the
shrouded summit of Sinai—was destined, in all the facts
which he regarded as most distinctive, to be superseded
by the loftier and more spiritual revelation of this crucified Messiah.   Lastly, he would have to resign without a
murmur those exclusive privileges, that religious haughtiness by which he avenged himself on the insults of his
adversaries, while he regarded God as being "a respecter
of persons," and himself as the special favourite of Heaven.

And fear would be mingled with hatred.   Under
certain conditions, in the secrecy of Oriental seraglios, in
the back-stairs intercourse of courts and *gynæcea*, in safe
places like the harem of Abennerig and the audience-room
of Helen of Adiabene, with Mary of Palmyra, or Fulvia,
the wife of Saturninus, or Poppæa in the Golden House,[1]
a Jew was glad enough to gain the ear of an influential
proselyte, and the more moderate Jews were fully content
in such cases with general conformity.   They found it easy
to devour widows' houses and make long prayers.   But
they were well aware that every widely successful attempt
to induce Gentile proselytes to practise the outward ceremonies of their religion would be fraught with the extremest

---

[1] Jos. *Antt.* xiii. 9, § 1; 11, § 3; 15, § 4; xviii. 3, § 5; xx. 2, § 4; *B. J.* ii.
17,   10; *c. Ap.* ii. 39; Tac. *Ann.* ii. 85; *H.* v. 5; Hor. *Sat.* I. iv. 142; Dion.
Cass. xxxvii. 17, &c.; Juv. *Sat.* vi. 546. See too Derenbourg, *Palestine*,
p. 223, *seq.*

peril to their communities,[1] and would lead in every city of the Empire to a renewal of such scenes as those of which Alexandria had lately been the witness. It is probable that they would have checked any impolitic zeal on the part of even an orthodox Rabbi; but it filled them with fury to see it displayed by one who, as a schismatic, incurred a deadlier odium than the most corrupted of the heathen. To them a Paul was even more hateful than a Flaccus, and Paul was all the more hateful because he had once been Saul. And that this audacious pervert should not only preach, but preach to the heathen; and preach to the heathen a doctrine which proposed to place him on a level with the Jew; and, worse still, to place him on this level without any acceptance on his part of the customs without which a Jew could hardly be regarded as a Jew at all— this thought filled them with a rage which year after year was all but fatal to the life of Paul, as for long years together it was entirely fatal to his happiness and peace.[2]

Yet even supposing these obstacles to be surmounted, supposing that the missionaries were successful in converting their own countrymen, and so were enabled, by means of the "Proselytes of the Gate," to obtain their first point of contact through the synagogue with the heathen world, might it not seem after all as if their difficulties had then first begun? What hopes could they possibly entertain of making even the slightest impression on that vast weltering mass of idolatry and corruption? Now and then, perhaps, they

---

[1] As early as B.C. 139 Jews had been expelled from Rome for admitting proselytes to the Sabbath (Mommsen, *Rom. Gesch.* ii. 429). On the wider spread of Sabbatism even among heathens, see Jos. c. *Ap.* ii. 11, § 29. There appear to be some traces of the Jews taking pains annually to secure *one* proselyte (ἵνα προσήλυτον, Matt. xxiii. 15), to *typify* the salvability of the Gentiles (Taylor, *Pirke Abhôth*, p. 36).

[2] See Excursus XIII., "Burdens laid on Proselytes."

might win the heart of some gentle woman, sick to death of the cruelty and depravity of which she was forced to be a daily witness ; here and there, perhaps, of some slave, oppressed and ignorant, and eager to find a refuge from the intolerable indignities of ancient servitude ;—but even if they could hope for this, how far had they then advanced in the conversion of Heathendom, with all its splendid worldliness and glittering fascination ?

For to the mass of the heathen, as I have said, their very persons were hateful from the mere fact that they were Jews.[1] And so far from escaping this hatred, the missionaries were certain to be doubly hated as Christian Jews. For during the first century of Christianity, the ancients never condescended to inquire what was the distinction between a Jew and a Christian.[2] To them a Christian was only a more dangerous, a more superstitious, a more outrageously intolerable Jew, who added to the follies of the Jew the yet more inexplicable folly of adoring a crucified malefactor. It is to the supposed turbulence of One whom he ignorantly calls Chrestus, and imagines to have been still living, that Suetonius attributes the riots which cost the Jews their expulsion from Rome. The stolid endurance of agony by the Christians under persecution woke a sort of astonished admiration ;[3] but even Pliny, though his candid account of the Christians in Bithynia refutes his own epithets, could only call Christianity "a distorted and outrageous superstition;" and Tacitus and Suetonius, using the substantive, only qualify it by the severer epithets of "deadly," "pernicious," and "new."[4]

---

[1] See Excursus XIV., "Hatred of the Jews in Classical Antiquity."

[2] In Dio (lxvii. 12—14) the Christian (?) martyr Acilius Glabrio is called a Jew.

[3] Marc. Aurel. xi. 3 ; Mart. x. 25 ; Epict. *Dissert.* iv. 8.

[4] Plin. *Ep.* x. 97, "superstitionem pravam et immodicam ;" Tac. *Ann.* xv. 44, "exitiabilis superstitio ;" Suet. *Nero.* 16, "novae et maleficae superstitionis." See Excursus XV., "Judgments of Early Pagan Writers on Christianity."

The heathen world into which, "as lambs among wolves," the Apostles were going forth, was at that moment in its worst condition. The western regions, towards which the course of missions took its way, were prevalently Greek and Roman; but it was a conquered Greece and a corrupted Rome. It was a Greece which had lost its genius and retained its falsity, a Rome which had lost its simplicity and retained its coarseness. It was Greece in her lowest stage of seducer and parasite; it was Rome at the epoch of her most gorgeous gluttonies and her most gilded rottenness. The heart of the Roman Empire under the Cæsars was "a fen of stagnant waters." Cæsarism has found its modern defenders, and even a Tiberius has had his eulogists among the admirers of despotic power; but no defence can silence the damning evidence of patent facts. No advocacy can silence the awful indictment which St. Paul writes to the inhabitants of the imperial city.[1] If such things were done in the green tree, what was done in the dry? What was the condition of the thistles, if this was the code of the forest-trees? If St. John in the Apocalypse describes Rome as the harlot city which had made the nations drunk with the cup of the wine of her fornications, he uses language no whit severer than that of Seneca, who speaks of Rome as a cesspool of iniquity;[2] or than that of Juvenal, who pictures her as a filthy sewer, into which have flowed the abominable dregs of every Achæan and Syrian stream.[3] Crushed under the ignominies inflicted on her by the despotism of madmen and monsters;[4] corrupted by the pollutions of the stage, and hardened by the cruelties of

[1] See Friedländer, *Sittengesch. Rome.* B. v. Denis, *Idées Morales dans l'Antiquité,* ii. 218—236.

[2] Cf. Sall. *Cat.* xxxvii. 5, "Hi Romam sicut in *sentinam* confluxerunt."

[3] Juv. iii. 62; Tac. *Ann.* xv. 44.

[4] Cf. Tac. *Ann.* ii. 85; iv. 55, 56; Suet. *Tib.* 35; Ov. *Fast.* ii. 497, *seq.*

the amphitheatre; swarming with parasites, impostors, poisoners, and the vilest slaves; without any serious religion; without any public education; terrorised by insolent soldiers and pauperised mobs, the world's capital presents at this period a picture unparalleled for shame and misery in the annals of the world. But, reduced as it was to torpor under the night-mare of an absolutism which it neither could nor would shake off, the Roman world had sought its solace in superstition, in sensuality, or in Stoicism. The superstition mainly consisted in the adoption of cunning systems of priestcraft, impassioned rituals, horrible expiations borrowed from the degrading mythologies of Egypt or from the sensual religions of Galatia and Phrygia.[1] So rife were these, and so dangerous to morality and order, that long before this age the Senate had vainly attempted the suppression of the rites offered to Sabazius, to Isis, and to Serapis.[2] The jingling of sistra, and the cracked voices of beardless Galli, were familiar in every Roman town.[3] The sensuality was probably more shameful, and more shameless, than has ever been heard of in history. And amid this seething corruption, it was the few alone who retained the virtue and simplicity of the old family life and worship. The Stoicism in which the greater and more suffering spirits of the epoch—a Cremutius Cordus, a Thrasea Paetus, an Helvidius Priscus, an Annaeus Cor-

---

[1] Such were the taurobolies and kriobolies— hideous blood baths.

[2] Valerius Maximus (I. iii. 3) relates that when the Senate had ordered the demolition of a Serapeum at Rome (A.U.C. 535), no workman could be induced to obey the order, and the Consul had himself to burst open the door with an axe (see, too, Liv. xxxix. 8—18; Cic. *De Legg.* ii. 8; Dion. Halic, ii. 20; Dio Cass. xl. 47; Tert. *Apol.* 6; *Adv. Nat.* i. 10, quoted by Renan, *Les Apôtres*, p. 316, and for Isis worship, Appul. *Metam.* xi.

[3] Firmicius Maternus, in the days of Constantine, did not think it worth while to refute Greek and Roman mythology (*De Errore Profanae Relig.*), but only the rites of Isis, Mithras, Cybele, &c.

nutus, a Musonius Rufus, a Barea Soranus—found refuge,
was noble and heroic, but hard and unnatural.   He who
would estimate the reaction of man's nobler instincts
against the profligacy of Pagan life—he who would judge
to what heights the Spirit of God can aid those who unconsciously seek Him, and to what depths the powers of
evil can degrade their willing votaries—must bridge over
the gulf which separates a Petronius and an Appuleius
from the sweetness and dignity of "minds naturally
Christian," like those of an Epictetus and an Aurelius.
He who would further estimate the priceless services
which Christianity can still render even to souls the most
naturally exalted, must once more compare the chill, the
sadness, the painful tension, the haughty exclusiveness,
the despairing pride of Stoicism with the warmth, the
glow, the radiant hope, the unbounded tenderness, the free
natural emotion, the active charities, the peaceful, infinite
contentment of Christianity as it shines forth with all
its living and breathing sympathies in the Epistles of
St. Paul.

And this difference between Stoicism and Christianity
is reflected in the lives of their disciples.   While the
last genuine representatives of Roman statesmanship and
Roman virtue were thinking it a grand thing to hold aloof
from the flatteries into which the other senators plunged
with such headlong baseness—while they were being regarded as models of heroism for such acts as rising and
walking out of the senate when some more than usually
contemptible flattery was being proposed—while they were
thus eating away their own hearts in the consciousness of
an ineffectual protest, and finding it difficult to keep even
their own souls from "the contagion of the world's slow
stain"—two Jews of obscure name, of no position, without
rank, without wealth, without influence, without either

literary, political, or military genius, without any culture
but such as a Roman noble would have despised as useless
and grotesque—but mighty in the strength of a sacred
cause, and irresistible in the zeal of a conscious inspiration—set forth unnoticed on the first of those journeys
which were destined to convert the world.   For He who
made and loved the world, and knew the needs of the
world which He died to save, had sent them forth; and
if He had sent them forth without any apparent means
for the fulfilment of His great design, it was because He
willed to choose "the foolish things of the world to confound the wise, and the weak things to confound the
mighty, and things which are not to bring to nought
things which are, that no flesh should glory in His
presence." [1]

Vast, then, as was the task before them, and hedged
around by apparently insuperable difficulties, the elders of
the Church of Antioch were convinced that Barnabas and
Saul had indeed been summoned on a Divine mission, and
that they dared no longer delay the distinct manifestation
of the will of the Spirit.   They held one more special
prayer and fast,[2] laid on the heads of their two great
brethren the hands of consecration, and sent them on their
way.   Already, in his vision, Paul had been predestined to
be an Apostle of the Gentiles;[3] henceforth, after this
solemn ordination, he receives the title of an Apostle in
its more special significance.[4]   For a time, as in his Epistles
to the Thessalonians, he modestly abstains from himself
adopting it; but when his name was vilified, when his

---

[1] 1 Cor. i. 27, 28.

[2] Acts xiii. 3, νηστεύσαντες . . . προσευξάμενοι.

[3] Acts xxvi. 17, ἐξαιρούμενός σε ἐκ τοῦ λαοῦ καὶ τῶν ἐθνῶν εἰς οὓς ἐγὼ σὲ
ἀποστέλλω.

[4] Acts xiv. 4, 14 (cf. John xvii. 18; Heb. iii. 1).

teaching was thwarted, when his authority was impugned, he not only adopted it,[1] but maintained his independent position as a teacher, and his right to be regarded as in nowise inferior to the very chiefest of the Twelve.

[1] Except in the few purely private lines which he wrote to Philemon, and in the letter to his beloved Philippians who needed no assertion of his claim.

Book VI.

THE FIRST MISSIONARY JOURNEY.

CHAPTER XIX.

CYPRUS.

Τί λέγεις; καὶ Παῦλος ἐφοβεῖτο κινδύνους; Ἐφοβεῖτο καὶ σφόδρα ἐδεδοίκει. Εἰ γὰρ καὶ Παῦλος ἦν ἀλλ' ἄνθρωπος ἦν . . . Εἰ γὰρ οὐκ ἐφοβεῖτο ποία καρτερία τὸ τοὺς κινδύνους φέρειν; Ἐγὼ γὰρ καὶ διὰ τοῦτο αὐτὸν θαυμάζω ὅτι φοβούμενος καὶ οὐχ ἁπλῶς φοβούμενος ἀλλὰ καὶ τρέμων τοὺς κινδύνους διὰ παντὸς ἔδραμε στεφανούμενος καὶ πανταχοῦ τὸ κήρυγμα σπείρων.—CHRYSOST. *Opp.* x. 44, ed. Montfaucon.

"The travelled ambassador of Christ, who snatched Christianity from the hands of a local faction, and turned it to a universal faith, whose powerful word shook all the gods from Cyprus to Gibraltar, who turned the tide of history and thought, giving us the organisation of Christendom for the legions of Rome, and for Zeno and Epicurus, Augustine, Eckhart, and Luther."—MARTINEAU, *Hours of Thought*, p. 88.

"SENT forth by the Holy Spirit"—more conscious instruments, perhaps, of God's will than has ever been the case before or since, and starting on a journey more memorable in its issues than any which had ever been undertaken by man — Saul and Barnabas, accompanied by their more youthful attendant, John Mark, started on their way. What thoughts were in their minds as they turned their backs on the street Singôn, where they had preached with such acceptance and success? There were myriads of heathen and thousands of Jews in that gay voluptuous city who had not accepted Christianity; but the two Apostles were summoned to other work. They passed between the theatre and the amphitheatre,[1]

---

[1] See the elaborate plans and pictures of ancient and modern Antioch in Mr. Lewin's *St. Paul*, i., pp. 92—95.

crossed the main thoroughfare of the city with its trees
and statues and colonnades, passed the Roman sentries
who guarded the residence of the Legate of Syria in
the old palace of the Seleucidæ, crossed the bridge over
the Orontes, and leaving the grove of Daphne on their
right upon the further bank of the river, made their way,
through the oleanders and other flowering shrubs which
form a gorgeous border to its purple rocks, along the sixteen miles which separated them from the port of Seleucia.
History has contemptuously obliterated from her annals
the names of countless kings who have set forth from
their capitals for the scourge or conquest of nations at
the head of armies, and with all the pomp and circumstance
of glorious war; but centuries after those conquerors are
in their turn forgotten whom she still deigns to com-
memorate, she will preserve in the grateful memory of
mankind the names of these two poor Jews, who started
on foot, staff in hand, with little, perhaps, or nothing in
their scrip but the few dates that suffice to satisfy the
hunger of the Eastern traveller.

From Antioch they might have made their way to
Tarsus. But Paul had in all probability preached already
in his native Cilicia,[1] and as Barnabas was by birth a
Cypriote, they bent their voyage thitherward. It was
towards the west, towards Chittim and the Isles of
the Gentiles, that the course of missions naturally
tended. All land routes were more or less dangerous
and difficult. Roads were, with few exceptions, bad;
vehicles were cumbrous and expensive; robbers were
numerous and insolent. But the total suppression of
piracy by Pompey had rendered the Mediterranean safe,
and in the growth of navigation it had become "the

---

[1] Gal. i. 21; Acts ix. 30; xi. 25. That there were churches in Cilicia
appears from Acts xv. 41.

W

marriage-ring of nations."[1] Along the eastern coast
of Asia Minor the Jews had long been scattered in numbers far exceeding those to be found there at the present
day; and while the extension of the Greek language
furnished an easy means of communication, the power of
Roman law, which dominated over the remotest provinces
of the Empire, afforded the missionaries a free scope and
a fair protection. Accordingly they descended the rocky
stairs which led down to the port of Seleucia,[2] and
from one of its two piers embarked on a vessel which
was bound for Cyprus. And thus began "the great
Christian Odyssey."[3] The Apostolic barque has spread
her sails; the wind breathes low, and only aspires to
bear upon its wings the words of Jesus. If Rome has
but too good reason to complain of the dregs of moral
contamination which the Syrian Orontes poured forth to
mingle with her yellow Tiber, on this occasion, at any
rate, the Syrian river made ample amends by speeding on
their way with its seaward current these messengers of
peace and love.

As they sail south-westward over the hundred miles of
that blue sea which one of them was destined so many
times to traverse—the sea which four times wrecked him
with its unregardful storms, and tossed him for a night
and a day on its restless billows; as they sit at the prow
and cast their wistful gaze towards the hills which overshadow the scene of their future labours,—or, resting
at the stern, not without a glance of disgust at its

[1] See some good remarks in Renan, *Les Apôtres*, p. 280, *seq.*; and for an
exhaustive treatment, Herzfeld, *Gesch. d. jüdischen Handels.*

[2] Polyb. v. 59.

[3] Renan, *Les Apôtres*, p. 386; cf. *St. Paul*, p. 13, "Ce fut la seconde poésie
du Christianisme. Le lac de Tibériade et les barques de pêcheurs avaient
fourni la première. Maintenant un souffle plus puissant des aspirations vers
les terres plus lointaines nous entraîne en haute mer."

heathen images, look back on the rocky cone of Mount
Casius, "on which three centuries later smoked the last
pagan sacrifice,"[1] they must have felt a deep emotion at
the thought that now for the first time the Faith, on
which depended the hopes of the world, was starting for
fresh regions from its native Syria. Little did St. Paul
know how trying in its apparent failures, how terrible in
its real hardships, was the future which lay before him!
That future—the fire of the furnace in which the fine
gold of his heroic spirit was to be purged from every
speck of dross—was mercifully hidden from him, though
in its broad outlines he must have been but too well able
to conjecture something of its trials. But had he foreseen *all* that was before him—had he foreseen the scourgings, the flagellations, the stoning, the shipwrecks,[2] the
incessant toilings on foot along intolerable and dangerous
roads, the dangers from swollen rivers and rushing water-
courses, the dangers from mountain brigands, the dangers
from Jews, from Gentiles, from false Christians in city
and wilderness and sea,—the frantic crowds that nearly
tore him to pieces, the weary nights, the chill, naked,
thirsty, famine-stricken days, the incessant wearing responsibility, the chronic disease and weakness,—all the
outrages, all the insults, all the agitating bursts of indignation against those who put stumbling-blocks in the
paths of the weak,[3] the severe imprisonments, the incessant death, and all ended by desertion, failure, loneliness,
chains, condemnation, the chilly dungeon,[4] the nameless
martyrdom—had he foreseen all this, could he have borne
it? His human spirit might indeed have shrunk at all

---

[1] El Djebel el Akrâ, "the *bald* mountain" (Chesney, *Euphrat.* i. 386;
Amm. Marcell. xxii. 14, § 8; Julian, *Misop.* 361).

[2] 2 Cor. xi. 23—33.

[3] 2 Cor. xi. 29, τίς σκανδαλίζεται, καὶ οὐκ ἐγὼ πυροῦμαι.

[4] Clem. Rom. *Ep. ad loc.* i. 5.

the efforts and the agonies which lay before him—greater probably than have ever fallen to the lot of man; yet even at this early phase of his missionary career I doubt not that the hero's heart would have boldly uttered, "I hold not my life dear unto myself," and the faith of the Christian would have enabled him to say, "I can do all things through Christ that strengtheneth me."

Yet to all human judgment how ill qualified, physically, was the Apostle for the vast and perilous work which lay before him. The strongest athlete might well have quailed as he thought of the toil, the sleeplessness, the manual labour, the mental anxiety. The most imposing orator might have trembled at the thought of facing so many hostile potentates and raging crowds. The finest moral courage might have entreated to be spared the combined opposition alike of false friends and furious enemies. But Paul was no Milo, no Demosthenes, no Scipio Africanus; he was physically infirm, constitutionally nervous, painfully sensitive. His bodily presence was weak, his speech despised, his mind often overwhelmed with fear. But over the feeble body and shrinking soul dominated a spirit so dauntless that he was ready all his life long to brave torture, to confront mobs, to harangue tribunals, to quail as little before frowning tyrants as before stormy seas. He might have addressed his ailing body in the words of the great hero as he rode into the thick of battle, "Aha, you tremble! but you would tremble far more if you knew whither I meant to take you to-day." [1]

The concurrent testimony of tradition, and the oldest attempts at representation, enable us to summon up before us the aspect of the man. A modern writer, who cannot conceal the bitter dislike which mingles with his

Marshal Turenne.

unwilling admiration, is probably not far wrong in characterising him as a small and ugly Jew.[1] You looked on a man who was buffeted by an angel of Satan. And yet when you spoke to him; when the prejudice inspired by his look and manner had been overcome; when, at moments of inspiring passion or yearning tenderness, the soul beamed out of that pale, distressful countenance; when with kindling enthusiasm the man forgot his appearance and his infirmity, and revealed himself in all the grandeur of his heroic force; when triumphing over weakness he scathed his enemies with terrible invective, or rose as it were upon the wings of prophecy to inspire with consolation the souls of those he loved—then, indeed, you saw what manner of man he was. It was Paul seated, as it were, on sunlit heights, and pouring forth the glorious paean in honour of Christian love; it was Paul withstanding Peter to the face because he was condemned; it was Paul delivering to Satan the insolent offender of Corinth; it was Paul exposing with sharp yet polished irony the inflated pretensions of a would-be wisdom; it was Paul rolling over the subterranean plots of Judaisers the thunders of his moral indignation; it was Paul blinding Elymas with the terror of his passionate reproof; it was Paul taking command, as it were, of the two hundred and seventy souls in the driven dismantled hulk, and by the simple authority of natural pre-eminence laying his injunctions on the centurion and the Roman soldiers whose captive he was; it was Paul swaying the mob with the motion of his hand on the steps of Antonia; it was Paul making even a Felix tremble; it was Paul exchanging high courtesies in tones of equality with governors and kings; it was Paul "fighting with wild beasts" at Ephesus, and facing "the lion"

[1] Even Luther described St. Paul as "ein armes dürres Männlein wie unser Philippus" (Melancthon)

alone at Rome. When you saw him and heard him, then you forgot that the treasure was hid in an earthen vessel; out of the shattered pitcher there blazed upon the darkness a hidden lamp which flashed terror upon his enemies, and shone like a guiding star to friends.

So that, if ugliness, and fear and trembling, and ill-health,[1] and the knowledge that he belonged to a hated sect, and was preaching a despised foolishness—if these were terrible drawbacks, they were yet more than counter-balanced by the possession of unequalled gifts. Among his slighter outward advantages were a thorough training in the culture of his own nation, a good mastery of Greek, the knowledge of a trade by which he could support himself, and familiarity with the habits of men of every class and nation, derived from long residence both in Jewish and Gentile cities. As widower and childless, he was unencumbered by any domestic ties, and could only suffer an individual anguish without risking those who depended on him. Lastly, the possession of the Roman citizenship, though inadequate to protect him against provincial tumults, and though he probably waived the appeal to it among his own countrymen, yet stood him in good stead in more than one dangerous crisis. But these would have been less than nothing without the possession of other and far higher gifts. Such were the astonishing endurance which no trials could exhaust, and which enabled the most physically weak of the Apostles[2] to become the most ceaselessly active; the high conviction that God had called him to a special Apostolate "to make the Gentiles obedient by word and deed;"[3] the "enthusiasm

---

[1] See 2 Cor. x. 10; Gal iv. 13; 1 Cor. ii. 3; 2 Cor. iv. 7; vii. 5; xi. 6; xii. *passim*.

[2] 'Ασθενὴς is the key-note of 2 Cor. xiii. 3—9.

[3] Rom. xv. 18.

of humanity," which made him ready to associate, for
their souls' sakes, whether with men who had once been
thieves and drunkards, or with sweet, innocent, and
gentle women;[1] the courtesy which made him equally
at home among slaves and among kings; the power of
style which rose or fell with the occasion, sometimes
condescending to the humblest colloquialism, sometimes
rising to the most impassioned eloquence; the clearness
of insight which always kept one end in view, and
sacrificed all minor points to attain it;[2] the total emancipation from that slavery to trifles which is the characteristic of small minds, and is ever petrifying religion
into formulæ, or frittering it away into ceremonial; the
spirit of concession; the tact of management; the
willingness to bear and forbear, descend and condescend;
the tolerance of men's prejudices; the contented acceptance of less than was his due.—And there were in the
soul of Paul qualities more precious for his life's work
than even these. There was the tenderness for his converts which makes his words ever sound as though he
were ready to break into sobs as he thinks on the one
hand of their affection, on the other of their ingratitude;[3] there was the conviction which makes him anticipate the very fiat of the throne of judgment,[4] and vehemently to exclaim that if an angel were to preach a different gospel it would be false;[5] there was the missionary
restlessness so often found in the great pioneers of salvation, which drives him from city to city and continent to
continent in the cause of God; there was the ardent
and imaginative impulse which made it the very poetry
of his life to found churches among the Gentiles as the

---

[1] 1 Cor. vi. 9—11.   [2] 1 Cor. ix. 19.
[3] 1 Thess. ii. 7, 11; Gal. iv. 19; 1 Cor. iv. 15; Philem. 10.
[4] Rom. ii. 16.   [5] Gal. i. 8.

first messenger of the Gospel of peace;[1] and last, but perhaps most important of all, there was the perfect faith, the absolute self-sacrifice, self-obliteration, self-annihilation, which rendered him willing, nay glad, to pour out his whole life as a libation—to be led in triumph from city to city as a slave and a captive at the chariot-wheels of Christ.

The immense personal ascendency of St. Paul has almost effaced the recollection of the fellow-workers to whose co-operation he owed so much; but we must not forget that throughout the perilous initiatives of this great work, he had Barnabas ever at his side, to guide him by his calm wisdom, and support him by his steady dignity. Barnabas, the friend of his youth, perhaps the school-fellow of his studies,—who had taken him by the hand; who had drawn him from his obscure retirement; who had laboured with him at Antioch; who had been his fellow-almoner at Jerusalem—was still sharing his difficulties, and never envied or murmured when he saw himself being gradually subjugated by the powerful individuality of a younger convert. To us Barnabas must always be a less memorable figure than Paul, but let us not forget that up to this time he had held a higher rank, and wielded a more authoritative influence. As a Levite, as a prophet, as one who for the needs of the community had cheerfully sacrificed his earthly goods, as one who enjoyed to a very high degree the confidence of the Apostles, Barnabas, in these early days, was enabled to lend to St. Paul's conceptions a weight which they could hardly otherwise have won. It is only when the work has actually begun that Barnabas seems naturally to sink to a subordinate position. No sooner

---

[1] Rom. x. 18; xv. 18; Gal. i. 16; 1 Cor. i. 1; iii. 10; ix. 16; 2 Cor. xi. 2.

have they left Salamis than the very order of the names is altered. Sergius Paulus sends for "Barnabas and Saul," but it is Saul who instantly comes to the front to meet the opposition of Elymas; it is "Paul and his company" who sail from Paphos to Perga; it is Paul who answers the appeal to speak at Antioch in Pisidia; it is Paul who is stoned at Lystra; and thenceforth it is "Paul and Barnabas" throughout the rest of the history, except in the circular missive from James and the Church at Jerusalem.[1]

Nor must we altogether lose sight of the younger of the three voyagers—John, whose surname was Mark, who went with them in the capacity of their minister, corresponding, perhaps, in part to our notion of a deacon.[2] The presence of an active attendant, who could make all arrangements and inquiries, would be almost necessary to a sufferer like Paul. If Barnabas shared with Paul the reluctance to administer in person the rite of baptism,[3] we may suppose that this was one of the functions in which Mark would help them. Nor was it an unimportant circumstance to both of them that Mark, as the avowed friend and *protégé* of Peter, would have been unlikely to share in any mission which did not command the entire approval of his illustrious leader. In this and many other ways, now as at the close of his life, Paul doubtless felt that Mark was, or could be, "profitable to him for ministry." His nature imperiously demanded the solace of companionship; without this he found his work intolerable,

---

[1] Acts xv. 25; and Acts xiv. 14, where Barnabas is taken for the superior deity.

[2] Acts xiii. 5, ὑπηρέτης. In Luke iv. 20 the ὑπηρέτης is the *Chazzan* of the Synagogue. Mark, like Barnabas, may have been connected with the tribe of Levi; on the name καλοβοδάκτυλος and traditions about him, see Ewald, *Gesch.* vi. 445.

[3] 1 Cor. i. 13—17.

and himself the victim of paralysing depression.[1] The
principles which he adopted, his determination that
under no circumstances would he be oppressive to his
converts, the missionary boldness which constantly led him
into such scenes of danger as none but a man could face,
deprived him of that resource of female society—a sister,
a wife—which other Apostles enjoyed, and which has been
found so conducive to the usefulness of even such devoted
missionaries as Adoniram Judson or Charles Mackenzie.
But Paul was a missionary of the type which has been
reproduced in Francis Xavier or Coleridge Patteson; and
whatever he may have been in the past, he was now, at
any rate, a lonely man.

Such were the three humble Christian emissaries whose
barque, bending its prow to the south-west, sailed towards
the mountains of Cyprus, and, leaving the long promontory of Dinaretum on the right, sailed into the bay
of Salamis.   The scene must have been very familiar to
Barnabas.   Before them lay the flourishing commercial
town, conspicuous for its temple of the Salaminian Jupiter,
which tradition assigned to Teucer, son of Telamon.
Beyond the temple there stretched away to the circle of
enclosing hills a rich plain, watered by the abundant
streams of the Pediaeus.   The site of the town, which
our recent acquisition of the island has rendered so
familiar, is now marked by a few ruins about four miles to
the north of the modern Famagosta.   The ancient town
never entirely recovered the frightful injuries which it
underwent, first from an insurrection of the Jews in the
reign of Trajan, and afterwards from an earthquake.   But

---

[1] 1 Thess. iii. 1; 2 Cor. ii. 13; Phil. ii. 19, 20; 2 Tim. iv. 11.   It has been
said that St. Paul "had a thousand friends, and loved each as his own soul,
and seemed to live a thousand lives in them, and to die a thousand deaths
when he must quit them."

when the Apostles stepped ashore, upon one of the ancient
piers of which the ruins are still visible, it was a busy
and important place, and we cannot doubt that Barnabas
would find many to greet him in his old home. Doubtless, too, there would be some to whom their visit was
peculiarly welcome, because, ever since the persecution of
Stephen, Cyprus had been connected with the spread of
Christianity.[1]

That Barnabas had had a considerable voice in thus
repaying to his native island the service which it had
rendered to Antioch,[2] may be conjectured from the fact
that subsequently, when he had parted from Paul, he
and Mark once more chose it as the scene of their missionary labours. After this first visit, Paul, often as he
passed in sight of it, seems never to have landed there,
disliking, perhaps, to build on other men's foundations;
nor does he allude to Cyprus or to other Cypriotes in any
of his Epistles. Whether there be any truth or not in
the legend which says that Barnabas was martyred in the
reign of Nero, and buried near Salamis, it is quite fitting
that the church and grotto near it should be dedicated to
him.

But apart from any facilities which may have been
derived from his connexion with the island, it was
without doubt an excellent place to form a starting-
point for the evangelisation of the world. One of the
largest islands in the Mediterranean, possessed of a fertile
soil, varied in physical formation, and within easy reach
of the three great continents, it had been marked out by
nature as a convenient centre for extensive traffic. The
trade in natural products—chiefly metals and wine—
together with the fact that Augustus had farmed the

---

[1] Acts xxi. 16.   [2] Acts xi. 20.

copper-mines to Herod the Great, had attracted a large
Jewish population. So vast, indeed, were their numbers,
that in the reign of Trajan (A.D. 116) they rose upon the
native inhabitants, under a certain Artemio, and slew
240,000 of them in one terrible massacre. The revolt
was suppressed by Hadrian with awful severity, and after
that time no Jew might set foot upon the shore of Cyprus
on pain of death.[1]

Of their work at Salamis we are told nothing, except
that "they continued preaching the word of God in the
synagogues of the Jews."[2] It appears from this that
Salamis was one of the towns where the Jews' quarter
was sufficiently populous to maintain several synagogues;
and if the Apostles came in contact with the heathen
at all, it would only be with proselytes. But the
notices of this part of their journey are scant, nor is
any indication given of the length of their stay in
Cyprus. Any work among the Gentiles was doubtless
hindered by the apotheosis of sensuality for which the
island was noted. The contact of Greeks with Phœnicians
had caused a fusion between the subtle voluptuousness of
the Hellenic race and the more burning passion of the Phœnicians and other Orientals; and the maritime population
who touched at the island from every civilised country
were ready learners in the school of degradation. Venus
was the presiding goddess; and as she received from this
fact her name of Cypris, so she was most commonly
alluded to in the poets as the Paphian, Amathusian, or
Idalian, from her temples in various parts of the island.

---

[1] Strabo, xiv. 682; Tac. H. ii. 2, 4; Jos. Antt. xiii. 10, § 4; xvi. 4, § 5; xvii.
12, §§ 1, 2; B. J. ii. 7, § 2; Philo, Leg., p. 587; Milman, Hist. of Jews, iii. 111.
For its ancient history see Meursius, Opp. iii; for its modern condition, now so
interesting to us, see General Cesnola's Cyprus.

[2] Acts xiii. 5, κατήγγελλον.

She was

> "Idalian Aphrodite, beautiful,
> Fresh as the foam, new bathed in Paphian wells."

It was hitherward that she came as Aphrodite Anadyomene, when

> "From the sea
> She rose and floated in her pearly shell,
> A laughing girl."

It was by these "purple island sides" that she first

> "Fleeted a double light in air and wave."

Yet in the Paphian temple, where no blood was offered, where her immemorial shrine, famous even in the days of Homer,[1] breathed from a hundred altars the odour of perpetual incense,[2] and where kings and emperors turned aside to do her homage, the image which was enshrined in her *adytum* was no exquisite female figure sculptured by the hand of a Pheidias or a Scopas, but a coarse truncated cone of white marble[3]—a sort of Asherah—such as might naturally serve as the phallic symbol of the Assyrian and Sidonian deity from whom this form of nature-worship was derived.[4] And as her temples had the right of asylum —a right which was certain to crowd their vicinity with criminals of every variety—we might have conjectured, apart from direct testimony, that the worship was to the last degree debasing; that the Paphian divinity

---

[1] Hom. *Od.* 8, 362. [2] Virg. *Æn.* i. 417.

[3] As it was white (τὸ δὲ ἄγαλμα οὐκ ἂν εἰκάσαις ἄλλῳ τῳ ἢ πυραμίδι λευκῇ) there cannot be much doubt that it was of marble, though Maximus Tyr. adds ἡ δὲ ὕλη ἀγνοεῖται (Diss. 8, 8). " Apud Cyprios Venus in modum umbilici, vel, ut quidam volunt, *Metae*, colitur " (Serv. *ad Æn.* i. 724).

[4] Tac. *H.* ii. 3 ; Strabo, xiv. 683 ; Athen. xv. 18. The crescent and star represented on coins as adorning the front of the Temple are perhaps a trace of the Phœnician origin of the worship, and of the connexion between the Paphian Venus and the Phœnician Asherah (Mövers. *Phön.* 607). The sun, at Emesa, had a similar κονοειδὲς σχῆμα (Herodian. v. 3), a sort of βαιτύλιον δυνατές. Models of it were sold (ἀγαλμάτιον σπιθαμιαῖον. Athen. xv. 18).

was no Aphrodite Ourania,[1] but the lowest kind of Aphrodite Pandemos; that her worship was simply the prostitution of religion to the excuse of lust. Nor is it strange that under such circumstances there should be deadly opposition between the Jews and the Greek or Phœnician inhabitants, such as existed of old between the Jews and Canaanites. The mutual hatred thus engendered culminated in the internecine war which so soon broke out between the rival populations; it may have been one of the reasons why in Cyprus we read of no preaching to the heathen.

After their residence in Salamis the three missionaries traversed the whole island.[2] It is about a hundred miles in length from Salamis to New Paphos; and they probably followed a main road along the coast, diverging to places like Citium, the birthplace of Zeno the Stoic; Amathus, one of the shrines of Venus; and any towns where they would find the little Ghettos, whose conversion to the faith was their prime object. But not one incident of their journey is preserved for us until they reached the town of Paphos. By this name is intended, as the narrative shows, not the old and famous Paphos, the modern Kuklia, to which wanton pilgrimages were yearly made in honour of the old shrine so "famous-infamous" for many ages, but Nea-Paphos,[3] the modern Baffa, now a decayed and mouldering village, but then a

---

[1] The Virgin Mary is adored by Cypriotes under the name *Aphroditissa!* (Löhber, *Cyprus*, p. 105.)

[2] Acts xiii. 6, διελθόντες δὲ ὅλην τὴν νῆσον, א, A, B, C, D, E.   In omitting ὅλην our version follows G, H.

[3] "The dance, music, and song of the sacred processions of 3,000 years ago have been replaced by the *coo-coo-vaie* of the owl, and wild cries of other night-birds, and the piteous bark of famished dogs, left behind by no less famished masters, to roam the Oriental village in search of carrion. This is the Paphos of to-day " (Cesnola's *Cyprus*, p. 216).

bustling haven, and the residence of the Roman Proconsul Sergius Paulus.[1]

It does not in any way impugn the claim of Sergius Paulus to be regarded as a person of intelligence that he had with him, apparently residing in his house, a Jewish impostor named Bar-Jesus, who had arrogated to himself the complimentary title of Elymas, the Ulemah, or Wizard.[2] A notorious infidel like Philippe Égalité, though in other respects a man of ability, could yet try to presage his fate by the sort of cup-augury involved in examining the grounds of coffee (Κυλικομάντεια; cf. Gen. xliv. 5). A belief in some personal Power, the arbiter of man's destiny, above and beyond himself, is a primary necessity of the human mind. Mankind can never dispense with this belief, however superfluous, in certain cases, and for a time, it may seem to be to the individual. The noble Romans who had lost all firm hold on the national religion felt themselves driven by a kind of instinctive necessity to get such a connexion with the unseen world as could be furnished them by the mysticism of Oriental quacks. A Marius had resorted to the prognostications of the Jewess Martha. At this particular epoch augurs, haruspices, Babylonians, mathematici, astrologers, magians, soothsayers, casters of horoscopes, fortune-tellers, ventriloquists, dream-interpreters,[3] flocked to Rome in such multitudes, and acquired such vogue, as to attract the indignant notice of both satirists and historians. A few of them —like Apollonius of Tyana, and at a later period, Alexander of Abonoteichos, and the cynic Peregrinus—

---

[1] See Excursus XVI., "The Proconsulate of Sergius Paulus."

[2] Renan, however, says, "Élim ou sage . . . . mot arabe dont le pluriel est *ouléma*. Le mot n'existe ni en hébreu ni en araméen; ce qui rend fort douteuse cette étymologie d'Élymas" (*St. Paul*, p. 15). Ewald thinks he was a Nabathaean (*Gesch.* vi. 453).

[3] Juv. iii. 27. "Augur, schoenobates, medicus, magus."

attracted universal attention.   There was scarcely a
Roman family that did not keep or consult its own fore-
teller of the future; and Juvenal describes the Emperor
Tiberius as seated "with a herd of Chaldæans" on his rock
at Capri.[1] Nothing would be more natural than that an
intelligent and inquiring Roman, in the *ennui* of the
smallest of the provinces, and finding himself amid a mixed
population, half of Phœnician origin, and devoted to
strange forms of religion, should have amused his leisure
by inquiries into the bizarre superstitions by which he was
surrounded.[2]   The prevalence of earthquakes in Cyprus
would be likely to give to the minds of the residents that
gloomy and credulous tinge which is often found in
countries liable to such terrible inflictions; and New
Paphos had been devastated by an earthquake sufficiently
recent[3] to have left a deep impression.   Perhaps from this,
perhaps from other causes, Bar-Jesus had acquired unusual
influence; but it is an additional confirmation of the accuracy of St. Luke—one of those remote and incidental, and
therefore unsuspected, confirmations which so often occur to
establish the veracity of the sacred writers—that we find
Cyprus to have been specially famous for its schools of
religious imposture, of which one was professedly Jewish.
Simon Magus was in all probability an inhabitant of
Citium.[4] There is a most singular passage of Pliny,
which, when we combine it with his reference to a
Sergius Paulus, may be regarded as a confused echo
in the mind of the Roman littérateur of these very

---

[1] Tac. *H.* v. 3; Hor. *Sat.* I. ii. 1; *Od.* I. xi. 2; Juv. *Sat.* iii. 42, 60; vi.
543, 553, 562; x. 93; Suet. *Tib.* 36, 69; Aul. Gell. i. 9; Jos. *Antt.* viii. 2;
xx. 5, § 1; *B. J.* vi. 5, § 1.   Compare Matt. xxiv. 23, 24; Acts viii. 9; xvi. 16;
xix. 19; 2 Tim. iii. 13 (γόητες); Rev. xix. 20.

[2] See Jos. *Antt.* xx. 7, § 2.

[3] In the reign of Augustus (Dio. Cass. liv. 23).

[4] *Supra*, p. 260.

events, heard from the very Proconsul about whom
we are at present reading. He tells us that there were
at Paphos two schools of soothsayers, one of which professed connexion with Moses, Jamnes, and Jotapes, who
were Jews, and a much more recent Cyprian one.[1] To this
school Bar-Jesus must have belonged, and Pliny's allusion
throws once more a singular light on the fidelity of the
careful Evangelist.[2]

The same feelings which had induced Sergius Paulus
to domicile the Jewish sorcerer in the proconsular residence would naturally induce him to send for the new
teachers, whose mission had evidently attracted attention
by that loving earnestness which differed so widely from
the contemptuous neutrality of the synagogue. But the
position of soothsayer to a Roman Proconsul — even
though it could only last a year[3]—was too distinguished
and too lucrative to abandon without a struggle. Elymas
met the Apostles in open controversy, and spared
neither argument nor insult in his endeavour to persuade Sergius of the absurdity of the new faith. Instantly
Saul—and this is the moment seized by the historian to
tell us that he was also called by the name of Paul,
which henceforth he exclusively uses—came to the front
to bear the full force of the sorcerer's opposition. A
less convinced or a less courageous man might well have
shrunk from individual collision with a personage who
evidently occupied a position of high consideration in the
immediate household of the noble Roman. But to a spirit

[1] Tac. *H.* v. 3. Plin. *H. N.* xxx. 2, 6, "Est et alia factio a Mose et Jamne
et Jotape Judaeis pendens, sed multis millibus post Zoroastrem. *Tanto
recentior est Cypria.*" In Jamnes and Jotapes there seems to be some dim
confusion of supposed Jews with the traditional Egyptian magicians Jannes
and Jambres (2 Tim. iii. 8).

[2] Luke i. 3, ἀκριβῶς παρηκολουθηκότι.

[3] Dio Cassius tells us that these senatorial appointments were ἐπετήσιοι καὶ
κληρωτοί (liii. 13).

X

like St. Paul's, while there could be infinite compassion
for ignorance, infinite sympathy with infirmity, infinite
tenderness towards penitence, there could, on the other
hand, be no compromise with imposture, no tolerance for
cupidity, no truce with Canaan. He stood up, as it were,
in a flame of fire, his soul burning with inspired indignation, against a man whose cowardice, greed, and worthlessness he saw and wished to expose. Fixing on the false
prophet and sorcerer that earnest gaze which was perhaps
rendered more conspicuous by his imperfect sight,[1] he
exclaimed, "O full of all guile and all villainy, thou son of
the devil,[2] thou foe of all righteousness, cease, wilt thou, thy
perversion of the Lord's straight paths." And then, perceiving the terror produced on the mind of the unmasked
hypocrite by this bold and blighting invective, he suddenly
added, "And now, see, the Lord's hand is upon thee, and
thou shalt be blind, not seeing the sun for a time."[3] The
denunciation instantly took effect; the sorcerer felt in a
moment that his impostures were annihilated, that he
stood in the presence of an avenging justice. A mist
swam before his eyes, followed by total darkness, and
groping with outstretched hands he began to seek for
some one to lead and guide him.

Nor was it strange that a display of spiritual power
so startling and so irresistible should produce a strong

---

[1] Cf. Acts xxiii. 1.

[2] Possibly in allusion to his name Bar-Jesus—as though he had said,
"called the son of the salvation of Jehovah, but really the son of the devil,
and the enemy of all righteousness." For διάβολος cf. John viii. 44.
The reading of the Peshito Bar-Shûma, "son of a wound" or "son of a
name," is hard to account for, unless it be by euphemism (Castell, Lex
Syr. s. v.).

[3] Acts xiii. 11, ἄχρι καιροῦ, literally, "until an opportunity," or, as we
should say, "for the present." "Sciebat Apostolus, sui memor exempli, de
tenebris oculorum, mentis posse resurgere ad lucem;" Bede,—following the
hint of St. Chrysostom that οὐ κολάζοντος ἦν τὸ ῥῆμα ἀλλ' ἐπιστρέφοντος.

conviction on the mind of the Proconsul.[1] How far his consequent belief was deep-seated or otherwise we have no evidence which would enable us to judge. But the silence of St. Luke would seem to indicate that he was not baptised, and we can hardly look on him as a deep and lifelong convert, since otherwise we should, in the rarity of great men in the Christian community, have as certainly heard of him in their records as we hear of the very few who at this period—like Flavius Clemens or Flavia Domitilla—joined the Church from the ranks of the noble or the mighty.

The question has been often asked why it is at this point in the narrative that the name Saul is finally replaced by the name Paul.[2] The old answer supplied by St. Jerome, that he took the name as a trophy of his conversion of Sergius Paulus, has long and deservedly been abandoned; there would have been in it an element of vulgarity impossible to St. Paul. Nor is there anything to urge in favour of the fancy that he took the name as a token of his humility, to signify that he was "the least of the Apostles."[3] It is much more probable that he had either possessed from the first an alternative name for facility of intercourse among the heathen, or

[1] Acts xiii. 12.

[2] "A primo ecclesiae spolio Proc. Serg. Paulo victoriae suae trophaea retulit, erexitque vexillum ut Paulus a Saulo vocaretur" (Jer. ad Philem. 1). In the Toldoth Jeshu the name is connected with שעל, "he worked." If so, both words being passive participles, the change would be like a change from "sought" to "wrought;" and I cannot help thinking that the true explanation may lie here. Heinrichs explains Σαῦλος δὲ, ὁ καὶ Παῦλος "der auch, so wie der Proconsul, ebenfalls Paulus hiess."

[3] Paulus, a contraction of Pauxillus, means "least." "Paulus enim parvus" (Aug. Serm. clxix.). "Non ob aliud, quantum mihi videtur hoc nomen elegit nisi ut se ostenderet tamquam minimum Apostolorum" (Aug. De Spir. et Lit. xii.). With his usual exuberance of fancy he contrasts the "little" Saul of Benjamin, with the tall persecuting king. But in Conf. viii. 4 he leans to the other theory, "Ipse minimus Apostolorum tuorum, &c. . . . Paulus vocari amavit ob tam magnae insigne victoriae."

x 2

that this Roman designation may point to his possession of the Roman franchise, and perhaps to some bond
of association between his father or grandfather and the
Æmilian family, who bore the cognomen of Paulus. If
he adopted the name on the present occasion it may
have been because it was to a slight extent alliterative
with his Hebrew name *Shaül*, which would, in its Grecised
form, be represented by *Saulos;* but that was a form
which he could not use in intercourse with the Greeks,
owing to the fact that the word in Greek would
be a sort of slang term for " uppish," or wanton.
The mere changing of his name was so little unusual
that it had been from the earliest ages a custom
among his countrymen. Joseph had been known to the
Egyptians as Zaphnath Paaneah; Daniel to the Assyrians
as Belteshazzar; Hadassah to the Persians as Esther;
Jesus, Hillel, Onias, Joseph, Tarpho to the Greeks as
Jason, Pollio, Menelas, Hegesippus, and Trypho. When
not assonant the name was sometimes a translation, as
Peter is of Cephas, and Didymus of Thomas. Sometimes,
however, this name for use among the Gentiles was due
to accidental relations, as when Josephus took the præ-
nomen of Flavius in honour of Vespasian. Of this we
have other instances, in the Acts of the Apostles, in the
persons of John and Joses, who were known by the Latin
designations of Marcus and Justus. In Paul's case, however, as ancient Christian writers have pointed out, the
change of name marks also a total change in all the conditions of his life. " Paul suffers what Saul had inflicted;
Saul stoned, and Paul was stoned; Saul inflicted scourgings
on Christians, and Paul five times received forty stripes
save one; Saul hunted the Church of God, Paul was let
down in a basket; Saul bound, Paul was bound." [1]

[1] *Ap. Aug. Append. Serm.* 204.

CHAPTER XX.

ANTIOCH IN PISIDIA.

"Respondebit tibi Evangelica tuba, Doctor Gentium, vas aureum in toto xrbe resplendens."—JER. *Adv. Pelag.* Dial. iii. p. 545.

HAVING now traversed Cyprus, "Paul and his company"—to use the expression by which St. Luke so briefly intimates that the whole force of the mission was now identified with one man—weighed anchor from Paphos for Perga in Pamphylia. Whether they chose Perga as their destination in accordance with any preconceived plan, or whether it was a part of "God's unseen Providence by men nicknamed chance," we do not know. It was not easy for an ancient traveller to go exactly in what direction he liked, and he was obliged, in the circumscribed navigation of those days, to be guided in his movements by the accident of finding vessels which were bound for particular ports.[1] Now between Paphos, the political capital of Cyprus, and Perga, the capital of Pamphylia, there was in that day a constant intercourse, as would probably still be the case between Satalia and the western port of Cyprus but for the dangerous character of the now neglected harbour of Baffa. For Perga, then, the missionaries embarked. They sailed into the deep bight of Attaleia, and up the broad, and in those days navigable, stream of the Cestrus,

---

[1] See the chapter on ancient modes of travel in Friedländer, *Sittengesch. Roms.*

and anchored under the cliffs, which were crowned by the
acropolis of the bright Greek city and the marble pillars
of its celebrated Temple of Artemis.

But at Perga they made no stay, and their visit
was only marked by a single but disheartening incident. This was the desertion by John Mark of the
mission cause; "separating from them, he returned to
Jerusalem." The causes which led him thus to look back
after he had put his hand to the plough are not mentioned,
but it is evident that to the ardent soul of Paul, at any
rate, they appeared blameworthy, for we shall see that he
subsequently refused the companionship of one who had
shown such deficient resolution.[1] It is, however, but too
easy to conjecture the mixed motives by which Mark
was actuated. He was young. The novelty of the
work had worn off. Its hardships, even under the favourable circumstances in Cyprus, had not been slight.
His mother was at Jerusalem, perhaps alone, perhaps
exposed to persecution. It may be, too, that the young
man saw and resented the growing ascendency of Paul
over his cousin Barnabas. And besides all this, Mark,
bred up in the very bosom of the Church at Jerusalem,
may have felt serious misgivings about the tendency of
that liberal theology, that broad universalism of proffered
admission into the Church, which seemed to throw into
the background the immemorial sanctity, not only of the
oral but even of the written Law. Such may have been
the yearnings, the misgivings, the half-unconscious
jealousies and resentments which filled his mind, and
whatever may have been the qualms of conscience which
might otherwise have troubled his desertion of the sacred
task, these excuses and arguments for doing so must

[1] Acts xv. 38.

have met with a powerful ally in the circumstances which were evidently before them.

For as Mark gazed on the mighty chain of Taurus, and remembered that they were now about to penetrate countries of shifting languages, of unsettled government, of semi-barbarous populations, of strangely mingled worships, the brigand fastnesses of Pamphylians, Selgenses, Pisidians, Lycaonians, Isaurians, Cilicians, Cliti, Homodanenses,[1] he may not have been sorry to conceal dislike to the task on which he had entered under the plea of filial duty. At the time his defection must have been to Paul, even more than to Barnabas, a positive misfortune. Barnabas, though he clung to his friend and fellow-labourer with entire whole-heartedness, must yet have missed the genial brightness, the graphic utterance, the quick spirit of observation with which his cousin relieved the sombre absorption of Paul in his immediate purpose; and Paul, who ever loved the personal services of younger companions, must have been a little embittered, as daily worries became more trying in the absence of a vigorous comrade. There must have been in his heart a feeling of indignation against one who forsook them at the very moment when he could least be replaced, and when the difficulties which he could so greatly have lightened began to assume their most formidable shape.

So Mark left them, and the Apostles at once made their way towards the interior. Although we are not told of any synagogue at Perga, yet, since they preached there on their return journey, there must have been some special reason for their now leaving the place. This reason has been found in the probability that they

[1] Strabo, xii. 6, 7; Euseb. *H. E.* iii. 23. See Lewin, i. 123.

reached the town towards the middle of spring,[1] when the
entire population of the cities on the plain and sea-coast
are in the habit of moving inland to the *yailahs*, or, as
they would be called in Switzerland, "*alps*," or mountain
pastures, which enable them to escape the fierce and
malarious heat of the lower regions.[2] It would be useless
to preach in Perga at the very time that its main population were deserting it; and any of the numerous cara-
vans or family-migrations, which were filling the roads
and passes with mules and camels and herds of cattle,
would furnish the Apostles with company and protection.
Without such escort it would have been imprudent, if not
impossible, for them to make their way by those dangerous
roads where it is probable that the snow-drifts still lay in
many places, and they might often find the bridges
shattered and swept away by the sudden spates of rushing
streams.

The few modern travellers who have visited these parts
of Asia Minor have furnished us with minute and picturesque descriptions of the abrupt stone-paved ascents;
the sarcophagi and sculptured tombs among the projecting
rocks; the narrowing valleys through which the rivers
descend, and over which frown precipices perforated with
many caves; the sudden bursts of magnificent prospect in
which you gaze "from the rocky steps of the throne of
winter upon the rich and verdant plain of summer, with
the blue sea in the distance;" the constant changes of
climate; the zones of vegetation through which the
traveller ascends; the gleam of numberless cascades
caught here and there amid the dark pine groves that

---

[1] Con. and Howson, i. 177, who quote Spratt and Forbes, *Travels in
Lycia*, i. 48, 242, 248; Fellows, *Lycia*, 238.

[2] A striking description of such a migration among the Kirghis Tartars
may be found in Mr. Atkinson's Travels.

clothe the lower slopes; the thickets of pomegranate and
oleander that mantle the river-beds; the wild flowers
that enamel the grass with their rich inlay; the
countless flocks of cattle grazing over pastures whose
interminable expanses are only broken by the goat's-
hair huts of the shepherd, made to this day of the
same material as that by the manufacture of which
St. Paul earned his daily bread. And when the
traveller has emerged on the vast central plateau of Asia
Minor they describe the enchanting beauty of the fresh
and salt water lakes by which the road often runs for
miles; the tortoises that sun themselves in the shallow
pools; the flights of wild swans which now fill the air with
rushing wings, and now "ruffle their pure cold plumes"
upon the waters; the storks that stand for hours patiently
fishing in the swampy pools. Such must have been the
sights which everywhere greeted the eyes of Paul and
Barnabas as they made their way from Perga to the
Pisidian Antioch. They would have filled a modern
missionary with rapture, and the feelings of gratitude and
adoration with which a Martyn or a Heber would have
"climbed by these sunbeams to the Father of Lights"
would have gone far to help them in the endurance of
their hard and perilous journeys. Mungo Park, in a
touching passage, has described how his soul, fainting
within him to the very point of death, was revived by
seeing amid the scant herbage of the desert a single
tuft of emerald moss, with its delicate filaments and amber
spores; and the journals of those whose feet in recent
days have been beautiful upon the mountains over which
they carried the message of peace, abound in passages
delightfully descriptive of the scenes through which they
passed, and which they regarded as aisle after aisle in the
magnificent temple of the one true God. But, as we

have already noticed, of no such feeling is there a single trace in the writings of the Apostle or of his historian. The love of natural scenery, which to moderns is a source of delight so continuous and so intense, was little known to the ancients in general, and in spite of a few poetic exceptions, was known perhaps to the Semites of that age least of all.[1] How often did Paul climb the mountain passes of the Taurus; how often had he seen Olympus

"Soaring snow-clad through its native sky;"

how often had he passed on foot by "the great rivers that move like God's eternity;" how often had his barque furrowed the blue waters of the Ægean, among those

"Sprinkled isles,
Lily on lily, which o'erlace the sea,
And laugh their pride when the light wave lisps Greece!"

But all these scenes of glory and loveliness left no impression upon his mind, or have at least left no trace upon his page.[2] We might pity the loss which he thus suffered, and regret the ineffectualness of a source of consolation which would otherwise have been ever at hand, were it not that to St. Paul such consolations were needless. The soul that lived in heaven,[3] the thoughts which were full of immortality, the conviction that the Lord was at hand, the yearning for the souls for

[1] St. Paul was eminently a *homo desideriorum*; a man who, like all the best Jews, lived in the hopes of the future (Rom. viii. 24; xv. 4; Tit. ii. 13, &c.).

[2] There are some excellent remarks on this subject in Friedländer. *Sittengesch. Roms.* vii. 5, 3. He shows that the ancients rather noticed details than general effects. They never allude to twilight colours, or the blue of distant hills, or aërial perspective. Landscape painting, the culture of exotic plants, and the poetry of natural history have developed those feelings in the moderns (Humboldt's *Cosmos*, ii.).

[3] Phil. iii. 20; Eph. ii. 6, &c

which Christ died—made up to him for all besides. God would have granted all other consolations had he needed them; but the steps which were ever on the golden streets of the New Jerusalem trod heedlessly over the volcanic soil of a world treasured up with the stores of fire which should hereafter reduce it to ashes.[1] The goblet which was full of the new wine of the kingdom of heaven had no room in it for the fruit of the vine of even those earthly pleasures which are of all others the most innocent, the most universal, and the most blest.

Nor must we fail to see that there was an advantage as well as a disadvantage in this absorption. If St. Paul never alludes to the transcendent beauties of the lands through which he travelled, so neither does one word escape him about the recurrent annoyances, the perpetual minor discomforts and vexations of travel. The journals of modern wanderers tell us of the drenching rains, the glaring heats, the terrible fatigues, the incessant publicity, the stings of insects, the blinding storms of dust, the trying changes of season, the scarcity and badness of provisions. But to Paul all these trivial burdens, which often, nevertheless, require more heroism for their patient endurance than those more serious perils which summon up all our fortitude for their conquest or resistance, were as nothing. He felt the tedium and the miseries of travel as little as he cared for its rewards. All these things had no bearing on his main purpose; they belonged to the indifferent things of life.

And so the Apostles made their way up the valley of the Cestrus, passed along the eastern shore of the large and beautiful lake Eyerdir, and after a journey of some forty leagues, which probably occupied about a week, they

---

[1] 2 Pet. iii. 7.

arrived at the flourishing commercial town of Antioch
in Pisidia, or Antiochia Cæsarea.   We learn from Strabo
that it had been founded by the Magnetes, re-founded by
Seleucus, and subsequently made a Roman colony, with
free municipal government, by Augustus.   The centrality
of its position on roads which communicated southwards
with Perga and Attaleia, westwards with Apamea, northwards with the great towns of Galatia, and eastwards with
Iconium and the Cilician gates, made it a great commercial emporium for the trade of Asia Minor in wood, oil,
skins, goat's hair, and Angola wool.   Its true position—
for it had long been confused with Ak-sher, the ancient
Philomelium—was discovered by Mr. Arundell in 1833.[1]
Conspicuous among its ruins are the remains of a noble
aqueduct, which shows its former importance.   Its coins
are chiefly remarkable for the prominence given on the
one hand to its colonial privileges, and on the other to its
very ancient worship of the moon as a masculine divinity
under the title of Mēn Archaios.   This worship had in
former days been very flourishing, and the temple of
Mēn had been thronged with Hieroduli, who lived on its
estates and revenues.   Strabo tells us that, some seventy
years before this time, on the death of King Amyntas, to
whom Pisidia had been assigned by Mark Antony, this
temple had been abolished; but though the worship may
have been entirely shorn of its ancient splendour, it
probably still lingered among the ignorant and aboriginal
population.

But the message of the Apostles was not in the first
instance addressed to the native Pisidians, nor to the

---

[1] It is near the insignificant modern town of Jalobatz, and its identity is
rendered certain by coins and inscriptions. (See Arundell, *Asia Minor*,
ch. xii.; Hamilton, *Researches in Asia Minor*, i., ch. xxvii.; in Con. and Hows.
i. 182.)

Greeks, who formed the second stratum of the population, nor to the Romans, who were the latest occupants, but primarily to the Jews who had come thither with the stream of Latin immigration, which secured them equal privileges with the other inhabitants. Doubtless the first care of the Apostles—and this was the work in which Mark might have been specially useful—was to repair to the "strangers' rooms" attached to the synagogue, and then to find convenient lodgings in the Jews' quarter, and to provide means of securing a sale for the *cilicium*, by the weaving of which Paul honourably lived. The trade only occupied his hands, without interrupting either his meditations or his speech, and we may reasonably suppose that not a few of the converts who loved him best, were won rather by the teaching and conversations of the quiet rooms where he sat busily at work, than by the more tumultuous and interrupted harangues in the public synagogues.

But the mission of Paul and Barnabas was not meant for the few alone. They always made a point of visiting the synagogue on the Sabbath Day, and seizing any opportunity that offered itself to address the congregation. The visit to Antioch in Pisidia is rendered interesting by the scenes which led to the first sermon of St. Paul of which the record has been preserved.

The town possessed but a single synagogue, which must, therefore, have been a large one. The arrangements were no doubt almost identical with those which exist in the present day throughout the East. As they entered the low, square, unadorned building, differing from Gentile places of worship by its total absence of interior sculpture, they would see on one side the lattice-work partition, behind which sat a crowd of veiled and silent women. In front of these would be the reader's desk, and in its immediate neighbourhood, facing the rest of the congregation, those chief seats which Rabbis and Pharisees were so eager to secure. The *Kibleh*, or sacred direction towards which all prayer was offered, was Jerusalem; and on that side would be the curtain, behind which was the ark containing the sacred rolls.[1] Paul, as a former Sanhedrist, and Barnabas, as a Levite, and both of them as men of superior Jewish education, might fairly have claimed to sit in the chairs or benches set apart for the elders. But perhaps they had been told what their Lord had said on the subject, and took their seats among the ordinary worshippers.[2]

Each as he entered covered his head with his *Tallíth*, and the prayers began. They were read by the *Sheliach*, or "angel of the synagogue,"[3] who stood among the standing congregation. The language employed was probably Greek. Hebrew had long been to the Jews a learned language, understood only by the few, and in remote places, like Antioch of Pisidia, known possibly to only one or two. In spite of the stiff conservatism of a few Rabbis, the Jews as a nation had the good sense to see that it would be useless to utter prayers unless they were "understanded of the people."[4] After the prayers followed the First Lesson, or *Parashah*, and this, owing to the sanctity which the Jews attached to the very sounds and letters of Scripture, was read in Hebrew, but was translated or paraphrased verse by verse by the *Meturgeman*, or interpreter. The *Chazzán*, or clerk of the synagogue, took the *Thorah*-roll from the ark, and handed it to the reader. By the side of the reader

---

[1] תיבה.

[2] Matt. xxiii. 6, πρωτοκαθεδρίαι, קרית. Philo makes frequent allusions to the order and arrangements of synagogue-worship at this period.

[3] שליח צבור.

[4] *Berachôth*, f. 3, 1; *Sota*, f. 21, 1.

stood the interpreter, unless he performed that function for himself, as could be easily done, since the Septuagint version was now universally disseminated. After the *Parashah*, was read the short *Haphtarah*, or what we should call the Second Lesson, from the Prophets, the translation into the vernacular being given at the end of every three verses. After this followed the *Midrash*, the exposition or sermon. It was not delivered by one set minister, but, as at the present day any distinguished stranger who happens to be present is asked by way of compliment to read the *Thorah*, so in those days the *Rosh ha-Kenéseth* might ask any one to preach who seemed likely to do so with profit to the worshippers.[1]

Accordingly on this occasion when the *Haphtarah* and *Parashah* were ended, the *Batlanim*—the "men of leisure" who managed the affairs of the synagogue, and corresponded to our churchwardens—sent the *Chazzân* to ask the strangers if they had any word of exhortation to the people. Some rumour that they were preachers of a new and remarkable doctrine must already have spread in the little Jewish community, and it was evidently expected that they would be called upon. Paul instantly accepted the invitation.[2] Usually a Jewish preacher sat down during the delivery of his sermon,[3] as is freely done by Roman Catholics abroad ; but Paul, instead of going to the pulpit, seems merely to have risen in his place, and with uplifted arm and beckoning finger[4]—in the attitude

---

[1] προελθὼν δὲ ὁ πρεσβύτατος καὶ τῶν δογμάτων ἐμπειρότατος διαλέγεται (Philo, *Quod Omn. Prob.* 12). Dr. Frankl, in his *Jews in the East*, tells us that he was constantly called upon to perform this function. Full details of synagogue worship may be found in Maimonides, *Jad Hachezaka* (*Hilch. Tephil.* viii. 10—12), and s. v. *Haphtarah* and *Synagogue* in Kitto's *Cyclopædia*, by Dr. Ginsburg.

[2] We can hardly imagine that he showed the feigned reluctance inculcated by the rabbis (*Berachôth*, 34, 1).

[3] Luke iv. 20.   [4] Cf. Acts xii. 17 ; xxi. 40 ; xxvi. 1.

of one who, however much he may sometimes have been
oppressed by nervous hesitancy, is proved by the addresses
which have been preserved to us, to have been in moments
of emotion and excitement a bold orator—he spoke to the
expectant throng.

The sermon in most instances, as in the case of our
Lord's address at Nazareth, would naturally take the form
of a *Midrash* on what the congregation had just heard
in one or other of the two lessons. Such seems to have
been the line taken by St. Paul in this his first recorded
sermon.   The occurrence of two words in this brief
address, of which one is a most unusual form,[1] and the
other is employed in a most unusual meaning,[2] and the
fact that these two words are found respectively in the
first of Deuteronomy and the first of Isaiah, combined
with the circumstance that the historical part of St. Paul's
sermon turns on the subject alluded to in the first
of these chapters, and the promise of free remission is
directly suggested by the other, would make it extremely
probable that those were the two chapters which he
had just heard read.   His sermon in fact, or rather
the heads of it, which can alone be given in the brief
summary of St. Luke,[3] is exactly the kind of masterly
combination and application of these two Scripture lessons
of the day which we should expect from such a preacher.

---

[1] Acts xiii. 18, ἐτροφοφόρησεν (A, C, E), "carried them as a man carries
his little son." LXX., Deut. i. 31; cf. Ex. xix. 4; Isa. lxiii. 9; Am. ii. 10,
&c. He is not here reproaching them, but only speaking of God's mercy to
them. The word also occurs in 2 Macc. vii. 27.

[2] Acts xiii. 17, ὕψωσεν, in the sense of "he brought them up" (Isa. i. 2);
whereas elsewhere it means "elevated" or "raised up" (Luke i. 52; 2 Cor. xi. 7).
In verse 19 he uses κατεκληρονόμησεν (א, A, B, C, D, E, G, H, &c.) in the
rare sense of "divided as an inheritance" (where our text follows the correction, κατεκληροδότησεν), as in Deut. i. 38.

[3] It should not be forgotten that no single address of St. Paul in the Acts
would take more than five minutes in delivery.

And when turning to the Jewish Lectionary, and bearing in mind its extreme antiquity, we find that these two very lessons are combined as the *Parashah* and *Haphtarah* of the same Sabbath, we see an almost convincing proof that those were the two lessons which had been read on that Sabbath Day in the synagogue of Antioch more than 1,800 years ago.[1] Here again we find another minute and most unsuspected trace of the close faithfulness of St. Luke's narrative, as well as an incidental proof that St. Paul spoke in Greek. The latter point, however, hardly needs proof. Greek was at that time the language of the civilised world to an extent far greater than French is the common language of the Continent. It is quite certain that all the Jews would have understood it; it is very doubtful whether more than a few of them would have understood the Pisidian dialect; it is to the last degree improbable that Paul knew anything of Pisidian; and that he suddenly acquired it by the gift of tongues, can only be regarded as an exploded fancy due to an erroneous interpretation.

St. Paul's sermon is not only interesting as a sign of the more or less extemporaneous tact with which he utilised the scriptural impressions which were last and freshest in the minds of his audience, but far more as a specimen of the facts and arguments which he urged in his first addresses to mixed congregations of Jews and Proselytes. The numerous and exclusively Pauline expressions[2] in which it abounds, show that either notes

[1] They are read on the Sabbath which, from the first word of the chapter in Isaiah, is called the Sabbath *Hason*. In the present list of Jewish lessons, Deut. i.—iii. 22 and Is. i. 1—22, stand forty-fourth in order under the Masoretic title of דברים. This brilliant conjecture is due to Bengel.

[2] See (in the Greek) Acts xiii. 25 compared with xx. 24; 2 Tim. iv. 7; 26 with xx. 32; 27 with xxiv. 21; 39 with Rom. vi. 7; 39 with Rom. v. 9, Gal. iii. 11, and others, in Alford's references. Compare, too, the thoughts and expressions of 33, 34 with Rom. i. 4, vi. 9; and 39 with Rom. viii. 3, Gal. iii. 11.

Y

of it must have been preserved by some Antiochene
Christian, or that he must himself have furnished an
outline of it to St. Luke.[1] It is further important as an
indication that even at this early period of his career Paul
had been led by the Spirit of God, if not to the full comprehension, at least to the germ, of those truths which
he afterwards developed with such magnificent force and
overwhelming earnestness. The doctrine of justification
by faith, and of the inutility of the works of the law
to procure remission of sins, lie clearly involved in this
brief but striking sermon, which also gives us some
insight into Paul's method of applying Scripture; into his
adoption of the current chronology of his nation;[2] and,

---

[1] Perhaps a better hypothesis is that in general outline the three main
sections of it (Acts xiii. 16—22, 23—31, 32—41) may have been often repeated.
(Ewald, vi. 658.)

[2] For instance, in verse 20 he makes the period of the Judges last 450
years. It is true that here the best uncial MSS. transpose the ἔτεσι
τετρακοσίοις καὶ πεντήκοντα to the previous verse (א, A, B, C, and the Coptic,
Sahidic, and Armenian versions). But this is exactly one of the instances in
which the "paradiplomatic" evidence entirely outweighs that of the MSS.
For the reading of the text is found in E, G, H, and many other MSS.; and
while we see an obvious reason why it should have been altered, we see none
why the other reading should have been tampered with. The case
stands thus. The chronology which gives a period of 450 years to the
Judges is in direct contradiction to 1 Kings vi. 1, which makes the fourth
year of Solomon's reign fall in the 480th year after the Exodus. Why, then,
do modern editors adopt it in spite of the oldest uncials? Not, as Bishop
Wordsworth says, out of "arbitrary caprice," or "to gratify a morbid appetite
of scepticism by contradictions invented by itself, and imputed to Holy Writ,"
or "an inordinate love of discovering discrepancies in Holy Scripture;" but
for reasons, of which he must surely have been aware—viz., because (1) the
same erroneous chronology is also found in Josephus (Antt. viii. 3, § 1, and
potentially in xx. 10, § 1), and is, therefore, obviously the current one among
the Jews; and was current (2) because it is the exact period given by the
addition of the vague and often synchronous periods given in the Book of
Judges itself. And (3) even if we accept the corrected reading—which can
only be done in the teeth of the rule, "Difficiliori lectioni praestat ardua "—
we only create fresh chronological difficulties. On such subjects the knowledge of St. Paul and the Apostles never professes to be more than the
knowledge of their time. To attribute to them a miraculous superiority to

lastly, into the effects which had been produced upon his mind by the speeches he had heard from St. Peter and from St. Stephen. From the latter of these he borrows his use of what may be called the historic method; from the former, the remarkable Messianic argument for the Resurrection which he founds on a passage in the Second Psalm.[1]

Beginning with a courteous address to the Jews and Proselytes, and bespeaking their earnest attention, he touched first on that providence of God in the history of Israel of which they had just been reminded in the Haphtarah. He had chosen them, had nurtured them in Egypt, had delivered them from its bondage, had carried them like a nursing father in the wilderness, had driven out seven nations of Canaan before them, had governed them by judges for 450 years, and then for forty years, as tradition said, had granted them for their king one whom—with an allusion to his own name and tribe which is inimitably natural—he calls "Saul, the son of Kish, of the tribe of Benjamin." Then fusing three separate passages of scriptural encomium on David into one general quotation (13–22) he announces the central truth which it was his mission to preach: that, of David's seed, God had raised up according to His promise One who, as His very name signified, was a Saviour, and to whom the great acknowledged prophet, John the Baptist, had borne direct witness. It was true

the notions of their day in subjects within the reach of man's unaided research, is an error which all the greatest modern theologians have rightly repudiated as pregnant with mischief. Similarly, in verse 33, ἐν τῷ πρώτῳ ψαλμῷ, though only found in D, is undoubtedly the right reading, as against δευτέρῳ, which is found in א and the other uncials, which is simply a correction, because the quotation is from Psalm ii. 7; and it was overlooked that among the Jews in St. Paul's time the *Second* Psalm was regarded as the First, the First being "an introduction to the Psalter."

[1] Compare Acts xiii. 35—37 with St. Peter's speech in Acts ii. 27.

that the rulers of Jerusalem—and on this painful side of
the subject he dwells but lightly—had, less from deliberate
wickedness than from ignorance, put Him to death, thereby
fulfilling the direct prophecies of Scripture.   But—and
this was the great fact on which he relied to remove the
terrible offence of the Cross—GOD HAD RAISED HIM FROM
THE DEAD (23–31).   This was an historic objective fact, to
which, as a fact tested by their living senses, many could
bear witness.   And lest they should hesitate about this
testimony, he proceeded to show that it was in accordance
with all those prophecies which had been for centuries the
most inspiring part of their nation's faith.   The Resurrection to which they testified was the highest fulfilment
of the Psalm in which God had addressed David as His
son.   And there were two special passages which foreshadowed this great truth.   One was in Isaiah, where
the Prophet had promised to God's true children the
holy, the sure, mercies of David; the other was that on
which St. Peter had dwelt in his speech at Pentecost—
the confident hope expressed in that *Michtam* or "Golden
Psalm"—that God would not leave his soul in hell, or
suffer His holy one to see corruption.   More must have
been involved in that yearning conviction than could
possibly affect David himself.   He had died, he had seen
corruption; but He of the seed of David whom God
had raised—of Him alone was it true that His soul was
not left in the unseen world, and His flesh had not seen
corruption.   What they had to preach, then, was forgiveness of sins through Him.   In the Mosaic Law—and
once more Paul touched but lightly, and in language least
likely to cause offence, upon this dangerous ground—
remission of sins was not to be found; but there was
not only remission, but *justification*, for all who believed
in Jesus.   A quotation from Habakkuk formed the

striking peroration of a sermon which had been thus weighted with awful truths and startling testimony. It warned them that however startling that testimony might be, yet if they disbelieved it as their fathers had disbelieved the threat of Chaldean retribution, the contempt of insolent derision might be followed by the astonishment of annihilating doom (32–41).[1]

Thus, from the standpoint of those who heard him—commenting on the passages which had just sounded in their ears—appealing to the prophecies in which they believed—quoting, or alluding to, the Scriptures which they held so sacred—relying on the history to which they clung with such fond affection, and pouring his flood of light on those "dark speeches upon the harp" which had hitherto wanted their true explanation—thus mingling courtesy and warning, the promises of the past and their fulfilment in the present—thus drowning the dark horror which lay in the thought of a crucified Messiah in the dawning light of His resurrection—did St. Paul weave together argument, appeal, and testimony to convince them of the new and mighty hope which he proffered, and to foreshadow that which was so difficult for them to accept—the doing away of the old as that which, having received its divine fulfilment, must now be regarded as ineffectual symbol and obsolete shadow, that in Christ all things might become new.[2]

---

[1] Acts xiii. 41, "ye despisers" corresponds to "among the heathen" in the original of Hab. i. 5, because the LXX. which St. Paul here quotes seems to have read בֹּגְדִים (bogĕdím), "arrogantes," for בַּגּוֹיִם (baggoím), by one of the numberless instances of variant readings in the Hebrew of which the Greek version affords so striking a proof.

[2] Paul speaks slightingly of his own eloquence; but we see by the recorded specimens of his sermons to barbarians in Pisidia, to philosophers at Athens, and to Jews at Jerusalem, how powerful was his method; and we are sure that there must also have been the "vividus vultus, vividae manus, vividi oculi, denique omnia vivida."

It was not surprising that a discourse so powerful should produce a deep effect. Even the Jews were profoundly impressed. As they streamed out of the synagogue, Jew and Gentile alike[1] begged that the same topics might be dwelt on in the discourse of the next Sabbath;[2] and after the entire breaking up of the congregation, many both of the Jews and of the Proselytes of the Gate followed Paul and Barnabas for the purpose of further inquiry and conversation. Both at that time and during the week the Apostles did all they could to widen the knowledge of these inquirers, and to confirm their nascent faith.[3] Meanwhile the tidings of the great sermon spread through the city. On the following Sabbath a vast crowd, of all ranks, nationalities, and classes, thronged the doors of the synagogue. Immediately the haughty exclusiveness of the Jews took the alarm. They were jealous that a single address of this dubious stranger, with his suspicious innovations, should have produced a greater effect than their years of proselytism. They were indignant that one who seemed to have suddenly dropped down among them from the snows of Taurus with an astonishing gospel should, at a touch, thrill every heart with the electric sympathy of love, and achieve more by one message of free salvation than they had achieved in a century by raising a prickly hedge around the exclusive sanctity of their Law. Paul—again the chief speaker—no longer met with attentive and eager listeners; he was inter-

---

[1] Acts xiii. 42. The E.V. has "the Gentiles besought;" but τὰ ἔθνη is an idle gloss, not found in א, A, B, C, D, E, &c.

[2] εἰς τὸ μεταξὺ σάββατον. The use of μεταξὺ for "next following" has puzzled commentators, and led them to such erroneous renderings as "for the intervening week;" but it is found in late Greek (Jos. B. J. v. 4, § 2; c. Ap. i. 21; Plut. Inst. Lac. 42), and is a mere extension of the classical Greek idiom. (See my Brief Greek Syntax, § 82, iv.)

[3] Acts xiii. 43, "urged them to abide by the grace of God;" cf. xx. 24. The expression is thoroughly Pauline. (1 Cor. xv. 10; 2 Cor. vi. 1, &c.)

rupted again and again by flat contradiction and injurious taunts.[1] At last both the Apostles saw that the time was come to put an end to the scene, and to cease a form of ministration which only led to excited recriminations. Summoning up all their courage—and few acts are more courageous than the unflinching announcement of a most distasteful intention to an infuriated audience—they exclaimed that now they had done their duty, and discharged their consciences towards their own countrymen. They had made to them the offer of eternal life, and that offer had been disdainfully repudiated.[2] "Lo! you may be astonished and indignant, but now we turn to the Gentiles. In doing so we do but fulfil the prophecy of Isaiah, who said of our Lord that He was ordained for a Light of the Gentiles, and for salvation to the ends of the earth."

Gladly and gratefully did the Gentiles welcome the mission which now to them exclusively made free offer of all, and more than all, the blessings of Judaism without its burdens. All who, by the grace of God, decided to range themselves in the ranks of those who desired eternal life[3] accepted the faith. More and more widely[4] the word of the Lord began to spread. But the Jews were too powerful to be easily defeated. They counted among their proselytes a large number of women, of whom some were of high rank.[5] Their commercial ability had

---

[1] Acts xiii. 45, ἀντέλεγον.

[2] Acts xiii. 46, οὐκ ἀξίους κρίνετε ἑαυτοὺς τῆς αἰωνίου ζωῆς.

[3] ὅσοι ἦσαν τεταγμένοι εἰς ζ. αι. Those only will find in this expression a hard Calvinism who overlook the half-middle usage of the participle which is found in xx. 13 (cf. ii. 47) and in Philo. In a Calvinistic sense, moreover, the words are in direct antinomy with xiii. 46. The E.V. followed Tyndale, but the Rhemish "pre-ordained" is even stronger. The close juxtaposition of the two phrases shows the danger of building unscriptural systems on the altered perspective of isolated expressions.

[4] Acts xiii. 49, διεφέρετο.

[5] Jos. B. J. ii. 20, § 2; cf. Strab. vii. 2; ἅπαντες τῆς δεισιδαιμονίας ἀρχηγοὺς εἶναι τὰς γυναῖκας; cf. Juv. Sat. vi. 542. In Ps. lxviii. 11, "The Lord gave the

also secured them friends among the leading people of the city, who were the municipal Roman authorities. Tolerant of every legalised religion, the Romans had a profound distaste for religious embroilments, and so long as the Jews behaved peaceably, were quite willing to afford them protection. Knowing that all had gone smoothly till these new-comers had appeared, they were readily induced to look on them with dislike, especially since they were viewed with disfavour by the ladies of their families.[1] They joined in the clamour against the Apostles, and succeeded in getting them banished out of their boundaries. The Apostles shook off their feet the deep dust of the parched roads in testimony against them,[2] and passed on to Iconium, where they would be under a different jurisdiction.[3] But the departure did not destroy the infant Church which they had founded. It might have been expected that they would leave gloom and despondency among their discouraged converts; but it was not so. They left behind them the joy of a new hope, the inspiration of a new faith, the outpouring of the Holy Spirit in the hearts of those who had learnt of the heavenly promise.

word: great was the company of the preachers" (lit. "the female messengers," εὐαγγελιστρίαι, LXX.), fantastic commentators of the literalist type find in the fact that מְבַשֶּׂרֶת is feminine, an indication of the prominent agency of women in the spread of the Gospel.

[1] αὐταὶ δὲ καὶ τοὺς ἄνδρας προκαλοῦνται (Strabo, l.c.). For the indulgence of the Romans towards the Jews in the provinces, Renan refers to Jos. Antt. xiv. 10, § 11; xvi. 6, §§ 2, 4, 6, 7; Cic. pro Flacco, 28, &c.

[2] Matt. x. 14.

[3] Antioch was a Roman colony, under the general jurisdiction of the Propraetor of Galatia. Iconium was under a local tetrarch. (Plin. H. N. v. 27.)

CHAPTER XXI.

THE CLOSE OF THE JOURNEY.

Ἄπιστοι γὰρ Λυκάονες ὡς καὶ Ἀριστοτέλης μαρτυρεῖ.—SCHOL. *in H.* iv. 88.

"WHEN they persecute you in this city, flee ye to another," our Lord had said to His twelve Apostles when He sent them forth as lambs among wolves.[1] Expelled from Antioch,[2] the Apostles obeyed this injunction. They might have crossed the Paroreian range to Philomelium, and so have made their way westwards to Synnada and the Phrygian cities, or eastwards to Laodicea. What circumstances determined their course we cannot tell, but they kept to the south of the Paroreia, and, following a well-traversed road, made their way to the pleasant city of Iconium. For a distance of about sixty miles the road ran south-westwards over bleak plains, scoured by wild asses and grazed by countless herds of sheep, until it reaches the green oasis on which stands the city of Iconium.[3] It is the city so famous through the Middle Ages, under the name of Konieh, as the capital of the Sultans of Roum, and the scene of the romantic siege by Godfrey of Bouillon. Here, on the edge of an interminable steppe, and nearly encircled by snow-clad hills, they had entered the district of Lycaonia, and found

---

[1] Matt. x. 25.

[2] Acts xiii. 51, ἐξέβαλον αὐτούς.

[3] Strabo, xii. 6. Mentioned in *Xen. Anab.* i. 2, 19; Cic. *ad Fam.* iii. 8; v. 20; xv. 4, as lying at the intersection of important roads between Ephesus and Tarsus, &c.

themselves in the capital city of an independent tetrarchy.
The diversity of political governments which at this time
prevailed in Asia Minor was so far an advantage to the
Apostles, that it rendered them more able to escape from
one jurisdiction to another. Their ejection from Antioch
must have received the sanction of the colonial authorities, who were under the Propraetor of Galatia; but
at Iconium they were beyond the Propraetor's province,
in a district which, in the reign of Augustus, belonged
to the robber-chief Amyntas, and was still an independent
tetrarchy of fourteen towns.[1]

Doubtless, as at Antioch, their first care would be to
secure a lodging among their fellow-countrymen, and the
means of earning their daily subsistence. On the Sabbath
they entered as usual the one synagogue which sufficed
the Jewish population. Invitations to speak were at first
never wanting, and they preached with a fervour which
won many converts both among Jews and proselytes.
The Batlanîm, indeed, and the Ruler of the Synagogue
appear to have been against them, but at first their opposition was in some way obviated.[2] Some of the Jews,
however, stirred up the minds of the Gentiles against
them.[3] Over the Proselytes of the Gate the Apostles
would be likely to gain a strong influence. It would
not be easy to shake their interest in such teaching, or
their gratitude to those who were sacrificing all that

---

[1] Plin. N. H. v. 25. Some doubt seems to rest on this, from the existence
of a coin of the reign of Nero in which it is called Claudiconium, and of a
coin of Gallienus in which it is called a colony; but the adoption of the name
of Claudius may have been gratuitous flattery, and the privilege conceded long
afterwards.

[2] Although not authentic, there may be some basis of tradition in the
reading of D and (in part) Syr. marg., οἱ δὲ ἀρχισυνάγωγοι τῶν Ἰουδαίων καὶ οἱ
ἄρχοντες τῆς συναγωγῆς ἐπήγαγον αὐτοῖς διωγμὸν κατὰ τῶν δικαίων . . . . ὁ δὲ κύριος
ἔδωκεν ταχὺ εἰρήνην.

[3] This seems to be suggested by the contrast of Ἑλλήνων in verse 1 with
ἐθνῶν in verse 2.

made life dear to their desire to proclaim it. But when Jewish indignation was kindled, when the synagogue became the weekly scene of furious contentions,[1] it would be easy enough to persuade the Gentile inhabitants of the city that these emissaries, who had already been ejected from Antioch, were dangerous incendiaries, who everywhere disturbed the peace of cities. In spite, however, of these gathering storms the Apostles held their ground, and their courage was supported by the evident blessing which was attending their labour. So long as they were able not only to sway the souls of their auditors, but to testify the power of their mission by signs and wonders, they felt that it was not the time to yield to opposition. Their stay, therefore, was prolonged, and the whole population of the city was split into two factions—the one consisting of their enemies, the other of their supporters. At length the spirit of faction grew so hot that the leaders of the hostile party of Jews and Gentiles made

---

[1] Renan compares the journey of the Apostles from Ghetto to Ghetto to those of the Arab Ibn Batoutah, and the mediæval traveller Benjamin of Tudela. A more recent analogy may be found in Dr. Frankl's *Jews in the East.* The reception of these Christian teachers by remote communities of Jews has been exactly reproduced in modern times by the bursts of infuriated curses, excommunications, mobs, and stone-throwings with which modern Jews have received missionaries in some of their larger Moldavian communities. Here is the description of one such scene by a missionary:— "Fearful excommunications were issued in the synagogue, pronouncing most terrible judgments on any Jew holding communication with us; or who, on receiving any of our publications, did not at once consign them to the flames. The stir and commotion were so great that I and my brother missionaries were obliged to hold a consultation, whether we should face the opposition or fly from the town. We resolved to remain and face the danger in the name of God, and the next day being Saturday, the Jewish Sabbath, we went out with a stock of our publications. When we got near the synagogue we were driven away by a yelling, cursing, blaspheming crowd, who literally darkened the air with the stones they threw at us. We were in the greatest danger of being killed. Ultimately, however, we faced them, and by dint of argument and remonstrance gained a hearing." (*Speech of the Rev. M. Wolkenberg at Salisbury,* August 8, 1876.)

a plot to murder the Apostles.[1] Of this they got timely notice, and once more took flight. Leaving the tetrarchy of Iconium, they still pursued the great main road, and made their way some forty miles into the district of Antiochus IV., King of Commagene, and to the little town of Lystra in Lycaonia.

The site of Lystra has never been made out with perfect certainty, but there is good reason to believe that it was at a place now known as Bin Bir Kilisseh, or the Thousand and One Churches,—once the see of a bishop, and crowded with the ruins of sacred buildings. It lies in the northern hollows of the huge isolated mass of an extinct volcano, "rising like a giant from a plain level as the sea."[2] It is called the Kara Dagh, or Black Mountain, and is still the haunt of dangerous robbers.

Both at Lystra and in the neighbouring hamlets the Apostles seem to have preached with success, and to have stayed for some little time. On one occasion Paul noticed among his auditors a man who had been a cripple from his birth. His evident eagerness[3] marked him out to the quick insight of the Apostle as one on whom a work of power could be wrought. It is evident on the face of the narrative that it was not every cripple or every sufferer that Paul would have attempted to heal; it was only such as, so to speak, met half-way the exertion of spiritual power by their own ardent faith. Fixing his eyes on him, Paul raised his voice to

---

[1] The *Acta Pauli et Theclae*, of which the scene is laid at Iconium, are so purely apocryphal as hardly to deserve notice. They are printed in Grabe, *Spicileg.* 1; Tischendorf, *Acta Apost. Apocr.* p. 40. Tertullian says that a presbyter in Asia was deposed for having forged the story out of love for Paul (*De Bapt.* 17); St. Jerome adds that it was St. John who deposed him.

[2] Kinneir, *Travels in Karamania*, p. 212.

[3] Acts xiv. 9, ἤκουε τοῦ Παύλου λαλοῦντος.

its full compass, and cried—" Rise on thy feet upright."
Thrilled with a divine power, the man sprang up; he
began to walk. The crowd who were present at the
preachings, which seem on this occasion to have
been in the open air, were witnesses of the miracle,
and reverting in their excitement, perhaps from a sense
of awe, to their rude native Lycaonian dialect[1]— just
as a Welsh crowd, after being excited to an overpowering degree by the English discourse of some great
Methodist, might express its emotions in Welsh—they
cried: 'The gods have come down to us in the likeness
of men. The tall and venerable one is Zeus; the other,
the younger and shorter one, who speaks so powerfully,
is Hermes.'[2] Ignorant of the native dialect, the Apostles
did not know what the crowd were saying,[3] and withdrew to their lodging. But meanwhile the startling
rumour had spread. Lycaonia was a remote region where
still lingered the simple faith in the old mythologies.[4] Not
only were there points of resemblance in Central Asia
between their own legends and the beliefs of the Jews,[5]
but this region was rendered famous as the scene of more
than one legendary epiphany, of which the most celebrated

---

[1] Jablonski, in his monograph *De Lingua Lycaonia*, concluded that it was
a corrupt Assyrian, and therefore Semitic dialect; Guhling, that it was Greek,
corrupted with Syriac. The only Lycaonian word we know is δέλβεια, which
means "a juniper," as we find in Steph. Byzant.

[2] It is hardly worth while to produce classical quotation to show that
Hermes was the god of eloquence (Hor. *Od.* i. 10; Macrob. *Saturn.* i. 8). Hence
his epithet Λόγιος (*Orph. Hymn.* xxvii. 6). " Quo didicit culte lingua favente
loqui " (Ov. *F.* v. 665).

[3] See Chrysost. *Hom.* xxx. The notion of St. Jerome, that the power of
the Apostles to speak to the Lycaonians in their own language was one of the
reasons why the people took them for gods, is utterly baseless.

[4] Some remarkable proofs are given by Döllinger (*Judenth. u. Heidenth.*
bk. viii. 2, § 5).

[5] For instance, the sort of dim tradition of the Deluge at Apamea
Kibôtos.

—recorded in the beautiful tale of Philemon and Baucis[1] —was said to have occurred in this very neighbourhood. Unsophisticated by the prevalent disbelief, giving ready credence to all tales of marvel, and showing intense respect for any who seemed invested with special sacredness,[2] the Lycaonians eagerly accepted the suggestion that they were once more favoured by a visit from the old gods, to whom in a faithless age they had still been faithful. And this being so, *they* at least would not be guilty either of the impious scepticism which had ended in the transformation into a wolf of their eponymous prince Lycaon, or of the inhospitable carelessness which for all except one aged couple had forfeited what might have been a source of boundless blessings. Before the gate of the town was a Temple of Zeus, their guardian deity. The Priest of Zeus rose to the occasion. While the Apostles remained in entire ignorance of his proceedings he had procured bulls and garlands, and now, accompanied by festive crowds, came to the gates to do them sacrifice.[3] Paul and Barnabas were the last to hear that they were about to be the centres of an idolatrous worship, but when they did hear it they, with their sensitive conceptions of the awful majesty of the one true God, were horror-stricken to an extent which a Gentile could hardly have understood.[4] Rending their garments, they sprang

[1] Ov. *Met.* viii. 626, seqq.; *Fast.* v. 495; Dio. Chrysost. *Orat.* xxxiii. 408. On the common notion of these epiphanies, see Hom. *Od.* xvi. 484; Hes. *Opp. et D.* 247; Cat. lxv. 384.

[2] Tyana, the birthplace of the contemporary thaumaturge, Apollonius, who was everywhere received with so deep a reverence, is not far to the east of Lystra and Derbe.

[3] Probably the gates of the house, cf. xii. 13, Jul. Poll. *Onomast.* i. 8, 77 (cf. Virg. *Ecl.* iii. 487; Tert. *De Cor. Mil.* x.).

[4] Menexenus, the physician of Alexander, claimed to be a god, as did Alexander of Abonoteichus, to say nothing of the *Divi Cæsares.*—Ἐξεπήδησαν, א, A, B, C, D, E, &c. Barnabas is put first because he is most reverenced as *Zeus Poliouchos.* In the story of Baucis and Philemon the miracle at once led to a sacrifice.

out with loud cries among the multitude, expostulating
with them, imploring them to believe that they were but
ordinary mortals like themselves, and that it was the
very object of their mission to turn them from these empty
idolatries to the one living and true God, who made the
heaven, and the earth, and the sea, and all that in them
is. And so, as they gradually gained more of the ear of
the multitude, they explained that during past generations
God had, as it were, suffered all the heathen to walk in
their own ways,[1] and had not given them special revelations; and yet even in those days He had not left Himself
without witness by the mercies which He then sent, as
He sends them now, "by giving us from heaven rains
and fruitful seasons, by filling our hearts with food and
gladness."

Such was the strong yet kindly and sympathetic
protest uttered by the Apostles against the frank superstition of these simple Lycaonians. It was no time
now, in the urgency of the moment, to preach Christ
to them, the sole object being to divert them from
an idolatrous sacrifice, and to show the futile character
of the polytheism of which such sacrifices formed a part.
Paul, who was evidently the chief speaker, does this
with that inspired tact which can always vary its utterances
with the needs of the moment. No one can read the
speech without once more perceiving its subtle and
inimitable coincidence with his thoughts and expressions.[2]

---

[1] Acts xiv. 16. πάντα τὰ ἔθνη.

[2] Compare xiv. 15, ἀπὸ τούτων τῶν ματαίων ἐπιστρέφειν ἐπὶ Θεὸν ζῶντα with 1
Thess. i. 9, ἐπεστρέψατε πρὸς τὸν Θεὸν ἀπὸ τῶν εἰδώλων, κ.τ.λ., and the anar-
throus Θεὸν ζῶντα with Rom. ix. 26, &c. Compare too the very remarkable
expression and thought of ver. 16 with the speech at Athens, xvii. 30, Rom. i.
20, ii. 15, &c., and ver. 17 with Rom. i. 19, 20. The readings "us" and
"our hearts" (ἡμῖν and ἡμῶν, A, B, G, H, and the Coptic and Ethiopian
versions) are not certain, since these are exactly points in which diplomatic

The rhythmic conclusion is not unaccordant with the style of his most elevated moods; and besides the appropriate appeal to God's natural gifts in a town not in itself unhappily situated, but surrounded by a waterless and treeless plain, we may naturally suppose that the "filling our hearts with food and gladness" was suggested by the garlands and festive pomp which accompanied the bulls on which the people would afterwards have made their common banquet. Nor do I think it impossible that the words may be an echo of lyric songs[1] sung as the procession made its way to the gates. To use them in a truer and loftier connexion would be in exact accord with the happy power of seizing an argument which St. Paul showed when he turned into the text of his sermon at Athens the vague inscription to the Unknown God.

But the Lystrenians did not like to be baulked of their holiday and of their banquet; and those who had been most prominent in proclaiming the new epiphany of Zeus and Hermes were probably not a little ashamed. M. Renan is right in the remark that the ancient heathen had no conception of a miracle as the evidence of a doctrine. If, then, the Apostles could work a miracle, and yet indisputably disclaim all notion of being gods in disguise, what were they, and what became of their miracle? The Lycaonians, in the sulky revulsion of their feelings, and with a somewhat uneasy sense that they had put themselves into a ridiculous position, were

evidence can hardly be decisive; but they are surely much more in St. Paul's manner, and illustrate the large sympathy with which he was always ready to become all things to all men, and therefore to Gentiles to speak as though he too were a Gentile.

[1] Mr. Humphry *in loc.* not unnaturally took this for the fragment of some lyric song, and though most editors have rejected his conjecture, I think that its apparent improbability may partly be removed by the suggestion in the text (*infra*, Excursus III., p. 630).

inclined to avenge their error on those who had innocently caused it. They were a faithless and fickle race,
liable, beyond the common wont of mobs, to sudden gusts
of feeling and impulse.[1] In their disappointment they
would be inclined to assume that if these two mysterious
strangers were not gods they were despicable Jews; and
if their miracle was not a sign of their divinity, it
belonged to the malefic arts of which they may well have
heard from Roman visitors. And on the arrival of the
Jews of Antioch and Iconium at Lystra, with the express
purpose of buzzing their envenomed slanders into the ears
of these country people, the mob were only too ripe for a
tumult. They stoned Paul and, when they thought he
was dead, dragged him outside their city gates, leaving
him, perhaps, in front of the very Temple of Jupiter to
which they had been about to conduct him as an incarnation of their patron deity. But Paul was not dead.
This had not been a Jewish stoning, conducted with fatal
deliberateness, but a sudden riot, in which the mode of
attack may have been due to accident. Paul, liable at
all times to the swoons which accompany nervous organi-
sations, had been stunned, but not killed; and while the
disciples stood in an agonised group around what they
thought to be his corpse, he recovered his consciousness, and raised himself from the ground. The mob meanwhile had dispersed; and perhaps in disguise, or under
cover of evening—for all these details were as nothing to
Paul, and are not preserved by his biographer—he re-
entered the little city.

Was it in the house of Eunice and Lois that he

---

[1] Commenting on the treachery of Pandarus, in *Il.* iv. 88—92, the Scholiast
quotes the testimony of Aristotle to the untrustworthy character of the
Lycaonians; and see Cic. *Epp. ad Att.* v. 21, &c., who speaks of the natives
of these regions with great contempt.

z

found the sweet repose and tender ministrations which he would need more than ever after an experience so frightful? If Lystra was thus the scene of one of his intensest sufferings, and one which, lightly as it is dwelt upon, probably left on his already enfeebled constitution its lifelong traces, it also brought him, by the merciful providence of God, its own immense compensation. For it was at Lystra that he converted the son of Eunice, then perhaps a boy of fifteen,[1] for whom he conceived that deep affection which breathes through every line of the Epistles addressed to him. This was the Timotheus whom he chose as the companion of his future journeys, whom he sent on his most confidential messages, to whom he entrusted the oversight of his most important churches, whom he summoned as the consolation of his last imprisonment, whom he always regarded as the son in the faith who was nearest and dearest to his heart. If Luke had been with St. Paul in this his first journey, he would probably have mentioned a circumstance which the Apostle doubtless regarded as one of God's best blessings, and as one which would help to obliterate in a feeling of thankfulness even the bitter memories of Lystra.[2] But we who, from scattered allusions, can see that it was here and now that St. Paul first met with the gentlest and dearest of all his converts, may dwell with pleasure on the thought that Timotheus stood weeping in that group of disciples who surrounded the bleeding missionary, whose hearts glowed with amazement and thankfulness when they saw him recover, who perhaps helped to convey him secretly to his mother's house, and there, it may be, not only bound his wounds,

---

[1] This can hardly be regarded as in any way doubtful if we compare 1 Tim. . 2, 18 and 2 Tim. ii. 1 with Acts xvi. 1.

[2] 2 Tim. iii. 11.

but also read to him in the dark and suffering hours some of the precious words of those Scriptures in which from a child he had been trained.

But after so severe a warning it was scarcely safe to linger even for a single day in a town where they had suffered such brutal violence. Even if the passion of the mob had exhausted itself, the malignity of the Jews was not so likely to be appeased. Once more the only safety seemed to be in flight; once more they took refuge in another province. From Lystra in Lycaonia they started, under the grey shades of morning, while the city was yet asleep, for the town of Derbe,[1] which was twenty miles distant, in the district of Isaurica. It is grievous to think of one who had been so cruelly treated forced to make his way for twenty miles with his life in his hand, and still all battered and bleeding from the horrible attack of the day before. But if the dark and rocky summit of Kara Dagh, the white distant snows of Mount Ægaeus,[2] and the silver expanse of the White Lake had little power to delight his wearied eyes, or calm his agitated spirit, we may be sure that He was with him whom once he had persecuted, but for whose sake he was now ready to suffer all; and that from hour

---

[1] It appears from the evidence of coins compared with Dio Cass. lix. 8 that both Derbe and Lystra were under Antiochus IV. of Commagene (Eckhel, iii. 255; Lewin, *Fasti Sacri*, p. 250). If the inference be correct they could not, even in a political sense, be called "Churches of Galatia."

[2] The site of Derbe is still doubtful. Strabo (xii. 6) calls it a φρούριον Ισαυρικῆς καὶ λιμήν, where it has long been seen that the true reading must be λίμνη, and if so the lake must be Ak Ghieul, or the "White Lake." Near this place Hamilton found a place called Divlé, which would be an easy metathesis for the name Δελβεία, by which the town was sometimes called; but another site much more to the north, where he found the ruins of an Acropolis, seems more likely. This, which is the site marked in Kiepert's map, answers the requirements of Strabo, xii. 6, since it is on the confines of Isaurica and Cappadocia, on a lake, and not far from Laranda (Karawan). See Lewin, i. 151.

z 2

to hour, as he toiled feebly and wearily along from the cruel and fickle city, "God's consolations increased upon his soul with the gentleness of a sea that caresses the shore it covers."

At Derbe they were suffered to rest unmolested. It may be that the Jews were ignorant that Paul was yet alive. That secret, pregnant with danger to the safety of the Apostle, would be profoundly kept by the little band of Lystrenian disciples. At any rate, to Derbe the Jews did not follow him with their interminable hate. The name of Derbe is omitted from the mention of places where he reminds Timothy that he had suffered afflictions and persecutions. His work seems to have been happy and successful, crowned with the conversion of those disciples whom he ever regarded as "his hope and joy and crown of rejoicing." Here, too, he gained one more friend in Gaius of Derbe, who afterwards accompanied him on his last visit to Jerusalem.[1]

And now that they were so near to Cybistra (the modern Eregli), through which a few stages would have brought them to the Cilician gates, and so through Tarsus to Antioch, it might have been assumed that this would have been the route of their return. Why did they not take it? There may be truth in the ingenious suggestion of Mr. Lewin,[2] "that the road—as is sometimes still the case—had been rendered impassable by the waters of Ak Ghieul, swollen by the melting of the winter snows, and that the way through the mountains was too uncertain and insecure."[3] But they may have had no other reason

---

[1] Acts xx. 4. The Gaius of xix. 29 was a Macedonian, and of Rom. xvi. 23 and 1 Cor. i. 14 a Corinthian.

[2] Referring to Hamilton (*Researches*, ii. 313), who found the road from Eregli impassable from this cause.

[3] Strabo, XII. vi. 2—5; Tac. *Ann.* iii. 48; xii. 55; Cic. *ad Att.* v. 20, 5, &c.

than their sense of what was needed by the infant Churches which they had founded. Accordingly they went back, over the wild and dusty plain, the twenty miles from Derbe to Lystra, the forty miles from Lystra to Iconium, the sixty miles from Iconium to Antioch. It may well be supposed that it needed no slight heroism to face once more the dangers that might befall them. But they had learnt the meaning of their Lord's saying, "He who is near Me is near the fire." Precautions of secrecy they doubtless took, and cheerfully faced the degrading necessity of guarded movements, and of entering cities, perhaps in disguise, perhaps only at late nightfall and early dawn. The Christians had early to learn those secret trysts and midnight gatherings and private watchwords by which alone they could elude the fury of their enemies. But the Apostles accomplished their purpose. They made their way back in safety, everywhere confirming the disciples, exhorting them to constancy, preparing them for the certainty and convincing them of the blessing of the tribulations through which we must enter the kingdom of God.[1] And as some organisation was necessary to secure the guidance and unity of these little bodies of converts, they held solemn meetings, at which, with prayer and fasting, they appointed elders,[2] before they bestowed on them a last blessing and farewell. In this manner they passed through Lycaonia, Iconium, and Pisidia, and so into Pamphylia; and since on their first journey they had been unable to preach in Perga, they did so now. Possibly they found no ship ready to sail down the Cestrus to their destination. They therefore made their way sixteen miles overland to the flourishing

---

[1] Acts xiv. 22. The ἡμᾶς may imply a general Christian sentiment. It cannot in this connexion be relied on as showing the presence of St. Luke.

[2] Acts xiv. 23, χειροτονήσαντες is perfectly general, as in 2 Cor. viii. 19.

seaport of Attaleia, at the mouth of the Katarrhaktes,
which at that time found its way to the sea over a range
of cliffs in floods of foaming waterfall ; and from thence—
for they never seem to have lingered among the fleeting
and mongrel populations of these seaport towns—they took
ship to Seleucia, saw once more the steep cone of Mount
Casius, climbed the slopes of Coryphæus, and made their
way under the pleasant shade of ilex, and myrtle, and
arbutus, on the banks of the Orontes, until once more
they crossed the well-known bridge, and saw the grim
head of Charon staring over the street Singôn, in which
neighbourhood the little Christian community were
prepared to welcome them with keen interest and
unbounded love.

So ended the first mission journey of the Apostle Paul
—the first flight as it were of the eagle, which was soon
to soar with yet bolder wing, in yet wider circles, among
yet more raging storms. We have followed him by the
brief notices of St. Luke, but we have no means of deciding
either the exact date of the journey, or its exact duration. It is only when the crises in the history of the
early Church synchronise with events of secular history,
that we can ever with certainty ascertain the date to
which they should be assigned.[1] We have seen that Paul
and Barnabas visited Jerusalem about the time of Herod
Agrippa's death, and this took place in April A.D. 44.
After this they returned to Antioch, and the next thing
we are told about them is their obedience to the spiritual
intimation which marked them out as Evangelists to the
heathen. It is reasonable to believe, therefore, that they
spent about a year at Antioch, since they could not easily
find vessels to convey them from place to place except

---

[1] See Chronological Excursus, *infra*, ii.

in the months during which the sea was regarded as open.
Now navigation with the ancients began with the rising
of the Pleiades, that is, in the month of March; and we
may assume with fair probability that March, A.D. 45, is
the date at which they began their evangelising labours.
Beyond this all must be conjecture. They do not seem
to have spent more than a month or two in Cyprus;[1] at
Antioch in Pisidia their stay was certainly brief. At
Iconium they remained "a considerable time;" but at
Lystra again, and at Derbe, and on their return tour, and
at Perga and Attaleia, the narrative implies no long
residence. Taking into account the time consumed in
travelling, we are hardly at liberty to suppose that the
first circuit occupied much more than a year, and they
may have returned to the Syrian Antioch in the late
spring of A.D. 46.[2]

---

[1] Acts xiv. 3, ἱκανὸν χρόνον. This may mean anything, from a month or two,
up to a year or more. It is a phrase of frequent occurrence in St. Luke (see
Acts viii. 11; xxvii. 9; Luke viii. 27; xx. 9).

[2] That Antioch in Pisidia, Iconium, Derbe, and Lystra were *not* the
churches of Galatia, as has been suggested by Böttger (*Beiträge*, i. 28, *sq.*),
Renan, Hausrath, and others, is surely demonstrable. Galatia had two meanings
—the first ethnographical, the second political. The ethnographic use was the
popular and the all but universal one. It meant that small central district of
Asia Minor, about 200 miles in length, which was occupied by the three Gallic
tribes—the Trocmi, the Tolistobogii, the Tectosages—with the three capitals,
Tavium, Pessinus, and Ancyra. Politically it meant a "department," an
"administrative group," a mere agglomeration of districts thrown into loose
cohesion by political accidents. In this political meaning the Roman province
of Galatia was based on the kingdom of Amyntas (Dio Cass. liii. 26), a
wealthy grazier and freebooter, who had received from Mark Antony the
kingdom of Pisidia, and by subsequent additions had become possessed of
Galatia Proper, Lycaonia, parts of Pamphylia, and Cilicia Aspera. On his
death various changes occurred, but when Paul and Barnabas were on their
first journey Pamphylia was under a propraetor; Iconium was a separate
tetrarchy; Lystra and Derbe belonged to Antiochus IV. of Commagene.
Galatia, Pisidia north of the Paroreia, and the greater part of Lycaonia
formed the Roman province of Galatia. But even if we grant that St. Paul
and St. Luke might have used the word Galatia in its artificial sense, even
then Antioch of Pisidia appears to be the only town mentioned in this circuit

But brief as was the period occupied, the consequences were immense. For though Paul returned from this journey a shattered man—though twenty years afterwards, through a vista of severe afflictions, he still looks back, as though they had happened but yesterday, to the "persecutions, afflictions, which came upon him at Antioch, at Iconium, at Lystra; what persecutions he endured, and yet from all the Lord delivered him "[1]—though the journeyings and violence, and incessant menace to life, which has tried even men of such iron nerves as Oliver Cromwell, had rendered him more liable than ever to fits of acute suffering and intense depression,[2] yet, in spite of all, he returned with the mission-hunger in his heart;

which is actually in the Roman province. This alone seems sufficient to disprove the hypothesis that in the first journey we have a narrative of the founding of the Galatian Church. Further, as far as St. Luke is concerned, it would be a confused method, unlike his careful accuracy, to use the words Pisidia, Lycaonia, Pamphylia, and later in his narrative Mysia, and other districts in their geographical sense, and then suddenly, without any notice, to use Galatia in Acts xvi. in its political sense, especially as this political sense was shifting and meaningless. It can hardly be supposed that since he must hundreds of times have heard St. Paul mention the churches of Galatia, he should, if *these* were the churches of Galatia, never drop a hint of the fact, and, ignoring the Roman province altogether, talk of Antioch "of Pisidia," and Lystra and Derbe, "cities of Lycaonia." I should be quite content to rest an absolute rejection of the hypothesis on these considerations, as well as on the confusion which it introduces into the chronology of St. Paul's life. The few arguments advanced in favour of this view—*e.g.*, the allusion to Barnabas in Galatians ii. 1—are wholly inadequate to support it against the many counter improbabilities. Indeed, almost the only serious consideration urged in its favour—namely, the very cursory mention in Acts xvi. 6 of what we learn from the Epistle was the founding of a most important body of churches—is nullified by the certainty which meets us at every step that the Acts does not furnish us with a complete biography. In other instances also—as in the case of the churches in Syria and Cilicia—he leaves us in doubt about the time and manner of their first evangelisation. The other form of this theory, which sees the founding of the Galatian churches in the words καὶ τὴν περίχωρον (Acts xiv. 6), escapes some of these objections, but offers far greater difficulties than the common belief which sees the evangelisation of Galatia in the cursory allusion of Acts xvi. 6.

[1] 2 Tim. iii. 11.   [2] Gal. i. 10; vi. 17.

with the determination more strongly formed than ever
to preach the word, and be instant in season and out of
season; with the fixed conviction that the work and
destiny in life to which God had specially called him was
to be the Apostle of the heathen.[1]

That conviction had been brought unalterably home
to his soul by the experience of every town at which
they had preached. Up to a certain point, and that point
not very far within the threshold of his subject, the
Jews were willing to give him a hearing; but when
they began to perceive that the Gospel was universal—
that it preached a God to whom a son of Abraham
was no whit dearer than any one in any nation
who feared Him and loved righteousness — that it
gave, in fact, to the title of "son of Abraham" a significance so purely metaphorical as to ignore all special
privilege of blood—their anger burnt like flame. It was
the scorn and indignation of the elder brother against the
returning prodigal, and his refusal to enjoy privileges
which henceforth he must share with others.[2] The deep-
seated pride of the Jews rose in arms. Who were these
obscure innovators who dared to run counter to the
cherished hopes and traditional glories of well-nigh
twenty centuries? Who were these daring heretics,
who, in the name of a faith which all the Rabbis had
rejected, were thus proclaiming to the Gentiles the
abandonment of all exclusive claim to every promise and

---

[1] 1 Cor. ix. 21; Gal. v. 11; Rom. xv. 16; Eph. iii. 6, &c.

[2] The Rabbis who spoke in truer and more liberal tones were rare. We
find, indeed, in *Berachôth*, f. 34, 2, a remarkable explanation of the verse
"Peace, peace to him that is far off, and to him that is near," which amounts
to an admission that penitents and prodigals are dearer to God (as being here
addressed first) than Pharisees and elder brothers; but it is the penitents of
Israel who are contemplated, just as some of the Fathers held out hopes to
Catholics and Christians (merely on the ground of that privilege) which they
denied to others. (Jer. *in* Isa. lxvi. 16, *in* Eph. iv. 12, &c.)

every privilege which generations of their fathers had held
most dear?

But this was not all. To abandon privileges was
unpatriotic enough; but what true Jew, what observer of
the *Halachah*, could estimate the atrocity of apostatising
from principles? Had not Jews done enough, by freely
admitting into their synagogues the Proselytes of the
Gate? Did they not even offer to regard as a son of
Israel every Gentile who would accept the covenant rite
of circumcision, and promise full allegiance to the Written
and Oral Law? But the new teachers, especially Paul,
seemed to use language which, pressed to its logical conclusion, could only be interpreted as an utterly slighting
estimate of the old traditions, nay, even of the sacred rite
of circumcision. It is true, perhaps, that they had never
openly recommended the suppression of this rite; but it
was clear that it occupied a subordinate place in their
minds, and that they were disinclined to make between
their Jewish and Gentile converts the immensity of
difference which separated a Proselyte of Righteousness
from a Proselyte of the Gate.

It is very possible that it was only the events of
this journey which finally matured the views of St.
Paul on this important subject. The ordinary laws
of nature had not been reversed in his case, and
as he grew in grace and in the knowledge of our
Lord Jesus Christ, so his own Epistles,[1] though each
has its own divine purpose, undoubtedly display the kind
of difference in his way of developing the truth which we
should ordinarily attribute to growth of mind. And it is
observable that St. Paul, when taunted by his opponents

---

[1] 2 Cor. v. 16; 1 Cor. xiii. 9—12. Bengel says that when the Epistles are
arranged chronologically, "*incrementum apostoli spirituale cognoscitur*"
(p. 583).

with having once been a preacher of circumcision, does not
meet the taunt by a denial, but merely by saying that at
any rate his persecutions are a sign that *now* that time is
over.   In fact, he simply thrusts aside the allusion to
the past by language which should render impossible any
doubts as to his sentiments in the present.   In the same
way, in an earlier part of his Epistle,[1] he anticipates the
charge of being a time-server—a charge which he knew
to be false in spirit, while yet the malignity of slander
might find some justification of it in his broad indifference
to trifles—not by any attempt to explain his former line of
action, but by an outburst of strong denunciation which
none could mistake for men-pleasing or over-persuasiveness.
Indeed, in the second chapter of the Galatians, St. Paul
seems distinctly to imply two things.   The one is that it
was the treacherous espionage of false brethren that first
made him regard the question as one of capital importance ;
the other that his views on the subject were at that time
so far from being final, that it was with a certain amount
of misgiving as to the practical decision that he went up
to the consultation at Jerusalem.   It was the result of
this interview—the discovery that James and Kephas had
nothing to contribute to any further solution of the
subject—which first made him determined to resist to the
utmost the imposition of the yoke on Gentiles, and to
follow the line which he had generally taken.   But he had
learnt from this journey that nothing but the wisdom of
God annihilating human foolishness, nothing but the
gracious Spirit of God breaking the iron sinew in the neck of
carnal obstinacy, could lead the Jews to accept the truths
he preached.   Paul saw that the husbandmen in charge of
the vineyard would never be brought to confess that they

[1] Gal. i. 10.

had slain the Heir as they had slain well-nigh all who went before Him. Though He had come first to His own possessions, His own people refused to receive Him.[1] Israel after the flesh would not condescend from their haughty self-satisfaction to accept the free gift of eternal life.

And, therefore, he was now more than ever convinced that his work would lie mainly among the Gentiles. It may be that the fury and contempt of the Jews kindled in him too dangerously for the natural man—kindled in him in spite of all tender yearnings and relentings—too strong an indignation, too fiery a resentment. It may be that he felt how much more adapted others were than himself to deal with these; others whose affinities with them were stronger, whose insight into the inevitable future was less clear. The Gentiles were evidently prepared to receive the Gospel. For these other sheep of God evidently the fulness of time had come. To those among them who were disposed for eternal life the doctrine of a free salvation through the Son of God was infinitely acceptable. Not a few of them had found in the Jewish teaching at least an approach to ease.[2] But the acceptance of Judaism could only be accomplished at the cost of a heavy sacrifice. Even to become a "Proselyte of the Gate" subjected a man to much that was distasteful; but to become a Proselyte of the Gate was nothing. It was represented by all the sterner bigots of Judaism as a step so insignificant as to be nearly worthless. And yet how

---

[1] John i. 11, εἰς τὰ ἴδια . . . οἱ ἴδιοι.

[2] Further than the outermost pale of Judaism they could not approach. Religious thoughtfulness in a Gentile was a crime, "A Gentile who studies the Law (beyond the seven Noachian precepts) is guilty of death;" for it is said (Deut. xxxiii. 4) "Moses commanded us a Law, even the inheritance of the congregation of Jacob;" but not of Gentiles (and, therefore, Rashi adds it is *robbery* for a Gentile to study the Law). (*Sanhedrin*, f. 59, 1.) This is embodied by Maimonides, *Dig. Hilchoth Menachin*, x. 9.

could any man stoop to that which could alone make him a Proselyte of Righteousness, and by elevating him to this rank, place on him a load of observances which were dead both in the spirit and in the letter, and which yet would most effectually make his life a burden, and separate him—not morally, but externally—from all which he had loved and valued most?[1] The sacrifices which an African convert has to make by abandoning polygamy— which a Brahmin has to make by sacrificing caste—are but a small measure of what a Gentile had to suffer if he made himself a Jew. How eagerly then would such an inquirer embrace a faith which, while it offered him a purer morality, and a richer hope for the future, and a greater strength for the present, and a more absolute remission for the past, offered him these priceless boons unaccompanied by the degradation of circumcision and the hourly worry of distinctions between meats! Stoicism might confront him with the barren inefficiency of "the categorical imperative;" the Gospel offered him, as a force which needed no supplement, the Spirit of the living Christ. Yes, St. Paul felt that the Gentiles could not refuse the proffered salvation. He himself might only live to see the green blade, or at best to gather a few weak ears, but hereafter he was confident that the full harvest would be reaped. Henceforth he knew himself to be essentially the Apostle of the Gentiles, and to that high calling he was glad to sacrifice his life.

[1] "A Gentile who offers to submit to all the words of the Law *except* one is not received." Rabbi Jose Ben Rabbi Jehudah said, "Even if he rejects one of the *Halachôth* of the Scribes" (*Bechorôth*, f. 30, 2).

CHAPTER XXII.

THE CONSULTATION AT JERUSALEM.

Ἐλεύθερος ὢν ἐκ πάντων, πᾶσιν ἐμαυτὸν ΕΔΟΤΛΩΣΑ, ἵνα τοὺς πλείονας κερδήσω.—
1 Cor. ix. 19.

THE first step of Paul and Barnabas on their arrival at
Antioch had been to summon a meeting of the Church,
and give a report of their mission and its success, dwelling
specially on the proof which it afforded that God had
now opened to the Gentiles "a door of faith." God
Himself had, by His direct blessing, shown that the
dauntless experiment of a mission to the heathen was in
accordance with His will.

For some time the two Apostles continued to rest
from their toils and perils amid the peaceful ministrations of the new metropolis of Christianity. But it is
not intended that unbroken peace should ever in this world
continue for long to be the lot of man. The Church soon
began to be troubled by a controversy which was not only
of pressing importance, but which seemed likely to
endanger the entire destiny of the Christian faith.

Jewish and Gentile converts were living side by side
at Antioch, waiving the differences of view and habit
which sprang from their previous training, and united
heart and soul in the bonds of a common love for their
common Lord. Had they entered into doubtful dispu-
tations,[1] they would soon have found themselves face to

---

[1] Rom. xiv. 1, μὴ εἰς διακρίσεις διαλογισμῶν.

face with problems which it was difficult to solve; but they preferred to dwell only on those infinite spiritual privileges of which they regarded themselves as equal sharers.

Into this bright fraternal community came the stealthy sidelong intrusion of certain personages from Judæa,[1] who, for a time, profoundly disturbed the peace of the Church. Pharisees scarcely emancipated from their Pharisaism— Jews still in bondage to their narrowest preconceptions— brethren to whom the sacred name of brethren could barely be conceded[2]—they insinuated themselves into the Church in the petty spirit of jealousy and espionage,[3] not with any high aims, but with the object of betraying the citadel of liberty, and reducing the free Christians of Antioch to their own bondage. St. Luke, true to his conciliatory purpose, merely speaks of them as "certain from Judæa;" but St. Paul, in the heat of indignant controversy, and writing under a more intense impression of their mischievous influence, vehemently calls them "the false brethren secretly introduced."[4] But though, throughout their allusions to this most memorable episode in the history of early Christianity, the Apostle and the Evangelist are writing from different points of view, they

---

[1] Gal. ii. 4, παρεισῆλθον; cf. Jude 4, παρεισέδυσαν, "sneaked in."

[2] This is expressly stated in the margin of the later Syriac version, and in two cursive MSS. 8, 137. Epiphanius says that "their leaders were Cerinthus, the subsequent Gnostic opponent of St. John, and 'Ebion'" (Haer. 28, 30). But Ebion is a mere "mythical eponymus" (Mansel, Gnostic Her. 125; Tert. De praescr. Haeret. 33). Ebionite is an epithet (Epiphan. Haeret. xxx.), and means "poor" (Orig. c. Cels. ii. 1; Neander, Ch. Hist. ii. 14).

[3] Gal. ii. 4, κατασκοπῆσαι. I suppose that the title ממחה (moomhah)—one authorised by a diploma to give decisions—would have been technically claimed by these visitors.

[4] Gal. ii. 4, τοὺς παρεισάκτους ψευδαδέλφους, "falsos et superinducticios fratres" (Tert. adv. Marc. v. 3). The strongly indignant meaning of παρεισάγειν may be seen in 2 Pet. ii. 1, "false teachers who shall privily bring in (παρεισάξουσιν) heresies of perdition."

are in complete accordance as regards the main facts. The combination of the details which they separately furnish enables us to reproduce the most important circumstances of a contest which decided for ever the future of the Gentile Church.[1]

These brethren in name, but aliens in heart, came with a hard, plausible, ready-made dogma—one of those shibboleths in which formalists delight, and which usually involve the death-blow of spiritual religion. It demanded obedience to the Law of Moses, especially the immediate acceptance of circumcision[2] as its most typical rite; and it denied the possibility of salvation on any other terms. It is possible that hitherto St. Paul may have regarded circumcision as a rule for Jews, and a charitable concession on the part of Gentiles. On these aspects of the question he was waiting for the light of God, which came to him in the rapid course of circumstances, as it came to the whole world in the fall of Jerusalem. But even among the Jews of the day, the more sensible and the more enlightened had seen that for a pious Gentile a mere external mutilation could not possibly be *essential*. Ananias, who had the honour of converting the royal family of Adiabene, had distinctly advised Izates that it was not desirable to risk his crown by external compliance to a needless rite.[3] It

---

[1] The addition in D and the margin of the Syriac, καὶ τῷ ἔθει Μωυσέως περιπατῆτε, and in the *Constitutiones Apostolicae*, καὶ τοῖς ἔθεσιν οἶς διετάξατο, though not genuine, yet show what was felt to be implied.

[2] Acts xv. 1, περιτμηθῆτε, "be *once* circumcised;" א, A, B, C, D. Even Josephus (see next note) seems to think that the horrible death of Apion was a punishment in kind for his *ridicule* of circumcision (c. *Ap.* ii. 14). From this anecdote we can measure the courage of St. Paul, and the intense hatred which his views excited.

[3] Josephus, as a liberal Pharisee, held the same view (*Antt.* xx. 2; *Vit.* 23, 31). The Talmud mentions a certain Akiles (whom some identify with Aquila, the Greek translator of the Bible) as having submitted to circumcision, and

was only when men like Eleazar—fierce and narrow literalists of the school of Shammai—intervened, that Proselytes of the Gate were taught that their faith and their holiness were valueless unless they assumed the badge of Proselytes of Righteousness.[1] Izates and Monobazus, as was sure to be the case with timid and superstitious natures, had risked all to meet the views of these uncompromising zealots, just as from baser motives Aziz, King of Emesa, and Polemo of Cilicia had yielded in order to win the hands of the wealthy and beautiful princesses of the house of Herod.[2] But it was quite certain that such an acceptance of Mosaism would continue to be, as it always had been, extremely exceptional; and Paul saw that if Christianity was to be degraded into the mere superimposition of a belief in Christ as the Jewish Messiah upon the self-satisfaction of Shammaite fanaticism,[3] or even on the mere menace of the Law, it was not possible, it was not even desirable, that it should continue to exist. The force of habit might, in one who had been born a Jew, freshen with the new wine of

also a Roman senator (*Abhôda Zara*, 10; Hamburger, *s.v.* "Beschneidung"). The Roman Metilius saved his life by accepting circumcision (Jos. *B. J.* ii. 17, § 10). Antoninus *forbade* it in the case of Gentile proselytes (Gieseler, i., § 38).

[1] "So great is circumcision," said Rabbi [Jehuda Hakkadosh], "that but for it the Holy One, blessed be He, would not have created the world; for it is said (Jer. xxxiii. 25), 'But for My covenant [*i.e.*, circumcision] I would not have made day and night, and the ordinance of heaven and earth'" (*Nedarim*, f. 31, 2). "Abraham was not called 'perfect' till he was circumcised. It is as great as all the other commandments" (Exod. xxxiv. 27), (*Id.* f. 32, 1). It was one of the laws in the case of which the Jews preferred death to disobedience (*Shabbath*, f. 130, 1). The "good king" in *Pseudo-Baruch* (§§ 61, 66) is one who does not allow the existence of an uncircumcised person on the earth.

[2] Izates and Monabazus would have been called "lion-proselytes," and Aziz and Polemo "Shechemite proselytes."

[3] "How many laws have you?" asked a Gentile of Shammai. "Two," said Shammai, "the written and the oral." "I believe the former," said the Gentile, "not the latter; accept me as a proselyte on condition of learning the written law only." Shammai ejected him with a curse (*Shabbath*, f. 31, 1).

A A

the Gospel the old ceremonialism which had run to the lees of Rabbinic tradition. In Jerusalem a Christian might not be sensible of the loss he suffered by chaining his new life to the corpse of meaningless *halachôth* ; but in Antioch, at any rate, and still more in the new mission-fields of Asia, such bondage could never be allowed.

We can imagine the indignant grief with which St. Paul watched this continuous, this systematic[1] attempt to undo all that had been done, and to render impossible all further progress. Was the living and life-giving spirit to be thus sacrificed to the dead letter ? Were these new Pharisees to compass sea and land to make one proselyte, only that they might add the pride of the Jew to the vice of the Gentile, and make him ten times more narrow than themselves ? Was the superstitious adoration of dead ordinances to dominate over the heaven-sent liberty of the children of God ? If Moses had, under Divine guidance, imposed upon a nation of sensual and stiff-necked slaves not only a moral law of which Christ Himself had indefinitely deepened the obligation, but also the crushing yoke of " *statutes which were not good, and ordinances whereby they could not live*,"[2] was this yoke—now that it had been abolished, now that it had become partly impossible and mostly meaningless—to be disastrously imposed on necks for which its only effect would be to madden or to gall ?[3] Was a Titus, young, and manly, and free, and pure, with the love of Christ burning like a fire on the altar of his soul, to be held at arm's length by some unregenerate Pharisee, who while he wore broad *tephillín*, and *tsitsith* with exactly the right number of

---

[1] Acts xv. 1, ἐδίδασκον.

[2] Ezek. xx. 25.

[3] " Circumcidere genitalia instituere *ut diversitate noscantur*," says Tacitus (*H. V.* 5), and adds it is an aggravation, " Transgressi in morem eorum idem usurpant."

threads and knots, was yet an utter stranger to the love
of Christ, and ignorant as a child of His free salvation?
Were Christians, who were all brethren, all a chosen
generation and a royal priesthood, to be treated by Jews,
who had no merit beyond the very dubious merit of
being Jews, as though they were unclean creatures with
whom it was not even fit to eat? The Jews freely indulged in language of contemptuous superiority towards
the proselytes, but was such language to be for one
moment tolerated in the brotherhood of Christ?[1]

It is easy to understand in what a flame of fire Paul
must often have stood up to urge these questions during
the passionate debates which immediately arose.[2] It may
be imagined with what eager interest the Gentile proselytes would await the result of a controversy which was
to decide whether it was enough that they should bring
forth the fruits of the Spirit—love, joy, peace, long-
suffering, gentleness, goodness, faith, meekness, temperance—or whether they must also stick up *mezuzôth*
on their houses, and submit to a concision, and abstain
from the free purchases of the market, and not touch perfectly harmless kinds of food, and petrify one day out of
every seven with a rigidity of small and conventionalised
observances. To us it may seem amazing that the utterances of the prophets were not sufficient to show that
the essence of religion is *faith*, not outward service; and
that so far from requiring petty accuracies of posture,
and dress, and food, what the Lord requires of us is

---

[1] Here is a specimen of the language of Jewish Rabbis towards proselytes:
"Proselytes and those who sport with children [the meaning is dubious] delay
the coming of the Messiah. As for proselytes it is explained by Rabh Chelbo's
remark, that they are as injurious to Israel as a scab (since in Isa. xiv. 1 it is
said, 'strangers' *will be joined* to them (נלוה), and ספחת means 'a scab');
because, said Rashi, they are not up to the precepts, and cause calamities to
Israel" (*Niddah*, f. 13, 2).   [2] Acts xv. 2.

A A 2

that we should do justice, and love mercy, and walk humbly with our God.[1]   But the Judaisers had tradition, authority, and the Pentateuch on their side, and the paralysis of custom rendered many Jewish converts incapable of resisting conclusions which yet they felt to be false.   So far as they were true Christians at all, they could not but feel that the end of the commandment was love out of a good heart and a pure conscience, and faith unfeigned; but when their opponents flourished in their faces the Thorah-rolls, and asked them whether they dared to despise the immemorial sanctities of Sinai, or diminish the obligation of laws uttered by Moses amid its burning glow, the ordinary Jew and the ordinary Gentile were perplexed.   On these points the words of Jesus had been but a beam in the darkness, certain indeed to grow, but as yet only shining amid deep midnight.   They did not yet understand that Christ's fulfilment of the Law was its abrogation, and that to maintain the type in the presence of the antitype was to hold up superfluous candles to the sun.   From this imminent peril of absorption in exclusive ritual one man saved the Church, and that man was Paul.   With all the force of his argument, with all the weight of his authority, he affirmed and insisted that the Gentile converts should remain in the free conditions under which they had first accepted the faith of Christ.[2]

When there appeared likely to be no end to the dispute,[3] it became necessary to refer it to the decision of the Church at Jerusalem, and especially of those Apostles who had lived with the living Jesus.   It is

---

[1] Mic. vi. 8; Deut. x. 12; Hos. vi. 6; 1 Sam. xv. 22.

[2] Comp. MS. D, ἔλεγεν γὰρ ὁ Παῦλος μένειν οὕτως κάθως ἐπίστευσαν διϊσχυριζόμενος.

[3] The expressions of Acts xv. 2, γενομένης οὖν στάσεως καὶ συζητήσεως οὐκ ὀλίγης, κ.τ.λ., are very strong.   Στάσις is "insurrection" (Mark xv. 7; Luke xxiii. 19). For συζήτησις see Acts vi. 9; xxviii. 29; Mark ix. 14.

far from improbable that this plan was urged—nay, demanded—by the Judaisers themselves,[1] who must have been well aware that the majority of that Church looked with alarm and suspicion on what they regarded as anti-Judaic innovations.   There may even have been a certain insolence (which accounts for the almost irritable language of St. Paul long afterwards) in their manner of parading the immensely superior authority of living witnesses of the life of Jesus like James and Kephas.   They doubtless represented the deputation to Jerusalem as a necessary act of submission, a going up of Paul and Barnabas to be judged by the Jerusalem synod.[2]   At this period Paul would not openly repudiate the paraded superiority of the Twelve Apostles.   When he says to the Galatians that "he consulted them about the Gospel he was preaching, lest he might be, or had been, running to no purpose," he shows that at this period he had not arrived at the quite unshaken conviction, which made him subsequently say that "whether he or an angel from heaven preached any other gospel, let him be anathema."[3]   In

[1] As is again asserted in D, παρήγγειλαν αὐτοῖς τῷ Παύλῳ καὶ τῷ Βαρνάβᾳ καί τισιν ἄλλοις ἀναβαίνειν πρὸς τοὺς ἀποστόλους, κ.τ.λ., ὅπως κριθῶσιν ἐπ᾽ αὐτοῖς περὶ τοῦ ζητήματος τούτου.

[2] See the previous extract from D.

[3] I have here assumed without hesitation that the visit to Jerusalem of Gal. ii. 1—10, though there mentioned as though it were a *second* visit, was identical with that of Acts xv., and therefore was in reality his *third* visit. There are in the Acts of the Apostles *five* visits of St. Paul to Jerusalem—viz., (1) after his conversion (ix. 26); (2) with the Antiochene contribution (xi. 30); (3) to consult the Apostles about the necessity of circumcision for the Gentiles (xv. 2); (4) after his second missionary journey (xviii. 22); (5) before his imprisonment at Cæsarea (xxi.).   Now this visit of Gal. ii. could not possibly have been the *first*; nor, as is proved by Gal. ii. 7, as well as by the whole chronology of his life, could it have been the *second*; nor, as we see from the presence of Barnabas (comp. Gal. ii. 1 with Acts xv. 39), could it have been the *fourth*; for no one can assume that it was, without accusing St. Paul of disingenuous suppression when he spoke to the Galatians of this sole intercourse which he had had with the Apostles; and that it was not the *fifth* is quite decisively proved by Gal. ii. 11.   By the exhaustive method.

point of fact it was at this interview that he learnt that his own insight and authority were fully equal to those of the Apostles who were in Christ before him; that they had nothing to tell him and nothing to add to him; that, on the contrary, there were spheres of work which belonged rather to him than to them, and in which they stood to him in the position of learners;[1] that Jesus had fulfilled His own promise that it was *better* for His children that He should go away, because His communion with them by the gift of His Holy Spirit was closer and more absolute than by His actual presence. But even now Paul must have chafed to submit the decision of truths which

---

therefore, we see that the visit dwelt on in Gal. ii. must have been the *third.* It would, indeed, be conceivable that it was some visit not recorded by the author of the Acts if there were any reason whatever for such a supposition; but when we consider how impossible it was that such a visit should have occurred without the knowledge of St. Luke, and how eminently the facts of it accorded with the views which he wished to further, and how difficult it is to find any other occasion on which such a visit would have been natural, we have no valid reason for adopting such an hypothesis. Nor, indeed, can anything be much clearer than the identity of circumstances in the visits thus described. In the two narratives the same people go up at the same time, from the same place, for the same object, in consequence of the same interference by the same agitators, and with the same results. Against the absolute certainty of the conclusion that the visits described were one and the same there is nothing whatever to set but trivial differences of detail, every one of which is accounted for in the text. As for St. Paul's non-allusion to the so-called "decree," it is sufficiently explained by its local, partial, temporary — and, so far as principles were concerned, indecisive—character; by the fact that the Galatians were *not asking for concessions,* but seeking bondage; and by the Apostle's determination not to settle such questions by subordinating his Apostolic independence to any authority which could be described as either " of man or by man," by any-thing, in short, except the principles revealed by the Spirit of God Himself. Prof. Jowett (*Gal.* i. 253) speaks of the unbroken image of harmony presented by the narrative of the Acts contrasted with the tone of Gal. ii. 2—6; but " an unbroken image of harmony " is not very accordant with the πολλὴ συζήτησις of Acts xv. 7, which is an obvious continuation of the στάσις καὶ ζήτησις οὐκ ὀλίγη of ver. 2. The *extent* to which the Acts " casts the veil of time over the differences of the Apostles " seems to me to be often exaggerated.

[1] Gal. ii. 7—9.

he felt to be true to any human authority. But for one circumstance he must have felt like an able Roman Catholic bishop—a Strossmeyer or a Dupanloup—who has to await a decision respecting tenets which he deems irrefragable, from a Pope in all respects his inferior in ability and in enlightenment. That circumstance was the inward voice, the spiritual intimation which revealed to him that this course was wise and necessary. St. Luke, of course, tells the external side of the event, which was that Paul went by desire of the Church of Antioch; but St. Paul himself, omitting this as irrelevant to his purpose, or regarding it as an expression of the will of Heaven, tells his converts that he went up "by revelation." From Paul also we learn the interesting circumstance that among those who accompanied himself and Barnabas was Titus, perhaps a Cretan Gentile whom he had converted at Cyprus during his first journey.[1] Paul took him as a Gentile representative of his own converts, a living pledge and witness that uncircumcised Greeks, seeing that they were equal partakers of the gift of the Holy Ghost, were not to be treated as dogs and outcasts. The declared approval of God was not to be set aside for the fantastic demands of man, and the supercilious tolerance or undisguised contempt of Jews for proselytes was at once a crime and an ignorance when displayed towards a brother in the faith.

Alike the commencement and the course of their overland journey was cheered by open sympathy with their views. From Antioch they were honourably escorted on their way; and as they passed through Berytus, Tyre, Sidon, and Samaria, narrating to the Churches the conversion of the Gentiles, they—like

---

[1] Ewald, *Gesch.* vi. 456.

Luther on his way to the Diet of Worms—were encouraged by unanimous expressions of approval and joy. On arriving at Jerusalem they were received by the Apostles and elders, and narrated to them the story of their preaching and its results, together with the inevitable question to which it had given rise. It was on this occasion apparently that some of the Christian Pharisees at once got up, and broadly insisted on the moral necessity of Mosaism and circumcision, implying, therefore, a direct censure of the principles on which Paul and Barnabas had conducted their mission.[1] The question thus stated by the opposing parties was far too grave to be decided by any immediate vote ; the deliberate judgment of the Church on so momentous a problem could only be pronounced at a subsequent meeting. Paul used the interval with his usual sagacity and power. Knowing how liable to a thousand varying accidents are the decisions arrived at by promiscuous assemblies—fearing lest the voice of a mixed gathering might only express the collective incapacity or the collective prejudice—he endeavoured to win over the leaders of the Church by a private statement of the Gospel which he preached. Those leaders were, he tells us, at this time, James,[2] who is mentioned first because of his position as head of the Church at Jerusalem, and Peter and John. These he so entirely succeeded in gaining over to his cause—he showed to them with such unanswerable force that they could not insist on making Gentile Christians into orthodox Jews without incurring the tremendous responsibility of damming up for ever the free river of the grace of God—that they

---

[1] The παρεδέχθησαν ὑπὸ τῆς ἐκκλησίας of Acts xv. 4 implies a preliminary meeting distinct from the συνήχθησάν τε of ver. 6.

[2] Not here characterised as " the Lord's brother," because James, the son of Zebedee, was dead, and James, the son of Alphæus, was an Apostle of whom nothing is known.

resigned to his judgment the mission to the Gentiles.
Eminent as they were in their own spheres, great as was
their force of character, marked as was their individuality,
they could not resist the personal ascendency of Paul.[1]
In the presence of one whose whole nature evinced the
intensity of his inspired conviction, they felt that they
could not assume the position of superiors or guides.[2]
Whatever may have been their original prejudices, these
noble-hearted men allowed neither their private predilec-
tions nor any fibre of natural jealousy to deter their
acknowledgment of their great fellow-workers. They
gave to Paul and Barnabas the right hands of fellowship, and acknowledged them as Apostles to the Gentiles.
One touching request alone they made. The Church of
Jerusalem had been plunged from the first in abject
poverty. It had suffered perhaps from the temporary
experiment of communism ; it had suffered certainly from
the humble rank of its first converts, the persecutions
which they had endured, and the chronic famine to
which their city was liable. Paul and Barnabas were
working in wealthy Antioch, and were likely to travel
among Gentiles, who, if not rich, were amply supplied
with the means of livelihood. Would they forget Jerusalem ? Would they suffer those to starve who had
walked with Jesus by the Lake of Galilee, and sat
beside His feet when He preached the Sermon on the
Mount ? Already once they had brought from Antioch
the deeply acceptable *Chaluka*,[3] which in the fiercest
moment of famine and persecution had as much relieved
the brethren as the royal bounties of Helena had sustained the Jews. Surely they would not let religious
differences prevent them from aiding the hunger-bitten

---

[1] See John xvi. 7.   [2] Gal. ii. 7, Ἰδόντες; 9, γνόντες.   [3] חלקה

Church? It might be that they had been treated by Jerusalem Christians of the Pharisaic party with surreptitious opposition and undisguised dislike, but surely this would not weigh with them for a moment. The three heads of the afflicted Church begged the missionaries to the luxurious world " that they would remember the poor." It was a request in every respect agreeable to the tender and sympathetic heart of Paul.[1] Apart from all urging, he had already shown spontaneous earnestness [2] in this holy work of compassion, and now that it came to him as a sort of request, by way of acknowledging the full recognition which was being conceded to him, he was only too glad to have such means of showing that, while he would not yield an inch of essential truth, he would make any amount of sacrifice in the cause of charity. Thenceforth Paul threw himself into the plan of collecting alms for the poor saints at Jerusalem with characteristic eagerness. There was scarcely a Church or a nation that he visited which he did not press for contributions, and the Galatians themselves could recall the systematic plan of collection which he had urged upon their notice.[3] In the very hottest moment of displeasure against those who at any rate *represented themselves* as emissaries of James, he never once relaxed his kindly efforts to prove to the Church, which more than all others suspected and thwarted him, that even theological differences, with all their exasperating bitterness, had not dulled the generous sensibility of a heart which, by many

---

[1] Gal. ii. 10, ὃ καὶ ἐσπούδασα αὐτὸ τοῦτο ποιῆσαι ; *lit.*, " which also I was eager to do at once that very thing." " *Quod* etiam sollicitus fui *hoc ipsum* facere." (Vulg.)

[2] Acts xi. 29.

[3] 1 Cor. xvi. 3; cf. 2 Cor. viii., ix. ; Rom. xv. 27. Even many years after we find St. Paul still most heartily fulfilling this part of the mutual compact (Acts xxiv. 17). Phrygia alone seems to have contributed nothing.

a daily affliction, had learnt to throb with sympathy for the afflicted.

One part, then, of his mission to Jerusalem was fulfilled when the Lord's brother, and he to whom He had assigned "the keys of the kingdom of heaven," and he who had leaned his head at the Last Supper upon His breast, had yielded to him their friendly acknowledgment. It is on this that he chiefly dwells to the Galatians. In their Churches brawling Judaisers had dared to impugn his commission and disparage his teaching, on the asserted authority of the mother Church and its bishop. It was Paul's object to prove to them that his sacred independence had been acknowledged by the very men who were now thrust into antagonism with his sentiments. There may be in his language a little sense of wrong; but, on the other hand, no candid reader can fail to see that a fair summary of the antagonism to which he alludes is this—"Separation, not opposition; antagonism of the followers rather than of the leaders; personal antipathy of the Judaisers to St. Paul rather than of St. Paul to the Twelve."[1]

But St. Luke is dealing with another side of this visit. To him the authority of Paul was not a subject of doubt, nor was it seriously questioned by those for whom he wrote; but with the *teaching* of Paul it was far different, and it was Luke's object to show that the main principles involved, so far from being dangerous, had received the formal sanction of the older Apostles. That there was a severe struggle he does not attempt to conceal, but he quotes an authentic document to prove that it ended triumphantly in favour of the Apostle of the Gentiles.

---

[1] Jowett, *Romans*, &c., i. 326. In this essay, and that of Dr. Lightfoot on "St. Paul and the Three" (*Gal.* 276—346), the reader will find the facts fairly appreciated and carefully stated.

A concrete form was given to this debate by the presence of Titus as one of Paul's companions. Around this
young man arose, it is evident, a wild clamour of controversy. The Judaisers insisted that he should be circumcised. So long as he remained uncircumcised they refused
to eat with him, or to regard him as in any true sense a
brother. They may even have been indignant with Paul
for his free companionship with this Gentile, as they had
previously been with Peter for sharing the hospitality of
Cornelius. The Agapæ were disturbed with these contentions, and with them the celebration of the Holy Communion. Alike Titus and Paul must have had a troubled
time amid this storm of conflicting opinions, urged with
the rancorous intensity which Jews always display when
their religious fanaticism is aroused.[1] Even after the lapse
of five or six years St. Paul cannot speak of this episode
in his life without an agitation which affects his language
to so extraordinary a degree as to render uncertain to us
the result, of which doubtless the Galatians were aware,
but about which we should be glad to have more complete
certainty. The question is, did Paul, in this particular
instance, yield or not? In other words, was Titus circumcised? In the case of Timothy, Paul avowedly took into
account his Jewish parentage on the mother's side, and
therefore circumcised him as a Jew, and not as a Gentile,
because otherwise it would have been impossible to secure
his admission among Jews. Even this might be enough
to give rise to the charges of inconsistency with which we
know him to have been assailed. But if he had indeed
bowed to the storm in the case of Titus—if he, the firmest
champion of Christian uncircumcision, the foremost
preacher of the truth that in Christ Jesus neither circum-

---

[1] The date of the "Council" at Jerusalem is about A.D. 51; that of the
Epistle to the Galatians about A.D. 58.

cision was anything nor uncircumcision, but faith which
worketh by love, had still allowed an adult Gentile convert
to submit to a Jewish rite which had no meaning except as
an acknowledgment that he was bound to keep the Mosaic
Law — then, indeed, he might be charged with having
sacrificed the very point at issue.   He might of course
urge that he had only done it for the moment by way of
peace, because otherwise the very life of Titus would have
been endangered, or because his presence in the Holy City
might otherwise have caused false rumours and terrible
riots, as the presence of Trophimus[1] did in later years.
He might say, "I circumcised Titus only because there
was no other chance of getting the question reasonably
discussed;" but if he yielded at all, however noble and
charitable may have been his motives, he gave to his
opponents a handle against him which assuredly they did
not fail to use.

Now that he was most vehemently urged to take this
step is clear, and perhaps the extraordinary convulsiveness
of his expressions is only due to the memory of all that he
must have undergone in that bitter struggle.[2]   In holding

[1] This element of the decision has been universally overlooked. Gentiles
of course there were in Jerusalem, but for a Jew deliberately to introduce an
uncircumcised Gentile *as a full partaker of all religious rites in a Judæo-
Christian community* was a terribly dangerous experiment. If all the power
and influence of Josephus *could hardly save from massacre two illustrious
and highly-connected Gentiles who had fled to him for refuge*—although there
was no pretence of extending to them any religious privileges—because the
multitude said that " they ought not to be suffered to live if they would not
change their religion to the religion of those to whom they fled for safety "
(*Vit.* 31), *how could Paul answer for the life of Titus ?*

[2] This is the view of Dr. Lightfoot (*Gal.,* p. 102), who says, " The
counsels of the Apostles of the circumcision are the hidden rock on which the
grammar of the sentence is wrecked ; " and "the sensible undercurrent of
feeling, the broken grammar of the sentence, the obvious tenour of particular
phrases, all convey the impression that, though the final victory was complete, it
was not attained without a struggle, in which St. Paul maintained, at one time
almost single-handed, the cause of Gentile freedom."   I give my reason after-

out to the last he had, doubtless, been forced to encounter the pressure of nearly the whole body of the Church at Jerusalem, including almost certainly all who were living of the twelve Apostles, and their three leaders. Perhaps even Barnabas himself might, as afterwards, have lost all firm grasp of truths which seemed sufficiently clear when he was working with Paul alone on the wild uplands of Lycaonia. Certainly St. Paul's moral courage triumphed over the severest test, if he had the firmness and fortitude to hold out against this mass of influence. It would have been far bolder than Whitefield standing before a conclave of Bishops, or Luther pleading his cause at Rome. As far as courage was concerned, it is certain that no fear would ever have induced him to give way; but might he not have yielded *ad interim*, and as a charitable concession, in order to secure a permanent result?

Let us consider, in all its roughness, his own language. "Then," he says, "fourteen years after,[1] I again went up to Jerusalem with Barnabas, taking with me also Titus.[2] Now, I went up in accordance with a reve-lation, and I referred to them[3] the Gospel which I am preaching among the Gentiles—privately, however, to those of repute, lest perchance I am now running,[4]

wards for adopting a different conclusion. The sense of a complete victory contemplated years afterwards would hardly produce all this agitation. It would have been alluded to with the calm modesty of conscious strength. Not so an error of judgment involving serious consequences though actuated by the best motives. *If Titus was not circumcised, why does not Paul plainly say so?*

[1] Gal. ii. 1—6. Fourteen years after his first visit. The "about" of the E.V. should be omitted.

[2] And some others, whom, however, he could hardly be said to " take with him" (Acts xv. 2).

[3] ἀνεθέμην αὐτοῖς, " communicated " or " referred to them "—not " placed in their hands " (cf. Acts xxv. 14). Tertullian says " *ad patrocinium Petri, &c.*," which is too strong.

[4] I take τρέχω as an *indic.*, but it may be the subjunctive, as in 1 Thess. iii. 5, and for the metaphor Phil. ii. 16.

or even had run, to no purpose.[1]   But not even Titus,
who was with me, Greek though he was, was *obliged* to
be circumcised; but [he was only circumcised?] because of
the stealthily-introduced false brethren—people who came
secretly in to spy out our liberty which we have in Christ
Jesus, in order that they shall[2] utterly enslave us, [(to
whom) not even][3] for an hour did we yield *by way of sub-*

---

[1] Dr. Lightfoot takes this to mean "that my past and present labours
might not be thwarted by opposition or misunderstanding."   So Theophylact,
ad loc., ἵνα μὴ στάσις γένηται καὶ ἵνα ἀρθῇ τὸ σκάνδαλον.   The context seems to me
to show that it implies a desire on St. Paul's part to know *whether anything
valid could be urged against* his own personal conviction.   And so Tert. *adv.*
Marc. i. 20; v. 3; iv. 2.   The admission of the possibility of a misgiving as
to the *practical* issue only adds strength to the subsequent confirmation.
To St. Paul's uncertainty or momentary hesitation I would compare that of
St. John the Baptist (Matt. xi. 3).

[2] καταδουλώσουσι (א, A, B, C, D, E).   I have literally translated the bold
solecism, which was not unknown to Hellenistic Greek, and by which it gains
in vividness (cf. iv. 17, ἵνὰ ζηλοῦτε).

[3] In the insertion, omission, or variation of these two words οἷς οὐδὲ the
MSS. and quotations become as agitated and uncertain as the style of the writer.
If we could believe that the word οὐδὲ—"not even"—was spurious it would
then, I think, be obvious that St. Paul meant to say, "Owing to these false
brethren *I did*, it is true, *make a temporary concession* (πρὸς ὥραν), but only
with a view of ultimately securing for you *a permanent liberty*" (διαμείνῃ
πρὸς ὑμᾶς); "ostendens," as Tertullian says, "*propter quid fecerit* quod nec
fecisset nec ostendisset, si illud propter quod fecit non accidisset " (*adv. Marc.*
v. 3).   But admittedly the evidence of the manuscripts is in favour of retaining
the negative, though it is omitted by Irenæus, is absent from many Latin copies,
is declared on the doubtful authority of Victorinus to have been absent from
the *majority* of Latin and Greek manuscripts, and is asserted by Tertullian
to have been fraudulently introduced by the heretic Marcion.   Surely the
uncertainty which attaches to it, joined to the fact that *even its retention* by
no means excludes the supposition that Paul, to his own great subsequent
regret, had given way under protest while the debate was pending, are arguments in favour of this having been the case.   If this view be right it would
give a far deeper significance to such passages as Gal. i. 10; iv. 11.   In that case
his vacillation was an error of policy, which we have no more reason to believe
was impossible in his case than a moral error was in that of St. Peter at Antioch;
but it would have been an error of practical judgment, not of unsettled principle; an error of noble self-abnegation, not of timid complaisance.   And surely
St. Paul would have been the very last of men to claim immunity from the
possibility of error.   "The fulness of divine gifts," says Dr. Newman, "did
not tend to destroy what is human in him, but to spiritualise and perfect it."

mission—in order that the truth of the Gospel may remain entirely with you;[1] from those, however, who are reputed[2] to be something—whatever they were[3] makes no matter to me—God accepts no man's face—well, to me those in repute added nothing." Such is a literal translation of his actual words in this extraordinary sentence; and he then proceeds to narrate the acknowledgment of the Three, that his authority was in no sense disparate with theirs; nay, that in dealing with the Gentiles he was to be regarded as specially endowed with Divine guidance.

But does he mean that, "I never for a moment yielded and circumcised Titus, in spite of the enormous pressure which was put upon me?" or does he mean, "I admit—grieved as I am to admit it—that in the case of Titus I *did* yield. Titus *was* circumcised, but not *under compulsion*. I yielded, but not out of *submission*. The concession which I made—vast as it was, mistaken as it may have been—was not an abandonment of principle, but a stretch of charity?"

It must be remembered that Paul "cared for *ideas*, not for forms;" the fact that circumcision was a matter in itself indifferent—the admitted truth that men could be saved by the grace of our Lord Jesus Christ, and by that alone—may have induced him, under strong pressure,[4] to concede that the rite should be performed—with the same kind of half-contemptuous indifference to the exaggeration of trifles which makes him say to the Galatians in a burst of bitter irony, "I wish that, while they are about it,

[1] διαμείνῃ.

[2] δοκούντες, "seem," not "seemed," as in E.V.

[3] Renan and others see in this a covert allusion to the former disbelief of James; this is utterly unlikely, seeing that the reference is also to Peter and John. It means, rather, "however great their former privilege in nearness to the living Christ" (cf. 2 Cor. vi. 16). Indeed, it is better to join the ποτε to the ὁποῖοί, "*qualescunque*."

[4] Acts xv. 10.

these Judaisers, who make so much of circumcision, would go a little farther still and make themselves altogether like your priests of Agdistis."[1] When Paul took on him the Nazarite vow, when he circumcised Timothy,[2] he did it out of a generous desire to remove all needless causes of offence, and not to let his work be hindered by a stiff refusal to give way in things unimportant. We know that it was his avowed principle to become all things to all men, if so be he might win some. His soul was too large to stickle about matters of no moment. Can we not imagine that in the wild strife of tongues which made Jerusalem hateful so long as the uncircumcised Titus was moving among the members of the Church, Paul might have got up and said, "I have come here to secure a decision about a matter of vast moment. If the presence of Titus looks to you like an offensive assertion of foregone conclusions—well, it is only an individual instance—and while the question is still undecided, I will have him circumcised, and we shall then be able to proceed more calmly to the consideration of the general question?" Might he not have regarded this as a case in which it was advisable "*reculer pour mieux sauter?*" and to his own friends who shared his sentiments might he not have said, "What does it matter in this particular instance? It *can* mean nothing. Titus himself is generous enough to wish it for the sake of peace; he fully understands that he is merely yielding to a violent prejudice. It may be most useful to him in securing future admission to Jewish assemblies. To him, to us, it will be regarded as 'concision,' not 'circumcision;' an outward observance submitted to from voluntary good nature; not by any means a solemn precedent, or a significant rite?"

---

[1] Gal. v. 12 (in the Greek).   [2] Acts xvi. 3.

B B

And would not Titus have also urged the Apostle not to be deterred by any consideration for him? Might he not naturally have said, "I am grieved that there should be all this uproar and heart-burning on my account, and I am quite willing to allay it by becoming a proselyte of righteousness?" If Titus took this generous line, Paul's reluctance to take advantage of his generosity might have been increased, and yet an additional argument would have been supplied to his opponents. "Moses," they would have said, "commanded circumcision; we cannot let this Gentile sit at our Agapæ without it; he is himself, much to his credit, quite ready to consent to it; why do you persist in troubling our Israel by your refusal to consent?"

For whatever may be urged against this view, I cannot imagine why, if Paul did *not* yield, he should use language so ambiguous, so involved, that *whether we retain the negative or not* his language has still led many—as it did in the earliest ages of the Church—to believe that he did the very thing which he is generally supposed to be denying. Nothing could have been easier or pleasanter than to say, "I did *not* circumcise Titus, though every possible effort was made to force me to do so. My not doing so—even at Jerusalem, even at the beginning of the whole controversy, even at the head-quarters of the Judæo-Christian tyranny, even in the face of the evident wish of the Apostles—proves, once for all, both my independence and my consistency." But it was immensely more difficult to explain why he *really had given way* in that important instance. It may be that Titus was by his side while he penned this very paragraph, and, if so, it would be to Paul a yet more bitter reminder of a concession which, more than aught else, had been quoted to prove his subjection and his insincerity.

He is therefore so anxious to show *why* he did it, and what were *not* his motives, that ultimately he unconsciously omits to say it in so many words at all.[1] And if, after the decision of the meeting, and the battle which he had fought, Paul still thought it *advisable* to circumcise Timothy merely to avoid offending the Jews whom he was about to visit, would not the same motives work with him at this earlier period when he saw how the presence of Titus threw the whole Church into confusion? If the false inferences which might be deduced from the concession were greater in the case of a pure-blooded Gentile, on the other hand the necessity for diminishing offence was also more pressing, and the obligatoriness of circumcision had at that time been less seriously impugned. And it is even doubtful whether such a course was not overruled for good. But for this step would it, for instance, have been possible for Titus to be overseer of the Church of Crete? Would any circumcised Jew have tolerated at this epoch the "episcopate" of an uncircumcised Gentile? I have dwelt long upon this incident because, if I am right, there are few events in the biography of St. Paul more illustrative alike of his own character and of the circumstances of his day. He would rather have died, would rather have suffered a schism between the Church of Jerusalem and the Churches of her Gentile converts, than admit that there could be no salvation out of the pale of

---

[1] "Cette transaction coûta beaucoup à Paul, et la phrase dans laquelle il en parle est une des plus originales qu'il ait écrites. Le mot qui lui coûte semble ne pouvoir couler de sa plume. La phrase au premier coup d'œil paraît dire que Titus ne fut pas circoncis, tandis qu'elle implique qu'il le fut " (Renan, *St. Paul*, p. 92). It need hardly be said that there is no question of *suppression* here, because I assume that the fact was perfectly well known. We find a similar characteristic of style and character in Rom. ix. Baur, on the other hand (but on very insufficient grounds), thinks that "nothing can be more absurd." Yet it was the view of Tertullian (*c. Marc.* v. 3), and Baur equally disbelieves the expressly asserted circumcision of Timothy.

Mosaism. In this or that instance he was ready enough —perhaps, in the largeness of his heart, too ready for his own peace—to go almost any length rather than bring himself and, what was infinitely more dear to him, the Gospel with which he had been entrusted, into collision with the adamantine walls of Pharisaic bigotry. But he always let it be understood that his *principle* remained intact—that Christ had in every sense abolished the curse of the Law—that, except in its universal moral precepts, it was no longer binding on the Gentiles—that the "traditions of the fathers" had for them no further significance. He intended at all costs, by almost unlimited concession in the case of individuals, by unflinching resistance when principles were endangered, to establish, as far at any rate as the Gentiles were concerned, the truth that Christ had obliterated the handwriting in force against us, and taken it out of the way, nailing the torn fragments of its decrees to His cross.[1]

And so the great debate came on. The Apostles—at any rate, their leaders—had to a great extent been won over in private conferences; the opponents had been partially silenced by a personal concession. Paul must have looked forward with breathless interest to the result of the meeting which should decide whether Jerusalem was still to be the metropolis of the Faith, or whether she was to be abandoned to the isolation of unprogressive literalism, while the Gospel of Christ started on a new career from Antioch and from the West. One thing only must not be. She must not swathe the daily-strengthening youth of Christianity in the dusty cerements of an abolished system ; she must not make Christianity a religion of washings and cleansings, of times and seasons, of meats and drinks, but a religion of

[1] Col. ii. 14.

holiness and of the heart—a religion in which men might eat or not as they pleased, and might regard every day as alike sacred, so that they strove with all their power to reveal in their lives a love to man springing out of the root of love to God.

We are not surprised to hear that there was much eager and passionate debate.[1] Doubtless, as in all similar gatherings of the Church to settle disputed questions, there were mutual recriminations and misunderstandings, instances of untenable argument, of inaccurate language, of confused conceptions. The Holy Spirit, indeed, was among them then, as now, in all gatherings of faithful Christian men: He was with them to guide and to inspire. But neither then nor now—as we see by the clearest evidence of the New Testament then, and as we see by daily experience now—did His influence work to the miraculous extinction of human differences, or obliteration of human imperfections. Those who supported the cause of Paul rendered themselves liable to those charges, so terrible to a Jew, of laxness, of irreligion, of apostasy, of unpatriotism, of not being believers in revealed truth. Was not Moses inspired? Was the Sacred Pentateuch to be reduced to a dead letter? Were all the curses of Ebal to be braved? Were the Thorah-rolls to be flung contemptuously into the Dead Sea? On the other hand, those who maintained the necessity of circumcision and of obedience to the Law, laid themselves open to the fatal question, "If the Law is essential to salvation, what, then, has been the work of Christ?"

But when the subject had been amply discussed, Peter arose.[2] Which side he would take could be hardly

---

[1] See on this dissension Hooker, *Eccl. Pol.* iv., xi.
[2] On the views of St. John, see Excursus XVII., "St. John and St. Paul."

doubtful.   He had, in fact, already braved and over-
borne the brunt of a similar opposition.   But an exceptional instance was felt to be a very different thing
from a universal rule.   It was true that Peter did not
now stand alone, but found the moral support, which
was so necessary to him, in the calm dignity of Barnabas
and the fervid genius of Paul.   But in all other respects
his task was even more difficult than it had been before,
and, rising to the occasion, he spoke with corresponding
boldness and force.[1]   His speech was in accordance with
the practical, forthright, non-argumentative turn of his
mind.   Filled with energetic conviction by the logic of
facts, he reminded them how, long ago,[2] the question had
been practically settled.   God had selected him to win over
the first little body of converts from the Gentile world; and
the gift of the Spirit to them had showed that they were
cleansed by faith.   To lay on them the burden of the Law
—a burden to the daily life which it surrounded with
unpractical and often all but impracticable observances—
a burden to the conscience because it created a sense of
obligation of which it could neither inspire the fulfilment
nor remedy the shortcoming—a burden which had therefore been found intolerable both by their fathers and themselves[3]—was simply to tempt God by hindering His
manifest purposes, and resisting His manifest will.   In
one doctrine all present were agreed;[4] it was that alike

---

[1] Acts xv. 7—11.   Again we have to notice the interesting circumstance
that in this brief speech the language is distinctly Petrine.   Such minute marks
of authenticity are wholly beyond the reach of a forger.

[2] The expression ἀφ' ἡμερῶν ἀρχαίων would naturally refer to the ἀρχὴ of the
Gospel (cf. xi. 15; xxi. 16; Phil. iv. 15).   But if the conversion of Cornelius
took place during the "rest" procured for the Church by the absorption of the
Jews in their attempt to rebut the mad impiety of Gaius, A.D. 40, that was
not twelve years before this time.

[3] Gal. v. 3.   The Law was a ζυγὸν δουλείας, the Gospel a ζυγὸς χρηστός, a
φορτίον ἐλαφρόν (Matt. xi. 29, 30).   [4] Cf. Acts xi. 17.

the Jews and the Gentile converts should be saved only by the grace of the Lord Jesus Christ. The inference then was obvious, that they were not and could not be saved by the works of the Law. In the observance of those works the Jews, on whom they were originally enjoined, might naturally persevere till fresh light came; but these hereditary customs had never been addressed to the Gentiles, and, since they were unnecessary to salvation, they must obviously be to the Gentiles not burdensome only, but a positive stumbling-block.

The weight of Peter's dignity had produced silence in the assembly. The excitement was now so far calmed that Paul and Barnabas were at least listened to without interruptions. Barnabas—who, in the Jewish Church, still retained his precedence, and who was as acceptable to the audience from his past liberality as Paul was unacceptable from his former persecutions—spoke first; but both he and Paul seem to have abstained from *arguing* the question. All the arguments had been urged at private conferences when words could be deliberately considered. They were not there to impress their own views, but to hear those of the Apostles and of the Church they governed. Barnabas never seems to have been prominent in debate, and Paul was too wise to discuss theological differences before a promiscuous audience. They confined themselves, therefore, to a simple history of their mission, dwelling especially on those "signs and wonders" wrought by their hands among the Gentiles, which were a convincing proof that, though they might not win the approval of man, they had all along enjoyed the blessing of God.

Then rose James. Every one present must have felt that the practical decision of the Church—Paul must have felt that, humanly speaking, the future of Christianity—depended on his words. A sense of awe clung about him

and all he said and did. Clothed with a mysterious and
indefinable dignity as "the brother of the Lord," that
dignity and mystery were enhanced by his bearing, dress,
manner of life, and entire appearance. Tradition, as embodied in an Ebionite romance, and derived from thence
by Hegesippus,[1] represents him as wearing no wool, but
clothed in fine white linen from head to foot, and—either
from some priestly element in his genealogy, or to symbo-
lise his "episcopate" at Jerusalem—as wearing on his forehead the *petalon*, or golden plate of High-priesthood.[2] It is
said that he was so holy, and so highly esteemed by the
whole Jewish people, that he alone was allowed, like the
High Priest, to enter the Holy Place; that he lived a
celibate[3] and ascetic life; that he spent long hours alone
in the Temple praying for the people, till his knees became
hard and callous as those of the camel; that he had the
power of working miracles; that the rain fell in accordance with his prayers; that it was owing to his merits
that God's impending wrath was averted from the Jewish
nation; that he received the title of "the Just" and
Obliam, or "Rampart of the People;" and that he was
shadowed forth in the images of the prophets.[4] Some of

---

[1] "The Ascent of James." The narrative of Hegesippus is quoted at length
by Eusebius, *H. E.* ii. 23. Other passages which relate to him are Epiphan.
Haer. lxxviii. 7, 13, 14; Jer. *De Vir. Illustr.* 2; Comm. in Gal. i. 19.

[2] Epiphan. *Haer.* xxix. 4. The same story is told of St. John, on the
authority of Polycrates, Bishop of Ephesus (Euseb. *H. E.* iii. 31; v. 24).
Either Polycrates has taken literally some metaphorical allusion, or John really
did sometimes adopt a symbol of Christian High-priesthood. The former
seems the more probable supposition.

[3] This is rendered doubtful by 1 Cor. ix. 5, unless he was an exception
to the other *Desposyni*.

[4] Dan. i. 8, 12; Tob. i. 11, 12. ὡς οἱ προφῆται δηλοῦσι περὶ αὐτοῦ (Heges.
ubi supr.). This, perhaps, refers to Isa. iii. 10. If he be the Jacob of Kephar
Sechaniah he is indeed regarded as a *Min*, yet he is represented as having
various dealings with orthodox Rabbis (Grätz, *Gnostic. u. Judaism*, p. 25). The
name Oblias, עובליא, is explained by Hausrath to mean "Jehovah my chain."

these details must be purely imaginative; but legends, as
has well been said, are like the clouds that gather upon the
mountain summits, and show the height and take the
shapes of the peaks about which they cling. We may
readily believe that he was a Nazarite, perhaps even an
ascetic—one who, by the past affinities of his character, was
bound rather to Banus, and John Baptist, and the strict
communities of the Essenes, than to the disciples of One
who came eating and drinking, pouring on social life the
brightness of His holy joy, attending the banquet of the
Pharisee at Capernaum, and the feast of the bridegroom
at Cana, not shrinking from the tears with which Mary of
Magdala or the perfumes with which Mary of Bethany
embathed his feet.

Such was the man who now rose to speak, with the
long locks of the Nazarite streaming over his white robe,
and with all the sternness of aspect which can hardly have
failed to characterise one who was so rigid in his convictions, so uncompromising in his judgments, so incisive
in his speech. The importance of his opinion lay in the
certainty that it could hardly fail to be, at least nominally,
adopted by the multitude, among whom he exercised an
authority, purely local indeed and limited, but within
those limits superior even to that of Peter. The most
fanatical of bigots could hardly refuse to be bound by the
judgment of one who was to the very depth of his being
a loyal Jew; to whom even unconverted Jews looked up
with reverence ; to whom the "Law," which neither St.
Peter nor St. John so much as mention in their Epistles,
was so entirely the most prominent conception that he
does not once mention the Gospel, and only alludes to it

with allusion to the Nazarite vow. **Hitzig** (*Kl. Propheten*) thinks the name
may refer to the staff, נֹעַם, in Zech. xi. 7. Is it possible that the name may
be some confusion of *Abh leam,* "father of the people?"

under the aspect of a law, though as "the perfect law of liberty."[1]

His speech—which, as in so many other instances, bears internal marks of authenticity[2]—was thoroughly Judaic in tone, and yet showed that the private arguments of the Apostles of the Gentiles had not been thrown away on a mind which, if in comparison with the mind of a Paul, and even of a Peter, it was somewhat stern and narrow, was yet the mind of a remarkable and holy man who would not struggle against the guidance of the Holy Spirit of God. Peter, in one of those impetuous outbursts of generous conviction which carried him beyond his ordinary self, had dauntlessly laid down broad principles which are, perhaps, the echo of thoughts which Paul had impressed upon his mind. It would have been too much to expect that James would speak with equal breadth and boldness. Had he done so, we should have felt at once that he was using language unlike himself, unlike all that we know of him, unlike the language of his own Epistle. But though his speech is as different from St. Peter's as possible—though it proposed restrictions where *he* had indicated liberty—it yet went farther than could have been hoped; farther than bigots either liked or cordially accepted; and, above all, it conceded the main point at issue in implying that circumcision and the ceremonial law were, as a whole, non-essential for the Gentiles.

Requesting their attention, he reminded them that Symeon[3]—as, using the Hebrew form of the name, he characteristically calls his brother Apostle—had narrated to them the Divine intimations which led to the call of the Gentiles, and this he shows was in accordance with ancient

---

[1] James i. 25; ii. 12.

[2] *E.g.*, "on whom my name has been called;" cf. James ii. 7.

[3] As in 2 Peter i. 1. This is the last mention of Peter in the Acts.

prophecy, and, therefore, with Divine fore-ordination.[1] But obviously—this was patent to all Jews alike—the Gentiles would never accept the whole Mosaic Law. His authoritative decision,[2] therefore, took the form of "a concession and a reserve." He proposed to release the converted Gentiles from all but four restrictions—which belonged to what was called the Noachian dispensation[3]— abstinence, namely, from things polluted by being offered to idols,[4] and from fornication, and from anything strangled, and from blood.[5] "For," he adds, in words which are pregnant with more than one significance, "Moses from of old hath preachers in the synagogues in every city, being read every Sabbath day." By this addition he probably meant to imply that since Moses was universally read in synagogues attended both by Jews and by Gentile converts, we will tell the Gentiles that this Law which they hear read is not universally binding on them, but only so far as charity to the Jew requires; and we will tell the Jews that we have no desire to abrogate *for them* that Law to whose ordinances they hear a weekly witness.

One of the most remarkable points in this speech is the

---

[1] Amos ix. 11, 12. The true reading here, among numberless divergences, seems to be γνωστὰ ἀπ' αἰῶνος (א, B, C), "it has been known of old." James affirms what Amos prophesied, but his speech is not free from difficulties. (See Baur, *Paul.* i. 124.)

[2] ἐγὼ κρίνω, but he was only *primus inter pares*. (See Acts xv. 6; xxi. 25.)

[3] See Gen. ix. 4.

[4] Acts xv. 20, ἀλισγήματα τῶν εἰδώλων = εἰδωλόθυτα (ver. 29; xxi. 25) 'Αλισγιέ = *gâal*, "to redeem with blood" (Dan. i. 8; Mal. i. 7). We are told that the Jews in the days of Antiochus were ready to die rather than εἰδωλο-θύτων ἀπογεύεσθαι.

[5] These two restrictions are practically identical, the πνικτὰ being only for-bidden because they necessarily involved the eating of the blood. Αἷμα cannot mean "the shedding of blood"—homicide, as some of the Fathers supposed. On "things strangled" and "blood," see Tert. *Apol.* ix.; Schöttgen, *Hor. Hebr. in loc.*; Kalisch on Gen. ix. 4.

argument deduced from the prophecy of Amos, which was primarily meant as a prophecy of the restoration of Israel from captivity, but which St. James, with a large insight into the ever-widening horizons of prophecy, applies to the ideal restoration, the reception of Jehovah as their common Father by the great family of man. In the re-building of the ruined tabernacle of David he sees the upraising of the Church of Christ as an ideal temple to which the Gentiles also shall be joined. Nor is it a little striking that in adducing this prophecy he quotes, not the Hebrew, but mainly the Septuagint.[1] The Greek differs essentially from the Hebrew, and differs from it in the essence of the interpretation, which lies not only in the ideal transference from the Temple to the Church, but in direct reference to the Gentiles—viz.:

"*That the residue of men might seek after the Lord,* and all the Gentiles upon whom My name is called, saith the Lord.*"

But the Hebrew says, much less appositely to the purpose of the speaker,

"*That they may possess the remnant of Edom,* and of all the heathen upon whom My name is called, saith the Lord."

The difference is due to one of those numberless and often extraordinary variations of the original text of which the Septuagint is so decisive a proof, and which makes that version so interesting a study.[2] This application of James may be regarded as implicitly involved even in the Hebrew, and is yet more directly supported by other passages;[3] but the fact that here and elsewhere the New

---

[1] παρενοχλεῖν (ver. 19) occurs only in the LXX.

[2] The LXX. seems clearly to have read אָדָם (*adâm*), "man," for אֱדוֹם (*edôm*). Dr. Davidson, *Sacr. Hermen.*, p. 462, goes so far as to suppose that the Jews have here altered the Hebrew text.

[3] *E.g.,* Ps. lxxxvi. 9; xxii. 31; cii. 18; Isa. xliii. 7.

Testament writers quote and argue from the undeniably variant renderings of the Septuagint, quoting them from memory, and often differing in actual words *both* from these and from the Hebrew, shows how utterly removed was their deep reverence for Scripture from any superstition about the literal dictation of mere words or letters.

The debate was now at an end, for all the leaders had spoken. The objections had been silenced; the voice of the chief elder had pronounced the authoritative conclusion. It only remained to make that conclusion known to those who were immediately concerned. The Apostles and Elders and the whole Church therefore ratified the decision, and selected two of their own body, men of high repute—Judas Barsabbas and Silas[1]—to accompany the emissaries from the Church of Antioch on their return, and to be pledges for the genuineness of their written communication. The letter which they sent embodied their resolutions, and ran as follows:—"The Apostles and Elders [2] and brethren to the brethren from the Gentiles in Antioch

---

[1] The Silas of Acts is, of course, the Silvanus—the name being Romanised for convenience—of the Epistles (1 Thess. i. 1; 2 Thess. i. 1), and perhaps of 1 Pet. v. 12. He is not mentioned in the Acts after the first visit of St. Paul to Corinth, and in undesigned coincidence with this his name disappears in the superscription of the Epistles after that time. (See Wordsworth, Phil. i. 1.)

[2] Although καὶ οἱ is omitted (א, A, B, C, the Vulgate and Armenian versions, Irenæus, and Origen, and the καὶ by D), I still believe them to be genuine. The diplomatic evidence seems indeed to be against them, the weight of the above Unciais, &c., being superior to that of E, G, H, the majority of Cursives, and the Syriac, Coptic, and Æthiopic versions. But objection to the apparent parity assigned to the brethren might have led, even in early days, to their omission, while if not genuine it is not easy to see why they should have been inserted. They also agree better with ver. 22, "with the whole Church," and ver. 24, "going out *from among us.*" The importance of the reading is shown by its bearing on such debates as the admission of laymen into ecclesiastical conferences, &c. Wordsworth quotes from Beveridge, *Codex Canonum Vindicatus*, p. 20, the rule "*Laici ad judicium de doctrina aut disciplina Ecclesiastica ferendum nunquam admissi sunt.*"

and Syria and Cilicia, greeting.[1]   Since we heard that some who went out from among us troubled you with statements, subverting[2] your souls, who received no injunction from us,[3] we met together, and decided to select men and send them to you with our beloved Barnabas and Paul,[4] persons[5] who have given up their lives for the name of our Lord Jesus Christ.[6]   We have therefore commissioned Judas and Silas to make in person the same announcement to you by word of mouth—namely, that it is our decision, under the guidance of the Holy Ghost,[7] to lay no further burden[8] upon you beyond these necessary things : to abstain from things offered to idols, and from blood, and from strangled, and from fornication, in keeping yourselves from which it shall be well with you.   Farewell."[9]

It will be observed that throughout this account I have avoided the terms "Council" and "decree."   It is only by an unwarrantable extension of terms that the meeting of

---

[1] χαίρειν, lit., "rejoice."   It is a curious circumstance that the *Greek* salutation—for the Hebrew salutation would be שׁלום, "Peace"—is only found in the letter of a Gentile, Claudius Lysias (xxiii. 26), and in the letter of him who must have taken a main part in drawing up this letter (James i. 1).

[2] ἀνασκευάζοντες, lit., "digging up from the foundations" (Thuc. iv. 116).

[3] This disavowal is complete, and yet whole romances about counter-missions in direct opposition to St. Paul, and organised by James, are securely built on the expression in Gal. ii. 12, τινὰς ἀπὸ Ἰακόβου, though it is very little stronger than the τινὲς κατελθόντες ἀπὸ τῆς Ἰουδαίας of xv. 1, and not so strong as the τινὲς ἐξ ἡμῶν ἐξελθόντες here.

[4] In order, of course, that no possible suspicion might attach to the letter as an expression of their real sentiments.

[5] I have expressed the difference of ἄνδρας and ἀνθρώπους, but the only difference intended is that the latter expression is more generic.

[6] They were martyrs at least in will (Alf.).

[7] Cf. Ex. xiv. 31 ; 1 Sam. xii. 18.   Hence the "Sancto Spiritu suggerente," commonly prefixed to decrees of Councils.

[8] This word (cf. ver. 10) seems to show the hand of Peter (cf. Rev. ii. 24).

[9] D, followed by some versions, and many Cursives, has the curious addition, "and whatsoever ye do not wish to be done to yourselves, do not to another. Farewell, walking in the Holy Spirit."   With these *minimum* requirements, intended to put Gentiles on the footing of Proselytes of the Gate, compare Lev. xvii. 8—16 ; xviii. 26.

the Church of Jerusalem can be called a "Council," and
the word connotes a totally different order of conceptions
to those that were prevalent at that early time. The
so-called Council of Jerusalem in no way resembled the
General Councils of the Church, either in its history, its
constitution, or its object. It was not a convention of
ordained delegates, but a meeting of the entire Church
of Jerusalem to receive a deputation from the Church of
Antioch. Even Paul and Barnabas seem to have had no
vote in the decision, though the votes of a promiscuous
body could certainly not be more enlightened than theirs,
nor was their allegiance due in any way to James. The
Church of Jerusalem might out of respect be consulted,
but it had no claim to superiority, no abstract prerogative
to bind its decisions on the free Church of God.[1] The
"decree" of the "Council" was little more than the wise
recommendation of a single synod, addressed to a particular district, and possessing only a temporary validity.[2]
It was, in fact, a local *concordat*. Little or no attention
has been paid by the universal Church to two of its
restrictions; a third, not many years after, was twice
discussed and settled by Paul, on the same general
principles, but with a by no means identical conclusion.[3]
The concession which it made to the Gentiles, in not
insisting on the necessity of circumcision, was equally
treated as a dead letter by the Judaising party, and cost
Paul the severest battle of his lifetime to maintain. If
this circular letter is to be regarded as a binding and final
decree, and if the meeting of a single Church, not by
delegates but in the person of all its members, is to be

---

[1] See Article xxi. Pope Benedict XIV. says, "*Speciem* quandam et
imaginem Synodi in praedicta congregatione eminere" (*De Synod.* i. 1—5; *ap*
Denton, Acts ii. 82).
[2] Hooker, *Eccl. Pol.* IV. xi. 5.   [3] Rom. xiv.; 1 Cor. viii.

regarded as a Council, never was the decision of a Council
less appealed to, and never was a decree regarded as so
entirely inoperative alike by those who repudiated the
validity of its concessions,[1] and by those who discussed, as
though they were still an open question, no less than three
of its four restrictions.[2]

The letter came to the Churches like a message of peace.
Its very limitation was, at the time, the best proof of its inspired wisdom. Considering the then state of the Church, no
decision could have more clearly evinced the guidance of the
Holy Spirit of God.[3] It was all the more valuable because
there were so many questions which it left unsolved. The
heads of the Church admitted—and that was something
—that circumcision was *non-essential* to Gentiles, and they
may seem to have indulged in an extreme liberality in
not pressing the distinction between clean and unclean
meats, and, above all, in not insisting on the abstinence
from the flesh of swine. By these concessions they undoubtedly removed great difficulties from the path of
Gentile converts. But, after all, a multitude of most
pressing questions remained, and left an opening for each
party to hold almost exactly the same opinions as before.
A Gentile was not to be *compelled* to circumcision and

---

[1] Gal. iii. 1; v. 2, and *passim.* It is astonishing to find that even Justin
declares the eating of εἰδωλόθυτα to be as bad as idolatry, and will hold no
intercourse with those who do it (*Dial. c. Tryph.* 35); but the reason was
that by that time (as in the days of the Maccabees) it had been adopted by
the heathen as a *test* of apostasy. And compare 1 Cor. x. 20, 21. (Ritschl,
Alt. Kath. Kirch 310, 2nd ed.)

[2] St. Paul discusses the question of meats offered to idols without the
remotest reference to this decree, and the Western Church have never held
themselves bound to abstain "from things strangled," and from blood (Aug.
c. Faust. xxxii. 13). St. Paul's silence about the decree when he writes to the
Romans perhaps rises from its provisional and partial character. It was only
addressed to the Gentile converts of "Antioch, Syria, and Cilicia."

[3] "Ils virent que le seul moyen d'échapper aux grands questions est de ne
pas les résoudre . . . de laisser les problèmes s'user et mourir faute de raison
d'être" (Renan, *St. P.* 93).

Mosaism. Good; but might it not be infinitely *better* for him to accept them? Might there not have been in the minds of Jewish Christians, as in those of later Rabbis, a belief that "even if Gentiles observe the seven Noachian precepts, they do not receive the same reward as Israelites?"[1] It is, at any rate, clear that neither now nor afterwards did the Judaisers admit Paul's dogmatic principles, as subsequently stated to the Galatians and Romans. Probably they regarded him, at the best, as the Ananias for future Eleazers.[2] Above all, the burning question of social relations remained untouched. Titus had been circumcised as the only condition on which the members of the Church at Jerusalem would let him move on an equal footing among themselves. It was all very well for them to decide with more or less indifference about *" choots learets,"* " the outer world," " people elsewhere," " those afar,"[3] as though they could much more easily contemplate the toleration of uncircumcised Christians, provided that they were out of sight and out of mind in distant cities; but a Jew was a Jew, even if he lived in the wilds of Isauria or the burnt plains of Phrygia; and how did this decision at Jerusalem help him to face the practical question, "Am I, or am I not, to share a common table with, to submit to the daily contact of people that eat freely of that which no true Jew can think of without a thrill of horror—the unclean beast?"

These were the questions which, after all, could only be left to the solution of time. The prejudices of fifteen centuries could not be removed in a day. Alike the more enlightened and the more bigoted of Jews and Gentiles continued to think very much as they had thought before,

---

[1] *Abhoda Zara,* f. 3, 1.
[2] See Pfleiderer, ii. 13.
[3] Acts ii. 39, οἱ εἰς μακράν; Col. iv. 5, οἱ ἔξω.

c c

until the darkness of prejudice was scattered by the broadening light of history and of reason.

The *genuineness* of this cyclical letter is evinced by its extreme naturalness. A religious romancist could not possibly have invented anything which left so much unsolved. And this genuineness also accounts for the startling appearance of a grave moral crime among things so purely ceremonial as particular kinds of food. There is probably no other period in the history of the world at which the Apostles would have found it needful to tell their Gentile converts to abstain from fornication, as well as from things offered to idols, things strangled, and blood. The first of these four prohibitions was perfectly intelligible, because it must have been often necessary for a Gentile Christian to prove to his Jewish brethren that he had no hankering after the "abominable idolatries" which he had so recently abandoned. The two next prohibitions were desirable as a concession to the indefinable horror with which the Jews and many other Eastern races regarded the eating of the blood, which they considered to be " the very life."[1] But only at such a period as this could a moral pollution have been placed on even apparently the same footing as matters of purely national prejudice. That the reading is correct,[2] and that the

---

[1] Gen. ix. 4; Lev. xvii. 14. So too Koran, Sur. v. 4. See Bähr, *Symbolik*, ii. 207. On the other hand, "the blood" was a special delicacy to the heathen (Hom. *Od.* iii. 470; xviii. 44; Ov. *Met.* xii. 154) ; and hence "things strangled" were with them a common article of food. Rutilius calls the Jew, "Humanis animal dissociale cibis " (*It.* i. 384). Even this restriction involved a most inconvenient necessity for never eating any meat but *kosher*, *i.e.*, meat prepared by Jewish butchers in special accordance with the laws of slaughtering (שחיטה). It would more or less necessitate what would be, to a Gentile at any rate, most repellent—the "cophinus foenumque supellex" (Juv. *Sat.* iii. 14), which were, for these reasons, the peculiarity of the Jew (Sidon. *Ep.* vii. 6).

[2] There is not the faintest atom of probability in Bentley's conjecture of πορκεια. At the same time, it must be noted as an extraordinary stretch of

thing forbidden is the sin of fornication,[1] not idolatry, or mixed marriages, or marriages between blood relations (1 Cor. v. 1), or second marriages (1 Tim. iii. 2), or any of the other explanations in which an astonished exegesis has taken refuge, must be regarded as certain. How, then, can the fact be accounted for? Only by the boundless profligacy of heathendom; only by the stern purity of Christian morals. The Jews, as a nation, were probably the purest among all the races of mankind; yet even they did not regard this sin as being the moral crime which Christianity teaches us to consider it;[2] and they lived in the midst of a world which regarded it as so completely a matter of indifference that Socrates has no censure for it,[3] and Cicero declares that no Pagan moralist had ever dreamt of meeting it with an absolute prohibition.[4]

liberality on the part of the Judaisers not to require the abstention from swine's flesh by their Gentile brethren ('Ιουδαῖος θᾶττον ἂν ἀποθάνοι ἢ χοιρείον φάγοι, Sext. Emp. Tac. H. V. 4; Sen. Ep. 108, 22; Macrob. Sat. ii. 4). This abstinence was common in the East (Dio. Cass. lxxix. 11).

[1] The notion that πορνεία can mean things sold (πέρνημι) in the market after idol feasts is also utterly untenable. See the question examined by Baur, Paul. i. 146, seq. Besides, the four prohibitions correspond to those attributed to Peter in Ps. Clem. Hom. vii. 4, where μὴ ἀκαθάρτως βιοῦν = πορνεία.

[2] In point of fact the Jews probably regarded the other three things with infinitely greater horror than this. The practice even of their own Rabbis, though veiled under certain decent forms, was far looser than it should have been, as is proved by passages in the Talmud (Gittin, f. 90; Joma, f. 18, 2; Selden, Ux. Hebr. iii. 17).

[3] Xen. Mem. iii. 13.

[4] This passage is remarkable as coming from one of the purest of all ancient writers (Cic. pro Cael. xx.; cf. Ter. Adelph. i. 2, 21). The elder Cato was regarded as a model of stern Roman virtue, yet what would be thought in Christian days of a man who spoke and acted as he did? (Hor. Sat. i. 2, 31.) If Cato could so regard the sin, what must have been the vulgar estimate of it? Nor must it be forgotten that the letter was addressed to Jews and Gentiles alike familiar with an epoch in which, as indeed for many previous centuries, this crime, and crimes yet more heinous, formed a recognised part of the religious worship of certain divinities (cf. Baruch vi. 43; Strabo, viii. 6); and in which the pages of writers who reek with stains like these formed a part of the current literature. Few circumstances can show more clearly the change which Christianity has wrought. But to every reader of

c c 2

What is it that has made the difference in the aspect
which sensuality wears to the ancient and to the modern
conscience?   I have no hesitation in answering that
the reason is to be found in the purity which every page
of the New Testament breathes and inspires, and specially
in the words of our Blessed Lord, and in the arguments of St. Paul.   If the blush of modesty on youthful
cheeks is a holy thing, if it be fatal alike to individuals
and to nations "to burn away in mad waste" the most
precious gifts of life, if debauchery be a curse and stain
which more than any other has eaten into the heart of
human happiness, then the saintly benefactor to whose
spirituality we owe the inestimable boon of having impressed these truths upon the youth of every Christian
land is he who—taught by the Spirit of the Lord—showed
more clearly, more calmly, more convincingly than any
human being has ever shown, the true heinousness, the
debasing tendency, the infusive virulence of sins which,
through the body, strike their venom and infix their
cancer into the soul; of sins which have this peculiar
sinfulness—that they not only destroy the peace and
endanger the salvation of the soul which is responsible for
itself, but also the souls of others, which, in consequence
of the sinner's guilty influence, may remain impenitent,
yet for the sake of which, no less than for his own,
Christ died.

the letter the immediate link of connexion between εἰδωλόθυτα and πορνεία
would be but too obvious. Further, it should be steadily observed that the
allusions—stern yet tender, uncompromising yet merciful—of St. Paul's own
Epistles to the prevalence of this sin, show most decidedly that if conversion
at once revealed to Christians its true heinousness, it often failed to shield
them against temptation to its commission.

CHAPTER XXIII.

ST. PETER AND ST. PAUL AT ANTIOCH.

"Separati epulis, discreti cubilibus."—TAC. *H.* v. 5.

"At ais Ecclesia est sancta, Patres sunt sancti Bene; sed Ecclesia quamlibet sancta tamen cogitur dicere Remitte nobis peccata nostra. Sic Patres quamlibet sancti per remissionem peccatorum salvati sunt."—LUTHER, *Comm. on Galat.* i.

SUCH, then, was the result of the appeal upon which the Judaisers had insisted; and so far as the main issue was concerned the Judaisers had been defeated. The Apostles, in almost indignantly repudiating the claim of these men to express their opinions, had given them a rebuff. They had intimated their dislike that the peace of Churches should be thus agitated, and had declared that circumcision was not to be demanded from the Gentiles. It needed but a small power of logic to see that, Christianity being what it was, the decision at least *implied* that converts, whether Jews or Gentiles, were to bear and forbear, and to meet together as equals in all religious and social gatherings. The return of the delegates was therefore hailed with joy in Antioch, and the presence of able and enlightened teachers like Judas and Silas, who really were what the Pharisaic party had falsely claimed to be—the direct exponents of the views of the Apostles—diffused a general sense of unity and confidence. After a brief stay, these two emissaries returned to Jerusalem.[1] On

[1] The true reading is not πρὸς τοὺς Ἀποστόλους, as in our version, but "to those who sent them" (πρὸς τοὺς ἀποστείλαντας αὐτούς—א, A, B, C, D).

Silas, however, the spell of Paul's greatness had been so powerfully exercised that he came back to Antioch, and threw in his lot for some time with the great Apostle of the Gentiles.[1]

Paul, in fact, by the intensity of his convictions, the enlightenment of his understanding, the singleness of his purpose, had made himself completely master of the situation. He had come to the very forefront in the guidance of the Church. The future of Christianity rested with the Gentiles, and to the Gentiles the acts and writings of Paul were to be of greater importance than those of all the other Apostles. His Apostolate had been decisively recognised. He had met Peter and John, and even the awe-inspiring brother of the Lord, in conference, and found himself so completely their equal in the gifts of the Holy Ghost, that it was impossible for them to resist his credentials. He had greatly enlarged their horizon, and they had added nothing to him. He had returned from Jerusalem more than ever conscious of himself, conscious of his own power, clear in his future purposes. He inspired into the Church of Antioch his own convictions with a force which no one could resist.

But since the letter from Jerusalem suggested so many inquiries, and laid down no universal principle, it was inevitable that serious complications should subsequently arise. A scene shortly occurred which tested to the extremest degree the intellectual firmness and moral courage of St. Paul. St. Peter seems about this time to have begun that course of wider

---

[1] The reading of our version, ver. 34, "Notwithstanding it pleased Silas to abide there still," is the pragmatic gloss of a few MSS., to which D adds μόνος δὲ 'Ιούδας ἐπορεύθη. It is not found in א, A, B, G, E, H. Of course, either this fact or the return of Silas is implied by ver. 40, but the separate insertion of it is exactly one of those trivialities which ancient writers are far less apt than moderns to record. ·

journeys which, little as we know of them, carried him in
some way or other to his final martyrdom at Rome. We
do not again hear of his presence at Jerusalem. John
continued there in all probability for many years, and
Peter may have felt his presence needless; nor is it
unlikely that, as Peter dwelt on the wider views which he
had learnt from intercourse with his brother Apostle, he
may have found himself less able to sympathise with the
more Judaic Christianity of James. At any rate, we find
him not long after this period at Antioch, and there so
frankly adopting the views of St. Paul, that he not only
extended to all Gentiles the free intercourse which he
had long ago interchanged with Cornelius, but seems
in other and more marked ways to have laid aside the
burden of Judaism.[1] Paul could not but have rejoiced
at this public proof that the views of the Apostle of
the circumcision were, on this momentous subject, identical with his own. But this happiness was destined to
be seriously disturbed. As the peace of the Church
of Antioch had been previously troubled by "certain
which came down from Jerusalem," so it was now broken
by the arrival of "certain from James." Up to this
time, in the Agapæ of Antioch, the distinction of Jew
and Gentile had been merged in a common Christianity,
and this equal brotherhood had been countenanced by
the presence of the Apostle who had lived from earliest
discipleship in the closest intercourse with Christ. But
now a cloud suddenly came over this frank intercourse.[2]
Under the influence of timidity, the plastic nature of
Peter, susceptible as it always was to the impress of the

---

[1] Gal. ii. 14, ἐθνικῶς καὶ οὐχ Ἰουδαϊκῶς ζῆς. Nothing definite can be made of
the tradition that St. Peter was first Bishop of Antioch.

[2] If the reading ἦλθεν in Gal. ii. 12 were right it could only point to James
himself; but this would have been a fact which tradition could not have
forgotten, and James seems never to have left Jerusalem.

moment, began to assume a new aspect. His attitude to the Gentile converts was altered. "He began to draw away and separate himself," in order not to offend the rigid adherents of the Lord's brother.[1] It is not said that they claimed any direct authority, or were armed with any express commission; but they were strict Jews, who, however much they might tolerate the non-observance of the Law by Gentiles, looked with suspicion—perhaps almost with horror—on any Jew who repudiated obligations which, for *him* at any rate, they regarded as stringent and sacred.[2] A false shame, a fear of what these men might say, dislike to face a censure which would acquire force from those accumulated years of habit which the vision of Joppa had modified, but not neutralised—perhaps too a bitter recollection of all he had gone through on a former occasion when he "had gone in unto men uncircumcised and eaten with them"—led Peter into downright hypocrisy.[3] Without any acknowledged change of view, without a word of public explanation, he suddenly changed his course of life, and it was almost inevitable that the other Jewish Christians should follow this weak and vacillating example. The Apostle who "seemed to be a pillar" proved to be a "reed shaken with the wind."[4] To the grief and shame of Paul, even Barnabas—Barnabas, his fellow-worker in the Churches of the Gentiles—even

---

[1] Gal. ii. 12, ὑπέστελλεν καὶ ἀφώριζεν ἑαυτόν.

[2] How anxious James was to conciliate the inflammable multitude who were "zealous for the Law" is apparent from Acts xxi. 24.

[3] The forger of the letter of Peter to James, printed at the head of the Clementine *Homilies*, deeply resents the expression, § 2. But St. Peter's "hypocrisy" consisted in "having implied an objection which he did not really feel, or which his previous custom did not justify" (Jowett, *Gal.* i. 245). It is idle to say that this shows the non-existence of the "decree;" that, as I have shown, left the question of intercourse with the Gentiles entirely undefined.

[4] See Hausrath, p. 252. "Boldness and timidity—first boldness, then timidity—were the characteristics of his nature" (Jowett, i. 243). See also Excursus XVII., "St. John and St. Paul."

Barnabas, who had stood side by side with him to plead for the liberty of the Gentiles at Jerusalem, was swept away by the flood of inconsistency, and in remembering that he was a Levite forgot that he was a Christian. In fact, a strong Jewish reaction set in. There was no question of charity here, but a question of principle. To eat with the Gentiles, to live as do the Gentiles, was for a Jew either right or wrong. Interpreted in the light of those truths which lay at the very bases of the Gospel, it was right; and if the Church was to be one and indivisible, the agreement that the Gentiles were not to put on the yoke of Mosaism seemed to imply that they were not to lose status by declining to do so. But to shilly-shally on the matter, to act in one way to-day and in a different way to-morrow, to let the question of friendly inter-course depend on the presence or absence of people who were supposed to represent the stern personality of James, could not under *any* circumstances be right. It was monstrous that the uncircumcised Gentile con-vert was at one time to be treated as a brother, and at another to be shunned as though he were a Pariah. This was an uncertain, underhand sort of procedure, which St. Paul could not for a moment sanction. He could not stand by to see the triumph of the Pharisaic party over the indecision of men like Peter and Barnabas. For the moral weakness which succumbs to impulse he had the deepest tenderness, but he never permitted himself to maintain a truce with the interested selfishness which, at a moment's notice, would sacrifice a duty to avoid an inconvenience. Paul saw at a glance that Kephas [1] (and the Hebrew name seemed best to suit the Hebraic defec-tion) was wrong—wrong intellectually, if not morally—

---

[1] Gal. ii. 11, Κηφᾶς (א, A, B, C).

and that he was mainly responsible for the wrong into which the others had been betrayed by his example. He did not, therefore, hesitate to withstand him to the face. It was no occasion for private remonstrance; the reproof must be as public as the wrong, or the whole cause might be permanently imperilled. Perhaps few things demand a firmer resolution than the open blame of those who in age and position are superior to ourselves. For one who had been a fierce persecutor of Christians to rebuke one who had lived in daily intercourse with Christ was a very hard task. It was still more painful to involve Barnabas and other friends in the same censure; but that was what duty demanded, and duty was a thing from which Paul never shrank.

Rising at some public gathering of the Church, at which both Jews and Gentiles were present, he pointedly addressed Peter in language well calculated to show him that he stood condemned.[1] "If thou," he said before them all, "being a born Jew, art living Gentile fashion and not Jew fashion, how[2] canst thou try[3] to compel the Gentiles to Judaise?"[4] So far his language complained of his brother Apostle's inconsistency rather than of his present conduct. It was intended to reveal the inconsistency which Peter had wished to hide. It directly charged him with having done the very thing

---

[1] Gal. ii. 11, κατεγνωσμένος ἦν. This is the word which gives such bitter offence to the forger of the Clementine *Homilies*, xvii. 18, 19. "Thou didst withstand me as an opponent (ἐνάντιος ἀνθέστηκάς μοι) . . . If thou callest me condemned (κατεγνωσμένος) thou accusest God who revealed Christ to me," &c., and much more to the same effect.

[2] πῶς.

[3] Gal. ii. 14. The wrong aspirate in οὐχ Ἰουδαϊκῶς may be a Cilicism. But surely the editors should give us Ἰουδαϊκῶς. The ἐφ' ἐλπίδι of the best MSS. in 1 Cor. ix. 10 is supported by the occurrence of ἐλπίς in inscriptions.

[4] ἀναγκάζεις, "are by your present conduct practically obliging." "He was half a Gentile, and wanted to make the Gentiles altogether Jews" (Jowett, *Galat.* i. 244).

which his present withdrawal from Gentile communion
was meant to veil. "You have been living as a Gentile
Christian in the midst of Gentile Christians; you may
alter your line at this moment, but such has been your
deliberate conduct. Now if it is unnecessary for you, a
born Jew, to keep the Law, how can it be necessary, even
as a counsel of perfection, that the Gentiles should do
so? Yet it must be necessary, or at least desirable, if, short
of this, you do not even consider the Gentiles worthy of
your daily intercourse. If your present separation means
that you consider it to be a contamination to eat with
them, you are practically forcing them to be like you
in all respects. Be it so, if such is your view; but let
that view be clearly understood. The Church must not
be deceived as to what your example *has* been. If
indeed that conduct was wrong, then say so, and
let us know your reasons; but if that conduct was
not wrong, then it concedes the entire equality and
liberty which in the name of Christ we claim for our
Gentile brethren, and you have left yourself no further
right to cast a doubt on this by your present behaviour."
It has been the opinion of some that St. Paul's actual
speech to Peter ended with this question, and that the
rest of the chapter is an argument addressed to the
Galatians. But though, in his eager writing, St. Paul
may unconsciously pass from what he said in the assembly
at Antioch to the argument which he addressed to apostatising converts in Galatia, yet he can hardly have
thrown away the opportunity of impressing his clear
convictions on this subject upon Peter and the Church of
Antioch. He wished to drive home the sole legitimate
and logical consequence of the points already established; and we can scarcely doubt that he used on
this occasion some of those striking arguments which

we shall subsequently examine in the Epistle to the Galatians.[1]

They all turn on the great truth over which the Holy Spirit had now given him so firm a grasp— the truth of Justification by Faith alone. If no man could see salvation save by means of faith, and on account of Christ's mercy, then even for the Jew the Law was superfluous. The Jew, however, might, on grounds of national patriotism, blamelessly continue the observances which were ancient and venerable,[2] provided that he did not trust in them. But the Gentile was in no way bound by them, and to treat him as an inferior because of this immunity was to act in contradiction to the first principles of Christian faith. The contrasted views of St. Paul and of the Judaists were here brought into distinct collision, and thereby into the full light on which depended their solution. Faith without the Law, said the Judaists, means a state of Gentile "sinfulness." Faith with the Law, replied St. Paul, means that Christ has died in vain.[3] Among good and holy men love would

[1] See on Gal. ii. 15—21, *infra*, ii., p. 147.

[2] See some admirable remarks on the subject in Augustine, *Ep.* lxxxii. He argues that, after the revelation of faith in Christ, the ordinances of the Law had lost their life; but that just as the bodies of the dead ought to be honourably conducted, with no feigned honour, but with real solemnity to the tomb, and not to be at once deserted to the abuse of enemies or the attacks of dogs—so there was need that the respect for the Mosaic Law should not be instantly or rudely flung aside. But, he says, that even for a Jewish Christian to observe what could still be observed of the Law after it had been abrogated by God's own purpose in the destruction of Jerusalem, would be to act the part, not of one who honours the dead, but of one who tears out of their resting-places the buried ashes of the slain.

[3] Holstein, *Protestantenbibel*, 729. This dissension—if dissension it could be called—between the two great Apostles will shock those only who, in defiance of all Scripture, persist in regarding the Apostles as specimens of supernatural perfection. Of course, the errors of good men, even if they be mere errors of timidity on one side and vehemence on the other, will always expose them to the taunts of infidels. But when Celsus talks of the Apostles

still be the girdle of perfectness; but when the controversy waxed fierce between inspired conviction on the one side, and designing particularism on the other, hard terms were used. " Your principle is a nullification of Moses, of inspiration, of religion itself," said the Judaists; "it is downright rationalism; it is rank apostasy." "Your Gospel," replied the Apostle, " is no Gospel at all; it is the abnegation of the Gospel; it is a bondage to carnal rudiments; it is a denial of Christ."

A reproof is intolerable when it is administered out of pride or hatred, but the wounds of a friend are better at all times than the precious balms of an enemy that break the head. We are not told the immediate effect of Paul's words upon Peter and Barnabas, and in the case of the latter we may fear that, even if unconsciously, they may have tended, since human nature is very frail and weak, to exasperate the subsequent quarrel by a sense of previous difference. But if Peter's weakness was in exact accordance with all we know of his character, so too would be the rebound of a noble nature which restored

---

"inveighing against each other so shamefully in their quarrels," he is guilty —so far as the New Testament account of the Apostles is concerned—of gross calumny (*ap.* Orig. *c. Cels.* v. 64). The " blot of error," of which Porphyry accused St. Peter, shows only that he was human, and neither Gospels nor Epistles attempt to conceal his weaknesses. The " petulance of language" with which he charges St. Paul finds no justification in the stern and solemn tone of this rebuke; and to deduce from this dispute "the lie of a pretended decree" is a mere abuse of argument. We may set aside at once, not without a feeling of shame and sorrow, the suggestion (Clem. Alex. *ap.* Euseb. *H. E.* i. 12) that this Kephas was not St. Peter, but one of the Seventy; and the monstrous fancy—monstrous, though stated by no less a man than Origen (*ap.* Jer. *Ep.* cxii.), and adopted by no less a man than Chrysostom (*ad loc.*), and for a time by Jerome—that the whole was a scene acted between the two Apostles for a doctrinal purpose! As if such dissimulation would not have been infinitely more discreditable to them than a temporary disagreement in conduct! The way in which St. Peter bore the rebuke, and forgave and loved him who administered it, is ten-thousandfold more to his honour than the momentary inconsistency is to his disgrace.

him at once to strength. The needle of the compass may
tremble and be deflected, but yet it is its nature to point
true to the north; and if Peter was sometimes swept
aside from perfectness by gusts of impulse and temptation; if after being the first to confess Christ's divinity
he is the first to treat Him with presumption; if at
one moment he becomes His disciple, and at another
bids Him depart because he is himself a sinful man;
if now he plunges into the sea all faith, and now sinks
into the waves all fear; if now single-handed he draws
the sword for His Master against a multitude, and now
denies Him with curses at the question of a servant-
maid—we are not surprised to find that one who on
occasion could be the boldest champion of Gentile equality
was suddenly tempted by fear of man to betray the cause
which he had helped to win.[1] But the best proof that
he regretted his weakness, and was too noble-hearted to
bear any grudge, is seen in the terms of honour and
affection in which he speaks of Paul and his Epistles.[2]
It is still more clearly shown by his adopting the very
thoughts and arguments of Paul, and in his reference,
while writing among others to the Galatians, to the very
words of the Epistle in which his own conduct stood so
strongly condemned.[3] The legend which is commemorated in the little Church of " *Domine quo vadis* " near
Rome, is another interesting proof either that this tendency to vacillation in Peter's actions was well understood
in Christian antiquity, or that he continued to the last
to be the same Peter—" consistently inconsistent," as he

[1] At such an epoch of transition it was inevitable that charges of inconsistency should be freely bandied about on both sides, and with a certain
amount of plausibility. Cf. Gal. vi. 13.

[2] 2 Pet. iii. 15.

[3] Comp. 1 Pet. ii. 16, 17 with Gal. v. 1, 13, 14, and 1 Pet. ii. 24 with a
passage of this very remonstrance (Gal. ii. 20).

has most happily been called—liable to weakness and error, but ever ready to confess himself in the wrong, and to repent, and to amend :—

> "And as the water-lily starts and slides
> Upon the level in little puffs of wind,
> Though anchored to the bottom—such was he."

But while to a simple and lofty soul like that of Peter there might almost be something of joy in the frank acknowledgment of error and the crushing down of all anger against the younger, and, at that period, far less celebrated man who had publicly denounced him, such was by no means the case with the many adherents who chose to elevate him into the head of a faction.[1] What may have been the particular tenets of the Kephas-party at Corinth, we have no means for deciding, and the only thing which we can imagine likely was that their views were identical with those of the least heretical Ebionites, who held the Mosaic Law to be binding in its entirety on all Jews. Whatever may have been the action of James, or of those who assumed his authority,[2] neither

[1] "And I of Kephas ;" but when Paul again refers to the parties, with the delicate consideration of true nobleness, he omits the name of Kephas.

[2] The minute accounts of a counter-mission *inaugurated by James* are nothing more or less than an immense romance built on a single slight expression (τινας ἀπὸ Ἰακόβου), applicable only with any certainty to the one occasion to which it is referred. In Gal. ii. 12; iv. 16; 1 Cor. i. 12; ix. 1, 3, 7; 2 Cor. iii. 1; x. 7; Phil. i. 15, 17, we see the traces of a continuous opposition to St. Paul by a party which, in the nature of things, must have had its head-quarters in Jerusalem ; and of course the leaders at Jerusalem could not remain wholly uninfluenced by the tone of thought around them, and the views which were in the very atmosphere which they daily breathed. Yet they publicly disavowed the obtrusive members of their community (Acts xv. 24), and towards St. Paul personally they always, as far as we know, showed the most perfect courtesy and kindness, and to them personally he never utters one single disrespectful or unfraternal word. There is not a trace of that stern or bitter tone of controversy between them and him which we find interchanged by Bernard and Abelard, Luther and Erasmus, Fénélon and Bossuet, Wesley and Whitefield. He always speaks of them with gentleness and respect (1 Cor. ix. 5; Eph. iii. 5, &c.).

in the New Testament, nor in the earliest Christian writings, is there any trace of enmity between Paul and Peter, or of radical opposition between their views.[1] The notion that there was, has simply grown up from the pernicious habit of an over-ingenious criticism which "neglects plain facts and dwells on doubtful allusions." Critics of this school have eagerly seized upon the Clementines—a malignant and cowardly Ebionite forgery of uncertain date—as furnishing the real clue to the New Testament history, while they deliberately ignore and set aside authority incomparably more weighty. Thus the silence[2] of Justin Martyr about the name and writings of St. Paul is interpreted into direct hostility, while the allusions of the *genuine* Clement, which indicate the unanimity between the Apostles, are sacrificed to the covert attacks of the forger who assumes his name. But St. Paul's whole argument turns, not on the supposition that he is setting up a counter-gospel to the other Apostles, but on Peter's temporary treason to *his own* faith, *his own* convictions, *his own* habitual professions; [3] and all subsequent facts prove that the two Apostles held each other in the highest mutual esteem; they were lovely and pleasant in their lives, and in death they were not divided.[4]

Thus, then, thanks to St. Paul, the battle was again

---

[1] Even the *Praedicatio Pauli* (preserved in Cyprian, *De Rebaptismate*) implies that they were reconciled at Rome before their martyrdom, "postremo in urbe, quasi tunc primum, invicem sibi esse cognitos."

[2] On the explanation of this silence, which does not, however, exclude apparent allusions, see Westcott, *Canon.*, p. 185; Lightfoot, *Gal.*, p. 310. Who can suppose that Justin's γινέσθε ὡς ἐγὼ ὅτι κἀγὼ ἤμην ὡς ὑμεῖς (*Cohort. ad Graec.*, p. 40) bears only an accidental resemblance to Gal. iv. 12?

[3] Maurice, *Unity*, 497.

[4] See Excursus XVIII., "The Attacks on St. Paul in the Clementines." In the Romish Church the commemoration of St. Paul is *never separated* from that of St. Peter. On the feast-days set apart to each saint, the other is invariably honoured in the most prominent way.

won, and the Judaisers, who were so anxious to steer
the little ship of the Church to certain wreck and ruin
on the rocks of national bigotry, could no longer claim
the sanction of the relapsing Peter. But no sooner
was all smooth in the Church of Antioch than the old
mission-hunger seized the heart of Paul, and urged him
with noble restlessness from the semblance of inactivity.
Going to his former comrade Barnabas, he said, "Come,
let us re-traverse our old ground, and see for ourselves
how our brethren are in every city in which we preached
the word of the Lord." Barnabas readily acceded to the
proposal, but suggested that they should take with them
his cousin Mark.[1] But to this Paul at once objected.
The young man who had suddenly gone away home from
Pamphylia, and left them, when it was too late to get any
other companion, to face the difficulties and dangers of
the journey alone, Paul did not think it right to take
with them. Neither would give way; neither put in
practice the exquisite and humble Christian lesson of
putting up with less than his due. A quarrel rose
between these two faithful servants of God as bitter as
it was deplorable,[2] and the only hope of peace under such
circumstances lay in mutual separation. They parted,
and they suffered for their common fault. They parted
to forgive each other indeed, and to love and honour each
other, and speak of each other hereafter with affection
and respect, but never to work together again; never to
help each other and the cause of God by the union of

---

[1] The true reading of Acts xv. 37 is ἐβούλετο, א, A, B, C, E, Syr., Copt.
Æth., &c. (Vulg. Volebat). The word is characteristically mild compared
with the equally characteristic vehemence of the ἠξίου . . . μὴ of St. Paul.

[2] Notice the emphatic tone of the original in Acts xv. 39. The word
παροξυσμὸς (="exacerbatio," "provocation") implies the interchange of sharp
language; but it also implies a temporary ebullition, not a permanent quarrel.
Elsewhere it only occurs in Heb. x. 24; Deut. xxix. 28 (LXX.).

their several gifts; never to share with one another in
the glory of Churches won to Christ from the heathen;
and in all probability to rue, in the regret of lifelong
memories, the self-will, the want of mutual concession, the unspoken soft answer which turneth away
wrath, which, in a few bitter moments, too late repented
of, robbed them both of the inestimable solace of a
friend.

Which was right? which was wrong? We are not
careful to apportion between them the sad measure of
blame,[1] or to dwell on the weaknesses which marred the
perfection of men who have left the legacy of bright
examples to all the world. In the mere matter of judgment each was partly right, each partly wrong;[2] their
error lay in the persistency which did not admit of mutual
accommodation. Each was like himself. St. Barnabas may
have suffered himself too strongly to be influenced by
partiality for a relative; St. Paul by the memory of personal indignation. Barnabas may have erred on the side
of leniency; Paul on the side of sternness. St. Paul's
was so far the worst fault, yet the very fault may have
risen from his loftier ideal.[3] There was a "severe earnestness" about him, a sort of intense whole-heartedness,
which could make no allowance whatever for one who, at
the very point at which dangers began to thicken, deserted
a great and sacred work. Mark had put his hand to the
plough, and had looked back; and, conscious of the serious
hindrance which would arise from a second defection, conscious of the lofty qualities which were essential to any
one who was honoured with such Divine responsibilities,

---

[1] " Viderint ii qui de Apostolis judicant; mihi non tam bene est, immo
non tam malè est, ut Apostolos committam " (Tert. De Praescr. 24).

[2] Paulus severior, Barnabas clementior; uterque in suo sensu abundat; et
tamen dissensio habet aliquid humanae fragilitatis " (Jer. Adv. Pelag. ii. 522).

[3] 'Ο Παῦλος ἐζήτει τὸ δίκαιον, ὁ Βαρνάβας τὸ φιλάνθρωπον (Chrys.).

St. Paul might fairly have argued that a cause must not be risked out of tenderness for a person.[1] Barnabas, on the other hand, might have urged that it was most unlikely that one who was now willing to face the work again should again voluntarily abandon it, and he might fairly have asked whether one failure was to stamp a life-time. Both persisted, and both suffered. Paul went his way, and many a time, in the stormy and agitated days which followed, must he have sorely missed, amid the provoking of all men and the strife of tongues, the repose and generosity which breathed through the life and cha-racter of the Son of Exhortation. Barnabas went his way, and, dissevered from the grandeur and vehemence of Paul, passed into comparative obscurity, in which, so far from sharing the immortal gratitude which embalms the memory of his colleague, his name is never heard again, except in the isolated allusions of the letters of his friend.

For their friendship was not broken. Barnabas did not become a Judaiser, or in any way discountenance the work of Paul. The Epistle which passed by his name is spurious,[2] but its tendency is anti-Judaic, which would not have been the case if, after the dispute at Antioch, he had permanently sided with the anti-Pauline faction. In the Acts of the Apostles he is not again mentioned. Whether he confined his mission-work to his native island, whither he almost immediately sailed with Mark, or whether, as seems to be implied by the allusion in the Epistle to the Corinthians, he extended it more widely, he certainly continued to work on the same principles as before, taking with him no female companion, and

[1] Prov. xxv. 19.
[2] It is examined and rejected, among others, by Hefele, *Das Sendschr. d. Ap. Barnabas* (Tübingen, 1840).

D D 2

accepting nothing from the Churches to which he preached.[1]

And though, so far as they erred, the Apostles suffered for their error, God overruled evil for good. Henceforth they were engaged in two spheres of mission action instead of one, and henceforth also the bearing and the views of Paul were more free and vigorous, less shackled by associations, less liable to reaction. Hitherto his position in the Church of Jerusalem had depended much upon the countenance of Barnabas. Henceforth he had to stand alone, to depend solely on himself and his own Apostolic dignity, and to rely on no favourable reception for his views, except such as he won by the force of right and reason, and by the large benefits which accrued to the Church of Jerusalem from the alms which he collected from Gentile Churches.

And Mark also profited by the difference of which he was the unhappy cause. If the lenient partiality of one Apostle still kept open for him the missionary career, the stern judgment of the other must have helped to make him a more earnest man. All that we henceforth know of him shows alike his great gifts and his self-denying energy. In his Gospel he has reflected for us with admirable vividness the knowledge and experience of his friend and master St. Peter, to whom, in his later years, he stood in the same relation that Timothy occupied

---

[1] 1 Cor. ix. 6; Gal. ii. 9. It has been inferred from the mention of Mark as known to the Churches of Bithynia, Pontus, Cappadocia, Galatia (1 Pet. i. 1; v. 13), and Colossæ (Col. iv. 10), and his presence long afterwards in Asia Minor (2 Tim. iv. 11), that, if he continued to accompany his cousin Barnabas, Asia Minor, and especially its eastern parts, may have been the scene of their labours (Lewin, i. 165). The allusion in Col. iv. 10 has been taken to imply that by that time (A.D. 63) Barnabas was no longer living. Nothing certain is known about the place, manner, or time of his death. The *Acta et Passio Barnabae in Cypro* is apocryphal. St. Mark is said to have been martyred at Alexandria.

towards St. Paul.[1]   But even St. Paul saw good cause
not only to modify his unfavourable opinion, but to
invite him again as a fellow-labourer.[2]   He urges the
Colossians to give him a kindly welcome,[3] and even writes
to Timothy an express request that he would bring him
to Rome to solace his last imprisonment, because he had
found him—that which he had once failed to be—" profitable to him for ministry."[4]

---

[1] 1 Pet. v. 13.   [2] Philem. 24.
[3] Col. iv. 10.   [4] 2 Tim. iv. 11, εἰς διακονίαν.

CHAPTER XXIV.

BEGINNING OF THE SECOND MISSIONARY JOURNEY: PAUL
IN GALATIA.

"Come, let us get up early to the vineyards; let us see if the vines
flourish."—CANT. vii. 12.

THE significant silence as to any public sympathy for
Barnabas and Mark, together with the prominent mention
of it in the case of Paul, seems to show that the Church
of Antioch in general considered that St. Paul was in
the right. Another indication of the same fact is that
Silas consented to become his companion. Hitherto
Silas had been so closely identified with the Church of
Jerusalem that he had been one of the emissaries chosen
to confirm the genuineness of the circular letter, and in
the last notice of him which occurs in Scripture we find
him still in the company of St. Peter, who sends him
from Babylon wi+h a letter to some of the very Churches
which he had visited with St. Paul.[1] His adhesion to
the principles of St. Paul, in spite of the close bonds
which united him with the Jewish Christians, is a
sufficient proof that he was a man of large nature;
and as a recognised prophet of Jerusalem and Antioch,
his companionship went far to fill up the void left in
the mission by the departure of Barnabas. His name
Silvanus,[2] and the fact that he, too, seems to have been a
Roman citizen,[3] may perhaps show that he had some

---

[1] 1 Pet. v. 12. The identity cannot, however, be regarded as certain.

[2] Silas may be of Semitic origin. Josephus mentions four Orientals of the
name (Krenkel, p. 78).

[3] Acts xvi. 20, 37.

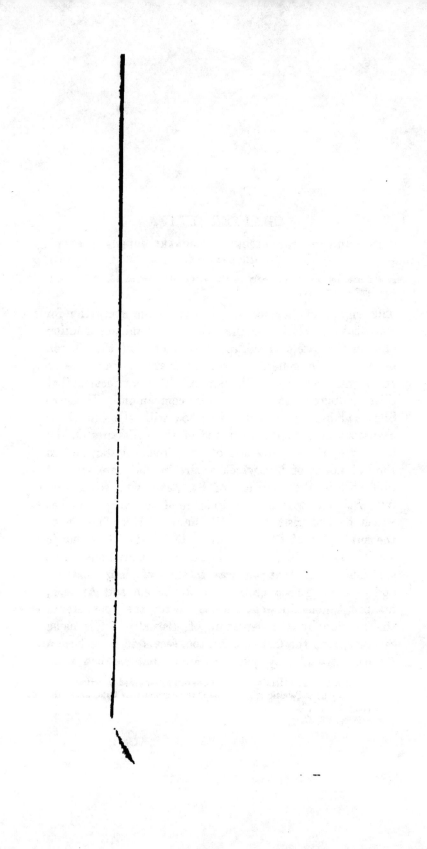

connexion with the Gentile world, to which, therefore,
he would be a more acceptable Evangelist. In every
respect it was a happy Providence which provided St.
Paul with so valuable a companion. And as they started
on a second great journey, carrying with them the hopes
and fortunes of Christianity, they were specially com-
mended by the brethren to the grace of God.

St. Paul's first object was to confirm the Churches
which he had already founded. Such a confirmation of
proselytes was an ordinary Jewish conception,[1] and after
the vacillations of opinion which had occurred even at
Antioch, Paul would be naturally anxious to know whether
the infant communities continued to prosper, though they
were harassed by persecutions from without, and liable
to perversion from within. Accordingly he began his
mission by visiting the Churches of Syria and Cilicia.
It is probable that he passed along the eastern coast of the
Gulf of Issus, and through the Syrian and Amanid Gates
to the towns of Alexandria and Issus.[2] There the road
turned westward, and led through Mopsuestia and Adana
to Tarsus. From Tarsus three routes were open to him—
one running along the shore of the Mediterranean to the
Cilician Seleucia, and then turning inland through the
Lycaonian Laranda to Derbe; the other a narrow and un-
frequented path through the mountains of Isauria; the
third, which in all probability he chose as the safest, the
most frequented, and the most expeditious, through the
famous Cilician Gates,[3] which led direct to Tyana, and then
turning south-westward ran to Cybistra, and so to Derbe,
along the southern shore of Lake Ak Ghieul.[4] And if,

[1] See Schleusner, *s.v.* στηρίζω.
[2] The Syrian gates are now called the Pass of Beylan; the Amanid Gates
are the Kara-Kapu.
[3] Now the Kü ek-Boghaz.
[4] For further geographical details, see Con. and Howson, ch. viii., and

indeed, Paul and Silas took this route and passed through the narrow gorge under its frowning cliffs of limestone, clothed here and there with pine and cedar, which to the Crusaders presented an appearance so terrible that they christened it the Gates of Judas, how far must they have been from imagining, in their wildest dreams, that their footsteps—the footsteps of two obscure and persecuted Jews—would lead to the traversing of that pass centuries afterwards by kings and their armies. How

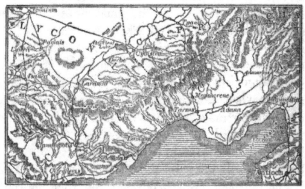

THE COUNTRY ROUND TARSUS.

little did they dream that those warriors, representing the haughtiest chivalry of Europe, would hold the name of Jews in utter execration, but would be sworn to rescue the traditional tomb of that Christ whom they acknowledged as their Saviour, from the hands of a mighty people who also recognised Him as a Prophet, though they did not believe Him to be Divine!

Whatever road was taken by Paul and Silas, they must

Lewin, ch. x. It is humiliating to think that the roads in St. Paul's day were incomparably better, and better kept, than they are at this moment, when the mere *débris* of them suffice for peoples languishing under the withering atrophy of Turkish rule.

have been their own messengers, and announced their own arrival. And we can well imagine the surprise, the emotion, the delight of the Christians in the little Isauric town, when they suddenly recognised the well-known figure of the missionary, who, arriving in the opposite direction, with the wounds of the cruel stonings fresh upon him, had first taught them the faith of Christ. Can we not also imagine the uneasiness which, during this visitation of the Churches which he loved so well, must often have invaded the heart of Paul, when almost the first question with which he must have been greeted on all sides would be, "And where is Barnabas?" For Barnabas was a man born to be respected and loved; and since Silas—great as may have been his gifts of utterance, and high as were his credentials [1]—would come among them as a perfect stranger, whom they could not welcome with equal heartiness, we may be sure that if Paul erred in that sad dissension, he must have been reminded of it, and have had cause to regret it at every turn.

From Derbe once more they passed to Lystra. Only one incident of their visit is told us, but it happily affected all the future of the great Apostle. In his former visit he had converted the young Timotheus, and it was in the house of the boy's mother Eunice,[2] and his grandmother Lois, that he and Silas were probably received. These two pious women were Jewesses who had now accepted the Christian faith. The marriage of Eunice with a Greek,[3] and the non-cir-

---

[1] προφήτης (Acts xv. 32).

[2] The name Eunice being purely Greek might seem to indicate previous association with Gentiles.

[3] At the same time, mixed marriages were far less strictly forbidden to women than to men. Drusilla and Berenice married Gentile princes, but compelled them first to accept circumcision. The omission of the covenant rite in the case of Timothy may have been owing to the veto of the child's Greek father.

cumcision of her son, indicate an absence of strict
Judaism which, since it was not inconsistent with "un-
-feigned faith," must have made them more ready to
receive the Gospel; and Paul himself bears witness to
their earnest sincerity, and to the careful training in the
Scriptures which they had given to their child.

We are led to suppose that Eunice was a widow, and if
so she showed a beautiful spirit of self-sacrifice in parting
with her only son. The youthful Timothy is one of the
best known and most lovable of that little circle of companions and followers—chiefly Gentile converts—who are
henceforth associated with the wanderings of St. Paul. Of
the many whom Paul loved, none were dearer to him than
the young disciple of Lystra. Himself without wife or
child, he adopted Timothy, and regarded him as a son in
all affectionate nearness. "To Timothy, my son;" "my
true son in the faith"—such are the terms in which he
addresses him;[1] and he reminds the Philippians how well
they knew "that, as a son with a father, he had slaved with
him for the Gospel."[2] And slight as are the touches
which enable us to realise the character of the young
Lystrenian, they are all wonderfully graphic and consistent. He was so blameless in character that both in his
native Lystra and in Iconium the brethren bore warm and
willing testimony to his worth.[3] In spite of a shyness

[1] 1 Tim. i. 2, 18; 2 Tim. ii. 2.

[2] Phil. ii. 22, ἐδούλευσεν εἰς τὸ εὐαγγέλιον.

[3] Whether Timothy belonged to Lystra or to Derbe is a matter of small
importance, but that in point of fact he did belong to Lystra seems so clear
from a comparison of Acts xvi. 1, 2; xx. 4; and 2 Tim. iii. 11, that it is strange
there should have been so much useless controversy on the subject. The
notion that "Gaius" in Acts xx. 4 could not be "of Derbe," because there is
a Gaius of Macedonia in xix. 29 (who may or may not be the Gaius of Rom.
xvi. 23; 1 Cor. i. 14), is like arguing that there could not be a Mr. Smith of
Monmouth and another Mr. Smith of Yorkshire; and the transference on this
ground of the epithet Δερβαῖος to Τιμόθεος in the absence of all evidence of
MSS. is mere frivolity.

and timidity which were increased by his youthfulness,[1] he was so entirely united in heart and soul with the Apostle that among his numerous friends and companions he found no one so genuine, so entirely unselfish, so sincerely devoted to the furtherance of the cause of Christ.[2] He was, in fact, more than any other the *alter ego* of the Apostle. Their knowledge of each other was mutual;[3] and one whose yearning and often lacerated heart had such deep need of a kindred spirit on which to lean for sympathy, and whose distressing infirmities rendered necessary to him the personal services of some affectionate companion, must have regarded the devoted tenderness of Timothy as a special gift of God to save him from being crushed by overmuch sorrow. And yet, much as Paul loved him, he loved his Churches more; and if any Church needs warning or guidance, or Paul himself desires to know how it prospers, Timothy is required to overcome his shrinking modesty,[4] to console the persecuted Churches of Macedonia,[5] or face the conceited turbulence of Corinth,[6] or to be the overseer of the Church of Ephesus,[7] with its many troubles from without and from within. In fact, no name is so closely associated with St. Paul's as that of Timothy. Not only were two Epistles addressed to him, but he is associated with St. Paul in the superscription of five;[8] he was with the Apostle during great part of his second missionary journey;[9] he was with him at Ephesus;[10] he accompanied him in his last

---

[1] Acts xvi. 2.

[2] Phil. ii. 20, οὐδένα γὰρ ἔχω ἰσόψυχον, ὅστις γνησίως τὰ περὶ ὑμῶν μεριμνήσει· οἱ πάντες γὰρ τὰ ἑαυτῶν ζητοῦσιν, οὐ τὰ Ἰησοῦ Χριστοῦ.

[3] 2 Tim. iii. 10, Σὺ δὲ παρηκολούθηκάς μου τῇ διδασκαλίᾳ, τῇ ἀγωγῇ, κ.τ.λ.

[4] 1 Cor. iv. 17; xvi. 10, ἀφόβως.

[5] Acts xix. 22; 1 Thess. iii. 2; Phil. ii. 18—20.

[6] 1 Cor. xvi. 10.

[7] 1 Tim. i. 3.　　　　　　　　　[8] 1, 2 Thess., 2 Cor., Phil., Col.

[9] Acts xvi. 3; xvii. 14; xviii. 5.　　[10] 1 Cor. iv. 17; xvi. 10.

voyage to Jerusalem;[1] he helped to comfort his first imprisonment at Rome;[2] he is urged, in the Second Epistle addressed to him, to hasten from Ephesus, to bring with him the cloak, books, and parchments which St. Paul had left with Carpus at Troas, and to join him in his second imprisonment before it is too late to see him alive.[3] Some sixteen years had elapsed between the days when Paul took Timothy as his companion at Lystra,[4] and the days when, in the weary desolation of his imprisoned age, he writes once more to this beloved disciple.[5] Yet even at this latter date St. Paul addresses him as though he were the same youth who had first accompanied him to the hallowed work. "To him," says Hausrath, " as to the Christian Achilles, the Timotheus-legend attributes eternal youth;" this being, according to the writer, one of the signs that the two pastoral Epistles addressed to Timothy were the work of a writer in the second century.[6] But surely it is obvious that if Timothy, when St. Paul first won him over to the faith of Christ, was not more than sixteen or seventeen years old, he would be still far short of the prime of life when the Second Epistle was addressed to him; and that, even if he were older, there is no more familiar experience than an old man's momentary forgetfulness that those whom he has known as boys have grown up to full manhood.[7]

---

[1] Acts xx. 4.   [2] Phil. ii. 18—20.   [3] 2 Tim. iv. 9, 13.
[4] *Circ.* A.D. 51.   [5] *Circ.* A.D. 66.
[6] Hausrath, p. 259. He admits that they "contain important historic indications."
[7] It has always been recognised as a most natural touch in Tennyson's poem, "The Grandmother," that she speaks of her old sons as though they were still lads. But even if Timotheus had reached the age of forty by the time he was appointed "Bishop" of Ephesus, there would be nothing incongruous in saying to him, Μηδείς σου τῆς νεότητος καταφρονείτω (1 Tim. iv. 12), or τὰς δὲ νεωτερικὰς ἐπιθυμίας φεῦγε (2 Tim. ii. 22), especially as these were written not many years after the μή τις οὖν αὐτὸν ἐξουθενήσῃ of 1 Cor. xvi. 11.

This was the youth whose companionship Paul now secured. Young as he was, the quick eye of Paul saw in him the spirit of loving and fearful duty—read the indications of one of those simple, faithful natures which combine the glow of courage with the bloom of modesty. When Jesus had sent forth His disciples He had sent them forth two and two; but this was only in their own native land. It was a very different thing to travel in all weathers, through the blinding dust and burning heat of the plains of Lycaonia, and over the black volcanic crags and shelterless mountain ranges of Asia. He had suffered from the departure of Mark in Pisidia, and henceforth we never find him without at least two associates—at this time Silas and Timothy; afterwards Titus and Timothy in Macedonia and Achaia, and Luke and Aristarchus in his journey to Rome.

It may surprise us that the first step he took was to circumcise Timothy; and that since the rite might be performed by any Israelite, he did it with his own hands.[1] We have, indeed, seen that he was in all probability driven to circumcise the Gentile Titus; but we are not told of any pressure put upon him to perform the same rite for Timothy, who, though the son of a Jewess, had grown up without it. Nothing is more certain than that, in St. Paul's opinion, circumcision was valueless. His conduct, therefore, can only be regarded as a second concession to, or rather a prevention and anticipation of, prejudices so strong that they might otherwise have rendered his work impossible. St. Luke says that it was done "on account of the Jews in those regions; for they all knew that his father was a Greek." Now, if this was generally known, whereas it was not so widely known that his mother was a

---

[1] By none, however, *except* an Israelite (*Abhôda Zara*, f. 27, 1).

Jewess, St. Paul felt that Timothy would everywhere be looked upon as an uncircumcised Gentile, and as such no Jew would eat with him, and it would be hopeless to attempt to employ him as a preacher of the Messiah in the synagogues, which they always visited as the beginning of their labours. If, on the other hand, it were known that he was by birth a Jewish boy—since the rule was that nationality went by the mother's side [1]—an uncircumcised Jew would be in every Ghetto an object of execration. If, then, Timothy was to be ordained to the work of the ministry, his circumcision was indispensable to his usefulness, and his Jewish parentage was sufficient to deprive the act of the dangerous significance which might much more easily be attached to it in the case of Titus. Obviously, too, it was better that Paul should do it spontaneously than that it should receive a factitious importance by being once more extorted from him in spite of protest. He did it, not in order to please himself, but that he might condescend to the infirmities of the weak.[2]

The circumcision was followed by a formal ordination. The whole Church was assembled; the youth made the public profession of his faith;[3] the elders and Paul himself solemnly laid their hands upon his head;[4] the prophetic voices which had marked him out for a great work[5] were confirmed by those who now charged him with the high duties which lay before him, and at the same time warned

---

[1] "Partus sequitur ventrem" is the rule of the Talmud (*Bechoroth*, 1, 4, &c.; Wetst. *ad loc.*). If the Jews knew that his mother was a Jewess, and yet that he had not received the "seal of the covenant," they would have treated him as a *mamzer*. (See Ewald, *Alterth.* 257.)

[2] Rom. xv. 1; 1 Cor. ix. 20.

[3] 1 Tim. vi. 12, ὁμολόγησας τὴν καλὴν ὁμολογίαν ἐνώπιον πολλῶν μαρτύρων.

[4] 1 Tim. iv. 14, τὸ χάρισμα ὃ ἐδόθη σοι διὰ προφητείας μετὰ ἐπιθέσεως τῶν χειρῶν τοῦ πρεσβυτερίου; 2 Tim. i. 6, ὃ ἐ τῆς ἐπιθέσεως τῶν χειρῶν μου.

[5] 1 Tim. i. 18, κατὰ τὰς προαγούσας ἐπὶ σὲ προφητείας. Compare the happy prognostications of Staupitz about the work of Luther.

him of the dangers which those duties involved;[1] the grace of the Holy Spirit descended like a flame into his heart,[2] and the gentle boy of Lystra was henceforth the consecrated companion of toils and wanderings, of which the issue was the destined conversion of the world.

The mission opened with every circumstance of encouragement. The threefold cord of this ministry was not quickly broken. At each city which they visited they announced the decisions arrived at by the Apostles and elders at Jerusalem,[3] and the Churches were strengthened in the faith, and grew in numbers daily.

In this way they traversed "the Phrygian and Galatian district."[4] There has been much speculation as to the towns of Phrygia at which they rested, but in the absolute silence of St. Luke, and in the extreme looseness of the term "Phrygian," we cannot be sure that St. Paul preached in a single town of the region which is usually included under that term. That he did not found any church seems clear from the absence of allusion to any Phrygian community in the New Testament. The conjecture that he travelled on this occasion to the far distant Colossæ is most improbable, even if it be not excluded by the obvious inference from his own language.[5] All that we can reasonably suppose is that after leaving Iconium he proceeded

---

[1] 1 Tim. i. 18, ἵνα στρατεύῃ ἐν αὐταῖς τὴν καλὴν στρατείαν ; cf. iv. 14; vi. 12.

[2] 2 Tim. i. 6, ἀναζωπυρεῖν (= "to fan into fresh flame," κυρίως τοὺς ἄνθρακας φυσᾶν, Suid.; σφοδρότερον τὸ πῦρ ἐργάζεσθαι, Theophyl.) τὸ χάρισμα τοῦ Θεοῦ, ὅ ἐστιν ἐν σοὶ, κ.τ.λ.

[3] In a loose way even Antioch and Iconium might be regarded as Churches of Cilicia, Tarsus (as appears from coins, Lewin, i. 171) being regarded as a capital of Lycaonia, Isauria, and even of Caria. Further, the circular letter had been drawn up with more or less express reference to what had taken place in these Churches (Acts xv. 12).

[4] The true reading is τὴν Φρυγίαν καὶ Γαλατικὴν χώραν (א, A, B, C, D).

[5] Col. i. 4, 6, 7; ii. 1.

to Antioch in Pisidia—since there could be no reason
why he should neglect to confirm the Church which he
had founded there—and then crossed the ridge of the
Paroreia to Philomelium, from which it would have
been possible for him either to take the main road to
the great Phrygian town of Synnada, and then turn
north-eastwards to Pessinus, or else to enter Galatia by
a shorter and less frequented route which did not run
through any Phrygian town of the slightest importance.
It does not seem to have been any part of St. Paul's
plan to evangelise Phrygia. Perhaps he may have originally intended to make his way by the road through
Apamea, to Colossæ and Laodicea, and to go down
the valley of the Mæander to Ephesus. But if so, this
intention was hindered by the guidance of the Holy
Spirit.[1] Such providential hindrances to a course which
seemed so obvious may well have been mysterious to
St. Paul; but they appear less so to us when, view-
ing them in the light of history, we see that otherwise
the Epistle to the Galatians might never have been
written, and that thus the whole course of Christian
theology might have been entirely changed.

Of any work in Phrygia, therefore, there was nothing
to narrate;[2] but we may well deplore St. Luke's non-
acquaintance with the details of that visit to Galatia,

---

[1] It will be seen that I take the clause κωλυθέντες, κ.τ.λ. (Acts xvi. 6) retro-
spectively—i.e., as the reason assigned for their divergence into the Phrygian
and Galatian district. If they entertained the design of preaching in Asia—i.e.,
in Lydia—the natural road to it would have been from Antioch of Pisidia, and it
is hardly likely that they would have intentionally turned aside to the semi-
barbarous regions of Phrygia and Galatia first; indeed, we have St. Paul's
own express admission (Gal. iv. 13) that his evangelisation of Galatia was the
result of an accidental sickness. The permission to preach in Asia was only
delayed (Acts xix. 10).

[2] That some converts were made is implied by Acts xviii. 23. The absence
of a definite Phrygian Church is seen in the silence about any collection there.

which were deeply interesting and important, and of which we are now left to discover the incidents by piecing the fragmentary notices and allusions of the Epistle.

We may suppose that on · finding it impossible to preach at this time in the great cities of Lydian Asia,[1] St. Paul and his companions next determined to make their way to the numerous Jewish communities on the shores of the Euxine. They seem to have had no intention to preach among a people so new to them, and apparently so little promising, as the Galatians. But God had other designs for them; they were detained in Galatia, and their stay was attended with very memorable results.

St. Luke, who uses the ordinary geographical term, must undoubtedly have meant by the term Galatia that central district of the Asian peninsula[2] which was inhabited by a people known to the ancient world under the names of Celts, Galatians, Gauls, and (more recently) Gallo-Greeks. Their history was briefly this. When the vast tide of Aryan migration began to set to the westward from the valleys of the Oxus and the plains of Turkestan, the Celtic family was among the earliest that streamed away from their native seats.[3] They gradually occupied a great part of the centre and west of Europe, and various tribes of the family were swept hither and thither by different currents, as they met with

[1] "Asia" in the Acts (cf. Catull. xlvi. 5) seems always to mean the region round the old "Asian meadow" of Homer (Il. ii. 461)—i.e., the entire valley and plain of the Cayster—i.e., Lydia. Every one of "the seven churches which are in Asia" (Rev. i.—iii.) is Lydian.

[2] The term Asia Minor is first used by Orosius in the fourth century (Oros. i. 2).

[3] On the Celtic migrations, see the author's *Families of Speech*, 2nd ed. (reprinted in *Language and Languages*), p. 329.

E E

special obstacles to their unimpeded progress. One of
their Brennuses,[1] four centuries before the Christian era,
inflicted on Rome its deepest humiliation. Another,
one hundred and eleven years later,[2] filled Northern Greece
with terror and rapine, and when his hordes were driven
back by the storms and portents which seconded the
determined stand of the Greeks at Delphi, they joined
another body under Leonnorius and Lutarius,[3] struggled
across the Hellespont in the best way they could, and
triumphantly established themselves in the western regions
of Asia Minor. But their exactions soon roused an opposition which led to an effectual curbing of their power,
and they were gradually confined in the central region

---

[1] B.C. 390. The word Brennus is a Latinised form of the title which
is preserved in the Welsh *brenin*, "king."

[2] B.C. 279.

[3] Lív. xxxviii. 16. These names—Celtic words of obscure origin with
Latin terminations—are eagerly seized on by German travellers and commentators, and identified with Leonard and Lothair (Luther), in order to
prove that the people of Galatia were not Celts, but Teutons. Why both
French and Germans should be so eager to claim affinities with these not very
creditable Galatians I cannot say; but meanwhile it must be regarded as
certain that the Galatæ were Celts, and not only Celts, but Cymric Celts.
The only other arguments, besides these two names, adduced by Wieseler and
other German writers are— (1) The name *Germanopolis*—a late and hideous
hybrid which, at the best, only points to the settlement of some Teutonic
community among the Gauls; (2) the tribe of Teutobodiaci, about whom we
know too little to say what the name means; and (3) the assertion of St.
Jerome that the Galatians (whom he had personally visited) spoke a language
like the people of Trèves (Jer. in *Ep. Gal.* ii. *praef.*). This argument, however, tells precisely in the opposite direction, since the expressions of Cæsar
and Tacitus decisively prove that the Treveri were Gauls (Tac. *Ann.* i. 43,
H. iv. 71; Cæs. *B. G.* ii. 4, &c.), though they aped Teutonic peculiarities
(Cæs. *B. G.* viii. 25; Tac. *Germ.* 28). Every trait of their character, every
certain phenomenon of their language, every proved fact of their history,
shows beyond the shadow of a doubt that the Galatæ, or Gauls, were not
Slavs, nor Teutons, but Celts; and it is most probable that the names Galatæ
and Celtæ are etymologically identical. The ingenuity which elaborately
sets itself to overthrow accepted and demonstrated conclusions leads to endless
waste of time and space. Any who are curious to see more on the subject
will find it in the Excursus of Dr. Lightfoot's *Galatians*, pp. 229—240.

which is partly traversed by the valleys of the San-
garius and the Halys. Here we find them in three
tribes, of which each had its own capital. Bordering on
Phrygia were the Tolistobogii, with their capital Pessinus; in the centre the Tectosages, with their capital
Ancyra; and to the eastward, bordering on Pontus, were
the Trocmi, with their capital Tavium.[1] Originally the
three tribes were each divided into four tetrarchies, but
at length they were united (B.C. 65) under Deiotarus,
tetrarch of the Tolistobogii, the Egbert of Galatian
history.[2] The Romans under Cn. Manlius Vulso had
conquered them in B.C. 189,[3] but had left them nominally independent; and in B.C. 36 Mark Antony made
Amyntas king. On his death, in B.C. 25, Galatia was
joined to Lycaonia and part of Pisidia, and made a
Roman province; and since it was one of the Imperial
provinces, it was governed by a Propraetor. This was
its political condition when Paul entered Pessinus, which,
though one of the capitals, lies on the extreme frontier,
and at that time called itself Sebaste of the Tolistobogii.[4]

The providential cause which led to St. Paul's stay in
the country was, as he himself tells us, a severe attack of
illness: and the manner in which he alludes to it gives us
reason to infer that it was a fresh access of agony from that
"stake in the flesh" which I believe to have been acute
ophthalmia, accompanied, as it often is, by violent cere-

---

[1] Tolistobogii, or Tolosatobogii, seems to combine the elements of Tolosa
(Toulouse) and Boii. The etymologies of Tectosages (who also occur in
Aquitaine, Cæs. *B. G.* vi. 24; Strabo, p. 187) and Trocmi are uncertain.
Other towns of the Galatæ were Abrostola, Amorium, Tolosochorion, towns of
the Tolistobogii; Corbeus and Aspona, of the Tectosages; Mithradatium and
Danala, of the Trocmi.

[2] Strabo, p. 567.

[3] Liv. xxxviii. 12. "Hi jam degeneres sunt; mixti et Gallograeci vere,
quod appellantur."

[4] It is now a mere heap of ruins.

bral disturbance.[1] In his letter to his Galatian converts he makes a touching appeal, which in modern phraseology might run as follows:[2]—"Become as I am, brethren, I beseech you" (*i.e.*, free from the yoke of external and useless ordinances), "for I, too, made myself as you are.[3] Jew that I was, I placed myself on the level of you Gentiles, and now I want you to stand with me on that same level, instead of trying to make yourselves Jews. I do not wish to speak by way of complaint about you. You never did *me* any personal wrong.[4] Nay, you know that when I preached the Gospel among you, on my first visit, it was in consequence of an attack of sickness, which detained me in the midst of a journey; you could not, therefore, feel any gratitude to me as though I had come with the express purpose of preaching to you; and besides, at that time

[1] On this subject see *infra*, Excursus XL, "The Stake in the Flesh."

[2] Gal. iv. 12—14. This passage may serve to illustrate the necessity of a new English version founded on better readings. Thus in verse 12, the "*be*" of our version should be rendered "become;" and the "*I am* as you are" should be "I became;" the "*have* not injured" should be "*did* not injure," since the tense is an aorist, not a perfect, and the allusion is to some fact which we do not know. In verse 13, the δὲ ought not to be left unnoticed; "through infirmity of the flesh" is a positive mistake (since this would require δι' ἀσθενείας, per) for "on account of an attack of illness," as in Thuc. vi. 102; τὸ πρότερον probably means "the former time," not "at the first." In verse 14 the best reading is not τὸν πειρασμόν μου, but τὸν π. ὑμῶν (א, A, B, C, D, F, G, &c., and "faciliori lectioni praestat ardua"); and ἐξεπτύσατε is stronger than "rejected." In verse 15, τοῦ, not τίς, is probably the right reading, and ἦν should certainly be omitted—and the meaning is not "where is *the blessedness ye spake of*," but "your self-congratulation on my arrival among you;" the ἂν should certainly be omitted with ἐξωρύξατε, as it makes the Greek idiom far more vivid, although inadmissible in English (cf. John xv. 22; xix. 11). In verse 16 the ὥστε draws a conclusion, "so that," which is suddenly and delicately changed into a question, "have I?" instead of "I have." It is only by studying the intensely characteristic Greek of St. Paul that we are able, as it were, to lay our hands on his breast and feel every beat of his heart.

[3] Gal. ii. 17; 1 Cor. ix. 21.

[4] Cf. 2 Cor. ii. 5, οὐκ ἐμὲ λελύπηκεν.

weak, agonised with pain, liable to fits of delirium, with my eyes red and ulcerated by that disease by which it pleases God to let Satan buffet me, you might well have been tempted to regard me as a deplorable object. My whole appearance must have been a trial to you—a temptation to you to reject me. But you did not; you were very kind to me. You might have treated me with contemptuous indifference;[1] you might have regarded me with positive loathing;[2] but instead of this you honoured, you loved me, you received me as though I were an angel—nay, even as though I were the Lord of angels, as though I were even He whom I preached unto you. How glad you were to see me! How eagerly you congratulated yourselves and me on the blessed accident— nay, rather, on the blessed providence of God, which had detained me amongst you![3] So generous, so affectionate were you towards me, that I bear you witness that to aid me as I sat in misery in the darkened rooms, unable to bear even a ray of light without excruciating pain, you would, if that could have helped me, have plucked out your eyes and given them to me."[4]

[1] Cf. 2 Cor.x.10. His bodily presence is ἀσθενὴς, and his speech ἐξουθενημένος.

[2] Lit., " Ye did not despise nor loathe your temptation in my flesh;" one of the nobly careless expressions of a writer who is swayed by emotion, not by grammar. It means "You did not loathe," &c., " me, though my bodily aspect was a temptation to you." "Grandis tentatio discipulis, si magister infirmetur" (Primas.). On the possible connexion of ἐξεπτύσατε with epilepsy see infra, p. 657). It would be most accurately explained by ophthalmia.

[3] The sufferings of St. Paul from travels when in a prostrate condition of body have been aptly compared by Dean Howson to those of St. Chrysostom and Henry Martyn in Pontus. They both lie buried at Tocat (Comana). (C. and H. i. 295.)

[4] No one disputes that this in itself may be a metaphorical expression for any severe sacrifice, as in Cat. lxxxii. :—

"Quinti si tibi vis oculos debere Catullum,
Aut aliud si quid carius est oculis."

But how incomparably more vivid and striking, and how much more germane to the occasion, does the expression become if it was an attack of ophthalmia from which Paul was suffering!

Nothing is more natural than that the traversing of vast distances over the burning plains and freezing mountain passes of Asia Minor—the constant changes of climate, the severe bodily fatigue, the storms of fine and blinding dust, the bites and stings of insects, the coarseness and scantness of daily fare—should have brought on a return of his malady to one whose health was so shattered as that of Paul. And doubtless it was the anguish and despair arising from the contemplation of his own heartrending condition, which added to his teaching that intensity, that victorious earnestness, which made it so all-prevailing with the warm-hearted Gauls.[1] If they were ready to receive him as Christ Jesus, it was because Christ Jesus was the Alpha and the Omega, the beginning and the end of all his teaching to them. And hence, in his appeal to their sense of shame, he uses one of his own inimitably picturesque words to say, " Senseless Galatians, what evil eye bewitched you?[2] before whose eyes, to avert them from such evil glances, I painted as it were visibly and large the picture of Jesus Christ crucified."[3]

[1] No doubt the Galatians with whom he had to deal were not the Gallic peasants who were despised and ignorant (" paene servorum loco habentur," Cæs. B. G. vi. 13); but the Gallo-græci, the more cultivated and Hellenised Galli of the towns. (Long in Dict. Geogr. s.v.)

[2] Gal. iii. 1. Omit τῇ ἀληθείᾳ μὴ πείθεσθαι with אּ, A, B, D, E, F, G, &c., and ἐν ὑμῖν with אּ, A, B, C.

[3] Gal. iii. 1, οἷς κατ᾽ ὀφθαλμοὺς Ἰησοῦς Χριστὸς προεγράφη ἐσταυρωμένος. It is true that προγράφειν is elsewhere always used in the sense of " to write before" (Rom. xv. 5; Eph. iii. 3), and not " to post" or " placard" (Ar. Av. 4;0), even in Hellenistic and late Greek (1 Macc. x. 36; Jude 4; Justin, Apol. ii. 52, B); but the sense and the context here seem to show that St. Paul used it—as we often find modern compounds used—in a different sense (προεζωγραφήθη). The large picture of Jesus Christ crucified was set up before the mental vision of these spiritual children of Galatia (" Dicitur fascinus proprie infantibus nocere"—Primas.) to avert their wandering glances from the dangerous witchery (τίς ὑμᾶς ἐβάσκανεν) of the evil eye (רַע עַיִן, Prov. xxiii. 6; Ecclus. xiv. 6, &c.; βάσκανοι, Ælian,

But the zealous readiness of the Galatians, their impulsive affection, the demonstrative delight with which they accepted the new teaching, was not solely due to the pity which mingled with the admiration inspired by the new teacher. It may have been due, in some small measure, to the affinities presented by the new religion to the loftiest and noblest parts of their old beliefs; and at any rate, being naturally of a religious turn of mind,[1] they may have been in the first instance attracted by the hearing of a doctrine which promised atonement in consequence of a shedding of blood. But far more than this, the quick conversion of the Galatians was due to the mighty outpouring of the Spirit which followed Paul's preaching, and to the new powers[2] which were wrought in his converts by their admission into the Church. But while these were the results among the truer converts, there must have also been many whose ready adhesion was due to that quick restlessness, that eager longing for change, which characterised them,[3] as it characterised the kindred family of Greeks with which they were at this time largely mingled. It was the too quick springing of the good

---

H. A. i. 53). We may be reminded of the huge emblazoned banner with which Augustine and his monks caught the eye of Ethelbert at Canterbury.

[1] "Natio est omnis Gallorum admodum dedita religionibus" (Cæs. B. G. vi. 16).

[2] Gal. iii. 5, ἐπιχορηγῶν (= abundantly supplying; cf. Phil. i. 19; 2 Pet. i. 5) ὑμῖν τὸ πνεῦμα καὶ ἐνεργῶν δυνάμεις ἐν ὑμῖν. The latter clause may undoubtedly mean "working miracles among you;" but the parallels of 1 Cor. xii. 10; Matt. xiv. 2, seem to show that it means "working powers in you." See, too, Isa. xxvi. 12; Heb. xiii. 21. ἐνέργημα means, as Bishop Andrewes says, "a work inwrought in us." In 1 Cor. xii. 10 the "operations of powers" are distinguished from the "gifts of healings."

[3] Cæsar complains of their "mobilitas," "levitas," and "infirmitas animi," and says, "in consiliis capiendis mobiles et novis plerumque rebus studentes" (B. G. ii. 1; iv. 5; iii. 10; and Liv. x. 28).

seed on poor and shallow soil; it was the sudden flaming
of fire among natures as light, as brittle, as inflammable
as straw. The modification of an old religion, the hearty
adoption of a new one, the combination of an antique
worship with one which was absolutely recent, and as
unlike it as is possible to conceive, had already been
illustrated in Galatian history. As Celts they had
brought with them into Asia their old Druidism, with its
haughty priestcraft, and cruel expiations.[1] Yet they
had already incorporated with this the wild nature-
worship of Agdistis or Cybele, the mother of the gods.
They believed that the black stone which had fallen
from heaven was her image, and for centuries after it
had been carried off to Rome[2] they continued to revere
her venerable temple, to give alms to her raving eunuchs,
to tell of the vengeance which she had inflicted on the
hapless Atys, and to regard the pine groves of Dindymus
with awe.[3] But yet, while this Phrygian cult was
flourishing at Pessinus, and commanding the services of
its hosts of mutilated priests, and while at Tavium the
main object of worship was a colossal bronze Zeus of the
ordinary Greek type,[4] at Ancyra, on the other hand, was
established the Roman deification of the Emperor Augustus, to whom a temple of white marble, still existing in
ruins, had been built by the common contributions of

---

[1] Strabo, xii. 5, p. 567, who tells us that they met in council at Dryne-
metum, or "Oak-shrine" (drw cf. δρῦς, and nemed, "temple"), as Vernemetum
= "Great-shrine" (Venant. Fortun. i. 9), and Augustonemetum = "Augustus-
shrine."

[2] B.C. 204. See Liv. xxix. 10, 11. The name of the town was dubiously
connected with Πισσῖν. (Herodian. i. 11.)

[3] Liv. xxxviii. 18: Strabo, p. 489; Diod. Sic. iii. 58. Julian found the
worship of Cybele still languishing on at Pessinus in A.D. 363, and made a
futile attempt to galvanise it into life (Amm. Marc. xxii. 9). The lucrative
features in the worship of Cybele—the sale of oracles and collection of alms
—may have had their attraction for the avaricious Gauls.

[4] Strabo, xii. 5. The very site of Tavium is unknown.

Asia.[1] Paul must have seen, still fresh and unbroken, the celebrated *Monumentum Ancyranum*, the will of Augustus engraved on the marble of the temple, and copied from the inscription set up by his own command upon bronze tablets in front of his mausoleum; but while he may have glanced at it with interest, and read with still deeper pleasure on one of the pillars the decree in which the Emperor had rewarded the friendliness of the Jews by a grant of religious immunity,[2] he must have thought with some pity and indignation of the frivolity of spirit which could thus readily combine the oldest and the newest of idolatrous aberrations— the sincere and savage orgies of Dindymene with the debasing flattery of an astute intriguer—the passionate abandonment to maddening religious impulse, and the calculating adoration of political success. In point of fact, the three capitals of the three tribes furnished data for an epitome of their history, and of their character. In passing from Pessinus to Ancyra and Tavium the Apostle saw specimens of cults curiously obsolete side by side with others which were ridiculously new. He passed from Phrygian nature-worship through Greek mythology to Roman conventionalism. He could not but have regarded this as a bad sign, and he would have seen a sad illustration of the poorer qualities which led to his own enthusiastic reception, if he could have read the description in a Greek rhetorician long afterwards of the Galatians being so eager to seize upon what was new, that if they did but get a glimpse of the cloak of a philo-

---

[1] Ancyra—then called Sebaste Tectosagum, in honour of Augustus—is now the flourishing commercial town of Angora. The Baulos-Dagh—Paul-Mountain—near Angora still reminds the traveller of St. Paul's visit to these cities, which is also rendered more probable by their having been early episcopal sees.

[2] Jos. *Antt.* xvi. 6, § 2. On Cæsar-worship see Tac. *Ann.* iv. 55, 56.

sopher, they caught hold of and clung to it at once, as
steel filings do to a magnet.[1] In fact, as he had bitter
cause to learn afterwards, the religious views of the Gauls
were more or less a reflex of the impressions of the
moment, and their favourite sentiments the echo of the
language used by the last comer. But on his first visit
their faults all seemed to be in the background. Their
tendencies to revelries and rivalries, to drunkenness and
avarice, to vanity and boasting, to cabals and fits of rage,
were in abeyance,[2]—checked if not mastered by the powerful influence of their new faith, and in some instances,
we may hope, cured altogether by the grace of the Holy
Spirit of God. All that he saw was their eagerness and
affection, their absence of prejudice, and willingness to
learn—all that vivacity and warmheartedness which were
redeeming points in their Celtic character.[3]

How long he was detained among them by his illness
we are not told, but it was long enough to found several
churches, one perhaps in each of the three capitals,
and it may be in some of the minor towns. His success
was clearly among the Gauls; and in the absence of all
personal salutations in his Epistle, we cannot tell whether
any of the aboriginal Phrygians, or Greek settlers, or of

---

[1] Themistius, *Or.* xxiii., p. 299; *ap.* Wetstein in Gal. i. 6. καὶ τριβωνίου
παραφανέντος ἐκκρέμανται εὐθὺς ὥσπερ τῆς λίθου τὰ σιδήρια.

[2] Gal. v. 7, 15, 21, 26. Diodorus Siculus says that they were so excessively drunken (κάτοινοι καθ᾽ ὑπερβολήν) that they drenched themselves with
the raw wine imported by merchants, and drank with such violent eagerness as either to stupefy themselves to sleep or enrage themselves to madness
(v. 26; cf. Ammian. Marc. xv. 12). He also calls them "extravagantly
avaricious" (v. 27; Liv. xxxviii. 27) and testifies to their disorderly and
gesticulative fits of rage (v. 31; Ammian. Marc. *l.c.*).

[3] The vitality of traits of character in many races is extraordinary, and
every one will recognise some of these Celtic peculiarities in the Welsh, and
others in the Irish. Ancient testimonies to their weaknesses and vices have
often been collected, but the brighter features which existed then, as they do
still, are chiefly witnessed to by St. Paul.

the Roman governing class, embraced the faith. But though he is avowedly writing to those who had been Gentiles and idolators,[1] there must have been a considerable number of converts from the large Jewish population[2] which had been attracted to Galatia by its fertility, its thriving commerce, and the privileges which secured them the free exercise of their religion. These Jews, and their visitors from Jerusalem, as we shall see hereafter, proved to be a dangerous element in the infant Church.

The success of this unintended mission may have detained St. Paul for a little time even after his convalescence; and as he retraced his journey from Tavium to Pessinus he would have had the opportunity which he always desired of confirming his recent converts in the faith. From Pessinus the missionaries went towards Mysia, and laid their plans to pass on to the numerous and wealthy cities of western Bithynia, at that time a senatorial province. But once more their plans, in some way unknown to us, were divinely overruled. The "Spirit of Jesus"[3] did not suffer them to enter a country which was

[1] Gal. iv. 8; v. 2; vi. 12, &c. On the other hand, iv. 9 has been quoted (Jowett, i. 187) as "an almost explicit statement that they were Jews;" this is not, however, necessarily the case. Doubtless, writing to a church in which there were both Jews and Gentiles, St. Paul may use expressions which are sometimes more appropriate to one class, sometimes to the other, but "the weak and beggarly elements" to which the converts are *returning* may include Gentile as well as Jewish ritualisms; and some of them may have passed through both phases.

[2] St. Peter in addressing the Diaspora of Galatia and other districts (1 Pet. i. 1) must have had Jews as well as Gentiles in view. The frequency of Old Testament quotations and illustrations in the Epistle to the Galatians is perhaps a proof that not a few of the converts had been originally proselytes. Otherwise it would be impossible to account for the fact that "in none of St. Paul's Epistles has the cast of the reasoning a more Jewish character" (Jowett, i. 186). Gal. iii. 27, 28 may allude to the existence of converts from both classes.

[3] Acts xvi. 7. This ἅπαξ λεγόμενον, which is the undoubtedly correct reading (א, A, B, C², D, E, and many versions and Fathers), perhaps indicates that St. Luke is here using some document which furnished him with brief notes of

destined indeed to be early converted, but not by them,
and which plays a prominent part in the history of early
Christianity.[1] Once more divinely thwarted in the fulfilment of their designs, they made no attempt to preach
in Mysia,[2] which in its bleak and thinly populated uplands
offered but few opportunities for evangelisation, but
pressed on directly to Troas, where an event awaited them
of immense importance, which was sufficient to explain
the purpose of Him who had shaped the ends which they
themselves had so differently rough-hewn.

From the slopes of Ida,[3] Paul and Silvanus with their
young attendant descended the ravine which separated
the mountain from the port and colony. They were on
classic ground. Every step they took revealed scenes to
which the best and brightest poetry of Greece had given
an immortal interest. As they emerged from the pine
groves of the many-fountained hill, with its exquisite
legend of Œnone and her love, they saw beneath them the

" Ringing plains of windy Troy,"

where the great heroes of early legend had so often

" Drunk delight of battle with their peers."

But if they had ever heard of

" The face that launched a thousand ships,
And sacked the topmost towers of Ilion,"

or looked with any interest on the Simois and the Sca-

this part of Paul's journeys. The remarkable fact that in the *Filioque* controversy neither side appealed to this expression shows how early the text
had been altered by the copyists.

[1] See Pliny's letter to Trajan (x. 97), when he was Proconsul of Bithynia,
asking advice how to deal with the Christians.

[2] This must be the meaning of παρελθόντες (=ἀφέντες, "neglecting"). It
cannot be *translated* "passing through," which would be διελθόντες, though a
glance at the map will show that they *must* have passed through Mysia without stopping. The absence of synagogues and the remote, unknown character
of the region account for this.   [3] Acts xvi. 8, κατέβησαν.

mander, and the huge barrows of Ajax and Achilles, they do not allude to them. Their minds were full of other thoughts.

The town at which they now arrived had been founded by the successors of Alexander, and had been elevated into a colony with the *Jus Italicum*. This privilege had been granted to the inhabitants solely because of the romantic interest which the Romans took in the legendary cradle of their greatness, an interest which almost induced Constantine to fix there, instead of at Byzantium, the capital of the Eastern Empire. Of any preaching in Alexandria Troas nothing is told us. On three separate occasions at least St. Paul visited it.[1] It was there that Carpus lived, who was probably his host, and he found it a place peculiarly adapted for the favourable reception of the Gospel.[2] On this occasion, however, his stay was very short,[3] because he was divinely commanded to other work.

St. Paul had now been labouring for many years among Syrians, Cilicians, and the mingled races of Asia Minor; but during that missionary activity he had been at Roman colonies like Antioch in Pisidia, and must have been thrown very frequently into the society of Greeks and Latins. He was himself a Roman citizen, and the constant allusions of his Epistles show that he, like St. Luke, must have been struck with admiration for the order, the discipline, the dignity, the reverence for law which characterised the Romans, and especially for the bravery, the determination, the hardy spirit of self-denial which actuated the Roman soldier.[4] He tells us, later in

[1] Acts xx. 1, 2, compared with 2 Cor. ii. 12; 1 Cor. xvi. 5—9; and Acts xx. 6; and 2 Tim. iv. 13.

[2] 2 Cor. ii. 12.

[3] Acts xvi. 10, εὐθέως ἐζητήσαμεν implies that they took the first ship which they could find for a voyage to Macedonia.

[4] This is shown by the many military and agonistic metaphors in his Epistles.

his life, how frequently his thoughts had turned towards
Rome itself,[1] and as he brooded on the divinely indicated
future of Christianity, we cannot doubt that while wandering round the then busy but now land-locked and
desolate harbour of Troas, he had thrown many a wistful
glance towards the hills of Imbros and Samothrace; and
perhaps when on some clear evening the colossal peak of
Athos was visible, it seemed like some vast angel who
beckoned him to carry the good tidings to the west. The
Spirit of Jesus had guided him hitherto in his journey,
had prevented him from preaching in the old and famous
cities of Asia, had forbidden him to enter Bithynia, had
driven the stake deeper into his flesh, that he might
preach the word among the Gauls. Anxiously must he
have awaited further guidance;—and it came. In the
night a Macedonian soldier[2] stood before him, exhorting
him with these words, "Cross over into Macedonia and
help us." When morning dawned Paul narrated the
vision to his companions,[3] "and immediately we sought,"
says the narrator, who here, for the first time, appears as
the companion of the Apostle, "to go forth into Macedonia, inferring that the Lord has called us to preach the
Gospel to them." With such brevity and simplicity is the
incident related which of all others was the most important
in introducing the Gospel of Christ to the most advanced
and active races of the world, and among them to those races
in whose hands its future destinies must inevitably rest.

[1] Acts xix. 21; cf. Rom. i. 13—"Oftentimes I purposed to come to you;"
xv. 23—"I have had a great desire these many years to come to you." These
passages were written from Achaia—probably from Corinth—six or seven
years after this date.

[2] The ἀνήρ and the ἑστώς, and the instant recognition that it was a
Macedonian, perhaps imply this. It is called an ὅραμα, which is used of
impressions more distinct than those of dreams. Acts x. 3, ἐν ὁράματι φανερῶς.
Matt. xvii. 9 (the Transfiguration).

[3] D. διεγερθεὶς οὖν διηγήσατο τὸ ὅραμα ἡμῖν (Acts xvi. 10).

The other incident of this visit to the Troas is the meeting of Paul with Luke, the author of the Acts of the Apostles and the Gospel. This meeting is indicated with profound modesty by the sudden use of the pronoun "we;" but even without this the vivid accuracy of detail in the narrative which immediately ensues, is in such striking contrast with the meagreness of much that has gone before, that we should have been driven to conjecture the presence of the writer on board the little vessel that now slipped its hawsers from one of the granite columns which we still see lying prostrate on the lonely shores of the harbour of Troas.

And this meeting was a happy one for Paul; for, of all the fellow-workers with whom he was thrown, Timotheus alone was dearer to him than Luke. From the appearance and disappearance of the first personal pronoun in the subsequent chapters of the Acts,[1] we see that he accompanied St. Paul to Philippi, and rejoined him there some seven years afterwards, never again to part with him so long as we are able to pursue his history. How deeply St. Paul was attached to him appears in the title "the beloved physician;" how entire was his fidelity is seen in the touching notice, "Only Luke is with me." He shared his journeys, his dangers, his shipwreck; he shared and cheered his long imprisonments, first at Cæsarea, then at Rome. More than all, he became the biographer of the Great Apostle, and to his allegiance, to his ability, to his accurate preservation of facts, is due nearly all that we

---

[1] The "we" begins in Acts xvi. 10; it ends when Paul leaves Philippi, xvii. 1. It is resumed at Philippi at the close of the third missionary journey, xx. 5, and continues till the arrival at Jerusalem, xxi. 18. It again appears in xxvii. 1, and continues throughout the journey to Rome. Luke was also with the Apostle during his first (Col. iv. 14; Philem. 24) and second imprisonments (2 Tim. iv. 11). It is far from certain that 2 Cor. viii. 18 refers to him.

know of one who laboured more abundantly than all the
Apostles, and to whom, more than to any of them, the cause
of Christ is indebted for its stability and its dissemination.

Of Luke himself, beyond what we learn of his movements and of his character from his own writings, we know
but little.   There is no reason to reject the unanimous
tradition that he was by birth an Antiochene,[1] and it is
clear from St. Paul's allusions that he was a Gentile
convert, and that he had not been circumcised.[2]   That he
was a close observer, a careful narrator, a man of cultivated intellect, and possessed of a good Greek style,[3] we
see from his two books; and they also reveal to us a
character gentle and manly, sympathetic and self-denying.
The incidental allusion of St. Paul shows us that he was a
physician, and this allusion is singularly confirmed by his
own turns of phrase.[4]   The rank of a physician in those

[1] Euseb. *H. E.* iii. 4; Jer. *De Virr. Illustr.*   Such allusions as "Nicolas, a
proselyte of Antioch," and the mention of Christians important there, but
otherwise unknown, lend probability to this tradition (cf. xi. 20; xiii. 1, &c.).
If we could attach any importance to the reading of D in Acts xi. 28
(συνεστραμμένων δὲ ἡμῶν), it would show that Luke had been at Antioch
during the year when Paul and Barnabas were working there before the famine.
The name Lucas is an abbreviation of Lucanus, as Silas of Silvanus; but the
notion that they were the same person is preposterous.

[2] Col. iv. 10, 11, 14.

[3] As an incidental confirmation that he was a Gentile, Bishop Wordsworth
(on 1 Thess. ii. 9) notices that he says "day and night " (Acts ix. 24), whereas
when he is reporting the speeches of St. Paul (Acts xx. 31; xxvi. 7, in the
Greek) he, like St. Paul himself (1 Thess. iii. 10; 2 Thess. iii. 8; 1 Tim. v. 5,
&c.), always says "night and day," in accordance with the Jewish notion that
the night preceded the day.   A more decisive indication that Luke was a
Gentile is Acts i. 19, τῇ ἰδίᾳ διαλέκτῳ αὐτῶν, slipped into St. Peter's speech.
"Lucas, medicus Antiochensis, ut scripta ejus indicant " (Jer.).

[4] See a highly ingenious paper by Dr. Plumptre on St. Luke and St. Paul
(*The Expositor*, No. xx., Aug., 1876).   He quotes the following indications of
medical knowledge :—The combination of feverish attacks with dysentery (Acts
xxviii. 8), and the use of τιμή in the sense (?) of *honorarium ; βάσεις* and *σφυρὰ*
in Acts iii. 7 (cf. Hippocrates, p. 637); the incrustation caused by ophthalmia
(Acts ix. 18) ; ἔκστασις (Acts x. 9, 10) ; σκωληκόβρωτος (Acts xii. 23) ; " Physician,
heal thyself," only in Luke iv. 23; θρόμβοι (Luke xxii. 44), &c.

days was not in any respect so high as now it is, and
does not at all exclude the possibility that St. Luke
may have been a freedman; but on this and all else
which concerns him Scripture and tradition leave us
entirely uninformed. That he was familiar with naval
matters is strikingly shown in his account of the shipwreck, and it has even been conjectured that he exercised
his art in the huge and crowded merchant vessels which
were incessantly coasting from point to point of the
Mediterranean.[1] Two inferences, at any rate, arise from
the way in which his name is introduced: one that he had
already made the acquaintance of St. Paul, perhaps at
Antioch; the other that, though he had some special connection with Philippi and Troas, his subsequent close
attachment to the Apostle in his journeys and imprisonments may have arisen from a desire to give him the
benefit of medical skill and attention in his frequent
attacks of sickness.[2] The lingering remains of that illness
which prostrated St. Paul in Galatia may have furnished
the first reason why it became necessary for Luke to
accompany him, and so to begin the fraternal companionship which must have been one of the richest blessings of
a sorely troubled life.

---

[1] Smith, *Voy. and Shipwreck*, p. 15, who shows that St. Luke's nautical
knowledge is at once *accurate* and *unprofessional*.

[2] Dr. Plumptre (*ubi supra*) tries to show that the intercourse of Luke, the
Physician, left its traces on St. Paul's own language and tone of thought—
e.g., the frequent use of ὑγιαίνω (1 Tim. i. 10; vi. 3, &c., in eight places), which
is found three times in St. Luke, and not in the other Gospels; νοσῶ (1 Tim.
vi. 4); γάγγραινα (2 Tim. ii. 17); τυφόω (1 Tim. iii. 6; vi. 4, &c.); κεκαυτηριασμένοι
(1 Tim. iv. 2); κνηθόμενοι (2 Tim. iv. 3); Hippocr., p. 444; γυμνασία (1 Tim.
iv. 8); στόμαχος (1 Tim. v. 23); the anti-ascetic advice of Col. ii. 23 (which
means that "ascetic rules have no value in relation to bodily fulness"—*i.e.*, are
no remedy against its consequences in disordered passions); κατατομή (Phil.
iii. 2); σκύβαλα (Phil. iii. 8, &c.). The facts are curious and noticeable, even if
they will not fully bear out the inference.

F F

Book VII.

CHRISTIANITY IN MACEDONIA.

CHAPTER XXV.

PHILIPPI.

"The day is short; the work abundant; the labourers are remiss; the reward is great; the master presses."—PIRKE ABHÒTH, ii.

So with their hearts full of the high hopes inspired by the consciousness that they were being led by the Spirit of God, the two Apostles, with Luke and Timotheus, set sail from the port of Troas. As the south wind sped them fast upon their destined course, they may have seen a fresh sign that He was with them who causes the east wind to blow in the heavens, and by His power brings in the south wind.[1] Owing to this favourable breeze, they traversed in two days the distance which occupied five days when they returned.[2] On the first day they ran past Tenedos and Imbros straight for Samothrace, and anchored for the night to leeward of it. Did Paul as he gazed by starlight, or at early dawn, on the towering peak which overshadows that ancient island, think at all of its immemorial mysteries, or talk to his companions about the Cabiri, or question any of the Greek or Roman

---

[1] See Con. and Hows. i. 305. The description of the voyage by St. Luke, however brief, is, as usual, demonstrably accurate in the minutest particulars.
[2] Acts xx. 6.

sailors about the strange names of Axiocheros, Axiochersos, and Axiochersa? We would gladly know, but we have no data to help us, and it is strongly probable that to all such secondary incidents he was habitually indifferent.

On the next day, still scudding before the wind,[1] they passed the mouth of the famous Strymon; sailed northward of Thasos amid the scenes so full to us of the memory of Thucydides; gazed for the first time on the "goldveined crags" of Pangaeus; saw a rocky promontory, and on it a busy seaport, over which towered the marble Maiden Chamber of Diana; and so, anchoring in the roadstead, set foot—three of them for the first time—on European soil. The town was Neapolis, in Thrace—the modern Kavala—which served as the port of the Macedonian Philippi. Here St. Paul did not linger. As at Seleucia, and Attaleia, and Perga, and Peiraeus, and Cenchreae, he seemed to regard the port as being merely a starting-point for the inland town.[2] Accordingly, he at once left Neapolis by the western gate and took the Egnatian road, which, after skirting the shore for a short distance, turns northward over a narrow pass of Mount Pangaeus, and so winds down into a green delicious plain,—with a marsh on one side where herds of large-horned buffaloes wallowed among the reeds, and with meadows on the other side, which repaid the snows of Hæmus, gathered in the freshening waters of the Zygactes, with the bloom and odour of the hundred-petal rose. At a distance of about seven miles they would begin to pass through the tombs that bordered the road-

---

[1] St. Luke most accurately omits the εὐθυδρομήσαμεν of the *second* day's voyage; a S.S.E. wind—and such are prevalent at times in this part of the Ægean—would speed them direct to Samothrace, but not quite in so straight a course from Samothrace to Neapolis.

[2] V. supra, p. 390.

sides in the neighbourhood of all ancient cities, and one mile further brought them to Philippi, whose Acropolis had long been visible on the summit of its precipitous and towering hill.[1]

The city of Philippi was a monumental record of two vast empires. It had once been an obscure place, called Krenides from its streams and springs; but Philip, the father of Alexander, had made it a frontier town, to protect Macedonia from the Thracians, and had helped to establish his power by the extremely profitable working of its neighbouring gold mines. Augustus, proud of the victory over Brutus and Cassius,—won at the foot of the hill on which it stands, and on the summit of which Cassius had committed suicide,—elevated it to the rank of a colony, which made it, as St. Luke calls it, if not the first yet certainly " a first city of that district of Macedonia." [2] And this, probably, was why St. Paul went directly to it. When Perseus, the last successor of Alexander, had been routed at Pydna (June 22, B.C. 168), Macedonia had been reduced to a Roman province in four divisions. These, in accordance with the astute and machiavellic policy of Rome, were kept distinct from each other by differences of privilege and isolation of interests which tended to foster mutual jealousies. Beginning

---

[1] *Appian*, iv. 105. On the site of it is a small Turkish village, called Filibedjik.

[2] The full title, " Colonia Augusta Julia Victrix Philippensium," is found on inscriptions (*Miss. Archéol.*, p. 18). A great deal has been written about ἥτις ἐστὶ πρώτη τῆς μερίδος τῆς Μακεδονίας πόλις κολωνία. A favourite explanation is that it means " the first city of Macedonia they came to," regarding Neapolis as being technically in Thrace. Both parts of the explanation are most improbable; if πρώτη only meant " the first they came to," it would be a frivolous remark, and would require the article and the imperfect tense; and Neapolis, as the port of Philippi, was certainly regarded as a Macedonian town. Πρώτη is justifiable politically—for Philippi, though not the capital of Macedonia Prima, was certainly more important than Amphipolis. Bp. Wordsworth makes it mean " the chief city of *the frontier* of Macedonia " (cf. Ezek. xlv. 7).

eastwards at the river Nestus, Macedonia Prima reached to
the Strymon; Macedonia Secunda, to the Axius; Macedonia Tertia, to the Peneus; and Macedonia Quarta, to
Illyricum and Epirus.[1] The capitals of these divisions
respectively were Amphipolis, Thessalonica,—at which the
Proconsul of the entire province fixed his residence,—Pella,
and Pelagonia. It is a very reasonable conjecture that
Paul, in answer to the appeal of the Vision, had originally
intended to visit—as, perhaps, he ultimately did visit—all
four capitals. But Amphipolis, in spite of its historic
celebrity had sunk into comparative insignificance, and the
proud colonial privileges of Philippi made it in reality the
more important town.

On the insignia of Roman citizenship which here met
his gaze on every side—the S.P.Q.R., the far-famed
legionary eagles, the panoply of the Roman soldiers which
he was hereafter so closely to describe, the two statues
of Augustus, one in the paludament of an Imperator, one
in the semi-nude cincture of a divinity—Paul could not
have failed to gaze with curiosity; and as they passed
up the Egnatian road which divided the city, they must
have looked at the figures of tutelary deities rudely scratched
upon the rock, which showed that the old mythology was
still nominally accepted. Can we suppose that they
were elevated so far above the sense of humour as not to
smile with their comrade Silvanus as they passed the
temple dedicated to the rustic god whose name he bore,
and saw the images of the old man,

"So surfeit-swollen, so old, and so profane,"

whom the rural population of Italy, from whom these

[1] Liv. xlv. 18—29. We cannot be sure that these divisions were still
retained.

colonists had been drawn, worshipped with offerings of fruit and swine?

They had arrived in the middle of the week, and their first care, as usual, was to provide for their own lodging and independent maintenance, to which Luke would doubtless be able to contribute by the exercise of his art. They might have expected to find a Jewish community sheltering itself under the wings of the Roman eagle; but if so they were disappointed. Philippi was a military and agricultural, not a commercial town, and the Jews were so few that they did not even possess a synagogue. If during those days they made any attempt to preach, it could only have been in the privacy of their rooms, for when the Sabbath came they were not even sure that the town could boast of a *proseucha*, or prayer-house.[1] They knew enough, however, of the habits of the Jews to feel sure that if there were one, it would be on the river-bank outside the city. So they made their way through the gate[2] along the ancient causeway which led directly to the Gangites,[3] and under the triumphal arch which commemorated the great victory of Philippi ninety-four years before.[4] That victory had finally decided the prevalence of the imperial system, which was fraught with such vast consequences for the world. In passing to the banks of the river the missionaries were on the very ground on which the battle had been fought, and near which the camps of Brutus and Cassius had stood, separated by the river from the army of Octavianus and Antony.

---

[1] Acts xvi. 13. This is the sense which I extract from the various readings of א, B (?), C, D, and from the versions.

[2] Acts xvi. 13, πύλης, א, A, B, C, D, &c.

[3] Perhaps from the same root as Ganges (Renan, p 145).

[4] Called Kiemer (*Miss. Archéol.*, p. 118).

But when they reached the poor open-air *proseucha*,[1] strange to say they only found a few women assembled there. It was clearly no time for formal orations. They simply sat down, and entered into conversation with the little group.[2] Their words were blessed. Among the women sat a Lydian proselytess, a native of the city of Thyatira, who had there belonged to the guild of dyers.[3] The luxurious extravagance of the age created a large demand for purple in the market of Rome, and Lydia found room for her profitable trade among the citizens at Philippi. As she sat listening, the arrow of conviction pierced her heart. She accepted the faith, and was baptised with her slaves and children.[4] One happy fruit her conversion at once bore, for she used hospitality without grudging. " If you have judged me," she said, " to be faithful to the Lord, come to my house, and stay there." To accede to the request, modestly as it was urged, was not in accordance with the principles which the great Apostle had laid down to guide his conduct. Fully acknowledging the right of every missionary of the faith be to maintained by those to whom he ministered, and even to travel about with a wife, or an attendant deaconess, he had yet not only foregone this right, but begged as a personal favour that it might not be pressed upon him, because he valued that proof of his sincerity

---

[1] *Proseuchae* were circular-shaped enclosures open to the air (Epiphan. *Haer.* lxxx. 1), often built on the sea-shore or by rivers (Phil. *in Flacc.* 14; Jos. *Antt.* xiv. 10, 23; Tert. *ad Nat.* i. 13; Juv. *Sat.* iii. 12), for the facility of the frequent ablutions which Jewish worship required.

[2] Acts xvi. 13, ἐλαλοῦμεν; 14, τοῖς λαλουμένοις.

[3] The province of Lydia was famous for the art of dyeing in purple (Hom. *Il.* iv. 141; Claud. *Rapt. Proserp.* i. 270; Strabo, xiii. 4, 14). Sir G. Wheler found an inscription at Thyatira mentioning "the dyers" (οἱ βαφεῖς).

[4] Acts xvi. 14, ἤκουεν . . . διήνοιξεν. How unlike invention is the narrative that, summoned by a vision to Macedonia, his first and most important convert is a woman of the Asia in which the Spirit had forbidden him to preach !

which was furnished by the gratuitous character of his ministry. Lydia, however, would not be refused, and she was so evidently one of those generous natures who have learnt how far more blessed it is to give than to receive, that Paul did not feel it right to persist in his refusal. The trade of Lydia was a profitable one, and in her wealth, joined to the affection which he cherished for the Church of Philippi beyond all other Churches, we see the probable reason why he made other Churches jealous by accepting pecuniary aid from his Philippian converts, and from them alone.[1]

There is some evidence that, among the Macedonians, women occupied a more independent position, and were held in higher honour, than in other parts of the world.[2] In his Epistle to the Philippians St. Paul makes prominent mention of two ladies, Euodia and Syntyche, who were well known in the Christian community, although unhappily they could not agree with each other.[3] The part that women played in the dissemination of the Gospel can hardly be exaggerated, and unless it was a mere accident that only women were assembled in the *proseucha* on the first Sabbath at Philippi, we must suppose that not a few of the male converts mentioned shortly afterwards[4] were originally won over by their influence. The only converts who are mentioned by name are Epaphroditus, for whom both Paul and the Philippian Church seem to have felt a deep regard; Clemens, and Syzygus, or "yokefellow,"[5] whom Paul

---

[1] 1 Thess. ii. 5, 7, 9; twice in Thessalonica, Phil. iv. 16; once in Athens, 2 Cor. xi. 9; once in Rome, Phil. iv. 10.

[2] See Lightfoot, *Philip.*, p. 55.

[3] Phil. iv. 2.   [4] Acts xvi. 40.

[5] It is true that the name does not occur elsewhere, but I cannot for a moment believe with Clemens Alex. (*Strom.* iii. 6, § 53) and Epiphanius (*H. E.* iii. 30) that the word σύζυγε means "wife." Lydia is not mentioned in

addresses in a playful paronomasia, and entreats him to help the evangelising toils—the joint wrestlings for the Gospel—of Euodia and Syntyche. But besides these there were other unnamed fellow-workers to whom St. Paul bears the high testimony that "their names were in the book of life."

Very encouraging and very happy must these weeks at Philippi have been, resulting, as they did, in the founding of a Church, to whose members he finds it needful to give but few warnings, and against whom he does not utter a word of blame. The almost total absence of Jews meant an almost total absence of persecution. The Philippians were heart-whole in their Christian faith. St. Paul's entire Epistle to them breathes of joy, affection, and gratitude. He seems to remember that he is writing to a colony, and a military colony—a colony of Roman "athletes." He reminds them of a citizenship loftier and more ennobling than that of Rome;[1] he calls Epaphroditus not only his fellow-worker, but also his fellow-soldier, one who had stood shoulder to shoulder with him in the new Macedonian phalanx, which was to join as of old in an advance to the conquest of the world. He derives his metaphorical expressions from the wrestling-ground and the race.[2] Alike St. Paul and St. Luke seem to rejoice in the strong, manly Roman nature of these converts, of whom many were slaves and freedmen, but of whom a large number had been soldiers, drawn from various parts of Italy in the civil wars—men

the Epistle, unless the name of this Lydian lady was Euodia or Syntyche. She may have died, or have returned to her native city in the intervening years. She most assuredly would have been named if the Epistle had been a forgery.

[1] Phil. i. 27, πολιτεύεσθε; iii. 20, πολίτευμα.

[2] Phil. i. 27, στήκετε; iii. 12, διώκω; 14, ἐπὶ τὸ βραβεῖον; iv. 3, συνήθλησαν; i. 27, συναθλοῦντες; iii. 16, τῷ αὐτῷ στοιχεῖν.

of the hardy Marsian and Pelignian stock—trained in the
stern, strong discipline of the Roman legions, and unsophisticated by the debilitating Hellenism of a mongrel
population. St. Paul loved them more and honoured them
more than he did the dreamy, superstitious Ephesians,
the fickle, impulsive Gauls, or the conceited, factious
Achaians. In writing to Thessalonica and Philippi he
had to deal with men of a larger mould and manlier
mind — more true and more tender than the men of
Corinth, with their boastful ignorance which took itself
for knowlege, or the men of Asia, with their voluptuous mysticisms and ceremonial pettiness. He was now
thrown for the first time among a race which has been
called the soundest part of the ancient world,[1] a race
which shone forth like torches in narrow and winding
streets, like stars that beamed their light and life in the
dark firmament—blameless children of God amid the
dwarfed and tortuous meanness of a degenerate race.[2]

Their stay in this fruitful field of labour was cut short
by an unforeseen circumstance, which thwarted the greed
of a few interested persons, and enlisted against Paul
and Silas the passions of the mob. For there is this
characteristic difference between the persecutions of Jews
and Gentiles—that the former were always stirred up by
religious fanaticism, the latter by personal and political
interests which were accidentally involved in religious
questions. Hitherto the Apostles had laboured without
interruption, chiefly because the Jews in the place, if there
were any at all, were few and uninfluential; but one day,
as they were on their way to the *proseucha*, they were met
by a slave-girl, who, having that excitable, perhaps
epileptic diathesis which was the qualification of the

---

[1] See the excellent remarks of Hausrath, p. 281, seqq.
[2] Phil. ii. 15.

Pythonesses of Delphi, was announced to be possessed by a Python spirit.[1] Nothing was less understood in antiquity than these obscure phases of mental excitation, and the strange flashes of sense, and even sometimes of genius, out of the gloom of a perturbed intellect, were regarded as inspired and prophetic utterances. As a fortune-teller and diviner, this poor girl was held in high esteem by the credulous vulgar of the town.[2] A slave could possess no property, except such *peculium* as his master allowed him, and the fee for consulting this unofficial Pythoness was a lucrative source of income to the people who owned her. To a poor afflicted girl like this, whose infirmities had encircled her with superstitious reverence, more freedom would be allowed than would have been granted, even in Philippi, to ordinary females in the little town; and she would be likely—especially if she were of Jewish birth—to hear fragments of information about Paul and his teaching. They impressed themselves on her

---

[1] Acts xvi. 16, πνεῦμα Πύθωνα (κ, A, B, C, D, &c.). The corresponding Old Testament expression is אוֹב *obh.* (Lev. xx. 6). It points to the use of ventriloquism, as I have shown, s.v. "Divination," in Smith, *Bibl. Dict.* At this period, and long before, people of this class—usually women—were regarded as prophetesses, inspired by the Pythian Apollo (πυθόληπτοί). Hence they were called Πύθωνες, and Εὐρυκλεῖς, from an ancient soothsayer named Eurycles and ἐγγαστρίμυθοι, from the convulsive heavings, and the speaking as ont of the depths of the stomach, which accompanied their fits (Sophocles Fr., στερνόμαντις). See Plutarch, *De Defect. Orac.* 9; Galen, *Gloss. Hippocr.* ('Εγγαστρίμυθοι· οἱ κεκλεισμένου τοῦ στόματος φθεγγόμενοι διὰ το δοκεῖν ἐκ τῆς γαστρὸς φθέγγεσθαι.) Hesych. s. v. Schol. *ad Ar. Vesp.* 1019, and Tertullian, *Apol.* 23, who distinctly defines them as people "qui de Deo pati existimantur, *qui anhelando praefantur.*" Neander quotes from Ellis the interesting fact that the Priest of Obo, in the Society Isles, found himself unable to reproduce his former convulsive ecstasies of supposed inspiration, after his conversion to Christianity (*Plantg.,* p. 176).

[2] We know that "an idol is nothing in the world," and therefore the expression that this girl had "a spirit of Pytho" is only an adoption of the current Pagan phraseology about her. Hippocrates attributed epileptic diseases to possession by Apollo, Cybele, Poseidon, &c., *De Morbo Sacr.* (C and H. i. 321).

imagination, and on meeting the men of whom she had
heard such solemn things, she turned round[1] and followed
them towards the river, repeatedly calling out—perhaps
in the very phrases which she had heard used of them—
"These people are slaves of the Most High God, and they
are announcing to us the way of salvation."[2] This might
be tolerated once or twice, but at last it became too
serious a hindrance of their sacred duties to be any longer
endured in silence.

In an outburst of pity and indignation[3]—pity for the
sufferer, indignation at this daily annoyance—Paul suddenly turned round, and addressing the Pytho by whom
the girl was believed to be possessed, said, "I enjoin
thee, in the name of Jesus Christ, to go out of her." The
effect was instantaneous. The calm authoritative exorcism
restored the broken harmony of her being. No more
paroxysms could be expected of her; nor the wild unnatural screaming utterances, so shrill and unearthly that
they might very naturally be taken for Sibylline frenzies.
Her masters ceased to expect anything from her oracles.
Their hope of further gain "went out" with the spirit.[4] A
piece of property so rare that it could only be possessed
by a sort of joint ownership was rendered entirely valueless.

Thus the slave-masters were touched in their pockets,
and it filled them with fury. They could hardly, indeed, go before the magistrates and tell them that Paul
by a single word had exorcised a powerful demon; but
they were determined to have vengeance somehow or

[1] Acts xvi. 16, ἀπαντῆσαι; 17, κατακολουθήσασα.

[2] Slaves; cf. Acts iv. 29; Rom. i. 1; Tit. i. 1.

[3] Acts xvi. 18, διαπονηθείς. The same word is used of the strong threats
of the priests at the teaching of the Apostles in Jerusalem (Acts iv. 2).

[4] Acts xvi. 19, ἐξῆλθεν ἡ ἐλπὶς τῆς ἐργασίας αὐτῶν. The use of the same
word after the ἐξῆλθεν (τὸ πνεῦμα) αὐτῇ τῇ ὥρᾳ is perhaps intentional.

other, and, in a Roman colony composed originally of discharged Antonian soldiers, and now occupied partly by their descendants, partly by enfranchised freedmen from Italy,[1] it was easy to raise a clamour against one or two isolated Jews. It was the more easy because the Philippians might have heard the news of disturbances and riots at Rome, which provoked the decree of Claudius banishing all Jews from the city.[2] They determined to seize this opportunity, and avail themselves of a similar plea.[3] They suddenly arrested Paul and Silas, and dragged them before the sitting magistrates.[4] These seem to have relegated the matter to the *duumviri*,[5] who were the chief authorities of the colony, and who, aping the manners and the titles of Imperial Rome, had the impertinence to call themselves "Prætors."[6] Leading

[1] This is proved by the inscriptions found at Philippi, which record the donors to the Temple of Silvanus, nearly all of whom are slaves or freedmen (*Miss. Archéol.*, p. 75).

[2] Acts xviii. 2; Suet. *Claud.* 25. See Ewald, vi. 488.

[3] Judaism was a *religio licita*, but anything like active proselytism was liable to stern suppression. See Paul. *Sentent,* 21; Serv. Virg. *Æn.* viii. 187; and the remarkable advice of Mæcenas to Augustus to dislike and punish all religious innovators (τοὺς δὲ ξενίζοντάς τι περὶ αὐτὸ [τὸ θεῖον] καὶ μίσει καὶ κόλαζε. Dio. Cass. vii. 36). "Quoties," says Livy, "hoc patrum avorumque aetate negotium est ut sacra externa fieri vetarent, sacrificulos vatesque foro, circo, urbe prohiberent" (Liv. xxxix. 16).

[4] Possibly the aediles (*Miss. Archéol.*, p. 71).

[5] Acts xvi. 19, εἵλκυσαν πρὸς τὴν ἀγορὰν ἐπὶ τοὺς ἄρχοντας; 20, καὶ προσαγαγόντες αὐτοὺς τοῖς στρατηγοῖς. The different verbs—of which the second is so much milder—and the different titles surely imply what is said in the text.

[6] Acts xvi. 20. στρατηγὸς is the Greek version of the originally military title "Prætor;" and it was also a Greek title in vogue for the chief magistrates in little cities (Ar. *Polit.* vii. 8). The fashion seems to have been set in Italy, where Cicero, a hundred years before this time, notices with amusement the "cupiditas" which had led the Capuan Duumviri to arrogate to themselves the title of "Prætors," and he supposes that they will soon have the impudence to call themselves "Consuls." He notices also that their "lictors" carried not mere staves (*bacilli*), but actual bundles of rods with axes inside them (*fasces*) as at Rome (*De Leg. Agrar.* 34). The name *stradigo* lingered on in some cities till modern days (Wetst. *in loc.*).

their prisoners into the presence of these "Prætors," they exclaimed, "These fellows are utterly troubling our city, being mere Jews; and they are preaching customs which it is not lawful for us, who are Romans, to accept or to practise."[1] The mob knew the real state of the case, and sympathised with the owners of the slave girl, feeling much as the Gadarenes felt towards One whose healing of a demoniac had interfered with *their* gains. In the minds of the Greeks and Romans there was always, as we have seen, a latent spark of abhorrence against the Jews. These sweepings of the Agora vehemently sided with the accusers, and the provincial duumvirs, all the more dangerous from being pranked out in the usurped peacock-plumes of "prætorian" dignity, assumed that the mob must be right, or at any rate that people who were Jews must be so far wrong as to deserve whatever they might get. They were not sorry at so cheap a cost to gratify the Roman conceit of a city which could boast that its citizens belonged to the Voltinian tribe.[2] It was another proof that—

> "Man, proud man,
> Dressed in a little brief authority,
> Plays such fantastic tricks before high heaven
> As makes the angels weep, who, with our spleens,
> Would all themselves laugh mortal."

Paul and Silas had not here to do with the haughty impartiality and supercilious knowledge which guided the decisions of a Gallio, but with the "justice's justice" of the Vibiuses and Floruses who at this time fretted their

---

[1] Acts xvi. 20, 'Ιουδαῖοι ὑπάρχοντες; 21, Ρωμαίοις οὖσι. Since neither "exorcism" nor "Judaism" (though they regarded Judæa as a "suspiciosa et maledica civitas," Cic. *pro Flacc.* 28, and generally *teterrima*, Tac. *H.* v. 8) were cognisable offences, the slave-owners have to take refuge in an undefined charge of innovating proselytism.

[2] *Miss. Archéol.*, p. 40.

little hour on the narrow stage of Philippi. Conscious of their Roman citizenship, they could not have expected so astounding a result of their act of mercy, as that their political franchise should be ignored, and they themselves, after condemnation without trial, ignominiously hurried off into the punishments reserved for the very meanest malefactors.[1] Such, however, was the issue of the hearing. Their Prætorships would imitate the divine Claudius, and wreak on these wandering Israelites a share of the punishment which the misdeeds of their countrymen had brought upon them at Rome. As the proceedings were doubtless in Latin, with which Paul and Silas had little or no acquaintance, and in legal formulæ and procedures of which they were ignorant, they either had no time to plead their citizenship until they were actually in the hands of the lictors,[2] or, if they had, their voices were drowned in the cries of the colonists. Before they could utter one word in their own defence, the sentence—" *summovete, lictores, despoliate, verberate* "—was uttered; the Apostles were seized; their garments were rudely torn off their backs;[3] they were hurried off and tied by their hands to the *palus*, or whipping-post in the forum; and whether they vainly called out in Greek to their infuriated enemies, " We are Roman citizens," or, which is far more likely, bore their frightful punishment in that grand silence which, in moments of high spiritual

---

[1] The Jews, who were so infamously treated by Flaccus, felt this, as Paul himself did (1 Thess. ii. 2, ὑβρισθέντες, ὡς οἴδατε, ἐν Φιλίπποις), to be a severe aggravation of their sufferings (Philo, *in Flacc.* 10, αἰκισθῆναι μάστιξιν ἃς ἔθος τοὺς κακούργων πονηροτάτους προσηλακί(εσθαι).

[2] Perhaps Paul's language in verse 20 is generic. If so he would be most unlikely to plead a privilege which would protect himself alone.

[3] On this tearing off of the garments see Liv. viii. 32; Tac. *H.* iv. 27; Val. Max. ii. 7, 8; Dion. Halic. ix. 39. The verbs used are *scindere, spoliare, lacerare* (also the technical word for the laceration of the back by the rods), περικαταῤῥῆξαι, showing that it was done with violence and contumely.

rapture, makes pain itself seem painless [1]—in that forum of which ruins still remain, in the sight of the lowest dregs of a provincial outpost, and of their own pitying friends, they endured, at the hands of these low lictors, those outrages, blows, strokes, weals, the pangs and butchery, the extreme disgrace and infamy, the unjust infliction of which even a hard-headed and hard-hearted Gentile could not describe without something of pathos and indignation.[2] It was the first of three such scourgings with the rods of Roman lictors which Paul endured, and it is needless to dwell even for one moment on its dangerous and lacerating anguish. We, in these modern days, cannot read without a shudder even of the flogging of some brutal garotter, and our blood would run cold with unspeakable horror if one such incident, or anything which remotely resembled it, had occurred in the life of a Henry Martyn or a Coleridge Patteson. But such horrors occurred eight times at least in the story of one whose frame was more frail with years of suffering than that of our English missionaries, and in whose life these pangs were but such a drop in the ocean of his endurance, that, of the eight occasions on which he underwent these horrible scourgings, this alone has been deemed worthy of even passing commemoration.[3]

---

[1] A much lower exaltation than that of the Apostle's would rob anguish of half its sting (cf. Cic. *in Verr.* ii. v. 62, "Hâc se commemoratione civitatis omnia verbera depulsurum, cruciatumque a corpore dejecturum arbitrabatur").

[2] Cato *ap.* Aul. Gell. x. 3.

[3] The five *Jewish* scourgings were probably submitted to without any protest (*v. supra*, p. 41.). From a fourth nearly consummated beating with thongs (?) he did protect himself by his political privilege (Acts xxii. 25). Both that case and this show how easily, in the midst of a tumult, a Roman citizen might fail to make his claim heard or understood; and the instance mentioned by Cicero, who tells how remorselessly Verres scourged a citizen of Messana, though "inter dolorem crepitumque plagarum," he kept exclaiming "*Civis Romanus sum,*" shows that in the provinces the insolence of power would sometimes deride the claim of those who were little likely to find an oppor-

Nor was this all. After seeing that a scourging of extreme severity had been inflicted, the Duumvirs, with the same monstrous violation of all law, flung Paul and Silas into prison, and gave the jailer special orders to keep them safely. Impressed by this injunction with the belief that his prisoners must have been guilty of something very heinous, and determined to make assurance doubly sure, the jailer not only thrust them into the dank, dark, loathsome recesses of the inner prison, but also secured their feet into "the wood." "The wood" was an instrument of torture used in many countries, and resembling our "stocks," or rather the happily obsolete "pillory," in having five holes—four for the wrists and ankles, and one for the neck.[1] The jailer in this instance only secured their feet; but we cannot be surprised that the memory of this suffering lingered long years afterwards in the mind of St. Paul, when we try to imagine what a poor sufferer, with the rankling sense of gross injustice in his soul, would feel who—having but recently recovered from a trying sickness—after receiving a long and frightful flagellation as the sequel of a violent and agitated scene, was thrust away out of the

---

tunity of enforcing it (Cic. *In Verr.* i. 47 ; v. 62, &c.). Moreover the reverence for the privilege must have been much weakened by the shameless sale of it to freedmen, &c., by Messalina Dio. Cass. lx., p. 676 ; cf. Tac. *H.* 12). Further than this, it would be quite easy to stretch the law so far as to make it appear that they had forfeited the privilege by crime. At any rate it is certain that under the Empire not citizens only, but even senators, were scourged, tortured, and put to death. without the slightest protection from the Porcian and Valerian laws (Tac. *H.* i. 6 ; ii. 10, &c.). And although Paul willingly—nay, gladly—endured the inevitable trials which came before him in the performance of duty (2 Cor. xi. 23), I do not believe that he would have accepted anguish or injustice which he had a perfect right to escape.

[1] Acts xvi. 24, ξύλον or ποδοκάκη (cf. Job xiii. 27). In Latin *nervus*. It had five holes, and is hence called πεντεσύριγγον (Schol. Ar. *Eq.* 1046 ; cf. Poll. viii. 72 ; Plaut. *Capt.* iii. 79 ; Euseb. *H. E.* vi. 39 ; Job xiii. 27 ; xxxiii. 11 ; Jer. xxix. 26).

jeers of the mob into a stifling and lightless prison, and
sat there through the long hours of the night with his
feet in such durance as to render it impossible except in
some constrained position to find sleep on the foul bare
floor.[1]

Yet over all this complication of miseries the souls
of Paul and Silas rose in triumph.   With heroic
cheerfulness they solaced the long black hours of midnight with prayer and hymns.[3]   To every Jew as to
every Christian, the Psalms of David furnished an in-
exhaustible storehouse of sacred song.   That night the
prison was wakeful.   It may be that, as is usually the
case, there was some awful hush and heat in the air—a
premonition of the coming catastrophe; but, be that as
it may, the criminals of the Philippian prison were
listening to the sacred songs of the two among them,
who deserving nothing had suffered most.   "The prison,"
it has been said, "became an Odeum;" and the guilty
listened with envy and admiration to the "songs in the
night," with which God inspired the innocent.   Never,
probably, had such a scene occurred before in the world's
history, and this perfect triumph of the spirit of peace
and joy over shame and agony was an omen of what
Christianity would afterwards effect.   And while they
sang, and while the prisoners listened, perhaps to verses

---

[1] If by the *Tullianum* at Rome we may judge of other prisons—
and it seems that the name was generic for the lowest or inmost prison,
even of provincial towns (Appul. *Met.* ix. 183; O. and H. i. 326)—there
is reason to fear that it must have been a very horrible place.   And, indeed,
what must ancient Pagan provincial prisons have been at the best, when we
bear in mind what English and Christian and London prisons were not fifty
years ago?

[3] "The leg feels nothing in the stocks," says Tertullian, "when the soul is
in heaven; though the body is held fast, to the spirit all is open."   Christian endurance was sneered at as "sheer obstinacy."   In a Pagan it would
have been extolled as magnificent heroism.

which "out of the deeps" called on Jehovah, or "fled to Him before the morning watch," or sang—

"The plowers plowed upon my back and made long furrows,
But the righteous Lord hath hewn the snares of the ungodly in pieces"—

or triumphantly told how God had "burst the gates of brass, and smitten the bars of iron in sunder"— suddenly there was felt a great shock of earthquake, which rocked the very foundations of the prison. The prison doors were burst open; the prisoners' chains were loosed from the staples in the wall.[1] Startled from sleep, and catching sight of the prison doors standing open, the jailer instantly drew his sword, and was on the point of killing himself, thinking that his prisoners had escaped, and knowing that he would have to answer for their production with his life.[2] Suicide was the common refuge of the day against disaster, and might have been regarded at Philippi as an act not only natural but heroic.[3] Paul, however, observed his purpose, and, always perfectly self-possessed even in the midst of danger, called out to him in a loud voice, "Do thyself no harm, for we are all here." The entire combination of circumstances—the earthquake, the shock of sudden terror, the revulsion of joy which diverted his intention of suicide, the serene endurance and calm forgiveness of his prisoners—all melted the man's heart. Demanding lights, he sprang into the inner prison, and flung himself, in a tremor of agitation, at the feet of Paul and Silas. Then, releasing their feet from the stocks, and leading them out of their dark recess, he exclaimed, "Lords ($Kύριοι$), what must I do to be saved?" His mode of address showed deep

[1] Acts xvi. 26.
[2] See the Dig. *De custodia et exhibitione reorum*, xlviii., iii. 12 and 16.
[3] Sen. *De Prov.* ii. 6; *Ep.* 58; Diog. Laert. vii. 130; Cic. *De Fin.* i. 15, &c

G G 2

reverence. His question echoed the expression of the demoniac.[1] And the Apostles answered him partly in the terms which he had used, "Believe," they said, "on the Lord (Κύριον) Jesus Christ, and thou shalt be saved, and thy house." Deeply impressed, the man at once assembled his household in a little congregation, and, worn and weary and suffering as they were, Paul and Silas spoke to them of Him by whom they were to find salvation.[2] Then the jailer, pitying their condition, washed their bruised backs, and immediately afterwards was, with his whole house, baptised in the faith.[3] All this seems to have taken place in the prison precincts. Not till then did they think of food or rest. Leading them upstairs into his house, he set a table before them, and in that high hour of visitation from the Living God, though he had but heard words and been told of a hope to come, he and his whole house felt that flow of elevated joy which sprang naturally from a new and inspiring faith.[4]

Day dawned, and the duumvirs were troubled. Whether they had felt the earthquake,[5] and been alarmed lest these "slaves of the Most High God" should be something more than the poor Jewish wanderers that they seemed to be, or whether the startling events of the

---

[1] Acts xvi. 17, ὁδὸν σωτηρίας; ver. 30, ἵνα σωθῶ.

[2] Acts xvi. 33, ἐν ἐκείνῃ τῇ ὥρᾳ.

[3] Ἔλουσεν καὶ ἐλούθη, "he washed and was washed," says Chrysostom. For the bearing of the expression οἱ αὐτοῦ πάντες (Acts xvi. 33), and ὁ οἶκος αὐτῆς (ver. 15), cf. xviii. 8; 1 Cor. i. 16, on infant baptism, see Coleridge, *Aids to Reflection*. The Church of England wisely makes no direct use of this argument in Art. xxvii. But though Bengel's remark, "Quis credat in tot familiis nullum fuisse infantem?" is not decisive, the rest of his observation "Et Judaeos circumcidendis, Gentiles lustrandis illis assuetos, non etiam obtulisse illos baptismo?" has much weight.

[4] Acts xvi. 34, ἠγαλλιᾶτο, impf. C, D various versions, &c. καίτοι οὐδὲν ἦν ἀλλὰ ῥήματα μόνον καὶ ἐλπίδες χρησταί.

[5] In Acts xvi. 35, D adds ἀναμνησθέντες τὸν σεισμὸν τὸν γεγονότα.

night had reached their ears—they had at any rate become heartily ashamed of their tumultuary injustice. They felt it incumbent on them to hush up the whole matter, and get rid as quickly as possible of these awkward prisoners. Accordingly, they sent their lictors, no longer to use their rods in outrageous violation of justice, but to "set those people free." The jailer hurried to Paul with the message of peaceful liberation, which no doubt he thought would be heartily welcomed. But Paul felt that at least some reparation must be offered for an intolerable wrong, and that, for the sake of others if not for his own, these provincial justices must be taught a lesson not to be so ready to prostitute their authority at the howling of a mob. Sending for the lictors themselves, he sternly said, in a sentence of which every word was telling, " After beating us publicly uncondemned, Romans though we are by right, they flung us into prison; and now they are for casting us out secretly. No such thing. Let them come in person, and conduct us out."[1] The lictors took back the message to the " Praetors," and it filled them with no small alarm. They had been hurried by ignorance, prejudice, and pride of office into glaring offences against the Roman law.[2] They had condemned two Roman citizens without giving them their chartered right to a fair trial;[3] and, on condemning them, had further outraged the birthright and privilege of

---

[1] Acts xvi. 37. The 'Ρωμαίους ὑπάρχοντας is perhaps an allusion to the insolent 'Ιουδαῖοι ὑπάρχοντες and Ρωμαίοις οὖσιν of the accusers (ver. 21). See the Lex Cornelia, *Dict. of Antt.*, p. 638; Paulus, *Instt.*, let. iv.; *De incuriis*, § 8.

[2] Zeller starts (*Hilgenfeld's Zeitsch.* 1864, p. 103) the amazing theory that this is a reproduction of the story found in Lucian's *Toxaris* (27—34), about a Greek medical student named Antiphilus, who is imprisoned in Egypt with his servant on a false charge of theft from a temple. Krenkel (p. 221) characterises it as " a subtle conjecture " that the narrative of the Acts is an imitation of this story. And this is criticism!

[3] Cic. *in Verr.* ii. 1, 9; Plaut. *Curcul.* v. 3, 16; Tac. *H.* 1, 6.

citizenship by having them bound and scourged; and they
had thus violated the Porcian law[1] in the presence of the
entire mob of the forum, and in sight of some at least
who would be perfectly able to take the matter up and
report their conduct in high quarters. Their worships
had simply flagellated in public the law and majesty of
Rome.[2] They did not at all like the notion of being
themselves summoned before the Proconsul's court to
answer for their flagrant illegality; so, trusting to the
placability of the Jewish character as regards mere personal wrongs, they came in person, accompanied, says one
manuscript, by many friends.[3] Entreating the pardon
of their prisoners, they urged them, with reiterated
requests, to leave the city, excusing themselves on the
plea that they had mistaken their true character, and
pleading that, if they stayed, there might be another
ebullition of public anger.[4] Paul and Silas, however, were
courageous men, and had no intention to give any colour
of justice to the treatment they had received by sneaking
out of the city. From the prison they went straight to
the house of Lydia; nor was it till they had seen the
assembled brethren, and given them their last exhortation,
that they turned their backs on the beautiful scenes where
a hopeful work had been rudely ended by their first experience of Gentile persecution. But, in accordance with a
frequent custom of St. Paul,[5] they left Luke behind them.[6]

[1] Cic. *pro Rabir.* 3.

[2] "Facinus est vinciri civem Romanum, *scelus* verberari," Cic. *in Verr.*
v. 66.

[3] Acts xvi. 39, D, παραγενόμενοι μετὰ φίλων πολλῶν εἰς τὴν φυλακήν.

[4] All this is intrinsically probable, otherwise I would not, of course, insert
it on the sole and fantastic authority of D, εἰπόντες Ἠγνόησαμεν τὰ καθ' ὑμᾶς ὅτι
ἐστε ἄνδρες δίκαιοι, &c., and μήποτε πάλιν συστραφῶσιν ἡμῖν ἐπικράζοντες καθ' ὑμῶν.

[5] Cf. xvii. 14; xviii. 19; Titus i. 5; 2 Tim. iv. 20.

[6] The third person is resumed in Acts xvii. 1, and the first person only
recurs in Acts xx. 5.

Perhaps at Philippi he had found favourable opportunities for the exercise of his art, and he could at the same time guide and strengthen the little band of Philippian converts, before whom days and years of bitter persecution were still in store.[1]

---

[1] Phil. i. 28—30. Although here and there the Apostles won a convert of higher rank, it was their glory that their followers wore mainly the babes and sucklings of human intellect—not many wise, not many noble, not many rich, but the weak things of the world. "Philosophy," says Voltaire, "was never meant for the people. The *canaille* of to-day resembles in everything the *canaille* of the last 4,000 years. *We have never cared to enlighten cobblers and maid-servants. That is the work of Apostles.*" Yes; and it was the work of Christ.

CHAPTER XXVI.

THESSALONICA AND BERŒA.

Μνημονεύετε γὰρ ἀδελφοὶ τόν κόπον ἡμῶν καὶ τὸν μόχθον (1 Thess. ii. 9).
"In oppidum devium Beroeam profugisti" (Cic. *in Pis.* 36).

LEAVING Philippi, with its mingled memories of suffering and happiness, Paul and Silvanus and Timotheus took an easy day's journey of about three-and-thirty miles to the beautiful town of Amphipolis. It lies to the south of a splendid lake, under sheltering hills, three miles from the sea, and on the edge of a plain of boundless fertility. The strength of its natural position, nearly encircled by a great bend of the river, the mines which were near it, and the neighbouring forests, which furnished to the Athenian navy so many pines, fit

> "To be the mast
> Of some great Ammiral,"

made it a position of high importance during the Peloponnesian wars. If St. Paul had ever read Herodotus he may have thought with horror of the human sacrifice of Xerxes[1]—the burial alive at this place of nine youths and nine maidens; and if he had read Thucydides—which is excessively doubtful, in spite of a certain analogy between their forms of expression—he would have gazed with peculiar interest on the sepulchral mound of Brasidas, and the hollowing of the stones in the way-worn city

[1] Hdt. vii. 114.

street which showed the feet of men and horses under the gate, and warned Kleon that a sally was intended.[1] If he could read Livy, which is by no means probable, he would recall the fact that in this town Paulus Æmilius[2]— one of the family from whom his own father or grandfather may have derived his name—had here proclaimed, in the name of Rome, that Macedonia should be free. But all this was little or nothing to the Jewish missionaries. At Amphipolis there was no synagogue, and therefore no ready means of addressing either Jews or Gentiles.[3] They therefore proceeded the next day thirty miles farther, through scenery of surpassing loveliness, along the Strymonic Gulf, through the wooded pass of Aulon, where St. Paul may have looked at the tomb of Euripides, and along the shores of Lake Bolbe to Apollonia. Here again they rested for a night, and the next day, pursuing their journey across the neck of the promontory of Chalcidice, and leaving Olynthus and Potidæa, with their heart-stirring memories, far to the south, they advanced nearly forty miles farther to the far-famed town of Thessalonica, the capital of all Macedonia, and though a free city,[4] the residence of the Roman Proconsul.

Its position on the Egnatian road, commanding the entrance to two great inland districts, and at the head of the Thermaic Gulf, had made it an important seat of commerce. Since the days when Cassander had re-founded it, and changed its name from Therma to Thessalonica in honour of his wife, who was a daughter of Philip of Macedon, it had always been a flourishing city, with many

[1] Thuc. iv. 103—107, v. 6—11.
[2] Liv. xlv. 30.
[3] The town had become so insignificant that Strabo does not even mention it.
[4] Plin. H. N. iv. 17.

historic associations. Here Cicero had spent his days of melancholy exile.[1] Here a triumphal arch, still standing, commemorates the victory of Octavianus and Antony at Philippi. From hence, as with the blast of a trumpet, not only in St. Paul's days,[2] but for centuries afterwards, the Word of God sounded forth among the neighbouring tribes. Here Theodosius was guilty of that cruel massacre, for which St. Ambrose, with heroic faithfulness, kept him for eight months from the cathedral of Milan. Here its good and learned Bishop Eustathius wrote those *scholia* on Homer, which place him in the first rank of ancient commentators. It received the title of "the orthodox city," because it was for centuries a bulwark of Christendom, but it was taken by Amurath II. in 1430. Saloniki is still a great commercial port of 70,000 inhabitants, of whom nearly one-third are Jews; and the outrage of Mohammedan fanaticism which has brought its name into recent prominence is but the beginning of events which will yet change the map and the destinies of Southern Europe.

At this city—blighted now by the curse of Islam, but still beautiful on the slopes of its vine-clad hills, with Pelion and Olympus full in view—the missionaries rested, for here was the one Jewish synagogue which sufficed for the entire district.[3] After securing the means of earning their daily bread, which was no easy matter, they found a lodging in the house of a Jew, who had Græcised the common name of Jesus into Jason.[4] Even

---

[1] Cic. *Pro. Planc.* 41.

[2] 1 Thess. i. 8, ἐξήχηται.

[3] Acts xvii. 1. ἡ συναγωγή is probably the right reading, though the ἡ is wanting in א, A, B, D. In any case it is evidently meant that there was but one synagogue, and tradition still points out the mosque—once the Church of St. Demetrius, which is supposed to stand upon its site. There are now nearly forty Jewish synagogues in Saloniki.   [4] Rom. xvi. 21 (?).

if their quarters were gratuitously allowed them, St. Paul, accepting no further aid, was forced to daily and nightly labour of the severest description[1] to provide himself with the small pittance which alone sufficed his wants. Even this was not sufficient. Poor as he was— for if he ever possessed any private means he had now lost them all[2]—the expenses of the journey from Philippi had probably left him and his companions nearly penniless, and but for the timely liberality of the Philippians it would have fared hardly with the Apostle, and he might even have been left without means to pursue his further journeys.[3] There is no contradiction between the two contributions from Philippi and the Apostle's account of his manual labours; for there is nothing to show that he only stayed in Thessalonica a little more than three weeks.[4] In addition to the fact that the second contribution would be partly wanted for his new journeys, we find that at this time a famine was raging, which caused the price of wheat to rise to six times its usual rate.[5] However much this famine may have enhanced the difficulties of St. Paul and his companions, it must have confirmed him in the purpose of placing the motives of his ministry above suspicion by making it absolutely gratuitous. Such disinterestedness added much to the strength of his position, especially in the "deep poverty" which must have prevailed in such times among the low-born proselytes of a despised

---

[1] 1 Thess. ii. 9, νυκτὸς γὰρ καὶ ἡμέρας ἐργαζόμενοι, πρὸς τὸ μὴ ἐπιβαρῆσαί τινα ὑμῶν, κ.τ.λ.

[2] Phil. iii. 8, τὰ πάντα ἐζημιώθην.

[3] Phil. iv. 15, 16.

[4] He can hardly have failed to stay much longer, for Philippi was a hundred miles from Thessalonica, and it would take time for news to travel and the to-and-fro journey to be made.

[5] Pointed out by Mr. Lewin, *Fasti Sacri*, p. 290; *St. Paul*, i. 231.

religion. If St. Paul did not refuse the contributions from Philippi, it was because they came spontaneously, at an hour of bitter need, from those who could spare the money, and who, as he well knew, would be pained by any refusal of their proffered aid. Yet all who knew him knew well that the aid came unsought, and that, as far as Paul's own personal life was concerned, he was utterly indifferent to privations, and set the example of an un-flinching endurance rendered easy by a perfect trust in God.[1]

For three Sabbaths in succession he went to the synagogue, and argued with the Jews. It might well have been that the outrage at Philippi, and its still lingering effects, would have damped his zeal, and made him shrink from another persecution. But, fresh as he was from such pain and peril, he carried on his discus-sions with undiminished force and courage,[2] explaining the prophecies, and proving from them that the Messiah was to suffer, and to rise from the dead, and that "this is the Messiah, Jesus, whom I am preaching to you."[3] The synagogue audience was mainly composed of Jews, and of these some were convinced and joined the Church.[4] Conspicuous among them for his subsequent devo-tion, and all the more conspicuous as being almost the only warmly-attached convert whom St. Paul won from the ranks of "the circumcision," was Aristarchus, the sharer of St. Paul's perils[5] from mob-violence at Ephesus,

---

[1] Phil. iv. 11, 12.

[2] 1 Thess. ii. 2, ἐπαῤῥησιασάμην; Acts xvii. 2, διελέγετο αὐτοῖς. The teaching of the synagogue admitted of discussions and replies (John vi. 25, &c.); as it does to this day in the Rabbinic synagogues.

[3] Acts xvii. 3, διανοίγων καὶ παρατιθέμενος.

[4] One of these was Secundus (Acts xx. 4), and, perhaps, a Gaius (xix. 29). The names are common enough, but it is a curious coincidence to find them, as well as the name Sosipater, inscribed among the Politarchs on the triumphal arch of Thessalonica.

[5] Acts xix. 29; xx. 4; Col. iv. 10, συναιχμάλωτος; Philem. 24.

of his visit to Jerusalem, of his voyage and shipwreck, and of his last imprisonment. A larger number, however, of proselytes and of Greeks accepted the faith,[1] and not a few women, of whom some were in a leading position. This inveterate obstinacy of the Jews, contrasting sadly with the ready conversion of the Gentiles, and especially of women, who in all ages have been more remarkable than men for religious earnestness, is a phenomenon which constantly recurs in the early history of Christianity. Nor is this wholly to be wondered at. The Jew was at least in possession of a religion, which had raised him to a height of moral superiority above his Gentile contemporaries; but the Gentile of this day had no religion at all worth speaking of. If the Jew had more and more mistaken the shell of ceremonialism for the precious truths of which that ceremonialism was but the integument, he was at least conscious that there *were* deep truths which lay enshrined behind the rites and observances which he so fanatically cherished. But on what deep truths could the Greek woman rest, if her life were pure, and if her thoughts had been elevated above the ignorant domesticism which was the only recognised virtue of her sex? What comfort was there for her in the cold grey eyes of Athene, or the stereotyped smile of the voluptuous Aphrodite? And when the Thessalonian Greek raised his eyes to the dispeopled heaven of the Olympus, which towered over the blue gulf on which his city stood—when his imagination could no longer place the throne of Zeus, and the session of his mighty deities, on that dazzling summit where Cicero had remarked

---

[1] In Acts xvii. 4, even if there be insufficient MSS. evidence in favour of the reading τῶν τε σεβομένων καὶ Ἑλλήνων (A, D, Vulg., Copt.), yet the Epistles prove decidedly that Gentiles predominated among the converts.

with pathetic irony that he saw nothing but snow and ice—what compensation could he find for the void left in his heart by a dead religion?[1] By adopting circumcision he might become, as it were, a Helot of Judaism; and to such a sacrifice he was not tempted. But the Gospel which Paul preached had no esoteric doctrines, and no supercilious exclusions, and no repellent ceremonials; it came with a Divine Example and a free gift to all, and that free gift involved all that was most precious to the troubled and despondent soul. No wonder, then, that the Church of Thessalonica was mainly Gentile, as is proved by the distinct language of St. Paul,[2] and the total absence of any Old Testament allusion in the two Epistles. In the three weeks of synagogue preaching, St. Paul had confined his argument to Scripture; but to Gentile converts of only a few months' standing such arguments would have been unintelligible, and they were needless to those who had believed on the personal testimony to a risen Christ.

After mentioning the first three Sabbaths, St. Luke furnishes us with no further details of the stay at Thessalonica. But we can trace several interesting facts about their further residence from the personal allusions of St. Paul's Epistles. The First Epistle to the Thessalonians —the earliest of all his letters which have come down to us—was written within a month or two of his departure. We trace in it the tone of sadness and the yearning for a brighter future which were natural to one whose habitual life at this time was that of a hated and hunted outcast. We see that the infant Church was remarkable for a faith-

---

[1] "Subversae Deorum arae, lares a quibusdam in publicum abjecti" (Suet. *Calig.* 5). "Plures nusquam jam Deos ullos interpretabantur" (Plin. *Epp.* vi. 20; *supra*, p. 28).

[2] 1 Thess. i. 9; ii. 14.

fulness, love, and patience which made it famous as a model
church in all Macedonia and Achaia.[1] It shone all the
more brightly from the fierce afflictions which from the
first encompassed the brethren, but failed either to quench
their constancy or dim their joy.[2] St. Paul dwells much
on his own bearing and example among them; the boldness
which he showed in spite of present opposition and past
persecutions; the total absence of all delusive promises in a
teaching which plainly warned them that to be near Christ
was to be near the fire;[3] the conviction wrought by the
present power of the Holy Spirit testifying to his words;[4]
the simplicity and sincerity which enabled him to appeal to
them as witnesses that his Gospel was not stained by the
faintest touch of deceitful flattery, or guilty motive, or
vain-glorious self-seeking;[5] the independence which he had
maintained;[6] the self-sacrificing tenderness which he had
showed; the incessant severity of his industry;[7] the
blameless purity of his life; the individual solicitude of
his instructions.[8] And this high example had produced
its natural effects, for they had embraced his teaching
with passionate whole-heartedness as a divine message,[9]
and inspired him with an affection which made their
image ever present to his imagination, though untoward
hindrances had foiled a twice-repeated attempt to visit
them again.

The Epistle also throws light on that special feature of
St. Paul's teaching which was ultimately made the ground
for the attack upon him. His sufferings had naturally

---

[1] 1 Thess. i. 2, 3, 6—8.
[2] 2 Thess. i. 4, 5; 1 Thess. ii. 14; i. 6.
[3] 1 Thess. iii. 4, "We told you before that we should suffer tribulation."
ὁ ἐγγὺς μου ἐγγὺς τοῦ πυρός (saying of our Lord. Orig. *Hom. in Jerem.*
iii. 778).
[4] *Id.* ii. 1, 2.   [5] *Id.* i. 5.   [6] *Id.* ii. 3—6.
[7] *Id.* ii. 6; 2 Thess. iii. 8—10.   [8] *Id.* ii. 9.   [9] *Id.* ii. 13.

turned his thoughts to the future; the cruelty of man had tended to fix his faith yet more fervently on the help of God; the wickedness of earthly rulers, and the prevalence of earthly wrongs, had combined with circumstances on which we shall touch hereafter, to fill his teaching with the hopes and prophecies of a new kingdom and a returning King. His expectation of the rapid revelation of that Second Advent had been a theme of encouragement under incessant afflictions.

Few indeed were the untroubled periods of ministry in the life of St. Paul. The jealousy and hatred which had chased him from city to city of Pisidia and Lycaonia pursued him here. The Jews from first to last—the Jews for whom he felt in his inmost heart so tender an affection —were destined to be the plague and misery of his suffering life. At Antioch and Jerusalem, Jews nominally within the fold of Christ opposed his teaching and embittered his days; in all other cities it was the Jews who contradicted and blasphemed the holy name which he was preaching. In the planting of his Churches he had to fear their deadly opposition; in the watering of them, their yet more deadly fraternity. The Jews who hated Christ sought his life; the Jews who professed to love Him undermined his efforts. The one faction endangered his existence, the other ruined his peace. Never, till death released him, was he wholly free from their violent conspiracies or their insidious calumnies. Without, they sprang upon him at every opportunity like a pack of wolves; within, they hid themselves in sheep's clothing to worry and tear his flocks. And at Thessalonica he had yet a new form of persecution against which to contend. It was not purely Jewish as in Palestine, or purely Gentile as at Philippi, or combined as at Iconium, but was simply a brutal assault of the mob, hounded on by Jews in the background. Jealous,[1] as usual, that the abhorred preaching of a crucified Messiah should in a few weeks have won a greater multitude of adherents than they had won during many years to the doctrines of Moses—furious, above all, to see themselves deprived of the resources, the reverence, and the adhesion of leading women—they formed an unholy alliance with the lowest dregs of the Thessalonian populace. Owing to the dishonour in which manual pursuits were held in ancient days,[2] every large city had a superfluous population of worthless idlers—clients who lived on the doles of the wealthy, flatterers who fawned at the feet of the influential, the lazzaroni of streets, mere loafers and loiterers, the hangers-on of forum,[3] the claqueurs of law-courts, the scum that gathered about the shallowest outmost waves of civilisation. Hiring the assistance of these roughs and scoundrels,[4] the Jews disturbed the peace of the city by a fanatical riot, and incited the mob to attack the house of Jason, in order to bring the Apostles before the popular Assembly. But Paul had received timely warning, and he and his companions were in safe concealment. Foiled in this object, they seized Jason and one or two others whom they recognised as Christians, and dragged them before the Politarchs,[5] or presiding magistrates of the free city of Thessalonica.

[1] This is sufficiently obvious, whether we read ζηλώσαντες in Acts xvii. 5 (A, B, E, and many versions) or not.

[2] " Illiberates autem et sordidi quaestus mercenariorum omniumque quorum operae non artes sunt; est enim ipsa merces auctoramentum servitutis " (Cic. De Off. i. 42).

[3] Subrostrani (Cic. Epp. Fam. viii. 1, 2), Subbasilicani (Plaut. Capt. iv. 2, 35), turba forensis. "Lewd" (A. S. Læwede) means (1) lay, (2) ignorant, (3) bad.

[4] Acts xvii. 5, τῶν ἀγοραίων ἄνδρας τινὰς πονηρούς. Cf. Ar. Eg. 181; Sen. De Benef. 7.

[5] This name is unknown to classical literature. It would have furnished fine scope for the suspicious ingenuity of Baur and Zeller, had it not been fortunately preserved as the title of the Thessalonian magistrates on a still legible

H H

" These fellows," they shouted, " these seditious agitators of the civilised world [1] have found their way here also. Jason has received them. The whole set of them ought to be punished on a *crimen majestatis*, for they go in the teeth of Cæsar's decrees, and say that there is a different king, namely Jesus." [2] But the mob did not altogether succeed in carrying their point. In dealing with the seven Politarchs, under the very shadow of the proconsular residence, they were dealing with people of much higher position, and much more imbued with the Roman sense of law, than the provincial *duumviri* of Philippi. Neither the magistrates nor the general multitude of the city liked the aspect of affairs. It was on the face of it too ludicrous to suppose that hard-working artisans like Jason and his friends could be seriously contemplating revolutionary measures, or could be really guilty of *laesa majestas*. [3] A very short hearing sufficed to

inscription over the triumphal arch at Thessalonica, known as the Vardár gate (Böckh. *Inscr.* 1967). This arch was recently destroyed, but the fragments were saved by our Consul, and were brought to the British Museum in 1876. There are *seven*, and among them the names of Sosipater, Gaius, and Secundus. There are no *soi-disant* στρατηγοί or ῥαβδοῦχοι in the *Urbs Libera* Thessalonica, as there were at the colony Philippi, but there was a δῆμος and πολιτάρχαι.

[1] The expression shows how widely Christianity was spreading, and perhaps alludes to the recent events at Rome, which may have been a sufficient reason for the Jews themselves to keep rather in the background, and incite the Gentiles to get the Apostles expelled.

[2] The half truth, which made this accusation all the more of a lie, is seen in St. Paul's preaching of the Second Advent (1, 2 Thess. *passim*) and the kingdom of Christ (1 Thess. ii. 12; 2 Thess. i. 5), and not impossibly in some distortion of what he had told them of ὁ κατέχων and τὸ κατέχον (2 Thess. ii. 6, 7). The " *nec Caesaribus honor* " is one of the complaints of Tacitus against the Jews (*Hist.* v. 5).

[3] We see in the pages of Tacitus that it was the endless elasticity of this charge—the *crimen majestatis*—which made it so terrible an engine of tyranny (*Ann.* iii. 38). The facts here mentioned strikingly illustrate this. Any one who chose to turn *delator* might thus crush an obscure Jew as easily as he could crush a powerful noble.

show them that this was some religious opinion entertained
by a few poor people, and so far from taking strong
measures or inflicting any punishment, they contented
themselves with making Jason and the others give some
pecuniary security[1] that they would keep the peace, and
so dismissed them.   But this was a sufficient sign that for
the present further mission work would be impossible.   No
magistrates like the presence of even an innocently dis-
turbing element in their jurisdiction, and if Paul and Silas
were brought in person before them, they might not
escape so easily.   Nor, in the defective police regulations
of antiquity, was it at all certain that the moderation of
the magistrates would be an efficient protection to two
poor Jews from the hatred and violence of a mob.   In any
case it is probable that they would be unwilling to run the
risk of impoverishing Jason and their other friends by
causing a forfeiture of the scant and much-needed earnings
which they had been obliged to pledge.   The brethren,
therefore, devised means to secure the escape of Paul and
Silas by night.   It is not impossible that Timotheus stayed
among them for a time, to teach and organise the Church,
and to add those last exhortations which should nerve
them to bear up against the persecutions of many years.[2]
For in the Church of the Thessalonians, which was in some
respects the fairest gain of his mission, St. Paul felt an
intense solicitude, manifested by the watchful care with
which he guarded its interests.[3]

---

[1] Acts xvii. 9, λαβόντες τὸ ἱκανόν sounds like a translation of the Latin
phrase "Satisdatione acceptâ."   Cf. Lev. xxv. 26 (LXX.).   It was the Jewish
sense that the Romans loved justice which made them all the more readily accept
their yoke (Jos. *Antt.* xvii. 9, § 4, and 13, § 1; *B. J.* vi. 6, § 2; Dio Cass. xxxvi.
p. 37).   Titus upbraided them with all the generous favours which they had
received from Rome (Jos. *B. J.* vi. 2, § 4).

[2] I agree with Alford in thinking that the mention of Timothy in the
superscription of both Epistles, and his mission to them from Athens, prove
that he was with St. Paul during this visit.   [3] 1 Thess. ii. 18.

H H 2

When night had fallen over the tumult which had been surging through the streets of Thessalonica, news of the issue of the trial before the Politarchs was brought to Paul and Silas in their concealment. The dawn might easily witness a still more dangerous outbreak, and they therefore planned an immediate escape. They gathered together their few poor possessions, and under the cover of darkness stole through the silent and deserted streets under the triumphal Arch of Augustus, and through the western gate. Whither should they now turn? From Philippi, the virtual capital of Macedonia Prima, they had been driven to Thessalonica, the capital of Macedonia Secunda. An accidental collision with Gentile interests had cost them flagellation, outrage, and imprisonment in the colony; the fury of Jewish hatred had imperilled their lives, and caused trouble and loss to their friends in the free city. Should they now make their way to Pella, the famous birthplace of the young Greek who had subdued the world, and whose genius had left an indelible impress on the social and political conditions which they everywhere encountered? To do this would be obviously useless. The Jewish synagogues of the dispersion were in close connexion with each other, and the watchword would now be evidently given to hound the fugitives from place to place, and especially to silence Paul as the arch-apostate who was persuading all men everywhere, as they calumniously asserted, to forsake the Law of Moses. Another and less frequented road would lead them to a comparatively unimportant town, which lay off the main route, in which their presence might, for a time at any rate, remain unsuspected. Striking off from the great Via Egnatia to one which took a more southerly direction, the two fugitives made their way through the darkness. A night escape of at least fifty miles, along

an unknown road, involving the dangers of pursuit and
the crossing of large and frequently flooded rivers like
the Axius, the Echidorus, the Lydias, and some of the
numerous affluents of the Haliacmon, is passed over with
a single word. Can we wonder at the absence of all
allusion to the beauties, delights, and associations of
travel in the case of one whose travels were not only
the laborious journeys, beset with incessant hardships, of
a sickly Jewish artisan, but also those of one whose life
in its endless trials was a spectacle unto the universe,
to angels and to men? [1]

The town which they had in view as a place of refuge
was Berœa,[2] and their motive in going there receives
striking and unexpected illustration from a passage of
Cicero. In his passionate philippic against Piso he says
to him that after his gross maladministration of Macedonia, he was so unpopular that he had to slink into
Thessalonica incognito, and by night;[3] and that from
thence, unable to bear the concert of wailers, and the
hurricane of complaints, he left the main road and fled
to the out-of-the-way town of Berœa. We cannot
doubt that this comparatively secluded position was the
reason why Paul and Silas chose it as safer than the
more famous and frequented Pella.

And as they traversed the pleasant streets of the town—
" dewy," like those of Tivoli, " with twinkling rivulets "—
it must have been with sinking hearts, in spite of all their
courage and constancy, that Paul and Silas once more made
their way, as their first duty, into the synagogue of the
Jews. But if the life of the Christian missionary has its
own breadths of gloom, it also has its lights, and after all

[1] 1 Cor. iv. 9.

[2] Berœa is perhaps a Macedonian corruption for Pherœa (cf. Βίλιππος for
Φίλιππος). It is now called Kara Pheria.

[3] Cic. in Pis. 36. Adduced by Wetstein ad loc.

the storms which they had encountered they were cheered
in their heaviness by a most encouraging reception.   The
Jews of this synagogue were less obstinate, less sophisticated,
than those whom St. Paul ever found elsewhere.   When
he had urged upon them those arguments from the
Psalms, and from Isaiah, and from Habakkuk, about a
Messiah who was to die, and suffer, and rise again, and
about faith as the sole means of justification, the Jews,
instead of turning upon him as soon as they understood
the full scope and logical conclusions of his arguments,
proved themselves to be " nobler "[1] than those of Thessalonica—more generous, more simple, more sincere and
truth-loving.   Instead of angrily rejecting this new
Gospel, they daily and diligently searched the Scriptures
to judge Paul's arguments and references by the word
and the testimony.   The result was that many Jews
believed, as well as Greeks—men and women of the more
respectable classes.   They must have spent some weeks
of calm among these open-minded Berœans, for twice
during the stay St. Paul conceived the design of going
back to his beloved Thessalonians.   Untoward obstacles
prevented this,[2] and so heavily did the interests of the
persecuted Church rest on his mind that either from
Berœa, or subsequently from Athens, he sent Timothy
to inquire into and report their state.   One permanent
friend, both to St. Paul and to Christianity, was gained
in the person of Sopater, of Berœa.

But it would have been too much to hope that all
should be thus open to conviction, and the news was soon
unfavourably reported to the Synagogue of Thessalonica.

---

[1] Acts xvii. 11, εὐγενέστεροι. The expression is interesting as an instance
of εὐγενής, used (as in modern times) in a secondary and moral sense. The
best comment on it is the "Nobilitas sola est atque unica virtus."
[2] 1 Thess. ii. 18.

The hated name of Paul acted like a spark on their inflammable rage, and they instantly despatched emissaries to stir up storms among the mob of Berœa.[1] Once more Paul received timely notice from some faithful friend. It was impossible to face this persistent and organised outburst of hatred which was now pursuing him from city to city. And since it was clear that Paul, and not Silas, was the main object of persecution, it was arranged that, while Paul made good his escape, Silas and Timothy —who may have joined his companions during their residence at Berœa—should stay to set in order all that was wanting, and water the good seed which had begun to spring.

And so—once more in his normal condition of a fugitive—St. Paul left Berœa. He was not alone, and either from the weakness of his eyesight or from his liability to epilepsy, all his movements were guided by others. "The brethren" sent him away to go seawards,[2] and there can be little doubt that they led him sixteen miles to the colony of Dium,[3] whence he sailed for Athens. That he did not proceed by land seems certain. It was the longer, the more expensive, the more dangerous, and the more fatiguing route. If St. Paul was so little able to make his way alone that, even by the sea route, some of the Berœan brethren were obliged to accompany him till they left him safe in lodgings at Athens, it is clear that by the land route their difficulties, to say nothing of

---

[1] Acts xvii. 13, σαλεύοντες τοὺς ὄχλους.

[2] Acts xvii. 14, ὡς ἐπὶ τὴν θάλασσαν is a mere pleonastic phrase for "in the direction of the sea" (Strabo, xvi. 2, &c.). Ἕως, the reading of א, A, B, E, and other variations of the text, seem to have arisen from the comparative rarity of the expression. The notion that he only made a feint of going to the sea, and then turned landwards to foil pursuit, arises from an erroneous interpretation of the phrase.

[3] Perhaps to Alorus or Methone. (Renan, St. Paul, p. 166, quoting Strabo, vii., pp. 20, 22; Leake, iii. 435.)

the danger of pursuit, would have been much increased. The silence of St. Luke as to any single town visited on the journey is conclusive,[1] and we must suppose that some time in autumn, St. Paul embarked on the stormy waves of the Mediterranean, and saw the multitudinous and snowy peaks of Olympus melt into the distant blue. He sailed along shores of which every hill and promontory is voiceful with heroic memories ; past Ossa and Pelion, past the coast of Thermopylæ, along the shores of Eubœa,[2] round the "marbled steep" of Sunium, where the white Temple still stood entire, until his eye caught the well-known glimpse of the crest and spear-head of Athene Promachos on the Acropolis,[3]—the helm was turned, and, entering a lovely harbour, his ship dropped anchor in full sight of the Parthenon and the Propylæa.

[1] The addition of D, παρῆλθεν δὲ τὴν Θεσσαλίαν ἐκωλύθη γὰρ εἰς αὐτοὺς κηρύξαι τὸν λόγον, throws no light on the question.

[2] Whether St. Paul sailed down the Euripus or to the east of Eubœa uncertain. The former route was the more common.

[3] Pausan. Attic. i. 28, 2; Herod. v. 77.

Book VIII.

CHRISTIANITY IN ACHAIA.

'Ω ταὶ λιπαραὶ καὶ ἰοστέφανοι καὶ ἀοίδιμοι
Ἑλλάδος ἔρεισμα, κλειναὶ 'Αθᾶναι, δαιμόνιον πτολίεθρον.—PIND. *Fr.* 47.

Τοιοῦτον αὐτοῖς 'Αρεος εὔβουλον πάγον
ἐγὼ ξυνήδη χθόνιον ὄνθ', ὃς οὐκ ἐᾷ
Τοιούσθ' ἀλήτας τῇδ' ὁμοῦ ναίειν πόλει.—SOPH. *Œd. Col.* 947.

Ποῦ νῦν τῆς 'Ελλάδος ὁ τῦφος; ποῦ τῶν 'Αθηνῶν τὸ ὄνομα; ποῦ τῶν φιλοσόφων ὁ
λῆρος; ὁ ἀπὸ Γαλιλαίας, ὁ ἀπὸ Βηθσαΐδα, ὁ ἄγροικος πάντων ἐκείνων περιεγίνετο.
CHRYS. *Hom.* iv. *in Act.* iii. (*Opp.* ix. 38, *ed.* Montfaucon).

CHAPTER XXVII.

ST. PAUL AT ATHENS.

"Immortal Greece, dear land of glorious lays,
 Lo, here the Unknown God of thine unconscious praise."—KEBLE.

ATHENS!—with what a thrill of delight has many a modern traveller been filled as, for the first time, he stepped upon that classic land! With what an eager gaze has he scanned the scenery and outline of that city

——————" on the Ægean shore,
Built nobly, pure the air, and light the soil,
Athens, the eye of Greece, mother of arts
And eloquence."

As he approached the Acropolis what a throng of brilliant scenes has passed across his memory; what processions of grand and heroic and beautiful figures have swept across the stage of his imagination! As he treads upon Attic ground he is in "the Holy Land of the Ideal;"

he has reached the most sacred shrine of the "fair humanities" of Paganism.   It was at Athens that the human form, sedulously trained, attained its most exquisite and winning beauty; there that human freedom put forth its most splendid power; there that human intellect displayed its utmost subtlety and grace; there that Art reached to its most consummate perfection; there that Poetry uttered alike its sweetest and its sublimest strains; there that Philosophy attuned to the most perfect music of human expression its loftiest and deepest thoughts.   Had it been possible for the world by its own wisdom to know God; had it been in the power of man to turn into bread the stones of the wilderness; had permanent happiness lain within the grasp of sense, or been among the rewards of culture; had it been granted to man's unaided power to win salvation by the gifts and qualities of his own nature, and to make for himself a new Paradise in lieu of that lost Eden, before whose gate still waves the fiery sword of the Cherubim,—then such ends would have been achieved at Athens in the day of her glory. No one who has been nurtured in the glorious lore of that gay and radiant city, and has owed some of his best training to the hours spent in reading the history and mastering the literature of its many noble sons, can ever visit it without deep emotions of gratitude, interest, and love.[1]

And St. Paul must have known at least something of the city in whose language he spoke, and with whose writers he was not wholly unfamiliar.   The notion that he was a finished classical scholar is, indeed, as we have

---

[1] We read the sentiments of Cicero, Sulpicius, Germanicus, Pliny, Apollonius, &c., in Cic. *Ep. ad Quint. fratr.* i. 1; *Epp. Fam.* iv. 5; *ad Att.* v. 10; vi. 1; Tac. *Ann.* ii. 53; Plin. *Ep.* viii. 24; Philostr. *Vit. Apoll.* v. 41; Renan, *St. Paul,* 167; but, as he adds, "Paul belonged to another world; his Holy Land was elsewhere."

shown already, a mere delusion; and the absence from his
Epistles of every historical reference proves that, like the vast
mass of his countrymen, he was indifferent to the history
of the heathen, though profoundly versed in the history
of Israel. He was, indeed, no less liberal and cosmopolitan
—nay, in the best sense, far more so—than the most advanced
Hellenist, the most cultivated Hagadist of his day. Yet he
looked at " the wisdom of Javan " as something altogether
evanescent and subsidiary—an outcome of very partial enlightenment, far from pure, and yet graciously conceded to
the ages of ignorance. It was with no thrill of rapture,
no loyal recognition of grace and greatness, that Paul
landed at Phalerum or Peiræus, and saw the crowning
edifices of the Acropolis, as it towered over the wilderness of meaner temples, stand out in their white lustre
against the clear blue sky. On the contrary, a feeling
of depression, a fainting of the heart, an inward unrest
and agitation, seems at once to have taken possession
of his susceptible and ardent temperament; above
all, a sense of loneliness which imperiously claimed the
solace of that beloved companionship which alone rendered his labours possible, or sustained him amid the
daily infirmities of his troubled life. As he bade farewell
to the faithful Berœan brethren who had watched over
his journey, and had been to him in the place of eyes,
the one message that he impresses on them is urgently
to enjoin Silas and Timotheus to come to him at once
with all possible speed. In the words of St. Luke we
still seem to catch an echo of the yearning earnestness
which shows us that solitude [1]—and above all solitude in
such a place—was the one trial which he found it the
most difficult to bear.

[1] Acts xvii. 15, λαβόντες ἐντολὴν πρὸς τὸν Σίλαν καὶ τὸν Τιμόθεον ἵνα ὡς
τάχιστα ἔλθωσιν πρὸς αὐτόν.

But even if his two friends were able instantly to set
out for Athens, a full week must, at the lowest compu-
tation, inevitably elapse before Silas could reach him
from Berœa, and a still longer period before Timothy
could come from Thessalonica; and during those days of
weary and restless longing there was little that he
could do.   It is probable that, when first he was guided
by his friends to his humble lodging, he would have
had little heart to notice the sights and sounds of
those heathen streets, though, as he walked through the
ruins of the long walls of Themistocles to the Peiraic
gate, one of the brethren, more quick-eyed than himself,
may have pointed out to him the altars bearing the inscription, *'ΑΓΝΩΣΤΟΙΣ ΘΕΟΙΣ*,[1] which about the same
time attracted the notice of Apollonius of Tyana, and
were observed fifty years afterwards by the traveller Pausanias, as he followed the same road.[2]   But when the
brethren had left him—having no opportunity during
that brief stay to labour with his own hands—he relieved
his melancholy tedium by wandering hither and thither,
with a curiosity [3] largely mingled with grief and indignation.[4]

The country had been desolated by the Roman
dominion, but the city still retained some of its ancient
glories.   No Secundus Carinas had as yet laid his greedy
and tainted hand on the unrivalled statues of the Athens
of Phidias.   It was the multitude of these statues in a
city where, as Petronius says,[5] it was more easy to meet

---

[1] Pausan. I. i. 4; Hesych. *s. v.*, 'Αγνῶτες θεοί; v. *infra*, p. 11.

[2] They lay on the road between the Phaleric port and the city, and St.
Paul may possibly have landed at Phalerum, the nearest though not the most
frequented harbour for vessels sailing from Macedonia.

[3] Acts xvii. 23, διερχόμενος καὶ ἀναθεωρῶν τὰ σεβάσματα ὑμῶν.

[4] *Id.* 16, παρωξύνετο τὸ πνεῦμα αὐτοῦ.   Cf. 1 Cor. xiii. 5, οὐ παροξύνεται, "is
not exasperated."

[5] Petron. *Sat.* 17.

a god than a man, which chiefly absorbed St. Paul's attention. He might glance with passing interest at the long colonnades of shops glittering with wares from every port in the Ægean ; but similar scenes had not been unfamiliar to him in Tarsus, and Antioch, and Thessalonica. He might stroll into the Stoa Pœcile, and there peer at the paintings, still bright and fresh, of Homeric councils of which he probably knew nothing, and of those Athenian battles about which, not even excepting Marathon,[1] there is no evidence that he felt any interest. The vast enlargement of his *spiritual* horizon would not have brought with it any increase of secular knowledge, and if Paul stood in these respects on the level of even the Gamaliels of his day, he knew little or nothing of Hellenic story.[2] And for the same reason he would have been indifferent to the innumerable busts of Greeks of every degree of eminence, from Solon and Epimenides down to recent Sophists and Cosmetae, and still more indifferent to the venal intrusions which Athenian servility had conceded to Roman self-importance. A glance would have been more than enough for Greek statues decapitated to furnish figures for Roman heads, or pedestals from which the original hero had been displaced to make room for the portly bulk and bloated physiognomy of some modern Proconsul. Some Jew might take a certain pride in

[1] Mr. Martineau, after remarking that modern lives of St. Paul have been too much of the nature of " illustrative guide-books, so instructive, that by far the greatest part of their information would have been new to St. Paul himself," adds that " in the vicinity of Salamis or Marathon he would probably recall the past no more than a Brahmin would in travelling over the fields of Edgehill or Marston Moor" (*Studies in Christianity*, p. 417).

[2] Nothing in the Talmud is more amazing than the total absence of the geographic, chronological, and historic spirit. A genuine Jew of that Pharisaic class in the midst of which St. Paul had been trained, cared more for some pedantically minute *Halacha*, about the threads in a *Tsitsith*, than for all the Pagan history in the world.

pointing out to him the statues of Hyrcanus, the Asmonæan High Priest, and of that beautiful Berenice before
whom he little thought that he should one day plead his
cause.[1] But his chief notice would be directed to the
bewildering multiplicity of temples, and to the numberless "idols" which rose on every side. Athens was the
city of statues.   There were statues of Phidias, and
Myron, and Lysicles, and statues without number of the
tasteless and mechanical copyists of that dead period of
the Empire; statues of antiquity as venerable as the
olive-wood Athênê which had fallen from heaven, and
statues of yesterday; statues colossal and diminutive;
statues equestrian, and erect, and seated; statues agonistic
and contemplative, solitary and combined, plain and
coloured; statues of wood, and earthenware, and stone,
and marble, and bronze, and ivory and gold, in every
attitude, and in all possible combinations; stautes starting
from every cave, and standing like lines of sentinels in
every street.[2] There were more statues in Athens, says
Pausanias, than in all the rest of Greece put together,
and their number would be all the more startling, and
even shocking, to St. Paul, because, during the long
youthful years of his study at Jerusalem, he had never
seen so much as one representation of the human form,
and had been trained to regard it as apostasy to give the
faintest sanction to such violations of God's express command.   His earlier Hellenistic training, his natural large-
heartedness, his subsequent familiarity with Gentile life,
above all, the entire change of his views respecting the
universality and permanence of the Mosaic Law, had
indeed indefinitely widened for him the shrunken horizon

[1] Jos. *Antt.* xiv. 8, § 5.
[2] "Athenae simulacra Deorum hominumque habentes omni genere et
materiae et artium insignia " (Liv. xlv. 27).

of Jewish intolerance. But any sense of the dignity and beauty of Pagan art was impossible to one who had been trained in the schools of the Rabbis.[1] There was nothing in his education which enabled him to admire the simple grandeur of the Propylæa, the severe beauty of the Parthenon, the massive proportions of the Theseum, the exquisite elegance of the Temple of the Wingless Victory. From the nude grace and sinewy strength of the youthful processions portrayed on frieze or entablature, he would have turned away with something of impatience, if not with something even of disgust. When the tutor of Charles the Fifth, the good Cardinal of Tortosa, ascended the Papal throne under the title of Adrian the Sixth, and his attendants conducted him to the Vatican to show him its splendid treasures of matchless statuary, his sole remark, in those uncouth accents which excited so much hatred and ridicule in his worthless subjects, was

"SUNT IDOLA ANTIQUORUM!"[2]

It was made a scoff and a jest against him, and doubtless, in a Pontiff of the sixteenth century, it shows an intensity of the Hebraising spirit singularly unsoftened by any tinge of Hellenic culture. But, as has been admitted even by writers of the most refined æsthetic sympathies, the old German Pope was more than half right. At any rate, the sort of repugnance which dictated his disparaging remark would have been not only natural, but inevitable, in a Pharisee in the capital of Judaism and under the very shadow of the Temple of the Most High. We who have learnt to see God in all that is refined and

---

[1] The reader will recall the censure passed on Gamaliel for having merely entered a bath in which was a statue of Aphrodite (*infra*, p. 645).

[2] He walled up, and never entered, the Belvedere (Symonds, *Renaissance*, p. 377).

beautiful; whom His love has lifted above the perils
of an extinct paganism; whom His own word has taught
to recognise sunbeams from the Fountain of Light in
every grace of true art and every glow of poetic inspiration, may thankfully admire the exquisite creations of
ancient genius;—but had Paul done so he could not have
been the Paul he was. "The prejudices of the icono-
clastic Jew," says Renan, with bitter injustice, "blinded
him; he took these incomparable images for idols. 'His
spirit,' says his biographer, 'was embittered within him
when he saw the city *filled with idols.*' Ah, beautiful and
chaste images; true gods and true goddesses, tremble!
See the man who will raise the hammer against you.
The fatal word has been pronounced: you are *idols*. The
mistake of this ugly little Jew will be your death-warrant."[1]

Yes, their death-warrant as false gods and false goddesses, as "gods of the heathen" which "are but idols,"[2]
but not their death-warrant to us as works of art; not their
death-warrant as the imaginative creations of a divinely
given faculty; not their death-warrant as echoes from within
of that outward beauty which is a gift of God; not in any
sense their death-warrant as standing for anything which
is valuable to mankind. Christianity only discouraged
Art so long as Art was the handmaid of idolatry and vice;
the moment this danger ceased she inspired and ennobled
Art. It is all very well for sentimentalists to sigh
over "the beauty that was Greece, and the glory that
was Rome;" but Paganism had a very ragged edge, and

---

[1] *St. Paul*, p. 172. The word κατείδωλον is, however, St. Luke's, not
St. Paul's.

[2] "The pagan worship of beauty . . . had ennobled art and corrupted
nature; extracted wonders from the quarries of Pentelicus, and horrors from
the populace of Rome and Corinth; perfected the marbles of the temple,
and degraded the humanity of the worshipper. Heathenism had wrought
into monstrous combination physical beauty and moral deformity" (Martineau,
Hours of Thought, p. 306).

it was *this* that Paul daily witnessed. Paganism, at
its *best*, was a form assumed by natural religion, and
had a power and life of its own; but, alas! it had not
in it enough salt of solid morality to save its own
power and life from corruption. St. Paul needed no
mere historical induction to convince him that the loftiest
heights of culture are compatible with the lowest abysses
of depravity, and that a shrine of consummate beauty could
be a sink of utter infamy. Nay, more, he knew by personal observation, what we may only be led to conjecture
by thoughtful comparison, that there was no slight connexion between the superficial brightness and the hidden
putrescence; that the flowers which yielded the intoxicating
honey of ancient art were poisoned flowers; that the perfectness of sculpture might have been impossible without
the nude athleticism which ministered to vice. For one
who placed the sublime of manhood in perfect obedience to
the moral law, for one to whom purity and self-control
were elements of the only supreme ideal, it was, in that
age, impossible to love, impossible to regard even with
complacence, an Art which was avowedly the handmaid
of Idolatry, and covertly the patroness of shame. Our
regret for the extinguished brilliancy of Athens will be
less keen when we bear in mind that, more than any other
city, she has been the corruptress of the world. She
kindled the altars of her genius with unhallowed incense,
and fed them with strange fires. Better by far the
sacred Philistinism—if Philistinism it were—for which
this beautiful harlot had no interest, and no charm, than
the veiled apostasy which longs to recall her witchcraft
and to replenish the cup of her abomination. Better
the uncompromising Hebraism which asks what concord
hath Christ with Belial and the Temple of God with idols,
than the corrupt Hellenism which under pretence of

T I

artistic sensibility or archæological information, has left
its deep taint on modern literature, and seems to be
never happy unless it is raking amid the embers of forgotten lusts.

Nor was Paul likely to be overpowered by the sense
of Athenian greatness. Even if his knowledge of past
history were more profound than we imagine it to have
been, yet the Greece that he now saw was but a shadow
and a corpse—"Greece, but living Greece no more."[1]
She was but trading on the memory of achievements not
her own; she was but repeating with dead lips the echo
of old philosophies which had never been sufficient to
satisfy the yearnings of the world. Her splendour was
no longer an innate effulgence, but a lingering reflex.
Centuries had elapsed since all that was grand and
heroic in her history had " gone glimmering down
the dream of things that were; " and now she was
the weak and contemptuously tolerated dependent of an
alien barbarism,[2] puffed up by the empty recollection of
a fame to which she contributed nothing, and retaining no
heritage of the past except its monuments, its decrepitude,
and its corruption. Among the things which he saw at
Athens there were few which Paul could naturally admire.

---

[1] See Apollonius, *Ep.* lxx. (*ubi supr.*). Ἕλληνες οἴεσθε δεῖν ὀνομάζεσθαι . . . ἀλλ
ὑμῶν γε οὐδὲ τὰ ὀνόματα μένει τοῖς πολλοῖς, ἀλλ' ὑπὸ νέας ταύτης εὐδαιμονίας (the
patronage of Rome), ἀπολωλέκασι τὰ τῶν προγόνων σύμβολα.

[2] The nominal freedom of Athens had been spared by successive conquerors. Though she had always been on the defeated side with Mithri-
dates, Pompey, Brutus and Cassius, and Anthony, yet the Roman Emperors
left her the contemptuous boon of an unfettered loquacity. This was her
lowest period. "She was no longer the city of Theseus; she was not yet the
city of Hadrian" (Renan, p. 178). About this very time the city was visited
by the thaumaturgist Apollonius, and, according to Philostratus, the estimate
which he formed of the city was most unfavourable . . . οὐ μένοντες Ἕλληνες
ὅπως δὲ οὐ μένοντες ἐγὼ φράσω, Γέρων σοφὸς οὐδεὶς Ἀθηναῖος . . . ὁ κόλαξ παρὰ ταῖς
πύλαις, ὁ συκοφάντης πρὸ τῶν πυλῶν, ὁ μαστροπὸς πρὸ τῶν μακρῶν τειχῶν, ὁ
παράσιτος πρὸ τῆς Μουνυχίης καὶ πρὸ τοῦ Πειραιοῦ, ἡ θεὸς δὲ οὐδὲ Σούνιον ἔχει (*Opp.*
Philostr. ed. Olear. ii. 406.)

He would indeed have read with interest the moral inscriptions on the Hermæ which were presented to her citizens by the tyrant Hipparchus,[1] and would have looked with something of sympathy on such altars as those to Modesty and to Piety. But, among the many altars visible in every street, there was one by which he lingered with special attention, and of which he read with the deepest emotion the ancient inscription—

ΑΓΝΩΣΤΩΙΘΕΩΙ.
" To the unknown God."[2]

The better-known altars, of which the inscriptions were in the plural, and which merely bore witness to the catholicity of Paganism, would have had less interest for him. It is merely one of the self-confident assertions which are too characteristic of Jerome[3] that St. Paul misquoted the singular for the plural. The inscription to which he called attention on the Areopagus was evidently an ancient one, and one which he had observed on a single altar.[4] Whether that altar was one of those which Epimenides had advised the Athenians to build to whatever god it might be — τῷ προσήκοντι θεῷ — wherever the black and white

---

[1] Such as Μνῆμα τόδ' Ἱππάρχου· στεῖχε δίκαια φρονῶν, or Μνῆμα τόδ' Ἱππάρχου μὴ φίλον ἐξαπάτα.

[2] This, and not " to an unknown God," is the right rendering.

[3] "Inscriptio arae *non ita erat ut Paulus asseruit* Ignoto Deo; sed ita; Diis Asiae et Europae et Africae, Diis ignotis et peregrinis. Verum quia Paulus non pluribus Diis ignotis indigebat sed uno tantum ignoto Deo, singulari verbo usus est." Jer. *ad Tit.* i. 12 (see Biscoe, p. 210).

[4] Acts xvii. 23, βωμὸν ᾧ ἐπεγέγραπτο. The fact that Pausanias (*Attic.* i. 1), Philostratus (*Vit. Apollon.* vi. 3), and others (Diog. Laert. i. x. 110, &c.), mention altars, ἀγνώστων δαιμόνων, does not of course prove that there was no altar with the singular inscription; nor, indeed, is it certain that these words may not mean altars on *each* of which was an inscription, 'Αγνώστῳ θεῷ, as Winer understands them. Dr. Plumptre favours the view that it means "to the Unknowable God;" and compares it with the famous inscription on the veil of Isis, and the Mithraic inscription found on an altar at Ostia, " *Signum indeprehensibilis Dei,*" and 1 Cor. i. 21.

I I 2

sheep lay down, which he told them to loose from the
Areopagus; or one dedicated to some god whose name had
in course of time become obliterated and forgotten;[1] or one
which the Athenians had erected under some visitation of
which they could not identify the source[2]—was to St. Paul
a matter of indifference.   It is not in the least likely that
he supposed the altar to have been intended as a recognition of that Jehovah[3] who seemed so mysterious to the
Gentile world.   He regarded it as a proof of the confessed
inadequacy, the unsatisfied aspirations, of heathendom.
He saw in it, or liked to read *into* it, the acknowledgment
of some divinity after whom they yearned, but to the
knowledge of whom they had been unable to attain; and
this was He whom he felt it to be his own mission to
make known.   It was with this thought that he consoled
his restless loneliness in that uncongenial city; it was
this thought which rekindled his natural ardour as he
wandered through its idol-crowded streets.[4]

His work among the Jews was slight.   He discoursed,[5]
indeed, not unfrequently with them and their proselytes
in the synagogue or meeting-room[6] which they frequented;

---

[1] Eichhorn.   [2] Chrysostom.

[3] Called by the Gentiles ὁ πάγκρυφος (Just. Mart. *Paraenet. ad Graecos*, 38;
Apol. ii. 10; Philo, *Leg.* § 44).

[4] Acts xvii. 16.   And yet his high originality was shown in the fact that
he did not, like his race in general, vent his indignation in insults, "Gens con-
tumelia numinum insignis" (Plin. *H. N.* xiii. 9; Cic. *p. Flacc.* § 67).   Claudius,
in confirming their privileges, warned them, μὴ τὰς τῶν ἄλλων ἐθνῶν δεισιδαιμονίας
ἐξουθενίζειν (Jos. *Antt.* xix. 5, 3).   κατείδωλον means "full of idols," not as in
the E.V., "wholly given to idolatry;" "non *simulacris dedita*, sed *simulacris
referta*" (*Herm. ad Vig.* p. 638) cf. κατάμπελος, κατάδενδρος.   The word receives
most interesting illustration from Wetstein, from whom all succeeding commentators have freely borrowed.

[5] Acts xvii. 17, διελέγετο, not "disputed," but "conversed."

[6] No trace of any building which could have been a synagogue has been
found at Athens.   It has been inferred from passages in the Talmud that Jews
were numerous in Athens; but these passages apply to a much later period,
and in any case the Talmud is perfectly worthless as a direct historic guide.

but it is probable that they were few in number, and we find no traces either of the teaching which he addressed to them or of the manner in which they received it. It was in the market-place of Athens—the very Agora in which Socrates had adopted the same conversational method of instruction four centuries[1] before him—that he displayed his chief activity in a manner which he seems nowhere else to have adopted, by conversing daily and publicly with all comers. His presence and his message soon attracted attention. Athens had been in all ages a city of idlers, and even in her prime her citizens had been nicknamed Gapenians,[2] from the mixture of eager curiosity and inveterate loquacity which even then had been their conspicuous characteristics. Their greatest orator had hurled at them the reproach that, instead of flinging themselves into timely and vigorous action in defence of their endangered liberties, they were for ever gadding about asking for the very latest news;[3] and St. Luke—every incidental allusion of whose brief narrative bears the mark of truthfulness and knowledge—repeats the same characteristic under the altered circumstances of their present adversity. Even the foreign residents caught the infection, and the Agora buzzed with inquiring chatter at this late and decadent epoch no less loudly than in the days of Pericles or of Plato.

Among the throng of curious listeners, some of the Athenian philosophers were sure, sooner or later, to be

---

[1] Socrates died B.C. 399.

[2] Κεχηναῖοι, Ar. Eg., 1262. Demades said that the crest of Athens ought to be a great tongue. "Alexander qui quod cuique optimum est eripuit Lacedaemona servire jubet, Athenas tacere" (Sen. Ep. 94; see Demosth. Phil. iv.) τὴν πόλιν ἅπαντες τῶν Ἑλληνες ὑπολαμβάνουσιν ὡς φιλόλογός τε ἐστιν καὶ πολύλογος (Plat. Legg. i. 11).

[3] καινότερον (cf. Matt. xiii. 52). "Nova statim sordebant, noviora quaerebantur" (Bengel). Gill says that a similar question אחד חדש was common in the Rabbinic schools (Bammidbar Babba, f. 212, 4).

seen. The Stoa Pœcile, which Zeno had made his school,
and from which the Stoics derived their name, ran along
one side of the Agora, and not far distant were the gardens
of Epicurus. Besides the adherents of these two philosophical schools, there were Academics who followed Plato,
and Peripatetics who claimed the authority of Aristotle,
and Eclectics of every shade.[1] The whole city, indeed, was
not unlike one of our University towns at the deadest
and least productive epochs of their past. It was full of
professors, rhetors, tutors, arguers, discoursers, lecturers,
grammarians, pedagogues, and gymnasts of every description; and among all these Sophists and Sophronists there
was not one who displayed the least particle of originality
or force. Conforming sceptics lived in hypocritical union
with atheist priests, and there was not even sufficient
earnestness to arouse any antagonism between the empty
negations of a verbal philosophy and the hollow profession of a dead religion.[2] And of this undistinguished
throng of dilettanti pretenders to wisdom, not a single
name emerges out of the obscurity. Their so-called philosophy had become little better than a jingle of phrases[3]—
the languid repetition of effete watchwords—the unintelligent echo of empty formulæ. It was in a condition of
even deeper decadence than it had been when Cicero, on

---

[1] " From whose mouth issued forth
  Mellifluous streams that watered all the schools
  Of Academics old and new, with those
  Surnamed Peripatetics, and the school
  Epicurean, and the Stoic severe."   (Milton, *Par. Reg.*)

[2] See Renan, *St. Paul*, p. 186, who refers to Cic. *ad Fam.* xvi. 21 ; Lucian,
Dial. Mort. xx. 5 ; Philostr. *Apollon.* iv. 17.

[3] Φιλοσοφία Ἑλλήνων λόγων ψόφος. Tertullian asks, "Quid simile philosophus
et Christianus ?" (Tert. *Apol.* 46) ; but Paul, catholic and liberal to all truth,
would have hailed the truths which it was given to Greek philosophers to
see (Clem. Alex. *Strom.* vi. 8, § 65, and *passim*). χρησίμη πρὸς θεοσέβειαν γίνεται
προπαιδεία τις οὖσα (*Id.* i. 5, § 28 ; Aug. *De Civ. Dei*, ii. 7).

visiting Athens, declared its philosophy to be all a mere chaos—*ἄνω κάτω*—upside down.[1] Epicureans there were, still maintaining the dictum of their master that the highest good was pleasure; and Stoics asserting that the highest good was virtue; but of these Epicureans some had forgotten the belief that the best source of pleasure lay in virtue, and of these Stoics some contented themselves with their theoretic opinion with little care for its practical illustration. With the better side of both systems Paul would have felt much sympathy, but the defects and degeneracies of the two systems rose from the two evil sources to which all man's sins and miseries are mainly due—namely, sensuality and pride. It is true indeed that—

> "When Epicurus to the world had taught
> That pleasure was the chiefest good,
> His life he to his doctrines brought,
> And in a garden's shade that sovran pleasure sought;
> Whoever a true Epicure would be,
> May there find cheap and virtuous luxury."

But the famous garden where Epicurus himself lived in modest abstinence[2] soon degenerated into a scene of profligacy, and his definition of pleasure, as consisting in the absence of physical pain or mental perturbation (*ἀταραξία*), had led to an ideal of life which was at once effeminate and selfish. He had misplaced the centre of

---

[1] We can the better estimate this after reading such a book as Schneider's *Christliche Klänge aus dem Griech. und Rom. Classikern* (1865). The independence, cheerfulness, royalty, wealth of the true Christian recall the Stoic "kingliness," *αὐτάρκεια*—the very word which St. Paul often uses (2 Cor. ix. 8; Phil. iv. 11—18; 1 Cor. iv. 8—10, &c., compared with Cic. *De Fin.* iii. 22; Hor. *Sat.* i.—iii., 124—136; Sen. *Ep. Mor.* ix.). But what a difference is there between these apparent resemblances when we look at the Stoic and Christian doctrines—i. in their real significance; and ii. in their surroundings.

[2] Juv. *Sat.* xiii. 172; xiv. 319.

gravity of the moral system, and his degenerate followers, while they agreed with him in avowing that pleasure should be the aim of mortal existence, selected the nearer and coarser pleasures of the senses in preference to the pleasures of the intellect or the approval of the conscience. The sterner and loftier Epicureans of the type of Lucretius and Cassius were rare; the school was more commonly represented by the base and vulgar Hedonists who took as their motto, "Let us eat and drink, for to-morrow we die."[1] On the other hand, their great Stoic rivals had little reason to boast the efficacy of their nobler theory. Aiming at the attainment of a complete supremacy not only over their passions, but even over their circumstances—professing a fictitious indifference to every influence of pain or sorrow,[2] standing proudly alone in their unaided independence and self-asserted strength, the Stoics, with their vaunted apathy, had stretched the power of the will until it cracked and shrivelled under the unnatural strain; and this gave to their lives a consciousness of insincerity which, in the worse sort of them, degraded their philosophy into a cloak for every form of ambition and iniquity, and which made the nobler souls among them melancholy with a morbid egotism and an intense despair. In their worst degeneracies Stoicism became the apotheosis of suicide, and Epicureanism the glorification of lust.[3]

---

[1] Cf. Eccles. v. 18; Wisd. ii. 7—9.

[2] "There never was philosopher
Who yet could bear the toothache patiently."

[3] The ancient philosophers in the days of the Roman Empire (ἐκ πάγκυρες σοφοί, Phoenicides ap. Memeke, Com. Fr. iv. 511; Lucian, Eun. 8; Lact. Instt. iii. 25; Bactroperitae, Jer. in Matt. xi. 10, &c.) had as a body sunk to much the same position as the lazy monks and begging friars of the Middle Ages (see Sen. Ep. Mor. v. 1, 2; Tac. Ann. xvi. 32; Juv. iii. 116; Hor. Sat. i. 3, 35, 133). The reproaches addressed to them by the Roman satirists bear a close resemblance to those with which Chaucer lashed the mendicant preachers, and Ulric von Hutten scathed the degenerate monks.

How Paul dealt with the views and arguments of these rival sects—respectively the Pharisees and the Sadducees of the pagan world[1]—we do not know. Perhaps these philosophers considered it useless to discuss philosophical distinctions with one whose formal logic was as unlike that of Aristotle as it is possible to imagine—who had not the least acquaintance with the technicalities of philosophy, and whom they would despise as a mere barbarous and untrained Jew. Perhaps he was himself so eager to introduce to their notice the good news of the Kingdom of Heaven, that with him all questions as to the moral standpoint were subordinate to the religious truth from which he was convinced that morality alone could spring. They may have wanted to argue about the *summum bonum*; but he wanted to preach Christ. At any rate, when he came to address them he makes no allusion to the more popularly known points of contrast between the schools of philosophy, but is entirely occupied with the differences between their views and his own as to the nature and attributes of the Divine. Even to the philosophers who talked with him in the market-place[2] the subject-matter of his conversation had been neither pleasure nor virtue, but Jesus and the Resurrection.[3] The

[1] Josephus evidently saw the analogy between the Pharisees and the Stoics (Jos. *Antt.* xiii. 1, 5; xviii. 1, 2; *B.J.* ii. 8, § 2—14); and "Epicureans" is a constant name for heretics, &c., in the Talmud.

[2] When Apollonius landed at the Peiraeus he is represented as finding Athens very crowded and intensely hot. On his way to the city he met many philosophers, some reading, some perorating, and some arguing, all of whom greeted him. παρῄει δὲ οὐδεὶς αὐτὸν, ἀλλὰ τεκμηράμενοι πάντες ὡς εἴη Ἀπολλώνιος συνανεστρέφοντό τε καὶ ἠσπάζοντο χαίροντες (Philostr. *Vit.* iv. 17).

[3] Acts xvii. 18. The word "virtue" occurs but once in St. Paul (Phil. iv. 8), and ἡδονή, in the classic sense only in Tit. iii. 3. The notion that the philosophers took "the Resurrection" to be a new goddess Anastasis, though adopted by Chrysostom, Theophylact, Œcumenius, &c., and even in modern times by Renan ("Plusieurs à ce qu'il paraît, prirent *Anastasis* pour un nom de déesse, et crurent que Jésus et Anastasis étaient quelque nouveau couple

only result had been to create a certain amount of curiosity—a desire to hear a more connected statement of what he had to say.   But this curiosity barely emerged beyond the stage of contempt.   To some he was "apparently a proclaimer of strange deities;"[1] to others he was a mere " sparrow," a mere " seed-pecker "[2]—a " picker-up of learning's crumbs," a victim of unoriginal hallucinations, a retailer of second-hand scraps.   The view of the majority of these frivolous sciolists respecting one whose significance for the world transcended that of all their schools would have coincided nearly with that of

> "Cleon the poet from the sprinkled isles,"

which our poet gives in the following words :—

> "And for the rest
> I cannot tell thy messenger aright,
> Where to deliver what he bears of thine,
> To one called Paulus—we have heard his fame
> Indeed, if Christus be not one with him—
> I know not nor am troubled much to know.
> Thou canst not think a mere barbarian Jew,
> As Paulus proves to be, one circumcised,
> Hath access to a secret shut from us !
> Thou wrongest our philosophy, O King,
> In stooping to enquire of such an one,
> As if his answer could impose at all.

divin que ces rêveurs orientaux venaient prêcher," *St. Paul,* p. 190), seems to me almost absurd.   It would argue, as has been well said, either utter obscurity in the preaching of St. Paul, or the most incredible stupidity in his hearers.

[1] It is almost impossible to suppose that St. Luke is not mentally referring to the charge against Socrates, ἀδικεῖ Σωκράτης . . . καινὰ δαιμόνια εἰσφέρων (Xen. *Mem.* I. i.).

[2] Σπερμολόγος, a seed-pecking bird, applied as a contemptuous nickname to Athenian shoplifters and area sneaks (Eustath. *ad Od.* v. 490), and then to babblers who talked of things which they did not understand.   It was the very opprobrium which Demosthenes had launched against Æschines (*Pro Coronâ,* p. 269, *ed. Reiske*).   Compare the terms gobemouche, engoulevent, &c.

He writeth, doth he? well, and he may write!
O, the Jew findeth scholars! certain slaves,
Who touched on this same isle, preached him and Christ;
And (as I gathered from a bystander)
Their doctrines could be held by no sane man."[1]

With some hearers, however, amusement and curiosity won the day. So far as they could understand him he seemed to be announcing a new religion. The crowd on the level space of the Agora rendered it difficult for all to hear him, and as the Areopagus would both furnish a convenient area for an harangue, and as it was there that the court met which had the cognizance of all matters affecting the State religion, it was perhaps with some sense of burlesque that they led him up the rock-hewn steps—which still exist—to the level summit, and placed him on the "Stone of Impudence," from which the defendants before the Areopagus were wont to plead their cause.[2] Then, with a politeness that sounds ironical, and was, perhaps, meant by the volatile ringleaders of the scene as a sort of parody of the judicial preliminaries, they began to question him as in old days their ancestors had tried and condemned Anaxagoras, Diagoras, Protagoras, and Socrates, on similar accusations.[3] They said to him, "May we ascertain from

---

[1] Browning, *Men and Women.*

[2] Acts xvii. 19, ἐπιλαβόμενοι αὐτοῦ. It is quite a mistake to suppose that any violence is intended. Cf. ix. 27. Pausanias (*Attic.* i. 28, 5) is our authority for the λίθος 'Αναιδείας.

[3] It was the express function of the Areopagus to take cognizance of the introduction of ἐπίθετα ἱερά. Many writers hold that this was a judicial proceeding, and Wordsworth that it might have been an *Anakrisis*; and our translators, from their marginal note, "it was the highest court in Athens," probably shared the same view. The narrative, however, gives a very different impression. The Athenians were far less in earnest about their religion than Anytus and Meletus had been in the days of Socrates, and if this was meant for a trial it could only have been by way of conscious parody, as I have suggested.

you what is this new doctrine about which you have been talking? You are introducing some strange topic to our hearing. We should like, then, to ascertain what these things might mean?" And so the audience, keenly curious, but brimming over with ill-suppressed contempt and mirth, arranged themselves on the stone steps, and wherever they could best hear what sort of novelties could be announced by this strange preacher of a new faith.

But it was in no answering mood of levity that St. Paul met their light inquiries. The "ugly little Jew," who was the noblest of all Jews, was, perhaps, standing on the very stone where had once stood the ugly Greek who was the noblest of all Greeks, and was answering the very same charge. And Socrates could jest even in immediate peril of his life; but St. Paul, though secure in the tolerance of indifference, had all the solemnity of his race, and was little inclined to share in any jest. His was one of those temperaments which are too sad and too serious for light humour; one of those characters which are always and overwhelmingly in earnest. To meet badinage by badinage was for him a thing impossible. A modern writer is probably correct when he says that in ordinary society St. Paul would certainly not have been regarded as an interesting companion. On the other hand, he was too deeply convinced of his own position as one to which he had been called by the very voice and vision of his Saviour to be in the least wounded by frivolous innuendos or disdainful sneers. He was not overawed by the dignity of his judicial listeners, or by the reputation of his philosophic critics, or by the stern associations of the scene in the midst of which he stood. Above him, to the height of one hundred feet, towered the rock of the Acropolis like the vast altar of Hellas—that Acropolis which was to the

Greek what Mount Sion was to the Hebrew, the splendid boss of the shield ringed by the concentric circles of Athens, Attica, Hellas, and the world.[1] Beneath him was that temple of the awful goddesses whose presence was specially supposed to overshadow this solemn spot, and the dread of whose name had been sufficient to prevent Nero, stained as he was with the guilt of parricide, from setting foot within the famous city.[2] But Paul was as little daunted by the terrors and splendour of Polytheism in the seat of its grandest memorials and the court of its most imposing jurisdiction, as he was by the fame of the intellectual philosophy by whose living representatives he was encompassed. He knew, and his listeners knew, that their faith in these gay idolatries had vanished.[3] He knew, and his listeners knew, that their yearning after the unseen was not to be satisfied either by the foreign superstitions which looked for their votaries in the ignorance of the gynæceum, or by those hollow systems which wholly failed to give peace even to the few. He was standing under the blue dome of heaven,[4] a vaster and diviner temple than any which man could rear. And, therefore, it was with the deepest seriousness, as well as with the most undaunted composure, that he addressed them: "Athenians!"[5] he said, standing forth amongst them, with the earnest gaze and outstretched hand which was his attitude when addressing a multitude, "I observe

---

[1] Aristid. *Panathen.* i. 99; O. and H. i. 383.

[2] The Semnae, or Eumenides. Suet. *Ner.* 34.

[3] It is hard to conceive the reality of a devotion which laughed at the infamous gibes of Aristophanes against the national religion (*Lysistr.* 750).

[4] Ὑπαίθριοι ἐδικάζοντο (Pollux. viii. 118).

[5] Ἄνδρες Ἀθηναῖοι, &c. It was the ordinary mode of beginning a speech, and it seems to be strangely regarded by the author of *Supernatural Religion*, iii. 82, as a sign that these speeches are not genuine

that in every respect you are unusually religious."[1] Their attention would naturally be won, and even a certain amount of personal kindliness towards the orator be enlisted, by an exordium so courteous and so entirely in accordance with the favourable testimony which many writers had borne to their city as the common altar and shrine of Greece.[2] "For," he continued, "in wandering through your city, and gazing about me on the objects of your devotion,[3] I found among them[4] an altar on which had been carved an inscription, "To THE UNKNOWN GOD."[5] That, then, which ye unconsciously[6] adore, that am I

---

[1] Acts xvii. 22, δεισιδαιμονεστέρους. "Quasi superstitiores," Vulg.; "someway religious," Hooker; "very devout," Lardner; "very much disposed to the worship of divine Beings," Whateley; "Le plus religieux de peuples," Renan; "exceedingly scrupulous in your religion," Humphry. The word is used five times by Josephus, and always in a respectful sense, as it is in Acts xxv. 19. Of the many unfortunate translations in this chapter "too superstitious" (allzu abergläubisch, Luth.) is the most to be regretted. It at once alters the key-note of the speech, which is one of entire conciliatoriness. The value of it as a model for courteous polemics—a model quite as necessary in these days as at any past period—is greatly impaired in the E. V. It is possible to be "uncompromising" in opinions, without being violent in language or uncharitable in temper. St. Paul, however, would not have been likely to act contrary to the caution which struck Apollonius as necessary—σωφρονέστερον καὶ τὸ περὶ πάντων Θεῶν εὖ λέγειν καὶ τοῦτο 'Αθήνῃσι οὗ καὶ ἀγνώστων δαιμόνων βωμοὶ ἵδρυνται (Philostr. Vit. vi. 3).

[2] ὅλη βωμὸς, ὅλη θῦμα Θεοῖς καὶ ἀνάθημα (Xen. De Rep. Athen.; Alcib. ii. p. 97; Pausan. Attic. 24). τοὺς εὐσεβεστάτους τῶν 'Ελλήνων (Jos. c. Ap. ii. 11; Isocr. Paneg. 33; Thuc. ii. 38; Ælian, Var. Hist. v. 17; Pausan. xxiv. 3). When Apollonius landed at Athens Philostratus says, τὴν μὲν δὴ πρώτην διάλεξιν ἐποίησε φιλοθύτας τοὺς 'Αθηναίους εἶδεν, ὑπὲρ ἱερῶν διελέξατο (Vit. vi. 2). φιλόθεοι μάλιστα πάντων εἰσί (Jul. Misopogon).

[3] Not, as in E.V., "your devotions" (cf. Philostr. Vit. Apollon. iv. 19, p. 156).

[4] καὶ. For ἀναθεωρῶν D reads διιστορῶν, perspiciens, d. The ἐπεγέγραπτο implies permanence, and perhaps antiquity.

[5] ὅ . . . τοῦτο, א, A, B, D, with Origen and Jerome. Cf. Hor. Epod. v. 1. "At O Deorum quicquid in caelo regit;" and the frequent piacular inscription, "Sei Deo Sei Deae." The vague expression "the Divine" is common in Greek writers.

[6] Ver. 23, ἀγνοοῦντες, not "ignorantly," which would have been unlike Paul's urbanity, but "without knowing Who He is," with reference to ἀγνώστῳ (cf. Rom. i. 20). The word εὐσεβεῖτε also implies genuine piety.

.declaring unto you.   The God who made the universe and all things in it, He being the natural[1] Lord of heaven and earth, dwelleth not in temples made with hands,[2] nor is He in need of anything[3] so as to receive service[4] from human hands, seeing that He is Himself the giver to all of life and breath and all things ; and He made of one blood[5] every nation of men to dwell on the whole face of the earth, ordaining the immutable limits to the times and extents of their habitation,[6] inspiring them thereby to seek God, if after all they might grope in their darkness[7] and find Him, though, in reality,[8] He is not far from each one of us; for in Him we live, and move, and *are*, as some[9] also of your own poets have said—

> "(We need Him all,)
> For we are e'en His offspring."

[1] ὑπάρχων.

[2] An obvious reminiscence of the speech of Stephen (vii. 48; cf. Eurip. *Fragm.* ap Clem. Alex. *Strom.* V. ii. 76).

[3] A proposition to which the Epicureans would heartily assent.

[4] Θεραπεύεται, "is served," not "is worshipped," which is meaningless when applied to "hands."   It means by offerings at the altar, &c. (cf. *Il.* i. 39, εἴ ποτέ τοι χαρίεντ᾽ ἐπὶ νηὸν ἔρεψα).

[5] αἵματος is, to say the least, dubious, being omitted in א A, B, the Coptic, and Sahidic versions, &c.   On the other hand, as Meyer truly observes, ἀνθρώπου would have been a more natural gloss than αἵματος ; and the Jews used to say that Adam was דמו של עולם, "the blood of the world."

[6] Job xii. 23.

[7] ψηλαφᾶν, to fumble, like a blind man, or one in the dark (Arist. *Pax.* 691; Gen. xxvii. 21; Isa. lix. 10; cf. Rom. i. 21, x. 6—8):—

> "I stretch lame hands of faith, and *grope*
> And gather dust and chaff, and call
> To what I feel is Lord of all,
> And faintly trust the larger hope."—*Tennyson.*

[8] He means to imply that the necessity for this groping was their own fault—was due to *their* withdrawal to a distance from God, not His withdrawal from them.

[9] The poet actually quoted is Aratus of Cilicia, perhaps of Tarsus, and the line comes from the beginning of his Φαινόμενα :—

> πάντη δὲ Διὸς κεχρήμεθα πάντες
> Τοῦ γὰρ καὶ γένος ἐσμέν.

But he says τινες, because the same sentiment, in almost the same words, is

Since, then, we are the offspring of God, we ought not to
think that the Divine is like gold or silver or brass, the
graving of art and of man's genius." [1]

Condensed as this speech evidently is, let us pause for
an instant, before we give its conclusion, to notice the
consummate skill with which it was framed, the pregnant
meanings infused into its noble and powerful sentences.
Such skill was eminently necessary in addressing an
audience which attached a primary importance to rhetoric,
nor was it less necessary to utilise every moment during
which he could hope to retain the fugitive attention of
that versatile and superficial mob.   To plunge into any
statements of the peculiar doctrines of Christianity, or
to deal in that sort of defiance which is the weapon of
ignorant fanaticism, would have been to ensure instant
failure; and since his sole desire was to win his listeners
by reason and love, he aims at becoming as a heathen to
the heathen, as one without law to them without law, and
speaks at once with a large-hearted liberality which would
have horrified the Jews, and a classic grace which
charmed the Gentiles.   In expressions markedly courteous,
and with arguments exquisitely conciliatory, recognising
their piety towards their gods, and enforcing his views
by an appeal to their own poets, he yet manages, with
the readiest power of adaptation, to indicate the fundamental errors of every class of his listeners.   While
seeming to dwell only on points of agreement, he yet

found in Kleanthes, *Hymn in Jov.* 5, ἐκ σοῦ γὰρ γένος ἐσμέν, and it was, not
improbably, a noble common-place of other sacred and liturgical poems. Cf.
Virg. *Georg.* iv. 221—225. Bentley remarked that this chapter alone proves
"that St. Paul was a great master in all the learning of the Greeks" (*Boyle
Lectures*, iii.). This is a very great exaggeration. See Exc. III., p. 630 *sq.*

[1] "Judaea gens Deum sine simulacro colit" (Varro, *Fr.* p. 229). Hence
the "Nil praeter nubes et caeli numen adorat" of Juv. xiv. 97 and "Dedita
sacris Incerti Judaea Dei" of Luc. ii. 592; Tac. *H.* v. 6.

practically rebukes in every direction their natural and intellectual self-complacency.[1] The happy Providence—others, but not St. Paul, might have said the happy *accident*[2]—which had called his attention to the inscription on the nameless altar, enabled him at once to claim them as at least partial sharers in the opinions which he was striving to enunciate. His Epicurean auditors believed that the universe had resulted from a chance combination of atoms; he tells them that it was their Unknown God who by His fiat had created the universe and all therein. They believed that there were many gods, but that they sat far away beside their thunder, careless of mankind; he told them that there was but one God, Lord of heaven and earth. Around them arose a circle of temples as purely beautiful as hands could make them—yet there, under the very shadow of the Propylæa and the Parthenon, and with all those shrines of a hundred divinities in full view with their pillared vestibules and their Pentelic marble, he tells the multitude that this God who was One, not many, dwelt not in their toil-wrought temples,[3] but in the eternal temple of His own creation. But while he thus denies the Polytheism of the multitude, his words tell with equal force against the Pantheism of the Stoic, and

---

[1] Paul had that beautiful spirit of charity which sees the soul of good even in things evil. Hostile as he was to selfish hedonism, and to hard "apathy," he may yet have seen that there was a good side to the philosophy both of Epicurus and Zeno, in so far as Epicurus taught "the happiness of a cultivated and self-contented mind," and Zeno contributed to diffuse a lofty morality. "Encore que les philosophes soient les protecteurs de l'erreur toutefois ils ont frappé à la porte de la vérité. (Veritatis fores pulsant. Tert.) S'ils ne sont pas entrés dans son sanctuaire, s'ils n'ont pas eu le bonheur de le voir et de l'adorer dans son temple, ils se sont quelquefois présentés à ses portiques, et lui ont rendu de loin quelque hommage" (Bossuet, *Panég. de St. Catherine*).

[2] The word Τύχη does not occur in the N.T.

[3] 2 Chron. vi. 82, 88. ποῖος δ' ἂν οἶκος τεκτόνων πλασθεὶς ὑπὸ Δέμας τό θεῖον περιβάλοι τοίχων πτυχαῖς; (Eur. ap. Clem. Alex. *Strom.* V. xi. 76).

J J

the practical Atheism of the Epicurean. While he thus
de-consecrated, as it were, the countless temples, the Stoics
would go thoroughly with him; [1] when he said that God
needeth not our ritualisms, the Epicurean would almost
recognise the language of his own school; [2] but, on the
other hand, he laid the axe at the root of their most
cherished convictions when he added that Matter was no
eternal entity, and God no impersonal abstraction, and
Providence no mere stream of tendency without us, which,
like a flow of atoms, makes for this or that; but that He
was at once the Creator and the Preserver, the living and
loving Lord of the material universe, and of all His children
in the great family of man, and of all the nations, alike
Jew and Gentile, alike Greek and barbarian, which had
received from His decrees the limits of their endurance and
of their domains. In this one pregnant sentence he also
showed the falsity of all autochthonous pretensions, and
national self-glorifications, at the expense of others, as well
as of all ancient notions about the local limitations of special
deities.   The afflicted Jew at whom they were scoffing
belonged to a race as dear to Him as the beautiful Greek;
and the barbarian was equally His care, as from His throne
He beholds all the dwellers upon earth. And when he
told them that God had given them the power to find Him,
and that they had but dimly groped after Him in the darkness—and when he clenched by the well-known hemistich
of Aratus and Cleanthes (perhaps familiar to them at their
solemn festivals) the truth that we are near and dear to
Him, the people of His pasture and the sheep of His hand,

---

[1] Seneca *ap.* Lact. *Instt.* vi. 25, and *Ep. Mor.* xxxi. 11.

[2] "Omnis enim per se Divom natura necesse est
Immortali aevo summâ cum pace fruatur . . .
Ipsa suis pollens opibus, nihil indiga nostri."—Lucr. ii. 650.

Cf. Sen. *Ep.* 95, 47. St. Paul, however, more probably derived the sentiment
if from any source, from 2 Macc. xiv. 35, or from Ps. l. 11, 12; Job. xli. 11.

they would be prepared for the conclusion that all these cunning effigies—at which he pointed as he spoke—all these carved and molten and fictile images, were not and could not be semblances of Him, and ought not to be worshipped[1] were they even as venerable as the "heaven-fallen image"—the Διοπετὲς ἄγαλμα—of their patron-goddess, or glorious as the chryselephantine statue on which Phidias had expended his best genius and Athens her richest gifts.

Thus far, then, with a considerateness which avoided all offence, and a power of reasoning and eloquence to which they could not be insensible, he had demonstrated the errors of his listeners mainly by contrasting them with the counter-truths which it was his mission to announce.[2] But lest the mere demonstration of error should end only in indifference or despair, he desired to teach the Stoic to substitute sympathy for apathy, and humility for pride, and the confession of a weakness that relied on God for the assertion of a self-dependence which denied all need of Him; and to lead the Epicurean to prefer a spiritual peace to a sensual pleasure, and a living Saviour to distant and indifferent gods. He proceeded, therefore, to tell them that during long centuries of their history God had overlooked or condoned[3] this ignorance, but that now the kingdom of heaven had come to them— now He called them to repentance—now the day of judg-

---

[1] See for the Pagan view Cic. *de Nat. Deor.* i. 18.

[2] The Epicurean notion of happiness as the result of coarser atoms was as material as Paley's, who considers it to be "a certain state of the nervous system in that part of the system in which we feel joy and grief . . . which may be the upper region of the stomach or the fine net-work lining the whole region of the *praecordia*" (*Moral Philos.* ch. vi.).

[3] Ver. 30, ὑπεριδών. "Winked at" is a somewhat unhappy colloquialism of the E.V. (cf. Rom. i. 24). It also occurs in Ecclus. xxx. 11. "Times of ignorance" is a half-technical term, like the Arabic *jahilujya* for the time before Mahomet.

ment was proclaimed, a day in which the world should be judged in righteousness by One whom God had thereto appointed, even by that Jesus to whose work God had set His seal by raising Him from the dead——

That was enough. A burst of coarse derision interrupted his words.[1] The Greeks, the philosophers themselves, could listen with pleasure, even with something of conviction, while he demonstrated the nullity of those gods of the Acropolis at which even their fathers, four centuries earlier, had not been afraid to jeer. But now that he had got to a point at which he mixed up mere Jewish matters and miracles with his predication—now that he began to tell them of that Cross which was to them foolishness, and of that Resurrection from the dead which was inconceivably alien to their habits of belief—all interest was for them at an end. It was as when a lunatic suddenly introduces a wild delusion into the midst of otherwise sane and sensible remarks. The "strange gods" whom they fancied that he was preaching became too fantastic even to justify any further inquiry. They did not deign to waste on such a topic the leisure which was important for less extraordinary gossip.[2] They were not nearly serious enough in their

---

[1] Acts xvii. 32. "The moment they heard the words 'resurrection of the dead,' some began to jeer." Ἐχλεύαζον, which occurs here only in the N.T., is a very strong word. It means the expression of contempt by the lips, as μυκτηρίζω by the nostrils. It is used by Aquila in Prov. xiv. 9, for "Fools make a mock at sin." Not that the ancients found anything ludicrous in the notion of the resurrection of the *soul*; it was the resurrection of the body which seemed so childish to them. See Plin. *N. H.* vii. 55; Lucian, *De Mort. Peregr.* 13. The heathen Cæcilius in Minucius Felix (*oct.* 11, 34), says, "Oraculis fabulas adstruunt. Renasci se ferunt *post mortem et cineres et favillas*, et nescio quâ fiduciâ mendaciis invicem credunt." See Orig. *c. Cels.* v. 14; Arnob. ii. 13; Athenag. *De Resurr.* iii. 4; Tert. *De Carn. Christi*, 15; &c.

[2] There is a sort of happy play of words in the εὐκαίρουν of Acts xvii. 21. It is not a classical word, but implies that they were too busy to spare time from the important occupation of gossiping.

own belief, nor did they consider this feeble wanderer
a sufficiently important person to make them care to
enforce against St. Paul that decree of the Areopagus
which had brought Socrates to the hemlock draught
in the prison almost in sight of them; but they instantly offered to the great missionary a contemptuous
toleration more fatal to progress than any antagonism.
As they began to stream away, some broke into open
mockery, while others, with polite irony, feeling that such
a speaker deserved at least a show of urbanity, said to him,
" Enough for one day. Perhaps some other time we will
listen to you again about *Him.*" But even if they were
in earnest, the convenient season for their curiosity recurred
no more to them than it did afterwards to Felix.[1] On that
hill of Ares, before that throng, Paul spoke no more. He
went from the midst of them, sorry, it may be, for their
jeers, seeing through their spiritual incapacity, but conscious that in that city his public work, at least, was over.
He could brave opposition; he was discouraged by indifference. One dignified adherent, indeed, he found—but
one only[2]—in Dionysius the Areopagite;[3] and one more in
a woman—possibly a Jewess—whose very name is uncertain:[4] but at Athens he founded no church, to Athens
he wrote no epistle, and in Athens, often as he passed
its neighbourhood, he never set foot again. St. Luke has

[1] Acts xxiv. 25.

[2] " Le pédagogue est le moins convertissable des hommes" (Renan, p. 199).
" C'est qu'il faut plus d'un miracle pour convertir à l'humilité de la croix un
sage du siècle " (Quesnel).

[3] Christian tradition makes him a bishop and martyr (Euseb. *H. E.* iii. 4;
iv. 23; Niceph. iii. 11), and he is gradually developed into St. Denys of
France. The books attributed to him, *On the Heavenly Hierarchy, On
the Divine Names,* &c., are not earlier than the fifth century.

[4] Δάμαλις, "heifer," would be a name analogous to Dorcas, &c.; Damaris
occurs nowhere else, and is probably a mere difference of pronunciation. It
can have nothing to do with δάμαρ, and has led to the conjecture that she
was a Syrian metic. Absolutely nothing is known about her.

no pompous falsehoods to tell us. St. Paul was despised and ridiculed, and he does not for a moment attempt to represent it otherwise; St. Paul's speech, so far as any immediate effects were concerned, was an all but total failure, and St. Luke does not conceal its ineffectiveness.[1] He shows us that the Apostle was exposed to the ridicule of indifferentism, no less than to the persecutions of exasperated bigotry.

And yet his visit was not in vain. It had been to him a very sad one. Even when Timotheus had come to cheer his depression and brighten his solitude, he felt so deep a yearning for his true and tried converts at Thessalonica, that, since they were still obliged to face the storm of persecution, he had sacrificed his own feelings, and sent him back to support and comfort that struggling Church.[2] He left Athens as he had lived in it, a despised and lonely man. And yet, as I have said, his visit was not in vain. Many a deep thought in the Epistle to the Romans may have risen from the Apostle's reflections over the apparent failure at Athens. The wave is flung back, and streams away in broken foam, but the tide advances with irresistible majesty and might. Little did those philosophers, in their self-satisfied superiority, suppose that the trivial incident in which they had condescended to take part was for them the beginning of the end.[3] Xerxes and his

---

[1] Yet we are constantly asked to believe, by the very acute and impartial criticism of sceptics, that St. Luke is given to inventing the names of illustrious converts to do credit to St. Paul. If any one will compare Philostratus's *Life of Apollonius* with the Acts of the Apostles he will soon learn to appreciate the difference between the cloudy romance of a panegyrist and the plain narrative of a truthful biographer.

[2] As may be inferred from 1 Thess. iii. 2. Did Silas also join him at Athens, and was he also sent back (to Berœa)? The ἡμεῖς is in favour of the supposition, the μόνοι is against it.

[3] Renan alludes to the Edict of Justinian suppressing the Athenian chair of Philosophy 474 years after.

Persians had encamped on the Areopagus, and devoted to the flames the temples on the Acropolis on the very grounds urged by St. Paul, "that the gods could not be shut within walls, and that the whole universe was their home and temple."[1] Yet the sword and fire of Xerxes, and all the millions of his vast host, have been utterly impotent in their effects, if we compare them to the results which followed from the apparent failure of this poor and insulted tent-maker. Of all who visit Athens, myriads connect it with the name of Paul who never so much as remember that, since the epoch of its glory, it has been trodden by the feet of poets and conquerors and kings. They think not of Cicero, or Virgil, or Germanicus, but of the wandering tent-maker. In *all* his seeming defeats lay the hidden germ of certain victory. He founded no church at Athens, but there—it may be under the fostering charge of the converted Areopagite—a church grew up. In the next century it furnished to the cause of Christianity its martyr bishops and its eloquent apologists.[2] In the third century it flourished in peace and purity. In the fourth century it was represented at Nicaea, and the noble rhetoric of the two great Christian friends St. Basil and St. Gregory of Nazianzus was trained in its Christian schools. Nor were many centuries to elapse ere, unable to confront the pierced hands which held a wooden Cross, its myriads of deities had fled into the dimness of outworn creeds, and its tutelary goddess, in spite of the flashing eyes which Homer had commemorated, and the mighty spear which had been moulded out of the trophies of Marathon, resigned her maiden chamber to the honour of that

---

[1] Cic. *Legg.* ii. 10.
[2] Publius, A.D. 179; Quadratus, Euseb. *H. E.* iv. 23; Aristides, A.D. 126; Athenagoras, *circ.* A.D. 177.

meek Galilæan maiden who had lived under the roof
of the carpenter of Nazareth—the virgin mother of the
Lord.[1]

[1] It was probably in the sixth century, when Justinian closed the schools
of philosophy, that the Parthenon was dedicated to the Virgin Mary, and the
Theseum to St. George of Cappadocia.

CHAPTER XXVIII.

ST. PAUL AT CORINTH.

" Men, women, rich and poor, in the cool hours
Shuffled their feet along the pavement white,
Companioned or alone; while many a light
Flared here and there from wealthy festivals,
And threw their moving shadows on the walls,
Or found them clustered in the corniced shade
Of some arched temple-door or dusky colonnade."
KEATS, *Lamia*.

" *Ecclesia Dei in Corintho :* laetum et ingens paradoxon."
BENGEL, in 1 Cor. i. 2.

UNNOTICED as he had entered it—nay, even more unnoticed, for he was now alone—St. Paul left Athens. So little had this visit impressed him, that he only once alludes to it, and though from the Acrocorinthus he might often have beheld its famed Acropolis, he never felt the smallest inclination to enter it again. This was his only recorded experience of intercourse with the Gentile Pharisaism of a pompous philosophy. There was more hope of raging Jews, more hope of ignorant barbarians, more hope of degraded slaves, than of those who had become fools because in their own conceit they were exceptionally wise; who were alienated by a spiritual ignorance born of moral blindness; who, because conscience had lost its power over them, had become vain in their imaginations, and their foolish heart was darkened.

He sailed to Corinth, the then capital of Southern Greece, which formed the Roman province of Achaia.

The poverty of his condition, the desire to waste no time, the greatness of his own infirmities, render it nearly certain that he did not make his way over those forty miles of road which separate Athens from Corinth, and which would have led him through Eleusis and Megara, but that he sailed direct, in about five hours, across the Saronic bay, and dropped anchor under the low green hills and pine-woods of Cenchreæ. Thence he made his way on foot along the valley of Hexamili, a distance of some eight miles, to the city nestling under the huge mass of its rocky citadel. Under the shadow of that Acrocorinthus, which darkened alternately its double seas,[1] it was destined that St. Paul should spend nearly two busy years of his eventful life.

It was not the ancient Corinth—the Corinth of Periander, or of Thucydides, or of Timoleon—that he was now entering, but Colonia Julia, or Laus Juli Corinthus, which had risen out of the desolate ruins of the older city. When the Hegemony had passed from Sparta and Athens, Corinth occupied their place, and as the leader of the Achæan league she was regarded as the light and glory of Greece. Flamininus, when the battle of Cynoscephalae had destroyed the hopes of Philip, proclaimed at Corinth the independence of Hellas.[2] But when the city was taken by L. Mummius, B.C. 146, its inhabitants had been massacred, its treasures carried off to adorn the triumph of the conqueror, and the city itself devastated and destroyed. For a hundred years it lay in total ruin, and then Julius Cæsar, keenly alive to the beauty and importance of its position, and desiring to call attention to the goddess for whose worship it had been famous, and whose descendant he professed to be, rebuilt it from its

---

[1] Stat. Theb. vii. 106.   [2] B.C. 196.

foundations, and peopled it with a colony of veterans and freedmen.[1]

It sprang almost instantly into fame and wealth. Standing on the bridge of the double sea, its two harbours—Lechæum on the Corinthian and Cenchreæ on the Saronic Gulf—instantly attracted the commerce of the east and west. The Diolkos, or land-channel, over which ships could be dragged across the Isthmus, was in constant use, because it saved voyagers from the circumnavigation of the dreaded promontory of Malea.[2] Jews with a keen eye to the profits of merchandise, Greeks attracted by the reputation of the site and the glory of the great Isthmian games, flocked to the protection of the Roman colony. The classic antiquities found amid the *débris* of the conflagration, and the successful imitations to which they led, were among the earliest branches of the trade of the town. Splendid buildings, enriched with ancient pillars of marble and porphyry, and adorned with gold and silver, soon began to rise side by side with the wretched huts of wood and straw which sheltered the mass of the poorer population.[3] Commerce became more and more active. Objects of luxury soon found their way to the marts, which were visited by every nation of the civilised world—Arabian balsam, Egyptian papyrus, Phœnician dates, Libyan ivory, Babylonian carpets, Cilician goats-hair, Lycaonian wool, Phrygian slaves. With riches came superficial refinement and literary tastes. The life of the wealthier inhabitants was marked by self-indulgence and intellectual restlessness, and the mass of the people, even down to the slaves, were more or less affected by the

---

[1] B.C. 44. Pausan. ii. 1, 3; Plut. *Caes.* 57; Strabo, viii. 6.

[2] Cape Matapan. The Greeks had a proverb, Μαλέας περιπλέων ἐπιλάθου τῶν οἰκάδε—as we might say, "Before sailing round Malea, make your will" (Strab. viii. p. 368). "Formidatum Maleae caput" (Stat. *Theb.* ii. 33).

[3] 1 Cor. iii. 12; Hausrath, p. 317.

prevailing tendency.   Corinth was the Vanity Fair of
the Roman Empire, at once the London and the Paris of
the first century after Christ.

It was into the midst of this mongrel and heterogeneous population of Greek adventurers and Roman
bourgeois, with a tainting infusion of Phœnicians—this
mass of Jews, ex-soldiers, philosophers, merchants, sailors,
freedmen,[1] slaves, tradespeople, hucksters, and agents
of every form of vice—a colony "without aristocracy,
without traditions, without well-established citizens"—
that the toilworn Jewish wanderer made his way.   He
entered it as he had entered Athens—a stricken and lonely
worker; but here he was lost even more entirely in the
low and careless crowd.   Yet this was the city from
which and to whose inhabitants he was to write those
memorable letters which were to influence the latest
history of the world.   How little we understand what is
going on around us!   How little did the wealthy
magnates of Corinth suspect that the main historic
significance of their city during this epoch would be
centred in the disputes conducted in a petty synagogue,
and the thoughts written in a tent-maker's cell by that
bent and weary Jew, so solitary and so wretched, so
stained with the dust of travel, so worn with the attacks
of sickness and persecution!   How true it is that the
living world often knows nothing of its greatest men!

For when we turn to the Epistles to the Thessalonians and Corinthians, and trace the emotions which
during this period agitated the mind of the Apostle, we
find him still suffering from weakness[2] and anxiety, from
outward opposition and inward agonies.   He reminds the
Thessalonians that he had prepared them for his tribula-

---

[1] Ἐποίκους τοῦ ἀπελευθερικοῦ γένους πλείστους (Strab. viii. 6).

[2] Probably another attack of his malady (1 Cor. ii. 3).

tions and their own, and speaks touchingly of the comfort which he had received from the news of their faith in the midst of his afflictions.[1] Had he possessed the modern temperament he might often have been helped to peace and calm as he climbed the steep Acrocorinthus and gazed from its lofty summit on the two seas studded with the white sails of many lands, or watched the glow of sunset bathing in its soft lustre the widespread pageant of islands and mountains, and groves of cypress and pine. But all his interest lay in those crowded streets where his Lord had much people, and in the varied human surroundings of his daily life. How deeply he was impressed by these may be seen in the Corinthian Epistles. His illustrations are there chiefly drawn from Gentile customs—the wild-beast fights,[2] which Athens would never admit while she had an Altar to Pity; the lovely stadium, in which he had looked with sympathy on the grace and strength and swiftness of many a youthful athlete; the race[3] and the boxing-matches,[4] the insulting vanity of Roman triumph,[5] the long hair of effeminate dandies,[6] the tribunal of the Proconsul,[7] the shows of the theatre,[8] the fading garland of Isthmian pine.[9]

But there was one characteristic of heathen life which would come home to him at Corinth with overwhelming force, and fill his pure soul with infinite pain. It was the gross immorality of a city conspicuous for its depravity even amid the depraved cities of a dying heathenism.[10] Its very name had become a synonym for reckless de-

---

[1] 1 Thess. iii. 4, 7.
[2] 1 Cor. xv. 32; Lucian Demonax, 57; Philostr. *Apollon.* iv. 22.
[3] 1 Cor. ix. 24.
[4] *Id.* ver. 27.   [6] 1 Cor. xi. 14.   [8] 1 Cor. iv. 9.
[5] 2 Cor. ii. 14—16.   [7] 2 Cor. v. 10.   [9] 1 Cor. ix. 25.
[10] Hesych. s. v. Κορινθιάζεσθαι. Wetstein (the great source of classical quotations in illustration of the New Testament, whose stores have been

bauchery. This abysmal profligacy of Corinth was due partly to the influx of sailors, who made it a trysting-place for the vices of every land, and partly to the vast numerical superiority of the slaves, of which, two centuries later, the city was said to contain many myriads.[1] And so far from acting as a check upon this headlong immorality, religion had there taken under its immediate protection the very pollutions which it was its highest function to suppress. A thousand Hierodouloi were consecrated to the service of Impurity in the infamous Temple of Aphrodite Pandemos. The Lais of old days, whose tomb at Corinth had been marked by a sphinx with a human head between her claws, had many shameless and rapacious representatives. East and west mingled their dregs of foulness in the new Gomorrah of classic culture,[2] and the orgies of the Paphian goddess were as notorious as those of Isis or of Asherah. It was from this city and amid its abandoned proletariate that the Apostle dictated his frightful sketch of Paganism.[3] It was to the converts of this city that he addressed most frequently, and with most solemn warning and burning indignation, his stern prohibitions of sensual crime.[4] It was to converts drawn from the reeking haunts of its slaves and artisans that he writes that they too had once been sunk in the lowest depths of sin and shame.[5] It is of this city that we

---

freely rifled by later authors) and others refer to Ar. Plut. 149; Hor. *Epp.* I. xvii. 36; Athen. vii. 13; xiii. 21, 32, 54; Strabo, viii. 6, 20—21; xii. 3, 36; Cic. *De Rep.* ii. 4; and Aristid. *Or.* III., p. 39, &c.

[1] On the numbers of slaves in ancient days, see Athenæus vi. p. 275 (ed. Casaubon).

[2] Juv. viii. 112; Hor. *Ep.* I. xvii. 36; Strabo, viii. 6; Athen. xiii. p. 573, ed. Casaubon. A reference to the immorality of the city may still be heard in the use of the word "Corinthians" for profligate idlers.

[3] Rom. i. 21—32.

[4] 1 Cor. v. 1; vi. 9—20; x. 7, 8; 2 Cor. vi. 14; vii. 1.

[5] 1 Cor. vi. 9—11; 2 Cor. xii. 21.

hear the sorrowful admission that in the world of heathendom a pure life and an honest life was a thing well-nigh
unknown.[1] All sins are bound together by subtle links
of affinity. Impurity was by no means the only vice for
which Corinth was notorious. It was a city of drunkards;[2]
it was a city of extortioners and cheats. But the worse
the city, the deeper was the need for his labours, and
the greater was the probability that many in it would be
yearning for delivery from the bondage of corruption into
the glorious liberty of the children of God.

In such a place it was more than ever necessary that
St. Paul should not only set an example absolutely blameless, but that he should even abstain from things which
were perfectly admissible, if they should furnish a handle
to the enemies of Christ. And therefore, lest these
covetous shopkeepers and traders should be able to charge
him with seeking his own gain, he determined to accept
nothing at their hands. There seemed to be a fair chance
that he would be able to earn his bread by tent-making in
a port so universally frequented. In this respect he was
unusually fortunate. He found a Jew of Pontus, named
Aquila,[3] who worked at this trade with his wife Priscilla.

---

[1] 1 Cor. v. 9, 10.

[2] Corinthians were usually introduced drunk on the stage (Ælian. V. H.
iii. 15; Athen. x. 438, iv. 137; 1 Cor. xi. 21; Hausrath, p. 323).

[3] The Aquila, a Jew of Pontus, who translated the Old Testament into
Greek more literally than the LXX., lived more than half a century later, and
may conceivably have been a grandson of this Aquila. Pontius Aquila was a
noble Roman name (Cic. ad Fam. x. 33; Suet. Jul. 78); but that Aquila may
have been a freedman of that house, and that Luke has made a mistake in connecting him with Pontus, is without the shadow of probability (cf. Acts ii. 9;
1 Pet. i. 1). His real name may have been Onkelos (Deutsch, Lit. Rem.,
p. 336), Hebraised from 'Ακυλας, or may have been עקילס, Latinised into Aquila;
but these are mere valueless conjectures. He was a tent-maker, married to
an active and kindly wife, who lived sometimes at Rome, sometimes at
Corinth, and sometimes at Ephesus (Acts xviii. 26; 1 Cor. xvi. 19; Rom.
xvi. 3; 2 Tim. iv. 19); and they were much beloved by St. Paul, and rendered

As nothing is said either of their baptism or their conversion, it is probable that they were already Christians, and
Paul formed with them a lifelong friendship, to which
he owed many happy hours. This excellent couple were
at present living in Corinth in consequence of the decree
of Claudius, expelling all Jews from Rome.[1] Tyrannous as
the measure was, it soon became a dead letter, and probably
caused but little inconvenience to these exiles, because the
nature of their trade seems to have made it desirable for

extraordinary services to the cause of Christianity. Priscilla was probably
the more energetic of the two, or she would not be mentioned first in Acts
xviii. 18, 26 ; Rom. xvi. 3 ; 2 Tim. iv. 19 (Ewald, vi., p. 489 ; Plumptre, *Bibl.
Studies*, p. 417).

[1] In A.D. 52 the relations of Judæa to Rome began to be extremely
unsettled (Tac. *Ann.* xii. 54), and just as the Gauls and Celts were expelled
from Rome (A.D. 9) on receipt of the news about the loss of Varus and his
legions, so the Jews were now ordered to quit Rome. Suetonius says,
" Judaeos impulsore Chresto assidue tumultuantes Româ expulit " (*Claud.* 25).
Whether Chrestos was some unknown ringleader of tumult among the
immense Jewish population of Rome—so immense, that from their Ghetto
across the Tiber no less than 8,000 had petitioned against the succession of
Archelaus (Jos. *Antt.* xvii. 11, § 1)—or an ignorant misreading of the name of
Christ, cannot be ascertained. We know that Christianity was very early
introduced into Rome (Rom. xvi. 7 ; Acts xxviii. 14), and we know that
wherever it was introduced, Jewish tumults followed (Acts xvii. 18, xiv. 19 ;
xiii. 50), and that the Romans never took the trouble to draw any distinction
between Jews and Christians. It is, therefore, quite possible that these
incessant riots may have arisen in disputes about the Messiah. Dion Cassius,
indeed, corrects Suetonius, and says that the Jews were so numerous that
they *could not be expelled* without danger, and that Claudius therefore contented himself with closing their synagogues (Dion, lx. 6). Perhaps the
decree was passed, but never really enforced ; and Aquila may have been
one of the Jews who obeyed it without difficulty for the reasons suggested in
the text. Nay, more, he may have been selected for special banishment as
a ringleader in the agitation, if, as some suppose, he and his wife were the
founders of Christianity at Rome. In any case its operation was brief, for
shortly afterwards we again find the Jews in vast numbers at Rome (Rom.
xvi. 3 ; Acts xxviii. 17). It is not at all impossible that the edict may have
been identical with, or a part of, that *De Mathematicis Italiâ pellendis* which
Tacitus mentions as *atrox et irritum*. Certainly that decree was passed
at this very period (Tac. *Ann.* xii. 52), and many of the Jews, addicted as
they were to all kinds of iniquities (Jos. *Antt.* xviii. 1), may easily have been
classed with the Mathematici. (See Lewin, *Fasti Sacri*, 1774, 5.)

them to move from place to place. At Corinth, as subsequently at Ephesus, Paul worked in their employ, and shared in their profits. Those profits, unhappily, were scanty. It was a time of general pressure, and though the Apostle toiled night and day, all his exertions were unable to keep the wolf from the door.[1] He knew what it was to suffer, even from the pangs of hunger, but not even when he was thus starving would he accept assistance from his Achaian converts. He had come to an absolute determination that, while willing to receive necessary aid from churches which loved him, and which he loved, he would forego at Corinth the support which he considered to be the plain right of an Apostle, lest any should say that he too, like the mass of traffickers around him, did but seek his own gain.[2] Contentedly, therefore —nay, even gladly, did he become a fellow-labourer with the worthy pair who were both compatriots and brethren; and even when he was working hardest, he could still be giving instruction to all who sought him. But now, as ever, the rest of the Sabbath furnished him with his chief opportunity. On that day he was always to be found in the Jewish synagogue, and his weekly discourses produced a deep impression both on Jews and Greeks.

But when the period of his solitude was ended by the arrival of Silas from Berœa, and Timotheus from Thessalonica, he was enabled to employ a yet more intense activity. Not only did he find their presence a support, but they also cheered him by favourable intelligence, and brought him a contribution from the Philippians,[3] which alleviated his most pressing needs. Accordingly, their arrival was followed by a fresh outburst of missionary

---

[1] 2 Cor. xi. 9; 1 Cor. iv. 11, 12; ix. 4.
[2] See Acts xx. 34; 1 Cor. ix. 12; 2 Cor. vii. 2; 1 Thess. ii. 9; 2 Thess. iii. 8.
[3] Phil. iv 15; 2 Cor. xi. 9.

K K

zeal, and he bore witness with a yet more impassioned earnestness to his Master's cause.[1]   At this period his preaching was mainly addressed to the Jews, and the one object of it was to prove from Scripture the Messiahship of Jesus.[2]   But with them he made no further progress.   Crispus, indeed, the governor of the synagogue, had been converted with all his house; and— perhaps during the absence of his companions—Paul abandoned his usual rule by baptising him with his own hands.[3]   But, as a body, the Jews met him with an opposition which at last found expression in the sort of language of which the Talmud furnishes some terrible specimens.[4] No further object could be served by endeavouring to convince them, and at last he shook off the dust of his garments, and calling them to witness that he was innocent of their blood,[5] he announced that from that day forth he should preach only to the Gentiles.

Already he had converted some Gentiles of humble and probably of slavish origin, the first among these being the household of Stephanas.[6]   With Crispus and these

---

[1] The undoubted reading of Acts xviii. 5 is συνείχετο τῷ λόγῳ, " was being constrained by the word " (ℵ, A, B, D, E, G), not τῷ πνεύματι, as in E. V., " was pressed *in spirit*."   Cf. for the word συνείχετο, Luke xii. 50; 2 Cor. v. 14. De Wette, &c., make it mean " was engrossed " (Vulg., *instabat verbo*), but less correctly.   " Sensus est, majore vehementiâ fuisse impulsum ut libere palamque de Christo dissereret " (Calvin).

[2] 1 Cor. xv. 3.

[3] 1 Cor. i. 14.

[4] Acts xviii. 6, ἀντιτασσομένων . . . καὶ βλασφημούντων.   See *Life of Christ*, ii. 452.

[5] Ezek. xxxiii. 4.

[6] 1 Cor. xvi. 15, " the firstfruits of Achaia " (in Rom. xvi. 5 the true reading is " of *Asia* ").   Fortunatus and Achaicus were probably slaves or freedmen, as were " Chloe's household "; Quartus and Tertius—who had the high honour of being the amanuensis of the Epistle to the Romans—were probably descendants of the Roman veterans who were the first colonists, and may have been younger brothers of Secundus.   Lucius, Jason, and Sosipater were Jews (Rom. xvi. 21).

faithful converts, he migrated from the synagogue to a room close by, which was placed at his disposal by a proselyte of the name of Justus.[1] In this room he continued to preach for many months. The entire numbers of the Corinthian converts were probably small — to be counted rather by scores than by hundreds. This is certain, because otherwise they could not have met in a single room in the small houses of the ancients, nor could they have been all present at common meals. The minute regulations about married women, widows, and virgins seem to show that the female element of the little congregation was large in proportion to the men, and it was even necessary to lay down the rule that women were not to teach or preach among them, though Priscilla and Phœbe had been conspicuous for their services.[2] And yet, small as was the congregation, low as was the position of most of them, vile as had been the antecedents of some, the method and the topics of the Apostle's preaching had been adopted with much anxiety. He was by no means at home among these eager, intellectual, disputatious, rhetoric-loving, sophisticated Greeks. They had none of the frank simplicity of his Thessalonians, none of the tender sympathy of his Philippians, none of the emotional susceptibility of his Galatian converts. They were more like the scoffing and self-satisfied Athenians. At Athens he had adopted a poetic and finished style, and it had almost wholly failed to make any deep impression. At Corinth, accordingly, he adopted a wholly different method. Ill and timid, and so nervous that he sometimes trembled while addressing them[3]—conscious that his bodily presence

---

[1] There is no sufficient ground for calling him Titius Justus on the strength of E and one or two versions; it seems to be simply due to the homœoteleuton in ὀνόματι. There is still less ground for identifying him with Titus.

[2] Rom. xvi. 1, 2. [3] 1 Cor. ii. 3.

K K 2

was mean in the judgment of these connoisseurs in beauty, and his speech contemptible in the estimation of these judges of eloquence[1]—thinking, too, that he had little in the way of earthly endowment, unless it were in his infirmities,[2] he yet deliberately decided not to avoid, as he had done at Athens, the topic of the Cross.[3]   From Corinth he could see the snowy summits of Parnassus and Helicon; but he determined never again to adorn his teaching with poetic quotations or persuasive words of human wisdom,[4] but to trust solely to the simple and unadorned grandeur of his message, and to the outpouring of the Spirit by which he was sure that it would be accompanied. There was, indeed, a wisdom in his words, but it was not the wisdom of this world, nor the kind of wisdom after which the Greeks sought.   It was a spiritual wisdom of which he could merely reveal to them the elements—not strong meat for the perfect, but milk as for babes in Christ. He aimed at nothing but the clear, simple enunciation of the doctrine of Christ crucified.[5]   But what was lacking in formal syllogism or powerful declamation was more than supplied by power from on high.   Paul had determined that, if converts were won, they should be won, not by human eloquence, but by Divine love.   Nor was he disappointed in thus trusting in God alone.   Amid all the sufferings which marked his stay among the Achaians, he appeals to their personal knowledge that, whatever they may have thought or said among themselves about the weakness of his words, they could not at least

[1] 2 Cor. x. 1, 10. Luther, who seems to have entered into the very life of St. Paul, calls him "Ein armes dürres Männlein wie unser Philippus" (Melancthon).

[2] 2 Cor. xii. 5, 9.

[3] 1 Cor. i. 23; ii. 2.

[4] 1 Cor. ii. 1—5. ἀνθρωπίνης is a good explanatory gloss of A, C, J, &c.

[5] 1 Cor. i. 17; ii. 2; 2 Cor. i. 18.

deny the "signs, and wonders, and powers"[1] which, by the aid of the Spirit, were conspicuous in his acts. They must have recalled many a scene in which, under the humble roof of Justus, the fountains of the great deep of religious feeling were broken up, the strange accents of "the tongues" echoed through the thrilled assembly, and deeds were wrought which showed to that little gathering of believers that a Power higher than that of man was visibly at work to convince and comfort them. And thus many Corinthians—the Gentiles largely exceeding the Jews in number—were admitted by baptism into the Church.[2] The majority of them were of the lowest rank, yet they could number among them some of the wealthier inhabitants, such as Gaius, and perhaps Chloe, and even Erastus, the chamberlain of the city. Nor was it in Corinth only that Christians began to be converted. Paul, like Wesley, "regarded all the world as his parish," and it is little likely that his restless zeal would have made him stay for nearly two years within the city walls. We know that there was a church at Cenchreæ, whose deaconess afterwards "carried under the folds of her robe the whole future of Christian theology;"[3] and saints were scattered in small communities throughout all Achaia.[4]

And yet, though God was thus giving the increase, it must have required no small courage in such a city to preach such a doctrine, and the very vicinity of the synagogue to the house of Justus must have caused frequent and painful collisions between the Jews and the little Christian community. Among all the sorrows to which St. Paul alludes whenever he refers to this long

[1] 2 Cor. xii. 12.
[2] Acts xviii. 8.
[3] Renan, p. 219.
[4] 2 Cor. i. 1; Rom. xvi. 1. The nearest Achaian towns would be Lechæum, Schœnus, Cenchreæ, Crommyon, Sicyon, Argos.

stay at Corinth, there is none that finds more bitter expression than his complaint of his fellow-countrymen. He speaks of them to the Thessalonians in words of unusual exasperation, saying that they pleased not God, and were contrary to all men, and that by their attempts to hinder the preaching to the Gentiles of the Christ whom they had murdered, they had now filled up the measure of their sins.[1] The rupture was open and decisive. If they had excommunicated him, and he was filled with such anger and despair when he thought of them, it is certain that the struggle between them must have been a constant source of anxiety and peril. This might even have ended in Paul's withdrawal to new fields of labour in utter despondency but for the support which again, as often at his utmost need, he received from a heavenly vision. The Lord whom he had seen on the road to Damascus appeared to him at night, and said to him: "Fear not, but speak, and hold not thy peace; for I am with thee, and no man shall set on thee to hurt thee; for I have much people in this city."

But at last the contest between the Jews and the Christians came to a head. The Proconsul of Achaia[2] ended his term of office, and the Proconsul appointed by the emperor was Marcus Annæus Novatus, who, having been adopted by the friendly rhetorician Lucius Junius Gallio, had taken the name of Lucius Junius Annæus Gallio, by which he is generally known. Very different was the estimate of Gallio by his contemporaries from the mis-

---

[1] 1 Thess. ii. 14—16.

[2] The term Proconsul is historically exact. The Government of Achaia had been so incessantly changed that a mistake would have been excusable. Achaia had been Proconsular under Augustus; imperial, for a time, under Tiberius (Tac. *Ann.* i. 76); Proconsular, after A.D. 44, under Claudius (Suet. *Claud.* xxv.); free under Nero (Suet. *Ner.* 24); and again Proconsular under Vespasian (Suet. *Vesp.* viii.). See *supra*, p. 351, and Excursus XVI.

taken one which has made his name proverbial for indifferentism in the Christian world. To the friends among whom he habitually moved he was the most genial, the most loveable of men. The brother of Seneca, and the uncle of Lucan, he was the most universally popular member of that distinguished family. He was pre-eminently endowed with that light and sweetness which are signs of the utmost refinement, and "the sweet Gallio" is the epithet by which he alone of the ancients is constantly designated.[1] "No mortal man is so sweet to any single person as he is to all mankind,"[2] wrote Seneca of him. "Even those who love my brother Gallio to the very utmost of their power yet do not love him enough,"[3] he says in another place. He was the very flower of pagan courtesy and pagan culture—a Roman with all a Roman's dignity[4] and seriousness, and yet with all the grace and versatility of a polished Greek.[5]

Such was the man on whose decision the fortunes of Paul were to depend. Whoever the former Proconsul had been, he had not been one with whom the Jews could venture to trifle, nor had they once attempted to get rid of their opponent by handing him over to the secular arm.

---

[1] "Dulcis Gallio" (Stat. *Sylv*. ii. 7, 32). See *Seekers after God*, 16—21. I need not here recur to the foolish notion that Gallio sent some of St. Paul's writings to his brother Seneca. On this see Aubertin, *Sénèque et St. Paul*, p. 117. Nor need I recur to the resemblance between the Roman philosopher and the Apostle, which I have examined in *Seekers after God*, 174—183, and which is fully treated by Dr. Lightfoot (*Phil*. pp. 268—331).

[2] "Nemo mortalium uni tam dulcis est quam hic omnibus" (Sen. *Quaest. Nat*. iv. *praef*. § 11). He dedicates to him his *De Irâ* and *De Vitâ Beatâ*, and alludes to him in *Ep*. civ. *Consol. ad Helv*. 16.

[3] "Gallionem, fratrem meum, quem nemo non parum amat etiam qui amare plus non potest" (*Nat. Qu*. iv. *praef*. § 10).

[4] Seneca (*Ep*. 104), in allusion to his high rank, playfully calls him "my Lord Gallio." He committed suicide after the ruin of his family in the plot against Nero, though his life had been spared (Tac. *Ann*. xv. 73; Dion Cass. lxii. 25; Euseb. *Chron. ad A.U.C*. 818).

[5] Dion Cass. lx. 35.

But now that a new Proconsul had arrived, who was perhaps
unfamiliar with the duties of his office, and whose desire
for popularity at the beginning of his government might
have made him complaisant to prosperous Jews, they
thought that they could with impunity excite a tumult.
They rose in a body, seized Paul, and dragged him before
the tesselated pavement on which was set the curule chair of
the Proconsul. It was evident that they had presumed
on his probable inexperience, and on his reputation for
mildness; and, with all the turbulent clamour of their
race, they charged Paul with "persuading men to worship
God contrary to the Law." Though Claudius had expelled them from Rome, their religion was a *religio
licita* — *i.e.*, it was licensed by the State; but the
religion of "this fellow," they urged, though it might
pass itself off under the name of Judaism, was not Judaism
at all—it was a spurious counterfeit of Judaism, which
had become a *religio illicita* by running counter to its
Mosaic Law.[1] Such was the charge urged by a hubbub
of voices, and, as soon as it had become intelligible, Paul
was on the point of making his defence. But Gallio was
not going to trouble himself by listening to any defence.
He took no notice whatever of Paul, and, disregarding
him as completely as though he had been non-existent,
replied to the Jews by a contemptuous dismissal of them
and their charge. With a thorough knowledge of,
and respect for, the established laws, but with a
genuinely Roman indifference for conciliatory language,
and a more than Roman haughtiness of demeanour
towards a people whom, like his brother, he probably
despised and detested, he stopped the proceedings with

---

[1] Hence though· παρὰ τὸν νόμον, ver. 13, means "contrary to the Jewish
law" (cf. ver. 15), it might in this way come under the cognisance of the
Roman law.

the remark that their accusation against St. Paul, as a violator of any law, Mosaic or otherwise, which he could recognise, was utterly baseless. "Had this been a matter of civil wrong or moral outrage[1] it would have been but right for me to put up with you, and listen to these charges of yours; but if it be a number of questions[2] about an opinion, and about mere names, and *your* law, see to it yourselves; for a judge of these matters I do not choose to be." Having thus, as we should say, quashed the indictment, "my Lord Gallio" ordered his lictors to clear the court. We may be sure they made short work of ejecting the frustrated but muttering mob, on whose disappointed malignity, if his countenance at all reflected the feelings expressed by his words, he must have been looking down from his lofty tribunal with undisguised contempt.[3] It took the Romans nearly two centuries to learn that Christianity was something infinitely more important than the Jewish sect which they mistook it to be. It would have been better for them and for the world if they had tried to get rid of this disdain, and to learn wherein lay the secret power of a religion which they could neither eradicate nor suppress. But while we regret this unphilosophic disregard, let us at least do justice to Roman

---

[1] Ver. 14, ἀδίκημα, a legal injury; ῥᾳδιούργημα, a moral offence.

[2] ζητήματα *infr.* A, B, D², E, Coptic, Sahidic, Armenian, &c. "My lord's" Roman disdain for the *gens sceleratissima* is heard in every accent.

[3] Perhaps no passage of the ancient authors, full as they are of dislike to the Jews (see *infra*, Excursus XIV.), expresses so undisguised a bitterness, or is so thoroughly expressive of the way in which the Romans regarded this singular people, as that in which Tacitus relates how Tiberius banished 4,000 freedmen "infected with that superstition" into Sardinia, to keep down the brigands of that island, with the distinct hope that the unhealthy climate might help to get rid of them—"et si, ob gravitatem caeli interissent, vile damnum" (*Ann.* ii. 85). Suetonius tells us, with yet more brutal indifference, that Tiberius, on pretext of military service, scattered them among all the unhealthiest provinces, banishing the rest on pain of being reduced to slavery (Suet. *Tib.* 36; Jos. *Antt.* xviii. 3, § 5).

impartiality. In Gallio, in Lysias, in Felix, in Festus, in the centurion Julius, even in Pilate,[1] different as were their degrees of rectitude, we cannot but admire the trained judicial insight with which they at once saw through the subterranean injustice and virulent animosity of the Jews in bringing false charges against innocent men. Deep as was his ignorance of the issues which were at stake, the conduct of Gallio was in accordance with the strictest justice when "he drave them from his judgment-seat."

But the scene did not end here. The volatile Greeks,[2] though they had not dared to interfere until the decision of the Proconsul had been announced, were now keenly delighted to see how completely the malice of the Jews had been foiled; and since the highest authority had pronounced the charge against St. Paul to be frivolous, they seized the opportunity of executing a little Lynch law. The ringleader of the Jewish faction had been a certain Sosthenes, who may have succeeded Crispus in the function of Ruler of the Synagogue, and whose zeal may have been all the more violently stimulated by the defection of his predecessor.[3] Whether the Corinthians knew that St. Paul was a Roman citizen or not, they must at least have been aware that he had separated from the synagogue, and that many Gentiles espoused his views. They thought it intolerable that Jews should try to trump up charges against one who in some measure belonged to themselves. The

---

[1] Acts xxiii. 29; xxv. 19. The ignorant provincialism of the justices at Philippi was of too low a type to understand Roman law.

[2] Acts xviii. 17, πάντες. The οἱ Ἕλληνες of D, E is a gloss, though a correct one. If this Sosthenes is identical with the Sosthenes of 1 Cor. i. 1, he must have been subsequently converted; but the name is a common one, and it is hardly likely that two rulers of the synagogue would be converted in succession.

[3] I give the view which seems to me the most probable, passing over masses of idle conjectures.

opportunity to show these Jews what they thought of them, and give them a lesson as to the way in which they should behave in the future, was too tempting. Accordingly they seized Sosthenes, and gave him a beating in the actual basilica in front of the tribunal, and under the very eyes of the Proconsul. An ancient gloss says that he pretended not to see what they were doing,[1] but the text implies that he looked on at the entire proceeding with unfeigned indifference. So long as they were not guilty of any serious infraction of the peace, it was nothing to him how they amused themselves. He had been familiar with similar disturbances in Rome. The Jews were everywhere a turbulent, fanatical race. What was it to him if the Greek *gamins* liked to inflict a little richly-deserved castigation? It would be so much the better if they taught this Sosthenes and any number more of these Jews a severe lesson. They would be more likely (he thought) to keep order in future, and less likely to trouble him again with their meanness and their malevolence, their riots and their rancours.[2]

There is one thing that we cannot but deeply regret. It is that Gallio's impatient sense of justice has deprived us of another speech by St. Paul which, delivered under such circumstances, and before such a judge, would have been of the deepest interest. But Gallio dismissed the whole scene from his mind as supremely unimportant. Had he ever thought it worth alluding to, in any letter to his brother Seneca, it would have been in some such terms as these:—"I had scarcely arrived when the Jews

---

[1] "Tunc Gallio fingebat enim non videre" (MS. *d*).

[2] Paley (*Hor. Paul.*) points out the honesty with which St. Luke narrates the supercilious indifference of great men to the circumstances which affected the life of the Apostle. The "things," however, for which Gallio "did not care" were not "the things of the kingdom of heaven," but the beating of a Jew by Greeks.

tried to play on my inexperience by dragging before me one Paulus, who seems to be an adherent of Chrestus, or Christus, of whom we heard something at Rome. I was not going to be troubled with their malefic superstitions, and ordered them to be turned out. The Greeks accordingly, who were favourable to Paulus, beat one of the Jews in revenge for their malice. You would have smiled, if you had been present, at these follies of the *turba forensis. Sed haec hactenus.*"

But the superficiality which judges only by externals always brings its own retribution. It adores the mortal and scorns the divinity; it welcomes the impostor and turns the angel from its door. It forms its judgment on trivial accidents, and ignores eternal realities. The haughty, distinguished, and cultivated Gallio, brother of Seneca, Proconsul of Achaia, the most popular man and the most eminent littérateur of his day, would have been to the last degree amazed had any one told him that so paltry an occurrence would be for ever recorded in history; that it would be the only scene in his life in which posterity would feel a moment's interest; that he would owe to it any immortality he possesses; that he would for all time be mainly judged of by the glimpse we get of him on that particular morning; that he had flung away the greatest opportunity of his life when he closed the lips of the haggard Jewish prisoner whom his decision rescued from the clutches of his countrymen; that a correspondence between that Jew Shaûl, or Paulus, and his great brother Seneca, would be forged and would go down to posterity;[1]

[1] No one in these days doubts that the letters of St. Paul and Seneca (Fleury, *St. Paul and Sénèque*, ii. 300; Aubertin, *Sénèque et St. Paul*, 409; Lightfoot, *Phil.* 327; Boissier, *La Religion Romaine*, ii. 52—104) are spurious. On the real explanation of the resemblances between the two, see *Seekers after God*, p. 270, *sq.*, and *passim*. It will there be seen how small ground there is for Tertullian's expression "Seneca *saepe noster.*"

that it would be believed for centuries that that wretched prisoner had converted the splendid philosopher to his own "execrable superstition," and that Seneca had borrowed from him the finest sentiments of his writings; that for all future ages that bent, ophthalmic, nervous, unknown Jew, against whom all other Jews seemed for some inconceivably foolish reason to be so infuriated, would be regarded as transcendently more important than his deified Emperors and immortal Stoics; that the "parcel of questions" about a mere opinion, and names, and a matter of Jewish law, which he had so disdainfully refused to hear, should hereafter become the most prominent of all questions to the whole civilised world.

And Paul may have suspected many of these facts as little as "the sweet Gallio" did. Sick at heart with this fresh outrage, and perhaps musing sadly on the utterance of his Master that He came not to send peace on earth but a sword, he made his way back from the Bema of the great Proconsul to the little congregation in the room of Justus, or to his lodging in the squalid shop of Aquila and Priscilla.

CHAPTER XXIX.

THE FIRST EPISTLE TO THE THESSALONIANS.

"Ergo latet ultimus dies ut observentur omnes dies."—AUG.

AT some period during his stay in Corinth, and probably before his arrest by the Jews early in the year 53, or at the close of A.D. 52, an event had taken place of immense significance in the life of the Apostle and in the history of the Christian faith. He had written to the Thessalonians a letter which may possibly have been the first he wrote to any Christian church,[1] and which certainly is the earliest of those that have come down to us. He had begun, therefore, that new form of activity which has produced effects so memorable to all generations of the Christian world.

We have already seen that Paul had left Timotheus in Macedonia, had been joined by him in Athens, and had once more parted from him, though with deep reluctance and at great self-sacrifice, because his heart yearned for his Thessalonian converts, and he had been twice prevented

---

[1] I only put this as a possibility. It will be seen hereafter (see 1 Cor. v. 9; 2 Cor. x. 9) that I regard it as certain that St. Paul wrote other letters, of which some—perhaps many—have perished; and it is difficult to believe that (for instance) he wrote no word of thanks to the Philippians for the contributions which they had twice sent to him at Thessalonica, or that he wrote nothing to the Thessalonians themselves when he sent Timothy to them from Athens. Does not the whole style of these Epistles show that they could not have been the first specimens of their kind? We cannot be surprised that, amid the disorders of the times, letters written on fugitive materials should have perished, especially as many of them may have been wholly undoctrinal. In 2 Thess. iii. 17 could St. Paul say ὅ ἐστι σημεῖον ἐν πάσῃ ἐπιστολῇ, if he had only written *one?*

from carrying out his earnest desire to visit them once
more. After doing all that he could to comfort and
support them in their many trials, Timotheus had returned,
in company with Silas, to Corinth, and doubtless there the
Apostle had talked with them long and earnestly about
the friends and brethren who had been won to Christ in
the Macedonian city. There was deep cause for thankfulness in their general condition, but there was some need
for advice and consolation. Paul could not send Timothy
again. There was other work to be done. Other
Churches required his own personal services. Nor could
he spare the companions of his toils in the midst of a
city which demanded his whole energy and strength. But
since he could neither come to the Thessalonians himself, nor send them back his truest and dearest fellow-
workers, he would at least write to them, and let his letter
supply, as far as possible, the void created by his absence.
It was a very happy Providence which inspired him with
this thought. It would come quite naturally to him,
because it had been a custom in all ages for Jewish communities to correspond with each other by means of
travelling deputations, and because the prodigious development of intercourse between the chief cities of Italy,
Greece, and Asia rendered it easy to send one or other of
the brethren as the bearer of his missives. And epistolary
correspondence was the very form which was of all others
the best adapted to the Apostle's individuality. It suited
the impetuosity of emotion which could not have been
fettered down to the composition of formal treatises. It
could be taken up or dropped according to the necessities
of the occasion or the feelings of the writer. It permitted
of a freedom of expression which was far more intense and
far more natural to the Apostle than the regular syllo-
gisms and rounded periods of a book. It admitted some-

thing of the tenderness and something of the familiarity of personal intercourse. Into no other literary form could he have infused that intensity which made a Christian scholar truly say of him that he alone of writers seems to have written, not with fingers and pen and ink, but with his very heart, his very feelings, the unbared palpitations of his inmost being;[1] which made Jerome say that in his writings the words were all so many thunders;[2] which made Luther say that his expressions were like living creatures with hands and feet. The theological importance of this consideration is immense, and has, to the deep injury of the Church, been too much neglected. Theologians have treated the language of St. Paul as though he wrote every word with the accuracy of a dialectician, with the scrupulous precision of a school-man, with the rigid formality of a philosophic dogmatist. His Epistles as a whole, with their insoluble antinomies, resist this impossible and injurious method of dealing with them as absolutely as does the Sermon on the Mount. The epistolary form is eminently spontaneous, personal, flexible, emotional. A dictated epistle is like a conversation taken down in shorthand. In one word, it best enabled Paul to be himself, and to recall most vividly to the minds of his spiritual children the tender, suffering, inspired, desponding, terrible, impassioned, humble, uncompromising teacher, who had first won them to become imitators[3] of himself and of the Lord, and to turn from hollow ritualisms or dead idols to serve the living and true God, and to wait for His Son from heaven, whom He raised from the dead, even Jesus who delivereth us from the coming wrath.

---

[1] Casaubon, *Adversaria ap. Wolf.* p. 135.

[2] Jer. *ad Pammach.* Ep. 48.

[3] 1 Thess. i. 6, μιμηταί, not "followers," as in E.V. See Excursus I., on "The Style of St. Paul as Illustrative of his Character," p. 619, *sq.*

And one cause of this vivid freshness of style which he imparted to his Epistles was the fact that they were, with few if any exceptions, not deeply premeditated, not scholastically regular, but that they came fresh and burning from the heart in all the passionate sincerity of its most immediate feelings. He would even write a letter in the glow of excited feeling, and then wait with intense anxiety for news of the manner of its reception, half regretting, or more than half regretting, that he had ever sent it.[1] Had he written more formally he would never have moved as he *has* moved the heart of the world. Take away from the Epistles of St. Paul the traces of passion, the invective, the yearning affection, the wrathful denunciation, the bitter sarcasm, the distressful boasting, the rapid interrogatives, the affectionate entreaties, the frank colloquialisms, the personal details—those marks of his own personality on every page which have been ignorantly and absurdly characterised as intense egotism —and they would never have been, as they are, next to the Psalms of David, the dearest treasures of Christian devotion;—next to the four Gospels the most cherished text-books of Christian faith. We cannot but love a man whose absolute sincerity enables us to feel the very beatings of his heart; who knows not how to wear that mask of reticence and Pharisaism which enables others to use speech only to conceal their thoughts; who, if he smites under the fifth rib, will smite openly and without a deceitful kiss; who has fair blows but no precious balms that break the head; who has the feelings of a man, the language of a man, the love, the hate, the scorn, the indignation of a man; who is no envious cynic, no calumnious detractor, no ingenious polisher of plausible hypocrisies, no

---

[1] 2 Cor. vii. 8.

L L

mechanical repeater of worn-out shibboleths, but who will, if need be, seize his pen with a burst of tears to speak out the very thing he thinks;[1] who, in the accents of utter truthfulness alike to friend and to enemy, can argue, and denounce, and expose, and plead, and pity, and forgive; to whose triumphant faith and transcendent influence has been due in no small measure that fearless and glad enthusiasm which pervaded the life of the early Church.

And thus, when Timothy had told him all that he had observed among the brethren of Thessalonica, we may feel quite sure that, while his heart was full of fresh solicitude, he would write to guide and comfort them,[2] and that many days would not elapse before he had dictated the opening words :—

"Paul, and Silvanus, and Timotheus to the Church[3] of the Thessalonians in God the Father and our Lord

---

[1] 2 Cor. ii. 4.

[2] That the external evidence to the genuineness of the Epistles to the Thessalonians is amply sufficient may be seen in Alford, iii., *Prolegom.*; Davidson, *Introduct.* i. 19—28 ; Westcott, *On the Canon*, 68, n., 168, &c. The internal evidence derived from style, &c., is overwhelming (Jowett, i. 15—26). The counter-arguments of Kern, Schrader, Baur, &c., founded, as usual, alike on divergences and coincidences, on real similarities and supposed discrepancies, on asserted references and imaginary contradictions to the Acts, are silently met in the text. They carry no conviction with them, and have found few followers; Baur (*Paul*, ii. 85—97), to a great extent, furnishing positive arguments against his own conclusion. (See Lünemann, *Br. an die Thessal.* 10—15.) Grotius, Ewald, Baur, Bunsen, Davidson, &c., consider that the First Epistle is really the second ; but the hypothesis is against external and internal evidence, is wholly needless, and creates obvious difficulties. It would require many volumes to enter into all these discussions for every Epistle ; but though I have no space for that here, I have respectfully and impartially considered the difficulties raised, and in many cases shown incidentally my grounds for disregarding them. One most inimitable mark of genuineness is the general resemblance of tone between the Epistle and that written ten years later to the other chief Macedonian Church—Philippi. (See Lightfoot in Smith's *Bibl. Dict.*)

[3] So in 1, 2 Thess., 1, 2 Cor., and Gal. But in the other Epistles τῇ ἀγίοις.

Jesus Christ, grace to you, and peace [from God our Father and the Lord Jesus Christ [1]]."

This opening address is in itself an interesting illustration of St. Paul's character. Though his letters are absolutely his own, yet with that shrinking from personal prominence which we often trace in him, he associates with himself in the introduction not only the dignified Silas,[2] but even the youthful Timothy;[3] and in these his earlier, though not in his later Epistles, constantly uses "we" for "I." By "we" he does not mean to imply that the words are conjointly those of his two fellow-labourers, since he adopts the expression even when he can only be speaking of his individual self;[4] but he is actuated by that sort of modesty, traceable in the language and literature of all nations, which dislikes the needlessly frequent prominence of the first personal pronoun.[5] In his letters to all other Churches, except to the Philippians, to whom the designation was needless, he calls himself Paul an Apostle, but he does not use the title directly[6] to the Thessalonians, because his claim to it in its more special sense had not yet been challenged by insidious Judaisers.[7] In his five earlier Epistles he always

---

[1] This addition is probably spurious. It belongs to 2 Thess. i. 2, and was added because the greeting is so short. As we have now reached St. Paul's first Epistle I must refer the reader to the Excursus which gives the Uncial Manuscripts of the Epistles, *infra*, Excursus II.

[2] Acts xv. 22, 32, 34.

[3] Silas and Timothy are associated with him in 2 Thess.; Sosthenes in 1 Cor.; Timothy in 2 Cor., Phil., Col., and Philem. Paul writes in his own name only to the Romans and Laodiceans, which Churches he had not personally visited. Origen says that the concurrence of Paul and Silas flashed out the lightning of these Epistles (*Hom.* v. *in Jerem.* 588 b).

[4] In 1 Thess. iii. 2, 6, and in Phil. ii. 19, Timothy is spoken of, though associated with Paul in the greeting. 1 Thess. ii. 18, " we . . even I Paul."

[5] "We" is chiefly characteristic of 1, 2 Thess. In 2 Thess. the only passage which relapses into "I" is ii. 5.

[6] See 1 Thess. ii. 6.

[7] It would have been inappropriate in the private note to Philemon.

addresses " the Church ; " in his later Epistles " the Saints," and the reason for this is not clear ; [1] but to all Churches alike he repeats this opening salutation, " Grace and peace."[2] It is a beautiful and remarkable blending of the salutations of the Jew and the Greek, the East and the West, with their predominant ideals of calm and brightness. The solemn greeting of the Jew was SHALÔM, " Peace be to you ; " the lighter greeting of the Greek was χαίρειν, " Rejoice ; " the Church of Christ—possessed of a joy that defied tribulation, heir to a Peace that passeth understanding—not only combined the two salutations, but infused into both a deeper and more spiritual significance.[3]

After this salutation[4] he opens his letter with that

[1] Another slight peculiarity is that in his first two Epistles he says " the Church of the Thessalonians;" whereas in the next three he prefers the expression " the Church in" such and such a city. This may be a mere trifle.

[2] In his Pastoral Epistles he adds the word ἔλεος, " mercy." We may thus sum up the peculiarities of the salutations :—i. " An Apostle," in all except Philem. and Phil. ii. "To the Church," in 1, 2 Thess., 1, 2 Cor., Gal. iii. "To the *Church of* the," 1, 2 Thess.; but "to the Church which is *in*," 1, 2 Cor., Gal. In all other Epistles, "To the *saints*." iv. "Grace and peace," in all but the Pastoral Epistles, which have " Grace, *mercy*, and peace."

[3] Χάρις, quae est principium omnis boni; εἰρήνη, quae est finale bonorum omnium (Thos. Aquin.).

[4] The Epistle, which is mainly personal and practical, may be analysed as follows :—I. i.—iii. Historical; II. iv.—v. Hortatory; each ending with a prayer. (I.) i. 1. Brief greeting. i. 2—10. Thanksgiving for their conversion and holiness. ii. 1—12. Appeal to them as to the character of his ministry. ii. 13—16. Renewed expression of thanksgiving for their constancy under persecutions, and bitter complaint of the Jews. ii. 17—iii. 10. His personal feelings towards them, and the visit of Timothy. iii. 11—13. His prayer for them. (II.) iv. 1—8. Warning against impurity. iv. 9—10. Exhortation to brotherly love; and 11, 12, honourable diligence. iv. 13—v. 11. The only doctrinal part of the Epistle. iv. 13—18. Consolation about the dead. v. 1—11. Duty of watchfulness, since the Lord's advent is near, and the time uncertain. v. 12—15. Their duties to one another. 16—22. Spiritual exhortations. 23, 24. His prayer for them. 25—28. Last words and blessing. The Epistle is characterised by simplicity of style, and the absence of controversy and of developed doctrine. Its keynote is " hope," as the keynote of the Epistle to the Philippians is " joy."

expression of thankfulness on their behalf which he addresses even to the Corinthians, whose deeds were so sad
a contrast to their ideal title of saints, and which is never
wanting, except in the burning letter to the apostatising
Galatians. So invariable is this characteristic of his mind
and style that it has acquired a technical description, and
German writers call it the *Danksagung* of the Epistles.[1]
It was no mere insincere compliment or rhetorical artifice.
Those to whom he wrote, however much they might sink
below their true ideal, were still converts, were a Church,
were saints, were brethren. There might be weak, there
might be false, there might be sinful members among
them, but as a body they were washed and sanctified
and justified, and the life of even those who were unworthy of their high vocation yet presented a favourable
contrast to the lives of the heathen around them. But
the expression of thankfulness on behalf of the Thessalonians is peculiarly full and earnest. It is an overflow
of heartfelt gratitude, as indeed the special characteristic
of the letter is its sweetness.[2] St. Paul tells them that
he is always giving thanks to God for them all, mentioning them in his prayers, filled with the ever-present
memory of the activity of their faith, the energy of their
love, the patience of their hope.[3] He reminds them of
the power and fulness and spiritual unction which had

[1] Ewald, *Die Sendschreiben des Ap. Paulus*, 19, 39, &c. It may perhaps
be urged that some of these peculiarities may be due to the ordinary stereotyped formula of correspondence in the humbler classes. Thus, in papyrus
rolls of the British Museum (edited for the Trustees by J. Forshall), we find
such phrases as εἴη ὡς ὡς τοῖς θεοῖς εὐχομένη διατελῶ, and even, apparently, σοῦ
διὰ παντὸς μνείαν ποιούμενοι. But St. Paul's incessant variations show how little
he was inclined to mere formulæ.

[2] " Habet haec Epistola meram quandam dulcedinem " (Bengel).

[3] Cf. Gal. v. 6. Thus in the very first lines which we possess from his
pen we meet with his fundamental trilogy of Christian virtues—faith, hope,
love. Cf. v. 8; Col. i. 4; Eph. i. 15, 18; iii. 17, 18, 20, &c. See Reuss, *Théol.
Chrét.* ii. 240.

accompanied his preaching of the Gospel, and how they
had become[1] imitators[2] of him and of Christ with such
spiritual gladness in the midst of such deep affliction[3]
that they had become models to all the Churches of
Northern and Southern Greece, and their faith had been
as a trumpet-blast[4] through all the Mediterranean coasts.
So universally was their belief in God known and spread
abroad, that there was no need for St. Paul or his companions to tell how they had worked at Thessalonica,
because every one had heard of their conversion from
idolatry to belief in the very and living God,[5] and to
the waiting for the return of that risen Saviour who
delivereth us from the coming wrath.[6]

---

[1] St. Paul, like many emotional and impressible writers, is constantly
haunted by the same word, which he then repeats again and again—ἥτις
ἀκούοντεσσι νεωτάτη ἀμφιπέληται ἀκούοντεσσι. He uses the verb γίνομαι no less
than eight times, although, as Bishop Ellicott points out, it only occurs twelve
times in all the rest of the New Testament, except in quotations from the
LXX. "Un mot l'obsède, il le ramène dans une page à tout propos. Ce n'est
pas de la stérilité : c'est de la contention de l'esprit et une complète insouciance
de la correction du style" (Renan, p. 233).

[2] μιμηταί, E.V. "followers."

[3] i. 6. The reader will notice the exquisite originality of conception in the
words ἐν θλίψει πολλῇ μετὰ χαρᾶς Πνεύματος Ἁγίου. It is no rhetorical oxymoron,
but the sign of a new aeon in the world's history.

[4] i. 8, ἐξήχηται. ὡς ἐπὶ σάλπιγγος λαμπρὸν ἠχούσης (Theoph.). Admitting for
the warmth of feeling which dictated the expression, it suggests no difficulty
when we remember that a year may have elapsed since his visit, and that
Thessalonica was "posita in gremio imperii Romani" (Cic.), and stood "on a
level with Corinth and Ephesus in its share of the commerce of the Levant."

[5] i. 10, Ἀληθινῷ (1 John v. 20). Ζῶντι as contrasted with dead men and
idols (Wisd. xiv. 15; Gal. iv. 8), which are mere elîlîm, "nullities" (Lev. xix. 4),
and habhâlim, "vapours." The expression shows that the Thessalonian Church
was mainly composed of Gentiles, which accords with Acts xvii. 4, if we read
καὶ Ἑλλήνων (supra, p. 509). If we omit καὶ there is still no contradiction, for
obviously many Gentiles, especially women, were converted, and even the
proselytes had once been idolaters.

[6] Not as in E. V., "who delivered (ῥυόμενον) us from the wrath to come"
(ἐρχομένης, not μελλούσης). The deliverance is continuous ("Christus nos
semel ἐλυτρώσατο semper ῥύεται."—Bengel); the wrath works as a normal law
(i. 1—10).

He appeals to them, therefore, as to unimpeachable witnesses of the earnestness of his visit to them, and of the boldness with which he had faced the dangers of Thessalonica, after such recent and painful experience of the outrages of Philippi. It has been evident, even through these opening sentences of thanksgiving, that there is in his words an undercurrent of allusion to some who would, if they could, have given a very different account of his conduct and motives.[1] These appeals to their knowledge of the life and character and behaviour of Paul and his two fellow-missionaries would have been needless if they had never been impugned. But it is easy to understand that alike the Jews in their eagerness to win back the few members of the synagogue who had joined the brethren, and the Gentiles vexed at the silent rebuke against their own sins, would whisper calumnies about the new teachers, and try to infuse into others their own suspicions. The cities of that age swarmed with every kind and denomination of quack and impostor. Might not these three poor Jews—that silent and digni-fied elder, the shy, gentle youth, and the short enthusiast of mean aspect—might they not be only a new variety of the genus *goës*—like the wandering Galli and worshippers of Isis, or Chaldaei, or Mathematici, or priests of Mithras?[2] Were they not a somewhat suspicious-look-ing trio? What was their secret object? Was it with sinister motives that they gathered into their communities these widows and maidens? Were they not surreptitiously

---

[1] 1 Thess. ii. 5, 9. These phrases are not accounted for by contrast with *heathen* deceptions. The ὑμῖν τοῖς πιστεύουσιν of verse 10 means "though *others* did not so regard our conduct."

[2] Hausrath, p. 300; μάγοι καὶ γόητες (Theoph.); ii. 3, ἐν δόλῳ (2 Cor. ii. 17; iv. 2; xi. 13). ἀκαθαρσία *may* only mean "impure motives" (*e.g.*, covetousness; cf. 2 Cor. xi. 8; 1 Tim. iii. 8; Titus i. 7); "Unlauterkeit, Beimischung men-schlicher Begehrnisse" (Ewald) ; verse 5, πλεονεξία (Acts xx. 33; 1 Cor. ix. 15; 2 Cor. xii. 14).

trying to get hold of money? or might it not be their own exaltation at which they were aiming?—Now there were some charges and attacks which, in after days, as we shall see, filled Paul with bitter indignation; but insinuations of this nature he can afford to answer very calmly. Such calumnies were too preposterous to be harmful; such innuendos too malevolent to be believed. In order to disprove them he had but to appeal at once to notorious facts; and, indeed, *no* elaborate disproof was needed, for his Thessalonian friends *knew,* and God was witness,[1] that there had been no deceit, no uncleanness, no base motives, no secret avarice, no desire to win favour, no fawning flattery in the exhortations of the missionaries. They had come, not for selfishness, but for sacrifice; not for glory, but to pour out their hearts' tenderness, and spend their very lives for the sake of their converts,[2] cherishing them as tenderly[3] as a nursing mother fosters her children in her warm bosom,[4] yet waiving their own rights, and taking nothing whatever from them, nor laying the smallest burden upon them.[5] The brethren knew that while they were preaching they regarded their mission as a glorious privilege;[6] and because their one desire was to please God, they endured and laboured[7] night and day[8] to win their own bread, setting blameless

---

[1] 1 Thess. ii. 5.

[2] ii. 8, *leg.* ὁμειρόμενοι, א, A, B, C, D, E, F, G, "clinging to you;" προσδεδεμένοι (Theoph.); ἀντεχόμενοι ὑμῶν (Œcumen.).

[3] ii. 7, ἤπιοι, found also in 2 Tim. ii. 24. The νήπιοι of א, B, C, D, F, G, is an obvious instance of mere homoeoteleuton.

[4] ii. 7, θάλπῃ.

[5] ἐν βάρει εἶναι, "oneri esse" (Vulg.). It may mean to be dictatorial (πολλῆς ἀπολαῦσαι τιμῆς—Chrys.), but see verse 9; 2 Cor. xi. 9; xii. 16; 2 Thess. iii. 8.

[6] ii. 4, δεδοκιμάσμεθα.

[7] ii. 9, κόπος, "active toil;" μόχθος, "steady endurance of toil."

[8] St. Paul uses the ordinary Hebrew expression (iii. 10; 2 Thess. iii. 8, &c.), which arose from the notion, found in an old border oath, that "God made

examples of holiness towards God, and righteousness towards men, and all the while exhorting their followers one by one[1] to live lives worthy of God and of the kingdom of His Christ.[2]

And this was why, thank God, the Thessalonians had accepted their preaching for what it was—a divine and not a human message; and had borne suffering at the hands of their Gentile neighbours with the same exemplary courage as the Churches of Judæa, who in like manner had been persecuted by the Jews. And here Paul, as he so constantly does, "*goes off at a word.*" The mere incidental mention of Jews makes him digress to denounce them, writing as he did in the very heat of those conflicts which ended in his indignant withdrawal from their synagogue at Corinth, and recalling the manner in which these murderers of the Lord and of the Prophets,[3] displeasing[4] to God and the common enemies of man,[5] chased him from city

---

the earth in six days and seven nights." Hence too the term νυχθήμερον. St. Luke, writing in his own person, says "day and night" (Acts ix. 24). The fact that there were wealthy and distinguished women among the proselytes (Acts xvii. 4) made this self-denial the more striking.

[1] ii. 11, ἵνα ἕκαστον ὑμῶν. Chrysostom says, βάβαι ἐν τοσούτῳ πλήθει μηδένα παραλιπεῖν; but probably the Christians in Thessalonica would have made an exceedingly small modern parish.

[2] ii. 1—12.

[3] Omit ἰδίους, א, A, B, D, &c. "*Suos* adjectio est haeretici" (*i.e.*, of Marcion)—Tert. *adv.* Marc. v. 15.

[4] μὴ ἀρεσκόντων. The μή, though "the prevailing New Testament combination with the participle" (Ellicott), is slightly less severe than if he had used οὐκ.

[5] The momentary exacerbation against the Jews in the mind of St. Paul must have been unusually intense to wring from him such words as these. We almost seem to catch the echo of the strong condemnation uttered against them by Gentiles as a God-detested race, who hated all men (" *odium generis humani*"—Tac. *H.* v. 5; Juv. *Sat.* xiv. 100), and such a view of them (which Lünemann here fails to overthrow) must have caused a deep pang to one who remained at heart a genuine patriot. (See Rom. ix. 1—5.) But the triumph of the Jews over the impious attempts of Caligula had caused a great recrudescence of fanaticism among them.

to city, and tried to prevent his mission to the Gentiles.
And it is thus, he says, that they are always filling up
the measure of guilt, and the wrath came upon them
to the end—potentially overtook them—in that sudden
consummation of their sins. Their very sin, he seems to
say, in hindering the proclamation of the Gospel, was itself
their punishment; their wrath against Christ was God's
wrath against them; their dementation would be, and was,
their doom.[1]

And having been thus diverted by his feeling of indignation against them from the topic of self-defence—on
which, indeed, nothing more was necessary to be said—he
goes on to tell them that regarding them as his glory
and joy and crown of boasting[2] at the coming of Christ—
feeling, in his absence from them, like a father bereaved of
his children[3]—he had twice purposed to come to them, and
had twice been hindered by Satan.[4] He had, however,

---

[1] ii. 14—16. Baur, in arguing that this could only have been written
after the destruction of Jerusalem, makes a double mistake. First, he takes
ἔφθασεν in the sense of ἴφθακεν (like the E. V. "has come"), which is the
erroneous gloss of B, D; and secondly, he does not see the ethical conception
which I have here tried to bring out. The wrath of God found its full consummation in the fulness of their criminality (Matt. xxvii. 25); the fiat of
their doom had then gone forth. It was not finally consummated till the fall
of Jerusalem, eighteen years later, but signs were already obvious that its
execution would not long be delayed. To the prescient eye of St. Paul the
commencing troubles in Palestine—and the recent expulsion of the Jews
from Rome—would be ample to justify his expression. In the true prophetic
spirit he regards the *inevitable* as the *actual.* It is possible, too, that St. Paul
may be alluding to the great discourse of Christ (Matt. xxiii. 37—39; xxiv.
6, 16; cf. Rom. i. 18; Dan. ix. 24).

[2] Ezek. xvi. 12 (LXX.).

[3] ii. 17, ἀπορφανισθέντες ἀφ' ὑμῶν.

[4] Once apparently at Berœa, once at Athens. The Satanic hindrance may
have been in Berœa Jewish persecutions, in Athens feeble health. (Cf. Rom.
xv. 22.) He is writing to Gentile converts, to whom it will be observed that he
does not adduce, in either Epistle, a single quotation from the Old Testament,
with which they could have been as yet but little familiar; but the immediate
reference of trials, sickness, and hindrances to Satan is found to this day in

done the next best thing he could. He had parted from
Timothy in Athens, and sent him to prevent them from
succumbing[1] to those fierce afflictions, of the certainty of
which they had been faithfully forewarned; and to ascertain
their faith, as shown by the dubious result of too definite
temptations.[2] When Timothy rejoined him at Corinth,
the news which he had brought back was so reassuring—
he was able to give so good an account of their faith, and
love, and steadfastness, and affection—that it had cheered
the Apostle in the midst of his own heavy afflictions, and
been to him like a fresh spring of life. No thanks to
God could be too hearty for this blessing, and it added
intensity to his prayer that God would yet enable him to
come and see them, and to perfect all deficiencies of their
faith. He concludes this historic or personal section of
his Epistle with the fervent prayer that God would
deepen the spirit of love which already prevailed among
them, and so enable them to stand before Him in blameless
holiness at the coming of our Lord Jesus with all His saints.[3]

all Oriental forms of speech. Even in the Bible the term Satan is sometimes
applied to "any adversary" or "opposing influence" (cf. 1 Chron. xxi. 1 with
2 Sam. xxiv. 1). "The devil," ὁ διάβολος, as distinguished from unclean spirits,
δαιμόνια, is only used by St. Paul in Eph. iv. 27; vi. 11; and three times in
the letters to Timothy. Where he regarded the hindrance as Satanic he
carries out his purpose another time, but where it is a divine prohibition
(Acts xvi. 6, 7) he finally gives it up. Acts xxi. 4 is only an apparent
exception.

[1] He here uses the metaphor σαίνεσθαι, derived from the fawning cowardice
of frightened animals; elsewhere he uses the metaphor στέλλεσθαι, "to furl
the sails in a high wind." He calls Timothy "a fellow-worker with God"
(συνεργὸν τοῦ Θεοῦ, D), an expression only altered in the MSS. because of its
boldness (1 Cor. iii. 9; 2 Cor. vi. 1).

[2] iii. 5, μή πως ἐπείρασεν . . . καὶ εἰς κενὸν γένηται.

[3] ii. 17—iii. 13. Parousia occurs six times in these two Epistles, and only
besides in 1 Cor. xv. 23. The word "advent" is said to occur first in Tert.
De Resurrect. 24. The "saints" seems to be a reference, not to angels
(Ps. lxxxix. 7; Matt. xvi. 27; Jude 14, &c.), because St. Paul does not use
this term of angels (kedoshîm, Ps. cxxxix. 7), but to those mentioned in iv. 16;
1 Cor. vi. 2.

From these earnest and loving messages he turns to
the practical part of his letter. He beseeches[1] and exhorts
them not to be stationary, but to advance more and more
in that Christian course which he had marked out for
them. And then he enters on those special injunctions
which he knew to be most needful. First and foremost
he puts the high virtue of purity. These converts had
but recently been called out of a heathenism which looked
very lightly on the sins of the flesh. The mastery over
lifelong habits of corruption was not to be won in a day.
They were still in danger of relapsing into sensual crime.
It was necessary to remind them that, however small
might be the censure which Gentiles attached to fornication,[2] and even to yet darker and deadlier sins,[3] they were
in direct opposition to the command, and would immediately
deserve the retribution of that God whose will was their
sanctification, and who laid on them the duty, however
difficult, of acquiring a secure and tranquil mastery over
their body and its lusts.[4] If then any one among them

---

[1] ἐρωτῶμεν, as in v. 12; 2 Thess. ii. 1; only elsewhere to his other Macedonian Church (Phil. iv. 3).

[2] Cic. pro Caelio, 48; Hor. Sat. I. ii. 32; Ter. Adelph. I. ii. 21; Jer. Ep. 77;
Aug. De Civ. Dei. xiv. 18.

[3] Ver. 7, ὃν . . . ἐπὶ ἀκαθαρσίᾳ ἀλλ' ἐν ἁγιασμῷ.

[4] iv. 4. The exact meaning of εἰδέναι ἕκαστον ὑμῶν τὸ ἑαυτοῦ σκεῦος κτᾶσθαι,
κ.τ.λ., must remain uncertain. It is wrongly translated in the E.V. "that
every one of you should know how to possess his vessel," &c., for κτᾶσθαι is "to
acquire." I have given what would be a very fine and forcible meaning of the
words, but it cannot be regarded as certain that σκεῦος means "body"(cf. 2 Cor.
iv. 7, Chrys., Theoph, Œcumen., Theod., Tert., and most moderns). I regard
it, however, as by far the most probable interpretation (cf. 1 Sam. xxi. 5;
2 Cor. iv. 7). So ἀγγεῖον is used for "body" in Philo, and vas in Latin writers
(see Cic. T. Disp. i. 22; Lucr. iii. 44). Theodore of Mopsuestia and Augustine
make it mean "his own wife;" and then it would be a recommendation to
the spirit of chastity at once preserved and continued in a holy marriage (Heb.
iii. 4). This view has been recently adopted by De Wette, Schott, &c., as it was
by Aquinas and Estius. In favour of it are the Hebrew יָד for wife (see
Rabbinic instances in Schoettgen, Hor. Hebr., ad loc.), and the phrase κτᾶσθαι
γυναῖκα (Ecclus. xxxvi. 29; cf. Eph. v. 28; 1 Cor. vii. 2; 1 Pet. iii. 7). But

professed to despise these precepts as though they were
merely those of the Apostle, he must now be reminded
that he was thereby despising, not any human teacher, but
God, who called them, not for uncleanliness, but in sanctification,[1] and by giving them His Holy Spirit, not only
deepened the duty, but also inspired them with the power
to sanctify His Temple in their hearts.[2]

The next Christian virtue of which he speaks is
brotherly love.   He feels it unnecessary to do so,[3] for God
Himself had taught them both to recognise that duty and
to put it in practice, not only towards the members of their
own church, but towards all Macedonian Christians (vs.
9, 10).

Further, they should make it their ambition to be
quiet,[4] working with their own hands,[5] and not to meddle
with others, and not to rely on the assistance of others,
but to present to the outer world a spectacle of honourable
and active independence (vs. 11, 12).

would the Thessalonians, whose women held a much higher and freer position
than Oriental women, have been aware of this somewhat repulsive Orientalism ? Would the use of it have been worthy of St. Paul's refinement ?
and is he not, as Theodoret observes, speaking to celibates and to women as
well as to men ?

[1] *Leg.* διδοντα, א, B, D, E, F, G.

[2] iv. 1—8. The dark warning of iv. 6 is lost in the E. V., because, though
it would be but too intelligible to Pagan converts, St. Paul veils it under the
delicate euphemisms, the *honesta aposiopesis,* familiar to his sensitive refinement (cf. 1 Cor. v. 1, 2; 2 Cor. vii. 11, &c.; Eph. v. 3, 12).   At any rate,
the Greek commentators, who would here be most likely to see his meaning,
take him to mean not only adultery, but yet deeper abysses of wickedness.
It cannot be "business," which would be τοῖς πράγμασιν. (See Döllinger,
Judenth. u. Heidenth.)

[3] This sort of παράλειψις (or praeteritio), noticed here by Theophylact, is a
rhetorical figure characteristic of St. Paul's kindliness (see v. 1; 2 Cor. ix. 1;
Philem. 19).   But the phrase also implies that it is *easier* to teach Christian
virtue than to eradicate habitual vice.

[4] One of St. Paul's happy turns of expression (*oxymoron,* Rom. xii. 11;
cf. Isa. xxx. 7).

[5] This shows that the Thessalonian converts were mainly artisans.

And now, by these moral exhortations, by thus recalling them from over-eschatological excitement to the quiet
fulfilment of the personal duties which lay nearest at hand,
he has prepared the way for the removal of a serious doubt
which had troubled some of them.   Since he left them
there had been deaths in the little community, and these
deaths had been regarded by some of the survivors with a
peculiar despondency.   They had been taught again and
again to hope for, to look unto, the coming of Christ.
That blessed Presence was to be for them the solution of all
perplexities, the righting of all wrongs, the consolation for
all sufferings. What the hopes of the birth of the Messiah
had been to the Jew, that the hope of His return with
all His saints was to the early Christian.   And it was
natural that such a topic should be prominent in the
addresses to a church which, from its very foundation, had
been, and for years continued to be, peculiarly afflicted.[1]
What, then, was to be said about those who had died, and
therefore had not seen the promise of Christ's coming?
What could be said of those whose life had ended like
the common life of men—no wrongs righted, no miseries
consoled?   Had not they been beguiled of their promise,
disappointed in their hope, deceived, even, as to the event
on which they had fixed their faith?   And if *they*, why
not *others?* If the dead were thus frustrated in their
expectation, why might not the living be?   St. Paul has
already given them the advice which would prevent them
from brooding too much on that one uncertain moment of
Christ's coming.   He has bidden them be pure, and loving,
and diligent, and live their daily lives in simple honour
and faithfulness.   He would have eminently approved the
quiet good sense of that president of the Puritan assembly,

[1] 2 Cor. vii. 5.

who, when a dense darkness came on, and some one proposed that they should adjourn because it might be the beginning of the Day of Judgment, proposed rather that candles should be lighted, because if it *was* to be the Day of Judgment, they could not be found better employed than in the quiet transaction of duty.   But Paul does not leave his converts in their perplexity about their departed friends.   He tells them, in words which have comforted millions of mourners since, not to sorrow as those that have no hope,[1] for that "if we believe that Jesus died and rose again, even so them also which had been laid asleep by Jesus will God bring with Him."[2]   He even enters into details.   He tells them "by the word of the Lord"[3] that death would practically make no difference whatever between the living and the dead, for that in the tremendous "NOW" of the Day of Judgment[4] the Lord Himself should descend from heaven with a cry of summons, with the voice of the archangel,[5] and with the trump of God,[6] and that

---

[1] That the Gentiles were at this time, as a rule, despondent in their views of death, in spite of dim hopes and splendid guesses, is certain. "Mortuus nec ad Deos, nec ad homines acceptus est" (*Corp. Inscr.* i. 118; Boissier, *La Rel. Rom.* i. 304, *seq.*).   See, for the more ancient Greek view, Æsch. *Eumen.* 648, &c.   The shade of Achilles says to Ulysses in Hades :—

> " 'Talk not of reigning in this dolorous gloom,
> Nor think vain words,' he cried, ' can ease my doom ;
> Better by far laboriously to bear
> A weight of woes, and breathe the vital air,
> Slave to the meanest hind that begs his bread,
> Than reign the sceptred monarch of the dead.' "

[2] iv. 14. If the διὰ τοῦ Ἰησοῦ be taken with κοιμηθέντας, "laid asleep by Jesus." Cf. Acts iii. 16; Rom. i. 8; v. 11; 2 Cor. i. 5, &c.

[3] "Quasi Eo ipso loquente" (Beza). As this can hardly be referred to Matt. xxiv. 31, and must be compared with the Hebrew phrase (1 Kings xx. 35, &c.), we can only understand it either of a traditional utterance of Christ or a special revelation to the Apostle. Ewald, however, says (*Sendschr.* 48), " Aus Christusworten die ihnen gewiss auch schriftlich vorlagen."

[4] Luther.

[5] Archangel only here and in Jud. 9.

[6] The imagery is borrowed from Ex. xix. 16.

then the dead in Christ should rise first, and we who are
alive and remain[1] be caught up to meet the Lord in the
air, and so be for ever with Him. "Wherefore," he
says, "comfort one another with these words."[2]

But *when* should this be?—after what period, at what
critical moment?[3] That was a question which he need not
answer, because they themselves knew precisely[4] the only
answer which could be given, which was that the day of
the Lord should come as a thief in the night, overwhelming those that chose darkness with sudden destruction.
But *they* were not of the darkness, but children of light;
so that, however suddenly it came, that day could not find
them unprepared.[5] For which purpose let them be sober
and vigilant, like soldiers, armed with faith and love for a
breastplate, and the hope of salvation for a helmet;[6] since
God had not appointed them for wrath, but to obtain salvation through Him who had died in order that they,
whether in life or in death, might live with Him for ever.[7]
The Thessalonians are bidden to continue edifying and
comforting one another with these words. Did none of
them ask, "But what will become of the Jews? of the
heathen? of the sinners and backsliders among ourselves?"
Possibly they did. But here, and in the Romans, and in
the Corinthians, St. Paul either did not anticipate such
questions, or refused to answer them. Perhaps he had

---

[1] These words will be explained *infra*.

[2] iv. 13—18. These verses furnish one leading *motive* of the Epistle.

[3] v. 1, περὶ δὲ τῶν χρόνων καὶ τῶν καιρῶν.

[4] v. 2, ἀκριβῶς.

[5] v. 4, A, B, read κλέπτας, which would be a slight change of metaphor.
" Weil der Dieb nur in und mit der Nacht kommt, vom Tage aber überrascht
wird " (Ewald). Cf. Matt. xxiv. 37; Rom. xiii. 11—14.

[6] The germ of the powerful and beautiful figure of the Christian's panoply
which is elaborated in Eph. vi. 13—17; Rom. xiii. 12. (Cf. Wisd. v. 18;
Baruch. v. 12).

[7] v. 1—11.

heard the admirable Hebrew apophthegm, "Learn to say, *'I do not know.'*" This at least is certain, that with him the idea of the resurrection is so closely connected with that of faith, and hope, and moral regeneration, that when he speaks of it he will speak of it mainly, indeed all but exclusively, in connection with the resurrection of the saints.[1]

To the thoughts suggested by St. Paul's treatment of this weighty topic we shall revert immediately. He ends the epistle with moral exhortations—all, doubtless, suggested by the needs of the Church—of extraordinary freshness, force, and beauty. There were traces of *insubordination* among them, and he bids them duly respect and love, for their work's sake, the spiritual labourers and leaders of their community,[2] and to be at peace among themselves. He further tells them—perhaps in these last verses especially addressing the presbyters—to warn those unruly brethren who would not obey. There was *despondency* at work among them, and he bids them " comfort the feebleminded, take the weak by the hand, be patient towards all men." They were to avoid all retaliations, and seek after all kindness[3] (vs. 12—15). Then follow little arrow-flights of inestimably precious exhortation. Was depression stealing into their hearts ? Let them meet it by remembering that God's will for them in Christ Jesus was perpetual joy, unceasing prayer, universal thanksgiving. Had there been any collisions of practice, and differences of opinion, among the excited enthusiasts whose absorption in the expected return of Christ left them neither energy nor wish to do their daily duties, while it made

---

[1] Pfleiderer, i. 275; Rom. vi. 23; 1 Cor. xv. 22, &c. See Reuss, *Théol. Chrét.* ii. 214.

[2] These vague terms seem to show that the ecclesiastical organisation of the Church was as yet very flexible.

[3] v. 15, contrast this with Soph. *Philoct.* 679.

M M

them also set very little store by the calmer utterances of moral exhortation? Then, besides the exhortation to peace, and the noble general rule to avoid every kind of evil,[1] he warns them that they should neither quench the Spirit nor despise prophesyings—that is, neither to stifle an impassioned inspiration nor to undervalue a calm address[2]—but to test all that was said to them, and hold fast what was good.[3]

Then, once more, with the affirmation that God's faithfulness would grant the prayer, he prays that God would sanctify them wholly, and preserve their bodies, their wills and affections, their inmost souls,[4] blamelessly till that coming of the Lord to which he has so often alluded. He asks their prayers for himself; bids them salute all the brethren with a holy kiss;[5] adjures them by the Lord[6]

[1] Not "every appearance of evil" (E. V.), grand as such an exhortation undoubtedly is. It may perhaps be "from every evil appearance," everything which has an ill look: possibly it refers to bad γένη of spiritual teaching.

[2] 1 Cor. xiv. 39.

[3] Verses 16—21. What they needed was the διάκρισις πνευμάτων (1 Cor. xii. 10; Heb. v. 14), and to be δόκιμοι τραπεζίται.

[4] v. 23, σῶμα, "body;" ψυχή, the entire human life and faculties; πνεῦμα the divinely imbreathed spirit, the highest region of life. ὁλοτελεῖς, ὁλόκληροι (James i. 4). Trench, *Synon.*, p. 70.

[5] The τοὺς ἀδελφοὺς πάντας must mean "one another," as in Rom. xvi. 16; 1 Cor. xvi. 20; 2 Cor. xiii. 12; 1 Pet. v. 14, unless these few concluding lines are addressed specially to the elders. On the "kiss of charity"—an Oriental custom—see Bingham, *Antiq.* iii. 3, 3; Hooker, *Pref.* iv. 4.

[6] The very strong adjuration may have been rendered necessary by some of the differences between the converts and the leading members of the community, at which the Apostle hints in v. 12—15. Some influential persons, to whom the letter was first handed, might be inclined to suppress any parts of it with which they disagreed, or which seemed to condemn their views or conduct. Timothy may have brought the news that some previous letter of the Apostle to this, or other churches, had not properly been made known. How easily such an interference was possible we see from 3 John 9, "I wrote to the Church, but Diotrephes, who loveth to have the pre-eminence among them, receiveth us not" (see Ewald, *Sendschr.* p. 51). Dionysius of Corinth deplores the falsification of his own letters (Euseb. *H. E.* iv. 23). St. Paul generally asked for a prayer himself towards the close of a letter (Eph. vi. 19; Col. iv. 3; 2 Thess. iii. 1).

that his letter be read to the entire community; and so concludes with his usual ending, "The grace of our Lord Jesus Christ be with you. Amen."[1] These last three verses were probably written in his own hand.

It may easily be imagined with what rapture the arrival of such a letter would be hailed by a young, persecuted, and perplexed community; how many griefs it would console; how many doubts it would resolve; how much joy, and hope, and fresh enthusiasm it would inspire. It could not but have been delightful in any case to be comforted amid the storm of outward opposition, and to be inspirited amid the misgivings of inward faithlessness, by the words of the beloved teacher whose gospel had changed the whole current of their lives. It was much to feel that, though absent from them in person, he was present with them in heart,[2] praying for them, yearning over them, himself cheered by the tidings of their constancy; but it was even more to receive words which would tend to heal the incipient disagreements of that small and loving, but inexperienced, and as yet but half-organised community, and to hear the divinely authoritative teaching which silenced their worst fears. And

---

[1] This γνώρισμα or badge of cognisance is found, with slight variations, at the close of all St. Paul's Epistles. Thus:—

(a) In 1 Thess. v. 28; 1 Cor. xvi. 23 we have, "The grace of our Lord Jesus Christ be with you," to which the word "all" is added in 2 Thess. iii. 18; Rom. xvi. 24; Phil. iv. 23.

(β) In Philem. 25; Gal. vi. 18 we have, "The grace of our Lord Jesus Christ be with your spirit" ("brethren," Gal.).

(γ) In Col. iv. 18; 1 Tim. vi. 21; 2 Tim. iv. 22 we have the shortest form, "Grace be with you" (thee), to which Titus iii. 15 adds "all."

(δ) In Eph. vi. 24 we have the variation, "Grace be with all them that love the Lord Jesus Christ in sincerity," and in 2 Cor. xiii. 14 alone the full "Apostolic benediction."

The *subscriptions* added to the Epistles at a much later period are mostly valueless (see Paley, *Horae Paulinae*, chap. xv.).

[2] 1 Thess. ii. 17.

M M 2

further than this, if the words of St. Paul shine so
brightly to us through the indurated dust of our long
familiarity, how must they have sparkled for them in their
fresh originality, and with heaven's own light shining on
those oracular gems!   "Having received the word *in much
affliction with joy of the Holy Ghost;"* [1]—that was no mere
artificial *oxymoron*, but an utterance which came from a
new world, of which they were the happy lords. "Jesus
which delivereth us from the coming wrath;" [2] "God
who called you unto His kingdom and glory;" [3] "This is
the will of God, even your sanctification;" [4] "So shall
we ever be with the Lord;" [5] "Ye are all the children of
the light and the children of the day;" [6] "See that none
render evil for evil unto any;" [7] "Rejoice evermore." [8]
What illimitable hopes, what holy obligations, what golden
promises, what glorious responsibilities, what lofty ideals,
what reaches of morality beyond any which their greatest
writers had attained, what strange renovation of the whole
spirit and meaning of life, lay hidden for them in those
simple words! [9]   The brief Epistle brought home to them

---

[1] i. 6.   [3] ii. 12.   [5] iv. 17.   [7] v. 15.
[2] i. 10.   [4] iv. 3.   [6] v. 5.   [8] v. 16.

[9] Baur (*Paul.* ii.), Kern (*Tüb. Zeitschr.* 1839), Van der Vaier (*Die beiden
Briefen aan de Thessal.*), De Wette (*Einleit.*), Volkmar, Zeller, &c., and
the Tübingen school generally, except Hilgenfeld (*Die Thessalonicherbriefe*),
reject both Epistles to the Thessalonians as ungenuine, and Baur calls the
first Epistle a "mattes Nachwerk." I have carefully studied their arguments,
but they seem to me so slight as to be scarcely deserving of serious
refutation. The difficulties which would be created by rejecting these
Epistles are ten times as formidable as any which they suggest. If an unbiassed scholar, familiar with the subject, cannot *feel* the heart of St. Paul
throbbing through every sentence of these Epistles, it is hardly likely that
argument will convince him. External evidence (Iren. *Haer.* v. 6, 1; Clem.
Alex. *Paedag.* i. p. 109, ed. Potter; Tert. *De Resurrect. Carnis*, cap. 24),
though sufficiently strong, is scarcely even required. Not only Bunsen,
Ewald, &c., but even Hilgenfeld (*l. c.*), Holtzmann (Thessalon. in Schenkel,
Bibel-lexikon), Pfleiderer (*Paulinism*, 29), Hausrath, Weisse, Schmidt, &c.,
accept the first.

the glad truth that they could use, for their daily wear, that glory of thought which had only been attained by the fewest and greatest spirits of their nation at their rarest moments of inspiration; and therewith that grandeur of life which, in its perfect innocence towards God and man, was even to these unknown.

It is a remarkable fact that in this Epistle St. Paul alludes no less than four times to the coming of Christ,[1] and uses, to describe it, the word *parousia*—"presence"—which also occurs in this sense in the second Epistle,[2] but in only one other passage of all his other Epistles.[3] Whether, after the erroneous conclusions which the Thessalonians drew from this letter, and the injurious effects which this incessant prominence of eschatology produced in their characters, he subsequently made it a less salient feature of his own teaching, we cannot tell. Certain, however, it is that the misinterpretation of his first letter, and the reprehensible excitement and restlessness which that misinterpretation produced,[4] necessitated the writing of a second very shortly after he had received tidings of these results.[5] It is equally certain that, from this time forward, the visible personal return of Christ and the nearness of the end, which are the predominant topics in the First Epistle to the Thessalonians, sink into a far more subordinate topic of reference; and that, although St. Paul's language in the letter was misunderstood, yet the

[1] ii. 19; iii. 13; iv. 15; v. 23.
[2] 2 Thess. ii. 1, 8.
[3] 1 Cor. xv. 23.
[4] We find in St. Paul's own words abundant proof that his teaching was distorted and slandered, and St. Peter gives us direct positive assurance that such was the case (2 Pet. iii. 16).
[5] Tradition should have some weight, and πρὸς Θεσσαλονικεῖς β′ is the reading of A, B, D, E, F, G. The internal evidences also, to some of which I have called attention, seem to me decisive.

misunderstanding was not a wilful but a perfectly natural one; and that in his later letters he anticipates his own death, rather than the second Advent, as his mode of meeting Christ. The divine and steady light of history first made clear to the Church that our Lord's prophetic warnings as to His return applied primarily to the close of the Jewish dispensation, and the winding up of all the past, and the inauguration of the last great aeon of God's dealings with mankind.

CHAPTER XXX.

"Δεῖ γὰρ ταῦτα γενέσθαι πρῶτον, ἀλλ' οὐκ εὐθέως τὸ τέλος."—Luke xxi. 9.

MANY months could not have elapsed before the Apostle heard that the Thessalonians, with all their merits and virtues, were still, and even more than previously, hindered in moral growth by eschatological enthusiasms. When he wrote to them before, they were tempted to despond about the death of friends, whom they supposed likely to be thus deprived of part at least of the precious hopes which were their main, almost their sole, support in the fiery furnace of affliction. The Apostle's clear assurance seems to have removed all anxiety on this topic, but now they regarded the immediate coming of Christ as a thing so certain that some of them were tempted to neglect his exhortations, and to spend their lives in aimless religious excitement.[1] St. Paul felt how fatal would be such a temperament to all Christian progress, and the main object of his second letter was to control into calm, and shame into diligence, the gossiping enthusiasm which fatally tended towards irregularity and sloth. They were not to desert the hard road of the present for the mirage which

---

[1] The reader will be struck with the close analogy of this temptation to that which did so much mischief among the Anabaptists and other sects in the days of the Reformation. The Thessalonian Church may have had its Carlstadts whom St. Paul felt it necessary to warn, just as Luther fought, with all the force of his manly sense, against the crudities of the religious errors which had derived their impulse from a perversion of his own teaching.

seemed to bring so close to them the green Edens of the future; they were not to sacrifice the sacredness of immediate duty for the dreamy sweetness of unrealised expectations. The Advent of Christ might be near at hand; but it was not so instant as they had been led to imagine from an erroneous view of what he had said, and by mistaken reports—possibly even by written forgeries—which ascribed to him words which he had never used, and opinions which he had never held.

The expression on which the Apocalyptic fanaticism of the less sensible Thessalonians seems to have fastened was that which occurs in 1 Thess. iv. 15—"WE, which are alive and remain to the presence of the Lord, shall certainly not anticipate those that have fallen asleep." It was not unnatural that they should interpret this to mean that their teacher himself expected to survive until the Epiphany of their Lord's presence.[1] If so, it must be very close at hand; and again, if so, of what use were the petty details of daily routine, the petty energies of daily effort? Was it not enough to keep themselves alive *anyhow* until the dawn of that near day, or the shadows of that rapidly approaching night, which might be any day or any night, on which all earthly interests should be dissipated for ever as soon as the voice of God and the trumpet of the dead should sound?

Now, we ask, had this been the real meaning of the words of St. Paul? The question has been voluminously and angrily debated. It has been made, in fact (and very needlessly), the battle-ground as to the question of verbal inspiration. Some have tried to maintain the desperate and scarcely honest position that neither St. Paul nor the Apostles generally had any expectation of the near visible

---

[1] Ἐπιφάνεια τῆς παρουσίας

advent of Christ; others that they were absolutely convinced that it would take place in their own generation, and even in their own lifetime.

Not in the interests of controversy, but in those of truth, I will endeavour to prove that neither of these extreme theses can be maintained. If the view of the Thessalonians had been *absolutely* groundless, it would have been easy for St. Paul to say to them, as modern commentators have said for him, " You mistook my general expression for a specific and individual one. When I said ' *we* which are alive and remain ' at the presence of Christ, I did not mean either myself, or you, in particular, but merely ' the living '—the class to which we at present belong—as opposed to the dead, about whose case I was speaking to you.[1] You are mistaken in supposing that I meant to imply a conviction that before my own death the Lord would reappear." Now, he does not say this at all;[2] he only tells them not to be drifted from their moorings, not, as he expresses it, to be tossed from their sound sense[3] by the supposition that he had spoken of the actual instancy[4] of the day of the Lord. He tells them plainly that certain events must occur before that day came; and these as certainly are events which precluded all possibility of the Second Advent taking place for them to-morrow or the next day. But, on the other hand, he does *not* tell them that the day of the Lord was not *near* (ἐγγύς). If he had done so he would have robbed of their meaning the exhortations which had formed the staple of his preaching at Thessalonica, as

[1] 1 Thess. iv. 15. ἡμεῖς . . . . οὐ περὶ ἑαυτοῦ φησίν—ἀλλὰ τοὺς πιστοὺς λέγει (Chrys).

[2] It is never his method to explain away his views because they have been perverted, but merely to bring them out in their full and proper meaning.

[3] μὴ ταχέως σαλευθῆναι ἀπὸ τοῦ νοὸς (2 Thess. ii. 2).

[4] ἐνέστηκεν.

they constituted the only prominent doctrinal statement
of his First Epistle.[1] If we are to judge of St. Paul's
views by his own language, and not by the preconceptions
of scholasticism, we can divine what would have been his
answer to the plain question, "Do you personally expect
to live till the return of Christ?" At *this* period of his
life his answer would have been, "I cannot speak positively on the matter. I see clearly that, before His
return, certain things must take place; but, on the whole,
I do expect it. But at a later period of his life he
would have said in substance, "It' may be so; I cannot
tell. On the whole, however, I no longer hope to
survive till that day; nor does it seem to me of any importance whether I do or not. At that day the quick
will have no advantage over the dead. What I now look
forward to, what I sometimes even yearn for, is my own
death. I know that when I die I shall be with Christ,
and it is for that pathway into His presence that I am
now watching. In the earlier years of my conversion we
all anticipated a speedier development of Antichrist, a
speedier removal of the restraining power, a speedier
brightening of the clouds about the flaming feet of our
Saviour. That for which I now look is far more the
spiritual union with my Lord than His visible manifestation. It may be, too, that He cometh in many ways.
If we ever mistook the nearer for the farther horizons of
His prophecy, it is but a part of that ignorance which, as
He Himself warned us, should, as regards the details of
this subject, be absolute and final. For said He not when
He was yet with us, '*Of that day and that hour knoweth*

---

[1] As Baur rightly observes (*Paulus*, ii. 94): but to assume that therefore
the Epistle cannot be St. Paul's is to the last degree uncritical. Moreover,
though there are no other "dogmatic ideas" brought forward with very
special prominence, there are "dogmatic ideas" *assumed* in every line.

no man; no, not the angels which are in heaven, neither the Son, but the Father'? But whether He come so soon as we have expected, or not, yet in one form or another assuredly now and ever 'the Lord is at hand;' and the lesson of His coming is that which He also taught us, and which we have taught from Him—'Take ye heed, watch and pray, for *ye know not when* the time is.'"

That these were the views of St. Paul and of other Apostles on "the crises and the periods" respecting which, if they ventured to hold any definite opinion at all, they could not but, according to their Lord's own warning, be liable to be mistaken, will, I think, be evident to all who will candidly weigh and compare with themselves the passages to which I here refer.[1]

Now so far as the fall of Jerusalem and the passing of doom upon the Jewish race was "a day of the Lord," so far even the most literal acceptation of their words is in close accordance with the actual results. Nor should this remarkable coincidence be overlooked. On December 19th, A.D. 69, the Capitoline Temple was burnt down in the war between Vitellius and Vespasian, which Tacitus calls the saddest and most shameful blow, and a sign of the anger of the gods. On August 10, A.D. 70, a Roman soldier flung a brand within the Temple of Jerusalem. "Thus,"

---

[1] Allusions to a near Advent, 1 Thess. i. 9, 10, "ye turned to God . . . . to wait for His Son from heaven;" 1 Cor. i. 7, "To wait for the coming of the Lord Jesus" (cf. 2 Thess. iii. 5); 1 Cor. xv. 51, "We shall not all sleep, but we shall all be changed " (cf. 1 Thess. iv. 15—17); James v. 8, 9, "The coming of the Lord draweth nigh. . . . . The judge standeth before the door;" 1 Pet. iv. 7, "The end of all things is at hand;" 1 John ii. 18, "Even now are there many antichrists, whereby we know that it is the last time;" Rev. xxii. 20, "Surely I come quickly." On the sayings of our Lord, on which the expectation was perhaps founded (Matt. xxiv. 29, 30, 34), see my *Life of Christ*, ii. 257 *sq.* On the other hand, if St. Paul contemplated the possibility of being alive at the Day of the Lord, he also was aware that though *near*, it would not be *immediate* (2 Cor. iv. 14; 2 Thess. ii.; Rom. xi. 24—27), and at a later period looked forward to his own death (Phil. i. 20—23).

says Döllinger,[1] " within a few months the national sanc-
tuary of Rome and the Temple of God, the two most
important places of worship in the old world, owed their
destruction to Roman soldiers—thoughtless instruments
of the decrees and judgment of a higher power. Ground
was to be cleared for the worship of God in spirit
and in truth. The heirs of the two temples, the Capitoline and the Jewish—a handful of artisans, beggars, slaves,
and women—were dwelling at the time in some of the
obscure lanes and alleys of Rome; and only two years
before, when they had first drawn public attention to
themselves, a number of them were sentenced to be burnt
alive in the imperial gardens, and others to be torn in
pieces by wild beasts."

We may, then, say briefly that the object of the Second
Epistle to the Thessalonians was partly to assure them that,
though St. Paul believed the day of the Lord to be near—
though he did not at all exclude the possibility of their
living to witness it—yet it was not so instantaneous as in
the least to justify a disruption of the ordinary duties of
life.[2] He had as little meant positively to assert that he
would survive to the Advent when he said " *we* that are
alive," than he meant positively to assert that he should
die before it occurred, when, years afterwards, he wrote,
" He which raised up the Lord Jesus shall raise up *us* also
by Jesus."[3] That the " we " in these instances was generic
is obvious from the fact that he uses it of the dead and of
the living in the same Epistle, saying in one place, " *We*

---

[1] *Judenth. u. Heidenth.* ix. *ad f.*

[2] The dread of some imminent world catastrophe, preluded by prodigies,
was at this time universal (Tac. *Ann.* vi. 28; xii. 43, 64; xiv. 12, 22; xv. 22;
Hist. i. 3; Suet. *Nero*, 36, 39; Dion Cass. lx. 35; lxi. 16—18, &c.). Hausrath,
N. Zeitgesch. ii. 108. Renan, *L'Antéchrist*, p. 35: " On ne parlait que de
prodiges et de malheurs."

[3] 2 Cor. iv. 14.

shall not all sleep,"[1] and in another, "God will also raise up *us* by His own power."[2]

On the nearness of the final Messianic Advent, the Jewish and the Christian world were at one; and even the Heathen were in a state of restless anticipation. The trials of the Apostle had naturally led him to dwell on this topic both in his preaching at Thessalonica, and in his earlier Epistle. His Second Epistle follows the general outlines of the First, which indeed formed a model for all the others. Nothing is more remarkable than the way in which the Epistles combine a singular uniformity of method with a rich exuberance of detail.[3] In this respect they are the reflex of a life infinitely varied in its adventures, yet swayed by one simple and supremely dominant idea. Except when special circumstances, as in the Epistles to the Corinthians, modify his ordinary plan, his letters consist, as a rule, of six parts, viz.:—i. a solemn salutation; ii. an expression of

---

[1] 1 Cor. xv. 51, on the reading, *v. infra*, ii.

[2] 1 Cor. vi. 14. Here, as in so many cases, a passage of the Talmud throws most valuable light on the opinions of St. Paul, which, on such a subject—where all special illumination was deliberately withdrawn—were inevitably coloured by the tone of opinion prevalent in his own nation:—"'When will Messiah come?' asked R. Joshua Ben Laive of Elijah the Tishbite. 'Go and ask Himself.' 'Where is He?' 'At the gateway of Rome.' 'How shall I know Him?' 'He sits among the diseased poor.' (Rashi quotes Isa. liii. 5.) 'All the others change the bandages of their sores simultaneously, but He changes them successively, lest, if called, His coming should be delayed.' R. Joshua Ben Laive went to Him, and saluted Him with the words 'Peace be to thee, my Rabbi, my teacher.' 'Peace be unto thee, Son of Laive,' was the answer of Messiah. 'When will the Master come?' asked the Rabbi. 'TO-DAY,' was the answer. By the time the Rabbi had finished telling the story to Elijah, the sun had set. 'How?' said the Rabbi; 'He has not come! Has He lied unto me?' 'No,' said Elijah, '*He meant* "TO-DAY, IF YE WILL HEAR HIS VOICE"' (Ps. xcv. 7)." *Sanhedrin*, f. 98. 1. This involves the same truth as the famous remark of St. Augustine, "Ergo latet ultimus dies, ut observentur omnes dies," which was also said by R. Eliezer.

[3] See Reuss, *Théol. Chrét.* ii. 11.

thankfulness to God for His work among those to whom
he is writing; iii. a section devoted to religious doctrine; iv. a section devoted to practical exhortation; v. a
section composed of personal details and greetings; and, vi.
the final autograph benediction which served to mark the
authenticity of the Epistle. We have already noticed that
this is the general structure of the First Epistle, and it
will be observed no less in the subjoined outline of the
Second.[1]

After the greeting, in which, as in the last Epistle, he
associates Silas and Timothy with himself,[2] he thanks God
once more for the exceeding increase[3] of their faith, and
the abounding love which united them with one another,
which enabled him as well as others[4] to hold them up in
the Churches of God[5] as a model of faith and patience, and

[1] i. The greeting, 2 Thess. i. 1, 2. ii. The thanksgiving, or Eucharistic
section, mingled with topics of consolation derived from the coming of Christ,
i. 3—12. iii. The dogmatic portion, which, in this instance, is the remarkable
and indeed unique section about the Man of Sin, ii. 1—12; the thanksgiving
renewed with exhortations and ending in a prayer, ii. 13—17. iv. The
practical part, consisting of a request for their prayers (iii. 1—5). v. Exhortations, and messages, also ended by a prayer, iii. 6—16. vi. The autograph conclusion and benediction, iii. 17, 18. These divisions, however, are not rigid and
formal; one section flows naturally into another, with no marked separation.
Each of the prayers (ii. 16; iii. 16) begins with the same words, Αὐτὸς δὲ ὁ
Κύριος.

[2] This accurately marks the date of the letter, as having been written at
Corinth shortly after the former. Silas ceases to be a fellow-worker with
Paul, and apparently joins Peter, after the visit to Jerusalem at the close of
the two years' sojourn at Corinth. It is probable that the mental and religious
affinities of Silas were more closely in accordance with the old Apostles who
had sent him to Antioch than with St. Paul.

[3] ὑπεραυξάνει. It is a part of St. Paul's emphatic style that he delights in
compounds of ὑπέρ, as ὑπεροχή, ὑπερλίαν, ὑπερβάλλω, ὑπερεκπερισσοῦ, &c.

[4] 2 Thess. i. 4, ἡμᾶς αὐτοὺς.

[5] This is a strong argument against Ewald's view that the Epistle was
written from Berœa; but it does not prove, as Chrysostom says, that a
considerable time must have elapsed. Writing from Corinth, there were
Churches both in Macedonia and Achaia to which St. Paul alludes. There
can be little doubt that the Epistle was written late in A.D. 53 or early in
A.D. 54.

that, too, under special tribulations. Those tribulations, he tells them, are an evidence that the present state of things cannot be final; that a time is coming when their persecutors will be punished, and themselves have relaxation from endurance[1]—which time will be at the Epiphany, in Sinaitic splendour,[2] of the Lord Jesus with his mighty angels, to inflict retribution on the Gentile ignorance which will not know God, and the disobedient obstinacy which rejects the Gospel. That retribution shall be eternal cutting off from the presence and glorious power of Christ[3] when He shall come to be glorified in His saints and to be wondered at in all that believed in Him.[4] And that they may attain to this glory, he prayed that God may count them worthy of their calling, and bring to fulfilment the goodness in which they delight,[5] and the activity of their faith, both

---

[1] ἄνεσιν.

[2] Ex. iii. 2; xix. 18; xxiv. 17; 2 Chr. vii. 1, &c. א, A, K, L, have πυρὶ φλογός. The comma should be after fire, not, as in E. V., after "angels."

[3] i. 9. It is clear that ἀπὸ here means "separation from," *not* "immediately after," or "by." This is the only passage in all St. Paul's Epistles where his eschatology even seems to touch on the future of the impenitent. When Chrysostom triumphantly asks, "Where, then, are the Origenists? He calls the destruction αἰώνιον;" his own remarks in other places show that he could hardly have been unaware that this rhetoric of "œconomy" might sound convincing to the ignorant and the superficial, but had no bearing whatever on the serious views of Origen. Observe, i. διδόναι ἐκδίκησιν (cf. 2 Sam. xxii. 48, LXX.) does not mean "take vengeance." ii. The fire is not penal fire, but is the Shechinah-glory of Advent (Dan. vii. 9; Ex. iii. 2). iii. Those spoken of are not sinners in general, but wilful enemies and persecutors. iv. The retribution is not "destruction," but "destruction-from-the-Presence of the Lord," *i.e.*, a cutting off from Beatific Vision. v. The "æonian exclusion" of this passage takes place at Christ's First Advent, not at the final Judgment Day.

[4] They will inspire wonder, because they will in that day reflect His brightness.

[5] i. 11, πληρώσῃ εὐδοκίαν ἀγαθωσύνης. Not as in E.V., "fulfil all the good pleasure of *his* goodness," but "honestatis dulcedinem"—*i.e.*, "honestatem, quâ recreemini." Εὐδοκία, indeed, is often referred to God (Eph. i. 5, 9, &c.); but ἀγαθωσύνη, used four times in St. Paul, is "moral and human goodness," the classic χρηστότης. It is borrowed from the LXX. (See Eccl. ix. 18.)

to the glory of their Lord and to their own glory, as
granted by His grace.[1]

Then follows the most remarkable section of the letter,
and the one for the sake of which it was evidently written.
He had, in his first letter, urged them to calmness and
diligence, but the eagerness of expectation, unwittingly
increased by his own words, had prevailed over his exhortations, and it was now his wish to give them further and
more definite instruction on this great subject. This was
rendered more necessary by the fact that their hopes
had been fanned into vivid glow, partly by prophecies
which claimed to be inspired, and partly by words or
letters which professed to be stamped with his authority.
He writes, therefore, in language of which I have attempted to preserve something of the obvious mystery
and reticence.[2]

"Now we beseech you, brethren, touching[3] the presence of our Lord
Jesus Christ and our gathering[4] to meet Him, that ye be not quickly
tossed from your state of mind,[5] nor even be troubled either by spirit,[6]
or by word, or by letter purporting to come from us,[7] as though the

---

[1] 2 Thess. i. 3—12.

[2] Neither this nor any other passage which I translate apart from the E.V.
is intended as a specimen of desirable translation. I merely try to translate
in such terms as shall most easily explain themselves to the modern reader,
while they reproduce as closely as possible the *form* of the orignal.

[3] ὑπέρ, not an adjuration in the New Testament, yet a little stronger
than περί.

[4] An obvious allusion to 1 Thess. iv. 17. The substantive ἐπισυναγωγή only
occurs in Heb. x. 25, but the verb in Matt. xxiii. 37; xxiv. 31, "as a hen
gathereth her chickens under her wings" (cf. John xi. 52).

[5] "Fro youre witte" (Wicl.); "from your sense" (Rhemish version).

[6] *i.e.*, by utterance professing to be inspired. The "discerning of spirits,"
or testing of what utterances were, and what were not, inspired, was one of
the most important χαρίσματα in the early Church.

[7] The commentators from Chrysostom and Theodoret downwards are almost
unanimous in taking this to mean that a letter on these subjects had been
forged in St. Paul's name, and had increased the excitement of the Thessalonians. It seems to me that the requirements of the expression are fulfilled

day of the Lord is here.[1] Let no one deceive you in *any* way, because[2]—unless the apostasy[3] come first, and the man of sin be revealed,[4] the son of destruction,[5] who opposeth,[6] and exalteth himself above and against every one who is called God,[7] or is an object of worship, so that he enters and seats himself in the shrine of God,[8] displaying himself that he is God. Do you not recall that, while I was still with you, I used to tell you this? And now the restraining power—you know what it is—which prevents his appearing—that he may appear in his own due time [and not before]. For the mystery of the lawlessness is already working, only he who restrains now—until he be got out of the way.[9] And then shall be revealed the lawless one, whom the Lord Jesus shall destroy with the breath of His mouth, and shall annihilate with the Epiphany of His presence ;[10] whose presence is in accordance with the energy of Satan in all power, and signs, and prodigies of falsehood, and in all deceitfulness of iniquity for the ruin of those who are perishing,[11] because they received not the love of the truth that they

---

if we make the surely more probable supposition that some letter had been circulated among them—perhaps anonymous, perhaps with perfectly honest intentions—which professed to report his exact opinions, while in reality it misunderstood them.

[1] This, rather than "is immediately imminent," seems to be the meaning of ἐνέστηκεν (Rom. viii. 38; Gal. i. 4, &c.). τινὲς γὰρ προφητείαν ὑποκρινόμενοι ἐπλάνων τὸν λαὸν ὡς ἤδη παρόντος τοῦ Κυρίου (Theod.). At any rate, the word implies the closest possible proximity. τὰ ἐνεστῶτα means "things present." (See Rom. viii. 38; 1 Cor. iii. 22.)

[2] He purposely suppresses the discouraging words "the Lord will not come."

[3] Certainly not "the revolt of the Jews."

[4] The apocalypse of the Antichrist.

[5] Whose end is destruction (Phil. iii. 19; John xvii. 12).

[6] A human Satan or adversary (Renan, p. 255).

[7] ὑπεραιρόμενος . . . ἐπί, perhaps "*exceedingly* exalteth himself against." Dan. xi. 36, speaking of Antiochus Epiphanes.

[8] καθίσαι . . . εἰς. A *constructio praegnans*. (See my *Brief Greek Syntax*, § 89.) Omit ὡς θεόν, א, A, B, D, &c. ναὸν stronger than ἱερόν, and could only be naturally understood of the Jewish Temple.

[9] "Tantum qui nunc tenet (teneat) donec de medio fiat" (Tert. *De Resur. Carn*. 25). I have attempted to preserve the unfinished clauses (*anakolutha*) of the original, which are full of meaning. The ὁ κατέχων may, however, be merely misplaced by hyperbaton.

[10] Isa. xi. 4; Wisd. xi. 20, 21. A rabbinic expression. "Prima adventus ipsius emicatio (Bengel).

[11] I so render τοῖς ἀπολλυμένοις because it is the dative of "disadvantage." Τhe is probably spurious, being omitted in א, A, B, D, F, G.

N N

might be saved.   And, because of this, God is sending[1] them an
energy of error, so that they should believe the lie[2] that all may be judged
who believed not the truth, but took pleasure in unrighteousness."[3]

Of this strange but unquestionably genuine passage,
which is nevertheless so unlike anything else in St. Paul's
Epistles, I shall speak immediately. He proceeds to tell
them that *their* case, thank God, was very different from
that of these doomed dupes of Antichrist, seeing that God
had chosen and called them from the beginning[4] to sanctification and salvation and glory.[5] He exhorts them therefore, to stand fast, and hold the teaching which they had
received from his words and his genuine letter, and prays
that our Lord Jesus Christ and God our Father may
comfort them and stablish them in all goodness.[6]

Beginning the practical section of the Epistle, he
asks their prayers that the Gospel may have free course

---

[1] *Leq.*, πέμπει, κ, A, B, D, F, G.   The "strong delusion" of the E.V. is
a happy expression; it is penal blindness, judicial infatuation, the dementation before doom.

[2] 1 Tim. iv. 1, 2.

[3] 2 Thess. ii. 1—12. In the E.V. there are the following five or six
obvious errors, which I have corrected:—Ver. 1, ὑπὲρ τῆς παρουσίας, "by the
coming;" ver. 2, ἀπὸ τοῦ νοὸς, "in mind;" ἐνέστηκε, "is at hand" (which is
not strong enough, and contradicts "Maranatha," ὁ κύριος ἐγγὺς); ver. 3,
ἡ ἀποστασία, "a falling away;" ver. 4, ἐπὶ πάντα, κ. τ. λ., "above all, &c.,"
instead of "against every one," though this is perhaps defensible—ὡς Θεὸν,
"as God," is probably spurious, not being found in κ, A, B, D; ver. 5, ἔλεγον,
"I told;" ver. 11, τῷ ψεύδει, "a lie;" ver. 12, κριθῶσι, "be damned."   There
are also minor inaccuracies. But while calling attention to these, let me not
be supposed to speak with any feeling but admiration and gratitude of our
English version.   It needs the revision which it is receiving, but it is magnificent with all its defects; and while those defects are far fewer than might
have been reasonably expected, there is incomparable merit in its incessant
felicity and noble rhythm.

[4] ἀπ' ἀρχῆς (Eph. i. 4). B, F, G have ἀπαρχήν, "as a firstfruit;" but this
was not a fact (Acts xvi.).

[5] εἰς περιποίησιν δόξης, "to the obtaining of glory;" cf. 1 Thess. v. 9;
Heb. x. 39.

[6] 2 Thess. ii. 13—17.

among others as among them, and that he may be delivered from perverse and wicked men ;[1] and expressing
his trust in God, and his confidence in them, prays that
the Lord may guide their hearts into the love of God and
the patience of Christ.[2] That patience was lacking to
some of them who, he had been told, were walking disorderly, not following the precepts he had given, or the
example he had set. The rule he had given was that a
man who would not work had no right to eat, and the
example he had set, as they well knew, had been one of
order, manly self-dependence, strenuous diligence, in that
he had voluntarily abandoned even the plain right of
maintenance at their hands.[3]

He therefore commands and exhorts[4] in the name of
Christ those who were irregular, and whose sole business was
to be busybodies,[5] to be quiet and diligent, and earn their
own living; and if, after the receipt of this letter, any one
refused obedience to his advice, they were to mark that man
by avoiding his company that he might be ashamed; not,
however, considering him as an enemy, but admonishing
him as a brother. As for the rest, let them not be weary
in fair-doing;[6] and he again concludes with a prayer that

[1] An allusion to his struggles with the Jews at Corinth. "Synagogas
Judaeorum fontes persecutionum" (Tert. *Scorp.* 10). ἄτοπος only in Luke
xxiii. 41, and Acts xxviii. 6.

[2] *i.e.*, a patience like His patience. The "patient *waiting for* Christ,"
of the E.V., though partially sanctioned by Chrysostom and Theophylact, can
hardly be tenable, and they prefer the meaning here given.

[3] iii. 1—11.

[4] These injunctions are more emphatic, authoritative, and precise
than those of the First Epistle; another sign that this followed it.
παραγγέλλω, so much stronger than ἐρωτῶ, occurs four times in this Epistle
(iii. 4, 6, 10, 12), and only elsewhere, of his Epistles, in 1 Thess. iv. 11;
1 Tim. vi. 13; 1 Cor. vii. 10; xi. 17.

[5] 2 Thess. iii. 11, οὐκ ἐργαζομένους ἀλλὰ περιεργαζομένους (see *infra*, p. 629,
" The Rhetoric of St. Paul ").

[6] Καλοποιοῦντες, " beautiful conduct;" not exactly ἀγαθόν, " well-doing " (cf.
2 Cor. viii. 21).

N N 2

the Lord of Peace Himself may give them peace perpetually, and in every way.   The Lord be with them
all![1]

And having dictated so far—probably to his faithful
Timothy—the Apostle himself takes the pen, for the use of
which his weak sight so little fitted him, and bending over
the papyrus, writes :—

" The salutation of me Paul with my own hand, which
autograph salutation is the proof of genuineness in every
Epistle.[2] This is how I write.   The Grace of our Lord
Jesus Christ be with you all."[3]

Valuable to us, and to all time, as are the practical
exhortations of this brief Epistle, the distinctive cause for
its being written was the desire to dispel delusions about
the instantaneous appearance of Christ, which prevented
the weak and excitable from a due performance of their
duties, and so tended to diminish that respect for them
among the heathen which the blamelessness of the early
Christians was well calculated to inspire.   To the Thessalonians the paragraph on this subject would have had
the profoundest interest.   To us it is less immediately
profitable, because no one has yet discovered, or ever will
discover, what was St. Paul's precise meaning; or, in
other words, because neither in his time, nor since, have
any events as yet occurred which Christians have unani-

---

[1] iii. 12—16.

[2] iii. 17, 18. This emphatic autograph signature, not necessary in the
first letter, had been rendered necessary since that letter was written by the
credence given to the unauthorised communication alluded to in ii. 2.   The
" *every* Epistle " shows that St. Paul meant henceforth to write to Churches
not unfrequently. Of course, Epistles sent by accredited messengers (*e.g.*,
2 Cor. and Phil.) would not need authentication. The ordinary conclusion of
letters was ἔρρωσθε, "farewell." On this authenticating signature see Cic. *ad
Att.* viii. 1 ; Suet. *Tib.* 21, 32.

[3] The " all " is only found in 2 Cor., Rom., and Tit. (cf. Eph. vi. 24 and
Heb. xiii. 25), but was peculiarly impressive here, because his last words have
been mainly those of censure.

mously been able to regard as fulfilling the conditions
which he lays down. We need not, however, be distressed if this passage must be ranked with the very few
others in the New Testament which must remain to us in
the condition of insoluble enigmas. It was most important for the Thessalonians to know that they did not need
to get up every morning with the awe-inspiring expectation that the sun might be darkened before it set, and the
air shattered by the archangelic trumpet, and all earthly
interests smitten into indistinguishable ruin. So far St.
Paul's assurance was perfectly distinct. Nor, indeed, is
there any want of clearness in his language. The difficulties of the passage arise exclusively from our inability
to explain it by subsequent events. But these one or two
obscure passages in no wise affect the value of St. Paul's
writings.[1] Since his one object is always edification, we
may be sure that subjects which are with him purely incidental, which are obscurely hinted at, or only partially
worked out, and to which he scarcely ever afterwards recurs,
are non-essential parts of the central truths, to the dissemination of which he devoted his life. To the Messianic
surroundings of a Second personal Advent he barely again
alludes. He dwells more and more on the mystic oneness
with Christ, less and less on His personal return. He
speaks repeatedly of the indwelling presence of Christ,
and the believer's incorporation with Him, and hardly at
all of that visible meeting in the air which at this epoch
was most prominent in his thoughts.[2]

We may assume it as a canon of ordinary criticism that
a writer intends to be understood,[3] and, as a rule, so writes

---

[1] See Reuss, *Théol. Chrét.* ii., p. 10.

[2] 1 Cor. viii. 6; Gal. iii. 28; Eph. iv. 6, &c.

[3] "No man writes unintelligibly on purpose" (Paley, *Hor. Paulinae*). He
acutely points out how the very obscurity of this passage furnishes one strong

as to be actually understood by those whom he addresses.
We have no difficulty in seeing that what St. Paul here
says to the Thessalonians is that Christ's return, however
near, was not so instantaneous as they thought, because,
before it could occur, there must come "the apostasy,"
which will find its personal and final development in the
apocalypse of "the man of sin"—a human Satan who
thrust himself into the temple of God and into rivalry
with Him.   Then, with an air of mystery and secrecy
which reminds us of the Book of Daniel and the Revelation of St. John,[1] and with a certain involved embarrass-
ment of language, he reminds them of his repeated oral
teachings about something, and some person,[2] whose power
must first be removed before this mystery of iniquity could
achieve its personal and final development.   They knew,
he says, what was "the check" to the full development of
this opposing iniquity, which was already working, and
would work, until the removal of "the checker."   After
that removal, with power and lying portents winning the
adherence of those who were doomed to penal delusion,
the Lawless One should be manifested in a power which
the breath and brightness of Christ's Presence should
utterly annihilate.   Between the saved, therefore, and the
Second Advent there lay two events—"the removal of the
restrainer," and the appearance of the Lawless One.   The

argument for the genuineness of the Epistle, which I note by way of curiosity
that Hilgenfeld regards as "a little Pauline Apocalypse of the last year of
Trajan" (*Einleit.* 642).

[1] These secrets and dim allusions (cf. Dan. xii. 10) current among the early
Christians (like the greeting and symbol Ἰχθύς), and the riddles of the number
of the beast (666=קסר נרון, Nero Cæsar: cf. Jos. *B. J.* vi. 5, 1; Suet. *Ner.* 40,
Vesp. 4; Tac. *H.* v. 13) in Rev. xiii. 18, and in the Sibylline books, were
necessitated by the dangers which surrounded them on every side.   The
years which elapsed between the Epistle and the Apocalypse had made
the views of the Christians as to Antichrist much more definite (Renan
L'Antechrist, p. 157, &c.).

[2] 2 Thess. ii. 6, 7, ὁ κατέχων – τὸ κατέχον.

destruction of the latter would be simultaneous with the event which they had so often been bidden to await with longing expectation.

This is what St. Paul plainly says; but how is it to be explained? and why is it so enigmatically expressed?

The second question is easily answered. It is enigmatically expressed for two reasons—first, because all that is enigmatical in it for us had been orally explained to the Thessalonians, who would therefore clearly understand it; and secondly, because there was some obvious danger in committing it to writing. This is in itself a sufficient proof that he is referring to the Roman Empire and Emperor. The tone of St. Paul is exactly the same as that of Josephus, when he explains the prophecy of Daniel. All Jews regarded the Fourth Empire as the Roman; but when Josephus comes to the stone which is to dash the image to pieces, he stops short, and says that " he does not think proper to explain it,"[1]—for the obvious reason that it would have been politically dangerous for him to do so.

Now this reason for reticence at once does away with the conjecture that " the check," or " the checker," was some distant power or person which did not for centuries come on the horizon, even if we could otherwise adopt the notion that St. Paul was uttering some far-off vaticination of events which, though they might find their fulfilment in distant centuries, could have no meaning for the Thessalonians to whom he wrote. When a few Roman Catholic commentators say that the Reformation was the Apostasy, and Luther the Man of Sin, and the German Empire " the check;" or when a mass of Protestant writers unhesitatingly identify the Pope with the Man of Sin—one

---

[1] See the instructive passage, Jos. Antt. x. 10, § 4.

can only ask whether, apart from traditional exegesis, they
have really brought themselves to hold such a view? If,
as we have seen, St. Paul undoubtedly held that the day
of the Lord was *at hand*, though not immediate, do they
really suppose, on the one hand, that St. Paul had any
conception of Luther? or, on the other, that the main
development of lawlessness, the main human representative
of the power of Satan, is the succession of the Popes?
Can any sane man of competent education seriously argue
that it is the Papacy which pre-eminently arrays itself in
superiority to, and antagonism against, every one who is
called God, or every object of worship?[1] that its essential
characteristic marks are lawlessness, lying wonders, and
blasphemous self-exaltation? or that the annihilation of
the Papacy—which has long been so physically and politically weak—" by the breath of His mouth and the brightness of His coming," is to be one main result of Christ's
return? Again, do they suppose that St. Paul had, during
his first visit, *repeatedly revealed* anything analogous to
the development of the Papacy—an event which, in their
sense.of the word, can only be regarded as having taken
place many centuries afterwards—to the Thessalonians
who believed that the coming of Christ might take place
on any day, and who required two epistles to undeceive
them in the notion? If these suppositions do not sink
under the weight of their own *intrinsic* unreasonableness
let them in the name of calm sense and Christian charity
be consigned henceforth to the vast limbo of hypotheses

---

[1] St. Paul's " Lawless One," and " Man of Sin," who is to be destroyed by
the advent of Christ must have some chronological analogy to St. John's Antichrist. Now St. John's Antichrist in the Epistles is mainly Gnostic heresy
("omnis haereticus Antichristus"—Luther), and the denial that Jesus Christ
is come in the flesh (1 John iv. 3). In the Apocalypse it is Nero. In the
Old Testament Antichrist is Antiochus Epiphanes. What has this to do
either with the Papacy or with the Reformation?

which time, by accumulated proofs, has shown to be utterly untenable.[1]

To that vast limbo of exploded exegesis—the vastest and the dreariest that human imagination has conceived—I have no intention of adding a fresh conjecture. That "the check" was the Roman Empire, and "the checker" the Roman Emperor, may be regarded as reasonably certain; beyond this, all is uncertain conjecture. In the Excursus I shall merely mention, in the briefest possible manner, as altogether doubtful, and most of them as utterly valueless, the attempts hitherto made to furnish a definite explanation of the expressions used; and shall then content myself with pointing out, no less briefly, the regions in which we must look for illustrations to throw such light as is possible on the meaning of St. Paul.[2] As to the precise details, considering the utter want of unanimity among Christian interpreters, I am content to say, with St. Augustine, "I confess that I am entirely ignorant what the Apostle meant."

---

[1] If it be urged that this was the view of Jewell and Hooker, Andrewes and Sanderson, &c., the answer is that the knowledge of the Church is not stationary or stereotyped. The Spirit of God is with her, and is ever leading her to wider and fuller knowledge of the truth. Had those great men been living now, they too would have enlarged many of their views in accordance with the advance now made in the interpretation of the Scripture. Few can have less sympathy than I have with the distinctive specialities of the Church of Rome; but in spite of what we hold to be her many and most serious errors she is, by the free acknowledgment of our own formularies, a Church, and a Christian Church, and has been pre-eminently a mother of saints, and many of her Popes have been good, and noble, and holy men, and vast benefactors of the world, and splendid maintainers of the Faith of Christ; and I refuse to regard them as "sons of perdition," or representatives of blasphemy and lawlessness, or to consider the destruction of their line with everlasting destruction from the presence of the Lord as the one thing to be looked forward to with joy at the coming of Him who we believe will welcome many of them, and myriads of those who accept their rule, into the blessed company of His redeemed.

[2] See *infra*, Excursus I., vol. ii., "The Man of Sin." For the symbols employed, see Ezek. xxxviii. 16, 17; Dan. vii. 10, 11, 23—26; xi. 31, 36.

APPENDIX.

EXCURSUS I. (p. 26).

THE STYLE OF ST. PAUL AS ILLUSTRATIVE OF HIS CHARACTER.

THE reader may be interested to see collected a very few of the varying estimates of the style of the great Apostle :—

LONGINUS [Paul as master of the dogmatic style]—

Κορωνὶς δ' ἐστιν λόγου παντὸς καὶ φρονήματος
Ἑλληνικοῦ Δημοσθένης κ.τ.λ. πρὸς τούτοις Παῦλος ὁ Ταρσεὺς
ὅντινα καὶ πρῶτόν φημι προϊστάμενον δόγματος ἀνυποδείκτου.

ST. CHRYSOSTOM [Paul a champion, and his Epistles a wall of adamant round the Church]—

ὥσπερ γὰρ τεῖχος ἐξ ἀδάμαντος κατασκευασθὲν οὕτω τὰς
πανταχοῦ τῆς οἰκουμένης ἐκκλησίας τὰ τούτου τειχίζει γράμματα· καὶ
κάθαπέρ τις ἀριστεὺς γενναιότατος ἕστηκε κ. τ. λ. (quoting 2 Cor. x. 5).
De Sacerdotio, 1, iv. 7.

ST. JEROME [Paul's words thunders].—"Paulum proferam quem quotiescunque lego, video mihi *non verba audire sed tonitrua* . . . Videntur quidem verba simplicis et quasi innocentis hominis et rusticani et qui nec facere nec declinare noverit insidias, *sed quocunque respexeris fulmina sunt.* Haeret in causâ; capit omne quod tetigerit; tergum vertit ut superet; fugam simulat ut occidat" (*Ep. ad Pammach.* 68, 13).

DANTE—

" Vidi due vecchi in abito dispari
    Ma pari in atto, ognuno onesto e sodo.
L' un [1] si monstrava alcun de famigliari
    Di quel sommo Ippocrate, che natura
Agli animali fe' ch' ella ha piu cari.
    Monstrava l' altro [2] la contraria cura

---

[1] St. Luke, "the beloved *physician.*"   [2] St. Paul.

Con una spada lucida ed acuta [1]
Tal che di qua dal rio mi fe' paura.

Purgatorio, xxix. 134.

Andovvi poi lo *vas d' elezione* [2]
Per recarno conforto a quella Fede
Ch' è principio alla via di salvazione.

Inferno, ii. 28.

LUTHER.—" Paulus meras flammas loquitur tamque vehementer ardet ut incipiat etiam quasi Angelis maledicere " (*in Gal.* i.).

" In S. Paulo und Johanne ist eine sonderliche fürtreffliche Gewissheit und *Plerophoria;* sie reden davon als sey es schon allbereit vor Augen " (*Tischreden*, iv. 399; ed. Forstemann).

Bishop HERBERT DE LOSINGA.—" Certe, fratres, verba Pauli, non verba hominis, sed aetheris tonitrua esse videntur " (*Life and Sermons*, ii. 309).

ERASMUS [Paul's style like a thunderstorm].—" Non est cujusvis hominis Paulinum pectus effingere; tonat, fulgurat, meras flammas loquitur Paulus " (*ad Col.* iv. 16).

And again [Paul's rhetorical skill like the course of a stream]— " Sudatur ab eruditissimis viris in explicandis poetarum ac rhetorum consiliis, at in hoc rhetore longe plus sudoris est ut deprehendas quid agat, quo tendat, quid velit; adeo stropharum plenus est undique, absit invidia verbis. Tanta vafrities est, non credas eundem hominem loqui. Nunc ut turbidus quidam fons sensim ebullit, mox torrentis in morem ingenti fragore devolvitur, multa obiter secum rapiens, nunc placide leniterque fluit, nunc late velut in lacum diffusus exspatiatur. Rursum alicubi se condit ac diverso loco subitus emicat; cum visum est miris maeandris nunc has nunc illas lambit ripas, aliquoties procul digressus, reciprocato flexu in sese redit " (Id. *Paraph.* Dedicat.).

CASAUBON.—" Ille solus ex omnibus scriptoribus non mihi videtur digitis, calamo, et atramento scripsisse, verum ipso corde, ipso affectu, et denudatis visceribus " (*Adversaria, ap.* Wolf., p. 135).

On the other hand, CALVIN, after alluding to his anakolutha, ellipses, &c., adds—" Quae sunt quidem orationis vitia sed quibus nihil majestati decedit caelestis sapientiae quae nobis per apostolum traditur. Quin potius singulari Dei providentia factum est, ut *sub contemptibili verborum humilitate* altissima haec mysteria nobis traderentur, ut

---

[1] The Epistles.

[2] σκεῦος ἐκλογῆς (Acts ix. 15). For other allusions see *Parad.* xviii. 131, xxi. 119.

non humanae eloquentiae potentia, sed solâ spiritus efficaciâ niteretur nostra fides."

HEMSTERHUSIUS [Character of St. Paul's flowers of speech].—"Eloquentia ejus non in flosculis verborum et rationis calamistratae pigmentis . . . sed indolis excelsae notis et pondere rerum. . . . In ejus epistolis nullae non exstant oratorum figurae, non illae quidem e rhetorum loculis et myrotheciis depromptae . . . Verum affectus animi coelesti ardore inflammatus haec scriptionis lumina sponte sub manum praevenientia pergignebat." [1]

REUSS.—"Ordinairement il débute par des phrases on ne peut plus embarrassées. . . . Mais dès qu'il a trouvé la bonne veine, combien son style n'est il pas le fidèle miroir de son individualité ! Il est ni correct, ni classique; il lui manque la cadence sonore. Des antithèses paradoxales, des gradations pleines d'effet, des questions pressantes, des exclamations passionnées, des ironies qui terrassent l'opposition, une vivacité, enfin, qui ne permet aucun repos au lecteur, tout cela alterne avec des épanchements naïfs et touchants, qui achèvent de gagner le cœur" (Théol. Chrét. ii. 11).

R. H. HUTTON.—" Who that has studied St. Paul at all has not noticed the bold soaring dialectic with which he rises from the forms of our finite and earthly thought to the infinite and the spiritual life embodied in them. What ease and swiftness and power of wing in this indignant upward flight from the petty conflicts of the Corinthian Church ; the upward flight which does not cease till the poor subjects of contention, though he himself was one of them, seem lost like grains of sand beneath the bending sky ! . . . The all but reckless prodigality of nature which made St. Paul now and then use a stratagem, and now and then launch a thunderbolt, in the fervour of his preaching, is the spring of all his finest touches, as when he wishes himself accursed from Christ if it could save his Jewish brethren " (Essays, 321—330).

The AUTHOR of "Saul of Tarsus."—" If he staggers under the greatness of his subject, if he is distracted by the infinity of the interests which he treats, if every word which rises to his lips suggests a host of profound and large associations, if the care of all the Churches, gives all the facts a varied but a real significance. . . Human speech must be blamed for its poverty ; human experience, which has developed speech, for its narrowness. His life was ever in his hand, his heart was on his lips. The heart was often too great for the speech " (p. 229).

MARTINEAU.—" What can be more free and buoyant, with all their variety, than his writings ? Brilliant, broken, impetuous as the moun-

[1] See next Excursus.

tain torrent freshly tilled, never smooth and calm but on the eve of some bold leap, never vehement but to fill some receptacle of clearest peace, they present everywhere the image of a vigorous joy. Beneath the forms of their theosophic reasonings, and their hints of deep philosophy, there may be heard a secret lyric strain of glorious praise, bursting at times into open utterance, and asking others to join the chorus. . . . His life was a battle from which in intervals of the good fight, his words arose as the song of victory" (*Hours of Thought*, p. 156).

PROF. JOWETT speaks of him as teaching his great doctrines "in broken words and hesitating form of speech, with no beauty or comeliness of style."

BAUR, after pointing out how the style is filled to overflowing with the forms and elements of thought, and that thoughts not only follow hard on thoughts, but that those thoughts succeed each other as determinations and *momenta* of some one conception that is greater than all of them, so that the thought unfolds itself, as it were, out of its own depths, and determines itself by taking up its own *momenta*, adds :— " Hence the peculiar stamp of the Apostle's language: it is distinguished on the one hand for precision and compression ; on the other hand it is marked by a harshness and roughness which suggests that the thought is far too weighty for the language, and can scarcely find fit form for the superabundant matter it would fairly express" (*Paul.* ii. 281).

HAUSRATH.—"Es est schwer diese Individualität zu charakterisiren in der sich Christliche Liebesfülle, rabbinischer Scharfsinn, und antike Willenskraft so wunderbar mischen. Wie wogt, strömt, drängt Alles in Seinen Briefen. Welch ein Wechsel glühender Ergüsse und spitzer Beweisführungen ! Hier überwindet er das Heidenthum mit der Liebesfülle Jesu. Dort knebelt er das Judenthum, mit dessen Eigenen Gürtel rabbinischer Scriftbeiwise. Am wenigsten hat die Phantasie Antheil an Seiner Innern Welt. Die Sprache ist oft hart und herb weil nur die Gedanke sie geboren hat. Die Bilder die er braucht sind meistens farblos. . . Das est die Schranke seines Geisteslebens. Darin blieb er stets ein Rabbi" (*Der Apostel Paulus*, 502).

RENAN [Paul's style like a conversation].—" Le style epistolaire de Paul est le plus personnel qu'il y ait jamais eu ; la langue y est si j'ose le dire, broyée ; pas une phrase suivie. Il est impossible de violer plus audacieusement, je ne dis pas le génie de la langue grecque, mais la logique du langage humain ; on dirait une rapide conversation sténographiée et reproduite sans corrections. . . . Un mot l'obsède. . . . Ce n'est pas de la stérilité ; c'est de la contention de l'esprit et une complète insouciance de la correction du style" (*St. Paul*, p. 232).

The less favourable of the above estimates shelter themselves in part under the assertion that St. Paul recognised the popular and vulgar character of his own style. But such passages as 2 Cor. xi. 6 do not bear out these remarks. His language was not indeed of a class which would have gained applause from pedantic purists and Atticising professors ; it bears about the same relation to the Greek of Plato as the Latin of Milton does to that of Cicero. But this fact constitutes its very life. It is a style far too vivid, far too swayed and penetrated by personal emotion, to have admitted of being polished into conformity with the artificial standards and accuracies of the schools. It more closely resembles the style of Thucydides than that of any other great writer of antiquity.[1] That many defects in it can be pointed out is certain ; but then in one important point of view these defects are better than any beauties, because they are due to Paul's individuality. In whole sections of his Epistle his very want of style is his style. His style, like that of every great man, has the defects of its qualities. "Le style," said Buffon, not (as he is usually quoted) *c'est l'homme*, but "*c'est de l'homme*."[2] He has, as every great writer has, " le style de sa pensée :" he has the style of genius, if he has not the genius of style.[3]

After quoting such remarkable and varied testimonies, it is needless for me to write an essay on the Apostle's style. That he could when he chose wield a style of remarkable finish and eloquence without diminishing his natural intensity, is proved by the incessant assonances and balances of clauses and expressions (parechesis, parisosis, paromoiosis) in such passages as 2 Cor. vi. 3—11. And yet such is his noble carelessness of outward graces of style, and his complete subordination of mere elegance of expression to the purpose of expressing his exact thought, that he never shrinks, even in his grandest outbursts of rhythmic eloquence, from the use of a word, however colloquial, which expresses his exact shade of meaning.[4]

All that has been written of the peculiarities of St. Paul's style may,

[1] See some good remarks of Baur:—"Such passages as 1 Cor. iv. 12, 13; vii. 29—31; 2 Cor. vi. 9, 10, have the true ring of Thucydides, not only in expression, but in the style of the thought. The genuine dialectic spirit appears in both, *in the love of antithesis and contrast, rising not unfrequently to paradox.* . . . . With both these men the ties of national particularism give way before the generalising tendency of their thought, and cosmopolitanism takes the place of nationalism" (*Paul.* ii. 281). He refers to Baur's *Philologia Thucydideo-Paulina*, 1773, which I have not seen.

[2] D'Alembert, *Œuvres* vi. 13. The "de" in Buffon's phrase occurs in later editions.

[3] Grimm, *Corresp.*, 1788.

[4] *E.g.*, ψωμίσω and περιπερεύεται in 1 Cor. xiii. 3, 4; κατανάρκησω, 2 Cor. xi. 8; ἀποκόψονται, Gal. v. 12.

I think, be summed up in two words—Intense Individuality. His style is himself. His natural temperament, and the circumstances under which that temperament found its daily sphere of action; his training, both Judaic and Hellenistic; his conversion and sanctification, permeating his whole life and thoughts—these united make up the Paul we know. And each of these has exercised a marked influence on his style.

1. The absorption in the one thought before him, which makes him state without any qualification truths which, taken in the whole extent of his words, seem mutually irreconcilable; the dramatic, rapid, overwhelming series of questions, which show that in his controversial passages he is always mentally face to face with an objection;[1] the *centrifugal* force of mental activity, which drives him into incessant digressions and goings off at a word, due to his vivid power of realisation; the *centripetal* force of imagination, which keeps all these digressions under the control of one dominant thought;[2] the grand confusions of metaphor;[3] the vehemence which makes him love the most emphatic compounds;[4] the irony[5] and sarcasm;[6] the chivalrously delicate courtesy;[7] the overflowing sympathy with the Jew, the Pagan, the barbarian—with saint and sinner, king and slave, man and woman, young and old;[8] the passion, which now makes his voice ring with indignation[9] and now break with sobs;[10] the accumulation and variation of words, from a desire to set forth the truths which he is proclaiming in every possible light;[11] the emotional emphasis and personal references of his style;[12] the depressed humility passing into boundless exultation;[13]—all these are due to his *natural temperament*, and the atmosphere of controversy and opposition on the one hand, and deep affection on the other, in which he worked.

2. The rhetorical figures, play of words, assonances, oxymora, antitheses, of his style, which are fully examined in the next Excursus; the

---

[1] Rom. x.; 2 Cor. vi., xi., and *passim.*

[2] 2 Cor. ii. 14—16; xii. 1—3, 12—16; Eph. iv. 8—11; v. 12—15; and Paley, *Hor. Paulinae,* vi. 3.

[3] 2 Cor. iii. 1; Col. ii. 6.

[4] Especially compounds in ὑπὲρ. *Supra*, p. 606

[5] 1 Cor. iv. 8; 2 Cor. xi. 16—20, and *passim.*

[6] Phil. iii. 2; Gal. iv. 17; v. 12, and *passim.*

[7] 1 Cor. i.—iii.; Philem. and Phil. *passim*; Acts xxvi. 29, &c.

[8] Rom. i. iv., and all the Epistles *passim.*

[9] Galatians, Corinthians, Phil., 2 Tim., *passim.*

[10] All the Epistles *passim.*

[11] All the Epistles *passim.*

[12] All the Epistles *passim.*

[13] 2 Cor. ii. 14; Rom. vii. 25, &c.

constant widening of his horizon ;[1] the traceable influence of cities, and even of personal companions, upon his vocabulary ;[2] the references to Hellenic life ;[3] the method of quoting Scripture ; the Rabbinic style of exegesis, which have been already examined [4]—these are due to his training at Tarsus and Jerusalem, his life at Corinth, Ephesus, and Rome.

3. The daring faith which never dreads a difficulty;[5] the un-solved antinomies, which, though unsolved, do not trouble him ;[6] "the bold soaring dialectics with which he rises from the forms of one finite and earthly thought to the infinite and spiritual life embodied in them ;" the "language of ecstasy," which was to him, as he meant it to be to his converts, the language of the work-day world; that "trans-cendental-absurd," as it seems to the world, which was the very life both of his conscience and intellect, and made him what he was ; the way in which, as with one powerful sweep of the wing, he passes from the pettiest earthly contentions to the spiritual and the infinite ; the "shrinking infirmity and self-contempt, hidden in a sort of aureole of revelation, abundant beyond measure "[7]—this was due to the fact that his citizenship was in heaven, his life hid with Christ in God.

EXCURSUS II. (p. 26).

RHETORIC OF ST. PAUL.

M. RENAN, in describing the Greek of St. Paul as Hellenistic Greek charged with Hebraisms and Syriacisms which would be scarcely intelligible to a cultivated reader of that period, says that if the Apostle had ever received even elementary lessons in grammar or rhetoric at Tarsus, it is inconceivable that he would have written in the *bizarre*, incorrect, and non-Hellenic style of his letters.

Now, I do not think that St. Paul would have made about his own

---

[1] "Eo (ordine Epistolarum chronologico) constituto . . . incrementum Apostoli spirituale) cognoscitur" (Bengel, *ad Rom.* i. 1).

[2] V. *supra*, pp. 481, 623.

[3] See Excursus III.

[4] See Excursus IV.

[5] See Ep. to Romans, *passim.*

[6] See vol. ii., Excursus, "The Antinomies of St. Paul."

[7] See 2 Cor. x.—xiii. *passim,* and some excellent remarks in Hutton's *Essays,* i. 325—330.

O O

knowledge of Greek the same remarks as Josephus does, who tells us that he had taken great pains to master the learning of the Greeks and the elements of the Greek language. St. Paul had picked up Greek quite naturally in a Greek city, and I think that I have decisively proved that he could not have possessed more than a partial and superficial acquaintance with Greek literature. But I have little doubt that he, like Josephus, would have said that he had so long accustomed himself to speak Syriac that he could not pronounce Greek with sufficient exactness, and that the Jews did not encourage the careful endeavour to obtain a polished Greek style, which they looked on as an accomplishment of slaves and freedmen.[1] Yet, after reading the subjoined list of specimens from the *syntaxis ornata* of St. Paul, few, I think, will be able to resist the conviction that he had attended, while at Tarsus, some elementary class of Greek rhetoric. I will here content myself with brief references; if the reader should feel interested in the subject, I have gone further into it in the *Expositor* for 1879.

Figures (σχήματα) are divided by Greek and Latin rhetoricians into Figures of Language (*figurae verborum, elocutionis*, λέξεως), and Figures of Thought (*sententiae*, διανοίας). They drew this distinction between them—that figures of language disappear, for the most part, when the words and their order are changed; whereas figures of thought still survive.[2] The distinction is superficial and unsatisfactory, and it would perhaps be more to the point to divide figures into :—1. Those of *colour*, dependent on the imagination; as metaphor, simile, allegory, personifications, metonyms, catachresis, &c. 2. Those of *form*, ranging over an immense field, from the natural expression of passions, such as irony, aposiopesis, erotesis, &c., down to mere elegancies of verbal ornament, and variations of style (such as zeugma, &c.) or of order (such as chiasmos, hysteron-proteron, &c.). 3. Those of *sound*, dependent on analogies of words, resemblance of sounds, unconscious associations of ideas, &c., such as alliteration, parisosis, paromoiosis, parechesis, paronomasia, oxymoron, plays on names, &c.

1. On figures of *Colour* I have already touched.[3] As specimens of the two other classes in St. Paul's Epistles we may take the following— referring to my *Brief Greek Syntax*, or to other books, for an explanation of the technical terms :—

2. Figures of *Form*.

Chiasmus—a crosswise arrangement of words or clauses, as in

[1] Jos. *Antt.* xx. 11, § 2.

[2] So Aquila, Rutilius, &c., following Cic. *De Orat.* 3. See Voss, *Instt. Orat.* v. 1; Glass, *Philologia Sacra*, p. 953, &c.

[3] *Supra*, i., pp. 17—21.

Rom. ii. 6, 10. (This figure is much more common in the Epistle to the Hebrews.) A good instance is—

1 Cor. iii. 17, εἴ τις τὸν ναὸν τοῦ Θεοῦ φθείρει, φθερεῖ αὐτὸν ὁ Θεός.

Euphemism.

1 Cor. v. 1, 2, ἔχειν . . . ὁ τὸ ἔργον τοῦτο ποιήσας.

2 Cor. vii. 11, ἐν τῷ πράγματι.

1 Thess. iv. 6, *supra*, p. 589.

Litotes.

Rom. i. 28, ποιεῖν τὰ μὴ καθήκοντα.

Eph. v. 4, τὰ οὐκ ἀνήκοντα.

1 Cor. xi. 22, ἐπαινέσω ὑμᾶς ἐν τούτῳ; οὐκ ἐπαινῶ.

Philem. 18, εἰ δέ τι ἠδίκησέ σε ἢ ὀφείλει.

Philem. 11, τόν ποτέ σοι ἄχρηστον.

Meiosis.[1] Rom. iii. 9, οὐ πάντως (comp. 1 Cor. xvi. 12).

1 Cor. i. 29, ὅπως μὴ καυχήσηται πᾶσα σάρξ.

Rom. iii. 20, ἐξ ἔργων νόμου οὐ δικαιωθήσεται πᾶσα σάρξ.

Antithesis, Parisosis, Paromoiosis,[2] *Paradox, Alliteration, Erotesis, Epexergasia*—all exhibited in such passages of deep emotion as 2 Cor. vi. 3—16; xi. 22—28; 1 Cor. iv. 8—11.

Epanaphora.

Phil. iv. 8, ὅσα . . . ὅσα . . . κ. τ. λ. εἴ τις, κ. τ. λ.

Phil. ii. 1, εἴ τις . . . εἴ τι . . . κ. τ. λ.

2 Cor. vii. 11, ἀλλὰ . . . . ἀλλὰ . . . κ. τ. λ.

Aposiopesis.

2 Thess. ii., *vide supra*, p. 609.

Proparaitesis, Protherapeia, Captatio, Benevolentiae, &c.

The Thanksgiving at the beginning of every Epistle except the "Galatians."

Rom. ix. 1—5.

Acts xxiv. 10 (before Felix), and xxvi. 2, 3, before Agrippa.

Paraleipsis (praeterita).

Philem. 19, ἵνα μὴ λέγω σοι.

1 Thess. iv. 9, οὐ χρείαν ἔχετε ὑμῖν γράφεσθαι (cf. v. 1; 2 Cor. ix. 1).

Intentional *Anakoluthon.*

Gal. ii. 6, ἀπὸ δὲ τῶν δοκούντων εἶναί τι . . .

2 Thess. ii. 3, ὅτι ἐὰν μὴ ἔλθῃ ἡ ἀποστασία πρῶτον . . .

2 Thess. ii. 7, μόνον ὁ κατέχων ἄρτι . . .

---

[1] These usages are, however, idiomatic (Winer, § 26).

[2] See Arist. *Rhet.* iii. 9, 9.

(The Anakolutha of mere inadvertence, due to the eager rapidity of thought, are incessant in St. Paul, as in Rom. ii. 17—21; xvi. 25—27, &c. &c.)

Climax.

Rom. v. 3—5.
Rom. viii. 29, 30.
Rom. x. 14, 15, &c.

Zeugma.

1 Cor. iii. 2, γάλα ὑμᾶς ἐπότισα καὶ οὐ βρῶμα.
1 Tim. iv. 3, κωλυόντων γαμεῖν, ἀπέχεσθαι βρωμάτων.

Oxymoron.

2 Cor. vi. 9, θανατούμενοι καὶ ἰδοὺ ζῶμεν (being slain, yet behold we live).

1 Tim. v. 6, ζῶσα τέθνηκεν (living she is dead).

Rom. i. 20, τὰ ἀόρατα αὐτοῦ . . . καθορᾶται (His unseen things are clearly seen).

Rom. xii. 11, τῇ σπουδῇ μὴ ὀκνηροί (in *haste* not sluggish).

1 Thess. iv. 11, φιλοτιμεῖσθαι ἡσυχάζειν (be *ambitious* to be *quiet*).

1 Thess. i. 6, ἐν θλίψει πολλῇ μετὰ χαρᾶς (joyous affliction).

1 Cor. viii. 10, οἰκοδομηθήσεται (ruinous edification).

Rom. i. 22, φάσκοντες εἶναι σοφοὶ ἐμωράνθησαν.

Eph. vi. 15, Gospel of *peace* part of panoply of *war*.

2 Cor. viii. 2, deep *poverty* abounding to *wealth* of liberality.

2 Cor. xii. 10, "When I am weak, then I am strong."

It will be sufficient to make the merest reference to *Anadiplosis* (Rom. ix. 30; Phil. ii. 8); *Epanodos* (Gal. ii. 16); *Epanorthosis* (Rom. viii. 34; Gal. ii. 20; iii. 4, &c.); *Asyndeton* (1 Cor. xv. 43; 1 Tim. i. 17; 2 Tim. iii. 2—5, 10, 11, &c.); *Antiptosis* (Col. iv. 17; Gal. vi. 1; iv. 11); *Hyperbaton* (2 Thess. ii. 5, &c.); *Alliteration* (1 Cor. ii. 13; 2 Cor. viii. 22; ix. 8, &c.); *Constructio praegnans* (2 Thess. ii. 4, &c.); and many minor figures.

3. Coming to figures of the third division—*Sound*—we find that St. Paul makes most remarkable and frequent use of paronomasia.

E.g. (α) Paronomasia, dependent on the change of one or two letters[1]:—

Rom. i. 29, πορνείᾳ πονηρίᾳ . . . φθόνου, φόνου.

Rom. i. 30, ἀσυνέτους, ἀσυνθέτους.

Rom. xi. 17, τινὲς τῶν κλάδων ἐξεκλάσθησαν.

Cf. Heb. v. 8, ἔμαθεν ἀφ' ὧν ἔπαθεν.

---

[1] See Cic. *De Orat.* ii. 63; Auct. *ad Herenn.* iv. 24; Quint. *Instt. Orat.* ix. 3, 66, &c. An instance in our Prayer Book is—"among all the changes and chances of this mortal life."

(β) Paronomasia, dependent on a play of words of similar sound or derivation.[1] This is St. Paul's most frequent rhetorical figure :—

2 Cor. iii. 2, γινωσκομένη καὶ ἀναγινωσκομένη.[2]

Rom. i. 28, οὐκ ἐδοκίμασαν (they *refused*) . . . ἀδόκιμον νοῦν (a *refuse* mind).

Phil. iii. 2, 3, κατατομή (*concision*) . . . περιτομή (*circumcision*).

Rom. ii. 1, κρίνεις . . . κατακρίνεις.

1 Cor. xi. 29, seq., διάκρισις . . . κρίμα . . . κατάκριμα.

Rom. xii. 3, "Not to be high-*minded* (ὑπερφρονεῖν) above what we ought to be minded (φρονεῖν), but to be *minded* so as to be sober-minded" (σωφρονεῖν). Cf. Thuc. ii. 62, οὐ φρονήματι μόνον ἀλλὰ καὶ καταφρονήματι.

1 Cor. vii. 31, χρώμενοι . . . καταχρώμενοι.

2 Cor. vi. 10, ἔχοντες . . . κατέχοντες.

2 Cor. iv. 8, ἀπορούμενοι . . . ἐξαπορούμενοι.

2 Tim. iii. 4, φιλήδονοι . . . φιλόθεοι.

2 Thess. iii. 11, not *busy* (ἐργαζομένους) but busybodies (περι εργαζομένους).[3]

1 Tim. v. 13, οὐ μόνον δὲ ἀργαί, ἀλλὰ καὶ περίεργοι (female toilers in the school of idleness).

Cornelius à Lapide and others have imagined a latent paronomasia in 1 Cor. i. 23, 24. If St. Paul thought in Syriac it might be "To the Jews a *micsol*, and to the Greeks a *mashcal*, but to those that are called —Christ the *secel* of God." But this is probably a mere ingenious fancy.[4]

(γ) A third class of paronomasias consists in plays on names, of which we find three in St. Paul :—

Philem. 11, 'Ονήσιμον . . . ἄχρηστον.[5]

Philem. 20, Ναί, ἐγώ σου ὀναίμην.

Phil. iv. 3, σύζυγε γνήσιε, "yoke-fellow by name and yoke-fellow by nature."[6]

St. Jerome imagines another in Gal. i. 6, where he thinks that "ye are being removed" (μετατίθεσθε) is a play on the name Galatæ and the Hebrew *Galal*, "to roll."

Since, then, we find upwards of fifty specimens of upwards of thirty

---

[1] A curious instance occurs in our E. V. of James i. 6, "He that *wavereth* is like a *wave* of the sea," where it does not occur in the original.

[2] Compare Acts viii. 30, and Basil's remark to the Emperor Julian, ἀνέγνως οὐκ ἔγνως, εἰ γὰρ ἔγνως οὐκ ἂν κατέγνως.

[3] So Domitius Afer, "Non agentes sed satagentes" (Quint. vi. 3, 54).

[4] Glass, *Philolog. Sacra*, p. 959.

[5] V. *infra*, vol. ii., *ad loc.*, where I have noticed the possible second paronomasia in ἄχρηστον, εὔχρηστον.   [6] V. *infra, ad loc.*

Greek rhetorical figures in St. Paul, and since they are far more abundant in his Epistles than in other parts of the New Testament, and some are found in him alone, may we not conclude that as a boy in Tarsus he had attended some elementary class in Greek rhetoric, perhaps as a part of his education in the grammatical knowledge of the language? Professional rhetoricians abounded in Tarsus, and if Paul's father, seeing the brilliant capacity of his son, meant him for the school of Gamaliel, he may have thought that an elementary initiation into Greek rhetoric might help to pave the way for his future distinction among the Hillelites of Jerusalem; since, as we see from the Talmud, this kind of knowledge opened to some Rabbis a career of ambition. If so, the lessons which the young Saul learnt were not thrown away, though they were turned to very different objects than had been dreamt of by one who intended his boy to be, like himself, a Pharisee of Pharisees and a Hebrew of Hebrews.

EXCURSUS III. (p. 39).

THE CLASSIC QUOTATIONS AND ALLUSIONS OF ST. PAUL.

1. THOSE who maintain the advanced classic culture of St. Paul, rely on the fact that he quotes from and alludes to Greek and Roman writers.

Three quotations are incessantly adduced. One is the hexameter written by the Cretan poet Epimenides in such stern and contemptuous depreciation of the character of his own countrymen—

Κρῆτες ἀεὶ ψεῦσται, κακὰ θηρία, γαστέρες ἀργαί.[1]

("Liars the Cretans aye, ill monsters, gluttonous idlers.")

Another is the half-hexameter in which he reminds his audience, in the speech on the Areopagus, that certain also of their native poets had said—

Τοῦ γὰρ καὶ γένος ἐσμέν.[2]

("For we are also his offspring.")

A third is the moral warning to the Corinthians—

Φθείρουσιν ἤθη χρηστὰ ὁμιλίαι κακά;[3]

("Evil communications corrupt good manners;")

or it may, perhaps, be more correctly rendered, "Evil associations destroy excellent characters."

---

[1] Tit. i. 12.   [2] Acts xvii. 28.   [3] 1 Cor. xv. 33.

Now, if we look a little closer at these quotations, we shall see how very little proof they furnish of anything more than the most superficial acquaintance with Greek writers. The first of them is just such a current national characterisation [1] as might pass everywhere from mouth to mouth, and which St. Paul might very well repeat without having read a line of the poem of Epimenides on *Oracles*, or Callimachus's *Hymn to Zeus*, in both of which it occurs.[2] The second is a recognised commonplace of heathen insight, to which many parallels might be quoted, but which is found in Cleanthes[3] nearly in the form in which St. Paul quotes it. The actual quotation is from one of those tedious poems which were most in vogue at this period, the *Phœnomena* of Aratus.[4] With the writings of this poet St. Paul may have become acquainted, both because they are entirely harmless—which is more than can be said of almost any other Pagan production which was popular at that time—and because Aratus was a Cilician, and very probably a Tarsian.[5] The third was one of those common sententious pieces of morality which had passed into a proverb, and which in all probability Menander, in his *Thais*, had appropriated from some lost tragedy of Euripides. St. Paul is far more likely to have heard it used in common parlance, or to have seen it inscribed on one of the Hermæ at Tarsus or Athens, than to have read it in Menander, or even—as Socrates[6] and Chrysostom seem to think—in one of the Greek tragedians. It is further remarkable about these quotations, first, that *all three* of them were so current, they are found in at least two poets each; and next, that two of them occur at the very beginning of *Hymns to Zeus*. If any collection of *Hymns to Zeus* was to be found on any bookstall at Athens, it is exactly the kind of book into which St. Paul's human sympathies may have induced him to dip in support of his

---

[1] See, as to the Cretans, Leonidas, *Anthol.* iii., p. 369; Polyb. vi. 47; Diod. Sic., xxxi. Fr.; Westst. *ad loc.*

[2] Callim. *Hymn. in Jov.*, 8. Κρῆτες ἀεὶ ψεῦσται, καὶ γὰρ τάφον ἃ ἀνα σεῖο Κρῆτες ἐτεκτήναντο. See Chrysostom and Jerome *ad* Tit. i. 12. Moreover, the line had originated one of the commonest syllogistic puzzles, called "the Liars." "Epimenides said that the Cretans were liars; but Epimenides was a Cretan; therefore Epimenides was a liar; therefore the Cretans were not liars; therefore Epimenides was not a liar," &c. &c. (Diog. Laert. ii. 108.) It was invented by Eubulides; cf. Cic. *Div.* ii. 4, "mentiens."

[3] Cleanthes, *Hymn. in Jov.*, 5.

[4] Aratus flourished about B.C. 270. His poems, considering that they only bear a sort of dull resemblance to Thomson's *Seasons*, acquired astonishing popularity. They were translated, among others, by Cicero, and by Cæsar Germanicus.

[5] Buhle, *Aratus*, ii. 429.

[6] *Hist. Ecc.* iii. 16.

liberal and enlightened view that God had revealed Himself even to
the heathen, to a degree sufficient for their happiness and their salvation,
had they chosen to make use of the light they had.[1] A third very
remarkable point is that in the quotation from Menander or Euripides,
whichever it may have been, the great majority of the best MSS. read
χρηστὰ, not χρῆσθ'[2]—a reading which may therefore be regarded as
certainly genuine, since no one would have dreamt of altering the
correct metre, if it had been given in the original manuscript. Now if
such be the case, it seems to indicate that the ear of St. Paul was
unfamiliar with—or, which comes to the same thing, was indifferent to
—even so common a rhythm as that of the iambic verse. Our conclusion,
therefore, is that St. Paul's isolated quotations no more prove a study
of Greek literature than the quotation of such a national epigram as

> "Inglese italianato, Diavolo incarnato,"

or of such a line as

> "Lasciate ogni speranza voi ch' entrate,"

would necessarily prove that an English writer was a proficient in the
literature of Italy, or had read the poems of Dante. St. Paul was a
man of remarkable receptivity, and, as we have seen, an habitual
quoter. Except in Epistles intended for readers to whom Old Testament quotations would have been unintelligible, he can hardly write
five sentences in succession without a Biblical reference. The utter
absence of any similar use of even the noblest of the classic writers, is a
proof either that he had intentionally neglected them, or that, at any
rate, they had left little or no mark on an intellect so sensitive to every
cognate influence. For that it was not only the Scriptures of the
Jewish canon which thus clung to his retentive memory, is apparent
from the free use which he makes of the Book of Wisdom, and perhaps
of other books of the Jewish Apocrypha.[3] It is also traceable in the

---

[1] Acts xiv. 17; xvii. 27; Rom. i. 20.

[2] ᾗ, A, B, D, E, F, G, &c., ἰαμβείῳ τραγικῷ. Clem. Alex. *Strom.* i. 14, 59;
Meineke, *Fr. Com.*, p. 75.

[3] See Hausrath, p. 23. He compares 1 Cor. vi. 2 with Wisd. iii. 8, the image of
the Christian armour with Wisd. v. 17, the metaphor of the potter making one
vessel to honour and another to dishonour with Wisd. xv. 7. The memorable
thrice-repeated saying, "Neither circumcision is anything, nor uncircumcision"
(Gal. v. 6; vi. 15; 1 Cor. vii. 19), is by Photius, Syncellus, and others said to be a
quotation from "Revelation of Moses." Dr. Lightfoot (on Gal. vi. 17) shows that
there is some reason to doubt this, and says that "a sentiment which is the very
foundation of St. Paul's teaching was most unlikely to have been expressed in any
earlier Jewish writing; and if it really occurred in the apocryphal work in

extent to which he is constantly haunted by a word,[1] and in the new and often rare expressions which are found in every one of the Epistles,[2] and which show us a mind keenly susceptible to impressions derived from the circumstances around him, and from the intercourse of those among whom he was habitually thrown.

2. But though the Greek culture of Tarsus had little or no influence on the current of the Apostle's thoughts, it would be a mistake to suppose that it produced no influence at all on his life or on his style. Besides the direct quotations, there is more than one isolated passage which may be the distant echo of classical reminiscences. Such, for instance, is the apologue of the self-asserting members in 1 Cor. xii., which reminds us at once of the ingenious fable of Menenius Agrippa ;[3] and the fearful metaphor of Rom. vii. 24, which has less probably been held to refer to a true story of the family of Regulus.[4] And it is far from improbable that it was in some "class of rhetoric" at Tarsus that the Apostle acquired the germs, at any rate, of that argumentative habit of mind, that gift of ready extempore utterance, and that fondness for chiasmus, paronomasia, paraleipsis, oxymoron, litotes, and other rhetorical figures, which characterise his style.[5] It was there, too, that he may have learnt that ready versatility, that social courtesy, that large comprehensiveness, that wide experience and capacity for dealing with varied interests and intricate matters of business, which made him, in the high and good sense of the word, a true gentleman, a Christian man of the world. He was, in heart and feeling, an ideal specimen of what the Greeks called the καλὸς κἀγαθός—"fair and good"—and his intercourse with polished Greeks may have tended to brighten that spirit of "entirely genuine Attic urbanity"[6]—a spirit more flexible

question, this work must have been either written or interpolated after St. Paul's time (See Lücke, *Offenb. d. Johan.* i., p. 232)." The same must be said of the Book of Wisdom on the ingenious hypothesis that it was written by Apollos (Plumptre, *Expositor,* i. 422, *sq.*).

[1] *e.g.* γίνομαι in 1 Thess. i.; τὰ ἐπουράνια in Eph. i.; χαίρω and χάρις in Phil.; μὴ γένοιτο in Rom.; φυσιόω in 1 Cor. iv.; καυχᾶσθαι in 2 Cor. xi.; παρακαλέω in 2 Cor. i.; λύπη in 2 Cor. ii., &c.

[2] As, for instance, καταναρκάω and ἡμέρα in 1 Cor.; πλήρωμα in the Epistles of the Captivity; ὑγιής in the Pastoral Epistles, &c.

[3] Liv. ii. 32. There is also a remarkable parallel in Sen. *De Irâ,* ii. 31.

[4] The ἐκ is against this supposed reference. On the other hand, the "*perikatharmata*" and *peripsema* of 1 Cor. iv. 13 *may* be an allusion to ancient piacular offerings (*v. infra ad loc.*).

[5] *E.g., Chiasmus,* Rom. ii. 7—10; *Paronomasia,* 2 Thess. iii. 11 (*infr. ad loc.*); *Paraleipsis,* 1 Thess. iv. 9, v. 1; *Oxymoron,* Rom. i. 20, Philem. 11; *Litotes,* 1 Cor. xi. 22, &c. (See Excursus II., "The Rhetoric of St. Paul.")

[6] Krenkel, p. 12. See Arist. *M. Mor.* ii. 9, 2.

and more charming than natural Semitic dignity—which breathes in every line of the Epistle to Philemon.

3. It is a remarkable proof of this natural liberality that, in spite of the burning hatred of idolatry which we have already noticed, he is yet capable of looking with sympathy, and even admiration, on some of those nobler and more innocent aspects of heathen life which his countrymen indiscriminately condemned.[1] The hallowing of heathen symbols, the use of metaphors derived from heathen life for the illustration of Christian truths and Christian duties, is a very remarkable feature of the style of St. Paul. There were few of the crimes of Herod which the strict Pharisees had regarded with more undisguised horror and hatred than his construction of a theatre at Cæsarea ; yet St. Paul quite freely, and without misgiving, adopting a metaphor which would have caused a shudder to any Palestinian Pharisee, compares the transient fashion of the world to the passing scene of a theatrical display, and in other places turns the whole Universe into a theatre, on the stage of which were displayed the sufferings of the Apostles as a spectacle to angels and to men.[2] We recognise, too, the more liberal son of the Dispersion—the man whose thoughts have been enlarged by travel and by intercourse with men of other training and other race—in the apparently vivid sympathy with which St. Paul draws some of his favourite metaphors from the vigorous contests of the Grecian games.[3] Those games constituted the brightest, the most innocently attractive feature of Hellenic life. During his long stay at Ephesus and at Corinth he had doubtless witnessed those wrestling bouts, those highly-skilled encounters of pugilism, those swift races to win the fading garlands of laurel or pine, which, for some of his heathen converts, and particularly for the younger among them, could not at once have lost their charm. We can well imagine how some young Ephesian or Corinthian might have pressed St. Paul to come

---

[1] The Talmud abounds in passages which utter nothing but unmixed scorn of the Gentiles, even of their very virtues. In *Babha Bathra*, f. 10, 2, there is a notable discussion on Prov. xiv. 34. It is rendered, "Righteousness exalteth a nation, and *the goodness of nations is sin.*" R. Eleasar explained it to mean, "Righteousness exalts Israel ; but the goodness of other nations is sin, being only due to their self-exaltation." Rabban Gamaliel said, "They were only good in order to heap reproach on the shortcomings of Israel ;" and Rabbi Nechunya Ben Hakanah punctuated the verse, "Righteousness exalteth a nation (Israel) and goodness : but the nations, a sin-offering." This explanation was adopted by Rabban Johanan Ben Zakkai.

[2] 1 Cor. vii. 31, παράγει τὸ σχῆμα τοῦ κόσμου. 1 Cor. iv. 9, θέατρον ἐγενήθημεν. (Cf. Heb. x. 33, θεατριζόμενοι.)

[3] 1 Cor. ix. 24; Phil. iii. 14; 1 Tim. vi. 12; 2 Tim. iv. 8; ii. 5; 1 Thess. ii. 19.

with him and see the struggle and the race; and how, for one whose
sympathies were so vividly human, there would have been a thrilling
interest in the spectacle of those many myriads assembled in the vast
stadium—in the straining eyes and eager countenances and beating
hearts—in the breathless hush with which they listened to the pro-
clamations of the herald—in the wild-eyed charioteers bending over
their steeds, with the hair blown back from their glowing faces—in
the resounding acclamations with which they greeted the youthful
victor as he stepped forward with a blush to receive his prize. Would
these fair youths do so much, and suffer so much, to win a poor withering chaplet of pine and parsley, whose greenness had faded before the
sun had set, and would they use *no* effort, make *no* struggle, to win a
crown of amaranth, a crown of righteousness which could not fade
away! And that, too, when here the victory of one was the shame
and disappointment of all the rest, while, in that other contest, each
and all might equally be victors, and the victory of each be a fresh
glory to all who were striving for the same high prize?[1] And as such
thoughts passed through his mind there was no Judaic narrowness,
but a genial sympathy in his soul, and a readiness to admire whatever
was innocent and beautiful in human customs, when he wrote to his
converts of Corinth—"Know ye not that they which run in a stadium
run all, but one receiveth the prize! So run that ye may grasp.'
Now every one that striveth is temperate in all things; they, however,
that they may receive a corruptible crown, but we an incorruptible.
I, then, so run, not as uncertainly; so box I, as one who beateth not
the air; but I bruise my body with blows and enslave it, lest perchance, after making proclamation to others, I myself should prove to
be a rejected combatant."[3]

4. But it was not only with Greek customs that St. Paul became
familiar during his residence at Tarsus. It is clear that he must also
have possessed some knowledge of Roman law. His thoughts often
have a juridical form. He speaks of the "earnest-money" of the
Spirit; of the laws of inheritance; of legal minority; of the rights of
wives and daughters.[4] The privileges and the *prestige* conferred upon

---

[1] See a close parallel in Sen. *Ep. Mor.* lxxviii. 16.
[2] καταλάβητε. Cf. Phil. iii. 12—14, κατὰ σκοπὸν . . . ἐπὶ τὸ βραβεῖον.
[3] 1 Cor. ix. 24—27. ἀδόκιμος, *vocabulum agonisticum* (Beng.; Philo, *de Cherub.*
§ 22). On the temperate training of competitors, see Hor. *A. P.* 412; Epict.
Enchir. 35; *Dissert.* iii. 15; Tert. *ad Mart.* 3. ἀέρα δέρειν is to fight a σκιαμαχία
(i.e., make mere feints), (Eustath, *ad Il.* xx. 446; Athen. 154, A, &c.; Virg. *Æn.*
v. 376). Κηρύξας, perhaps "heralding the laws of the contest" (*Æsch. Eum.* 566).
[4] Gal. iii. 17, 18; iv. 1, 2; Rom. vii. 2, &c.

him by his rights of *Civitas* would have inevitably turned his thoughts
in this direction. The Laws of the Twelve Tables had defined the
authority which might be exercised by fathers over sons even after
they have come of age (*patria potestas*) in a manner which Gaius tells
us was peculiar to Roman jurisprudence, with the single exception that
it also existed among the *Galatæ*. If this means the Galatians it would
give peculiar significance to the illustration in Gal. iv. 1, which in any
case proves St. Paul's familiarity with Roman institutions which had
no existence among the Jews. So, too, we are told by Sir H. Maine
that "a true power of testation" was nowhere provided for in the
Jewish Code of Laws, and that the Romans "invented the will." Yet
to the rules of testamentary bequests, and their irrevocability in certain
cases, St. Paul seems to make an express allusion (Gal. iii. 15). Again,
he gives prominence to the Roman idea of artificial "adoption," even
to the extent of making an apparent reference to the fact that a son,
fully adopted, abandoned the domestic rites (*sacra*) of his own family,
and attached himself to those of his new parent (Gal. iv. 5 ; Eph. i. 5).[1]

5. We may select one more passage—though in this case it involves
no admiration or sympathy—to show how accurately the customs of
the Pagan life had been observed by St. Paul in that varied experience
which made him, in the best sense, a citizen of the world. It is a
passage which, from the absence of this knowledge, has often been
entirely misunderstood. It occurs in 2 Cor. ii. 14—16 : "Now thanks
be to God, who always leadeth us everywhere in triumph [2] in Christ,
and who by us maketh manifest the odour of the knowledge of Him
in every place. For we are to God a sweet odour of Christ among
those who are being saved, and among those who are perishing. To
the latter we are an odour of death to death, to the former an odour
of life to life."

Here, though the details of the metaphor are intricately involved
the general conception which was in the thoughts of the Apostle, and
swayed his expression, is derived from the customs of a Roman triumph.

---

[1] These instances are pointed out by Dean Merivale, *Boyle Lectures*, and in *St.
Paul at Rome*, pp. 172—180. The passages of Gaius referred to are *Instt*. i. 55 (cf.
Cæsar, *B. G.* vi. 19) and 189 ; *Digests*, xxvi. 3 ; but I cannot pretend to say that
the conclusions formed are indisputable.

[2] The rendering of the E. V., "which always *causes us to triumph* in Christ," is
both philologically impossible (cf. Col. ii. 15), and confuses the metaphor to such
an extent as to render it entirely unintelligible. St. Paul may well have heard of
the famous triumph of Claudius over the Britons a few years before (A.D. 51), in
which Caractacus had walked as a prisoner (θριαμβευθείς), but "had passed from
the ranks of the 'lost' to those of the 'saved'" (Tac. *Ann.* xiii. 36). (See Dr.
Plumptre, *ad loc.*) Cleopatra had proudly said, οὐ θριαμβευθήσομαι.

It was one main feature of such "insulting vanities" that the chief captives were paraded before the victor's path, and sweet odours were burnt in the streets while his car climbed the Capitol.[1] But when he reached the foot of the Capitoline hill there was a fatal halt, which, in the utter deadness of all sense of pity, might be a moment of fresh exultation to the conqueror, but which was death to the captive; for at that spot the captives ceased to form any part of the procession, but were led aside into the rocky vaults of the Tullianum, and strangled by the executioner in those black and fetid depths. And thus the sweet odours, which to the victor—a Marius or a Julius Cæsar—and to the spectators were a symbol of glory and success and happiness, were to the wretched victims—a Jugurtha or a Vercingetorix—an odour of death. Reminded of this by his use of the words "leadeth us in triumph," St. Paul for an instant fancies himself a captive before the chariot of God—a captive in connexion with Christ; and then another passing fancy strikes him. The preachers of Christ are like that burning incense whose perfume filled the triumphant streets,[2] but they were not an odour of life and hope to all. As light is light yet pains the diseased eye, as honey is honey yet palls on the sated taste,[3] so the odour retained its natural fragrance, although to many—through their own sins and wilfulness—it might only breathe of death. The tidings of salvation were glad tidings, but to the guiltily hardened and the wilfully impenitent they might prove to be tidings of wrath and doom.[4]

Little, perhaps, did it occur to St. Paul as he wrote those words, that the triumph of God, in which he was being led along from place to place as a willing victim, might end for him also in the vaults of that very Tullianum[5]—the description of which must have been mingled in his thoughts with the other details of the Roman pomp—and that if not from the Mamertine, yet from some other Roman prison he would only be dragged forth to die.

---

[1] Dio Cass. lxxiv.; Hor. *Od.* iv. 2, 50; Plut. *Æmil.* p. 272.

[2] St. Paul rises superior to the vulgar prejudice of the Rabbis, who said that " a man is a sinner who while walking in a part of a town inhabited by idolaters inhales purposely the odour of incense offered up by them" (*Berachôth*, f. 53, 1).

[3] See Theophyl. *ad loc.*

[4] Similarly the Rabbis spoke of the law as an "aroma of life to those who walk on the right, an "aroma of death" to those on the left (*Shabbath*, f. 88, 2).

[5] The Tullianum is, according to old tradition, the scene of the last imprisonment, before martyrdom, both of St. Peter and St. Paul. It was the rock-hewn lower dungeon added by Servius Tullius to the *carcer* of Ancus Martius. Excavations within the last few months prove that it was much larger than has been hitherto supposed.

EXCURSUS IV. (p. 58).

St. Paul a Hagadist: St. Paul and Philo.

There are two large divisions of Rabbinic lore, which may be classed under the heads of *Hagadôth*, or unrecorded legends, and *Halachôth*, or rules and precedents in explanation of dubious or undefined points of legal observance.[1] It is natural that there should be but few traces of the latter in the writings of one whose express object it was to deliver the Gentiles from the intolerable burden of legal Judaism. But though there is little trace of them in his writings, he himself expressly tells us that he had once been enthusiastic in their observance.[2] "I was making," he says to the Galatians, "continuous advance in Judaism above many who were my equals in age in my own race, being very exceedingly a zealot for the traditions handed down from my fathers."[3] And there are in the Epistles abundant signs that with the *Hagadôth* he was extremely familiar, and that he constantly refers to them in thought. Thus in 2 Tim. iii. 8 he traditionally names Jannes and Jambres, two of the Egyptian magicians who withstood Moses. He adopted the current Jewish chronologies in Acts xiii. 20, 21. He alludes to the notion that the Adam of Gen. i. is the ideal or spiritual, the Adam of Gen. ii. the concrete and sinful Adam.[4] The conception of the last trumpet,[5] of the giving of the Law at Sinai by angels,[6] of Satan as the god of this world and the prince of the power of the air,[7] and of the celestial and infernal hierarchies,[8] are all recurrent in Talmudic writings. When, in 1 Cor. xi. 10, he says that "a woman

---

[1] I have tried fully to explain the nature of the *Halachah* and the *Hagadah* in the *Expositor*, October, 1877. The former dealt mainly with the Pentateuch, the latter with the Hagiographa. Dr. Deutsch (Smith's *Dict.* s. v. "Versions" says, "If the Halachah used the Scriptural word as a last and most awful resort against which there was no further appeal, the Hagadah used it as the golden nail on which to hang its gorgeous tapestry. If the former was the iron bulwark round the nationality of Israel, the latter was a maze of flowery walks within those fortress walls."

[2] Gal. i. 14.

[3] The παράδοσις did not mean the written Law, but the Oral Law, the πάτρια ἔθη of which Josephus speaks so much; the germ, in fact, of the *Halachôth* of the Mishna and Gemara.

[4] 1 Cor. xv. 47. This is also found in Philo, *De Opif. Mund.* i. 32.

[5] 1 Cor. xv. 52; 1 Thess. iv. 16.

[6] Gal. iii. 19.

[7] Eph. ii. 2.

[8] Eph. i. 21, iii. 10; vi. 12; Col. i. 16; ii. 15.

ought to have a veil [1] on her head because of the angels," there can, I
think, be no shadow of doubt in the unprejudiced mind of any reader
who is familiar with those Jewish views of the subject in which St. Paul
had been trained, that he is referring to the common Rabbinic interpretations of Gen. vi. 2 (LXX. Cod. A, "the angels"), where the Targum, and,
indeed, all Jewish authorities down to the author of the Book of Enoch
(quoted in the Epistle of Jude),[2] attribute the Fall of the Angels to their
guilty love for earthly women. St. Paul could not have been unaware
of a notion which for many ages seems to have been engrained in the
Jewish mind[3]—a notion which is found over and over again in the
Talmud, and which is still so prevalent among Oriental Jews, as also
among Mohammedans,[4] that they never allow their women to be
unveiled in public lest the *Shedîm*, or evil spirits, should injure them
and others.[5] To this very day, for this very reason, Jewish women in

[1] Such, however arrived at, or whatever be the special shade of thought about
the use of the word—which may be a mere provincialism—is the obvious meaning
of ἐξουσία in 1 Cor. xi. 10. St. Paul gives three reasons for his rule—(1) our
instinctive sense that an uncovered head, like a shaven head, is a dishonour to
a woman, whose hair is a glory to her; (2) the fact that woman's hair indicates her
subordinate position towards man, as man's covered head denotes his subordination
to God; (3) "because of the angels."

[2] 2 Pet. ii. 4; Jude 6, 14.

[3] The argument that οἱ ἄγγελοι is never used in the New Testament except for
good angels is quite valueless, for the fallen angels were supposed to have been good
angels until they fell, and, if they had fallen thus, there was nothing to show the
impossibility that others might similarly fall. This interpretation is given quite
unhesitatingly by Tertullian, *de Virg. Vel.* 7, "propter angelos, scilicet quos
legimus a Deo et coelo excidisse ob concupiscentiam feminarum." I have
thoroughly examined this point in a paper in the *Homiletic Quarterly* of 1878, and
quoted many Rabbinic illustrations. (*Tanchuma,* f. 51, 4; Abhoth of Rabbi
Nathan, c. 34.)

[4] See the very remarkable story of Khadijah, who discovers that it is really
Gabriel who has appeared to Mohammed by his flying away directly she takes off her
veil, "knowing from Waraka that a good angel must fly before the face of an
unveiled woman" (Weil, *Mohamed,* 48). (See Dean Stanley's exhaustive note,
Cor. p. 187.)

[5] See *Berachôth,* f. 6, 1: "Abba Benjamin says that if we had been suffered to
see them, no one would stand before the hurtful demons. Rav Huna that each of
us has 1,000 at his left and 10,000 at his right hand (Ps. xci. 7)," &c. &c. The
reason why Solomon's bed was guarded by sixty valiant men with drawn swords
was "because of fear in the night" (Cant. iii. 7, 8). "Walk not alone at night,
because Egrath, daughter of Machlath, walks about—she and 180,000 destroying
angels, and every one of them individually has permission to destroy" (*Pesachim,*
112, 2). They are called *ruchin, shedim, lilin, tiharim,* &c. (Hamburger, *s.v.*
"Gespenster"). The only other view of the passage which seems to me even
possible (historically) is that of St. Chrysostom, "because good angels present at
Christian worship rejoice to see all things done decently and in good order."

some Eastern cities wear an inconceivably hideous headdress, called the *khalebi*, so managed as to entirely conceal the hair. It exposes them to derision and inconvenience, but is worn as a religious duty, "because of the spirits."

Again, in Rom. iv. 5, 13, Paul evidently accepts the tradition, also referred to by St. Stephen, that Abraham had been an uncircumcised idolater when he first obeyed the call of God, and that he then received a promise—unknown to the text of Scripture—"that he should be the heir of the world."[1] In Rom. ix. 9 it has been supposed, from the form of his quotation, that he is alluding to the Rabbinic notion that Isaac was created in the womb by a fiat of God; in Gal. iv. 29 to the Hagadah that Ishmael not only laughed, but jeered, insulted, and mistreated Isaac;[2] and in 2 Cor. xi. 14 to the notion that the angel who wrestled with Jacob was an evil angel assuming the semblance of an Angel of Light. These three latter instances are slight and dubious; but there is a remarkable allusion to the smitten rock in the wilderness, which in 1 Cor. x. 4 is called "a spiritual *following* rock." The expression can have but one meaning. Among the many marvellous fancies which have been evolved from the thoughts of Jewish teachers, occupied for centuries in the adoring and exclusive study of their sacred books, was one to which they repeatedly recur, that the rock, from which the water flowed, was round and like a swarm of bees, and rolled itself up and went with them in their journeys. When the Tabernacle was pitched, the rock came and settled in its vestibule. Then came the princes, and standing near it exclaimed, "Spring up, O well; sing ye unto it,"[3] and it sprang up. How are we to regard these strange legends? Can we suppose that wise and sensible Rabbis like Hillel and Gamaliel took them literally? There is no ground whatever for supposing—indeed, it is essentially impossible—that any one could have accepted, *au pied de la lettre*, all the fables of the Talmud, which are in many instances both senseless and contradictory. Many of them were doubtless regarded as mere plays of pious fancy — mere ingenious exercises of loving inference. Others were only an Oriental way of suggesting mystic truths—were, in fact, intentional allegories. Others, in their broad outlines, were national traditions, which may often have corresponded with fact, and which, at any rate, had passed into general and unquestioned credence in ages little troubled by the spirit of historical criticism.[4] Though St. Paul might quite naturally glance at,

---

[1] Rom. iv. 13. Cf. Josh. xxiv. 15.

[2] *Sanhedr.* f. 89, 2.

[3] Num. xxi. 17.

[4] The Rabbis themselves draw a distinction between passages which are to be accepted literally (פשוטו כמשמעו) and those which are meant to be "hyperbolical," in

allude to, or even make use of some of these latter, it would be an utter mistake to assume that he necessarily attached to them any objective importance. If he alludes to the simplest and most reasonable of them, he does so ornamentally, incidentally, illustratively, and might in all probability have attributed to them no value beyond their connexion with loving reminiscences of the things which he had learnt in the lecture-hall of Gamaliel, or in his old paternal home. In this very passage of the Corinthians the word "following" (ἀκολουθούσης) is only a graceful allusion to the least fantastic element of a legend capable of a spiritual meaning; and St. Paul, in the instant addition of the words "and this rock was Christ," shows how slight and casual is the reference to the purely *Hagadistic* elements which, in the national consciousness, had got mingled up with the great story of the wanderings in the wilderness.[1] Meanwhile—since it is the spiritual and not the material rock which is prominent in the thoughts of St. Paul—is there any one who holds so slavish and unscriptural a view of inspiration as to think that such a transient allusion either demands our literal acceptance of the fact alluded to, or, if we reject it, weakens the weight of apostolic authority? If a modern religious writer glanced allusively at some current legend of our own or of ancient history, would it be at once assumed that he meant to support its historical certainty? If he quotes Milton's line about Aaron's breastplate "ardent with gems oracular," is he held to pledge himself to the Rabbinic theory of the light which moved upon them? Does any one think himself bound to a literal belief in seven heavens, because St. Paul, in direct accordance with Jewish notions, tells us that he was caught up into Paradise as far as the third?[2]

There is one respect in which these traces of Judaic training are specially interesting. They show the masterly good sense of the Apostle, and they show his inspired superiority to the influences of his training. That he should sometimes resort to allegory is reasonable and interesting; but when we study the use which he makes of the allegorising method

ordinary Oriental fashion (שׁבֵי הֶחָכָם), (Reland, *Antt. Hebr.*, p. 140). It must further be remembered that much of the Talmud consists of cryptographs which designedly concealed meanings φωνᾶντα συνετοῖσιν from "persecutors" and "heretics." Space prevents any further treatment of these subjects here, but I may refer those who are interested in them to my papers on the Halacha and the Hagada, Talmudic cryptographs, &c., in the *Expositor* for 1877.

[1] Seven such current national traditions are alluded to in St. Stephen's speech. (See *supra*, p. 163.)

[2] 2 Cor. xii. 2, 4; Eph. iv. 10. Many other passages and expressions of St. Paul find their illustration from the Talmud—*e.g.*, 1 Cor. xv. 37, 45, γυμνὸν κόκκον; Eph. ii. 14 (the *Chel*); 1 Cor. v. 2 (*arātsôth*, "other lands"); 2 Cor. ii. 16, ὀσμὴ θανάτου; 2 Cor. v. 2, ἐπενδύσασθαι, &c. (See Meyer on these passages.)

P P

in the case of Sarah and Hagar, we see at once its immense superiority
to the fantastic handling of the same facts by the learned Philo.   How
much more soberly does St. Paul deal with the human and historic
elements of the story ; and how far more simple and natural are the conclusions which he derives from it !   Again, when he alludes to the
legends and traditions of his nation, how rational and how purely incidental is his way of treating them !   Compare St. Paul with Philo, with
the Talmudists, with any of the Fathers in the first three centuries, and
we can then more clearly recognise the chasm which separates the Apostle
from the very greatest writers both of his own nation and of the early
Christian Church.

The question as to whether St. Paul had or had not read Philo is not
easy to answer.   Gfrörer's work on Philo might seem a decisive proof
that he had done so.   Undoubtedly many passages may be adduced
from the voluminous pamphlets of the eloquent Alexandrian which
might lead us to repeat the old remark that "either Paul Philonises, or
Philo is a Christian."   Philo, like St. Paul, speaks of the Word of God
as the antitype of the manna, and the smitten rock, and the pillar of
cloud and fire ; and as a Mediator, and as begotten before the worlds,
and as the Heavenly Man.   He speaks of the strife between the fleshly
and the rational soul ; of the assisting grace of God ; of the milk of
doctrine ; of seeing God as through a mirror ; of the true riches ; and of
the faith of Abraham.   And, besides agreement in isolated phrases,
Philo resembles St. Paul in his appeal to overwhelming revelations,[1] in
modes of citing and interpreting Scripture, in his use of allegory, in the
importance which he attaches to the spiritual over the carnal meaning
of ordinances, and in many other particulars.   But when we look closer
we see that many of these expressions and points of view were not
peculiar to Philo.   They were, so to speak, in the air.   They fall under
the same category as the resemblances to Christian sentiments which may
be adduced from the writings of Seneca, Epictetus, and Marcus
Aurelius, and may therefore be explained as having been due rather to
the prevalent currents of moral and religious sentiment, than to any
imitation or conscious interchange of thought.   And side by side with
these resemblances, the differences between Paul and Philo are immense.
The cardinal conception of Philo is that of the Logos, and it is one
which, in *this* sense, is never used by St. Paul.   St. Paul makes but one
or two distant and slighting allusions to the ancient Greek philosophy,
which Philo regarded as of transcendent importance.   St. Paul makes
but the most subordinate use of the allegoric method, which with Philo

[1] *De Cherubim,* i. 443.

is all in all. To Philo the Patriarchs become mere idealised virtues; to St. Paul they are living men. Philo addresses his esoteric eclecticism to the illuminated few; St. Paul regards all alike as the equal children of a God who is no respecter of persons. Philo clings to the Jewish ritualisms, though he gives them a mystic significance; St. Paul regards them as abrogated for Gentiles, and non-essential even for Jews. Philo still holds to the absolute superiority of the Jew over the Gentile; St. Paul teaches that in Christ Jesus there is neither Jew nor Gentile. In Philo we see the impotence of Hellenising rationalism; in St. Paul the power of spiritual truth. Philo explains and philosophises in every direction; St. Paul never recoils before a paradox, and leaves antinomies unsolved side by side. Philo, like St. Paul, speaks much of faith; but the "faith" of Philo is something far short of a transforming principle,[1] while that of St. Paul is a regeneration of the whole nature through mystic union with Christ. The writings of Philo are a collection of cold abstractions, those of St. Paul a living spring of spiritual wisdom. "Philo," says Professor Jowett, "was a Jew, St. Paul a Christian. Philo an eclectic, St. Paul spoke as the Spirit gave him utterance. Philo was an Eastern mystic, St. Paul preached the resurrection of the body. Philo was an idealiser, St. Paul a spiritualiser of the Old Testament. Philo was a philosopher, St. Paul a preacher; the one taught a system for the Jews, the other a universal religion. The one may have guided a few more solitaries to the rocks of the Nile, the other has changed the world. The one is a dead, unmeaning literature, lingering amid the progress of mankind; the other has been a principle of life to the intellect as well as to the heart. While the one has ceased to exist, the other has survived, without decay, the changes in government and the revolutions in thought of 1,800 years."[2]

Of the Apocryphal books there was one at least with which St. Paul was almost certainly acquainted—namely, the Book of Wisdom. No one, I think, will question this who compares his views of idolatry, and the manner in which he expresses them, with the chapters in which that eloquent book pursues the worship of heathenism with a concentrated scorn hardly inferior to that of Isaiah; or who will compare together the passages to which I have referred in a former note. If the books for which St. Paul wrote from his last imprisonment were any but sacred books, we may feel a tolerable confidence that the Book of Wisdom was among their number.[3]

[1] Philo's highest definition of faith is "a bettering in all things of the soul, which has cast itself for support on the Author of all things" (*De Abraham*, ii. 39).

[2] *Romans*, i. 416.

[3] Comp. Rom. v. 12; xi. 32; 1 Cor. vi. 2; 2 Cor. v. 4, &c., respectively, with Wisd. ii. 24; xi. 23—26; iii. 8; ix. 15, &c. But see *supra*, p. 633.

P P 2

EXCURSUS V. (p. 114).

GAMALIEL AND THE SCHOOL OF TÜBINGEN.

I SHALL not often turn aside to meet what seem to me to be baseless objections; but as the name of Gamaliel will always be associated with that of St. Paul, it may be worth while to do so for a moment in this instance. It seems, then, to me that this accusation of St. Luke is founded on a mass of errors.[1] Gamaliel, like St. Paul, was a Pharisee, the son of Pharisees, and it was doubtless his nobleness and candour of disposition which impressed the Apostle with the better elements of Pharisaism. The fiery zeal of a youthful Tarsian may have led him for a time to adopt the more violent tone of the school of Shammai, and yet might have been very far from obliterating the effects of previous teaching. But, in point of fact, even a Hillel and a Gamaliel, in spite of their general mildness, would have described themselves without hesitation as "exceedingly zealous for the traditions of the fathers." Their concessions to expediency were either concessions in their conduct to the heathen, or concessions to necessity and the general interest.[2] The difference between the two Pharisaic schools was not nearly so wide as that between the two great Jewish sects. The Pharisees were beyond all question allied to the Zealots in political sympathies, while the Sadducees had natural affinities with the Herodians. In what we know of Gamaliel, we trace a spirit, a tone, a point of view, which eminently resembles that of his far greater pupil. His decision that soldiers in war time, and all people engaged in works of mercy, duty, or necessity, might be exempted from the more stringent Sabbatical traditions; his concession of rights of gleaning to the poorer brethren;[3] his direction that the "Peace be with you" should be addressed even to pagans on their feast days[4]—are all exactly analogous to the known sentiments of

---

[1] The precept of Gamaliel, "Get thee a teacher, eschew that which is doubtful, and do not multiply uncertain tithes" (*Pirke Aboth*, 1, 15), might have emanated from Shammai himself. In fact, the difference between the two schools existed far more in infinitesimal details than in fundamental principles.

[2] מפני תקון העולם, "for the good order of the world," *Gittin*, v. 5. (Derenbourg, *Palestine*, p. 189.) It is difficult, however, to account for Gamaliel I. having a figure engraved on his seal if that story belongs to him.

[3] See Dr. Ginsburg, s. v., in Kitto's *Cycl.*, and Grätz, *Gesch. d. Juden*, iii. 274, sq.; Jost, *Gesch. d. Judenthums*, i. 281; Frankel, *Hodegetica in Mischnam*, 57; Derenbourg, *Palestine*, 239, sq.

[4] In *Jer. Berachôth*, ix. (Schwab, p. 159), there is a story that meeting a beautiful Pagan woman he uttered to her the *Shalôm alaikh*. "Is it possible?" is the amazed remark of the Gemara. "Did not R. Zeira say, on the authority of R. José bar

the Apostle ; while the just, humane, and liberal regulations which he
laid down to prevent the unfairness of husbands towards divorced wives,
and of disobedient children towards their mothers, are identical in spirit
to those which St. Paul applies to similar subjects.   The story that he
bathed in a bath at Ptolemais which was adorned with a statue of
Aphrodite, and answered the reproaches of a *min* with the remark that
the statue had evidently been made for the bath, and not the bath for
the statue, belongs not to him but to his grandson, with whom he is
perpetually confused.[1]   To the latter is also due the wise and kindly
rule of burying the dead in simple white linen, instead of in costly
robes.   Yet so close was the unity of doctrine which bound together
the successive hereditary presidents of the school of Hillel, that we may
look on any anecdote of the younger Gamaliel as fairly illustrative of
the views of the elder ; and the argument of Gamaliel II., that, if he
were to be excluded from the enjoyment of every place which had been
defiled by the rights of idolatry, he would not be able to find any place
to live in at all, reminds us of more than one passage in St. Paul's
argument about meats offered to idols.   We may therefore regard it as
a significant fact that, in spite of these liberal principles, Gamaliel of
Jabne sanctioned the use of the " curse against heretics," [2] which is given
twelfth in order in the *Shemone Ezre.*[3]   It is probable that his grand-

R. Hanina, and R. Ba or R. Hiya, on the authority of R. Jochanan, that one ought
not to express admiration for Pagans?" (a rule based on a sort of *jeu des mots*
derived from Deut. vii. 3).   The answer is that Gamaliel only admired her as he
might have admired a beautiful horse or camel, exclaiming that Jehovah had made
beautiful things in the universe.   The Talmudist then proceeds to excuse Gamaliel
for the enormity of looking at a woman, on the ground that it could only have been
unexpectedly in a narrow street.

[1] *Abhoda Zara*, f. 44, 2.   Conybeare and Howson, Krenkel, Lewin, and others,
confuse the anecdotes of this Gamaliel (*Ha-zaken*, or " the Elder ") and Gamaliel
II., as also does Otho, *Lex. Rabb.*, s. v. (Etheridge, *Hebr. Lit.*, p. 45).

[2] ברכת המינים, *Berachôth*, f. 28, 2.   Its first sentence is, " Let there be no hope to
them that apostatize from the true religion ; and let heretics (*minîm*), how many
soever they be, all perish as in a moment."   The actual author of this prayer was
Samuel the Little (*Ha-katôn*).   (Grätz, iv. 105, 434.)   The notion that this Samuel
the Less (for his name is, perhaps, given to distinguish him from the prophet
Samuel : cf. ὁ μέγας, as the title of Herod, *Life of Christ*, i., p. 48, *n.*) has anything
to do with Saul (Shaûl being a contraction of Shamuel, and Paulus being supposed
to mean *the little*; Alting, *Schilo*, iv. 28 ; Basnage, Bk. III. i., pp. 12, 13) is an
absurdity hardly worthy of passing notice.   (Eisenmeng. *Entd. Judenth.*, ii. 107 ;
Buxtorf, *Lex. Talm.*, 1,201, 2,662 ; Wolf, *Bibl. Hebr.*, i. 1,119.)

[3] In point of fact, there is a considerable amount of obscurity about this prayer.
The *Shemone-ezre* or *amida* is a prayer recited after the *Shema*.   It is named from
the " eighteen blessings," or sections, of which it is composed, and is recited three
times a day, or oftener on feast days.   It *actually* contains nineteen sections, the

father, who was equally liberal in many of his sentiments, would yet have been perfectly willing to authorise a similar prayer. His sense of expediency was so little identical with any indifference to pure Mosaism, that when he died it was said that the purity and righteousness of Pharisaism was removed, and the glory of the Law ceased.[1] Neither, then, in St. Paul's original zeal for the oral and written Law, nor in the liberality of his subsequent views and decisions about Mosaic observances, do we find any reason whatever to doubt the statement of his relation to Gamaliel, but on the contrary we find it confirmed by many minute and, at first sight, counter indications. And as far as the speech of Gamaliel is concerned, it seems probable that his toleration would have had decided limits. As it is by no means clear that he did not *afterwards* sanction the attempt to suppress the Christians, so it is by no means improbable that up to this time even Saul of Tarsus, had he been present at the debate, might have coincided with the half-tolerant, but also half-contemptuous, views of his great teacher. Although the Pharisees, in their deadly opposition to the Sadducees, were always ready to look with satisfaction on that one part of Christianity which rested on the belief in the Resurrection, the events of the next few months greatly altered the general relations of the Church, not only towards them, but also towards the entire body of the Jewish people, of whom, up to this time, a great multitude had welcomed its early manifestations with astonishment and joy.

12th, which is numbered 11 *bis*, being the celebrated *Birkath ha-Minim*, or prayer against the *minim*, or heretics. Now, in *Jer. Berachôth*, ch. iv., § 3, we are expressly told that this prayer was added to the *Amida* at Jabne, and therefore by Gamaliel II. in the second century, long after the destruction of Jerusalem (Cahen, *Hist. de la Prière*, p. 30, sq.; and *Megillah*, f. 17, 2). How this can be reconciled with the asserted death of Samuel the Little, before the destruction of Jerusalem, is only one of the confusions and contradictions which meet us in every stage of Talmudic literature. Hallel (quoted by Schwab) says that the prayer is sometimes called "the *blessing* (by euphemism) of the Sadducees," and is intended as a protest of the Pharisees against the mixture of temporising and severity by which the Sadducees ruined their country. Chronology shows this to be futile.

[1] *Sotah*, f. 49, 1. He, or his grandson, are cited with high respect for various minute decisions in the *Berachôth*. (See Schwab's *Traité des Berachôth*, pp. 1, 11, 12, &c.)

EXCURSUS VI. (p. 165).

CAPITAL PUNISHMENTS: THE STONING OF ST. STEPHEN.

GENERALLY speaking the Sanhedrin were not a sanguinary tribunal. They shuddered at the necessity of bloodshed, and tried to obviate its necessity by innumerable regulations. So great was their horror at putting an Israelite to death, that any means of avoiding it seemed desirable. Simeon Ben Shatach is the only conspicuous Rabbi who, for his cruelty in deciding causes, is said "to have had hot hands." Josephus expressly marks it as disgraceful to the Sadducees that, unlike the rest of their nation, they were savage in their punishments. We are told that if even once in seven years—Rabbi Eleazar Ben Azariah went so far as to say that if once in seventy years—a Sanhedrin inflicted capital punishment it deserved the opprobrious title of "sanguinary."[1] The migration of the Sanhedrin forty years before the destruction of Jerusalem, from their "Hall of Squares," which was beside the great Court of the Temple to the Chanujôth or "shops" which were under two cedars on the Mount of Olives, is expressly stated to have been due to their desire to get to a greater distance from the sacred precincts, in order that they might not feel it so sternly incumbent upon them to inflict the strict punishments of the Law.[2] But if, after strict and solemn voting, a man was condemned to any of the four capital punishments, the utmost care was taken to remove from the punishment all semblance of vindictive haste. In the case of a convicted blasphemer the death assigned by the Law was stoning, and in Leviticus it is ordained that the witnesses should lay their hands upon his head, and all the congregation should stone him.[3] In Deuteronomy we read the further regulations that the hand of the witnesses was first to be upon him[4]—and this horrible duty was one of the deterrents from false or frivolous accusation. But if we may accept the authority of the *Mishna*, the process was an elaborate one. On pronunciation of the sentence the condemned was handed over to the *Shoterim* or Lictors of the Sanhedrin, and led to the place of execution. An

---

[1] מכות, *Macooth*, f. 7, 1; Derenbourg, p. 201.

[2] The *Dini Kenasôth* or punitive decisions (*Abhôda Zara*, f. 8, 2; *Shabbath*, f. 15, 1). Rashi inferred from Deut. xvii. 10, that minor Sanhedrins outside Jerusalem could not pronounce capital sentences (*Dini Nephashôth*) unless the greater Sanhedrin was seated on the Temple Mount.

[3] Lev. xxiv. 14.

[4] Deut. xvii. 7.

official stood at the door of the Judgment Hall[1] holding in his hand a handkerchief; a second on horseback was stationed just in sight of the first, and if, even at the last moment, any witness could testify to the innocence of the condemned, the first shook his handkerchief, and the second galloped at full speed to bring back the accused, who was himself allowed to be led back as many as four or five times if he could adduce a single solid proof in his own favour. Failing this he was led on with a herald preceding him, who proclaimed his name, his crime, and the witnesses on whose testimony he had been condemned. At ten paces' distance from the place of death he was bidden to confess, because Jewish no less than Roman law valued the certainty derived from the "confitentem reum," and the Jews deduced from the story of Achan that his punishment would be, as regards the future world, a sufficiently complete expiation of his crime.[2] A bitter draught containing a grain of frankincense was then given him to stupefy his senses and take away the edge of terror. At four cubits' distance from the fatal spot he was stripped bare of his upper garments, and according to the older and simpler plan of procedure was then stoned, the witnesses simultaneously hurling the first stones.[3] But the later custom seems to have been more elaborate. The place of execution[4] was twelve feet high, and one of the witnesses flung the criminal down, back foremost, from the top, the other immediately hurling a heavy stone upon his chest. If this failed to produce death, all who were present joined in stoning him, and his body was subsequently hung by the hands on a tree until the fall of evening.[5]

We may be quite sure that none of these elaborate prescriptions were followed in the martyrdom of Stephen. He was murdered in one of those sudden outbursts of fury to which on more than one occasion the life of our Lord had been nearly sacrificed.

EXCURSUS VII. (p. 166).

THE POWER OF THE SANHEDRIN TO INFLICT DEATH.

A QUESTION has often been raised how the Sanhedrin at this time had the power of inflicting death at all? The well-known passage of

---

[1] All these particulars, except when otherwise stated, I derive from the tract Sanhedrin of the *Mishna*, cap. vi. (Surenhus. ii., p. 234, seqq.)

[2] *Tanchuma*, f. 39, § 3; Schöttg. *Hor. Hebr. ad* Acts vii. 58.

[3] *Tanchuma, ubi supr.;* Deut. xvii. 7.

[4] Called הסקילה בית.

[5] Deut. xxi. 22, 23.

St. John, "It is not lawful for us to put any man to death," has been asserted to be in direct contradiction to the narrative. The explanation of that passage to mean "it is not lawful at the time of the feast" is both philologically and historically untenable, and there seems to be little doubt that there is truth in the statement of the Talmud that about forty years—a well-known vague term in Jewish writers—before the fall of Jerusalem, the Sanhedrin had relinquished—it would be truer to say, had been deprived of—the power of death.[1] That deprivation was due to the direct interference of the Romans, who would not extend the highest judicial functions to men so likely to abuse them for seditious ends. It is, perhaps, only an attempt of the Rabbis to veil their national humiliation, when they attribute the diminished glories of their "House of Judgment" to their own leniency; to their reluctance to shed the blood of a descendant of Abraham; to the consequent increase of crimes; and to the migration from the Hall of Squares to the "Shops" of the Beni Hanan. But, on the other hand, we know the astute connivance which the Romans were always ready to extend to acts which were due to religious excitement and not to civil rebellion.[2] They rarely interfered with national superstitions. Even Pilate, though by no means void of a sense of justice, had been quite willing to hand over Jesus to any extreme of ecclesiastical vengeance, provided only that the direct responsibility did not fall upon himself. Further than this, there is every reason to believe that St. Stephen's martyrdom finds its counterpart in the murder of James, the Lord's brother. That was brought about by the younger Hanan during a High Priesthood of only three months' duration, in which he seized his opportunity, and availed himself of a brief interregnum which followed on the death of Festus, and preceded the arrival of his successor Albinus. It was at just such an interregnum that the death of Stephen is believed to have taken place. Pontius Pilate had been sent to Rome by his official chief, Vitellius, the Præfect of Syria, to answer to the Emperor for the complaints of cruelty and insult brought against him by the inhabitants of every division of his Procuratorship. Before his arrival the Emperor Tiberius died. An event of this magnitude relaxed the sternness of government in every province of the Empire,[3]

---

[1] *Abhodah Zara,* f. 8, 2.

[2] The policy of Rome towards her Oriental subjects was a policy of contemptuous tolerance in all matters that affected the local cult.

[3] That there was at this very time a special desire to conciliate the Jews, who had been so much exasperated by the cruelties of Pilate, is clear from the circumstance that Vitellius, after a magnificent reception at Jerusalem, had just restored to the Jews the custody of the pontifical vestments, which since the days of Herod

and though Vitellius appointed Marcellus as a brief temporary *locum tenens* until the arrival of Marullus, who was appointed Procurator by Gaius,[1] the Sanhedrin may have met while there was no Procurator at all, and in any case would have found it easy to persuade a substitute like Marcellus, or a new-comer like Marullus, that it would be useless to inquire into a mere riot which had ended in the richly deserved punishment of a blaspheming Hellenist. In short, we find that the possibility of tumultuous outbreaks which might end in a death by stoning is constantly recognised in the New Testament;[2] and it would have been easy for the Sanhedrin to represent the stoning of St. Stephen in such a light.

EXCURSUS VIII. (p. 179).

DAMASCUS UNDER HARETH.

HARETH was the father-in-law of Herod Antipas, and from the day when the weakness of that miserable prince had beguiled him into his connexion, at once adulterous and incestuous, with Herodias, his brother Philip's wife, Hareth had been the implacable foe of the Tetrarch of Galilee. Their quarrel had ended in a battle, in which the troops of Hareth won a signal victory. After this defeat, in which the Jews saw a retribution for the murder of John the Baptist,[3] Antipas applied to the Emperor Tiberius, who sent Vitellius to chastise the audacious Emir who had dared to defeat an ally of Rome. But when Vitellius had reached Jerusalem, he heard the news of the death of Tiberius. The death of a Roman emperor often involved so immense a change of policy, that Vitellius did not venture, without fresh instructions, to renew the war. The details of what followed have not been preserved. That Hareth ventured to seize Damascus is improbable. Vitellius was too vigorous a legate, and the Arab had too wholesome a dread of imperial Rome, to venture on so daring an

---

the Great had been kept in the Tower of Antonia (Jos. *Antt.* xv. 11, 4 ; xviii. 4, 2). The privilege was again forfeited, and again restored to them by Claudius, at the request of Agrippa II. (*id.* xx. 1, 2). The power of inflicting *minor* punishments seems always to have rested with the Jews, as it does with many religious communities of *raïas*, even under the tyranny of Turkish misrule (Renan, *Les Apôtres*, p. 144).

[1] Jos. *Antt.* xviii. 6, 10 (cf. 4, 2).

[2] John viii. 59 ; x. 31—33 ; Matt. xxiii. 37 ; Acts v. 26. See Orig. *ad Africam.* § 14, *apud* Wordsworth.

[3] Jos. *Antt.* xviii. 5, § 1.

act of rebellion. On the other hand, it is not impossible that the Emperor Gaius—who was fond of distributing kingdoms among princes whom he favoured, and whose mind was poisoned against Antipas by his friend and minion Agrippa I.—should have given back to Hareth a town which in old days had belonged to the Nabathæan dynasty.[1] The conjecture receives some independent confirmation. Coins of Damascus are found which bear the image of Augustus, of Tiberius, and again of Nero, but none which bear that of Gaius or of Claudius. This would lead us to infer that during these reigns Damascus was subject to a local sway.[2]

EXCURSUS IX. (p. 213).

SAUL IN ARABIA.

FEW geographical terms are more vaguely used by ancient writers than "Arabia," and some have seen the explanation of St. Luke's silence about the retirement of St. Paul, in the possibility that he may scarcely have gone beyond the immediate region of Damascus. Justin Martyr challenges Trypho to deny that Damascus "belongs and did belong to Arabia, though now it has been assigned to what is called Syrophœnicia." Some shadow of probability may be, perhaps, given to the view that St. Paul did not travel far from Syria, because the Arabic translator of the Epistle to the Galatians renders the clause in Gal. i. 17, &c., "Immediately I went to *El Belka;*" and in Gal. iv. 25, mistaking the meaning of the word συστοιχεῖ (which means "answers to," "corresponds with," "falls under the same row with"), he says that "Mount Sinai or El Belka is contiguous to Jerusalem."[4] But since Sinai is certainly not in the El Belka with which alone we have any acquaintance —namely, the region to the north and east of the Dead Sea—this curious version does not seem worthy of any further notice. Doubtless,

---

[1] Thus in A.D. 38 he gave Ituræa to Soheym; Lesser Armenia to Cotys; part of Thrace to Rhæmetalces; Pontius, &c., to Polemo II. (Dio Cass. lix. 12). Keim thinks that Aretas may have had a sort of *partial* jurisdiction in Damascus.

[2] Jos. *Antt.* xiii. 5, §§ 2, 3; Wieseler, *Chron. des Apost. Zeitalt.* 174.

[3] Wieseler, in his article on Aretas in Herzog's *Encycl.*, refers to Mionnet, p. 204, as his authority for the existence of a coin of Aretas, which bears the date 101 (.A.D). Now, if this date refer to the Pompeian era, the coin would belong to A.D. 37—38, about the very time in which Saul's mission to Damascus took place.

[4] Lightfoot, *Galatians*, p. 81.

in the then disturbed and fluctuating relations between the Roman Empire and the various Eastern principalities, St. Paul might have found himself far beyond the range of interruption by taking but a short journey from the neighbourhood of Damascus.

But is it not more probable that when St. Paul speaks of his visit to Arabia, he means Arabia in that Hebrew sense in which the word would be understood by the majority of his readers? We cannot, indeed, accept the proof of his familiarity with these regions which is derived from the reading of our Received text, "for this Hagar is Mount Sinai in Arabia," and from the supposition that Hagar was a local name for the mountain itself.[1] For the true reading of that verse seems to be, "for Sinai is a mountain in Arabia;" and, as Dr. Lightfoot has shown, there is no adequate authority for the assertion—perhaps originally a mistake of St. Chrysostom—that Mount Sinai was ever called Hagar. Moreover, it is doubtful whether, even by way of allegoric paronomasia, St. Paul would have identified *Hagar*, " a wanderer," with *chadjar*, " a stone ; " especially since Philo, who also has an allegory about Hagar and Sarah, had already extracted a moral meaning from the correct derivation. But setting this ancient argument aside, nothing can seem more natural than that St. Paul, possibly already something of a fugitive, almost certainly a sufferer in health and mind, driven by an imperious instinct to seek for solitude, should have turned his lonely steps to a region where he would at once be safe, and unburdened, and alone with God.

EXCURSUS X. (p. 221).

St. Paul's " Stake in the Flesh."

THERE are two main passages on which our inferences about the " stake in the flesh" must be founded, and the impression which they leave is only strengthened by more isolated allusions. These two passages, to give them in their chronological order, are : 2 Cor. xii. 1—10[2] and Gal. iv. ;[3] and I translate them in all their ruggedness, and the interchanges of thought which render it almost impossible to explain the rapid transition of their causal connexions.

---

[1] Gal. iv. 25.
[2] Written not earlier than the autumn of A.D. 57.
[3] Written perhaps in the spring of A.D. 58.

i. The first of them runs as follows :—After showing that, however weak and unworthy he may be, he has yet laboured and suffered more than "the super-pre-eminent Apostles,"—a boastfulness the very semblance of which he loathes, but which, again and again, he says has been forced upon him by the intrigues and slanders of interested opponents—he mentions his perilous escape from Damascus, which had made a deep impression on his memory, and then continues : "Boasting, evidently, is not expedient for me; for I will come to visions and revelations of the Lord.[1] I know a man in Christ fourteen years ago—(whether in the body I know not, or whether out of the body I know not : God knoweth)—caught up, such a one as far as the third heaven. And I know such a man—(whether in the body, or apart[2] from the body, I know not : God knoweth)—that he was caught up into Paradise and heard unutterable things which it is not lawful for man to speak. About such a one I will boast; but about myself I will not boast except in mine infirmities. For if I should wish to boast, I shall not be a fool, for I shall speak the truth ; but I forbear, that no one may reckon about me more than what he seeth me or heareth anything from me. And, that I may not be puffed up by this abundance of revelations, there was given me a stake in the flesh an angel of Satan,[3] that it may buffet me that I may not be puffed up. For this, thrice did I entreat the Lord that it might depart from me. And He hath said to me : My grace sufficeth for thee; for power is being perfected in weakness.[4] Most gladly, then, rather will I boast in my infirmities, that the power of Christ may spread its tent over me. Therefore, I am content in infirmities, in insults, in necessities, in persecutions, in distresses, for Christ's sake, for when I am weak then I am powerful."[5]

ii. The other passage is Gal. iv. 12—16. St. Paul has been vehemently urging the Galatians not to sink to the low level of their previous bondage from the freedom of the Gospel, and in the midst of his reasonings and exhortations he inserts this tender appeal :—

"Become as I am, for I too have become as you, brethren, I beseech you. In no respect did ye wrong me. Yea, ye know that because of infirmity of the flesh I preached to you the first time, and your temptation in my flesh[6] ye despised not nor loathed, but as an angel of God

---

[1] The reading of this verse is extremely doubtful; *v. infra, ad loc.*

[2] χωρίς, B, D, E, which is more likely to have been altered into the ἐκτὸς of the previous verse (א, F, G).

[3] Cf. 1 Cor. v. 5.

[4] Omit μου (א, A, B, D, F, G).

[5] 2 Cor. xii. 1—10.

[6] The true reading is τὸν πειρασμὸν ὑμῶν ἐν τῇ σαρκί μου.

ye received me, as Christ Jesus. What, then, was your self-congratulation? For I bear you witness that, if possible, ye dug out your eyes [1] and gave them me. So, have I become your enemy by telling you the truth?"

iii. The most prominent *allusions* to the same bodily affliction are—Gal. vi. 17: "Henceforth let no man trouble me, for I carry in my body the brands of Jesus;"[2] 2 Cor. iv. 10: "Always bearing about in the body the putting to death of the Lord Jesus;" and perhaps indirectly, Col. i. 24: "Now I rejoice[3] in my sufferings for you, and I supplement in Christ's stead the deficiences of the afflictions of Christ in my flesh for His body which is the Church." When, too, we remember that the word for "stake" is only a more contemptuous form of the word for "cross,"[4] there may be a further allusion to this special trial in the words, "I have been crucified with Christ."[5]

α. Now, from the first of these passages we see that St. Paul, so far from boasting of exceptional revelations, will only mention them because they are connected with infirmities so painful as to render it ridiculous as well as sinful for him to boast at all, unless he might boast that his very weakness was but a more signal proof of that strength of Christ which had enabled him to do and to suffer more than the very chiefest Apostles.

β. We gather that his trial was something agonising, or it would not be called a stake in the flesh;[6] mysterious in its nature, or it would not be described as an angel of Satan; intermittent, as is implied in the word "buffet," and as is also apparent from various special paroxysms to which St. Paul alludes; and a direct consequence of, or at any rate intimately connected with, his most exalted moments of revelation and ecstasy.

γ. From the second passage, we have the additional particulars, that it was in consequence of some sharp attack of his malady that he had been detained in Galatia; that this malady was of such a nature as to

---

[1] The omission of the ἄν (cf. John xix. 11; Matt. xxvi. 28) gives far more vividness to the expression. (See my *Brief Greek Syntax*, § 137.)

[2] Leg. τοῦ Ἰησοῦ (all but Uncials).

[3] Leg. Νῦν χαίρω (A, B, C).

[4] Lipsius *De Cruce*, i. 4. Hence σκολοπίζω = σταυρόω (cf. *stipes*).

[5] Gal. ii. 20, Χριστῷ συνεσταύρωμαι. This epistle is full of the "cross," and was written with vivid reminiscence (at least) of the "stake." The allusion of 1 Thess. ii. 18, "but Satan hindered us," is too vague to be referred with any special probability to this affliction.

[6] Ἄκανθαι καὶ σκόλοπες ὀδύνας σημαίνουσι διὰ τὸ ὀξύ (*Artemid.* iii. 33, Meyer); (cf. Num. xxxiii. 55; Josh. xxiii. 13; Ezek. xxviii. 24; σκόλοψ πικρίας, Hos. ii. 6; LXX.). Hence perhaps the rendering "thorn."

form an actual trial to the Galatians, and naturally dispose them to look on him with contempt, if not with positive loathing ; but that they had so completely triumphed over this feeling as to receive him with almost divine respect, and that they had so congratulated themselves on his visit as to have been ready, had it been possible, to dig out their very eyes and give them to their suffering teacher.

3. The other references confirm these conclusions. In one of them we learn that St. Paul looked on his physical infirmities as sacred stigmata by which Jesus had marked him out as His slave, that he might be secured from molestation;[1] and in the others that he regarded his living death as a sort of continuation of his Lord's crucifixion, and a supplement to those sufferings for the sake of His Church, in which Christ allowed His servants to participate by taking up their cross and following after Him for the service of mankind.[2]

Now these passages at once exclude nine-tenths of the conjectures which have been so freely hazarded, and which could not have been hazarded at all by those who had carefully considered the conditions of the question. Many of these conjectures would not have even deserved a passing mention if they had not, on the one hand, possessed a certain archæological interest as belonging to the history of exegesis, and on the other brought to light some fragments of old tradition, or pointed to certain features in the character of the Apostle.

1. It is, for instance, abundantly clear that the stake in the flesh was nothing of a spiritual nature. If we find such men as Jean Gerson,[3] and Luther, and Calvin more or less confidently deciding that the expression alludes to *high spiritual temptations,* such as shrinking from his duties as an Apostle, tormenting doubts, and stings of conscience for the past, the decision is only interesting as a proof that these great and holy men could so well sympathise with these painful hindrances. Yet such an explanation is wholly impossible. It is excluded at once by the references to the infirmity as being of a physical description. It is excluded also by St. Paul's character, and by the circumstances of his life. There is much in his Epistles about weariness and sorrow, about fightings without and fears within, but there is not the faintest trace that the fire of zeal burnt low, even at his moments of deepest discouragement, on the altar of his heart. Nor could tormenting doubts have had much reality in the soul of one who had seen

---

[1] Gal. vi. 17.

[2] 2 Cor. iv. 10; Col. i. 24; Phil. iii. 10; Gal. ii. 20.

[3] Perhaps the author, or part author, of the *Imitatio Christi.* (See *Companions of the Devout Life,* p. 8, *sq.*)

the risen Christ, and to whom were constantly vouchsafed the vivid revelations which not only solved the problems, but even guided the movements of his life.[1]

2. And while we reject this view of some great Reformers, we must reject quite as decidedly the fixed opinion of the most eminent Roman Catholics. Vague expressions in St. Jerome, St. Augustine, and Gregory the Great seem to have led to an opinion that the stake in the flesh was *some form of carnal temptation.*[2] This view, repeated by the Venerable Bede, has been continued through Aquinas, Bellarmine, Cornelius à Lapide, and other Roman Catholic writers down to Van Est in the sixteenth century, till it has become almost a stereotyped part of the exegesis of the Roman Catholic Church. It is due to the ambiguous rendering of "stake in the flesh," by *stimulus carnis* in the Vulgate translation. Now, in this case also—though we may observe with sorrowful interest that the struggles of ascetics to subdue by unwise methods their carnal passions made them glad to believe that even in the case of St. Paul such an infirmity was never wholly removed—we are nevertheless obliged on every ground to reject the explanation. It in no way satisfies the general tenor of St. Paul's expressions. It is not an infirmity of which by any possibility he could boast. We cannot conceive so revolting a stain on the character of the Apostle as that which would be involved in the supposition that such tendencies, if he had been cursed with them, should have so manifested themselves as to be a hindrance to his ministry, and a source of loathing to those who heard him. It is still more outrageous to imagine that such criminal concupiscence would have been implanted or strengthened in him as a counterpoise to the spiritual pride which might otherwise have resulted from special revelations. But besides all this, it fixes on the memory of the Apostle a weakness from which we may well believe that he was most exceptionally free. It is true that in the Epistle to the Romans he describes, in language of intense emotion, the struggle in the soul between the good and the evil impulse—the *Yetser ha-tôbh* and *Yetser ha-râ* of which he had heard so much in the Beth Midrash of his education. But it is idle to imagine that a strife so multiform must be referred to one only of its manifestations. And we judge that St. Paul had very early subdued every motion of rebellious sensuality, not only because no man who ever lived has uttered words of loftier purity; not only because upon his principles more than upon those of any human moralist have been founded the very bases of Christian abstinence; not only because, to an extent unparalleled in literature, he

[1] See Acts xvi. 7; xxi. 4; xxii. 17; Gal. ii. 2, &c.
[2] Greg. *Moral.* x. 8, 315. See the authorities in Tillemont, i. 222 (ed. 1693).

has the high gift of being able to brand the shamelessness of impurity without wounding the delicacy of Christian thought;[1] but more than this, because he is able to appeal to others that they should learn by his example how possible it was to live by the rule of a holy continence. Admitting as he does to the Corinthians that it is better once for all to marry than to be consumed by the slow inward fires of concupiscence,[2] he yet says to the unmarried, "it is good for them to abide even as I," and that "he would that all men were even as he himself."[3] There would be hypocrisy, and something worse than hypocrisy, in such language if the "stake in the flesh," which was still unremoved when he wrote the Second Epistle, were that which this long succession of commentators have supposed it to be.[4]

3. It may, then, be regarded as certain that the stake in the flesh was some physical malady; for the fancy first mentioned by Chrysostom and adopted by the Greek fathers, as well as by Hilary and Augustine, that it means the *opposition and persecution* with which St. Paul met at the hands of Judaists, and perhaps especially of one leader among them who was "a thorn in his side,"[5] is too entirely at variance with the conditions of the question to deserve further notice. But when, in our anxiety to understand and sympathise as far as possible with the Apostle's personality, we still ask what was this malady, we are left in uncertainty. To omit the more futile conjectures, neither attacks of headache nor earache mentioned traditionally by Tertullian and Jerome, nor the stone which is the conjecture of Aquinas, present those features of external repulsiveness to which the Apostle evidently alludes as the concomitants of his trial. The only conjectures which have much intrinsic probability are those which suppose him to have suffered from epilepsy or from ophthalmia.

4. There is something to be said in favour of the view that it was *Epilepsy*. It is painful; it is recurrent; it opposes an immense difficulty to all exertion; it may at any time cause a temporary suspension of

---

[1] Rom. i.; Eph. v., &c.

[2] 1 Cor. vii. 9, κρεῖσσον γαμῆσαι ἢ πυροῦσθαι.

[3] 1 Cor. vii. 7, 8.

[4] It is difficult to believe that 2 Cor. vii. 2; xi. 8; and 1 Thess. ii. 3 are intended to refute charges which had been even brought against Paul himself. They may be intended to contrast his own conduct with that of other teachers, and indeed the first two passages do not necessarily refer to unchastity at all. The ἀκαθαρσία 1 Thess. ii. 3 is explained, even by Chrysostom, of vile and juggling arts; and Olshausen, Lünemann, Alford, Ellicott, and others all suppose it to refer primarily to αἰσχροκέρδεια and similar impure motives.

[5] A special person may be indicated in 2 Cor. x. 7, 10, 11, 18; xi. 4, 20; and in Gal. i. 9; iii. 1; vi. 7, 12.

Q Q

work; it is intensely humiliating to the person who suffers from it; it exercises a repellent effect on those who witness its distressing manifestations. Moreover, it was regarded in ancient days as supernatural in its character, was surrounded with superstitious fancies, and was directly connected by the Jews with demoniacal possession.[1] Further, St. Paul himself connects his infirmity with his trances and visions, and the soul of man is so constituted that any direct intercourse with the unseen world—even, in a lower order, any deep absorption in religious thought, or paroxysms of religious feeling—does tend to a violent disturbance of the nervous organism.[2] It would be specially certain to act in this way in the case of one whose temperament was so emotional as was that of St. Paul. It is not impossible that the prostration which followed his conversion may have been induced by the shock which his system received from his miraculous conversion on the road to Damascus; and that the recurrence of this shock, involving a chronic liability to its attacks, accompanied that second trance in the Temple, which determined his future career as the Apostle of the Gentiles. His third ecstasy happened fourteen years[3] before he wrote the Second Epistle to the Corinthians, and therefore at some period during his second residence in Tarsus. If we take the words, "thrice I besought the Lord," literally, we may then further believe that it was at each of these recurrences of anguish upon the renewals of special revelations that he had made his most earnest entreaty to be delivered from the buffets of this angel of Satan; and that it was only during, or after, his third and most memorable vision that his Lord pointed out to him the meaning of the trial, and told him that, though it could not be removed, he should be strengthened with grace sufficient to enable him to bear it.[4]

---

[1] *Morbus Comitialis*, Dio Cass. xlvi. 33; Gell. xix. 2. In Welsh it is called *gwialen Christi*, "the rod of Christ," and *cledyt bendigaid*, "blessed disease." A curious Celtic tradition to this effect is preserved in the old Irish name for epilepsy, *in galar Poil* (Stokes, *Old Irish Glossary*, p. 120; *Anc. Laws of Ireland*, iii. 506). Krenkel, in Hilgenfeld's *Zeitschr.* xvi. (ii.) 233—244, notices the curious fact that the evil omen of epilepsy was averted by *spitting*. Hence Plautus calls it the "morbus qui sputatur" (*Captiv.* iii. 4, 15; cf. Plin. *H. N.* x. 23, 33; xxviii. 4, 7). He connects this with ἐξεπτύσατε (as though it meant "neither did ye spit") of Gal. iv. 14.

[2] The trances of Sokrates, the fits of Mohammed, accompanied by foaming at the mouth, and followed by the sleep of exhaustion, the faintings and ecstasies of St. Bernard, St. Francis, and St. Catherine of Siena, have been adduced as parallels (Hausrath, pp. 52—56). We may add the cases of George Fox, of Jacob Boehme, of Swedenborg, &c.

[3] The "about" in the E. V. is interpolated.

[4] Compare the interesting parallels of Alfred and of St. Bernard.

5. But even if this was the actual "stake in the flesh," there is the strongest reason to believe that St. Paul suffered further from *acute Ophthalmia*, which also fulfils in every particular the conditions of the problem. This, too, would have the advantage of following the analogy of God's dealings, by being a trial not arbitrarily inflicted, but one which might have resulted naturally—or, to use the more exact term, let us say, providentially—from the circumstances through which Paul had passed. We know that he was physically blinded by the glare of light which surrounded him when he saw the risen Lord. The whole circumstances of that event—the noonday journey under the fierce Syrian sun, the blaze of light which outshone even that noonday brightness, and the blindness which followed it—would have been most likely to leave his eyes inflamed and weak. His stay in the desert and in Damascus—regions notorious for the prevalence of this disease—would have tended to develop the mischief when it had once been set up; and though we are never told in so many words that the Apostle suffered from defective sight, there are yet so many undesigned coincidences of allusion all pointing in this direction, that we may regard it as an ascertained fact. Apart from the initial probability that eyes which had once been so seriously affected would be liable to subsequent attacks of disease, we have the following indications:—(i.) When speaking of his infirmity to the Galatians, St. Paul implies that it might well have rendered him an object of loathing; and this is pre-eminently the case with acute ophthalmia. The most distressing objects, next to the lepers, which the traveller will ever see in the East—those who will most make him inclined to turn away his face with a shudder of pity and almost involuntary disgust—are precisely those who are the victims of this disease.[1] (ii.) And this would give a deeper pathos and meaning to the Apostle's testimony that the Galatians in the first flush of their Gospel joy, when they looked on the preacher of those good tidings as an angel of God, would, had it been possible, *have dug out their eyes* in order to place them at the sufferer's service. (iii.) The term, "a stake in the flesh," would be most appropriate to such a malady, because all who have been attacked with it know that the image which it recalls most naturally is that of a sharp splinter run into the eye.[2] (iv.) Moreover, it would be extremely likely to cause

[1] When Dr. Lightfoot, who rejects this theory, says that "St. Paul's language implies some more *striking* complaint," he is probably thinking of the milder forms of ophthalmia with which alone we are familiar in England, and not of those virulent attacks which are but too common in Syria, and which make such terrible havoc of the human countenance.

[2] Alford's remark that ophthalmic disorders are not usually painful is singularly mistaken.

Q Q 2

epileptic or other symptoms, since in severe attacks it is often accompanied by cerebral disturbance. (v.) In spite of the doubt which has been recently thrown on the commonly accepted meaning of the expression which St. Paul uses to the Galatians, "Ye see in what large letters I write to you with my own hand," it must at any rate be admitted that it suits well with the hypothesis of a condition which rendered it painful and difficult to write at all. That this was St. Paul's normal condition seems to result from his almost invariable practice of employing an amanuensis, and only adding in autograph the few last words of greeting or blessing, which were necessary for the identification of his letters in an age in which religious forgeries were by no means unknown. (vi.) It is obvious, too, that an ocular deformity, caused as this had been, might well be compared to the brand fixed by a master on his slave. (vii.) Lastly, there is no other reasonable explanation of the circumstance that, when St. Paul had uttered an indignant answer to the High Priest, and had been rebuked for it, he at once frankly offered his apology by saying that " he had not recognised the speaker to have been the High Priest." Now, considering the position of the High Priest as *Nasi* of the Sanhedrin, seated at the end of the hall, with the *Ab Beth Din* on one side of him, and the *Chacham* on the other,[1] it is almost inconceivable that Paul should not have been aware of his rank if he had not suffered from defective sight. All that his blurred vision took in was a white figure, nor did he see this figure with sufficient clearness to be able to distinguish that the overbearing tyrant was no less a person than the High Priest himself.[2]

But if these conjectures are correct—and to me they seem to be almost certain—how immensely do they add to our conception of Paul's heroism; how much do they heighten the astonishment and admiration which we feel at all that he endured and all that he accomplished This man, who almost single-handed carried the Gospel of Christ from Damascus to Rome, was so great a sufferer from inflammation of the eyes that he was often pitiable to look upon; was unable to write except with pain, and in large letters; was liable to attacks of severe agony, accompanied at times with loss of consciousness. He was so

---

[1] Acts xxiii. 5. It is possible that the presence of Roman officials disturbed this order.

[2] The expression "fixing an earnest gaze" (ἀτενίσας) has often been adduced as yet another sign that St. Paul's eyesight was weak, and therefore that he had acquired the intent stare so common in short-sighted people. This argument is, however, untenable, since the word is a favourite one with St. Luke (Acts xiii. 9: xxiii. 1) and is applied not only to St. Paul, but also to St. Peter, St. Stephen, and even to whole bodies of men (Luke iv. 20 xxii. 56; Acts i. 10; iii. 2—4; vi. 15; vii. 55).

weak and ailing that under circumstances of danger he was personally helpless; that he had to be passively conducted from place to place; that it was almost impossible for him, I will not say only to preach, but even to get through the ordinary routine of life without companions to guide, and protect, and lead him by the hand.[1] We can then see how indispensable it was that St. Paul should have some "that ministered unto him;" how strongly he would feel the necessity of being always accompanied upon his missions by faithful friends;[2] how much anguish might lie in his remark that in his strong affection for the Thessalonians he was even ready for their sakes to part with his beloved Timotheus, and to be left at Athens *alone*.[3] How close, then, and how tender would be the bond of mutual gratitude and affection which would inevitably grow up under such circumstances between himself and the little band of disciples by whom he was usually accompanied! With what deepened bitterness would he feel the cruelty of neglect and ingratitude when, at his first answer, no man stood with him, but all forsook him![4]

EXCURSUS XI. (p. 226).

ON JEWISH SCOURGINGS.

EVEN a single Jewish scourging might well entitle any man to be regarded as a martyr. Thirty-nine blows were inflicted, unless, indeed, it was found that the strength of the patient was too much exhausted to admit of his receiving the full number. Both of his hands were tied to what is sometimes called a column, but which was in reality a stake a cubit and a half high.[5] The public officer then tore down his robe until

[1] Acts xvii. 14, τὸν Παῦλον ἐξαπέστειλαν οἱ ἀδελφοί; 15, οἱ δὲ καθιστάνοντες (καθιστῶντες, E, G, H) τὸν Παῦλον ἤγαγον ἕως Ἀθηνῶν. These phrases seem more specific than those in Gen. xviii. 16; Rom. xv. 24 (προπεμφθῆναι).

[2] Mr. Lewin (*St. Paul*, i. 189, third edition) was, I believe, the earliest to point out that these passages bear on the question. They are not in themselves conclusive; but when we find the same words used in Acts ix. 30 (to which Mr. Lewin does not refer), when we may well suppose that a fresh attack had followed a fresh revelation, they not improbably point to some such state of things as that which I have inferred.

[3] 1 Thess. iii. 1.

[4] 2 Tim. iv. 16.

[5] Marble "columns," traditionally assigned to this purpose, are shown among the relics of Roman Catholic churches; *e.g.*, the column of the flagellation in the Church of the Holy Sepulchre; that of the scourging of St. Paul in *S. Paolo fuori de' Muri* at Rome, &c.

his breast was laid bare. The executioner stood on a stone behind the criminal. The scourge consisted of two thongs, one of which was composed of four strands of calf-skin, and one of two strands of ass's-skin, which passed through a hole in a handle. The executioner, who was ordinarily the *Chazzan* of the synagogue, could thus shorten or lengthen them at will, so as not to strike too low.[1] The prisoner bent to receive the blows, which were inflicted with one hand, but with all the force of the striker, thirteen on the breast, thirteen on the right, and thirteen on the left shoulder. While the punishment was going on, the chief judge read aloud Deut. xxviii. 58, 59, "If thou wilt not observe to do all the words of this law that are written in this book, that thou mayest fear this glorious and fearful name, the Lord thy God; then the Lord will make thy plagues wonderful, and the plagues of thy seed." He then read Deut. xxix. 9, "Keep therefore the words of this covenant, and do them, that ye may prosper in all ye do;" and lastly, Ps. lxxviii. 38, 39, "But He, being full of compassion, forgave their iniquity, and destroyed them not: yea, many a time turned He His anger away, and did not stir up all His wrath." If the punishment was not over by the time that these three passages were read, they were again repeated, and so timed as to end exactly with the punishment itself. Meanwhile a second judge numbered the blows, and a third before each blow exclaimed "*Hakkehu*" (strike him). All these particulars I take from the Treatise on Punishments (מכות, *Makkôth*) in the Mishna.[2] The severity of the pain may best be estimated by the brief addition: "*If the criminal die under the infliction*, the executioner is not accounted guilty unless he gives by mistake a single blow too many, in which case he is banished."

These facts have an interest far deeper than archæological. They not only show how awful were the trials which St. Paul had to endure, if such as these were hardly counted worthy of narration amongst them, but also they illustrate to a singular degree the minute scrupulosity which reigned through all Jewish observances. If, for instance, only thirty-nine blows were inflicted instead of forty, it was not only, as is usually stated, to avoid the possibility of error in the counting, but also (such at least is the reason assigned by Maimonides[3]) because the Law says, "in number, forty,"[4] not "forty in number;" whence they concluded that they might assign a smaller but not a larger number; and, perhaps, also because the word "thy brother" (אחיך) stands by Gematria

---

[1] This was not strictly in accordance with Deut. xxv. 2; but it is strange to see how traditional laxity was mingled by the Jews with unintelligent literalism.

[2] See Surenhusius, *Mishna*, vol. iv., p. 286, seqq.

[3] Maimon. *Sanhedr.* 17

נמסטר אינעים.

for thirty-nine.[1] Another assigned reason is that the passage of the Psalm (lxxviii. 38, 39) which was recited on the occasion ends at verse 39. The scourge was made partly of ox-hide, partly of ass's-hide, for the astounding reasons that immediately after the passage in Deuteronomy which orders the infliction of scourging follows the verse, " Thou shalt not muzzle the ox when he treadeth out the corn ; "[2] and that in Isa. i. 3 we find, " The ox knoweth his owner, and the ass his master's crib ; but Israel doth not know, my people doth not consider." And thus it was thought right that those who do know should punish him who does not know ![3] The criminal was to receive only thirteen blows on his breast, but twenty-six on his shoulders, because it was inferred from Deut. xxv. 2 that it was only on the back that he was to be beaten, " according to his fault," so that the back received a double number of blows. The duty of reading aloud while the scourging continued was also a minute inference from the words of Scripture.[4]

A person was liable to this penalty if he wilfully violated any of the negative precepts of the Law, and inadvertently any of those which, if deliberately transgressed, involved the threat of excision from among the people,[6] or "death by the visitation of God."[7] Under which of the numerous offences for which this punishment was assigned Paul five times suffered, is by no means easy to say. Looking through them all as enumerated in the treatise *Makkôth*,[8] and as expanded by Maimonides,[9] I cannot find any of which the Apostle could possibly have been guilty. Where, however, the will to punish him existed, the

---

[1] *Gematria* (Geomatria) was one of the Kabbalistic methods of drawing interpretations from the numerical value of letters. I have given many instances in *Rabbinic Exegesis* (*Expositor*, May, 1877). Thus because both *Mashiach* and *nachash*, "serpent," numerically represent 358, they inferred that it was the Messiah who would bruise the serpent's head, &c.

[2] Deut. xxv. 4.

[3] So Maimonides and R. Ob. de Bartenora, *ap.* Surenhus. *l. c.*

[4] Buxtorf, *Synag.*, p. 523. See also *Praef. Libr. de Abbreviaturis*. This was one of the numerous instances in which the Jews were more legal than the Law itself. Similarly they extended the Sabbath into a Little Sabbath, an hour before and an hour after the true Sabbath. They were forbidden to have leaven in their houses during the Passover, and they abstained from even using the word. Being forbidden swine's flesh, they avoid the word pig altogether, and call the pig דָּבָר אַחֵר, *dabhar acheer*, "the other thing," &c. (Godwyn, *Moses and Aaron*, viii. 12.) These are specimens of the "*hedge* of the Law."

[5] Deut. xxv. 4, בקרא חרשׁ, "hinc colligimus plagas infigi debere inter legendum" (R. Ob. de Bartenora, *ap.* Surenhus. *Mishna*, iv. 290).

[6] כרת.

[7] מיתה בידי שמים.

[8] III., 1, 2, 3, 4.

[9] *Hilkoth Senhedr.* xviii., xix.

pretext would not long be wanting. His flagellation must have been that minor but still terrible punishment which was called "the legal scourging" or the "scourging of forty,"[1] because the yet deadlier flagellation with rods, which was called the Rabbinic, or the flagellation of contumacy,[2] was never inflicted within the limits of the Holy Land, and is expressly stated to have been a beating to death.

When once an offender had been scourged this punishment was considered to remove the danger of "cutting off,"[3] and not only so, but it was regarded as leaving no ignominy behind it. The humane expression of Moses that forty stripes were not to be exceeded "lest thy brother seem vile unto thee," was interpreted to mean that when the punishment was over the sufferer was "restored to his integrity." So completely was this the case that even the High Priest himself might be thus scourged, and afterwards be "restored to his majesty." But although it was assumed that he would suffer no ulterior injury, but rather be sure to win an inheritance in the future, yet, of course, if he again offended he was again scourged.[4] It was even possible that for one offence, if it involved the disobedience to several negative precepts, he might incur several consecutive scourgings, care being only taken that he had sufficiently recovered from the first before the next was inflicted. It is, therefore, by no means impossible, or even improbable, that during those "many days" which Paul spent in Damascus in trying to convince these passionate disputants, he may have incurred this torture several times.

To have refused to undergo it by sheltering himself under the privilege of his Roman citizenship would have been to incur excommunication, and finally to have cut himself off from admission into the synagogues.

EXCURSUS XII. (p. 250).

APOTHEOSIS OF ROMAN EMPERORS.

THE early Emperors rather discouraged than stimulated this tendency to flatter them by a premature apotheosis. If temples had been built to them in their lifetime, they had always been to their "genius,"

---

[1] *Malkooth*, מלקות, or מכות.
[2] מרדות. See Carpzov. *App. Crit.*, p. 589. The Greek τυμπανισμός.
[3] 2 Macc. iii. 35.
[4] They quoted Lev. xviii. 29; 2 Macc. iii. 15.

or had at least been associated—as at Athens—with the divinity of Rome.[1] Augustus, with these restrictions, had yielded to the earnest entreaties of the people of Pergamos and Nicomedia, but had expressly forbidden the Romans to take any part in this new cult. The base example spread rapidly in the provinces, and though it is probable that in secret Augustus was not displeased at so astonishing a proof of his own power, he affected to smile at it as a man of the world.[2] In the frenzy of flattery, which is the disease of despotisms, it was but too likely that this deification of a living man would creep from the provinces into Italy, and, in spite of the assertion of Dion Cassius, that in Italy no one ventured to worship Augustus, it is certain from the *Corpus Inscriptionum* that at his death there had sprung up, either by his permission or without his interference, priests of Augustus at Pompeii, flamens at Præneste, an Augusteum at Pisa, and a Cæsareum at Puteoli; and this—though it was due far more to the religious degradation of the age than to the phrenetic pride of the autocrat—was made a source of bitter blame against him when he was dead. Even at Rome,[3] though no temple rose to him till he was dead, yet we need go no further than the poetry of Virgil, Horace, and Ovid,[4] to show that he was commonly addressed as a deity (*numen*) and a god, and that sacrifices were offered either to him or in his name; and, as appears from inscriptions, even at Rome, if they did not worship him directly, they did so indirectly, by rearing altars to his virtues and his laws, and by inserting his name among those of ancient deities in the songs of the Arval brothers. After his death the worship was extended without limit. He was known universally as the Divine Augustus, a phrase which became as common as *feu le roi*.[5]

---

[1] Dion. li. 20 ; Suet. *Aug.* 52. Though he knew that even Proconsuls had in the provinces been honoured with temples, yet in "nullâ provinciâ, *nisi communi suo Romæque nomine* recepit." See the excellent chapter on "L'Apothéose Impériale," in Boissier, *La Religion Romaine*, i. 123—205.

[2] Quintil. *Instt. Orat.* vi. 3, 77.

[3] Tac. *Ann.* i. 10, "Nihil deorum honoribus relictum, cum se templis et effigie numinum per flamines et sacerdotes coli vellet;" Aurel. Vict. *de Cæsar.* 1, "Huicque, uti Deo, Romae provinciisque omnibus, per urbes celeberrimas vivo mortuoque templa sacerdotes et collegia sacravere." This seems, however, to be a positive mistake, though Pliny, *Nat. Hist.* xii. 19, mentions a temple which Livia erected to him after his death (Divo) on the Palatine. Suetonius, a very high authority on such a subject, says that he most obstinately refused this honour Rome when it was pressed upon him (*Aug.* 52, "In urbe quidem pertinacissime abstinuit hoc honore").

[4] See Bentley's note on Hor. *Epp.* II. i. 16 ; Virg. *Ecl.* i. 7 ; *Georg.* i. 42 ; Hor. *Od.* i. 2, 41 ; iii. 5, 1 ; iv. 5, 16 ; Ov. *Trist.* ii. 8, 9 ; iv. 9, 111. (Boissier, i. 153.)

[5] Tac. *Ann.* 1, 73, "Caelum decretum."

Tiberius, for political reasons, patronised, and even to a certain extent enforced, this new worship, but he also discouraged the extravagance which endeavoured to extend divine honours to his *living self*, and by doing so he at once gratified his undisguised cynicism and showed his strong good sense. But the tendency to apotheosis was in his time firmly established. He was, as a matter of course, deified a..er his death, and his panegyrist, Velleius Paterculus, tells us a story that when he was in the midst of a campaign among the Chauci, a barbarian chief obtained permission to see him, and after crossing the river in order to do so, gazed at him for a long time in silence, and exclaiming that he had now seen the gods,[1] asked to touch his hand, and then pushed off his boat towards the opposite shore, gazing to the last on the living deity. So rapidly did the disease of adulation grow that, according to Suetonius, Domitian actually used to begin his letters with the words "Dominus et Deus noster sic fieri jubet"—"Thus orders our Lord and God, Domitian!"[2]

EXCURSUS XIII. (p. 329).

BURDENS LAID ON PROSELYTES.

WE are told in the Talmud that if a Gentile wished to become a proselyte he was asked his reasons for the wish, and informed that Israel is now afflicted, persecuted, and cast down with all kinds of sufferings. If he replies that he knows it, and is not worthy to share in their sufferings, he is admitted, but is told enough of the "light" and the "heavy" precepts to warn him to desist in time if he is not sincere, since, as Rabh Chelbo said, "proselytes are as injurious to Israel as a scab." He is told about the rules respecting gleaning, and tithes, and the penalties attached to any transgression of the Law, and is informed that henceforth if he desecrates the Sabbath he is liable to death by stoning. If he submits he is circumcised, and even circumcised a second time, if there were any neglect or carelessness in the first performance of the rite. After his recovery he is immersed without delay by way of baptism, and two "disciples of the wise" stand by him, repeating some of the "light" and "heavy" precepts.[3] In fact, a Gentile could only

---

[1] Vell. Paterc. ii. 107, "Quos ante audiebam hodie vidi deos."
[2] Suet. *Domit.* 13.   [3] *Yebhamoth,* f. 47, 1.

become a proselyte by submitting himself to the whole yoke of Rabbinism, the tyranny of archaic, puerile, and wearisome halachôth which year by year was laid more heavily on Jewish shoulders by the pedantry of their theologic schools. It was the fault of the Jews that the Gentiles usually concentrated their attention on mere transient Jewish *rites,* and not on the eternal *principles* which God had revealed to them. Can we be surprised at this when we find R. Eleazar Ben Chasmah saying that the rules about birds' nests (*kinim*), and the "uncleanliness" of women (*niddah*) are *essentials* of the Law?[1]

EXCURSUS XIV. (p. 330).

HATRED OF THE JEWS IN CLASSICAL ANTIQUITY.

IT is at once curious and painful to perceive how strange was the mixture of curiosity, disgust, and contempt, with which the Jews were regarded in pagan antiquity. From Manetho the Egyptian priest, with whom seems to have originated the calumny that they were a nation of lepers,[2] down to Annæus Florus, who brands them as an impious race,[3] the references to them in secular literature are a tissue of absurd calumnies or biting sarcasms. Chæremon alludes to them as unclean and polluted;[4] Lysimachus, as diseased and unsocial;[5] Diodorus Siculus, as addicted to strange rites, and hostile to strangers;[6] Apollonius Molon, a Greek rhetorician of the time of Cicero, as "godless and misanthropical;"[7] Cicero heaps scorn and indignation upon them in his Oration for the extortionate and tyrannous Flaccus,[8] and in that on the

---

[1] *Pirke Abhoth,* iii. 28. In partial defence of the Jews it may be said that some were inclined to become proselytes to avoid military service (Tac. *Ann.* ii. 85; Suet. *Tib.* 36; Jos. *Antt.* xviii. 3, 5), others were *Shechemite* proselytes —*i.e.*, to marry rich Jewesses (*id.* xvi., 7, 5; xx. 7, 2, 3), others were "*lion*-proselytes"—*i.e.*, out of fear (2 Kings xvii. 26; Jos. *B. J.,* ii. 17, 10). Herzog. *Real. Enc.,* s. v.

[2] *Ap.* Jos. *c. Ap.* i. 26.

[3] Speaking of Pompey, Florus says, "Et vidit illud grande impiae gentis arcanum.

[4] Jos. *c. Ap.* i. 32.

[5] *Id.* i. 34.

[6] Diod. Sic. xl.

[7] Jos. *c. Ap.* ii. 14.

[8] Cic. *pro. Flacco,* xxviii.

consular provinces calls them "a race born for slavery;"[1] Horace sneers at their proselytism, and their circumcision, and their Sabbaths;[2] Seneca calls them "a most abandoned race;"[3] Martial, besides odious allusions to their national rite, pours his contempt on their poverty, their mendicancy, their religion, and their low trade of selling sulphur matches and buying broken glass, and he seems to be the first to originate the slander repeated by Sir Thomas Browne in his "Popular Errors;"[4] Quintilian, gentle as he was, yet admits a very bitter remark against the Jews and Moses;[5] Lucan alludes to their "uncertain Deity;"[6] Petronius Arbiter seems to think, as did many of the ancients, that the Jews did not abhor, but actually worshipped the pig;[7] Tacitus, in his History, reproaches them with gross sensuality, low cunning, and strong hatred of all nations but their own, and gives at full length, and with all gravity, the preposterous story about their veneration for the ass.[8] In his Annals he speaks with equal horror and equal ignorance of Jews and Christians, and considers that if the thousands of Jews who were deported to Sardinia died it would be a cheap loss;[9] Juvenal flings scornful allusion at their squalor, beggary, turbulence, superstition, cheatery, and idleness;[10] Celsus abused them as jugglers and vagabonds;[11] Ammianus Marcellinus as "disgusting and noisy;"[12] Rutilius Numatianus closes the long line of angry slanderers by a burst of abuse, in which he characterises Judæa as a "lying slave-cage."[13] Jeremiah had bidden the Jews to seek the peace of, and to pray for, the city

---

[1] *De Prov. Cons.* v.

[2] Hor. *Sat.* i. iv. 143; v. 100; ix. 69.

[3] *Ap.* Aug. *De Civ. Dei.* vii. 36, "Usque eo sceleratissimae gentis consuetudo convaluit [the Sabbath] ut," &c.

[4] Mart. *Ep.* i. 42; xii. 30, 35, 57; iv. 4; vii. 82; xi. 94, i. 4. Cf. Stat. *Silv.* i. 6. The relation of the Herods to the Cæsars had attracted a large share of attention to the Jews in the Imperial epoch. Pers. v. 179—184; Juv. vi. 157.

[5] *De Instt. Orat.* iii. 7.

[6] *Pharsal.* ii. 593, "incerti Judaea Dei."

[7] *Satiric.* Büchler, p. 221, "Judaeus licet et *porcinum* numen, adoret," &c. (Cf. Plut. *Synop.* iv. 5.)

[8] Tac. *Hist.* v. 2—5; Diod. Sic. i. 28; Plut. *Synop.* iv. 5. On this story see Geiger, *Juden und Judenthum, Illustr. Monatsch d. Judenth,* Oct., 1865.

[9] *Ann.* xv. 44; ii. 85, "si ob gravitatem caeli interissent, vile damnum." (Cf. Suet. *Tib.* 36; Jos. *Antt.* xviii. 3, 5; Philo, *Leg.* 24.)

[10] *Sat.* vi. 542—547, 156—160; xiv. 96—107. See, for other allusions, *id.* iii. 13, 296.

[11] *Ap.* Orig. *c. Cels.* i. 33, γοήτων.

[12] Ammian. Marc. xxii. 5, "fetentes Judaei." (See "Gentiles" in Kitto.)

[13] *Itinerar.* i. 3, 89. In the above quotations and references I have made free use (with certain additions) of Dr. Gill's *Notices of the Jews by Classic Authors* see also Meier's *Judaica,* and the article of Geiger, above quoted).

of their captivity, "for in the peace thereof shall ye have peace."[1] Better had it been for the ancient Jews if they had lived in the spirit of that large advice. But the Gentiles were well aware that in the Jewish synagogues there was an exception to the dead uniformity of the Romish Empire, and that they and their customs were there treated with open and bitter scorn, which they repaid tenfold.[2]

EXCURSUS XV. (p. 330).

JUDGMENTS OF EARLY PAGAN WRITERS ON CHRISTIANITY.

SUETONIUS (died circ. A.D. 110).

"Judaeos impulsore Chresto assidue tumultuantes Româ expulit" Claud. 25).[3]

"Afflicti suppliciis Christiani genus hominum superstitionis novae et maleficae" (Nero, 16).

"Percrebuerat Oriente toto vetus et constans opinio, esse in fatis, ut eo tempore, Judaea profecti rerum potirentur" (Vesp. 4).

TACITUS (Consul suffectus, A.D. 97).

"Ergo abolendo rumori Nero subdidit reos, et quaesitissimis poenis affecit, quos per flagitia invisos vulgus Christianos appellabat. Auctor ejus nominis Christus Tiberio imperitante per procuratorem Pont. Pilatum supplicio affectus est; repressaque in praesens exitiabilis superstitio rursum erumpebat non modo per Judaeam originem ejus mali, sed per urbem etiam quo cuncta undique atrocia aut pudenda confluunt celebranturque. Igitur primum correpti qui fatebantur, deinde indicio eorum multitudo ingens, haud perinde in crimine incendii quam odio generis humani convicti sunt. Et pereuntibus addita ludibria, ut ferarum tergis contecti laniatu canum interirent, aut crucibus affixi aut flammandi, atque ubi defecisset dies, in usum nocturni luminis urerentur . . . unde quamquam adversus sontes et novissima exempla

---

[1] Jer. xxix. 7.

[2] Ps. Heraclit. Ep. vii.; Hausrath, N. T. Gesch. ii. 79. Specimens of this scorn may be seen in Jos. c. Ap. ii. 34, 35.

[3] According to Sulpic. Severus (Hist. Sacr. ii. 30), Titus decided that the Temple should be destroyed that Christianity and Judaism might be eradicated together. "Quippe has religiones, licet contrarias sibi, iisdem tamen auctoribus profectas; Christianos ex Judaeis exstitisse; radice sublatâ, stirpem facile perituram." This is believed by Bernays to be a quotation from Tacitus.

meritos miseratio oriebatur tamquam non utilitate publicâ sed in saevitiam unius absumerentur" (*Ann.* xv. 44).

Gentiles in the Letter of the Churches of Vienne and Lyons complain, ξένην τινα καὶ καινὴν ἡμῖν εἰσάγουσι θρησκείαν (ap. Euseb. *H. E.* v. 1).

PLINY THE YOUNGER (died circ. A.D. 117).

His famous letter to Trajan is too long for insertion. He asks whether he is to punish persons for simply being Christians, or for crimes involved in the charge of being so (*nomen ipsum, si flagitiis careat, an flagitia cohaerentia nomini*). He says that he has punished those who, after threat of punishment, still declared themselves Christians, because he considers that in any case their "inflexible obstinacy" should be punished. Others equally infatuated (*similis amentiae*) he determined to send to Rome, being Roman citizens. Having received an anonymous accusation which inculpated many, he tested them, if they denied the charge of being Christians, by making them call on the gods, and offer incense and wine to the Emperor's image, and curse Christ. If they did this he dismissed them, because he was told that no true Christian would ever do it. Some said that they had long abjured Christianity, but declared that the head and front of their "fault" or "error" had simply been the custom of meeting before dawn, and singing antiphons to Christ as a God, and binding themselves with an oath [1] not to steal, rob, commit adultery, break their word, or deny the trust committed to them; after which they separated, meeting again for a harmless meal—a custom which they had dropped after Pliny's edict forbidding guilds. Scarcely crediting this strange account of their innocent life, he had put two deaconesses (ex duabus ancillis quae *ministrae* dicebantur) to the torture, but discovered nothing beyond perverted and immoderate superstition (*pravam, immodicam*). He therefore consults Trajan, because of the multitude of the accused, who were of every age, rank, and sex, both in the city and in the country. So widely had "the contagion of that wretched superstition" spread that the temples were almost deserted, and there was scarcely any one to buy the victims (*Ep.* x. 97).

To this letter Trajan briefly replies that the Christians are to be punished if convicted, but not to be sought out; to be pardoned if they sacrifice, and not to be tried on anonymous accusations.

EPICTETUS (died A.D. 117).

"Then through madness it is possible for a man to be so disposed towards these things" (*i.e.*, to be indifferent to the world), "and the Galilæans through habit" (*Dissert.* iv. 7).

---

[1] Interesting as the earliest Christian application of the word "Sacrament" (Waterland *On the Eucharist*, i.).

M. AURELIUS ANTONINUS (died A.D. 180).

Speaking of readiness to die, he says that it is noble, "so that it comes from a man's own judgment, not from mere obstinacy (διὰ ψιλὴν παράταξιν), as with the Christians, but considerately, and with dignity" (*Encheir.* xi. 3).

LUCIAN (died circ. A.D. 200).

His sneers and parodies of what he calls the θαυμαστὴ σοφία of the Christians are to be found in the *Ver. Historia*, I. 12, 30; II. 4, 11—12 (*Alexand.* (Pseudomantis) xxv. 38). The *Philopatris* is not by Lucian, but a hundred years later.

GALEN, the great writer on Physic (died A.D. 200).

In his book, *De different. pulsuum,* he alludes twice to the obstinacy of Christians.

EXCURSUS XVI. (p. 351).

THE PROCONSULATE OF SERGIUS PAULUS.

THE title of "Proconsul"[1] given to this insular governor is one of those minute touches of accuracy which occur on every page of the Acts of the Apostles.

It might have been a serious difficulty that the name of Sergius Paulus does not occur in the *Fasti* of the Consuls till long after this period,[2] but the difficulty vanishes when we find that the title of Proconsul was given to the Governor of a senatorial province, whatever may have been his previous rank.[3] But another and more serious difficulty was once urged. There were two kinds of provinces, the imperial and the senatorial, both of which were called Eparchies (ἐπαρχίαι). The imperial were those to which the governors were sent by the Emperor, because their circumstances involved the necessity of military command. Augustus, under pretence of relieving the Senate from the burden of the more disturbed provinces, had astutely reserved for his personal administration those regions of the empire where the presence of an army was required. As the title Praetor (in Greek, Στρατηγὸς, or general) still retained some shadow of its old military significance, the Governors

---

[1] E. V. "Deputy."

[2] Serg. Paulus, cousul suffectus, A.D. 21, and another, Consul, A.D. 168.

[3] Dio Cass. liii. 13, καὶ ἀνθυπάτους καλεῖσθαι μὴ ὅτι τοὺς δύο τοὺς ὑπατευκότας (ex-Consuls) ἀλλὰ καὶ τοὺς ἄλλους τῶν ἐστρατηγηκότων (ex-Praetors) κ. τ. λ.

of these provinces were called Propraetors, or 'Αντιστρατηγοι, for which, in the New Testament, the more general term 'Ηγεμών is often used. This Greek word for "Governor" serves as an equivalent both for "Procurator" and also for *Praeses* or *Legatus*, which was, for instance, the ordinary designation of the Governor of Syria. These *Praesides*, *Legati*, or *Propraetors* held their commands at the Emperor's pleasure, and, especially in the reign of Tiberius, were often left for years undisturbed in their tenure of office. The Proconsuls, or 'Ανθύπατοι, on the other hand, who were appointed by the Senate, only held their posts for a single year. Now it appears from Strabo that when, in B.C. 27, Augustus divided the provinces between himself and the Senate, Cyprus was reserved as one of the imperial districts (στρατηγικὴ ἐπαρχία), and with this Dion Cassius agrees.[1] Consequently even eminent writers like Grotius thought that St. Luke had here fallen into an error; and Baronius supposes that Cyprus must at this time have been an honorary adjunct to the Proconsulship of Cilicia, while Grotius suggests that Greek flattery might have often given to a Propraetor the more distinguished title of Proconsul, and that St. Luke might have used it in accordance with the common parlance. But a little more research has resulted in the discovery that though Cyprus originally was an imperial province, and ultimately reverted to the same condition, yet Augustus restored both it and Gallia Narbonensis to the Senate in exchange for Dalmatia, because he found that they did not need the presence of many soldiers.[2] And to set the matter finally at rest, copper coins and inscriptions of this very epoch have been found at Curium and Citium in which the title of Proconsul is given to Cominius Proclus, Julius Cordus, and L. Aunus Bassus, who must have been immediate predecessors or successors of Sergius Paulus.[3]

The name Sergius Paulus is itself interesting. Of this particular Proconsul, indeed, we know nothing beyond the eulogy of the sacred historian that he was a man of sense,[4] and that he was deeply impressed by the teaching of St. Paul. But Pliny the Elder, in his Natural History, three times refers to a Sergius Paulus as a person interested in intelligent researches; and it is not impossible that this Sergius Paulus may be none other than our Cyprian Proconsul.[5] If so, the character

---

[1] Dio Cass. liii. 12; Strabo, xiv. 685; Suet. *Aug.* 47.

[2] Dio Cass. liii. 13, τὴν Κύπρον . . . τῷ δήμῳ ἀπέδωκεν ; liv. 4, καὶ οὗτω ἀνθύπατοι καὶ ἐς ἐκεῖνα τὰ ἔθνη πέμπεσθαι ἥρξαντο.

[3] Eckhel, iii. 84; Akerman, *Numism. Illustr.*, pp. 39, 42; Boeckh, *Corp. Inscr.* 2631, 2632.

[4] Acts xiii. 7, ἀνδρὶ συνετῷ. The name of a Procunsul Paulus has been found on an inscription at Soli (Cesnola, *Cyprus*, p. 495).

[5] Plin. *H. N.* i. Pliny is writing only twenty years after this period.

given him in one passing word by St. Luke will be confirmed, and we
feel additional pleasure in tracing similar characteristics in others of the
same name who may well have been his descendants; for instance, in
the Sergius Paulus who, more than a hundred years afterwards, receives
the encomium of the physician Galen for his eminence both as a theoretic
and a practical philosopher.[1]

EXCURSUS XVII. (p. 440).

St. John and St. Paul.

Of the three "seeming pillars," John appears to have taken no part
in the synod at Jerusalem, or if he did it was not sufficiently decisive to
be recorded. He belonged, it is clear, at this time to the Church of the
Circumcision, and, so far as we know, this was the only occasion on
which he was thrown into the society of St. Paul. But we have St.
Paul's express testimony—in the only passage in which he is mentioned
in the Epistles—that he recognised his apostolate; and the Apocalypse,
his earliest writing, so far from showing that irreconcilable hatred to the
doctrines of St. Paul which has been assumed on grounds inconceivably
frivolous, and repeated subsequently with extraordinary recklessness,
offers a close parallelism to St. Paul's Epistles in thoughts and principles,
which is all the more striking from the marked differences of tone and
expression. We are calmly assured, without even the condescension of
an attempted proof, that the "false Jew," the "false Apostle," the
"false prophet," the "Balaam," the "Jezebel," the "Nicolas," the "chief
of the synagogue of Satan," alluded to in the Apocalypse,[2] are as indu-
bitably intended for St. Paul as are the savage allusions covertly made
to him under the name of Simon the Magician in the Pseudo-Clementines.
Now, on what basis is this conclusion founded? Simply on the resemblance in tone of a spurious Ebionite romance (the Clementines) to the
phrases, "those which say they are Apostles and are not," "those which
say they are Jews and are not," and the allusions to some who held the

---

[1] Renan, *St. Paul*, p. 15, who refers to Orelli, 2414, 4938. Galen, *De Anatom.* 1
(*apud* Wetstein), ἀνδρὸς τὰ πάντα πρωτεύοντος ἔργοις τε καὶ λόγοις τοῖς ἐν φιλοσοφίᾳ.
[2] Rev. ii. 2, 6, 9, 14, 15, 20, 24; iii. 9. (See Renan, *St. P.*, 302—305. who quietly
asserts this as if it were indisputable.) Yet St. Paul himself was the first to use this
very comparison with Balaam (1 Cor. x. 7, 8), and to denounce the extreme wickedness of putting a stumbling-block before others (Rom. xiv. 21; 2 Cor. xi. 29).

doctrine of Balaam, and of "that woman Jezebel," who taught people
"to commit fornication, and to eat things sacrificed unto idols." It is
true that there were Judaisers who attacked St. Paul's claim to be an
Apostle; but to assert that St. John was one of them is to give the
direct lie to St. Paul, while to class St. Paul with them "that say they
are Jews and are not" is to falsify the most notorious facts concerning
one who was a Pharisee of Pharisees, and a Hebrew of the Hebrews.
Again, to assert boldly that St. Paul ever taught people to eat things
offered to idols, or anything which could be so described without the
grossest calumny, is a distinct contradiction of his own words, since he
expressly warned his converts *not* to do this, and assigns for his warning
the very reason that to do so would be "to cast a stumbling-block before
the children of Israel."[1] In fact, though St. Paul would have denied
that to eat them was *wrong in itself*, his concessions on this point went
very little beyond those which are sanctioned in the Talmud itself.[2] Once
more, what conceivable excuse could there be for saying that St. Paul
ever taught men "to commit fornication?"—a sin against which, whether
literally or metaphorically understood, he has urged considerations more
deeply seated, more likely to touch the heart, more likely to bind the
conscience, than all the other writers in the New Testament put together.
That even in earliest days there did spring up antinomian sects which
were guilty of such accursed teaching, we know from Church history,
and find traces even in the sacred writers; and it is therefore probable
that the allusions of the Apocalypse are as literal as the Old Testament
analogies to which St. John no less than St. Paul refers.[3] That
"the fornication" of the Apocalypse means "mixed marriages" there
is not even a shadow of reason to believe, nor if it did would there
be any ground for saying that St. Paul encouraged them. Though he
used, on that as on all such topics, the language of wisdom and of
charity, the whole tendency of his teaching is to discourage them.[4]
Moreover, if Paul had been aimed at, and if St. John, the Apostle of
Love, really had been the slanderous and rabid Judaiser which these
allusions would then imply, it is inconceivable that no word should be
said about the points respecting which, to a Judaiser, he must have

---

[1] 1 Cor. viii. 13 (cf. x. 32).

[2] *Ketubhôth*, f. 15, 1, which, almost in the very language of St. Paul, lays down
the rule that if a man has bought meat, and is doubtful whether it is legally clean,
he must not eat it; but if he lights upon it accidentally, he may eat it without
further inquiry. Meat declared to be legally clean (*tâhor*) is stamped with a leaden
seal, on which is the word *kashar* ("lawful," καθαρὸν). (L. Disraeli, *Genius of
Judaism*, p. 154.)

[3] 1 Cor. x. 7, 8. (See some excellent remarks in Lightfoot's *Gal.*, pp. 290, 335.)

[4] See especially 2 Cor. vi. 14.

seemed infinitely more assailable—namely, St. Paul's very low estimate
of circumcision, and his declared conviction that by the works of the
Law no man can be justified in God's sight.   Now, in the Apocalypse
neither circumcision, nor the Law, nor Moses, nor oral tradition are
once so much as mentioned or alluded to, while redemption by the
blood of the Lamb, and the universality of that redemption as extending to "every kindred and tongue and people and nation,"[1] are
asserted as absolutely and unconditionally as they could have been
by Paul himself.   Further, it needs but a casual study of St. John and
St. Paul to see that "Jesus Christ" is in both of them the divine secret
and the fundamental conception of all Christianity.   St. John at this
time was the more contemplative, the less prominently active, St. John
of the Gospels.   "The hidden fires of his nature" had not yet "burst
out into a flame."   Two incidents preserved for us in the Gospels had
indeed shown that those fires were there ;[2] but it was not till James the
Lord's brother, and Peter, and Paul himself had passed away that he
became the bold and uncompromising leader whose counsels were as
oracles to the Asian Church.   Nevertheless, we may be sure that St.
John was *not* found among the opponents of St. Paul.   That opposition
is always connected with the adherents and the influence of James.
During the lifetime of Jesus James had not fully accepted His mission,
and seems only to have been converted by the Resurrection.   He had
not therefore lived, as the other Apostles had lived, in daily contact with
the mind and influence of Jesus, and was in consequence more deeply
imbued with the beliefs of his early Jewish training, and less entirely
permeated in intellect by the breath of the new life.   But Peter and
John, more than any living men, must have known what was the mind
of Christ.   We know that they were one in heart, and we may be sure
that they who had gone together to visit and confirm the detested
Samaritans and witness their participation in the gifts of the Holy
Ghost, would be little likely to look with rabid jealousy on the equal
freedom of a yet wider extension of the Kingdom of God.

EXCURSUS XVIII. (p. 448).

The Attacks on St. Paul in the Clementines.

That Paul, in consequence of the death-blow which he gave to Jewish
Pharisaism, was pursued by a particular section of the Judæo-Christian

---

[1] Rev. v. 9; vii. 9.   [2] Luke ix. 54; Matt. xx. 21

Church with unrelenting opposition, is a matter of history.   It needs no further proof than the large sections in his Epistles which are occupied with arguments against Pharisaic or Gnostic Judaism, such as had invaded the Churches of Corinth, Galatia, Colossæ, and Crete. But true though it is that he was obliged to contend in lifelong struggle with a *party*, it is not true that he remained long unrecognised by the Church at large.   The supposition that he was, has merely originated from the exceptional literary activity of a single section of Christian Ebionites.   Dr. Lightfoot, in his essay on "St. Paul and the Three," has shown, by patient and entirely candid investigation, that even the Church of Judæa was not exclusively anti-Pauline, and that the anti-Pauline faction within it, so far from representing the tendencies of the whole Christian Church, did not even represent the Christians of Palestine.   The Christian Jews of the Holy Land naturally continued, as a body, to observe the Mosaic Law—as was done by St. Paul himself so far as he could do so without compromising the emancipation of the Gentiles—until the fall of Jerusalem rendered all such observance a mere mockery and sham.[1] If the Passover, the very central ordinance of Mosaism, was rendered simply impossible, God had Himself demonstrated that the *aeon* of the Law was closed.   The withdrawal of the Church to Pella, caused by a recollection of the warnings of Jesus, would look to the Jews like an unpatriotic desertion of their cause ; and the frantic denunciations of the *Mins*, which date from this epoch, were but signs of the gathering detestation of Jew for Christian which culminated in the savage massacres by Bar-cochba of those Christians who refused to apostatise and blaspheme.   When the name of Jerusalem had given way to that of Ælia Capitolina, and Christians were allowed to live where no Jew might set his foot, the Church of the new city became predominantly Gentile, and was for the first time governed by a Gentile bishop.[2] It is not till after this period that we hear of two sects distinct from each other, but often confused.   These were the Nazarenes and the Ebionites. The NAZARENES were not in any way hostile to the work and memory of Paul, and they differed from other Christians only in holding that the Law was still binding on Jewish converts.   "The Testaments of the Twelve Patriarchs"—a book which, whether written by a Nazarene or not, expresses their general tenets so far as we can gather them—not only does not oppose the doctrines of St. Paul, but, though written from the Judæo-Christian standpoint, puts into the mouth of Benjamin a splendid eulogy of Paul, as one who is to arise from that

[1] Grätz, *Gesch. d. Juden*, iv. 112.
[2] Marcus, B.C. 132. Just. Mart. *Apol.* i. 31, p. 72.

tribe " beloved of the Lord, listening to His voice, enlightening all the
Gentiles with new knowledge." The EBIONITES, on the other hand—a
powerful and zealous sect—breathed the exact spirit of Paul's
Judaising enemies, and the views of many of them became deeply
tinged with the Gnostic tendencies of the more advanced Essenes. To
this section of the Ebionites we owe the forgeries known as the
Clementine Homilies, the Clementine Recognitions, extant in a Latin
paraphrase of Rufinus,[1] and a spurious letter of Peter to James. In
the Homilies St. Paul is surreptitiously attacked in the guise of Simon
Magus.[2] The allusion to his reproof of St. Peter at Antioch is too
plain to be overlooked, and discredit is thrown on his doctrine, his
revelations, and his independent attitude towards James. In the letter
of St. Peter he is still more severely, though still covertly slandered,
as " the enemy " whose teaching was antinomian and absurd, and who
calumniously asserted that St. Peter held one view and sanctioned
another. In the Recognitions these attacks do not appear, but " the
enemy " sent by Caiaphas to arrest St. Peter at Antioch, and who
throws St. James down the Temple steps, is evidently meant for St.
Paul, and this notable story is believed to have been borrowed from a
prating fiction called the " Ascents of James," which is also the source
of the venomous calumny that Paul was a Gentile who had accepted
circumcision in hopes of marrying the High Priest's daughter, and
had only apostatised from Mosaism when his hopes were disappointed.[3]

It is on trash of this kind, at once feeble and virulent, at once
baseless and malignant, that some have based the belief that there was
deadly opposition between Paul and the Twelve, and that his work was
not fully recognised till the close of the second century. The fact, however, is that these Ebionite slanders and forgeries are representative
of none but an isolated sect. Justin lived in Samaria in the earlier half
of the second century, and shows no trace of these views. Hegesippus
was a Jewish Christian who travelled to Rome in the middle of the
second century, visiting many Christian Churches; and Eusebius, who
knew his writings, vouches for his perfect orthodoxy.[4] Such being the
case, it is hardly even necessary to prove that the other churches of the
second century were in no sense anti-Pauline. It may be true that for

---

[1] And partly in Syriac.

[2] The English reader may see these passages translated in Baur's *First Three
Centuries*, i. pp. 89—98.

[3] Epiphan. *Haeres*, xxx. 16. Renan also refers to Massechta, *Gêrîm*, 1, ed.
Kirchheim.

[4] It is no disproof of this that he borrows the Ebionite account of St. James;
and his supposed condemnation of St. Paul for using the expression "Eye hath
not seen," &c., seems to rest on an entire misapprehension (Lightfoot, *Gal.*, p. 311).

a short time there were two sections—a Jewish and a Gentile—in the Church of Rome, and even that each section had its own bishop, the possible successors respectively of the Apostles of the circumcision and of the uncircumcision.[1] But if so, these two sections were, at the close of the first century, united under the gentle and orthodox Clement; and even on the doubtful hypothesis that the Clementines had a Roman origin, their indirectness—the cautious, subterranean, timid sort of way in which they attack the great Apostle—is alone a decisive proof that the forger *could by no means rely on the general sympathy of the readers into whose hands his writings fell.* And yet on this very attenuated apex is built the huge inverted pyramid of inference, which finally declares the Epistle of St. Jude to be a specimen of one of the letters, breathing sanguinary hatred and atrocious falsehood, which are supposed to have been despatched from Jerusalem in the name of the Apostles, and in the composition of which, "since James and Jude probably could not speak Greek," they probably employed Greek secretaries![2] Let any one read the Epistle of St. Jude, and consider, verse by verse, how it could be possibly applied to St. Paul, and how absolutely such a theory contradicts every really authentic fact of his relation to the Apostles, as well as the character and bearing of the Apostles themselves, and he will be able to estimate the validity of the criticism which calmly represents as reasonable history this darkening fume of inferences from the narrow aperture of a worthless forgery.

[1] Some such fact may lie behind the remark of Tertullian that Clement was ordained bishop by St. Peter, whereas Irenæus places Linus and Anencletus before him.

[2] Renan, *St. Paul*, p. 300. "En quittant Antioche les agents du parti hiérosolomyte jurèrent de bouleverser les fondations de Paul, de détruire les Eglises, de renverser ce qu'il avait édifié avec tant de labeurs. Il semble qu'à cette occasion de nouvelles lettres furent expédiées de Jérusalem, au nom des apôtres. Il se peut même qu'un exemplaire de ces lettres haineuses nous ait été conservé dans l'Epître de Jude, frère de Jacques, et comme lui 'frère du Seigneur,' qui fait partie du canon," &c. The apparent array of authorities quoted in support of such inferences has no real bearing on them, and upon examination dwindles into the narrow limits indicated below. Nor does M. Renan adduce a single proof, or anything remotely resembling a proof, that by πορνεία the Apocalypse and the Epistle of Jude imply the doctrine of St. Paul (*id.* p. 300), or that the relative moderation of Michael (Jude 9) is contrasted with the impertinence of St. Paul (!), or, in fact, any other of the utterly wild conclusions into which he has exaggerated the perverted ingenuity of Tübingen theorists. See further the Excursus on St. John and St. Paul.

CPSIA information can be obtained
at www.ICGtesting.com
Printed in the USA
LVHW081557260921
698753LV00012B/530

9 780341 946977